CONTENTS

RETHINKING
DEVELOPMENT
ECONOMICS

Edited by
Ha-Joon Chang

Anthem Press

This edition first published by Anthem Press 2003

Anthem Press is an imprint of
Wimbledon Publishing Company
75–76 Blackfriars Road
London SE1 8HA

British Library Cataloguing in Publication Data
Data available

Library of Congress Cataloging in Publication Data
A catalog record has been applied for

ISBN 1 84331 110 0

1 3 5 7 9 10 8 6 4 2

Typeset by Regent Typesetting, London
Printed in the Czech Republic by Newton Printing

CONTRIBUTORS

Ha-Joon Chang, Assistant Director of Development Studies, University of Cambridge

John Toye, Professor of Economics, University of Oxford

Deepak Nayyar, Vice Chancellor, Delhi University

Jose Antonio Ocampo, Executive Secretary, Economic Commission for Latin America and the Caribbean (ECLAC)

Gabriel Palma, University Lecturer in Economics, University of Cambridge

Howard Stein, Professor of Economics, Roosevelt University

Michael Ellman, Professor of Economics, University of Amsterdam

Ben Fine, Professor of Economics, School of Oriental and African Studies (SOAS), University of London

Amit Bhaduri, Senior Fellow, Institute for Advanced Studies, University of Bologna

Terry Byres, Professorial Research Associate, Department of Economics, School of Oriental and African Studies (SOAS), University of London

Sanjaya Lall, Professor of Development Economics, University of Oxford

Peter Nolan, Sinyi Professor of Chinese Management, Judge Institute of Management, University of Cambridge

Ilene Grabel, Associate Professor of International Finance, Graduate School of International Studies, University of Denver

Ajit Singh, Professor of Economics, University of Cambridge

John Sender, Professor of Economics, School of Oriental and African Studies (SOAS), University of London

Andrea Cornia, Professor of Development Economics, Faculty of Economics, University of Florence

Erik Reinert, Centre for Development and Environment, University of Oslo

Barbara Harriss-White, University Professor of Development Studies, University of Oxford

Martin Khor, Director, Third World Network

RETHINKING DEVELOPMENT ECONOMICS: AN INTRODUCTION

Ha-Joon Chang

Neoliberalism has been the dominant economic doctrine of the last quarter century. As its name implies, neoliberalism sees itself as the heir to liberalism, the dominant economic doctrine of the late nineteenth and the early twentieth century. Neoliberals see the latter period as the 'golden age' of capitalism, when the world prospered thanks to the absence of state owner-ship and regulation of industry and finance, flexible labour markets, rigid anti-inflationary macroeconomic policy (institutionally guaranteed by the Gold Standard) and free international flows of trade and capital.[1] In an attempt to return the world to that golden age, neoliberals have strongly pushed for 'reform' programmes made up of extensive privatization, radical deregulation, total opening-up of goods and capital markets, and tightening of macroeconomic policy.

While more or less the whole world has been touched by it, neoliberalism has been particularly rigorously implemented in the developing countries. What made this possible was the 1982 debt crisis. Coming after a decade of increasing self-confidence on the part of the developing countries, which culminated in the call for the New International Economic Order (NIEO), the debt crisis was seen by the neoliberals – who by then had come to control the governments of the major developed countries and the international financial institutions (IFIs: the International Monetary Fund and the World Bank) – as an opportunity to put the developing countries back on to the 'correct' path. As a result, stringent conditions intended to remould the developing countries in the neoliberal image have been attached to the bi-lateral aid from the developed country governments and to the concessional loans made by the IFIs.

During the 1990s, neoliberal reform programmes were pushed even more widely and even harder. First of all, the reforms implemented in the 1980s utterly failed to turn around the economies of the countries concerned, intensifying their financial dependence on the developed countries and on the IFIs. Second, the fall of Communism opened up a vast area of the world that was willing to implement the most extreme versions of neoliberal reform programmes. Third, the launch of the World Trade Organization (WTO) in 1995 has further restricted the ability of the developing countries to deviate from the neoliberal agenda. Finally, during the last few years of the 1990s the (now-fading) economic boom in the USA – the home of neoliberalism – and the relative stagnation of Japan and Germany – countries which were previously seen by some as providing alternatives to the US system – allowed the neoliberals to push their agenda, that there existed no alternative to American-style free-market capitalism, even harder on the ground.

Of course, it would be wrong to describe the advance of neoliberalism in the developing world purely as an imposition from the outside. Neoliberal reforms in these countries had their local defenders from the beginning; over time their number has multiplied and their influence has increased. An increasing number of developing-country companies have carved out positions as subcontractors or intermediaries of transnational corporations (TNCs) based in the developed countries. Moreover, neoliberal reforms have created a vast army of a new professional class that derives a large part of its wealth and power from its ability to understand and articulate the idioms of neoliberalism. This does not simply include the 'usual suspects', such as fund managers, international lawyers, accountants and management consultants. It also includes those who are working for NGOs financed by the rich country governments and international financial institutions, journalists with foreign links, government officials with experience in the IFIs and, last but not least, academic economists.

Reflecting these developments in the international and national politics of money and power, neoliberalism has established a near-total worldwide intellectual dominance during the last 25 years. In political debate, critics of neoliberalism are routinely dismissed as 'economically illiterate' or worse, as those who are trying to defend their 'vested interests' to the detriment of society – even when they are, say, garment workers in Mexico resisting plant closure or urban poor in Indonesia protesting against cuts in food subsidies. In this way, serious debates are avoided and dissenters systematically excluded.

Even in academia, where one would expect a more open intellectual atmosphere, there has been a remarkable degree of intolerance of dissenting views. While the economics profession has been dominated by the neoclassical school since the early twentieth century, it was more tolerant of dissenting views before the rise of neoliberalism. During the 1920s, the birth of welfare economics (or the 'market failure' approach) showed that neoclassical economics need not be in favour of the free market. In the 1930s and 1940s, Keynesian economics and (initially very non-neoclassical) development economics were born, further challenging neoclassical dominance. In the 1960s and 1970s more radical approaches, such as post-Keynesian economics and the dependency theory, were developed, while there was a revival of Marxian economics. Until the 1970s, therefore, being an economist did not necessarily mean being a neoclassical economist; moreover, being a neoclassical economist did not necessarily mean being a supporter of free-market capitalism.

However, with the rise of neoliberalism, this has completely changed. Neoliberalism does also use neoclassical analytical tools, but in the service of a narrow-minded free-market agenda of a nineteenth-century vintage, and therefore has a much lower tolerance level for dissenting views.[2] Being an economist therefore came to mean being a neoclassical economist (heterodox economists are frequently dismissed as 'sociologists' – a term of abuse among today's neoclassical economists), which in turn is often equated with supporting free-market policies.

As a result, since the 1980s, all the major economics departments in the USA and the UK – which lead the economics profession – have almost completely stopped making the few non-orthodox appointments they used to make, by reasserting the sanctity of neoclassical methodology in defining what constitutes good research, and thereby classifying dissenting economists as incompetents, rather than as dissenters. The heterodox economists who still remain in academia have been increasingly marginalized, finding it more and more difficult to get promoted, acquire research grants, and get new research students (as they have lower prestige and smaller budgets to support the research students).

The academic rollback has been particularly vicious in development economics, as, unlike in other branches of economics, the very existence of the subject resulted from the questioning of the assumptions and methodologies of the dominant neoclassical tradition. The main elements of this rollback were as follows.

First, a series of arguments were developed to 'explain' how some apparently 'irrational' behaviours of economic agents in developing countries that do not fit neoclassical assumptions are really nothing more than rational attempts to maximize their wealth, given the particular risk profile they face. In this way, the crucial 'rational self-seeking' assumption of neoclassical economics was restored.[3]

Secondly, the so-called 'government failure' argument was deployed in order to denounce state intervention, even where the neoclassical logic of market failure dictates it.[4] The argument, typical in early development economics, that developing countries need more state intervention than do developed countries because their markets fail more dramatically and frequently, was neatly replaced by the argument that developing countries should have less state intervention than developed countries, because their governments fail more dramatically and frequently due to the weakness of their political institutions. In other words, state intervention in developing countries was cast as a cure that is worse than the disease.

Thirdly, a sea of ink was spilled in order to 'prove' empirically that countries which had followed neoliberal policies did well. Many studies 'found' positive statistical correlation (which then got deceptively equated with causation) between a country's growth rate, on the one hand, and its trade openness or the smallness of its government, on the other.[5] Many case studies also argued that the economic successes of the East Asian economies were due to their 'good' (for which read 'neoliberal') policies, while the economic failures of Latin America and Sub Saharan Africa should be blamed on 'bad' policies inspired by the non-neoclassical development economics of the 1960s and 1970s.[6]

Once the key propositions of non-neoclassical development economics were disposed of, it was a short step towards the assertion that development economics does not deserve a separate existence. The existence of development economics, based on different assumptions and methodologies than the ones used in the rest of economics, was denied on the grounds that economics is a universal 'science', with laws that apply across time and place. In this view, development economics is distinguished from other (more legitimate) branches of economics only by the fact that the data sources used happen to come from developing countries. As a result, an increasing number of economics departments, not just in the developed countries but also in some developing countries, are no longer offering development economics courses. Once you train students in the 'core' subjects of microeconomic, macroeconomics and econometrics, the argument goes, there is really no need to teach them separate development economics, as it is merely an application of the 'core' subjects to developing-country data sets.

Once development economics was redefined in this way, acquisition of knowledge of particular countries' economic structures, institutions, politics and socio-cultural factors that used to be regarded as a highly-valued – even essential – asset for development economists in the early days of the subject, was denounced as a waste of valuable training time.[7] Indeed, many of those who hold the 'economics-as-a-universal-science' view would go a step further and argue that the possession of detailed knowledge about a country is a sign of intellectual failure. In their view, it is a sign that the researcher has sought refugee in intellectually 'soft' areas like languages and other social sciences because he/she was incapable of dealing with the 'hard' logical concepts required of rigorous economic analysis.

In developing countries, the resurgence of neoclassical economics has been systematically helped by the intellectual and monetary influences of developed countries and IFIs. First of all, in many developing countries the reputation of a 'good' economist is determined largely by the recognition that he gets through publication in the 'top' journals published in the developed countries (mostly the USA), most of which have a very narrow view of economics – this tendency has been particularly accentuated following the loss of intellectual confidence following the last two decades of development crisis. Also, the vast consultancy budgets that IFIs have at their disposal enable them to influence the evolution of economics in developing countries. Given the pitiful level of academic remuneration, a World Bank or IMF consultancy can be worth a few years' academic salaries in most developing countries. This presents a stark choice to all but the most strong-willed or financially fortunate non-orthodox economists in developing countries. Unless they 'convert' and start taking up consultancy contracts from the IFIs, they are condemned to a life of poverty.

Despite the apparent total intellectual and political victory of neoliberalism, there has been an increasing dissatisfaction with it. During the last few years, politicians opposed to neoliberal reforms have won electoral victories in a number of countries – the best example being the victory of Ignacio 'Lula' da Silva in the Brazilian presidential election of 2002. In many countries, riots and armed revolts against neoliberal policies have erupted – the Chiapas revolt in Mexico being the most prominent and prolonged example of the latter. The IMF, the World Bank and the WTO cannot hold their meetings without heavy security arrangements that remind us of war zones. The World Social Forum in Porto Alegre is now drawing almost as much media attention as the World Economic Forum in Davos, as a counterpoint to which it was set up. The cracks in the neoliberal edifice have also appeared from within, as best exemplified by the recent 'defection' of Joseph Stiglitz, the former World Bank Chief Economist and an Economics Nobel Laureate, to the 'other side'.[8]

The most important reason behind the spreading revolt against neoliberalism is its miserable economic record, especially in the developing countries. It is not simply that economic growth during the last two decades of neoliberal global capitalism has come at the cost of growing inequality, intensified social tension, emasculation of democratic institutions,[9] environmental degradation and other 'social' problems, as many critics have pointed out. The more serious, although not as widely-discussed, problem is that the growth we have gained at such costs has been disappointingly low – not only low in comparison with some ideal standards, but in comparison with the growth in the previous interventionist period between the 1950s and 1970s, upon which pro-growth neoliberalism was supposed vastly to improve.

The popular impression, largely created by neoliberal propaganda, is that neoliberalism is a doctrine that is able to generate rapid growth, albeit often at the cost of worsening other 'social' problems. However, this cannot be further from the truth. Neoliberalism simply has not been able to generate rapid growth.[10]

Per capita income growth in the developed countries slowed from 3.2% to 2.2% between the interventionist period 1960–80 and the neoliberal period of 1980–99, while that in the developing countries halved from 3% to 1.5%[11] – and without the strong growth performance during the last two decades by China and India, two countries that have definitely *not* followed the neoliberal recipe, the 1.5% rate would have been close to 1%. Moreover, this average growth rate does not fully convey the magnitude of the development crisis that many developing countries have been experiencing during the last two decades. In this period, economic growth basically evaporated in Latin America, with the annual growth rate of per capita income crashing from 3.1% in the period 1960–80 to 0.6% between 1980 and 1999. The crisis has been even deeper in other regions. Per capita income has actually been shrinking in the Middle East and North Africa (at the annual rate of -0.2%) and in Sub Saharan Africa (at the annual rate of -0.7%) during the last two decades, whereas they grew at the rates of 2.5% and 2% respectively during 1960–80. Most former Communist countries have experienced arguably the fastest falls in living standards in modern history since the start of their transition to capitalism, with many of them not having yet recovered even half their per capita income level under Communism.[12] Development crises in many developing countries have reached a scale that is now threatening the basic fabric of their societies.

This is a particularly damning record for an economic doctrine that has prided itself in being single-mindedly focused on economic growth, on the grounds that 'we first have to generate wealth before we can redistribute it'. This fact has not been widely acknowledged; however, thanks to the efforts of some researchers, notably those who are associated with the Washington-based think-tank, the Center for Economic and Policy Research (CEPR),[13] it is increasingly recognized by more and more people that neoliberalism is not working even in the area where it is supposed to work best, namely, in the generation of economic growth.

While the continued failure of neoliberalism, especially in developing countries, is generating greater demands for alternatives to it in both theory and policy, the supply-side conditions are not favourable. As I have pointed out above, the political and intellectual dominance of neoliberalism during the last two decades have left the alternative camps badly depleted in terms of financial, institutional and human resources, particularly in the developing countries.

Today, there are only a few developing countries – such as Brazil, India and Turkey – where heterodox development economics, or for that matter heterodox economics of any kind, has a significant presence. In other countries, heterodox economists are few in number and isolated. The prospect for the future is even bleaker. Few young economists are exposed to heterodox approaches during their training and thus are denied the chance to choose between alternative approaches with full knowledge of their relative intellectual merits. This means that they are made to adopt the orthodox approach even when they are not very happy with it, in the belief that there is no alternative to what they learn.

It is to make a contribution to changing this deplorable state of affairs that I took the initiative of organizing the Cambridge Advanced Programme on Rethinking Development Economics (CAPORDE), in which the lectures forming the basis of the chapters in this volume were delivered in 2001 and 2002. The workshop, made possible by generous financial support from the Ford Foundation and kindly hosted by the Development Studies Committee of the University of Cambridge, was intended to educate a new generation of independent-minded development economists with critical minds. Each year about 25 young economists (including some non-economists with a strong economics background) are invited from developing countries to attend around two dozen lectures by leading heterodox development economists. The lectures were originally pitched at the advanced graduate level; the chapters in this volume have been written in a more accessible manner than the lectures themselves, so they can be used for lower-level graduate, and advanced undergraduate level, courses.

For the convenience of readers, the chapters in the volume have been organized into seven parts covering different themes, each made up of three to four chapters.

Part I contains chapters that provide overviews of the main issues in development economics, such as the meaning of development, globalization and the role of the state, the market and institutions in economic development. While not short on details and finer logical points, overall these chapters are of a 'broad-brushstroke' nature, and provide theoretical and historical backgrounds for the discussions in subsequent chapters.

In chapter 1, 'Changing Perspectives in Development Economics', John Toye provides a highly erudite and lucid account of the history of development economics. After discussing the influence of Keynesianism in the birth of development economics, Toye discusses the main themes of early development economics – the Lewis model, development planning and project appraisal – and their critics. He then reviews the debates surrounding trade policy and 'government failure' that led to the rise of neoliberalism. This is followed by a discussion of how the failures of neoliberal structural adjustment programmes, and increasing recognition of the importance of institutional factors in economic development, are challenging the neoliberal orthodoxy. Toye concludes his chapter by pointing out that, despite the neoliberal contention to the contrary, the role of the state in economic development remains critical (and can be positive), and therefore that we need a more balanced and sophisticated 'political economy' than that offered by neoliberalism.

In chapter 2, 'The Market, the State and Institutions in Economic Development', Ha-Joon Chang starts his discussion with a highly unconventional interpretation of the history of capitalism. He argues that, contrary to the conventional wisdom, state intervention has played a critical role in the development of all of today's developed economies, including in particular the allegedly free-market, free-trade economies of the UK and the USA. Chang then critically reviews the dominant neoliberal theory of the market, the state and institutions, revealing some of its fundamental conceptual shortcomings. On the basis of this critical review, and partially in response to Toye's call for a 'better' political economy in chapter 2, Chang proposes an 'institutionalist political economy' that he believes can overcome the serious shortcomings of neoliberal theories and allows us to have a more balanced and realistic understanding of the state, the market and institutions.

In chapter 3, 'Globalization and Development', Deepak Nayyar provides an overview of globalization that is profound in its historical and theoretical insights and that contains a wealth of useful information. After an examination of the evolution of thinking on development over the last half century, Nayyar carefully documents the characteristics of globalization and the forces behind it during the last 25 years. He then puts the recent episode of globalization into historical perspective by comparing it with the earlier episode of the late nineteenth century. This is followed by a discussion of the consequences of recent globalization, especially the marginalization and exclusion of a large number of countries and of people. The chapter concludes by discussing how national strategies and global governance mechanisms can be restructured in order to promote more inclusive development.

In chapter 4, 'Development and the Global Order', Jose Antonio Ocampo offers a comprehensive and powerful critique, at both national and global levels, of the dominant neoliberal policy agenda, and comes up with innovative and measured alternatives. Ocampo starts his discussion by examining the state of international disparities and the critical influence of the global economic hierarchy on them. He then examines how the current global order is characterized by a number of asymmetries that hamper the progress of the developing countries, and proposes that it is necessary to change these through a reform of global governance. He then argues that at the national level a broader conception of macroeconomic stability, a better productive development strategy and improved social linkages are needed to promote development. He concludes his chapter by arguing how a broader conception of development and a dose of humility in advancing it are needed.

Part II comprises chapters that discuss the development experiences of the main developing regions of the world – East Asia, Latin America, Africa and the transition economies. This part provides empirical backdrops to the later 'thematic' chapters which inevitably have to rely on certain 'stylized facts' about the development experiences of different regions of the developing world.

In chapter 5, 'The East Asian Development Experience', Ha-Joon Chang considers the development experience of East Asia, which has witnessed the fastest economic and social transformations in human history over the last few decades, and thus has naturally generated some of the most heated debates in development economics. After discussing some definitional issues and the comparative performance of the region, Chang critically examines various debates surrounding the East Asian 'miracle'. He then looks at a set of very different (but related) debates generated by the recent economic troubles in the region, that is, the Japanese stagnation and the 1997 financial crisis in Korea, Hong Kong and South East Asia. The chapter concludes by critically reexamining the issue of 'replicability' of the East Asian experience in other developing countries with different political, social and cultural conditions.

In chapter 6, 'The Latin American Economies during the Second Half of the Twentieth Century – from the Age of "ISI" to the Age of "The End of History"', Gabriel Palma provides a fertile and sophisticated discussion of the developing region with the most dramatic developmental history. After putting the Latin American experience into historical and comparative perspectives, Palma defines the 1980s as the watershed in Latin American history, where the continent 'threw in the towel' and made a headlong dash to implement the neoliberal model with the zeal of a convert. He then examines the history of the region between the 1950s and 1970s, a period preceding this dramatic conversion, and critically assesses the region's record under neoliberalism. Palma concludes the chapter by discussing two endogenous factors that he believes to have hampered the region's development, namely, what he calls 'manic-depressive ideological cycles', and the unproductive nature of the capitalist elite.

In chapter 7, 'Rethinking African Development', Howard Stein considers the experience of Africa, a continent that has been mired in a developmental crisis during the last two decades, in a way that combines detailed factual knowledge with a sophisticated theoretical understanding. After reviewing the quantitative evidence on the continent's developmental crisis, Stein focuses on what he believes to be the most fundamental problem behind it, namely, the nature of the African states. After criticizing various orthodox views on the role of the state in Africa, Stein provides an alternative theoretical formulation that allows us to understand the African experience from a completely new and more convincing angle. The last two sections of the chapter critically examine the failures of the orthodox strategy in developing African agriculture and industry, and outline alternative policy proposals.

In chapter 8, 'Transition Economies', Michael Ellman takes an authoritative look at the experience of the transition economies. Unlike most other 'transition experts', Ellman is an authority on the Communist era and his analysis is therefore based on deep historical and institutional knowledge of the countries in question. After presenting a concise and informative review of the overall transition experience, he devotes most of the chapter to the experience of Russia, which is, in his words, 'the largest, most populous, most heavily armed, and most politically important, of the successor states of the former Soviet Union and the former Eastern Europe'. After reviewing the process of transition in Russia under Yeltsin in some detail, Ellman provides a fascinating discussion of the role of western economic advice in the Russian transition process, where the combination of international power politics, ideological prejudice, poor economic analysis and even personal greed led to advice which has been largely, if not entirely, negative for Russia.

Part III deals with structural and sectoral issues, which used to be at the foundation of early development economics but which have more recently been neglected or, even worse, reinterpreted in order to fit the orthodox framework.

In chapter 9, 'New Growth Theory', Ben Fine offers a devastating critique of the so-called new growth theory, which has emerged as the central plank of mainstream development economics during the last decade or so. After examining the basic theoretical premises of the old growth theory, which new growth theory is supposed to have enhanced, Fine discusses the theoretical and empirical limitations of new growth theory. The final part of the chapter places the critique in a broader perspective by examining the political and ideological contexts in which new growth theory emerged. Fine concludes his chapter by outlining an alternative approach to the study of economic growth and development that focuses upon history- and country-specific social relations, structures and processes.

In chapter 10, 'Structural Change and Development: The Relative Roles of Effective Demand and the Price Mechanism in a "Dual" Economy', Amit Bhaduri revisits one of the key issues in early development economics, namely, the role of intersectoral relationship between agriculture and industry in economic development. Bhaduri combines the Lewis model based on classical concepts with post-Keyneisan insights (of Kaldor and Kalecki) and develops a deceptively simple but highly sophisticated model of structural change. He then uses this model to explain a key modern paradox, namely, the fact that the Green Revolution has not solved the problem of widespread under-nutrition (and starvation), while increasing the inventories of food grains in government storage. Bhaduri argues that this was because the Green Revolution has not been complemented by policies to guarantee the expansion of domestic industries at a pace rapid enough to absorb the additional agricultural surplus that it generates.

In chapter 11, 'Agriculture and Development: The Dominant Orthodoxy and an Alternative View', Terry Byres offers a trenchant criticism, from a Marxist perspective, of the mainstream view on the issue of agriculture and development. After providing a brief but lucid review of the debates on some agrarian issues that led to the demise of what he calls the 'old' neoclassical economics and the rise of the 'new' neoclassical economics – surplus labour, relative price movements, rural interest rates and sharecropping – Byres critically examines the main tenets of today's orthodoxy in the area of agriculture and development. He then criticizes the orthodox position on the key issues in the area – such as the homogeneity of peasantry, the power relationship underlying production and exchange relationships, the causes of agrarian backwardness, and the role of the state in agricultural development – and offers alternative theoretical interpretations and policy recommendations.

Part IV discusses trade, industry and technology issues. These are issues that have arguably generated the most heated controversies in development economics during the last few decades, and are continuously generating new ones, especially following the establishment of the WTO and the dramatic global restructuring of many industries.

In chapter 12, 'Trade and Industrial Policy Issues', Ha-Joon Chang looks at a number of key trade and industrial policy issues. After critically reviewing two 'older' debates in the area, namely, the debates on trade policy orientation and on (selective) industrial policy, Chang looks at some of the 'newer' issues in the area. These include the debate on foreign direct investment (FDI) in the context of globalization, the implications of the new world trading order instituted through the WTO, and the trade-related intellectual property rights (TRIPS) agreement of the WTO. Whether they deal with 'older' or 'newer' issues, all sections of the chapter provide a critical discussion of the theories and stylized facts underlying the orthodox positions, and shed some new theoretical and empirical lights on the issues with which they deal.

In chapter 13, 'Technology and Industrial Development in an Era of Globalization', Sanjaya Lall offers a fascinating discussion of how the recent changes in technology, liberalization of economic policy and the spread of globalized production systems are creating new opportunities and challenges for industrial development in developing countries. After providing an overview of the newly-emerging global technological and industrial land-scape, Lall provides a comprehensive and highly knowledgeable discussion of the main structural determinants of technological development in developing countries. He then shows how his approach, which focuses on technological capability, enables us to understand the conditions for successful trade and industrial policies in developing countries. He concludes the chapter by point-ing out the limits to the 'passive' industrial policy that is preferred by the architects of the current global order, and then argues for a new global frame-work that will facilitate more 'active' trade and industrial policies in develop-ing countries, aimed at building more advanced technological capabilities.

In chapter 14, 'Industrial Policy in the Early Twenty-first Century: The Challenge of the Global Business Revolution', Peter Nolan challenges us with his bold and eye-opening analysis of what he calls the 'global business revolu-tion'. Nolan argues that during the 1990s a number of factors – especially neoliberal policy reforms, the collapse of Communism and technological changes – have created a new business landscape. Firms of unprecedented scale – and thus spending power – on brand-building and R&D have been created across industries, particularly (although not solely) through mergers and acquisitions. In this way, Nolan argues, it has become very unlikely that developing country governments can nurture national firms that can challenge the currently dominant firms based in the developed countries, particularly in the USA. Nolan concludes his chapter by calling for a more strategic and pragmatic approach on the part of the developing countries in deciding to what extent to fight the global giants, and how much to accept their dominance and try to become junior partners with them.

Part V discusses the issues of finance and corporate governance. These are issues that have attracted particular attention in recent years, in light of the eruption of some major financial crises – those of East and South East Asia, Russia, Brazil and Argentina – and the consequent attempts to restructure global and national systems of finance and corporate governance.

In chapter 15, 'International Private Capital Flows and Developing Countries', Ilene Grabel looks at the uncontrolled surge of international private capital flows, which in her view were behind the recent financial crises, and comes up with an innovative but realistic set of proposals to control them in a way that enhances economic stability and promotes development. After discussing some definitional issues and main empirical trends, Grabel critically compares orthodox and heterodox views on the benefits and costs of these flows. She then presents a number of policy measures that can be used in order to control these flows in a way that promotes stability and development. These measures include what she calls 'trip wires and speed bumps' (the introduction of graduated capital control when the risk factors rise above certain thresholds), the 'Chilean' model (centred around a compulsory deposit system that penalizes short-term flows) and restrictions on currency convertibility. She concludes the chapter by calling for more development-friendly international and national financial architectures.

In chapter 16, 'The "Three Routes" to Financial Crises: Chile, Mexico and Argentina [1]; Brazil [2]; and Korea, Malaysia and Thailand [3]', Gabriel Palma offers an innovative and informative comparative analysis of major financial crises in the developing world during the neoliberal era. Through a careful quantitative analysis, supplemented by detailed knowledge of the international financial market and the countries in question, Palma identifies three different routes to financial crisis that followed capital market opening and liberalization in a number of developing countries – Mexico (1988–94), Brazil (1994–9) and Korea (1988–97) respectively constituting the archetypal case of each route. According to Palma, the comparison between these three routes shows that the surge of capital inflow following capital market opening almost inevitably leads to a financial crisis sooner or later, regardless of the policy measures that are adopted to deal with the surge. In his view, this suggests that the developing countries should avoid opening up their capital markets.

In chapter 17, 'The New International Financial Architecture, Corporate Governance and Competition in Emerging Markets: New Issues for Developing Countries', Ajit Singh provides path-breaking analyses of the issues of corporate governance and competition policy – issues which have risen to the top of international policy agenda following the Asian crisis. After briefly summarizing the mainstream view, which blames the 1997 Asian crisis and various economic problems of the more advanced developing countries (typically known as 'emerging markets') on their pathological corporate governance system and the lack of competition in their product markets, Singh sets out to demolish it through his razor-sharp theoretical criticism and on the basis of his pioneering empirical works. In the process he shows that, contrary to the conventional wisdom, emerging market corporations are more exposed to the disciplines of the stock market and of the product market than are their developed country counterparts, thereby exposing some fundamental problems with the mainstream recommendation for a stock-market-based corporate governance system and a US-style competition policy.

Part VI explores the issues of poverty and inequality. These issues have of course been at the centre of development economics from the very beginning, but they have recently attracted even more attention, as people are beginning to assess the results of neoliberal reforms that appear to have had a particularly bad impact on them.

In chapter 18, 'Rural Poverty and Gender: Analytical Frameworks and Policy Proposals', John Sender offers a very powerful criticism of the orthodox view on poverty in developing countries. Sender shows that the mainstream programme for poverty alleviation is designed on the premise that most poor people in developing countries belong to a homogeneous group of self-employed small farmers, especially female-headed households. Given this, a strengthening of price incentives and an improvement in the access to producer inputs (especially producer credits) are seen as the key policy measures to alleviate poverty. However, Sender points out, this characterization is fundamentally flawed, as the poorest people are in fact female casual-wage labourers, and not self-employed farmers (female or not). He argues therefore that a more effective poverty reduction programme should target them. In particular, he recommends stabilization of basic food grain prices (given that the poorest are, being wage-earners, net buyers of food) and investment in irrigation (as this allows multiple cropping and thus increases demand for hired labour).

In chapter 19, 'Globalization and the Distribution of Income between and within Countries', Andrea Cornia provides a sophisticated and highly knowledgeable discussion of this contentious issue. After carefully reviewing the existing empirical studies, Cornia concludes that, during the last two decades of neoliberalism, between-country inequality has continued to grow, though much less rapidly than before. He also finds that within-country inequality rose in two thirds of the 73 countries reviewed, contradicting the orthodox view that it has remained stable throughout the post-World War II period. He then points out that much of this rising within-country inequality owes to the nature of the neoliberal reform programme. Of the policies that make up this programme, the negative distributive impact is particularly strong in the case of capital account opening, followed by domestic financial liberalization, labour market deregulation and tax reform. The distributional impacts of privatization and trade liberalization turn out to be more context-dependent. Cornia concludes his chapter by calling for measures to correct the negative distributional impacts of neoliberal policies.

In chapter 20, 'Increasing Poverty in a Globalized World: *Marshall Plans* and *Morgenthau Plans* as Mechanisms of Polarization of World Incomes', Erik Reinert looks at the issue of poverty from a rather unconventional angle, namely, that of national productive development. Likening the neoliberal reform programme to the Morgenthau Plan, which attempted a forced deindustrialization of Germany after the Second World War, Reinert argues that, in the same way that the Marshall Plan that replaced the Morgenthau Plan, poverty should be alleviated by helping the developing countries develop their productive capabilities. He argues that orthodox economics fails to see the difference between economic activities (especially in terms of productivity growth potential) and therefore treats all forms of productive specialization as equally good, when in reality the type of economic activity in which a country specializes is critical in determining its wealth and poverty. Reinert concludes his chapter by calling for a total recasting of the anti-poverty agenda through the revival of the 'productivist' tradition in economic theory – or what he calls the 'Other Canon'.

The final part, Part VII, looks at the issues of institutions and governance. These are issues to which the orthodox economists, previously dismissing them as mere details, have increasingly had to pay attention, as they have had to come up with an explanation as to why their programme has failed to deliver for so long. Many orthodox economists have started arguing that their policies failed not because they were wrong but because the developing countries implementing them did not have the 'right' institutions. Critics naturally point out that a sensible policy recommendation should have already taken this fact into account. This development has made institutions the new battleground in development economics.

In chapter 21, 'On Understanding Market as Social and Political Institutions in Developing Economies', Barbara Harriss-White provides a concise but penetrating review of the main theories of institutions. Harriss-White critically examines four main theories of institution, namely, the New Institutional Economics (NIE), economic sociology, the literature on the 'politics of market', and the social system of accumulation (SSA) school. All of these approaches, she points out, have inevitable limitations in that they privilege certain institutions at the expense of others. However, she finds that the NIE, which is today's orthodox theory of institutions, particularly wanting on a number of grounds: its failure to see markets as bundles of institutions which are also nested in other institutions; its inability to address the question of power and authority; and its detachment from historical and locational specificities. She concludes the chapter by arguing that markets are complex social and political constructs whose proper understanding requires inter-disciplinary work that takes into account political and social ideologies as well as 'material' conditions.

In chapter 22, 'Institutions and Economic Development in Historical Perspective', Ha-Joon Chang critically examines today's orthodox agenda for institutional reform in the developing countries from an unusual angle, the historical perspective. Criticizing the unrealistic nature of the orthodox agenda, which wants the developing countries to adopt 'global standard' institutions with a very short (5–10 year) transition period, Chang sets out to find out how today's developed countries *actually* developed their own institutions in the past. He shows that all the institutions regarded by orthodox economists as essential components of a 'good governance' structure are in fact products of lengthy processes of institutional development involving political struggles, ideological battles and legal reforms. He argues that, while institutional copying is often possible and desirable, institutions are not things that can be easily copied by every country regardless of its conditions. He concludes the chapter by calling for a complete rethinking of the so-called 'good governance' agenda.

In chapter 23, 'Globalization, Global Governance and the Dilemmas of Development', Martin Khor looks at the issue of global governance. This chapter provides a unique combination of academic sophistication and practical knowledge, as Khor, a former academic economist, is one of the world's leading NGO activists. After critically reviewing the record of recent globalization, Khor discusses why the developing countries need to integrate into the world economy selectively, rather than unconditionally, as the mainstream economists argue. He argues that, given the weak position of the developing countries in the global political-economic system, this need cannot be fulfilled without changing the current system of global governance dominated by the 'trinity' of the IMF, the World Bank and the WTO, as this system constrains national economic management by the developing countries in a way that hampers their development. Khor concludes the chapter by presenting some innovative and pragmatic proposals for the reform of the global governance system.

As should be clear from the above summaries, the chapters in this volume do not toe a single 'party line'. They are informed by a number of different approaches – institutionalist, structuralist, post-Keynesian, Marxist and others. They are influenced by, and cross over into, a number of related social sciences – political science, sociology and anthropology, among others. And their policy recommendations, while sharing substantial common ground, differ from each other in their details and nuances. However, this diversity is a strength, rather than a weakness, in a subject which has been characterized by a worrying degree of intellectual intolerance over the last quarter of a century.

Together, the chapters in this volume provide a set of powerful theoretical and empirical critiques of neoliberal development economics and show that, contrary to popular belief, there *do* exist sophisticated and balanced theoretical alternatives to the neoliberal orthodoxy. I hope that this volume convinces other researchers, especially young economists from developing countries, that it is necessary and possible to end the intellectual dominance of neoliberalism, and stimulates them into further advancing the ideas and visions that it sets out.

Notes

1 Of course, the reality was much more complex than this. For example, there may have been relatively few fully state-owned enterprises during the liberal period, but many governments invested in and subsidized enterprises in key industries, especially in infrastructure. To cite another example, it may be true that international trade was freer during the liberal period than it is today, but there were exceptions like the USA, which had an average manufacturing tariff rate of 45–55% during the period. More importantly, during this period most of the poorer economies were practising free trade only because they were forced into it by colonialism and unequal treaties. See this volume, chapter 2 (Chang), and for further details, see Chang 2002b, chapter 2. It should also be noted that the world economy performed much more poorly during the liberal period than during the *real* 'golden age' of capitalism, which was in fact the height of regulated capitalism (1950–73). The world economy grew at around 1–1.5% during the liberal golden age, whereas it grew at more than 3% during the 'real' golden age.

2 On the exact relationship between neoliberalism and neoclassical economics, see this volume, chapter 2 (Chang) and Chang 2002c. On the rise and fall of different schools of economic thought during the twentieth century, see Chang 2003, chapter 1.

3 See this volume, chapters 11 (Byres) and 18 (Sender).

4 See this volume, chapters 1 (Toye) and 2 (Chang).

5 See this volume, chapters 1 (Toye) and 12 (Chang).

6 See chapters 5 (Chang), 6 (Palma) and 7 (Stein).

7 This kind of view is well reflected in the practice of the IMF and the World Bank of usually making their new employees with PhDs work on countries and issues that are *not* related to their thesis topics on the grounds that a well-trained economist can work on any problem.

8 For a fuller discussion of the events leading to, and the controversies surrounding, Stiglitz's 'defection', see Chang 2001; 2002a.

9 This has happened because the neoliberals recommend that we create politically independent policymaking bodies, such as independent central banks or independent

competition commissions, in order to take power away from corrupt politicians and
self-seeking bureaucrats. See this volume, chapter 2 (Chang) for a critique of this view.

10 There are good reasons for it. Most importantly, it creates high economic instability
(which discourages long-term investment), promotes speculative activities (which drain
talents from more productive activities), encourages luxury consumption (which can
drain away investible surplus), and intensifies social tension (which discourages social
cohesion and diverts resources into anti-criminal expenditure).

11 The data in this paragraph are from the World Bank data sources, as cited in Chang
2002 (table 4.2 and 4.3). Also see Weisbrot et al. 2000, which draws the same picture
with a different data set.

12 For criticisms of the transition experiences, see this volume, chapter 8 (Ellman); Stiglitz
(2001).

13 Various papers discussing this point can be found at the Center's website,
www.cepr.net.

References

Chang, H-J, 2001, 'Introduction' in H-J Chang, ed., *The Rebel Within: Joseph Stiglitz and the
World Bank*, London, Anthem Press.

——, 2002a, 'The Rebel Within: Joseph Stiglitz, the World Bank, and the Nobel Prize',
Challenge, 2002, vol. 45, no. 2.

——, 2002b, *Kicking Away the Ladder: Development Strategy in Historical Perspective*, London,
Anthem Press.

——, 2002c, 'Breaking the Mould: An Institutionalist Political Economy Alternative to the
Neo-liberal Theory of the Market and the State', *Cambridge Journal of Economics*, vol. 26,
no. 5.

——, 2003, *Globalization, Economic Development and the Role of the State*, London, Zed Books,
and Penang, Third World Network.

Stiglitz, J, 2001, 'Whither Reform? – Ten Years of the Transition' in H-J Chang, ed., *The
Rebel Within: Joseph Stiglitz and the World Bank*, London, Anthem Press.

Weisbrot, M, Naiman, R and Kim, J, 2000, 'The Emperor Has No Growth: Declining
Economic Growth Rates in the Era of Globalisation', Briefing Paper, September 2000,
Washington, DC, Center for Economic and Policy Research.

PART I

OVERVIEWS

1

CHANGING PERSPECTIVES IN DEVELOPMENT ECONOMICS

John Toye

1. The early Keynesian influences

The objective of this chapter is to convey a sense of the major changes of perspective that the study of economic development has undergone since the Second World War. This is a useful preliminary to locating areas for fruitful new research. Of particular interest are the changes in the ways in which development economists have envisaged the link between the economics of development and politics.[1] Identifying major shifts is necessarily to some extent a personal judgement, and the changes in perspective noted here are changes relative to the path through the economics of development that I have trodden. Those following a different path would have seen perspectives shifting somewhat differently, although, one hopes, not entirely differently.

It was the war-torn decade of the 1940s that saw development economics emerge as a sub-discipline of academic economics, although there had been many anticipations.[2] This new sub-discipline was distinguished, above all, by its exploration of the problem of government-engineered economic transformation. Therefore, the study of economic development did not primarily focus on how economic development had occurred previously. Although Simon Kuznets and others later produced much valuable statistical work on past patterns of development this was a subordinate endeavour.[3] The key assumption behind the new economics of development was that governments needed guidance from economists on how to make economic development happen differently – and, especially, faster – in the future.

At that time, the Western liberal democracies shared a consensus that the economic world should not or could not continue to go on as it had in the 1930s. The harsh experience of the Great Depression and the failure to prevent the recurrence of world war had persuaded American and European electorates that a new start had to be made. The better postwar world was to include the operation of a new set of multilateral international economic institutions within the United Nations that would promote both prosperity and peace. The world, however, was still a very unequal place. Any hope that their colonial masters would lead poorer countries to greater prosperity flickered and died, as the rise of the US to global power called time on European as well as Japanese colonialism. Newly-independent countries in Asia, and later Africa, would soon join Latin America in the search for how to conjure up security and prosperity for themselves.

The inequality of world income tended to be seen as a reflection of the division between rich industrial and poor agricultural countries, brushing aside the anomalies of the likes of Australia, New Zealand, Argentina and Denmark. In the 1930s it seemed perfectly obvious to most people that the route to greater prosperity was to embark on industrialization. Stalin's drive for heavy industry appeared to be transforming the economy of old Russia. Meanwhile, the prices of primary products exports had crashed in the Depression, leaving Latin Americans either to learn to make manufactures or do without. Moreover, modernity was generally identified with industrialization, which, for that reason, was sometimes even advocated, not as a means to development, but as a national objective in its own right.

The poor agricultural economies had few economists and little economic expertise of their own. Foreigners, knowledgeable in the new Keynesian theory of the aggregate economy, initiated thinking about how economic policy might transform poor agricultural countries. The Keynesian revolution had shown why governments no longer needed to tolerate the scourge of involuntary unemployment. Paul Rosenstein-Rodan argued that a significant share of the labour force in the poor agricultural economies of East and South East Europe was in a state of 'disguised unemployment'.[4] This meant that they were in low productivity occupations that added little to either aggregate output or aggregate demand.

If world income inequality were to be reduced, this agrarian excess population either had to migrate to find capital to work with (an option not favoured), or capital had to be brought in to create more productive and better paid occupations – through industrialization. In this context, Rosenstein-Rodan made the point for which he is best remembered: that the industrial investment should be large, but diversified across a wide range of labour-intensive light-wage goods industries, so as to generate an increased supply that was well matched to the additional demand created by the investment.[5] The induced growth, through higher real wages in industry, would then decrease poverty.

Industrialization in this mode was something new. It was not driven by technical progress, but was an attempt to apply existing technology in the 'international depressed areas'. It depended on the engineering of complementary demand, and would therefore not happen – or would not happen anything like as quickly – if left to private sector initiatives. It had to be planned by the state, and partly funded from international sources. It provided a regional solution that did not rely on other parts of the international trade system absorbing the new output, in order to avoid disrupting the broader international division of labour. Here was a way to engineer 'a quick forward advance' in industrialization,[6] a method that is quite correctly described as *dirigiste* in conception.

In Latin America, however, industrialization was already well in train. The contribution of Raul Prebisch and the economists of the UN Economic Commission for Latin America in the 1950s was not, as many seem to believe, to advocate import-substituting industrialization as the path to economic development. While affirming that it was necessary to industrialize, given Hans Singer's discovery of the declining tendency in the terms of trade of primary producers,[7] Prebisch was more concerned with the limits of import-substituting industrialization. The creation of artificial industries by tariff protection was a much-discussed problem, and Prebisch needed no. persuasion that the actual tariff structures of Latin American governments were excessive and chaotic. The purpose of ECLA was never to endorse the existing protective schemes that national governments had adopted. Rather, it was to encourage them to construct a regional free-trade area to allow the development of a range of complementary light industries on a continent-wide basis.

2. The Lewis model and its critics

Apart from regional economic commissions like ECLA, the central economic organs of the UN took up the issue of international measures to maintain full employment and combat the spread of depression. Underdeveloped countries (to use the label of the day) felt excluded from the industrial countries' concern with how best to maintain full employment, which was something that they had never had. They sought UN action to overcome underemployment in underdeveloped countries.

W Arthur Lewis was the main inspiration for the subsequent UN report on *Measures for the Economic Development of Under-developed countries* (1951). The report does not discuss underemployment as such, but simply asserts that it will disappear once the process of economic development gathers pace. Lewis spelled out the political, institutional and social preconditions of economic development at some length. He stressed that the political leadership of the country in question must be committed to a strategy for development, rather than seeking the entrenchment of its own privileges. He did not assume that all governments are benevolent, far from it. Nor did he assume that the government alone must be the agent of development: the capitalists who do the job may be either public officials or private entrepreneurs.

The report, like the subsequent major works of Lewis,[8] does however make three economic assumptions, which are adopted from Rosenstein–Rodan. The first is that underdeveloped countries can draw on an ever-increasing stock of technologies for the purpose of catching up with other countries. The second is that the marginal productivity of capital must be higher in underdeveloped countries because of its scarcity relative to labour. The third is that gross underemployment of labour provides an opportunity to bring low-cost labour and additional capital together to produce labour-intensive manufactures.

These three assumptions underpin Lewis's model of economic development. It is a classical model of capitalist accumulation in the long run, which harks back to an older political economy. 'Excess agrarian population' becomes 'surplus labour', to be transferred progressively into industrial employment. It is assumed that this transfer can take place without any increase in the industrial real wage, and without any diminution of agricultural production. The transfer continues as long as any surplus labour remains in the agricultural sector, because the industry wage rate maintains a fixed premium over the rural wage, and the capitalists in the industrial sector reinvest their profits, thereby expanding both their demand for labour and their output.

During the transfer process, the share of industry in national output, the share of profits in national income and the share of savings and investment in national expenditure all rise markedly. The increasing profit share implies a rise in income inequality, even though a rising percentage of the labour force is in industrial occupations with higher average earnings. These changes to the structure of the economy come to an end as the real wage in industry begins to rise, and an increasing labour share of output reduces the incentive for the reinvestment of capital in industry. Income inequality now begins to decrease, consistently with the U-curve hypothesis of Kuznets.

During the 1960s, there was much work in development economics on this model of economic development, as its assumptions were explored and tested. Three lines of criticism produced major areas of new research activity. One reaction to the Lewis model was to question the link between capital investment and economic growth, which was mechanically derived from a fixed incremental capital/output ratio. If extra physical capital and extra standard labour generated extra output in this way, what was the function in economic development of the improvement of labour skills? Was not the improvement of human resources the central means, if not also the end, of economic development?

For Rosenstein-Rodan, the 'skilling' of labour was the first task of industrialization, but one that had to be undertaken by the state, because it does not pay firms to train potentially mobile workers. By contrast, TW Schultz raised the question of individuals' and families' own investments in what he called human capital – a stock of skills that could be used be deployed to earn future income.[9] This question led to a host of studies on the economics of investing in education and health in poor countries, and on the effects of health and education status on participation in the labour market. One important result has been to identify female education as a key policy variable in social and economic development.

Another element of the Lewis model that was queried was the dynamics of rural–urban migration. Harris and Todaro argued that the rural–urban differential in the real wage would generate an excess supply of job seekers migrating to towns in search of urban employment: the greater the wage differential, the more migrant job seekers there would be, and the lower the probability of securing an urban job.[10] Here was a neat explanation of the obvious phenomenon of urban unemployment in developing countries, but the explanation made all sorts of assumptions – for example, that the recruitment of industrial labour gangs does not take place in the rural areas – and these needed to be investigated in turn. Migration studies have since shown what a complex affair migration is, involving families and their income strategies rather than lone individuals, motivated by push factors as well as the pull of the rural–urban wage gap, and generating sophisticated schemes of urban–rural and foreign remittances.

Perhaps the most important reaction was to begin to correct the negative view of agriculture that was implicit in the Lewis model, and of which Bauer complained in an early review.[11] Why should agriculture be viewed only as a sector from which resources were to be drained? Why should agricultural investment and improvement not be a starting point of economic growth? Was it not both inefficient and inequitable to pour more resources into the sector that was already relatively well endowed with them?[12] Interest in the mechanics of peasant agriculture greatly intensified. Some doubted the existence of rural surplus labour, in the strict sense of its having zero marginal product. Others asked why peasants who did not migrate and whose incomes rose did not consume more food, thus reducing the marketed surplus and improving the rural–urban terms of trade.

Agricultural stagnation ceased to be a plausible assumption with the arrival of the new seed-fertilizer-irrigation technology in the early 1960s. Gauging the results of the Green Revolution caused much controversy, but it also stimulated the better study of rural institutions (share-cropping, interlocking markets), which in turn pointed to the importance of accounting for transaction costs in economic models.[13]

3. Practical applications: planning and project appraisal

Development economics had been conceived as a policy science. It was intended to furnish both the governments of poor countries and international economic organizations with tools of economic transformation. The practical problem was how to go beyond the development plans of colonialism, which were incoherent lists of possible investment projects. Newly-independent governments hired development economists to write plans, and they often worked out new planning methods on site and in the heat of the moment. They were the product of direct experience, and only later were they written up for the purpose of academic study.

New techniques were borrowed from the armoury of macroeconomics that economists in industrial countries had developed in the wake of the Keynesian revolution. In particular, a framework for development planning was provided by the system of national accounts that linked together the sources and uses of the aggregate product, investment and saving, the government budget and the balance of payments. A complementary tool was the inter-industry input–output table, by which the intermediate demands arising in the course of economic growth could be projected. Used in conjunction, the national accounts and the input–output table allowed planners to calculate in a consistent way the implications of a given rate of growth for the composition of both final demand and inter-industry demand.

Consistency is a minimum requirement of good planning: the skill in it is to identify correctly the constraints that will bind in the course of growth, and to judge the maximum feasible rate of growth that the country concerned can achieve. This calls for sensitivity to economic facts, such as the elasticity of the food supply and latent inflationary pressures, but more importantly to political facts, such as the goals of leaders and popular expectations. On both scores, the practice of planning tended to come unstuck. In the frequent absence of reliable economic statistics, practice tended towards planning without facts, not least in Africa.[14] Political leaders' desire to comply with the wishes of foreign aid agencies and local public opinion led to the making of some plans that the leaders concerned had no serious intention of implementing.[15] Economically-primitive planning models could not be made operational in the political contexts in which they were being applied.

Making a sensible macroeconomic plan could indicate the appropriate amount of investment in aggregate, but it did not bring coherence to the list of investment projects. For this to be achieved, what was needed was a technique that would rank projects in order of their economic desirability, so that they could be adopted in rank order until the investment budget was exhausted. Previously, development economists had argued the merits of different criteria for deciding on project investment – the degree of capital intensity, the rate of reinvestment, the size of the externalities and so on. The integration of these various investment criteria within a single procedure of appraisal of net present value was the work of Little and Mirrlees.[16]

A major issue of project appraisal was to measure the true cost of transferring a marginal unit of rural labour to urban employment, rather than assuming (with Lewis) that the transfer was costless. At the same time, however, it became clear that the valuation of a project's non-labour inputs and outputs also posed difficult problems, as a result of the interventions by governments that affected price formation in developing countries. If many and complex, these interventions made deviations from market-clearing prices hard to identify. Deviations were referred to as price distortions, but the idea of a price distortion made sense only relative to some standard of undistorted prices. Little and Mirrlees proposed 'world prices' as their 'sheet anchor', though not without meeting some scepticism. The use of world prices as a norm marked a significant shift in economic thinking about development, even though in practice the social cost-benefit appraisal techniques were scarcely more successful than macroeconomic planning.

The appraisal procedure for projects was a complex one, even with short cuts. Moreover, no procedure could preclude all opportunities for manipulating the numbers to show the results that political leaders wanted on non-economic grounds. Moreover, a more fundamental problem lurked. The SCBA technique was an attempt to use 'shadow' prices to select investments, that is, to invest as if free market prices ruled, when in fact they did not. Investments chosen in this way would not necessarily be financially viable in the existing price environment. That implied that the profitability of the project would depend on the government's continuing ability to give them subsidies, something that became more difficult as the politico-economic turbulence of the 1970s unfolded. The alternative – and this was the recommended option – was for government to dismantle the interventions that prevented the investment project from being profitable.

4. Trade regimes, international and national

Ever since the Havana Conference of 1947–8, representatives of developing countries had argued that an international trade regime based on rules of reciprocity and non-discrimination would be inadequate, in a world of gross inequalities between nations, to support their economic development. Development economists like Rosenstein-Rodan and Prebisch did not advocate autarky, but they did envisage growing regional free trade areas. GATT[17] disapproved of them, and while it provided a forum in which industrial countries could reduce their industrial tariffs, it had little to offer the countries that had yet to undergo industrialization.

In search of an international framework for trade that would better serve the late developers, Prebisch lobbied both for a new international organization (UNCTAD) and a new policy programme.[18] Among the measures sought were industrial preferences for developing countries and increased world liquidity linked to development finance. These, and other related proposals much discussed in the 1960s, did succeed in changing public policy.[19] Despite being universally agreed in principle, in the 1970s they were either deficiently implemented or else rendered completely abortive.

The culmination of the developing countries' drive to modify the institutions of international trade to accommodate the interdependence of trade and development was the call for a New International Economic Order in the 1970s. The policy centrepiece of the NIEO was an integrated programme of international commodity agreements, to be financed from a new Common Fund. The economics of commodity price stabilization was still a relatively under-researched area, however, and the demand for the integrated programme, because of its fragile basis in both economics and politics, hardly materialized, although a small Common Fund was set up in the early 1980s.

The commodity power of the OPEC oil producers' cartel did not persuade industrial countries to sign international agreements on commodities across the board. Together with the alarmist predictions of resource exhaustion, it promoted a public mood (outside the US) in favour of energy saving and the conservation of exhaustible resources. It also cast doubt on the wisdom of taking GNP growth as the indicator of development, since it ignored the resource depletion that such growth often involved. As environmentalism became a focus of utopian enthusiasm in the same way that economic development once had been, the very possibility of living standards in developing countries ever catching up was questioned, in the light of the resource use and pollution implications. Meanwhile, critics of the GNP measure pointed out that growth was compatible with chronic poverty, while the goal of development was the abolition of poverty. So the ideal of economic development became ever more diffuse and blurred, and the solidarity of the oil and non-oil developing countries weakened.

Nevertheless, the policy activism of the developing countries in the international economic arena provoked a tart response from the industrial countries.

Their message was that the main obstacles impeding development were internal, not external. The OECD, which represented the industrial countries, funded a series of studies designed to substantiate this thesis.[20] Their analytical key was the measurement of the effective rate of protection. This concept, like product valuation in project appraisal, was anchored in 'world prices': it is the difference between value-added at domestic and at world prices, divided by value-added at world prices. This rate differs from the nominal rate of protection for a product that is inscribed in the government tariff book, to the extent that imported inputs for the product are themselves free of tariffs. What matters is not just the height of individual tariffs, but the structure of protection.[21]

The OECD studies of trade and industry thus threw a new light on the nature of protection in the national trade regimes of nine developing countries. The effective rate of protection of some industries was at times twice as high as the nominal rate, which in many cases was around 100%. The studies found examples of industries with negative value-added: their inputs were worth more than the manufactured product. In agriculture, protection was often negative, however, since its inputs were taxed while imports of the product were let in free. These results suggested that governments were not just neglecting agriculture, but exploiting it in order to build up uncompetitive industries. That the use of protection by developing countries was excessive was already widely believed, but these studies provided a startlingly clear picture of the problem.

Coupled with this was a critique of governments' use of quantitative restrictions on imports (QRs) to maintain an overvalued exchange rate. It depressed exports, leading to loss of scale economies in industry. It cheapened imports and encouraged excessively capital-intensive methods of industrial production, thereby limiting job creation in industry. Nonetheless, industry was highly profitable because of high rates of effective protection, and the combination of artificially high profits and artificially low employment of labour worsened the distribution of income. Discrimination against exports caused under-investment in agriculture, while cheaper imports did little for a sector with low import requirements. QRs were singled out as a major obstacle to the rational management of the economy, responsible for a syndrome of slow growth and income inequality.

This bleak picture did not immediately translate into a prescription for trade liberalization. The static gains from dismantling QRs were unlikely to be large, so change had to be motivated by research on dynamic gains. Another multi-volume study sponsored by the US National Bureau of Economic Research found that, while reducing QRs did increase exports, and therefore growth (because exports are part of GNP), no increase was discernible in the elasticity of output with respect to exports.[22] The dynamic case for trade liberalization remained to be established.

These trade studies played a significant part in changing the perspective on development in the 1970s.[23] World prices were used to anchor detailed microeconomic analysis of government policy, which had been neglected in the earlier grand macroeconomic theories. The economy should no longer be treated as closed; foreign aid should no longer be assumed automatically to fill any balance of payments gap. Responsibility for the good management of foreign trade was pushed back to developing country governments. This was reasonable in the sense that many were evidently not making the best use of the trading opportunities that they faced. At the same time, it conveniently distracted attention from the fact that world prices were by no stretch of the imagination ideal scarcity prices. They reflected all the restraints on free trade that the industrial countries were imposing for their own purposes, such as agricultural subsidies and textile import quotas – in other words, all the distortions that needed to be removed in any negotiations for a true new international economic order.

5. Neoliberalism: less state, more market

The 1970s witnessed a groundswell of negative views on the performance of the state, not least in developing countries. The growing negativity about the state came from all parts of the ideological compass, and was by no means the monopoly of the political right wing. The closeness of the relation between planners and economic advisers and government machinery is perhaps the best explanation for the spreading frustration of the hope for a rational and benevolent state. Whereas errors of economic policy might once have been attributed to ignorance and honest mistakes, more sinister motives were now cited. Analysts began to explain the failure of development policies in terms not just of the conflict between development and other governments' public objectives but of conflict between development and the state's hidden agenda. The nature of the hidden agenda then began to be explored in a variety of political-economic analyses of the nature of the state.

The resurgence of neo-Marxism related the hidden agenda of the state to the interests of the capitalist class, and then examined class formations in developing countries and their links with the bourgeoisie of the industrialized world. The failure to develop was related to the non-emergence of a domestic bourgeoisie of the classical type, the consequent relative autonomy of the state and its domination by the metropolitan bourgeoisie in a system of neo-colonialism. The prognosis was pessimistic: nothing could be done before a wholesale socio-political change had taken place. To seek progressive change from existing state structures was naïve, and doomed to disappointment.

Non-Marxist political economy lightly dispensed with class and with international linkages, except for the supply of aid. One formulation was that the state was dominated by an urban coalition, unified by location but cutting across class lines, whose collective interest was the exploitation of the rural hinterland. Its policies systematically discriminated against agriculture in a way that was both inefficient and inequitable, a discrimination that was operated by maintaining an artificially high exchange rate and a state monopoly of agricultural exports. The Lewis model was accused of helping to legitimize this system of urban bias.[24] Progress could be made only by weakening the power of urban elites. This required a thorough reversal of political and administrative culture and priorities, and a widespread willingness to 'put the last first'.[25]

However, the form of political economy that won approval, once conservative governments were installed in the US, Germany and the UK after 1980, was centred on the collusion between the state in developing countries and rent-seeking domestic interest groups. The QR-overvalued exchange-rate syndrome was linked to the administrative allocation of import licences, which was linked in turn with the spawning of 'rent-seeking activities' that were unproductive and corrupting.[26] Using this analysis as a prime exhibit, a general case was made that government failure was worse than market failure, thus challenging the original justification for the expansion of government beyond its nightwatchman role and into the role of development entrepreneur.[27]

Based in the Research Department of the World Bank, this doctrine animated a policy programme of minimizing the role of the state in development and of 'getting prices right'. No longer was it a matter of governments selecting their industrial investments with the correct shadow prices. Governments were now adjured to divest themselves of state-owned industries and to liberalize comprehensively – in goods markets, labour markets, financial markets, capital markets and foreign-trade markets. They were encouraged to concentrate their efforts on law and order, education and health. This view became codified in what was called the Washington Consensus on economic policy for developing countries, ten precepts to which all sensible economists were expected to agree. Although intended modestly as a set of minimum aims, it was taken as the neoliberals' standard policy prescription, with the implication that 'one size fits all'.[28]

Although 'reduce poverty' was not one of the ten precepts of the Washington Consensus, the shrinking of the state had its own distributional justification. A smaller state would be good for growth, and growth would be good for poverty reduction. Also, because poverty is more severe in rural areas, and state economic regulations and organizations disadvantage agriculturists and advantage industrialists, a minimalist state would tend to reduce the inequality of distribution of income and wealth. The manifesto of the counter-revolution in development was not simply about greater efficiency: it contained a promise of poverty reduction through growth and greater equity as well.[29]

Champions of the free price mechanism highlighted and celebrated the newly industrializing countries of Asia as examples of the fast growth and good income distribution resulting from economic liberalization. Particularly in South Korea, they interpreted the dismantling of trade and payments restrictions in the mid-1960s as the trigger for developmental success. When closer inspection revealed considerable evidence of remaining government intervention in trade, industry and finance, ardent liberalizers brushed it aside with the assertion that the different interventions cancelled each other out, or that they were counter-productive and growth would have been even faster without them.[30] This claim now seems increasingly implausible. Despite inter-country differences, the East Asian growth story seems to be about government and businesses coordinating to secure high investment, high saving and reinvestment and rapid growth of competitive exports in a joint strategy of national development.[31] The debate now centres on whether a similar strategy could succeed equally well elsewhere.

6. From structural adjustment to poverty reduction

After 1980, the industrial countries increasingly backed away from the economic activities of the UN, while devising new functions for more malleable instruments like the IMF and the World Bank. In the wake of the Latin American debt crisis, the G7 used the Fund and Bank to engineer the 'structural adjustment' of the economies of developing countries. The shift was profound: instead of industrial countries changing their economic structure to accommodate additional output of the late developers, developing countries had to change their economic structure to accommodate more imports and private investment from the G7.

For countries whose balance of payments gap could no longer be filled by expanding aid grants, adjustment meant reducing aggregate demand to equal aggregate supply, plus whatever amount sustainable borrowing could finance. A simple reduction in absorption would, however, typically create an imbalance between the supply of and demand for non-traded goods, so that contraction of demand would have to be accompanied by currency devaluation. Contraction was not intended to be the end of the story: after successful macroeconomic stabilization, supply side measures were intended to promote the resumption of growth. The removal of price distortions, plus the shrinkage of the public sector, was intended to provide the impulse to resumed growth. The justification and criticism of this type of adjustment policy provided a major theme for development economists throughout the 1980s.

Stabilization was, relatively speaking, less controversial because often there was no feasible alternative: the only choice was between a planned and a chaotic contraction. Interest thus centred on measuring the size and duration of negative growth, plus how the different genders and socio-economic groups were affected.[32] More controversial were the effects of liberalization. Research trying to show that trade liberalization increased the rate of economic growth was dogged by the difficulty of applying an unambiguous measure of trade liberalization. Changes in effective rates of protection, though theoretically preferable, are extremely laborious to calculate, and other measures can be misleading in various ways. The World Bank wasted large sums on massive tomes on this topic that were tendentious and inconclusive.[33]

The case for financial liberalization rested on work done in the 1970s on financial repression.[34] Although the use of low-interest rate ceilings on formal sector lending could be criticized as an open door for the political allocation of loans in a context of excess demand, the expectation of rapid growth after their removal relied on some strong assumptions, including severe technological dualism within agriculture. Moreover, institutional aspects of changing from a rationed to a free market in credit were neglected, especially the (previously superfluous) issue of bankers' ability to judge and manage risk. One of the most prescient aphorisms of this period was Carlos Diaz-Alejandro's remark: 'goodbye financial repression, hello financial crisis', the overture to many analyses of the Southern Cone 1982–3, Mexico 1994 and the Asian crisis 1997–8.

In general, the verdict on structural adjustment in the 1980s was that it delivered much less than its advocates had claimed for it. Exports and overall growth grew slightly as a result, while the share of investment to GDP declined somewhat.[35] Structural adjustment was a very large policy package, since it comprised stabilization, liberalization and privatization, and each of these sub-categories of policy consisted of many different specific actions that, for success, should have been pursued in a coordinated programme. Development economics was not well equipped to resolve the practical issue of sequencing this package of policies. Some accordingly argued that sequencing did not matter: why not do everything at once in one big bang? Others urged gradualism.[36] Others still said: just get started and do what you can. Later evaluations showed up important sequencing errors as one of the factors that blunted the effectiveness of reforms.[37]

Excessive confidence was invested not only in the reforms themselves, but also in the Bank's ability to persuade countries to undertake them. The Fund and the Bank relied on making some of their loans conditional on the borrowing countries agreeing to implement the reform package. Apparently a powerful lever over countries in need of finance, loan conditionality in fact turned out to give the Bank rather little leverage. Game theory and principal-agent analyses explained this in terms of the Bank's conflict of objectives and the costs of supervision.[38]

By the end of the 1980s, the effort expended on structural adjustment seemed to have distracted attention from other central issues of development, especially poverty reduction. The willingness to let poverty reduction wait upon increased growth eroded as the growth record of structural adjustment policies was shown to be unimpressive. Greater credence was given to the idea that growth itself depended on poverty reduction. It was argued (once again) that better health and education services for the poor would permit the formation of socially-desirable human capital that would not otherwise take place, and thus make the economy more productive. These claims could be rationalized by reference to new theories of growth that installed human capital accumulation as the engine of growth.[39]

The complexity of the condition of poverty gained greater recognition. Although economists for convenience defined poverty as being below a given level of income or consumption, this excluded many elements that contribute to a standard of living. Assets, access to public services, rights to use common resources and the nexus of family, kin and social obligations all contribute to sustaining the livelihoods of the poor, and come into particular play in subsistence crises.[40] The phenomenon of livelihood diversification was at odds with the increasing specialization and division of labour that is conventionally seen as the hallmark of development. It testified to the dominance of severe risk in the economic calculations of the poor.[41]

The World Bank acknowledged the new interest in poverty reduction in its *World Development Report 1990*, which stressed the need to ensure that growth was labour intensive and that basic social services were effective. Also in 1990, UNDP began its *Human Development Report* series, featuring a statistically questionable but well-intentioned index of human development that was an equal-weight combination of GNP figures with life expectancy and literacy data.

7. Reintroducing institutions into economic development

In the 1990s, thinking on economic development became more flexible and more adventurous, even though neoliberalism by no means faded from the scene. Much of the intellectual preparation for these innovations had been done earlier, but the end of the Cold War warmed the climate for their fuller fruition. Three new strands of thinking about the role of institutions in development were particularly noteworthy. Early development economists like Arthur Lewis were well aware of the importance of sound institutions in making economic development possible, and wrote many wise words on this subject. They tended to be forgotten, however, because they were not integral to the economic development model that he also constructed. At that time, virtually all economists thought of institutions as fixed frameworks within which economic transactions took place, and that were not themselves amenable to, or part of, economic analysis.

The New Institutional Economics annulled this analytical divorce between institutions and economics.[42] The key insight was that all economic transactions have a cost. This sets up the requirement to minimize the sum of production and transactions costs, and a choice of making a transaction at arm's length on the market, or making it inside an institution – such as a firm, family, cooperative or government agency. The question then concerns what the market does, or is able to, supply to facilitate its own functioning, and what is better supplied by non-market institutions. The possibility of substitution of market for non-market institutions presents both with a challenge: to align incentives in ways that reduce transaction costs.

Much of the difficulty experienced with financial liberalization, for example, arises because it is more costly for depositors and regulators outside banks to acquire relevant information on bank operations than it is for the managers inside the bank to do so. This asymmetry of information creates perverse incentives for risky lending that may in turn provoke financial crises.[43] The logic of transaction costs has many applications, both analytical and prescriptive. It helps to explain why certain types of contract are designed in the way that they are – such as sharecropping contracts in agriculture and labour contracts in fishing. It also guides the design of more effective contracts for public service delivery.

The concept of social capital draws in part on the same logic. Networks of personal relationships can be used for economic transactions when people are too poor to support formal institutions or markets. Knowledge of the personal reputation of others can be acquired through personal contacts and then used to keep transaction costs low, facilitating transactions that would not otherwise take place.[44] In such a context, it makes sense to talk about investing in personal relationships, no less than in education and health care.

However, 'social capital' has another aspect that clearly belongs within the tradition of methodological individualism. Transactions conducted through personal networks are likely to be quite limited, given the amount of network-ing that any individual can afford to do. A more profound problem therefore is specifying the conditions for the creation of a climate of impersonal trust that would improve the working of formal institutions, or permit a much wider expansion of economic activity in countries where formal institutions are still weak.[45] How are social norms born, strengthened or changed? This remains a challenging and controversial area of research, with much potential relevance to development economics.

One recent response has been to reject the tradition of methodological individualism. The evolution of development economics has for the most part occurred inside this tradition. There is, however, an alternative way of under-standing the role of institutions in development. It is possible to accord the analytical primacy to politics, which determines the ways in which markets are constituted; which recognizes a temporal and causal priority of institu-tions to individuals; and which thus considers how institutions influence the motivations of individuals, and not just how they constrain their behaviour in situations in which their motives are fixed.[46] To think about economic development in this way would indeed be to break the mould, and embark on a radical departure from past perspectives.

8. Conclusion

The main changes of perspective that have affected development economics are the same as those that have affected economics as a whole. On the wider intellectual canvas of economics, too, the role of the state began to be seen as more problematic; the divorce between macroeconomics and micro-economics began to be seen as unsustainable; and the recognition of transaction costs enriched the understanding of why institutions exist and why incentives matter.

However, these broad changes had a greater significance for development economics, given its initial vision. We may no longer speak of 'international depressed areas', but there are still many parts of the world where modern economic activity has as yet hardly got going. So the question still remains – what should the state do to improve the lot of the people? The state that contents itself with holding the ring within which economic actors contend no longer provides a convincing image of the state that will achieve sustainable development. The regrettably rare quick forward advances in economic development seen in the last sixty years have not been achieved by that means. It might at best provide a default setting for economic policy in small open economies that cannot conjure up the political and bureaucratic skills to do anything more.

However, the clearest lesson of the past is that future development economists will need to consider not just what they want the state to do in the cause of development, but also how states might be formed to do what they prescribe. If development economists ever aspired to leave the realms of political economy, they had surely been frustrated by the start of the 21st century.

Notes

1 Thus I have omitted many important topics. Fuller reports on the state of development economics are in Ranis and Schultz 1988 and Meier and Stiglitz 2001.
2 See, for example, Meek 1976, Arndt 1987, chapter 1, and Cowen and Shenton 1996.
3 Kuznets 1971.
4 Rosenstein-Rodan 1943.
5 Hirschman 1958 later argued instead for 'unbalanced growth', i.e. investing in a few sectors with strong linkages, and relying on disequilibrium effects to create the incentives for investment elsewhere.
6 The phrase is from Buchanan 1946.
7 See Toye and Toye 2003.
8 Lewis 1954 and Lewis 1955.
9 Schultz 1961.
10 Harris and Todaro 1970.
11 Bauer 1956.
12 This was the burden of Lipton 1977.
13 Stiglitz 1974.
14 Stolper 1966.
15 Lewis 1965, p. 151.
16 Little and Mirrlees 1974.
17 The General Agreement on Tariffs and Trade was the residual framework for international trade after the failure to launch the International Trade Organisation.
18 UNCTAD 1964.
19 For example, by Johnson 1967 and Pincus 1967.
20 The OECD studies were summarised in Little, Scitovsky and Scott 1970.
21 Balassa 1971.
22 Bhagwati and Krueger 1978.
23 Backhouse 2002, p. 305.
24 The term 'urban bias' is due to Lipton 1977.
25 Chambers 1983.
26 Krueger 1974.
27 Lal 1983.
28 Williamson 1994, pp. 11–28.
29 These issues were further explored in Toye 1993 [1987].
30 Little 1979.
31 Wade 1990; Chang 1994; Akyuz 1998.
32 Khan; Elson 1995.
33 For example, the seven volumes of Papageorgiou, Michaely and Choksi 1991.
34 McKinnon 1973.
35 Mosley, Harrigan and Toye 1995 [1991].

36 Cornia, Jolly and Stewart 1987.
37 Collier and Gunning 1999.
38 Killick 1998; Collier 2000.
39 Lucas 1988; Scott 1989.
40 Sen 1981.
41 Ellis 1998.
42 Harriss, Hunter and Lewis 1995.
43 Stiglitz and Weiss 1981.
44 Fafchamps and Minten 1999.
45 Putnam 1993.
46 Chang 2002.

References

Akyuz, Y, 1998, ed., 'East Asian Development: New Perspectives', *Journal of Development Studies*, vol. 34, no. 6, 1–137.

Arndt, HW, 1987, *Economic Development. The History of an Idea*, Chicago, University of Chicago Press.

Backhouse, RE, 2002, *The Penguin History of Economics*, London, Penguin Books.

Balassa, B, 1971, *The Structure of Protection in Developing Countries*, Baltimore, Johns Hopkins University Press.

Bauer, PT, 1956, 'Lewis' *Theory of Economic Growth*. A Review Article', *American Economic Review*, vol. XLVI, no. 4, 632–41.

Bhagwati, J and AO Krueger, 1978, *Anatomy and Consequences of Exchange Control Regimes*, Cambridge, Mass., Ballinger.

Buchanan, NS, 1946, 'Deliberate Industrialisation for Higher Incomes', *Economic Journal*, vol. 56, 533–53.

Chambers, R, 1983, *Rural Development: Putting the Last First*, Harlow, Longmans.

Chang, H-J, 2002, 'Breaking the mould: an institutionalist political economy alternative to the neo-liberal theory of the market and the state', *Cambridge Journal of Economics*, vol. 26, no. 5, 539–59.

Collier, P, 2000, 'Conditionality, Dependence and Coordination: three current debates in aid policy', in Christopher L Gilbert and David Vines, 2000, ed., *The World Bank: Structure and Policies*, Cambridge, Cambridge University Press.

Collier, P and JW Gunning 1999, 'Explaining African Economic Performance', *Journal of Economic Literature*, vol. xxxvii, 64–111.

Cornia, A, R Jolly and F Stewart, 1987, *Adjustment with a Human Face*, Oxford, Clarendon Press.

Cowen, MP and RW Shenton, 1996, *Doctrines of Development*, London, Routledge.

Ellis, F, 1998, 'Household Strategies and Rural Livelihood Diversification', *Journal of Development Studies*, vol. 35, no. 1, 1–38.

Elson, D, 1995, ed., 'Gender, Adjustment and Macroeconomics', *World Development*, vol. 23, no. 11, 1825–2017.

Fafchamps, M and B Minten, 1999, 'Relationships and Traders in Madagascar', *Journal of Development Studies*, vol. 35, no. 6, pp. 1–35.

Harris JR and MP Todaro, 1970, 'Migration, Unemployment and Development: a Two-sector Analysis', *American Economic Review*, vol. lx, 126–42.

Harriss, J, J Hunter and CM Lewis, 1996, eds, *The New Institutional Economics and Third World Development*, London, Routledge.

Hirschman AO, 1958, *The Strategy of Economic Development*, New Haven, Yale University Press.

Johnson, HG, 1967, *Economic Policies Towards Less Developed Countries*, London, George Allen and Unwin Ltd.

Khan, MS and MD Knight, 1985, *Fund-supported Adjustment Programmes and Economic Growth*, Occasional Paper 41, Washington DC, International Monetary Fund.

Killick, T, 1998, *Aid and the Political Economy of Policy Change*, London, Routledge.

Krueger, AO, 1974, 'The Political Economy of the Rent-seeking Society', *American Economic Review*, vol. lxiv, 291–303.

Kuznets, S, 1971, *Economic Growth of Nations: total output and production structure*, Cambridge, Mass., Harvard University Press.

Lal, D, 1983, *The Poverty of Development Economics*, London, Institute of Economic Affairs.

Lewis, WA, 1954, 'Economic Development with Unlimited Supplies of Labour', *The Manchester School*, vol. 22, 139–91.

———,1955, *The Theory of Economic Growth*, London, George Allen and Unwin Ltd.

———, 1965, *Development Planning. The Essentials of Economic Policy*, London, George Allen and Unwin Ltd.

Lipton, M, 1977, *Why the Poor Stay Poor*, London, Maurice Temple-Smith.

Little, IMD, 1979, 'An Economic Renaissance', in W Galenson, ed., *Economic Growth and Structural Change in Taiwan*, Ithaca NY, Cornell University Press.

Little, IMD and J Mirrlees, 1974, *Project Appraisal and Planning for Developing Countries*, London, Heinemann Educational.

Little, IMD, T Scitovsky and MFG Scott, 1970, *Industry and Trade in Some Developing Countries*, Oxford, Oxford University Press.

Lucas, RE, 1988, 'On the Mechanics of Economic Development', *Journal of Monetary Economics*, vol. 22, no. 1, 3–42.

McKinnon, RI, 1973, *Money and Capital in Economic Development*, Washington DC, Brookings Institution.

Meek RL, 1976, *Social Science and the Ignoble Savage*, Cambridge, Cambridge University Press.

Meier, GM and JE Stiglitz, 2000, eds, *Frontiers of Development Economics. The Future in Perspective*, New York, World Bank and Oxford University Press.

Mosley, P, J Harrigan and J Toye, 1995 [1991], *Aid and Power. The World Bank and Policy-based Lending*, 2 vols, London, Routledge.

Papageorgiou, D, M Michaely and A Choksi, 1991, *Liberalizing Foreign Trade*, 7 vols, London, Oxford University Press.

Pincus, J, 1967, *Trade, Aid and Development. The Rich and Poor Nations*, New York, McGraw-Hill Book Company.

Putnam, RD, 1993, *Making Democracy Work: Civic Traditions in Modern Italy*, Princeton, Princeton University Press.

Ranis, G and TP Schultz, 1988, *The State of Development Economics: progress and perspectives*, Oxford, Basil Blackwell.

Rosenstein-Rodan, P, 1943, 'Problems of Industrialization in Eastern and South-Eastern Europe', *Economic Journal*, vol. liii, 202–11.

Scott, MFG, 1989, *A New Theory of Economic Growth*, Oxford, Oxford University Press.

Schultz, TW, 1961, 'Investment in Human Capital', *American Economic Review*, vol. li, 1–17.

Sen, AK, 1981, *Poverty and Famines. An Essay on Entitlement and Deprivation*, Oxford, Clarendon Press.

Stiglitz, JE, 1974, 'Incentives and Risk Sharing in Sharecropping', *Review of Economic Studies*, vol. 41, 219–55.

Stiglitz, JE and A Weiss, 1981, 'Credit Rationing in Markets with Imperfect Information', *American Economic Review*, vol. 71, 393–410.

Stolper, WF, 1966, *Planning Without Facts: lessons in resource allocation from Nigeria's development*, Cambridge, Mass., Harvard University Press.

Toye, J, 1993 [1987], *Dilemmas of Development*, Oxford, Basil Blackwell.

Toye, J and R Toye, 2003, 'The Origins and Interpretation of the Prebisch–Singer Thesis', *History of Political Economy*, forthcoming.

UNCTAD 1964, *A New Trade Policy for Development*, New York, United Nations.

Wade, R, 1990, *Governing the Market*, Princeton, Princeton University Press.

Williamson, J, ed., 1994, *The Political Economy of Policy Reform*, Washington DC, Institute of International Economics.

2

THE MARKET, THE STATE AND INSTITUTIONS IN ECONOMIC DEVELOPMENT

Ha-Joon Chang

1. Introduction

Defining the appropriate roles of the market and the state has been a central concern for policymakers since the beginning of capitalism. Indeed, economics itself was conceived as a practical policy science for the rulers of early capitalism.[1] However, the rise of development economics in the 1940s and the 1950s made this aspect of economics even more important. As Toye points out in chapter 1 of this volume, the very identity of development economics was determined by its concern for 'government-engineered economic transformation'.

The interest in the role of institutions in economic development is more recent. Although some early development economists acknowledged the (often negative) role of social institutions in the development process, such as traditional culture, it was not central to their arguments. However, through the debate on the role of the market and the state since the 1980s, a new consensus has emerged: that the simplistic market–state dichotomy obscures more than enlightens our understanding of the developmental process. However, despite the recent theoretical developments in institutional economics (especially in the so-called New Institutional Economics), which have furthered our understanding in this area, there still remains a lot of confusion and disagreement on how to theorize the role of institutions, in particular their relationship with the market and the state.

In this chapter, I will discuss the historical and theoretical backgrounds to this fundamental but still contentious area in development economics. In section 2, I will examine the historical evolution of the theory and practice of state intervention, in order to provide context to the subsequent discussion.

Section 3 will critically examine the currently dominant neoliberal view on the role of the market and the state. In section 4, taking these criticisms of the neoliberal approach as a point of departure I will outline an alternative: one that allows us to have a richer understanding of the market, the state and institutions, and the relationships that are formed between them. Section 5 will sum up the discussion and conclude.

2. The historical background: from the rise of capitalism to the early post-World War II years

According to what I call the 'official history of capitalism' that informs the current debate on economic development, the world economy has developed in the following way over the last few centuries.[2]

From the eighteenth century onward, Britain proved the superiority of free-market and free-trade policies by overtaking interventionist France, its main competitor at the time, and establishing itself as the supreme world economic power. Especially once it had abandoned its deplorable agricultural protection (the Corn Law) and other remnants of old mercantilist protectionist measures in 1846, it was able to play the role of the architect and hegemon of a new 'Liberal' world economic order. This Liberal world order, perfected around 1870, was based on: (a) laissez-faire industrial policies at home; (b) low barriers to the international flows of goods, capital and labour; and (c) macroeconomic stability, both nationally and internationally, guaranteed by the Gold Standard and the principle of balanced budgets. A period of unprecedented prosperity followed.

Unfortunately, according to this story, things started to go wrong with the onset of the First World War. In response to the ensuing instability of the world economic and political system, countries started to erect trade barriers again. In 1930, the USA also abandoned free trade and raised tariffs with the infamous Smoot–Hawley tariff, which the famous free-trade economist Jagdish Bhagwati called 'the most visible and dramatic act of anti-trade folly'.[3] The world free-trade system finally ended in 1932 when Britain, hitherto the champion of free trade, succumbed to temptation and reintroduced tariffs. The resulting contraction and instability in the world economy, and then World War II, finally destroyed the last remnants of the first Liberal world order.

After World War II, so the story goes, some significant progress was made in trade liberalization through the early GATT (General Agreement on Trade and Tariffs) talks. However interventionist approaches to economic management unfortunately dominated the policymaking scene in the developed world until the 1970s – and until the early 1980s in the developing world (and the Communist world until its collapse in 1989). According to the widely-cited article by Sachs and Warner, a number of factors contributed to the pursuit of protectionism and interventionism in developing countries.[4] There were 'wrong' theories, such as the infant industry argument, the 'big push' theory and Latin American structuralism, not to speak of various Marxist theories. There were also political dividends to protectionist policies such as the need for nation building and the need to buy off certain interest groups. There were also legacies of wartime controls.

Fortunately, it is said, interventionist policies have been largely abandoned across the world since the 1980s with the rise of neoliberalism, which emphasized the virtues of small government, laissez-faire policies and international openness. In the developing world in particular, economic growth had by the late 1970s begun to falter in most countries outside East and South East Asia, which were already pursuing 'good' (i.e. free-market and free-trade) policies. This growth failure, which often manifested itself in the economic crises of the early 1980s, exposed the limitations of old-style interventionism and protectionism. As a result, most developing countries have come to embrace 'policy reform' in a neoliberal direction. When combined with the establishment of new global governance institutions represented by the WTO, these policy changes at the national level have created a new global economic system, comparable in its (at least potential) prosperity only to the earlier 'golden age' of Liberalism (1870–1914). Renato Ruggiero, the first Director-General of the WTO, argues that thanks to this new world order we now have 'the potential for eradicating global poverty in the early part of the next [21st] century – a utopian notion even a few decades ago, but a real possibility today'.[5]

However, this is a fundamentally misleading portrayal of the history of capitalism in a number of ways. First of all, contrary to the official history of capitalism, virtually all now-developed countries (NDCs) have actively used tariffs, subsidies and other measures of intervention, especially in the early days of their economic development.[6] Virtually all of them used infant-industry protection when they were trying to develop new industries. And contrary to the conventional wisdom, trade protection was much more seriously practised in the supposed 'free trade' economies of the UK and the USA than in the supposedly 'interventionist' economies like France, Germany and Japan (see table 1).[7] Many states financed and subsidized large-scale and/or risky investments, especially in railroads but also in key manufacturing industries (e.g. steel). Many of them sponsored technology acquisition – through both legal (e.g. funding studies abroad) and illegal (e.g. the poaching of skilled workers, industrial espionage) means – and made attempts to raise 'awareness' about advanced technologies by, for example, setting up 'model

Table 1. **Average tariff rates on manufactured products for selected developed countries in their early stages of development**
(weighted average; in percentages of value)

	1820[1]	1875[1]	1913	1925	1931	1950
Austria[2]	R	15–20	18	16	24	18
Belgium[3]	6–8	9–10	9	15	14	11
Denmark	25–35	15–20	14	10	n.a.	3
France	R	12–15	20	21	30	18
Germany[4]	8–12	4–6	13	20	21	26
Italy	n.a.	8–10	18	22	46	25
Japan[5]	R	5	30	n.a.	n.a.	n.a.
Netherlands[3]	6–8	3–5	4	6	n.a.	11
Russia	R	15–20	84	R	R	R
Spain	R	15–20	41	41	63	n.a.
Sweden	R	3–5	20	16	21	9
Switzerland	8–12	4–6	9	14	19	n.a.
United Kingdom	45–55	0	0	5	n.a.	23
United States	35–45	40–50	44	37	48	14

Source: Chang 2002a, p. 17, table 2.1.

Notes:

R = Numerous and important restrictions on manufactured imports existed and therefore average tariff rates are not meaningful.

1 These are very approximate rates, and give range of average rates, not extremes.
2 Austria-Hungary before 1925.
3 In 1820, Belgium was united with the Netherlands.
4 The 1820 figure is for Prussia only.
5 Before 1911, Japan was obliged to keep low tariff rates (5% or below) through a series of unequal treaties with the European countries and the USA. A table in *World Development Report 1991* by the World Bank (1991, p. 97, box table 5.2) gives Japan's *unweighted* average tariff rate for *all goods* (and not just manufactured goods) for the years 1925, 1930, 1950 as 13%, 19%, 4%.

factories' and organising 'expos'. Many of them invested in R&D by setting up and subsidizing the establishment of universities, technical schools and science academies.

In short, it is simply not true that state interventionism in the early postwar years was an anomaly in the historical march of free-market global capitalism.

All countries have used interventionist measures when necessary and possible (I say 'possible' because the weaker countries have often faced restrictions in using those measures due to colonialism, bilateral unequal treaties and, today, intervention by multilateral institutions).

Having said this, it is true that there existed some important limits to the scope of state intervention until the early twentieth century, for institutional reasons. Most states had a fairly limited budgetary capability, mainly because there was no income tax, while the balanced budget doctrine constrained their ability to engage in deficit financing. They also had limited monetary policy capability. Most countries did not have a central bank until the late nineteenth century, and the Gold Standard constrained the scope of monetary policy anyway. They had limited command over investment resources, as there was little state ownership of financial institutions and few nationalized industries existed; moreover, there was little industrial regulation (such as anti-trust regulation or environmental regulation) and investment planning was non-existent.[8]

However, from the end of the nineteenth century onward the scope for state intervention started broadening: this culminated in a dramatic swing to interventionist policy regimes across the world after World War II.[9] What is important to note is that this swing was the result of the real failures of laissez-faire capitalism, and not of 'wrong theories', populist pressures and political manoeuvring, as the neoliberals suggest.

From the late nineteenth century onward, central banking and financial regulations were introduced in order to deal with the financial instability inherent in unregulated capitalism, while social welfare legislation and anti-trust regulation were introduced in order to restrain the worst distributional outcomes of laissez-faire capitalism. Subsequently, the spectacular failure of advanced capitalism since the Great Depression made the advanced capitalist economies build national and international institutions in order to soften business cycle (e.g. the strengthening of the central bank, and the Bretton Woods international financial system). The failure of laissez-faire capitalism in the colonies naturally convinced their postcolonial leaders that their states needed to take an active role after independence.

The last – but not least – misleading aspect is the neoliberal portrayal of the interventionist period of the third quarter of the twentieth century as a period of inefficiency and stagnation.[10] Contrary to what the neoliberals say, the world economy performed much better during this period than during the more 'liberal' regimes that preceded and followed it.

During the (old) 'liberal golden age' (1875–1913) that neoliberals so fondly look back upon, per capita income in the developed countries grew at around 1.5% per annum, with the colonies and semi-colonies in Asia and Africa at best stagnating and at worst contracting.[11] During the height of state interventionism in the 1960s and 1970s, both developed and developing countries grew at about 3% p.a. in per capita terms (3.2% and 3.0%, respectively). In contrast, during the neoliberal age of the 1980s and the 1990s, when many of the allegedly inefficient and growth-retarding interventionist measures were rolled back, per capita income growth was much slower. In the developed countries it slowed down from 3.2% per annum to 2.2% per annum, while growth in the developing countries collapsed from 3.0% to 1.5%. And even this 1.5% growth is largely due to the rapid growth of countries in East and South Asia, especially China and India, which did not follow the neoliberal prescription during this period. Per capita income stagnated in Latin America (down from 3.1% to 0.6% per annum), and shrank at an alarming rate in Sub Saharan Africa (down from 2.0% to –0.7%). Living standards in most ex-Communist countries have experienced a dramatic collapse during this period. Many of these countries have not even recovered their levels of income during the Communist period.

So, the neoliberal portrayal of the interventionist period of the third quarter of the twentieth century as a time of inefficiencies and stagnation is exactly the opposite of what has in fact happened. Capitalism has not done better either before or after that period, when more 'liberal' policies dominated. Indeed, one of the biggest public relations victories of neoliberalism is this portrayal of what was the real golden age of capitalism (1950–75) as the 'bad old days', and the liberal period of 1875–1913 as 'good old days', to which we should strive to return.

3. Neoliberal reaction and its limits[12]

There were broadly two strands in the neoliberal critique of the interventionist model of economic development that dominated the early post-World War II years, commonly known as the 'import substitution industrialization' (ISI) strategy.

The first was the so-called 'get the prices right' argument. This says that state intervention creates allocative inefficiencies, which in their view also leads to slower growth. The second was the 'political economy' argument. This rejects the perception of the state as a benevolent and omnipotent social guardian (epitomized in Plato's vision of the Philosopher King) found in various pro-interventionist theories. It then goes on to argue that economic policy will be determined by the sectional interests of politicians, bureaucrats and powerful interest groups, almost always at the cost of inefficiency and slow growth.[13]

Of these, the first argument was more influential in the early days of neoliberal reaction. However, there are a number of problems with this argument: first, there is no theoretical reason for a more liberalized economy to achieve higher allocative efficiency unless price liberalization is total (the so-called Second Best Theorem). Moreover, there is no theoretical reason why an economy with greater allocative efficiencies should grow faster, as even one of the leading proponents of 'get the prices right' argument admits.[14] Neoclassical price theory is a theory of allocating currently available resources, and it is therefore quite possible that an economy that is allocatively efficient grows slowly. Indeed, Schumpeter would have said that this is likely, as an allocatively efficient economy cannot by definition create the monopoly profit that is necessary to motivate people to innovate.[15] Also, empirically, it was pointed out that countries such as Japan, Korea and Taiwan, which 'got the prices wrong', in Alice Amsden's famous parodying,[16] did very well while the alleged econometric evidence linking the degree of price distortion with economic growth proved to be very fragile.[17]

In the long run, the more powerful element in the neoliberal reaction has proved to be the 'political economy' argument, rather than the 'get the prices right' argument. By fundamentally changing the very way in which we view the state itself, neoliberal political economy has completely shifted the terms of debate in this area. In this section, therefore, we critically examine the theoretical underpinnings of this argument.

3.1 Internal inconsistencies of neoliberal political economy

Neoliberalism was born out of an 'unholy alliance' between neoclassical economics and Austrian-Libertarian tradition. I say unholy, because there is no inevitable reason that these should go together. Neoclassical economics, with its logic of market failure, can be and has been used to justify a wide range of state intervention.[18] However, through this alliance, the Libertarians got the academic respectability and neoclassical economics got the political appeal (whoever died in the name of General Equilibrium?). In return, the interventionist potential of neoclassical economics had to be kept within a boundary acceptable to the neoliberal *political* agenda.

One such way is to argue that market failures, while logically possible anywhere, in reality exist only in a few limited areas – such as defence, law and order, and the provision of some large-scale physical infrastructure – and therefore only a 'minimal state' is necessary. The second way is to limit the spillage of the logic of market failure into policy actions by separating 'serious' academic discourse from 'popular' policy discourse. So, for example, neoclassical economists in universities may be doing research justifying stringent anti-trust policy, but policymakers may justify their lax anti-trust policy in terms of some other logic which has no place in neoclassical economics – say, by citing the need 'not to discourage entrepreneurship'. The third way of taming the neoclassical logic of market failure is to accept it fully and build models that may have strong interventionist policy conclusions, but later downplay the relevance of such models on the ground that real-life states cannot possibly be entrusted with such policies that are technically difficult (due to informational demands) and politically dangerous (due to bureaucratic abuse and/or interest group capture).[19]

These strategies of reconciling the two elements of the 'unholy alliance' inevitably create inconsistencies and tensions. However, these internal tensions are actually the least of the problems with the neoliberal view on the role of the market and the state, as this view suffers from some fundamental conceptual problems.

3.2 Defining the free market

Neoliberal economists argue that free markets produce the best outcome under just about all circumstances, and this argument seems straightforward, if empirically questionable. However, it is not such a straightforward argument, because defining the free market is a very complex exercise.

Let me illustrate this point with a couple of examples. First, take the case of child labour. Few people in today's developed countries would consider the ban on child labour as a state 'intervention' artificially restricting entry into the labour market, whereas many developing-country capitalists regard it as just that (as, until the early twentieth century, did capitalists in the now-advanced countries). This is because in the developed countries the right of children not to toil is more or less universally regarded as having precedent over the right of producers to employ whoever they find most profitable. As a result, in these countries, the ban on child labour is no longer even a legitimate subject of policy debate. By contrast, in the developing countries, both now and historically, this fundamental right of children is not so totally accepted, and therefore the state ban on child labour is considered an 'intervention', whose impact on economic efficiency is still a legitimate subject of policy debate. The same argument can be applied to the case of slavery. In societies in which the right to self-ownership is not universally accepted (in, say, the early-nineteenth-century USA), an attempt by the state to ban slavery can be disputed as an efficiency-reducing intervention, but once such a right is accepted as one of the fundamental rights of all members of the society, the ban will no longer be considered an 'intervention'.

More examples could be given, but the salient point is that the same state action might be considered an 'intervention' in one society and not in another, depending on which rights and obligations are regarded as legitimate and what kind of hierarchy between these rights and obligations is (explicitly and implicitly) accepted by members of the society.

I would even go further and say that defining a free market is fundamentally a pointless exercise: no market is in the end 'free', as all markets have some state regulations on who can participate in which markets and on what terms (more on this later). It is only because some state regulations – and the rights and the obligations that they support, or even create – can be so totally accepted that some markets appear to have no 'intervention' at all and are therefore considered 'free'.

3.3 Defining market failure

Despite its contention that market failures are rare and usually not as bad as government failure, the neoliberal discourse is still conducted in the languages of market failure. However, defining market failure is not as simple as it looks.

Market failure refers to a situation where the market does not work in a way expected of the ideal market. In the neoliberal framework, in turn, the ideal market is equated with the 'perfectly competitive market' of neoclassical economics. However, the neoclassical theory of the market is only one of many legitimate theories of market – and not a particularly good one at that. There are, to borrow Hirschman's phrase, many 'rival views of market society'.[20] Thus, the same market could be seen as failing by some, while others regard it as normally functioning, depending on their respective theories of the market. So, depending on the theory of the ideal market they have, some may perceive market failures where others see none.

For example, many think that one of the biggest 'failures' of the market is its tendency to generate an unacceptable level of income inequality (whatever the criteria for acceptability may be). However, in neoclassical economics this is not considered a market failure, because the ideal neoclassical market (at least in the Paretian version of it) is *not* supposed to generate equitable income distribution in the first place. This is not to deny that many well-intentioned neoclassical economists may dislike the income distribution prevailing in, say, Brazil, and may support some 'non-distortionary' lump-sum income transfers to reduce inequality. However, even these economists would argue that an equitable income distribution is not what we should expect from the ideal market, and therefore that, in this sense, there is no market failure in Brazil.

In short, therefore, when we talk about market failures, we need to make it clear what we expect from this ideal market, against which the failures of the existing markets can be defined. Otherwise, the concept of market failure becomes empty, and one person may see perfection in the same market where another person might see a miserable failure, and vice versa. Only when we clearly define our own theory of the market can we make clear our notion of market failure.

3.4 The market primacy assumption

One fundamental assumption behind neoliberal economics, which is also shared by neoclassical economists without a neoliberal leaning, is what I call the market primacy assumption – or the assumption that, in the words of Oliver Williamson, 'in the beginning, there were the markets'.[21]

The market primacy assumption implies that markets are natural institutions, and states or other institutions are man-made substitutes. However, in the real world, emergence of markets often needed heavy state involvement. In his classic work *The Great Transformation*, Polanyi emphasizes how even in the case of Britain, where the free market is believed by many to have emerged spontaneously,

> [t]he road to the free market was opened and kept open by *an enormous increase in continuous, centrally organised and controlled interventionism* [my italics]. To make Adam Smith's 'simple and natural liberty' compatible with the needs of a human society was a most complicated affair. Witness the complexity of the provisions in the innumerable enclosure laws; the amount of bureaucratic control involved in the administration of the New Poor Laws which for the first time since Queen Elizabeth's reign were effectively supervised by central authority; or the increase in governmental administration entailed in the meritorious task of municipal reform ....'[22]

My criticism is not just of historical interest. Even in the most advanced capitalist economies of today, which on the whole already have well-developed market systems, the state is constantly involved in creating new markets (e.g. the creation and the restructuring of markets by the state in mobile telecommunication, computer software, electricity, and internet service provision). More importantly, the severe economic crisis that many former Communist countries opting for a 'big bang' reform have experienced during the last several years is a striking example of how the establishment of a well-functioning market economy is impossible without a well-functioning state.[23] Likewise, the developmental crises that many developing countries have gone through during the last two decades or so also show how dangerous it is to assume the primacy of the market and believe that it will naturally develop so long as the state does not interfere with its evolution.

3.5 *Market and politics*

The neoliberal view is that politics interferes with economic rationality and therefore that a maximum degree of depoliticization of the policymaking process is necessary. It is therefore recommended that we reduce the scope of the state and reduce policy discretion even in those few areas where it is allowed to intervene.

However, I would argue that the market itself is a political construct, and therefore that the neoliberal proposal for its depoliticization is at best self-contradictory and at worst dishonest. What do I mean when I say the market itself is a political construct?

To begin with, the establishment and distribution of property rights and other entitlements that define the 'endowments' possessed by market participants, which neoliberal economists take as given, is a highly political exercise (e.g. the various episodes of 'original accumulation'). Even a basic knowledge of the history of the advanced countries over the last two centuries reveals how many of those now 'fundamental' rights, which very few of their citizens will today question, were in fact perfectly contestable and often fiercely contested in the past. Examples include the right to self-ownership (denied to slaves), the right to vote (and thus to have a say in the political modification of market outcomes), the right to minimum working hours, the right to organize, and the right not to be subject to physical abuse in the workplace. More recent struggles regarding rights in areas such as the environment, equal treatments across sexes or ethnicities, and consumer protection are reminders that the political struggles surrounding the establishment, sustenance and modification of the rights-obligations structures underlying markets will never end.

Moreover, even when we accept the existing rights-obligations structure as incontestable, there are in reality practically no prices which are not subject to 'political' influences, including those that are *not* perceived as such even by many neoliberals. To begin with, two critical prices which affect almost every sector – namely, wages and interest rates – are politically determined to a very great extent. Wages are politically modified not simply by minimum wage legislation but also by various regulations regarding union activities, labour standards, welfare entitlements and, most importantly, immigration control. Interest rates are also highly political prices, even when they are determined by a 'politically independent' central bank.[24] When we add to them those numerous regulations in the product markets regarding safety, pollution, import contents and so on, there is virtually no price which is free from politics.

In other words, the 'market rationality' that neoliberals want to rescue from the 'corrupting' influences of politics can only be meaningfully defined with reference to the existing institutional structure, which is itself a product of politics. And if this is the case, what the neoliberals are really doing when they talk of depoliticization of the market is to assume that the particular boundary between market and the state *they* wish to draw is the correct one, and that any attempt to contest that boundary is a 'politically-minded' one. If there appears to be a fixed boundary between the two in certain instances, it is only because those concerned do not even realize that the rights-obligations structure which underpins that boundary is potentially contestable.

Moreover, in calling for depoliticization of the economy, the neoliberals are not only dressing up their own political views as 'objective' and 'above politics', but are also undermining the principle of democratic control. The neoliberal call for depoliticization is often justified in populist rhetoric as an attempt to defend the so-called 'silent majority' from the corrupt politicians, fiefdom-building bureaucrats and powerful interest groups. However, the diminution of the legitimate domain of politics that the neoliberal proposal for depoliticization will bring about only serves to further diminish what little political influence the 'silent majority' have in modifying the market outcomes.

The market is therefore ultimately a political construct, and thus a full depoliticization of the market is not only an impossibility but also has danger-ous anti-democratic undertones. Note, however, that by saying this we are not denying that a certain degree of depoliticization of the resource allocation process may be necessary. Indeed, an excessive politicization of the resource allocation process made the management of the Communist economies difficult. However, this is not the same as arguing, as the neoliberals do, that no market should under any circumstances be subject to political modifi-cations, because in the final analysis, there is no market which can be really free from politics.

4. An alternative view: an institutionalist political economy approach

In the previous section, I have provided a critique of the prevailing neoliberal approach to the understanding of the market, the state and institutions (and the interrelationship between them). In this section, I will outline an alterna-tive approach, which I call the institutionalist political economy approach, that I think allows us to overcome the conceptual limitations and the covert political biases of the neoliberal approach.

4.1 Analysis of the market

The international political economy (henceforth IPE) framework emphasizes that markets need a complex set of formal and informal institutions in their definition and operation. Many of these institutions are 'invisible' because the rights-obligations structures that underlie them are taken so much for granted that they are seen as inalienable components of naturally-ordered free markets. However, no institution, however 'natural' it may look, can be regarded as such, and although in many cases we may choose to accept many institutions as given, in the final analysis we should be willing and able to subject all institutions that support markets to analytical and political scrutiny.

To begin with, all markets are based on institutions that regulate who can participate. For example, laws may stipulate that certain types of individuals (e.g. slaves, foreigners) cannot own property. Banking laws or pension laws may limit the range of assets that banks or pension funds own, and therefore limit the range of asset markets that they can enter. Who can participate in which labour market will be affected not only by formal state regulations and by private sector agents (e.g. laws regulating professional qualifications, rules of unions and professional associations) but also by social conventions regarding caste, gender and ethnicity. Company laws and industrial licensing rules will decide who can participate in the product market, while stock-market listing rules and brokerage regulations determine who can participate in the stock market.

Second, there are institutions which determine the legitimate objects of market exchange (and, by implication, ownership). In all countries, there are laws illegalizing transactions in things like addictive drugs, 'indecent' publications, human organs, or firearms (although different societies have different views on what count as, say, addictive drugs or indecent publications). Laws on slavery, child labour and immigration will stipulate, respectively, that human beings, labour service of children and labour service of illegal immigrants may not be legitimate objects of exchange.

Third, even when the legitimate participants in, and the legitimate objects of, exchange have been stipulated, we need institutions that define what exactly each agent's rights and obligations are in which areas. So, for instance, zoning laws, environmental regulations (e.g. those regarding pollution or noise), fire regulations and so on, define how property rights in land can be exercised (e.g. what kinds of building can be built where). To give another example, laws regarding health, safety, and grievance resolution in workplaces will define the rights and the obligations of workers and employers.

Fourth, there are numerous institutions that regulate the process of exchange itself. For example, there are rules regarding fraud, breach of contract, default, bankruptcy and other disruptions in the exchange process; these rules are backed up by the police, the court system and other legal institutions. Consumer and liability laws will stipulate when and how buyers of unsatisfactory or faulty products may annul the act of purchase and/or claim compensation from the sellers. Social conventions (e.g. those regarding fairness and probity) or codes of conduct issued by trade associations (e.g. bankers' associations) may also influence the way economic agents behave in economic transactions.

Emphasizing the institutional nature of the market requires that we have to bring politics explicitly into the analysis of the market, not just into the analysis of the state, and stop pretending – as the neoliberals do – that markets need to be, and can be, 'depoliticized'. Markets are in the end political constructs, in the sense that they are defined by a range of formal and informal institutions that embody certain rights and obligations, whose legitimacy (and therefore contestability) is ultimately determined in the realm of politics. This is why the 'political economy' in IPE is political economy in a much more fundamental sense than the neoclassical political economy that neoliberal economists deploy.

4.2 Analysis of the state

The neoliberal analysis of the state starts by questioning the 'public' nature of the motivations of the agents, such as politicians and state bureaucrats, that comprise the state. The theory of human motivation and behaviour underlying this analysis, and for that matter neoliberalism as a whole, asserts that self-aggrandizement is the only 'genuine' human motivation, except perhaps that vis-a-vis family members.[25]

However, as many critics have pointed out, human motivations are multifaceted and there are just too many kinds of non-selfish human behaviour that cannot be explained without admitting a range of non-selfish motivations and assuming a complex interaction between them.[26] This criticism applies even more to the analysis of the state and other aspects of public life, not only because individuals often join public life with commitments to certain non-selfish values (e.g. the public-service ethic, social reform, liberalism, party loyalty, nationalism) but also because, operating in an explicitly 'public' sphere of life, they end up internalizing many 'publicly-oriented' values.

A more fundamental criticism of the neoliberal view of human motivation is that it treats individual motivations (or what they call 'preferences') as the ultimate data. In this analysis, institutions may be able to shape individual *behaviour* by punishing or rewarding particular types of behaviour, but they are not able to change the *motivation* itself.[27] In contrast, IPE does not see these motivations as given, but as being fundamentally shaped by the institutions surrounding the individuals. This is because institutions embody certain 'values' and, by operating under these institutions, individuals inevitably internalize some of these values, thereby altering themselves. This is what I call the 'constitutive role of institutions', and it is a central hallmark of a truly 'institutionalist' approach, different from the neoliberal institutionalism of the so-called New Institutional Economics (NIE), which sees institutions as products of maximizing behaviour by individuals with pre-formed preferences.

Of course, if IPE is not to lapse into an unwarranted structural determinism, we need to accept that individuals also influence the way institutions are formed and run, as is typically the case in the NIE models. However, IPE differs from NIE in that it postulates a two-way causation between individual motivation and social institutions, rather than a one-way causation from individuals to institutions.[28] How can the IPE view of human motivation improve our theory of the state and the state reform policy that follows from it?

Neoliberal commentators have typically recommended the introduction of more individualistic and materialistic reward and sanction mechanisms to improve the workings of the bureaucracy (more monitoring, higher salaries, tougher punishments). IPE acknowledges the usefulness of these institutions that target *behaviours* directly, but would argue that behavioural standards can be also improved, and in some cases more effectively improved, by changing the *motivations* of public personages. This, in turn, can happen through direct ideological exhortation (e.g., emphasizing the public-service ethic in bureaucratic training), but also more indirectly, given the constitutive role of institutions, through changing the institutions that surround them (e.g. devising incentive systems that reward teamwork in the bureaucracy in order to boost *esprit de corps*).

Indeed, I would go a step further and argue that some of the measures that the neoliberals recommend as ways of improving the behavioural standards of public personages may be downright counterproductive, if they undermine the non-selfish motivations that had previously motivated the people in question – that is, if they lead to what Ellerman calls the 'atrophy of intrinsic motivation'.[29] These measures may make government officials behave in a more 'moral' way in areas where monitoring is easier (e.g. diligently documenting their expenses for business trips). However, it may make them less *motivated* to behave in a moral way and take initiatives in areas where monitoring is difficult (e.g. taking intellectual initiatives without material compensations), because it will make them feel that they are not trusted as 'moral' agents any more and therefore that they are under no moral obligations to behave morally unless they are forced to do so.

4.3 Analysis of politics

Neoliberal political economy has made an important contribution to the debate on the role of the state by bringing politics back into the analysis of state action. However, its claim that politics inevitably generates state actions that go against market 'rationality' is highly problematic.

First of all, neoliberals are claiming that markets should and can be free from politics. However, as I have argued, it is a myth that markets can be free from politics. I accept that this myth may be useful, or even necessary, in containing the potentially disruptive effects of a very high degree of contestation of the rights-obligation structure underlying existing markets. However, its usefulness does not alter the fact that it is still a myth. IPE argues that markets are fundamentally political constructs and therefore that it is not possible, or even desirable, to try to completely rid markets of politics as the neoliberals wish (see section 3.5).

Second, by portraying the particular boundary of the market that they are advocating (beyond which, they argue, political influences should not be allowed) as the 'rational' one, the neoliberals are claiming an objectivity that no theory can claim. However, once we accept the political nature of the market, we can see that there is no 'objective' way to decide the 'correct' boundary between the market and the state, as one's political view will deeply influence whether one sees a particular boundary as a legitimate (or, in their language, 'rational') one. In contrast, IPE argues that we need to see politics as a process through which people with different, and equally legitimate, views on the contestability of the existing rights-obligations structure vie with each other, rather than as a process in which interest groups try to change the 'natural' order of 'free markets' according to their own particular interests.

Therefore, IPE treats politics not as something alien and damaging to the market but as an integral part of its construction, operation and change, although it acknowledges the harm that excessive politicization can do. It also emphasizes that there is no such thing as a 'correct' political view and therefore that no one should be able to claim the boundary between the market and the state that he/she believes in to be the 'correct' one.

I would go even further and criticize the neoliberal analysis of politics for its failure to recognize the extent to which politics itself is an institutionally-structured process.[30] Of course, I am not here saying that institutions do not feature in the neoliberal analysis of politics. On the contrary, it has tried to analyze, often with success, how the formal and informal institutions that govern the way in which interests are organized and power exercized affect political actions (e.g. electoral rules, rules regulating the behaviour of public figures, rules on agenda formation and voting in parliamentary committees). However, like the other neoliberal analyses involving institutions, it has not gone beyond seeing institutions as 'constraining' factors on human behaviour and fails to see that institutions are also 'constitutive', namely that they can influence politics not only by affecting human actions but also by influencing individual motivations and worldviews.[31] Three related, but different, mechanisms are involved here.

First of all, institutions influence the very perception of their interests by individuals. So, for example, in societies containing political parties with more class-conscious organizations (e.g. formal affiliations between political parties and trade unions or employers' associations), many more voters will vote along 'class lines' than in societies without such parties.

Second, institutions influence people's views on what kinds of issues are legitimate targets of political action. So, for example, in societies where child labour is no longer a legitimate policy issue, not even people who will potentially benefit from such practice will start lobbying for its reintroduction, not simply because they fear some formal or informal sanctions but more significantly because they do not even think the issue to be a legitimate item on the agenda for political action by any group.[32]

Third, institutions influence how individuals perceive the legitimacy of particular types of political actions. So, for example, rent-seeking is likely to be less widespread in societies where open lobbying is, even if legal, considered to be in 'poor taste' than in societies where it is not, even if both societies have the same scope for rent-seeking.

As we can see from the above discussion, unless we break the neoliberal mould and see institutions both as constraining people's behaviour and as being constitutive of their motivations and perceptions, our understanding of politics will remain biased and incomplete.

5. Concluding remarks

This chapter has pointed out that the dominant neoliberal view on the role of the state in economic development suffers from a host of problems. It is based on a very biased reading of the history of capitalism and globalization. It not only suffers from the tension between its two key components – neoclassical economics and Libertarian-Austrian political philosophy – but also from some fundamental conceptual deficiencies that stem from the very ways in which it theorizes about the market, the state and other institutions. This chapter has outlined an alternative theoretical framework, which takes institutions and politics seriously and is thus called institutional political economy (IPE). It is hoped that this new theory will help us break the conceptual shackles of neoliberal political economy that has dominated the debates on the role of the state in economic development during the last two decades.

Notes

1 Deane 1989.
2 Chang 2002a, pp. 13–19.
3 Bhagwati 1985, p. 22, n. 10.
4 Sachs and Warner 1995, pp. 11–21.
5 Ruggiero 1998, p. 131.
6 Chang 2002a.
7 Indeed, the infant industry argument was first systematically developed in the USA by the country's first Treasury Secretary, Alexander Hamilton, and the economist Daniel Raymond. Friedrich List, the German economist who is widely regarded as the father of the infant industry argument, first learned of the argument when he was in exile in the USA during the 1820s (Chang 2002a, p. 25).
8 One somewhat paradoxical consequence of all these limitations was that tariff protection was far more important as a policy tool in the nineteenth century than it is in our time.
9 Chang and Rowthorn 1995.
10 All the data in this and the following paragraphs are from Chang 2002a, chapter 4, unless stated otherwise.
11 For example, during the first half of the twentieth century, per capita incomes in the postwar 'miracle' economies of Korea, Thailand, and Taiwan grew at 0.1%, 0.1%, and 0.4% p.a. respectively. During the same period, per capita income actually *contracted* at the rate of 0.1% p.a. in India and Indonesia, while that in China contracted at the rate of 0.3% p.a.. The data comes from Maddison 1989.
12 This and the next section draw heavily on Chang 2002b.
13 For example, the celebrated 'urban bias' argument of Lipton (1977) argued that the political strengths of the urban groups (e.g., industrialists, trade unions) in developing countries inevitably induce their governments to siphon resources from agriculture, where the countries have a comparative advantage, and channel them into internationally-uncompetitive, protected industries, whose owners and workers benefit from the resulting 'rents'. See Byres 1979 for a criticism.
14 Krueger 1980.
15 Schumpeter 1987.
16 Amsden 1989.
17 Helleiner 1990.
18 Indeed, the famous Polish political economist Oskar Lange justified his model of 'market socialism' using neoclassical economic theory.
19 Works of the American trade economist Paul Krugman provide some of the best examples. In many of his articles, a few paragraphs of 'pop political economy' analysis dismissing the integrity and ability of the state are deployed to discredit his own elaborate strategic trade-theory models endorsing state intervention that make up the bulk of the article. A leading neoliberal economist, Robert Lucas, reviewing Krugman's book with Helpmann, asked why they had written the book in the first place, if they were going to conclude that the interventionist policies that follow from their models cannot be recommended because of the political dangers that they carry (see Lucas 1990). This example shows that, in this neoliberal age, an economist may build models that recommend state intervention as far as they are 'technically competent', but, if he is to remain in the mainstream, he has to prove his political credentials by rubbishing his own models on political grounds.

20 Hirschman 1982.
21 Williamson 1975, p. 20. Williamson argues this is an innocent assumption, because you will get the same result if you started with the assumption that 'in the beginning there was central planning' (pp. 20–1), but this is not true. That this is not the case will become clearer later in our chapter.
22 Polanyi 1957, p. 140.
23 Chang and Nolan 1995; Stiglitz 2001.
24 For further discussions on the issue of central bank independence, see Grabel 2000.
25 Williamson 1993 is a recent and passionate defence of this theory.
26 Simon 1983; McPherson 1984; Frey 1997.
27 Ellerman 1999; Hodgson 2000.
28 IPE would, in addition, argue that in the final analysis a truly institutionalist analysis should see institutions as at least 'temporally prior' to individuals (Hodgson 2000).
29 Ellerman 1999.
30 See Chang and Evans 2000 for further discussions. March and Olsen 1989 argues along this line from a political science perspective.
31 Chang and Evans 2000.
32 See Goodin 1986 for further discussions of the issue of 'public agenda formation'.

References

Amsden, A, 1989, *Asia's Next Giant*, New York, Oxford University Press.
Bhagwati, J, 1985, *Protectionism*, Cambridge, Massachusetts, The MIT Press.
Byres, T, 1977, 'Of Neo-Populist Pipe Dreams: Daedalus in the Third World and the Myth of Urban Bias', *Journal of Peasant Studies*, vol. 6, no. 2.
Chang, H-J, 2002a, *Kicking Away the Ladder: Development Strategy in Historical Perspective*, London, Anthem Press.
——, 2002b, 'Breaking the Mould: An Institutionalist Political Economy Alternative to the Neo-liberal Theory of the Market and the State', *Cambridge Journal of Economics*, vol. 26, no. 5.
Chang, H-J and Evans, P, 2000, 'The Role of Institutions in Economic Change', a paper prepared for the meetings of the 'Other Canon' Group, Venice, January, 2000 and Oslo, August 2000.
Chang, H-J and Nolan, P, 1995, 'Europe versus Asia – Contrasting Paths to the Reform of Centrally Planned Systems of Political Economy', in H-J Chang and P Nolan, eds., *The Transformation of the Communist Economies – Against the Mainstream*, London, Macmillan.
Chang, H-J, and Rowthorn, R, 1995, 'Introduction' in H-J Chang and R Rowthorn, 1995, eds., *Role of the State in Economic Change*, Oxford, Oxford University Press.
Deane, P, 1989, *The State and the Economic System*, Oxford, Oxford University Press.
Ellerman, D, 1999, 'Helping Others to Help Themselves: The Challenge of Autonomy-Compatible Development Assistance,' mimeo., Washington, DC, The World Bank.
Frey, B, 1997, *Not Just for the Money – An Economic Theory of Personal Motivation*, Cheltenham, Edward Elgar.
Goodin, R, 1986, 'Laundering Preferences', in J Elster and A Hylland, 1986, eds., *Foundations of Social Choice Theory*, Cambridge, Cambridge University Press.
Grabel, I, 2000, 'The Political Economy of "Policy Credibility": The New-Classical

Macroeconomics and the Remaking of Emerging Economies', *Cambridge Journal of Economics*, vol. 24, no. 1.

Hodgson, G, 2000, 'Structures and Institutions: Reflections on Institutionalism, Structuration Theory and Critical Realism', mimeo., The Business School, University of Hertfordshire.

Helleiner, G, 1990, 'Trade Strategy in Medium-term Adjustment', *World Development*, vol. 18, no. 6.

Hirschman, A, 1982, 'Rival Views of Market Society', *Journal of Economic Literature*, vol. 48, no. 4.

Krueger, A, 1980, 'Trade Policy as an Input to Development', *American Economic Review*, vol. 80, no. 2.

Lucas, R, 1990, 'Review of *Trade Policy and Market Structure* by E Helpman and P Krugman (1989, Cambridge, Massachusetts, MIT Press)', *Journal of Political Economy*, vol. 98, no. 3.

Lipton, M, 1977, *Why Poor People Stay Poor*, London, Temple Smith.

Maddison, A, 1989, *The World Economy in the 20th Century*, Paris, OECD.

March, J and Olsen, J, 1989, *Rediscovering Institutions – The Organizational Basis of Politics*, New York, The Free Press.

McPherson, M, 1984, 'Limits of Self-Seeking: The Role of Morality in Economic Life' in D Colander, 1984, ed., *Neoclassical Political Economy*, Cambridge, Massachusetts, Balliger Publisher.

Polanyi, K, 1957, *The Great Transformation*, Boston, Beacon Press.

Sachs, J and Warner, A, 1995, 'Economic Reform and the Process of Global Integration', *Brookings Papers on Economic Activity*, 1995, no. 1.

Schumpeter, J, 1987, *Capitalism, Socialism and Democracy*, 6th edition, London, Unwin Paperbacks.

Simon, H, 1983, *Reasons in Human Behaviour*, Oxford, Basil Blackwell.

Stiglitz, J, 2001, 'Whither Reform? – Ten Years of the Transition', in H-J Chang, 2001, ed., *Joseph Stiglitz and the World Bank – The Rebel Within*, London, Anthem Press.

Williamson, O, 1975, *Markets and Hierarchies*, New York, The Free Press.

——, 1993, 'Calculativeness, Trust, and Economic Organisation', *Journal of Law and Economics*, vol. 36.

3

GLOBALIZATION AND DEVELOPMENT*

Deepak Nayyar

This chapter endeavours to situate the process of globalization in the wider context of development. In doing so, it explores the implications of globalization for development in retrospect and prospect. The structure of the chapter is as follows. Section 1 sets out the essential meaning of development, in light of the very uneven development experience and the fundamental change in thinking about development strategies over the past fifty years. Section 2 outlines the dimensions and characteristics of globalization in our times. Section 3 examines the economic factors, the political conjuncture and the intellectual rationale underlying globalization. Section 4 explores the historical origins of globalization, comparing current trends in globalization with those of the late nineteenth century, and highlighting similarities and differences between the two. Section 5 discusses how globalization led to uneven development in the late nineteenth century. Section 6 considers the development experience of the world economy during the last quarter of the twentieth century, which suggests that the exclusion of countries and of people, attributable partly to the logic of markets, is a fact of life. It suggests that, without correctives, it would lead to uneven development now. Section 7 argues that sensible strategies of development in a world of globalization should create economic space for the pursuit of national interests and development objectives. In this task there is a strategic role for the nation state, both in the national and international context.

---

* This essay draws upon some earlier work of the author. See Nayyar 1995; 1997; 2000; 2001. The author would like to thank Ram Singh for helpful suggestions and valuable assistance.

1. Conception of development

There is a vast literature on economic development which is rich in both its range and depth. Yet there is not enough clarity about what development actually means. There are in fact many different views of what it constitutes, and these perceptions have changed over time. There is, however, an irreducible objective which may be construed as the essential meaning: development must bring about an improvement in the living conditions of people. It should, therefore, ensure the provision of basic human needs for all – not just food and clothing, but also shelter, health care and education. This simple but powerful proposition is often forgotten in the pursuit of material wealth and the conventional concerns of economics. Early literature on development emphasized economic growth and capital accumulation at a macro level; contemporary literature on development stresses economic efficiency and productivity increases at a micro level. Industrialization has always been seen as an essential attribute of development: emphasis has simply shifted from the pace of industrialization to the efficiency of industrialization.

The underlying presumption is that economic growth and economic efficiency are not only necessary but also sufficient to bring about an improvement in the living conditions of people. From time to time, dissenting voices questioned conventional wisdom about using economic growth, or increases in per capita income, as a measure of development, and instead suggested other indicators of development, such as reductions in poverty, inequality and unemployment, that would indicate changes in the quality of life.[1] But these aspects of development were largely ignored by mainstream economics because it did not make this distinction. Economic growth and economic efficiency, or for that matter industrialization, are means. It is development which is an end. Thus, in order to attain development, growth and efficiency need to be combined with full employment, poverty eradication, reduced inequality, human development and a sustainable environment. The purpose of development, after all, is to create a milieu that enables people, ordinary people, to lead a good life.

In conventional terms, the world has made enormous economic progress during the second half of the twentieth century. Over the past fifty years, world GDP has multiplied tenfold while per capita income has trebled.[2] The growth has been impressive even in the developing world, particularly when compared with the underdevelopment and the stagnation of the colonial era during the first half of the twentieth century. But such aggregates might conceal more than they reveal, for development has been very uneven between countries and within countries. The pattern of development has been such that it has led to an increase in the economic distance between the industrialized world and much of the developing world. It has also led to an increase in the economic distance between the newly industrializing countries, at one end, and the least developed countries, at the other. At the same time, economic disparities between regions and between people within countries have also registered an increase. In other words, many parts of the world and a significant proportion of its people have been largely excluded from development. This may be attributable to the logic of markets, which give to those who have and take away from those who have not, as the process of cumulative causation leads to market-driven virtuous circles and vicious circles. This may be the outcome of patterns of development where economic growth is uneven between regions and the distribution of its benefits is unequal between people, so that there is growing affluence for some combined with persistent poverty for many. This may be the consequence of strategies of development, as a similar economic performance in the aggregate could lead to egalitarian development in one situation, and growth which bypasses the majority of people in another situation.

Uneven development has its consequences. Poverty, inequality and deprivation persist. And there is poverty everywhere. One eighth of the people in the industrialized world are affected by, or live in, poverty. Almost one third of the people in the developing world – an estimated 1.5 billion – live in poverty and experience absolute deprivation insofar as they cannot meet their basic human needs. The same number does not have access to clean water. As many as 840 million people suffer from malnutrition. More than 260 million children who should be in school are not. Nearly 340 million women are not expected to survive to the age of 40. And, as we enter the 21st century, more than 850 million adults remain illiterate. Most of them live in the developing world. But, in a functional sense, the number of illiterate people in the industrialized countries – 100 million – is also large.[3]

It is clear that the development experience of the world economy since 1950 has been uneven and mixed. The attempts to analyse what turned out right and what went wrong have led to both diagnosis and prescription. This in turn has meant a fundamental change in thinking about development strategies.[4] In the postcolonial era, which began soon after the end of World War II, most underdeveloped countries adopted strategies of development which provided a sharp contrast with those of the first half of the twentieth century. For one, there was a conscious attempt to limit the degree of openness and integration with the world economy, in pursuit of a more autonomous development. For another, the state was assigned a strategic role in development because the market, by itself, was not perceived as sufficient to meet the aspirations of latecomers to industrialization. Both represented points of departure from the colonial era, which was characterized by open economies and unregulated markets. In the early 1950s, this new approach also represented a consensus in thinking about the most appropriate strategy of industrialization. Despite a few voices of dissent it was, in effect, the development consensus at the time. 40 years later, in the early 1990s, perceptions about development apparently arrived at the polar opposite. Most countries in the developing world, as also in the erstwhile socialist bloc, began to reshape their domestic economic policies so as to integrate much more with the world economy and to enlarge the role of the market vis-a-vis the state. This was partly a consequence of internal crisis situations in economy, polity and society. It was also significantly influenced by the profound transformation in the world economic and political situation. The widespread acceptance of this approach, it would seem, represented a new consensus in thinking about development, which came to be known as the Washington Consensus. Although there was considerable dissent, this remained the dominant view, in part because it was propagated by the IMF and the World Bank, which exercized enormous influence on economies in crisis. However, this belief system was somewhat shaken by the financial crisis in Asia, and the Washington Consensus has also lost some of its lustre as the development experience during the 1990s has belied expectations. Its prescriptions are now subjected to question.[5] And the questions have not come from its critics alone.[6]

In spite of the paradigm shift from the development consensus of the 1950s to the Washington Consensus of the 1990s, the degree of openness vis-a-vis the world economy and the degree of intervention by the state in the market have remained the critical issues in the debate on development. The past fifty years have of course witnessed a complete swing of the pendulum in thinking about these issues. But the complexity of reality is not captured by either consensus. The reality, however, is clear. The exclusion of countries and of people from development has become much less acceptable with the passage of time. The proposition that economic growth, or economic efficiency, will ultimately improve the lot of the people is, obviously, far less credible 50 years later.

2. Contours of globalization

Globalization means different things to different people, and the word 'globalization' is used in two ways, which is itself a source of some confusion. It is used in a *positive* sense to *describe* a process of increasing integration into the world economy. It is used in a *normative* sense to *prescribe* a strategy of development based on a rapid integration with the world economy: some see this as salvation, while others see it as damnation.

Even its characterization, however, is by no means uniform. Globalization can be described, simply, as the expansion of economic activities across national boundaries. In this elementary sense, the world economy has experienced a progressive international economic integration since 1950. However, there has been a marked acceleration in this process of globalization during the last quarter of the twentieth century. There are three economic manifestations of this phenomenon – international trade, international investment and international finance – which also constitute its cutting edge. But there is much more to globalization than this. The term refers to the expansion of economic transactions and the organization of economic activities across political boundaries of nation states. More precisely, it can be defined as a process associated with increasing economic openness, growing economic interdependence and deepening economic integration in the world economy.

Economic *openness* is not simply confined to trade flows, investment flows and financial flows. It also extends to flows of services, technology, information and ideas across national boundaries. But the cross-border movement of people is closely regulated and highly restricted. Economic *interdependence* is asymmetrical. There is a high degree of interdependence among countries in the industrialized world, but considerable dependence of developing countries on the industrialized countries, and much less interdependence among countries in the developing world. It is important to note that a situation of interdependence is one where the benefits of linking and costs of delinking are about the same for both partners; where such benefits and costs are unequal between partners, a situation of dependence is implied. Economic *integration* straddles national boundaries as liberalization has diluted the significance of borders in economic transactions. Globalization is, in part, an integration of markets (for goods, services, technology, financial assets and even money) on the demand side, and, in part, an integration of production (horizontal and vertical) on the supply side.

The gathering momentum of globalization has brought about profound changes in the world economy. It is worth highlighting the characteristics of these changes.[7] An increasing proportion of world output is entering into world trade, while an increasing proportion of world trade is made up of intra-firm trade. Between the early 1970s and the late 1990s, the share of world exports in world GDP rose from 1/8 to almost 1/5.[8] The share of intra-firm trade in world trade, which was 1/5 in the early 1970s, rose to 1/3 in the early 1990s.[9] The significance of international investment flows also registered a rapid increase. Between 1980 and 1996, the stock of direct foreign investment in the world as a proportion of world output rose from less than 5% to more than 10%, while world direct foreign investment flows as a proportion of world gross fixed capital formation rose from 2% to almost 6%.[10]

The growth in international finance has been explosive, so much so that, in terms of magnitudes, trade and investment are now dwarfed by finance. The expansion of international banking is phenomenal, while the international market for financial assets has experienced a similar growth. There is a growing international market for government bonds;[11] the size of international foreign exchange markets is staggering. Global foreign exchange transactions have soared from $60 billion per day in 1983 to $1500 billion per day in 1997.[12] By comparison, in 1997, world GDP was $82 billion per day and world exports were $16 billion per day, while the foreign exchange reserves of all central banks put together were $1550 billion.[13]

3. Origins and foundations

The origins of globalization need to be analysed in terms of the economic factors underlying the process, the political circumstances that have enabled it to gather momentum and the intellectual rationale that is now almost prescriptive. We will consider each of these issues in turn.

The economic factors which have made globalization possible are: the dismantling of barriers to international economic transactions; the development of enabling technologies; and emerging forms of industrial organization. Globalization has followed the sequence of deregulation in the world economy. Trade liberalization came first, which led to an unprecedented expansion of international trade between 1950 and 1970. The liberalization of regimes for foreign investment came next, while a surge in international investment began in the late 1960s. Financial liberalization came last, starting in the early 1980s. This had two dimensions: the deregulation of the domestic financial sector in the industrialized countries and the introduction of convertibility on capital account in the balance of payments. These did not occur simultaneously. The United States, Canada, Germany and Switzerland removed restrictions on capital movements in 1973, while Britain and Japan did so in 1979 and 1980 respectively, and France and Italy made the transition as late as 1990. The globalization of finance, which has happened at a scorching pace since the mid-1980s, is not unrelated to the dismantling of regulations and controls.

The technological revolution in transport and communications has been a crucial factor in globalization. The second half of the twentieth century has witnessed the advent of jet aircraft, computers and satellites. The synthesis of communications technology, which is concerned with the transmission of information, and computer technology which is concerned with the processing of information, has created information technology that is remarkable in both scope and speed. These technological developments have had a dramatic impact on reducing geographical barriers. The time needed is a tiny fraction of what it was earlier, while cost incurred has been sharply reduced.

New forms of industrial organization have played a role in making globalization possible. The emerging flexible production system, shaped by the nature of technical progress, the changing output mix and the organizational characteristics (based on Japanese management systems) is forcing firms to constantly choose between trade and investment in their drive to expand activities across borders. The declining share of wages in production costs, the increasing importance of proximity between producers and consumers and the growing externalization of services are exercising a strong influence on the strategies and behaviour of firms in the process of globalization.

The politics of hegemony or dominance is conducive to the economics of globalization. The process of globalization, beginning in the early 1970s, has coincided with the political dominance of the United States as superpower. This political dominance has grown stronger with the collapse of communism and the triumph of capitalism, while political circumstances have transformed the concept of globalization into a 'virtual ideology' for our times. Dominance in the realm of politics is associated with an important attribute in the sphere of economics. For globalization requires a dominant economic power with a national currency which is accepted as the equivalent of international money: as a unit of account, a medium of exchange and a store of value. This role is being performed by the US dollar.

Economic theorizing often follows in the footsteps of political reality. It should come as no surprise, then, that recent years have witnessed the formulation of an intellectual rationale for globalization that is almost prescriptive. Globalization is perceived as a means of ensuring not only efficiency and equity but also growth and development in the world economy, and the analytical foundations of this world view are provided by the neoliberal model. Orthodox neoclassical economics suggests that intervention in markets is inefficient, while neoliberal political economy argues that governments are incapable of intervening efficiently. The essence of the neoliberal model, then, can be stated as follows. First, the government should be rolled back wherever possible so that it approximates to the ideal of a minimalist state. Second, the market is not only a substitute for the state but also the preferred alternative because it performs better. Third, resource allocation and resource utilization must be based on market prices which should conform as closely as possible to international prices. Fourth, national political objectives, domestic economic concerns or even national boundaries should not act as constraints. In conformity with this world view, governments everywhere, particularly in the developing countries and the former communist countries, are being urged or pushed into a comprehensive agenda of privatization (to minimize the role of the state) and liberalization (of trade flows, capital flows and financial flows). It is suggested that such policy regimes would provide the foundations for a global economic system characterized by free trade, unrestricted capital mobility, open markets and harmonized institutions. The ideologues believe that such globalization promises economic prosperity for countries that join the system and economic deprivation for countries that do not.[14] It needs to be stressed that this intertwined normative and prescriptive view of globalization is driven in part by ideology and in part by hope. It is not borne out by experience.

4. Historical parallel

There is a common assumption that the present set of circumstances, with globalization changing the character of the world economy, is altogether new and represents a fundamental departure from the past. However, such an assumption is incorrect: globalization is in fact nothing new. There was a similar phase of globalization which began a century earlier, around 1870, and gathered momentum until 1914, when it came to an abrupt end. The period from 1870 to 1914 was also the age of *laissez-faire*. Government intervention in economic activity was minimal and the movement of goods, capital and labour across national boundaries was almost unhindered. It was believed that the virtuous circle of rapid economic growth and the process of international economic integration in this era were closely related.

In many ways, the world economy in the late twentieth and early 21st centuries resembles the world economy in the late nineteenth century.[15] The parallels between the two periods are striking. The integration of the world economy through international trade at the turn of the nineteenth century was about the same as it was towards the end of the twentieth. For 16 major industrialized countries, now in the OECD, the share of exports in GDP rose from 18.2% in 1900 to 21.2% in 1913, even though tariffs were then much higher.[16] The story was about the same for international investment. In 1913, the stock of direct foreign investment in the world economy was 9% of world output.[17] At constant prices, total foreign investment in the world economy in 1914 was 4/5 of what it was in 1980.[18] What is more, the stock of foreign investment in developing countries was probably equal to about 1/4 their GDP at the turn of the century, and at constant prices, in 1914, this stock was almost double what it was in 1980.[19] The integration of markets for international finance was also comparable. The cross-national ownership of securities, including government bonds, reached very high levels.[20] International bank lending was substantial and, in relative terms, net international capital flows were much bigger than they are now. The only missing dimension was international transactions in foreign exchange (given the regime of fixed exchange rates under the gold standard).

There are striking similarities in the underlying factors which made globalization possible then and now.[21] There were almost no restrictions on the movement of goods, capital and labour across national boundaries, so that there was no need to dismantle barriers or liberalize regimes for international economic transactions. The advent of the steamship, the railway and the telegraph brought about a revolution in transport and communications.[22] This led to an enormous reduction in the time needed, and the cost incurred, in traversing geographical distances. Emerging forms of industrial organization performed a critical role. In the late nineteenth century, the advent of mass production was characterized by a rigid compartmentalization of functions and a high degree of mechanization. Mass production realized economies of scale and led to huge cost reductions compared with craft manufacturing.[23] Apart from dominance in the realm of politics, *Pax Britannica* provided a reserve currency, the pound sterling, which was the equivalent of international money. For this was 'the age of empire' when Britain more or less ruled the world.[24]

There are also important differences between the two phases of globalization. I would like to highlight four such differences: in trade flows, in investment flows, in financial flows and most important, perhaps, in labour flows, across national boundaries.

There are differences in the composition of trade and in the channels of trade. During the period from 1870 to 1913, an overwhelming proportion of international trade was constituted by inter-sectoral trade, where primary commodities were exchanged for manufactured goods. The trade was to a significant extent based on absolute advantage derived from natural resources or climatic conditions. Although trade flows were in the domain of large international firms, it was not intra-firm trade.

Differences also exist in the geographical destination and the sectoral distribution of investment flows. In 1914, the stock of long-term foreign investment in the world economy was distributed as follows: 55% in the industrialized world (30% in Europe, 25% in the United States) and 45% in the underdeveloped world (20% in Latin America and 25% in Asia and Africa). It is clear that developing countries are now far less central to the process.[25]

In 1913, the primary sector accounted for 55% of long-term foreign investment in the world, while transport, trade and distribution accounted for another 30%; the manufacturing sector accounted for only 10% and much of this was concentrated in North America or Europe.[26] The primary sector is now far less significant, while the manufacturing sector is much more important. In financial flows, there are substantial differences in the destination, the object, the intermediaries and the instruments. In the last quarter of the nineteenth century, capital flows were a means of transferring investible resources to underdeveloped countries or newly-industrialized countries with the most attractive growth opportunities. The object was to find avenues for long-term investments in search of profits. Banks were the only intermediaries between lenders and borrowers in the form of bonds with very long maturities. Securitization of long-term bonds with sovereign guarantees was provided by the imperial powers or the governments in the borrowing countries.

But there is a fundamental difference between the two phases of globalization. It is in the sphere of labour flows. In the late nineteenth century, there were no restrictions on the mobility of people across national boundaries. Passports were seldom needed, and immigrants were granted citizenship with ease. Between 1870 and 1914, international labour migration was enormous. During this period, about 50 million people left Europe, of whom 2/3 went to the United States while the remaining 1/3 went to Canada, Australia, New Zealand, South Africa, Argentina and Brazil.[27] This mass emigration from Europe amounted to 1/8 of its population in 1900. But that was not all: beginning somewhat earlier, following the abolition of slavery in the British empire, about 50 million people left India and China to work as indentured labour on mines, plantations and construction in Latin America, the Caribbean, Southern Africa, South East Asia and other distant lands.[28] The destinations were mostly British, Dutch, French and German colonies. In the second half of the twentieth century, there was a limited amount of international labour migration from the developing countries to the industrialized world during the period 1950–1970. Since then, however, international migration has been reduced to a trickle because of draconian immigration laws and restrictive consular practices. The present phase of globalization has found substitutes for labour mobility in the form of trade and investment flows. For one, industrialized countries now import manufactured goods that embody scarce labour. For another, industrialized countries export capital which employs scarce labour abroad to provide such goods.

5. Uneven development

The ideologues believe that globalization led to rapid industrialization and economic convergence in the world economy during the late nineteenth century. In their view, the promise of the emerging global capitalist system was wasted for more than half a century, first by three decades of conflict and autarchy that followed World War I and subsequently, for another three decades, by the socialist path and a statist world view. The return of globalization in the late twentieth century is thus seen as the road to salvation. The conclusion drawn is that globalization now – as much as then – promises economic prosperity for countries that join the system and economic deprivation for countries that do not.[29] For those who recall the development experience in the late nineteenth century, it should be obvious that the process of globalization will not reproduce or replicate the United States everywhere, just as it did not reproduce Britain everywhere a century earlier. This historical example reveals how globalization was already associated with uneven development, and is bound to produce uneven development now, not only between countries but also within countries.

The economic consequences of globalization in the late nineteenth century were, to say the least, asymmetrical. In this era, most of the gains from international economic integration accrued to the imperial countries which exported capital and imported commodities. There were a few countries like the United States and Canada – new lands with temperate climates and white settlers – which also derived some benefits. In these countries, the preconditions for industrialization were already being created; this process was strengthened by international economic integration, and was reinforced by direct foreign investment in manufacturing activities stimulated by rising tariff barriers, combined with technological and managerial flows. The outcome – industrialization and development – did not happen everywhere. Development was uneven in the industrial world, and much of southern and eastern Europe lagged behind. This meant divergence rather than convergence in terms of industrialization and growth.[30] There was, in fact, an increase in economic inequalities between countries and within countries. The income gap between the richest and the poorest countries, for instance, which was just 3:1 in 1820, more than doubled to 7:1 in 1870 and increased further to 11:1 in 1913.[31] Countries in Asia, Africa and Latin America, particularly the colonized, which were also a part of this process of globalization, were even less fortunate. Indeed, during the same period of rapid international economic integration, some of the most open economies in this phase of globalization – India, China and Indonesia – experienced deindustrialization and underdevelopment. We need to remind ourselves that, in the period from 1870 to 1914, these three countries practised free trade as much as the United Kingdom and the Netherlands, where average tariff levels were close to negligible (3–5%); by contrast, tariff levels in Germany, Japan and France were significantly higher (12–14%), and tariff levels in the United States were very much higher (33%).[32] What is more, these three countries were also among the largest recipients of foreign investment.[33] But their globalization did not lead to development. The outcome was similar elsewhere: in Asia, Africa and Latin America. So much so, that between 1860 and 1913 the share of developing countries in world manufacturing output declined from over 1/3 to under 1/10.[34] In these economies, export-oriented production in mines, plantations and cash-crop agriculture created enclaves which were integrated with the world economy in a vertical division of labour. But there were almost no backward linkages. Productivity levels outside the export enclaves stagnated at low levels. They simply created dualistic economic structures where the benefits of globalization accrued mostly to the outside world and in small part to the local elites.

The growing inequalities between and within countries, particularly in the industrial world, were perhaps a significant factor underlying the retreat from globalization after 1914. The following passage, written by John Maynard Keynes in 1919, vividly highlights the benefits of globalization for some people and some countries, but also recognizes how economic and political conflicts associated with the process stopped what had seemed irreversible at the time.

What an extraordinary episode in the economic progress of man that age was which came to an end in August 1914. The greater part of the population, it is true, worked hard and lived at a low standard of comfort, yet were, to all appearances, reasonably contented with this lot. But escape was possible, for any man of capacity or character at all exceeding the average, into the middle and upper classes, for whom life offered, at a low cost and with the least trouble, conveniences, comforts, and amenities beyond the compass of the richest and most powerful monarchs of other ages. The inhabitant of London could order by telephone, sipping his morning tea in bed, the various products of the whole earth, in such quantity as he may see fit and reasonably expect their early delivery upon his doorstep; he could at the same moment and by the same means adventure his wealth in the natural resources and new enterprises of any quarter of the world, and share, without exertion or trouble, in their prospective fruits and advantages; or he could decide to couple the security of his fortunes with the good faith of the townspeople of any substantial municipality in any continent that fancy or information might recommend. He could secure forthwith, if he wished it, cheap and comfortable means of transit to any country or climate without any passport or other formality, could despatch his servants to the neighbouring office of a bank for such supply of the precious metals as might seem convenient, and could then proceed to foreign quarters, without knowledge of their religion, language or customs, bearing coined wealth upon his person, and could consider himself greatly aggrieved and much surprised at least interference. But most important of all, he regarded this state of affairs as normal, certain, and permanent, except in the direction of further improvement, and any deviation from it as aberrant, scandalous and avoidable. The projects and politics of militarism and imperialism, of racial and cultural rivalries, of monopolies, restrictions and exclusions, which were to play the serpent to this paradise, were little more than amusement of his daily newspaper, and appeared to exercise almost no influence at all on the ordinary course of social and economic life, the internationalization of which was nearly complete in practice[35]

The process of globalization has led to uneven development, now as much as then. The reality that has unfolded so far clearly belies the expectations of the ideologues.

6. Globalization, development and exclusion

The development experience of the world economy from the early 1970s to the late 1990s, which could be termed the 'age of globalization', provides cause for concern, particularly when it is compared with the period from the late 1940s to the early 1970s, which has been described as the golden age of capitalism. Any such periodization is obviously arbitrary, but it serves an analytical purpose.[36]

Available evidence suggests that the past 25 years have witnessed a divergence, rather than convergence, in levels of income between countries and between people. Economic inequalities have increased during the last quarter century as the income gap between rich and poor countries, between the rich and the poor within countries, as well as between the rich and the poor in the world's population, has widened,[37] and income distribution has worsened.[38] The incidence of poverty increased in most countries of Latin America and Sub Saharan Africa during the 1980s and in much of Eastern Europe during the 1990s. Many countries in East Asia, South East Asia and South Asia, which experienced a steady decline in the incidence of poverty, constitute the exception. However, the recent financial meltdown and economic crisis in South East Asia has led to a marked deterioration in the situation. In the developing countries, employment creation in the organized sector continues to lag behind the growth in the labour force, so that an increasing proportion of workers are dependent upon low productivity and casual employment in the informal sector. Unemployment in the industrialized countries has increased substantially since the early 1970s and remained at high levels since then, except in the United States, while there has been almost no increase in the real wages of a significant proportion of the workforce in many industrialized countries. Inequality in terms of wages and incomes has registered an increase almost everywhere in the world. Over the same period, the rate of growth in the world economy has also registered a discernible slowdown. And the slower growth has been combined with greater instability. It would seem that, in some important respects, the world economy fared better in the golden age than it has done in the age of globalization.

It is obviously not possible to attribute cause-and-effect simply to the co-incidence in time. But it is possible to think of mechanisms through which globalization may have accentuated inequalities. Trade liberalization has led to a growing wage inequality between skilled and unskilled workers not only in industrialized countries but also in developing countries.[39] As a consequence of privatization and deregulation, capital has gained at the expense of labour almost everywhere, for profit shares have risen while wage shares have fallen.[40] Structural reforms, which have cut tax rates and brought flexibility to labour markets, have reinforced this trend. The mobility of capital combined with the immobility of labour has changed the nature of the employment relationship and has reduced the bargaining power of trade unions. The object of managing inflation has been transformed into a near-obsession by the sensitivity of international financial markets, so that governments have been forced to adopt deflationary macroeconomic policies that have squeezed both growth and employment. The excess supply of labour has repressed real wages. Financial liberalization, which has meant a rapid expansion of public as well as private debt, has been associated with the emergence of a new rentier class, and the inevitable concentration in the ownership of financial assets has probably contributed to a worsening of income distribution.[41] Global competition has driven large international firms to consolidate market power through mergers and acquisitions, a process which has made market structures more oligopolistic than competitive. The competition for export markets and foreign investment between countries has intensified in what is termed 'a race to the bottom', leading to an unequal distribution of gains from trade and investment.

Globalization has indeed created opportunities for some people and some countries that could not have been considered three decades ago. But it has also introduced new risks, if not threats, for many others. It has been associated with a deepening of poverty and an accentuation of inequalities. The distribution of benefits and costs is unequal. There are some winners: more in the industrialized world than in the developing world. There are many losers: numerous both in the industrialized world and in the developing world. It is perhaps necessary to identify, in broad categories, the winners and the losers.[42]

The winners are asset-owners, profit-earners, rentiers, the educated, the mobile and those with professional, managerial or technical skills, whereas asset-less, wage-earners, debtors, the uneducated, the immobile and the semi-skilled or unskilled are the losers. If we think of firms, large, international, global, risk-takers and technology-leaders are the winners, whereas small, domestic, local, risk-averse and technology-followers are the losers. If we think of economies, capital-exporters, technology-exporters, net lenders, those with a strong physical and human infrastructure, and those endowed with structural flexibilities are the winners, whereas capital-importers, technology-importers, net borrowers, those with a weak physical and human infrastructure, and those characterized by structural rigidities are the losers. It should be said that this classification is suggestive rather than definitive, for it paints a broad-brush picture of a more nuanced situation. But it does convey the simultaneous, yet asymmetrical, inclusion and exclusion that characterizes the process of globalization. It is not surprising, then, that the spread of globalization is uneven and limited both among people and across countries.[43]

Joan Robinson once said: 'There is only one thing that is worse than being exploited by capitalists. And that is not being exploited by capitalists.' Much the same can be said about markets and globalization, which may not ensure prosperity for everyone but may in fact exclude a significant proportion of people. Markets exclude people as consumers or buyers if they do not have any incomes, or sufficient incomes, which can be translated into purchasing power. Such people are excluded from the consumption of goods and services which are sold in the market. This exclusion is attributable to a lack of entitlements.[44] Markets also exclude people as producers or sellers if they have neither *assets* nor *capabilities*; people experience such exclusion if they do not have assets, physical or financial, which can be used (or sold) to yield an income in the form of rent, interest or profits. Even those without assets, however, people can enter the market as sellers, using their labour, if they have some capabilities. Such capabilities that are acquired through education, training or experience are different from natural abilities which are endowed. But the distribution of capabilities may be just as unequal, if not more so. It is these capabilities which can, in turn, yield an income in the form of wages. Hence, people without capabilities, the poor, who cannot find employment, are excluded. In fact even people with capabilities may be excluded from employment if there is no demand for their capabilities in the (labour) market. In the ultimate analysis, such capabilities are defined by the market: that is the problem.

Globalization has introduced a new dimension to the exclusion of people from development. Exclusion is no longer simply about the inability to satisfy basic human needs in terms of food, clothing, shelter, health care and education for large numbers of people. It is much more complicated. For, coupled with globalization, the consumption patterns and lifestyles of the rich have increasingly powerful demonstration effects. People everywhere, even the poor and the excluded, are exposed to these ever-expanding frontiers of consumer choice because the electronic media has spread the consumerist message far and wide. This creates both expectations and aspirations. But the simple fact of life is that those who do not have the incomes cannot buy goods and services in the market. When the paradise of consumerism is unattainable, which is the case for common people, frustration or alienation is often created. The reaction of people who experience such exclusion differs. Some seek short cuts to the consumerist paradise through drugs, crime or violence. Some seek refuge in ethnic identities, cultural chauvinism or religious fundamentalism.[45] Such assertion of traditional or indigenous values is often the only thing that poor people can assert, for these values contribute identity and meaning to their lives. Outcomes do not always take these extreme forms, although globalization inevitably tends to erode social stability.[46] Thus, economic integration with the world outside may accentuate social tensions or provoke social fragmentation within countries.

7. The state and development in the context of globalization

At the start of the 21st century, the facts of life in the world economy are clear. The name of the game is globalization , and no country wishes to be excluded from it: even large countries cannot afford to opt out. The choice, then, is between a market-driven, passive, insertion into the world economy and a selective, strategic, integration into the world economy. The sensible choice would be to opt for the latter. But is it possible to contemplate correctives that would make this market-driven process more people-friendly so that the outcome is globalization with a human face? The object of such a design should be to provide more countries with opportunities to improve their development prospects and more people within these countries with opportunities to improve their living conditions.

Globalization has reduced the autonomy of the nation state in matters economic, if not political, but there remain degrees of freedom which must be exploited in the pursuit of development. The ideology of globalization seeks to harmonize not only policy regimes but also institutions, including the economic role of the state, across the world. This is a mistake, because the role of the state in an economy depends on both level of income and stage of development. The object of any sensible strategy of development in a world of liberalization and globalization should be to create economic space for the pursuit of national interests and development objectives. In this task, there is a strategic role for the nation state, not only in the sphere of domestic economic policies but also in the arena of economic and political interaction with the outside world.[47]

Consider the national context. First, in countries that are latecomers to industrialization, the state must create the conditions for the development of industrial capitalism. In the earlier stages of industrialization, this means creating a physical infrastructure through government investment, investing in the development of human resources through education and catalysing institutional change, say, through agrarian reform. In the later stages of industrialization, this means using strategic industrial policy for the development of technological and managerial capabilities at a micro level, establishing institutions that would facilitate, regulate and govern the functioning of markets, and evolving strategic interventions interlinked across activities to guide the market in the pursuit of long-term development objectives. It must be emphasized that the benefits of integration with the world economy would accrue only to those countries which have laid these requisite foundations. Indeed, creating the preconditions and using strategic intervention are essential for internalizing (maximizing) the benefits and externalizing (minimizing) the costs of globalization.

Second, in the search for foreign investment, the state must resist the temptation to provide incentives and concessions. Indeed, wherever possible, the state must bargain with large international firms. Such an approach would not only improve the distribution of gains from economic transactions with transnational firms but also ensure that their activities are conducive to development. The reason for this is simple. Transnational corporations are in the business of profit while governments are in the business of development. For large countries, this means strategic negotiations in the sphere of trade and investment. For small countries, this means a conscious decision to opt out of 'a race to the bottom'. But this can only be done by governments and not by individuals or firms.

Third, the state must ensure a prudent macro management of the economy, particularly in the sphere of government finance, for two reasons. First, it saves governments from being forced into stabilization and adjustment programmes that come with high conditionality which, in turn, reduces degrees of freedom in the pursuit of development objectives. For another, it reduces the vulnerability and problems associated with rapid integration into international financial markets through portfolio investment or capital account convertibility. The bottom line is that such prudence can enable a country to avoid some of the costs of integration through globalization and, at the same time, to obtain some of the benefits by retaining the freedom to create the necessary conditions.

Consider the international context. In a world of unequal partners, it is not surprising that the rules of the game are asymmetrical in terms of construct and inequitable in terms of outcome. The strong have the power to make, and the authority to implement the rules. Conversely, the weak can neither set nor invoke the rules. The problem, however, takes different forms: there are different rules in different spheres, there are rules for some and not for others, and the agenda for new rules is partisan.

The existing (and prospective) rules of the WTO regime allow few exceptions and provide little flexibility to countries that are latecomers to industrialization. In comparison, there was more room for manoeuvre in the erstwhile GATT, *inter alia*, because of special and differential treatment for developing countries. The new regime is much stricter in terms of law and its implementation. The rules on trade in the new regime will make the selective protection or strategic promotion of domestic firms vis-a-vis foreign competition much more difficult. The tight system for the protection of intellectual property rights might pre-empt or stifle the development of domestic technological capabilities. The possible multilateral agreement on investment, when it materializes, will almost certainly reduce the possibilities of strategic bargaining with transnational firms. Similarly, commitments on structural reform, an integral part of stabilization and adjustment programmes with the IMF and the World Bank, inevitably prescribe industrial deregulation, privatization, trade liberalization and financial deregulation. Taken together, such rules and conditions are bound to curb the use of industrial policy, technology policy, trade policy and financial policy as strategic forms of intervention to foster industrialization. It must be recognized that such state intervention was crucial for development in the success stories among late industrializers during the second half of the twentieth century.[48]

In the changed international context, nation states in the developing world must endeavour to influence the rules of the game so that the outcome is more equitable. It need hardly be said that the nature of the solution depends upon the nature of the problem. Where there are different rules in different contexts, it is necessary to make such rules consistent. Where there are rules for some but not for others, it is necessary to ensure that the rules are uniformly applicable to all. Where the agenda for new rules is partisan, it is imperative to redress the balance in the agenda. However, fair rules are necessary but not sufficient. For a game is not simply about rules; it is also about players. And, if one of the teams or one of the players does not have adequate training and preparation it would simply be crushed by the other. In other words, the rules must be such that newcomers or latecomers to the game – for example, developing countries – are provided with the time and the space to learn so that they are competitive players rather than pushover opponents.

There is a clear need for greater consistency in the rules of the multilateral trading system embodied by the WTO. If developing countries provide access to their markets, this access should be matched with some corresponding access to technology. If there is almost complete freedom for capital mobility, the draconian restrictions on labour mobility should at least be reduced. Similarly, the rules of the multilateral financial institutions, implicit in the conditionalities of the IMF and the World Bank, applicable only to deficit countries or to borrowing countries, should be reshaped so that the standardized and inflexible package of policies is not imposed on countries irrespective of time and space, particularly where some elements of this package are not consistent with national development objectives in the long term.

It needs to be said that governing globalization is just as important as reducing asymmetries in its rules. The momentum of globalization is such that the power of national governments is being reduced through incursions into hitherto sovereign economic and political space, without a corresponding increase in effective international cooperation or supra-national government which could regulate this market-driven process. Global governance, however, is not so much about world government as it is about institutions and practices combined with rules that facilitate cooperation among sovereign nation states.[49]

Notes

1 See, for example, Baster 1972, Seers 1972 and Morris 1979. In recent years, this view has been put forward strongly by the UNDP in its *Human Development Reports*.

2 Cf. UNDP 1999, p. 25.

3 The evidence in this paragraph is from UNDP 1999.

4 For an analysis of contending views on openness and intervention, see Nayyar 1997.

5 See, for example, Killick 1984, Cornia et al. 1987, Taylor 1988, Bhaduri 1992, Cooper 1992, Taylor 1993 and Bhaduri and Nayyar 1996.

6 See Stiglitz 1998.

7 For a detailed discussion, see Nayyar 1995 and 1997.

8 The export-GDP ratios are from UNCTAD, *Handbook of International Trade and Development Statistics* and UN, *Yearbook of National Accounts Statistics*, various issues.

9 UNCTAD 1994, p. 143.

10 UNCTAD 1998, pp. 385, 399.

11 For evidence on the growth of international finance, see Nayyar 1995 and 1997. See also UNDP 1999, p. 25.

12 Bank for International Settlements, *Survey of Foreign Exchange Market Activity*, various issues.

13 The value of world GDP and exports in 1997, reported by the UN, has been converted into an average daily figure for the purpose of comparison. The figure on foreign exchange reserves is from the IMF *Annual Report 1998*.

14 See, for example, Sachs and Warner 1995.

15 This historical parallel was the theme of my Presidential Address to the Indian Economic Association in December 1995 (Nayyar 1995).

16 Cf. Bairoch 1982 and Maddison 1989.

17 UNCTAD 1994, p. 130.

18 At 1980 prices, total foreign investment in 1914 was $347 billion (Maddison 1989). The actual stock of direct foreign investment in 1980 was $448 billion (UNCTAD 1994).

19 See Nayyar 1997.

20 In 1913, foreign securities constituted 59% of all securities traded in London. Similarly, in 1908, the corresponding proportion was 53% in Paris. See Morgenstern 1959.

21 For a discussion of these underlying factors, see Nayyar 1995.

22 For example, the substitution of steam for sails, and of iron for wooden hulls in ships, reduced ocean freight by 2/3 between 1870 and 1900 (Lewis 1977).

23 The production of perfectly interchangeable parts, the introduction of the moving assembly line by Ford, and methods of management evolved by Taylor, provided the foundations for this new form of industrial organization. See Oman 1994.

24 Cf. Hobsbawm 1987.

25 The total foreign investment of $44 billion was distributed as follows: $14 billion in Europe, $10.5 billion in the USA, $8.5 billion in Latin America, and $11 billion in Asia and Africa (UNCTAD , *World Investment Report*, 1994, p. 415).

26 See Dunning 1983.

27 Cf. Lewis 1978.

28 See Tinker 1974 and Lewis 1977.

29 The best example is Sachs and Warner 1995.

30 See Bairoch and Kozul-Wright 1996.

31 Maddison 1995.

32 See Maddison 1989 and Bairoch 1982.

33 Cf. Maddison 1989.

34 Cf. Bairoch 1982.

35 Keynes 1919, pp. 9–10.

36 The quarter century that followed World War II was a period of unprecedented prosperity, earning the title of the *golden age of capitalism*. See Marglin and Schor 1990 and Maddison 1982. The *age of globalization*, a phrase that has not been used, is suggested by the author in order to facilitate comparison.

37 For evidence, see UNCTAD 1997, UNDP 1999 and IMF 1997.

38 The ratio of the average GNP per capita of the richest quintile of the world's population to that of the poorest quintile rose from 31:1 in 1965 to 60:1 in 1990 (UNCTAD 1997, p. 81) and 74:1 in 1997 (UNDP 1999, p. 3). The ratio of per capita income in the richest country to that in the poorest rose from 35:1 in 1950 to 44:1 in 1973 and 72:1 in 1992 (Maddison 1995 and UNDP 1999).

39 See UNCTAD 1997; Wood 1994 and 1997; Stewart 2000.

40 Some evidence is reported in UNCTAD 1997. See also Stewart 2000.

41 This argument is developed in UNCTAD 1997.

42 Cf. Streeten 1996, who draws up a balance sheet of globalization.

43 For a discussion, and evidence, on this issue, see Nayyar 2000.

44 This term was first used by Sen 1981 in his work on poverty and famines.

45 See Streeten 1996, who also cites Benjamin Barber (*Jihad vs McWorld*, New York, Random House, 1995) on this issue.

46 See Rodrik 1997.

47 For a more detailed analysis, see Nayyar 1997 and 2000.

48 See Amsden 1989, Wade 1990 and Chang 1996.

49 Global governance is analyzed, at some length, in Nayyar 2002.

References

Amsden, A, 1989, *Asia's Next Giant*, New York, Oxford University Press.

Bairoch, P, 1982, 'International Industrialization Levels from 1750 to 1980', *Journal of European Economic History*, vol. 11, 269–310.

Bairoch, P and Kozul-Wright, R, 1996, 'Globalization Myths: Some Historical Reflections on Integration, Industrialization and Growth in the World Economy', Discussion Paper, no. 13, Geneva, UNCTAD.

Baster, N 1972, 'Development Indicators', in Baster, N, ed., *Measuring Development*, London, Frank Cass, pp. 1–20.

Bhaduri, A, 1992, 'Conventional Stabilization and the East European Transition', in Richter, S, ed, *The Transition from Command to Market Economies in East-Central Europe*, San Francisco, Westview Press, pp.13–32.

Bhaduri, A and Nayyar, D, 1996, *The Intelligent Person's Guide to Liberalization*, New Delhi, Penguin Books.

Chang, H-J,1996, *The Political Economy of Industrial Policy*, London, Macmillan.

Cooper, RN, 1992, *Economic Stabilization and Debt in Developing Countries*, Cambridge, The MIT Press.

Cornia, GA, Jolly, R and Stewart, F, 1987, eds, *Adjustment with a Human Face*, Oxford, Clarendon Press.

Dunning, J H , 1983, 'Changes in the Level and Structure of International Production', in M Casson, ed., *The Growth of International Business*, London, Allen and Unwin, pp. 84–139.

Hobsbawn, E, 1987, *The Age of Empire,* London, Weidenfeld and Nicolson.

IMF, 1997, *Globalization: Opportunities and Challenges, World Economic Outlook*, Washington DC, IMF.

Keynes, JM, 1919, *The Economic Consequences of the Peace*, London, Macmillan.

Killick, T, 1984, *The Quest for Economic Stabilization*, London, Overseas Development Institute.

Lewis, WA, 1977, *Evolution of the International Economic Order*, Princeton, Princeton University Press.

——, 1978, *Growth and Fluctuations: 1870–1913,* London, Allen and Unwin.

Maddison, A, 1982, *Phases of Capitalist Development*, Oxford: Oxford University Press.

——, 1989, *The World Economy in the Twentieth Century*, Paris, OECD.

——, 1995, *Monitoring the World Economy: 1820–1992*, Paris, OECD.

Marglin, S and Schor, J, eds, 1990, *The Golden Age of Capitalism*, Oxford, Clarendon Press.

Morgenstern, O, 1959, *International Financial Transaction and Business Cycles*, Princeton, Princeton University Press.

Morris, MD, 1979, *Measuring the Conditions of the World's Poor*, Oxford, Pergamon Press.

Nayyar, D, 1995, 'Globalization: The Past in Our Present', Presidential Address to the Indian Economic Association, reprinted in *Indian Economic Journal*, vol. 43 no.3, 1–18.

——, 1997, 'Themes in Trade and Industrialization', in Nayyar, D, ed., *Trade and Industrialization*, New Delhi, Oxford University Press, pp. 1–42.

——, 2000, 'Globalization and Development Strategies', *High-level Roundtable on Trade and Development, UNCTAD X,* TD(X)/ RT.1/4, New York and Geneva, United Nations.

——, 2001, 'Globalization: What does it mean for Development?', in KS Jomo and S Nagaraj, eds., *Globalization versus Development*, London, Palgrave.

——, 2002, ed, *Governing Globalization: Issues and Institutions*, Oxford, Oxford University Press.

Oman, C, 1994, *Globalization and Regionalisation*, Paris, OECD.

Rodrik, D, 1997, *Has Globalization Gone Too Far?*, Washington DC, Institute for International Economics.

Sachs, J and Warner, A, 1995, 'Economic Reform and the Process of Global Integration', *Brookings Papers on Economic Activity*, no.1, 1–118.

Seers, D, 1972, 'What are we Trying to Measure?', in Baster, N, ed., *Measuring Development*, London, Frank Cass, pp. 21–36.

Sen, AK, 1981, *Poverty and Famines*, Oxford, Clarendon Press.

Stewart, F, 2000, 'Income Distribution and Development', *High-Level Roundtable on Trade, UNCTAD X,* TD(X)/RT.1/3, New York and Geneva, United Nations.

Stiglitz, JE, 1998, 'More Instruments and Broader Goals: Moving toward the Post-Washington Consensus', *WIDER Annual Lectures 2*, Helsinki, WIDER.

Streeten, PP, 1996, 'Governance of the Global Economy' paper presented to a Conference on Globalization and Citizenship, 9–11 December, Geneva, UNRISD.

Taylor, L, 1988, *Varieties of Stabilization Experience*, Oxford, Clarendon Press.

——, 1993, *The Rocky Road to Reform*, Cambridge, The MIT Press.

Tinker, H, 1974, *A New System of Slavery: The Export of Indian Labour Overseas, 1830–1920*, Oxford, Oxford University Press.

UNCTAD, 1994, *World Investment Report 1994*, Geneva, United Nations.

——, 1997, *Trade and Development Report 1997*, Geneva, United Nations.

——, 1998, *World Investment Report 1998*, Geneva, United Nations.

UNDP, 1999, *Human Development Report 1999*, New York, Oxford University Press.

Wade, R, 1990, *Governing the Market*, Princeton, Princeton University Press.

Wood, A, 1994, *North–South Trade, Employment and Inequality*, Oxford, Clarendon Press.

——, 1997, 'Openness and Wage Inequality in Developing Countries: The Latin American Challenge to East Asian Conventional Wisdom', *The World Bank Economic Review*, vol. 11 no.1, pp. 33–57.

4

DEVELOPMENT AND THE GLOBAL ORDER

José Antonio Ocampo

Globalization and its accompanying instrument, economic liberalization, have been heralded over the past quarter century as the gateway to an era of unprecedented prosperity. The Washington Consensus provided the best-known summary of this reform agenda, although it certainly did not reflect its more radical versions, calling for a minimalist State.[1]

During the last few years, the wisdom behind this vision has been called into question. Trade and foreign direct investment have boomed, but the 'Promised Land' of high growth rates is increasingly regarded as a mirage. International divergence of income levels has accelerated and distributive tensions have increased in the developed and the developing world alike. High financial volatility and a broad regulatory deficit are now evident even in the industrial world.

The call to 'civilize' the global economy[2] in order to generate a more inclusive form of globalization or, in the words of the United Nations Millenium Declaration, 'to ensure that globalization becomes a positive force for all the world's people'[3] has now become standard. This has been the strong view of international civil society since Seattle. Disenchantment with liberalization in the developing world and pluralist viewpoints in the economic debate are on the rise.[4] However, these positive processes have so far led to limited action.

Indeed, as the controversy surrounding liberalization has developed, the terminology used in the debate has become increasingly obscure. There is a great deal of talk about the need to consolidate the 'first generation' of reforms, and to supplement them with a 'second generation' aimed at strengthening institutions and social safety nets. In this regard, there is a basic substratum of agreement on the following issues: the need for strong macroeconomic frameworks, openness to the opportunities offered by the international economy, increased participation by the private sector, a more efficient state and, certainly, stronger institutions and active social policies. However, beyond these agreements, profound differences of opinion exist as to the exact meanings of all these terms.

In fact, the 'reform fetishism' implicit in the idea of the 'generation of reforms' is an intrinsic part of the problem. Its major underlying assumption is that development processes are linear and universal in nature. Thus, according to this view, the steps that have been taken during the early stages of the process constitute the foundation upon which additional parts of the building should be erected. This, however, is surely an inappropriate framework given that the precariousness of parts of those foundations leads to problems that have to be resolved during subsequent stages. In such cases, it becomes necessary to 'reform the reforms'.

Against the second assumption, that of universality, it can be argued that there is no single model of economic management that would guarantee macroeconomic stability, nor is there only one method of integration into the international economy or of designing economic and social institutions. In the terminology of Albert and Rodrik,[5] there are different 'varieties of capitalism', as the experience of developed and developing countries alike indicates. This is fortunate, as it implies that democracy has a role to play, and that 'ownership' of development policies has a positive meaning.

This paper presents an alternative view of the development agenda and the corresponding reforms in global arrangements that are required. It is divided into four sections. The first takes a look at global disparities. The second presents the broad brushstrokes of a global agenda, which assigns a critical role to regional institutions. The third looks at national development strategies. The fourth places development issues in a broader framework.

1. Global historical disparities

History demonstrates that international 'convergence' in income levels has been the exception rather than the rule. The only strong case of convergence in per capita income levels occurred among developed countries during the postwar 'golden age', 1950–73.[6] The process proceeded steadily until 1990, albeit at a slower pace, and came to a halt in the final decade of the twentieth century. The other historical period in which convergence took place was the second half of the nineteenth century. O'Rourke and Williamson[7] have demonstrated that during this period the United States and Europe witnessed a convergence of wage levels, basically as a result of the mass migration of European labour to the New World. Within Western Europe, a process of wage equalization also occurred, though it did not encompass countries of the

European periphery. Hence, even within the group of now industrialized countries, there was a divergence in per capita GDP trends.

This subject has been examined thoroughly in the recent literature on economic growth. In general, these analyses confirm that there has been a long-term divergence of per capita income levels over the past two centuries, and that the pace of this divergence was particularly rapid in the nineteenth and the first half of the twentieth centuries, slowed down in the period 1950–73, and has since been renewed. Thus, using per capita GDP levels for the 141 countries included in Angus Madisson's historical series,[8] the mean log deviation increased from 0.56 in 1973 to 0.65 in 1998 (Figure 1). However, various studies also indicate that there is some, though not systematic, evidence of 'conditional convergence', when other factors that influence the growth of countries – including education, infrastructure, macroeconomic stability and institutional development – are taken into account. Taken together, these two pieces of evidence indicate that those determinants of economic growth are distributed just as unequally – or even more so – as per capita GDP. This casts significant doubts on the validity of the concept of 'conditional convergence'.

An analysis of the same data source reveals another phenomenon: the marked and growing dispersion of growth rates during the last quarter of the twentieth century – in other words, the coexistence of 'winners' and 'losers' in all groups of countries. Indeed, the standard deviation of per capita GDP growth increased for the same sample of 141 countries from 1.73 in the period 1950–73 to 2.50 in 1973–90 and to 3.09 in the 1990s (Figure 2).

Figure 1. **Average log deviation of GDP per capita**

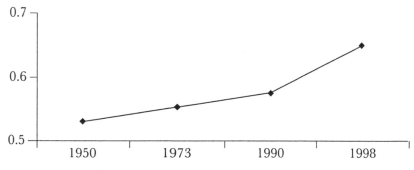

Source: Estimates based on Maddison 2001.

Figure 2. **Standard deviation of GDP per capita growth**

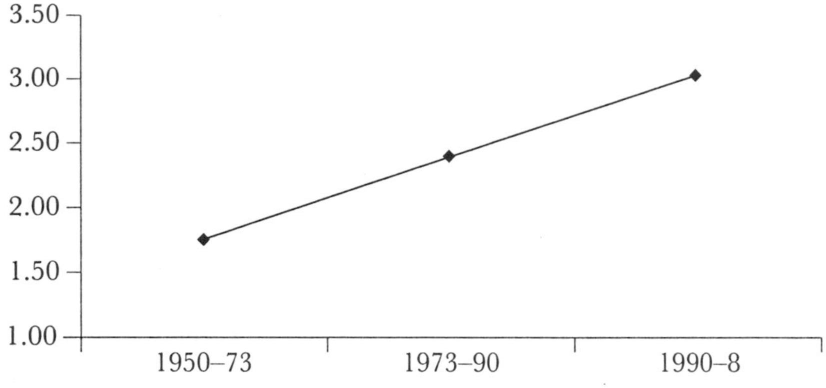

Source: Estimates based on Maddison 2001.

These trends are part of a larger process of a worsening distribution of income at the world level. The most comprehensive analysis of this issue, by Bourgignon and Morrison,[9] concludes that international inequalities increased significantly between 1820 and 1910, remained stable from 1910 to 1960, and grew again from 1960 to 1992. Deepening international disparities in per capita GDP levels have played a central role throughout the past two centuries. These disparities have been linked with experiences of open divergence in income levels (Africa), but also stagnation at middle income levels (the average experience of Latin America from 1870 to 1973) and several experiences of 'truncated convergence' (for example, Argentina after its 1880–1913 boom, Brazil and Mexico after their successful period of state-led industrialization and, more recently, Indonesia after its export-led growth was cut short by the Asian crisis). However, the trend in recent decades towards an amplification of international inequalities can be attributed not only to growing international disparities, but also to a fairly widespread increase in inequalities within countries. In point of fact, in the period 1975–95, 57% of the population in a sample of 77 nations were living in countries in which income distribution was worsening, whereas only 16% lived in nations in which it was improving.[10]

The strong renewal of the trend towards income divergence in recent decades goes against the expectation that economic liberalization would accelerate convergence by providing ample opportunities for developing countries. Thus, the attempt to draft simplistic links between economic liberalization and growth has been misguided. The best stylized fact in this regard is that, although trade policy, capital market liberalization and market incentives do matter, there are no single rules that can be applied to all countries at any point in time, nor to any single country in different time periods, a conclusion which is evident from comparative analyses of development experiences.[11] Therefore, in certain countries and periods, protection has been shown to be a source of growth; in others, it has blocked growth. The same thing can be said of freer trade. Mixed strategies have proven to be the most favourable in many circumstances. As Chenery and many others have observed, successful experiences of manufacturing export growth in the developing world since the mid-1960s were generally preceded by periods of import substitution industrialization, and the very successful integration of Asian NICs into the world economy was matched by strong state intervention.[12] Interestingly, Bairoch[13] came to similar views regarding the relations between protection and economic growth in the period preceding World War I; indeed, he came to the paradoxical conclusion that the fastest periods of growth of world trade prior to the war were not those characterized by the most liberal trade regimes, and therefore that economic growth led the expansion of world trade, not vice versa.

The growth and persistence of substantial inequalities in the world economy make it useful to think of the latter as a system in which opportunities are unevenly distributed between the centre of the world economy and its periphery – or, perhaps more accurately, peripheries – a point made by Latin American structuralist thinkers half a century ago.[14] Indeed, the best simple manifestation of this fact is that, despite some changes, the world hierarchy of per capita GDP levels has been remarkably stable over the past century, as demonstrated by the fact that about 60% of current income disparities in the world can be simply explained by the same disparities existing in 1913. This is also reflected in other crucial features of the world economic order: the very high concentration of the generation of core technology in a few countries, and the equally high concentration there of world finance and the headquarters of multinational firms.

The major implications of this fact are that, although national economic, social and institutional factors obviously do matter, economic opportunities are largely determined by position within the world hierarchy. Essential international asymmetries help to explain why the international economy is, in fact, an 'unlevelled playing field', implying that, unless such asymmetries are systemically addressed, world inequalities will be maintained or may deepen through time.

This implies, in turn, that economic development is not a question of going through 'stages' within a uniform pattern linked to the rise in income per capita: it is about succeeding in the required structural transformations and the appropriate macroeconomic and financial strategies, within the restrictions created by a country's positioning within the world hierarchy, and its internal economic and sociopolitical structures. This is the essential insight of the Latin American structuralist school, as well as of the literature on 'late industrialization' since Gerschenkron.[15]

2. The global order

2.1 Three essential objectives of international cooperation

An essential lesson of history is that resistance to any process as powerful as current globalization will eventually fail. But this does not mean that current trends can be taken as immutable realities. Although forceful technological and economic processes underlie it, globalization can be shaped, and indeed the form that it has been assuming has largely been shaped by explicit policy decisions.

The deficiencies shown by the current globalization process have demonstrated the need to work towards three key objectives:[16]

- Guaranteeing an adequate supply of global public goods;
- Building a human rights-based world system (i.e., global citizenship); and
- Gradually overcoming the asymmetries that characterize the world economic system.

The first of these objectives emphasizes the management of interdependence between nations. The other two focus on equity, in its two dimensions: between citizens and between nations. After some remarks on the first two objectives, I will concentrate on the third, which plays the essential role in guaranteeing equitable economic development at global level.

In the recent literature, the concept of global public goods has been understood in a broad sense that goes beyond the traditional definition of welfare economics – goods that are non-excludable and non-rivalrous in consumption – to include goods and services that have high externalities but whose benefits can be privately appropriated, and global commons (which are rivalrous in consumption). In this broad sense, it includes, among others: international peace and justice, human knowledge, cultural diversity, the fight against international pandemics, environmental sustainability, the regulation of the use of global commons, rules that regulate international economic transactions, and world macroeconomic and financial stability. What should be emphasized is the huge gap between recognition of the growing importance of interdependence and thus of global public goods, and the weakness of the existing international structures – decision-making, financing and management – that guarantee that they are adequately supplied.[17]

On the other hand, building global citizenship in a heterogeneous international community implies both respect for basic human rights and for cultural diversity, thus reconciling the principle of equality with the 'right to be different'. In this view, civil and political rights form an indivisible, interdependent whole with economic, social and cultural rights. It is recognized, however, that the exercise of economic and social rights is not automatic and will continue to be an essentially national responsibility. Consequently, it is necessary to move gradually to a clearly-defined 'political enforceability' of economic and social rights within the context of international forums and, most importantly, representative national forums where international assessments of the countries' fulfilment of their commitments are discussed. This political enforceability can gradually lead, under certain conditions, to a legal enforceability within the context of the corresponding national and international courts – a step which only the European Union has so far taken.

The commitments made, and their enforceability, must at all times be commensurate with each country's level of development, in order to preclude the emergence of both voluntarism and populism. Given the sharp inequalities that characterize the global order, a central element in the material expression of such rights is the fulfilment of official development assistance (ODA) commitments made within the framework of the United Nations. In the long run, this should lead to the design of a true 'global social cohesion fund' that facilitates the fulfilment of economic and social rights of the poorest members of the international community.

The third objective implies that, just as redistributive actions by the state are essential at the national level to ensure equality of opportunity, national efforts can succeed only if they are complemented by international cooperation aimed at gradually overcoming the basic asymmetries of the global order, which are at the root of profound international inequalities in income distribution.

These asymmetries fall into three basic categories. The first is associated with developing countries' greater macroeconomic vulnerability to external shocks and their limited effective macroeconomic policy autonomy. The net effect of this situation is that, whereas industrialized countries have greater manoeuvering room to adopt counter-cyclical policies and elicit a stabilizing response from financial markets, the developing economies have almost no such room at all, since financial markets tend to accentuate cyclical variations, and market agents expect national authorities to behave pro-cyclically as well.

The second type of asymmetry is the concentration of technical progress in developed countries. Following Prebisch's 50 year-old verdict, the spread of technical progress from the originating countries to the rest of the world continues to be 'slow and irregular'.[18] This reflects prohibitive entry costs into technological dynamic activities, as well as the constraints faced by developing countries in entering mature sectors, where opportunities are largely restricted to the attraction of multinationals operating in those sectors. In turn, the transfer of technology is subject to the payment of innovation rents, which are being afforded increasing protection by the international spread of intellectual property rights. The combined effect of all these factors explains why, at world level, the production structure has continued to exhibit a high degree of concentration of technical progress in the industrialized countries, which thus maintain their predominant position in the fastest-growing branches of international trade and their hegemony in the formation of major transnational corporations.

A third asymmetry is associated with the contrast between the high degree of capital mobility and the limited international mobility of labour, especially of low-skilled workers. This asymmetry is a distinctive feature of the current stage of globalization, since it was not observed in the nineteenth and early twentieth century (when all factors of production were highly mobile), or in the first quarter century following World War II (when all experienced limited mobility). This element is essential, given that asymmetries in the mobility of production have a regressive impact, as they work to the benefit of the more mobile factors of production – that is, capital and skilled labor – and to the detriment of the less mobile factors.[19]

Due to the inequalities generated by international asymmetries, 'levelling the playing field' by regulatory means is an inappropriate guide to international reform. Thus, the principle of 'common but differentiated responsibilities' enshrined in the Rio Declaration on Environment and Development, and the principle of 'special and differential treatment' incorporated in the trade agenda, are more appropriate guidelines for building a more equitable global order.

This analysis establishes essential elements of international reform vis-à-vis developing countries. Correcting the first of these asymmetries implies that a comprehensive approach should be adopted to reduce the segmentation and volatility of developing countries' access to international financial markets, and to provide them with more scope for the adoption of counter-cyclical macroeconomic policies. Correcting the second implies that the trading system should facilitate the smooth transfer of raw material production, technological mature industries and standardized services to developing countries. It should also accelerate the access of developing countries to technology (thus avoiding excessive protection of intellectual property rights) and guarantee developing countries' participation in technology generation and in higher-technology branches of production. To facilitate these processes, the trading system should provide adequate room for the adoption of active domestic productive strategies in developing countries. Finally, overcoming the third asymmetry implies that labour migration should be fully included in the international agenda, both through a global agreement on migration policy as well as regional and subregional agreements, while complementary mechanisms that facilitate migration (such as the recognition of educational achievements and the transferability of pension and other social security benefits) should also be adopted.

2.2 *Improved governance structures*

In the absence of suitable institutions, globalization is proving to be a highly disintegrative force, both at the international and the national level. This places an enormous demand on governance at all levels. There is now a broad consensus as to the decisive role played by national strategies and governance in determining how successful a country will be in forming strong links with the international community. However, without a suitable international framework, the insufficient supply of global public goods and the inequality-generating forces spawned by international asymmetries will hinder national development.

This implies that attempts to build strong institutions for a better global order should be based on a network of world, regional and national institutions, rather than being limited to one or a few international institutions. Such a system would be both more efficient and more balanced in terms of power relations. Action at the regional level plays a critical role as a midway point between the global and national orders for four main reasons: the complementarities between global and regional institutions in a heterogeneous international community; the unequal size of the actors involved in global processes, which means that the countries' voices will be better heard if expressed as a regional voice; the greater sense of ownership of regional institutions by small countries; and the fact that the scope for effective economic policy autonomy has shifted in some areas (e.g., macroeconomic and regulatory policies) from the national arena to the regional level.

Ultimately, however, international institutions would continue to rely on national responsibilities and policies, an essential characteristic of an international system where political processes continue to be built on nation states. A basic corollary of this is that global institutions should be firmly respectful of diversity. Furthermore, this is the only rule that is consistent with the promotion of democracy at the world level. Indeed, promoting democracy as a universal value entails ensuring that national processes providing for representation and participation are allowed to influence the definition of economic and social development strategies and to mediate the tensions inherent in the globalization process. This principle is embodied in the more recent thinking on cooperation for development, which emphasizes that its effectiveness will depend on strong national policy 'ownership' of development policies.

It is convenient to recall, in this regard, that successful multilateralism under Bretton Woods was precisely based on a judicious mix of international rules and cooperation, which provided sufficient degrees of freedom for national authorities to pursue their growth and development goals. It was based on strong and effective national authorities, not on weak ones. In this light, the current mix of incomplete international arrangements and weakened national policy effectiveness must be seen as the most inappropriate of all possible combinations.

Steps taken to restructure the international order should also ensure the participation of developing countries on an equitable basis, and the adoption of appropriate rules of governance. Achieving this will require positive discrimination in support of poor and small countries, as well as an effort on the part of those countries to organize themselves within the framework of regional institutions. Another implication of this principle is that preference should be given to institutional schemes having the largest possible number of active participants.

Finally, the adoption of appropriate rules of governance is another essential element in ensuring the basic rights of developing countries in the international order, institutionalizing accountability and strengthening auditing functions carried out by institutions that enjoy credibility with all relevant actors. This approach involves placing limits on the power of the countries having the most influence over those institutions. However, this is not necessarily to their detriment, as it will also increase the legitimacy of the global institutional order and the commitment to it by developing countries.

3. National strategies

Any national development strategy must be founded upon solid social covenants that ensure political stability, non-discretionary legal systems and practices that provide security of contracts and an impartial, efficient state bureaucracy. These broad institutional requirements, which have been correctly emphasized in recent literature, are essential elements of an appropriate investment environment and, as such, may be regarded as necessary conditions for growth. However, neither of them accounts for the specific forces that drive economic growth, nor do they provide means of dealing with old and new forms of vulnerability. Thus, the strategies adopted by developing countries should incorporate at least three additional elements: macroeconomic policies designed to reduce external vulnerability and facilitate productive investment, productive development strategies aimed at guaranteeing a dynamic restructuring of productive structures, and active social policies. There are no universally valid models in any of these areas, and there is consequently a great deal of scope for institutional learning and, most importantly, for the exercise of democracy.

3.1 A broad view of macroeconomic stability

The concept of macroeconomic stability has undergone considerable changes in economic discourse over the past decades. During the postwar years dominated by Keynesian thinking, this concept was basically defined as full employment and stable economic growth, accompanied by low inflation and sustainable external accounts. Over time, however, fiscal balance and price stability moved to centre stage, replacing the Keynesian emphasis on real economic activity.

Contrary to this trend, the consistency that ought to characterize macro-economic policies should be based on a broad definition of stability that recognizes that there is no single correlation between its alternative definitions, and that significant tradeoffs may be involved. Two lessons from recent history are particularly important in this regard. The first is that real instability is very costly. Recessions entail a significant loss of resources that may have long-term effects: firms may incur irreparable losses of both tangible and intangible assets (tacit technological and organizational knowledge, commercial contacts, etc.) and the human capital of the unemployed or the underemployed may be eroded or permanently lost. Volatile growth leads to a high average rate of underutilization of production capacity, reducing productivity and profits and thus adversely affecting investment. The uncertainty associated with variability in growth rates also encourages 'defensive' microeconomic strategies (i.e., those aimed at protecting the existing corporate assets of firms) rather than the 'offensive' strategies that lead to high investment rates and rapid technical change.

The second lesson is that private deficits are just as costly as public-sector ones, and that risky private balance sheets may be as damaging as flow imbalances. In financially liberalized economies, both may interact in non-linear ways with boom–bust cycles, which are an inherent characteristic of financial markets. Private spending booms and risky balance sheets tend to accumulate during periods of financial euphoria, implying that economic agents underestimate the intertemporal inconsistency that may be involved in their spending and financial strategies. When crises lead to a financial meltdown, the associated costs are extremely high. Asset losses may wipe out years of capital accumulation. The socialization of losses may be the only way to avoid a systemic crisis, but this will affect future fiscal (or quasi-fiscal) performance.

Restoring confidence in the financial system takes time, and the financial sector itself becomes risk-averse, a feature that undermines its ability to perform its primary economic functions.

These two lessons are basically interconnected, as financial boom–bust cycles have become a major source of business cycles in the developing world. The essential task of macroeconomic policy is thus to manage them with appropriate counter-cyclical tools, combining three policy packages, whose relative importance will vary depending on the structural characteristics and the macroeconomic policy tradition of each country.[20] The first such package comprises consistent and flexible macroeconomic – fiscal, monetary and exchange-rate – policies aimed at preventing public or private agents from accumulating excessive levels of debt, and at forestalling imbalances in key macroeconomic prices (exchange and interest rates) and in the prices of fixed and financial assets. The second is a system of strict prudential regulation and supervision with a clear counter-cyclical orientation. This means that prudential regulation and supervision should be tightened during periods of financial euphoria to counter the mounting risks incurred by financial intermediaries. The third element is a 'liability policy' aimed at ensuring that appropriate maturity profiles are maintained with respect to domestic and external public and private commitments. Preventive capital account regulations (i.e., those applied during periods of euphoria to avoid excessive borrowing) can play an essential role, both as a liability policy – encouraging longer-term flows – and as an instrument that provides additional degrees of freedom for the adoption of counter-cyclical monetary policies.

Managing counter-cyclical macroeconomic policies is no easy task, as financial markets generate strong incentives for developing countries to overspend during periods of financial euphoria and to overadjust during crises. Moreover, globalization places objective limits on national autonomy and exacts a high cost for any loss of credibility when national policy instruments are poorly administered. For this reason, it may be necessary for macroeconomic policy management to be supported by institutions and policy instruments that help to provide credibility, including fiscal rules and stabilization funds, and independent but politically accountable central banks. On the other hand, the explicit renunciation of policy autonomy (e.g., by adopting hard pegs or a foreign currency) is hardly a solution to this dilemma, as it may simply predetermine the nature of the adjustment, generating stronger business cycles. Indeed, the recent Argentine experience indicates that macroeconomic authorities' credibility can be strengthened more effectively through prudently-managed flexibility than through the adoption of overtly rigid rules.

The basic solution to the dilemma created by the lack of adequate degrees of freedom to undertake counter-cyclical macroeconomic policies lies in the international arena.[21] This means that an essential role of international financial institutions, from the point of view of developing countries, is to counteract the procyclical effects of financial markets. This can be achieved by smoothing out boom–bust cycles at source through adequate regulation, and by providing developing countries with additional degrees of freedom to adopt counter-cyclical policies (e.g. adequate surveillance and incentives to avoid the build-up of risky macroeconomic and financial conditions during periods of financial euphoria, together with mechanisms to smooth out adjustments in the event of abrupt interruptions in private capital flows). A second, equally essential role, is to counter the concentration of lending by providing access to finance to those countries and agents that tend to be rationed in private international capital markets.

In the long run, economic growth hinges on a combination of sound fiscal systems that provide the necessary resources for the public sector to do its job, a competitive exchange rate, moderate real interest rates and deep financial markets. Macroeconomic policy should be focused on ensuring the first three elements. The objective of financial deepening is to provide suitably-priced investment finance with sufficiently long maturities. The liberalization of financial systems in developing countries has not deepened financial markets or reduced the regions' high intermediation costs as much as had been expected. Consequently, the public sector still has an important role to play in furnishing financial services and promoting the emergence of new agents and segments in capital markets. Meanwhile, efforts to increase public-sector saving, the creation of corporate savings incentives and special mechanisms to foster household saving (for retirement, in particular) may be useful means of raising national savings rates.

3.2 Macroeconomic policies are not enough: the role of productive development strategies

The idea that the combination of open economies and stable macroeconomics – in the limited sense in which this term has come to be used, that is to say, fiscal balances and low inflation – would be sufficient to spur rapid economic growth has not so far been borne out. This has sparked an unresolved debate concerning the underlying reasons for this result. The orthodox interpretation is that markets have not been sufficiently liberalized. This reading is contradicted by the fact that the longest-lasting episodes of rapid growth in the developing world (e.g. the East Asian or, most recently, the Chinese and Indian 'miracles' or, in the past, the periods of rapid growth in Brazil or Mexico), involved a mix of 'local heresies' and more orthodox policy prescriptions.[22] Alternative interpretations emphasize the role of insufficient institutional development, or market failures – particularly in the functioning of technology and capital markets – as the explanation for slow growth. However, this line of reasoning must explain why rapid growth was possible in the past in many developing countries that faced even higher constraints on these accounts.

A more promising line of inquiry draws upon the different historical variants of structuralism in economic thinking, broadly defined. This view emphasizes the close connection among structural dynamics, investment and economic growth. According to this view, economic growth is a very dynamic process in which some sectors and firms grow and move ahead while others fall behind, thereby completely transforming economic structures. This process involves a repetitive phenomenon of 'creative destruction', to use Schumpeter's metaphor.[23] Not all sectors have the same ability to inject dynamism into the economy, to 'propagate technical progress'.[24] The complementarities (externalities) between enterprises and production sectors, along with their macroeconomic and distributive effects, can produce sudden jumps in the growth process or can block it[25] and, in so doing, may generate successive phases of disequilibria.[26] Since technical know-how and knowledge in general are not available in fully-specified blueprints, the growth path of firms entails an intensive process of adaptation and learning, closely linked to production experience, which largely determines the accumulation of technical, commercial and organizational know-how.[27]

The common theme in all these theories is the idea that economic growth is intrinsically tied to the structural context, which is made up of productive and technological apparatuses, the configuration of factor and product markets, the characteristics of entrepreneurial agents, and the way in which these markets and agents relate to the external environment. The leadership exercised by certain sectors and firms is, in this case, the essential dynamic factor that drives economic growth. In the developing world, many of the dynamic forces are associated with the successful adaptation of activities previously developed in the industrialized world, through import substitution, export promotion or a combination of the two.

Although alternative formulations can be used, one particularly promising approach in terms of its policy orientation emphasizes two essential concepts: (a) innovations and the learning processes associated with them; and (b) complementarities (linkages).[28] In this formulation, innovations are viewed as any economic activity that introduces new ways of doing things. The best definition was provided by Schumpeter[29] almost a century ago: new goods and services, or new qualities of goods and services; new production methods or marketing strategies; the opening of new markets; new sources of raw materials; and new market structures. All these innovations involve active learning and diffusion processes, characterized by dynamic scale economies. The second concept emphasizes the role of strategic synergies that, through the externalities that the various economic agents generate among themselves,[30] determine the degree of 'systemic competitiveness' of the relevant production structures.[31] In this light, institutional development may be viewed as an innovation, but also as an essential ingredient for the appropriate materialization of both innovation and complementarities.

These ideas have recently been used by several authors to emphasize the need for a productive development strategy as a basic component of a dynamic, open developing economy, a long-standing theme in the literature of 'late industrialization' (or, more precisely, 'late development'). Thus, Rodrik[32] has made a strong argument for a 'domestic investment strategy' to kick-start growth, and ECLAC[33] has referred to the need for a 'strategy of structural transformation'. The essential role of strong state/business sector partnerships is emphasized by Amsden,[34] who also underlines the need for 'reciprocal control mechanisms' that tie incentives to results in order to ensure that the former do not merely lead to rent-seeking behaviour. The need to reduce the 'costs of coordination' that characterize the development of new economic activities subject to important complementarities is the essential insight behind the classical defence of industrial policies.[35]

This interpretation highlights a central feature of successful development experiences in the past: a strong industrialization drive built on solid state/business sector partnerships. On the opposite side, recent experiences of several regions in the developing world indicate that opening markets with 'neutral' incentives, arms-length government–business relations and multilateral constraints on traditional development policy instruments do not provide an adequate substitute for active production development strategies.[36]

The use of explicit productive development strategies aimed at encouraging innovation and helping to build up complementarities are thus a better route to take. The international community should regard such strategies as an essential ingredient of successful development and should continue to search for instruments to implement such strategies, subject to the rule that they do not degenerate into 'beggar-thy-neighbour' competition for footloose production. This is the essential rule on which multilateral development-friendly trade and investment regulations should be built.

In the developing countries, a significant institutional and organizational effort is required to devise appropriate instruments for active production policies, as the old apparatuses of intervention were either dismantled or significantly weakened during the phase of liberalization in many of these countries. An effort must also be made to design instruments that, aside from being consistent with the open economies of today, avoid the 'government failures' that characterized some of the tools used in the past. Such government failures, including rent-seeking and cronyism, have obviously not been a monopoly of interventionist regimes: they have been equally present in the current liberal economic order (e.g. in the way the privatization process is managed).

3.3 Improved social linkages

In economic terms, social progress may be thought of as the result of three interrelated factors: a long-term social policy aimed at improving equity and guaranteeing inclusion; economic growth that generates quality employment in adequate quantities; and the reduction of the structural heterogeneity (dualism) of production sectors in order to narrow the productivity gaps between different economic agents. As the last section of this paper indicates, economic considerations are obviously not the only criteria to be used in designing social policy.

In a slightly revised formulation to that of the World Bank,[37] it may be that equity and inclusion should be based on broad access to resources, basic protections, voice and participation. Access to resources is the key to equal opportunity. In the case of human capital, it brings out the essential character of social spending as a productive investment. Basic protections are necessary to free people from 'negative risks' (sickness, unemployment and, worst of all, hunger) in order to allow and encourage them to undertake 'positive risks', particularly those associated with innovation. Voice is essential to guarantee that the interests of the poor are adequately taken into account in decisions that affect them. Through participation, poor people become central actors in building their own future. In many instances, organized communities have been shown to be a basic instrument of social and economic change.

To achieve these objectives, social policy should be guided by three basic principles: universality, solidarity and efficiency.[38] This subject has been surrounded by a great deal of confusion in recent years, as instruments – targeting, equivalency criteria between contributions and benefits, decentralization, private-sector participation – rather than principles have been guiding social-sector reforms. Moreover, these guiding principles emphasize the fact that social policy is a basic instrument of social cohesion, and that policy tools should be clearly subordinated to broader principles. Thus, targeting should be seen as an instrument for attaining universal coverage of basic services, and certainly not as a substitute for universality. Equivalency criteria should be applied in a way that is not inconsistent with solidarity. Properly managed, such criteria, along with decentralization and private-sector participation, are instruments for achieving efficiency.

To enhance equity, social policy should act upon the structural determinants of income distribution: education, employment, wealth distribution and demographic dependence, as well as their gender and ethnic dimensions. Education is essential for equitable growth, particularly in the knowledge/information age. But its objectives clearly go beyond these human capital dimensions: it is also a key factor to democratic development, strong citizenship and, more broadly, to self-realization. Its effects on equity may, however, have been overemphasized in recent discussions, since in highly segmented societies, education is also an instrument of segmentation. This factor has to be taken into serious consideration if education is to be used to improve equity. Moreover, failure to create sufficient quality jobs will defeat efforts made in the area of education, in terms of both the accumulation of human capital (in extreme cases, workers migrate; under more general circumstances, they remain underemployed) and equity (occupational segmentation then compounds the effects of educational segmentation). The link between economic growth and social progress is thus particularly crucial in this regard.

In the rapidly-changing environment that characterizes modern economies, the adaptability of labour to technical change and the business cycle is increasingly important. The crucial contributing factors in this regard are: strong labour-training schemes; institutions that enhance cooperation, both at the national level (social dialogue) and within firms; adequate social protection, both of a long-term nature and of the type needed to cope with adverse events; and a prudent minimum-wage policy. While flexibility may be an ingredient, provided it is accompanied by greater protection, it is only one of a number of alternative instruments. In this regard, it should be remembered that more flexible labour markets may adversely impact on other factors that have positive effects on adaptability, particularly labor–business cooperation. Most importantly, flexibility should not be seen as a substitute for adequate macroeconomic policies. Indeed, in an unstable macroeconomic environment, or in the presence of slow economic growth, job creation will be weak in any case, and additional flexibility may lead to a rapid deterioration in the quality of employment. In other words, flexibility has negative externalities, as it undermines jobs that would otherwise be stable.

Poor economic growth affects equity in another way that plays a crucial role in developing countries: it increases heterogeneity (dualism) in productive structures, as in the absence of job creation in dynamic activities, low-productivity (informal) activities mushroom. In the absence of adequate domestic linkages, or if the 'destructive' effects of productive restructuring predominate, there is in fact no automatic mechanism which guarantees that rapid technological innovation in dynamic activities will fuel economic growth: it may simply increase structural heterogeneity. If this happens, the growth effects will be weak and additional tensions will be created in relation to equity.

The links between the modernization of leading economic sectors and the rest of the economy are thus crucial. This also underscores the importance of a good distribution of production assets. Indeed, there is strong evidence that an appropriate distribution of production assets that generates a universe of strong small firms is associated with a better distribution of income (and less concentration of power in general). Policies aimed at democratizing access to production assets (capital, technology, training and land) are thus critical for both growth and equity.

The interaction between human capital and quality employment, and the effects of a better distribution of production assets, constitute only some of the positive connections between development and equity. There may also be favourable political economy linkages, as well as positive effects through the capital market and through the interaction between social cohesion, investment and productivity.[39]

Given the crucial linkages between economic and social development, integrated policy frameworks should be designed to take such connections into consideration, as well as those of social policy linkages (the supportive effects of different social policies in integrated poverty eradication programs, for example) and economic policy (particularly those that facilitate the development of dynamic small business sectors). A major weakness in this regard is the lack of appropriate coordination between economic and social authorities. Coordination should start by creating mechanisms that facilitate the 'visibility' of the social effects of economic policies and provide effective systems for mainstreaming social priorities into economic policy. This implies that macroeconomic authorities (including central banks) should be asked to evaluate, on a regular basis, the social effects of their policies, and that budgets and tax reform proposals should include analyses of their distributive effects.

Some of these ideas have been gradually incorporated into more orthodox analyses, but crucial differences in emphasis remain. Indeed, the 'leader/ follower' model, in which macroeconomic policy is determined first and social policy is left to address the social consequences, is still dominant.[40] The emphasis on 'social safety nets' and targeted social spending, rather than the broader views of social security, with their emphasis on universality and solidarity, is also a reflection of the continued view of social policy as an 'add-on' to market-based reforms.

4. Broader goals

One of the most positive aspects of debates in recent years has been the full realization that development comprises broader goals.[41] The concept of 'human development' or the more recent concept of 'development as freedom'[42] give expression to this perspective, but it is clearly a long-standing and deeply-rooted element of development thinking. Its most important manifestation is the gradual spread of global ideas and values, such as those of human rights, social development, gender equity, respect for ethnic and cultural diversity, and environmental protection, through the United Nations and the struggle of international civil society. These 'global values' should be regarded as the ethical framework for designing development policies today.

The implications of this perspective run more deeply than current economic thought is willing to recognize. The central implication, drawing on Polanyi's work,[43] is that the economic system must be subordinated to broader social objectives. A central issue, in this regard, is the need to confront the strong centrifugal forces that characterize private affairs today. Indeed, in many parts of the developing (and industrialized) world, people are losing their identification with collective goals and their awareness of the need to develop ties of solidarity. This fact drives home how important it is to foster those bonds in order to 'create society' and to arrive at a more widespread awareness of the social responsibilities of individuals and groups.

Either the state or civil society can take the initiative. In this sense, 'public affairs' should be viewed as the sphere in which collective interests come together, rather than as a synonym for state actions. It means, in other words, that all sectors of society need to participate more actively in democratic political institutions and that a wide range of mechanisms need to be developed within civil society itself to strengthen relationships of social solidarity and responsibility and, above all, to consolidate a culture of collective development founded upon tolerance of differences and a willingness to compromise.

The enormous intellectual challenges and practical tasks that are involved in the recognition of these factors should foster a sense of humility. The idea that 'we already know what must be done' is nothing more than a sign of arrogance on the part of the economics profession, which has only worsened since the rise to dominance of orthodox development thinking in the 1980s. A consideration of the unsatisfactory results of reforms and of the existing level of social discontent should – and is – leading many experts to rethink the development agenda for a more equitable global order. This is most welcome, but it is at best an incomplete, ongoing process.

Notes

1 Williamson 1997.
2 Helleiner 2000.
3 United Nations 2000.
4 See, for example, Rodrik 2001 and Stiglitz 2002.
5 See Albert 1991; Rodrik 1999.
6 Maddison 1991.
7 O'Rourke and Williamson 1999.
8 Maddison 2001.
9 Bourgignon and Morrison 2002.
10 Cornia 1999.
11 See, for example, Helleiner 1994.
12 See, for example, Chenery et al. 1986.
13 Bairoch 1993.
14 See, for example, Prebisch 1951.
15 For a recent restatement, see Amsden 2001.
16 ECLAC 2002.
17 Kaul, Grunberg and Stern 1999; Kaul et al. 2002.
18 Prebisch 1951.
19 Rodrik 1997.
20 Ocampo 2002a.
21 Eatwell and Taylor 2000; Ocampo 2002b.
22 Rodrik 1999.
23 Schumpeter 1962.
24 Prebisch 1951.
25 Rosenstein-Rodan 1943; Taylor 1991; Ros 2000.
26 Hirschman 1958.
27 Katz 1987; Amsden 2001.
28 Ocampo 2002c.
29 Schumpeter 1961, chapter II.
30 Hirschman 1958.
31 ECLAC 1990.
32 Rodrik 1999.
33 ECLAC 2000.
34 Amsden 2001.
35 Chang 1994.
36 Ocampo and Taylor 1998; UNCTAD 2002; ECLAC 2000 and 2002.
37 World Bank 2000.
38 ECLAC 2000.
39 Ros 2000, chapter 10.
40 Mkandawire 2001.
41 Stiglitz 1998.
42 Sen 1999.
43 See Polanyi 1957.

References

Albert, M, 1991, *Capitalisme contre capitalisme*, Paris, Éditions du Seuil.

Amsden, A, 2001, *The Rise of 'The Rest': Challenges to the West from Late Industrializing Countries*, New York, Oxford University Press.

Bairoch, P, 1993, *Economics and World History: Myths and Paradoxes*, Chicago, Illinois, University of Chicago Press.

Bourgignon, F, and Morrison, C, 2002, 'The Size Distribution of Income Among World Citizens: 1820–1990', *American Economic Review*, forthcoming.

Chang, H-J, 1994, *The Political Economy of Industrial Policy*, London, Macmillan, and New York, St. Martin's Press.

Chenery, H, Robinson, S, and Syrquin, M, 1986, *Industrialization and Growth: A Comparative Study*, New York, World Bank, Oxford University Press.

Cornia, GA, 1999, 'Liberalization, Globalization and Income Distribution', Working Papers, no. 157, Helsinki, United Nations University (UNU)/World Institute for Development Economics Research (WIDER), March.

Eatwell, J, and Taylor, L, 2000, *Global Finance at Risk: The Case for International Regulation*, New York, The New Press.

ECLAC (Economic Commission for Latin America and the Caribbean), 2002, *Globalization and Development*, Santiago, Chile.

——, 2000, *Equity, Development and Citizenship*, Santiago, Chile.

——, 1990, *Changing Production Patterns with Social Equity*, Santiago, Chile.

Helleiner, GK, 2000, 'Markets, Politics and Globalization: Can the Global Economy be Civilized?', *The Tenth Raúl Prebisch Lecture*, Geneva, 11 December.

——, ed., 1994, *Trade Policy and Industrialization in Turbulent Times*, New York, United Nations University (UNU)/World Institute for Development Economics Research (WIDER), New York, Routledge.

Hirschman, AO, 1958, *The Strategy of Economic Development*, New Haven, CT, Yale University Press.

Katz, J, 1987, 'Domestic Technology Generation in LDCs: A Review of Research Findings', in J Katz, ed, *Technology Generation in Latin American Manufacturing Industries*, London, Macmillan.

Kaul, I, Grunberg, I, and Stern, MA, eds, 1999, *Global Public Goods: International Cooperation in the 21ˢᵗ Century*, New York, Oxford University Press.

——, Conceição, P, Le Goulven, K, and Mendoza, R U, eds, 2002, *Providing Global Public Goods: Managing Globalization*, forthcoming.

Maddison, A, 2001, *The World Economy. A Millennial Perspective*, Paris, Development Centre Studies, Organisation for Economic Cooperation and Development (OECD).

——, 1991, *Dynamic Forces in Capitalist Development: A Long-Run Comparative View*, New York, Oxford University Press.

Mkandawire, T, 2001, 'Social Policy in a Development Context', *Social Policy and Development Paper* no. 7, United Nations Research Institute for Social Development.

Ocampo, JA, 2002a, 'Developing Countries' Anti-Cyclical Policies in a Globalized World', in A Dutt and Ros, J, eds, *Development Economics and Structuralist Macroeconomics: Essays in Honour of Lance Taylor*, Aldershot, UK, Edward Elgar.

——, 2002b, 'Recasting the International Financial Agenda', in J Eatwell and Taylor, L, eds, *International Capital Markets: Systems in Transition*, Oxford University Press, New York.

——, 2002c, 'Structural Dynamics and Economic Development', in V FitzGerald, ed., *Social Institutions and Economic Development: A Tribute to Kurt Martin*, Institute of Social Studies, Dordrecht, Kluwer.

Ocampo, JA and Taylor, L, 1998, 'Trade Liberalisation in Developing Economies: Modest Benefits but Problems with Productivity Growth, Macro Prices, and Income Distribution', *The Economic Journal*, vol. 108, no. 450.

O'Rourke, KH, and Williamson, JG, 1999, *Globalization and History. The Evolution of a Nineteenth-Century Atlantic Economy*, Cambridge, Massachusetts, The MIT Press.

Polanyi, K, 1957, *The Great Transformation: The Political and Economic Origins of Our Time*, Boston, Beacon Press.

Prebisch, R, 1951, 'Crecimiento, desequilibrio y disparidades: interpretación del proceso de desarrollo', *Estudio Económico de América Latina 1949*, New York, United Nations.

Rodrik, D, 2001, 'Development Strategies for the Next Century', in B Pleskovic and Stern, N, eds, *Annual World Bank Conference on Development Economics 2000*, World Bank, Oxford University Press.

——, 1999, *Making Openness Work: The New Global Economy and the Developing Countries*, Washington, DC, Overseas Development Council.

——, 1997, *Has Globalization Gone Too Far?*, Washington, DC, Institute for International Economics.

Ros, J, 2000, *Development Theory and The Economics of Growth*, University of Michigan Press.

Rosenstein-Rodan, P N, 1943, 'Problems of industrialization of Eastern and South-Eastern Europe', *The Economic Journal*, vol. 53.

Schumpeter, J, 1962, *Capitalism, Socialism and Democracy*, third edition, New York, Harper Torchbooks.

Schumpeter, J, 1961, *The Theory of Economic Development*, Oxford, Oxford University Press.

Sen, A, 1999, *Development as Freedom*, New York, Alfred A Knopf.

Stiglitz, JA, 2002, *Globalization and its Discontents*, New York, WW Norton.

——, 1998, 'More Instruments and Broader Goals: Moving Toward the Post-Washington Consensus', *WIDER Annual Lectures 2*, Helsinki.

Taylor, L, 1991, *Income Distribution, Inflation and Growth*, Cambridge, MIT Press.

UNCTAD (United Nations Conference on Trade and Development), 2002, *Trade and Development Report, 2002*, Geneva.

United Nations, 2000, 'United Nations Millennium Declaration', New York, General Assembly (Millennium Summit, New York, 6–8 September).

Williamson, J, 1997, 'The Washington Consensus revisited', in L Emmerij, ed., *Economic and Social Development into the XXI Century*, Washington, DC, IDB, Johns Hopkins University Press.

World Bank, 2000, *World Development Report 2000–2001. Attacking Poverty*, New York, Oxford University Press.

PART II

DEVELOPMENT EXPERIENCES

5

THE EAST ASIAN DEVELOPMENT
EXPERIENCE

Ha-Joon Chang

1. Introduction

During the second half of the twentieth century, East Asia was the most dynamic region in the world economy. At the same time, its policy practices and institutions have often significantly diverged from those that are regarded by many – including many East Asians themselves – as 'best practice', to be found chiefly in the Anglo–American economies. As a result, the East Asian economies, starting with the case of Japan and subsequently involving other economies in the region, have been at the centre of the debate in development economics since the 1960s.

More recently, of course, the decade-long economic stagnation in Japan, and the financial crises of 1997 in countries such as Korea, Indonesia, Thailand and Malaysia, took some gloss off the region's achievements. The crises immediately prompted claims that the East Asian miracle had never taken place, and that the economies in question were in fact inefficient and corrupt economies propped up by government bail-outs. Whatever one's view on the recent events, they should not obscure the fact that over the last few decades the region has achieved the fastest economic and social transformation in human history, which is why East Asia is such a key case in many debates in development economics.

2. The Definition Issue

Unusually for a geographical category, the very definition of 'East Asia' is a matter of controversy. The most widely-accepted definition, which is adopted in this chapter, incorporates Japan and the so-called first-tier NICs (Newly-Industrializing Countries) of South Korea (henceforth Korea), Taiwan, Hong Kong and Singapore. The origin of this definition is rather obvious, given that the debate has its origins in the spectacular performance of these economies between the mid-1960s and the mid-1980s.

However, since the early 1990s it has become increasingly common to include the so-called second-tier NICs of South East Asia – such as Thailand, Malaysia, and Indonesia – in the discussion of East Asia. More recently, others have come to believe that China and Vietnam should also be included, given that since the 1980s these economies have moved away from Communist isolationism and have enjoyed rapid growth of the kind observed only in the abovementioned countries.

This definition issue is not a matter of pedantry; rather, it has an important practical implication. For, depending on one's definition of 'East Asia', the lessons that we draw from it can vary significantly. For example, if we were to include only what I call the 'original five' of Japan and the first-tier NICs in this category, we are likely to conclude that active state intervention is beneficial for economic development (Hong Kong being the exception that proves the rule). On the other hand, the inclusion of the South East Asian second-tier NICs, which developed on the basis of far less state activism than the 'original four' (the 'original five' minus Hong Kong), makes it possible to argue that a high degree of state activism may not in fact be necessary for rapid development.

In this chapter I use the term East Asia to mean the 'original five' for two reasons. First, only during the 1990s have people started to define East Asia to include the second-tier NICs and the former Communist economies of China and Vietnam, and therefore most of the existing debates have been conducted with specific reference to the 'original five'. Introducing the new countries can therefore blur the focus of many existing debates, which some people have exploited in an attempt to discredit the 'East Asian model' as originally conceived.[1] Second, while the performances of the 'new wave' economies are very impressive, they are still no match for those of the 'original five'. The latter grew faster and for longer than have the 'new wave' countries and have broken into the rank of the advanced economies, while none of the 'new wave' countries have yet done so (and are unlikely to do so in the near future).

3. Comparative Performance

During the second half of the twentieth century, per capita incomes in the East Asian economies as we define them (the 'original five') have grown at 5 to 6% per year. Given that the per capita income growth rates of the European and the North American economies were typically not much above 1% during the Industrial Revolution and just over 3% even during the so-called 'Golden Age of Capitalism' (roughly 1950–75), this means that growth during this 50-year period in East Asia has been literally the fastest in human history.

What is especially notable about the growth records of the East Asian economies is that their rapid growth is an entirely postwar phenomenon. Estimates of earlier performance are not totally reliable, but Maddison's highly respected historical study of the 32 largest economies of the world[2] puts the yearly per capita income growth figures of Japan, Taiwan, and Korea for the period 1900–50 at 1%, 0.4%, and 0.1% respectively. Not only are these very low by their own postwar standards, they are also quite low by international standards of the time.

During this period, the Japanese per capita income growth rate of 1% was not only below average among the 17 major industrial countries (including the USSR) that were included in Maddison's study – Japan ranked joint 11th (with Germany and the Netherlands) among the 17 countries – but it was also lower than those of the six largest Latin American countries covered in the study (ranging from 1.8% for Brazil and Chile to 1.2% for Mexico and Peru). The Taiwanese and the Korean performances were even worse. Taiwan ranked joint 24th (with the Philippines) and Korea joint 26th (with Thailand) among the 32 countries included in the Maddison study – the last five places were taken up by Indonesia, India, Pakistan, Bangladesh (all of them grew at -0.1% per annum) and China (-0.3% per annum). The rapid postwar growth of the East Asian economies was, therefore, completely unexpected from a historical point of view.

The postwar growth in the East Asian economies is also notable in that it has resulted in remarkable improvements in social indicators, something to which not all experiences of rapid growth have led. The records of these economies in terms of improvements in infant mortality, life expectancy, educational achievement and other indicators of 'human development' have been very impressive. Of course, this is not to say that everything has been rosy in these countries: political authoritarianism, human rights violations, corruption, union repression, gender discrimination, mistreatment of ethnic minorities and so on, have all been problems to one degree or another in most of them. Despite these blemishes, it would however be fair to say that during the second half of the twentieth century the citizens of the East Asian economies have experienced improvements in income and general well-being that are unparalleled in human history.

4. Debates on the East Asian miracle

4.1 The debate on Japan

Outside interest in East Asia obviously began with Japan. The initial debate on Japan was strongly influenced by the fact that, until the mid-1970s, it remained the only industrialized country of non-European extraction. Some participants in the famous debate among Marxist historians regarding the 'transition from feudalism to capitalism' tried to attribute this fact to the uniquely 'European' (that is, decentralized) nature of Japanese feudalism.[3] By contrast, others tried to explain it in terms of the uniquely 'collectivist' nature of the Japanese variety of Confucianism, which puts emphasis on group loyalty over the system of personal edification that had been emphasized by the Chinese and the Korean varieties of Confucianism.[4] The subsequent industrialization of other parts of Asia as well as recent academic debate have revealed some problems with these early emphases on Japan's unique circumstances, but the earlier debates were useful in bringing to our attention the role of social structure and moral values in economic development.

During the late 1970s and the early 1980s, Japan's spectacular industrial success and the decline of many other industrialized countries generated a heated debate, especially in the USA, on the role of Japanese-style industrial policy.[5] Some argued that the centralized coordination of investment and technological upgrading (but not 'planning' in the Soviet sense) helped the Japanese firms aggressively invest in 'sunrise' industries with large productivity growth potential and widespread externalities.[6] Others argued that the Japanese industrial policy was not very extensive and not very effective, even in those few areas where it existed. They also pointed out that the success of industrial policy in Japan could not be emulated elsewhere, as it depended greatly on the unique bureaucratic structure and the collectivist nature of the country's culture.[7]

Numerous studies that followed have revealed that the pro-industrial policy authors had empirical facts on their side. Moreover, increasingly sophisticated theoretical arguments were provided to make sense of the Japanese-style industrial policy, which could not easily be comprehended through the dominant framework of neoclassical economics.[8]

4.2 The early debate on the East Asian NICs[9]

In contrast to the debate on Japan, during the early debate on the first-tier NICs, the very existence of state intervention was a controversial topic. Initially, many mainstream economists argued that the spectacular success of these economies was mainly indebted to their free-trade and free-market policies. Of course, these days, few people believe that the East Asian NICs – except Hong Kong – developed on the basis of a free market. However, I will start this section with the free-market view, because the more recent mainstream explanations are basically attempts to save the policy conclusions of the early mainstream explanation, while recognizing the existence of state intervention in these countries.

According to the early mainstream explanation, Taiwan and Korea initially pursued the import-substitution industrialization (ISI) policy that was popular in the early postwar period. However, this quickly ran out of steam, and, unlike many other developing countries that stuck to ISI, these countries switched to free-trade, free-market policies – Taiwan in the late 1950s and Korea in the mid-1960s. They introduced a unified, realistic exchange rate regime and liberalized trade.[10] These policies were regarded as having radically improved the performances of their economies. First of all, it was said, realistic exchange rates allowed them to follow their comparative advantages in labour-intensive industries, and therefore to reap more gains from trade. Second, trade liberalization improved the efficiency of the economy by exerting greater competitive pressures on domestic producers.

However, a number of researches published in the early- to mid-1980s revealed that this was a fundamentally misleading picture.[11] They showed that the extent of trade liberalization was rather limited, while foreign-exchange rationing, which had a persistent balance of payments problem continued, especially in Korea. The researches also documented the extensive array of trade and industrial policy measures deployed by these governments with a view to upgrading their industries. Also, as Chang later pointed out,[12] the early neoclassical explanation was not convincing even on its own theoretical terms. First of all, a more liberalized economy is not necessarily more efficient, even in purely neoclassical terms – the Second Best Theorem of Lipsey and Lancaster states that the removal of market distortions in some – but not all – markets does not guarantee that the economy achieves higher allocative efficiency. More importantly, as even one of the leading neoclassical trade economists, Anne Krueger, admits,[13] there is nothing in neoclassical theory that tells us that an allocatively more efficient economy will grow faster. Indeed, from a Schumpeterian point of view, where 'monopoly rent' (or 'entrepreneurial profit' as Schumpeter calls it) is necessary for people to invest in innovation, allocative *inefficiency* is an inevitable feature of a dynamic economy (of course, the reverse is not true).

4.3 More recent debates on the East Asian miracle

In response to the abovementioned criticism, some mainstream economists argued that the widespread import protection in the East Asian countries did not have ill effects, because their governments countered them with export subsidies, thus maintaining a 'virtual free trade' regime where there existed incentive neutrality between exports and production for the domestic market.[14] Others, however, have shown that there was nothing 'neutral' about trade regimes in these countries. They argued that the trade regimes which prevailed in these countries were a deliberate mixture of infant industry protection, relatively free trade in inputs (especially inputs for exports) and export subsidies, rather than a simulation of free trade, as the theory of virtual free trade would have us believe.[15]

In the late 1980s, there was a full-frontal attack by a group of heterodox economists and other social scientists on the then orthodoxy of 'free market, free trade East Asia'.[16] This group emphasized that all the first-tier NICs except Hong Kong practised Japanese-style strategic industrial policy. It argued that these countries promoted industries with high growth potential and widespread externalities through an array of means, which included: infant industry protection; export subsidies, including tariff rebates on imported inputs used for exports; coordination of complementary investments; regulation of firm entry, exit, investments, and pricing intended to 'manage competition'; subsidies and restriction of competition intended to help technology upgrading. They also argued that these countries could successfully import and assimilate foreign technologies because they could: skilfully integrate their education and training policies with industrial policy; effectively initiate and subsidize private-sector R&D while also providing public-sector R&D in key areas; and deliberately regulate technology licensing and foreign direct investments in a way that maximizes technology spillover.

Many of those who emphasize the importance of industrial policy in the first-tier NICs draw our attention to the existence of what Chalmers Johnson calls the 'developmental state' in these economies.[17] The proponents of the developmental state thesis argue that what distinguishes the East Asian states from other states most clearly is not the policy tools that they used, but their greater degree of autonomy from interest groups, which enabled them to discipline the recipients of their support when performance lagged. Evans advanced this argument further and developed the notion of 'embedded autonomy'.[18] He argued that the state autonomy possessed by the East Asian states was particularly beneficial because it was embedded in a dense policy network that linked them with the private sector, which provided a vital channel for information collection and interactive learning in the policy process.

The 'heterodox' attack of the late 1980s onward prompted the World Bank, as the leading proponent of the orthodox interpretation of the East Asian experience emphasizing the role of market forces, to respond with the famous *East Asian Miracle* Report (henceforth EAM) in the early 1990s.[19] The EAM acknowledged that there had been extensive state interventions in the East Asian economies and that some of these have been beneficial. However, it argued that industrial policy in these economies had been largely unsuccessful, with the partial exception of Japan. It also put great emphasis on the fact that the second-tier NICs of South East Asia grew rapidly without such policy, thus suggesting that East Asian-style industrial policy is not necessary for successful economic development. It then questioned whether the East Asian-style industrial policy could be practised in other developing countries that have underdeveloped bureaucracies and that are operating in an international environment much less tolerant of interventionist industrial and trade policies than it was in the 1960s or 1970s.

The EAM has been subject to a wide range of criticisms.[20] Many people found misleading its 'dilution' tactic of including the South East Asian economies as an integral part of East Asia. The critics argued that this deliberately blurred the focus of the earlier debate of which the EAM was supposed to be part, which after all was about the 'original five' or even the 'big three' (Japan, Korea, and Taiwan). A number of commentators have also questioned the theoretical framework and empirical methods underlying the study, especially those concerning the assessment of industrial policy.[21]

One positive contribution of the EAM was to emphasize the issue of policy implementation. It especially drew our attention to the role of high-quality bureaucracies and institutions that link the government and the private sector (e.g. Japan's deliberation council). However, the EAM took this one step too far, arguing that other developing countries which do not have such institutions should not attempt East Asian-style industrial policy. In its view, the 'good' institutions of East Asia cannot be emulated elsewhere because they are largely products of idiosyncratic historical factors (e.g. Confucian bureaucratic tradition, ethnic homogeneity). However, this argument ignores that many of the allegedly idiosyncratic institutions in the East Asian countries were in fact recent constructs, which were created 'along the way' rather than before they embarked on industrial policy experiments (more on this later).[22]

Shortly following the debate surrounding the EAM, there was a brief period when the so-called 'productivity debate' was in the limelight. This debate was prompted by the celebrated article by the American economist Krugman.[23] Krugman cited a number of growth-accounting studies allegedly showing that the East Asian economies – again with the exception of Japan – have grown almost exclusively on the basis of factor accumulation (greater investment and larger labour inputs) rather than of productivity growth. He then argued that, as they will soon exhaust the possibility of accumulation-based growth, these economies will grind to a halt in the near future – in a manner similar to the Eastern European economies, another set of accumulation-led economies, since the 1970s. He asserted that this apparent parallel between the two groups of 'Eastern' economies shows the limitations of 'collectivist' economic systems and the superiority of individualistic 'Western' economies.

Against Krugman, we should first of all point out that there are many growth-accounting studies, for what they are worth, that contradict the studies that Krugman uses. I say 'for what they are worth', because growth-accounting exercises are riddled with serious theoretical and statistical problems.[24] More importantly, economic history shows that economies at earlier stages of development are bound to rely more on factor accumulation than innovation and productivity growth, but that they are able to make the transition to a productivity-driven growth regime – indeed, estimates show that in Japan, Korea and Singapore, productivity growth accelerated over time. Even more important is the fact that it is precisely with the help of the organizational and institutional capabilities that had been accumulated in the earlier stage of development that economies are later able (or not) to make a transition to a productivity-driven growth regime. It is precisely because Krugman fails to understand the role of organizational and institutional factors in the process of economic development that he could lump the East Asian economies together with the Eastern European socialist economies.

5. Explaining the East Asian development experience

Before moving onto the debate on the recent Asian crisis, let me synthesize the debates up to now and summarize what I regard as the essence of the 'traditional' East Asian model.[25] Three major policy areas – that is, macroeconomic, external and industrial – are discussed.

5.1 Macroeconomic management

Mainstream accounts of the East Asian miracle (EAM) puts great emphasis on the prudent macroeconomic management of the East Asian countries. It is argued that their policymakers put emphasis on the attainment of macroeconomic stability (defined as low inflation), which provided the basis for the high investment that drove their economies.

This is a very misleading interpretation of East Asian macroeconomic policy. In East Asia, industrial upgrading, not macroeconomic stability (still less low inflation), was the overarching aim of economic policy.[26] Especially until the 1970s the East Asian – in particular the Japanese and Korean – governments pursed what Chang calls 'pro-investment macroeconomic policy', which resulted in considerable inflation.[27] For example, average rates of inflation (measured by the average annual growth of consumer price index) in Korea were 17.4% in the 1960s and 19.8% in the 1970s, which were higher, or not much lower, than those found in many Latin American countries during the same periods. In the 1960s, the Korean inflation rate was higher than those of Venezuela (1.3%), Bolivia (3.5%), Mexico (3.6%), Peru (10.4%) and Colombia (11.9%), and was not much lower than that of

Argentina (21.7%). In the 1970s, it was higher than those found in Venezuela (12.1%), Ecuador (14.4%), and Mexico (19.3%), and was not much lower than those found in Colombia (22.0%) or Bolivia (22.3%).[28]

At the same time, until these countries became quite rich, serious policy attempts were also made to repress consumption demand so that more resources could be released for investments.[29] The banks, which had been owned and/or controlled by the state, were instructed not to make consumer loans, and heavy taxes were imposed on luxury consumption goods. Controls were even stricter when it came to consumption that involved foreign exchange expenditure. In the earlier stages of development, luxury goods imports were either banned or subject to high tariffs and inland taxes. In the Korean case, foreign holidays were banned until the late 1980s.

5.2 External policy (or the question of 'openness')

Given their export successes, it is often uncritically assumed that the East Asian economies were wide open to the outside world on every front, but their openness has in fact been highly selective. They were more open in areas like trade, technology and debt, but less open to foreign direct investment, and almost completely closed in relation to the capital market. Even within the relatively open areas like trade and technology, the degree of openness differed across sectors and changed according to the changes in industrial policy.

There were various restrictions on the areas in which foreign direct investment (FDI) was allowed, and even when it was, foreign-majority ownership was practically banned outside the Free Trade Zones (FTZs). As of the mid-1980s, for example, only 6% of multinationals in Korea (including the ones in the FTZs) were wholly-owned subsidiaries, compared to 50% in Mexico and 60% in Brazil.[30] In the Taiwanese case, where the absence of large private-sector firms resulted in the relative lack of credible joint-venture partners with TNCs the ratio, at around 30%, was considerably higher than that in Korea, but still much lower than in Mexico or Brazil. Even technological licensing, which was preferred to foreign direct investment, was put under heavy restrictions.

This is not to say that the East Asian policymakers were against importing foreign technology; on the contrary, they have always been keen to acquire it. However, restrictions on technology imports were imposed because the East Asian policymakers have regarded the accumulation of technological capabilities by domestic firms as a vital condition for effective industrial upgrading.

5.3 *Industrial Policy*

The basic idea behind the East Asian industrial policy is that, in a world where technologies are not blueprints (and learning is therefore important), it makes sense for the state to create temporary protective barriers to give the firms the incentives to start new industries and the resources to invest in learning-related activities (e.g. training, R&D).

Typically, the East Asian states have chosen several industries at a time as 'priority sectors' and provided supports designed according to the particular needs of these sectors. These sectors had priority in acquiring rationed (and often subsidized) credits and foreign exchange, state investment funds, preferential tax treatments (e.g. tax holidays, accelerated depreciation allowances) and other supportive measures. In return for these supports, they became subject to state controls on technology (e.g. production methods, product variety), entry, capacity expansion and reduction, and pricing.

Given that the industrial policy measures used in the East Asian countries were actually quite similar to the ones used in other developing countries where such policies were less successful, many people have asked why the East Asian countries were particularly successful in using these measures.

The first reason is policy realism. Although the final goals were often ambitious, the choice of priority sectors were made only after careful consideration had been given to factors such as world market conditions and the state of local technological capabilities.

The second is policy flexibility. Like any businessman trying to move into new sectors, East Asian policymakers often made mistakes. However, they were quite willing to acknowledge mistakes and redirect their policies if they did not at first work.

Last but not least, their states had more 'autonomy'. The key to the success of industrial policy is that state support for an industry should be withdrawn when necessary (e.g., when performance is lagging or when the industry has outgrown its need for protection). Otherwise, the support becomes permanent featherbedding that produces no improvement in productivity. What differentiates East Asia from other countries is that the East Asian states have been willing and able to withdraw such support whenever necessary, because they were highly autonomous states. The point is that, as the state-created incentives dampen the disciplinary forces of the market, the success of an industrialization strategy based on such incentives critically depends on the willingness and ability of the state to discipline the recipients of such support. And in this conjunction, we should also note the role played by the emphasis on exports, which provided the state with relatively 'objective' criteria that it could use in disciplining the recipients of its support. Another important point to note in relation to the issue of state autonomy in East Asia was that this autonomy was deeply embedded in a dense network of institutions that enabled productive public–private sector interactions (deliberation councils, policy study groups, etc.).[31] In this way, the state could exercise its autonomy in a way that is attentive to, but not swayed by, private sector interests.

6. Japanese stagnation and the Asian financial crisis

With the bursting of the asset bubble in the early 1990s, the Japanese economy entered a period of prolonged recession – in fact, the longest in its modern history. In the meantime, some East and South East Asian economies (Thailand, Malaysia, Indonesia, Korea and Hong Kong) experienced major financial crises in 1997.

These two events together, especially when set against the strong performance of the US economy during the last half of the 1990s, have prompted many people to argue that 'Asian capitalism' was in the end a house of cards. By the late 1990s, it was widely argued that the East Asian economies were in trouble because of structural inefficiencies. These inefficiencies are said to be due to factors such as excessive state intervention, market-defying private-sector institutions (such as lifetime employment and pathological corporate-governance institutions), corruption, and a lack of transparency in the management of government and corporations.[32]

In addressing this view, it should first all be emphasized that there never existed such a thing as 'Asian capitalism'. We can certainly talk about the 'East Asian model', practised by the 'big three' and to a lesser extent by Singapore, but this model did not extend either to Hong Kong or the South East Asian economies. It is interesting, then, to note that it is mostly the more market-oriented economies of Hong Kong and South East Asia that were in crisis, rather than the countries that have practised the 'East Asian model'. The economies of Taiwan and Singapore were somewhat affected by the crises in the region but survived them more or less unscathed. Japan may have had a prolonged recession during most of the 1990s, but this is by no means a crisis situation, except perhaps in terms of wounded national pride and the spreading sense of uncertainty about the country's future. The obvious exception in this regard is Korea. However, given that the country had moved to a much more market-oriented model since the early 1990s, it is probably more accurate to attribute its crisis to the demise of the 'East Asian model' in the country rather than to its perpetuation.[33]

The fundamental problem with the arguments that try to explain the Asian crisis in terms of institutional deficiencies is that they never clearly specify these deficiencies except in broad and vague terms, often summarized in the catch-all term of 'moral hazard'.[34] Moreover, these arguments are not very well supported by facts.[35] First of all, if anyone had cared to look, all the necessary information predicting trouble in these countries was available at least for a couple of years before the crisis (e.g. the BIS reports in the years leading to the crisis), so the 'lack of transparency' argument is suspect. Second, there is no evidence for the existence of extensive government guarantees. There were bail-outs, but they were – especially in Korea – often accompanied by punishments of the managers responsible. Even in cases like Indonesia, where state discipline was weak, it does not make sense to argue that 'cronyism' was the main cause of the crisis. Given that cronyism by definition works only if it is confined to a small group, it is not plausible to argue that the 3,000-plus Indonesian manufacturing firms that borrowed from abroad all had cronyistic connections. As for corruption, it was ever-present in abundant quantities in all the countries concerned, and was if anything diminishing in the run-up to the crisis.

Although no-one would deny that certain economic and institutional weaknesses helped bring about the crisis economies of Asia, an increasing number of people across the ideological spectrum see the origins of the crisis elsewhere.[36] Many now believe that the main causes of the Asian crisis lie in factors such as: the deficiencies in the international financial architecture (e.g. unstable exchange rates, the absence of lenders of last resort); instability in the international capital markets due to increasing financial deregulation and globalization; premature capital-market liberalization and opening in the absence of proper supervisory mechanism in the crisis countries. They argue that the crisis occurred because the abovementioned factors have magnified the famous Kindlebergerian cycle of financial 'manias, panics, and crashes' that have been present in virtually all financial crises since the seventeenth century.[37]

Finally, whatever one's view on the Asian crisis, the Japanese case needs to be discussed separately. Above all, it should be noted that, while poor by its own historical standards (Japan's per capita income grew at over 6% between the 1950s and the 1970s, and at around 3.5% even during the 1980s), the Japanese economic performance during the 1990s is by no means a disaster by international standards. For example, during the 1990s a number of advanced economies (Canada, Switzerland, Italy and Sweden) have grown more slowly than Japan in per capita terms. Once again in per capita terms, Japan's performance during the 1990s was not far behind that of the US, which is supposed to have entered a new 'golden age' (however, note that, contrary to popular myth, the US growth rate over the last decade is actually below its historical average). According to the World Bank data, between 1990 and 1999 the US grew at 2.4% and Japan at 1.5% in per capita terms –

hardly an earth-shattering difference. And since the spring of 2001, with the bursting of the internet bubble and the revelation of major corporate corruption scandals, the US economy has been experiencing continued trouble, with no immediate end in sight.

7. The Question of Replicability

The question of replicability has been a persistent theme in the debate on East Asia. In the early days of the debate, when the mainstream economists recommended the supposedly 'free market-free trade' model of East Asia to other developing countries, many Dependency theorists pointed out that there were too many historical, geopolitical and perhaps cultural idiosyncrasies that made the model generally inapplicable, although they did not question the mainstream characterization of the model itself.[38] Later, when it became clear that the East Asian countries did not succeed on the basis of 'free market-free trade' policy, the mainstream economists adopted the Dependency-style argument that they had earlier disparaged, arguing that the model cannot be replicated because its success was based on certain unique conditions which other countries do not possess.[39] How plausible is this argument?[40]

It has often been argued that the Confucian culture that has dominated East Asia generated hard work, high savings propensity, zeal for education, and acceptance of authoritarian measures, thus making economic development easier. It is also pointed out that, largely because of Confucian tradition, the East Asian countries were uniquely endowed with high-quality bureaucracy from the early days of their economic development.

The basic problem with this argument is that Confucian culture has been there for centuries but did not lead to development earlier. Indeed, until the 1950s, many people blamed Confucianism for holding East Asia back. Confucianism, like all other cultures, contains many elements that are beneficial for growth and others that are harmful for growth – for example, it has a deep-seated contempt for commercial and industrial activities, while its emphasis on hierarchy is seen as impeding creativity.[41] The point is that Confucian culture *became* supportive of economic development, not by nature but because it had been deliberately refashioned to promote economic development.

In response to the argument emphasizing the role of historically-endowed high-quality bureaucracy in East Asia, it should be pointed out that such bureaucracy was a recent creation. The East Asian countries, especially Korea and Taiwan, had to spend a lot of time and energy in reforming their bureaucracies and training their bureaucrats before they could establish the kind of bureaucracies that they have now.[42] In this context, it is instructive to note that Korea was sending its bureaucrats for training to the Philippines and Pakistan until the late 1960s.

Given this, it is interesting to note that many people who express scepticism about the transferability of the East Asian model are quite cavalier when it comes to the transferability of the 'market-dominated models' of the Anglo–American economies. There may be an element of Anglocentrism here, but the more important problem is the implicit assumption behind this argument, which holds that markets are easy to create and therefore can be transplanted anywhere, while other institutions are not so.

However, markets are *not* natural phenomena that develop spontaneously, and like other institutions, have to be deliberately constructed.[43] Therefore, it is not that replicating the East Asian model requires institution-building (and so is next to impossible) while replicating the Anglo–American model does not require it (and therefore is easy). Rather, both just require different sets of institutions to be built. Indeed, if the free market system is so 'natural' and easy to replicate, the former socialist countries should not have had so much trouble establishing the market economy during the 1990s.

In other words, the argument that the East Asian model cannot be replicated elsewhere, because of its unique institutions, is one that perceives institutions as something fixed and underestimates the possibility of institutional transfer, adaptation and innovation. In fact, if there is one lesson to be drawn from the East Asian economies that is transferable everywhere, it is that the growth of a late-developing country depends critically on how successfully it can engage in the importation, adaptation, assimilation and innovation of institutions, not just of technologies.

The early Japanese experience is particularly instructive here. When the Japanese first embarked on the industrialization process, they had to import a lot of foreign institutions, picking what they thought were the most suitable among the 'best practice' institutions. If we look at the early Meiji period, for example, we find an institutional patchwork. Their commercial law system was from France, their criminal law from Germany, the Central Bank from Belgium, the Navy from Britain, the Army from Germany, the education system first from America but later from Germany, and so on.[44] These imported institutions were adapted to local conditions, while new institutions (e.g. lifetime employment, just-in-time production system) were subsequently invented. If the Japanese gave up on institutional learning on the grounds that their historical and cultural backgrounds are too different from 'Western' ones, we would not have had the East Asian miracle in the first place.

I would agree with those who express scepticism about the replicability of the East Asian model, if all they mean is that countries with different conditions may have to find different solutions to similar problems. However, they often have a very exaggerated view about the superiority of the 'initial conditions' of the East Asian countries, and have an unduly pessimistic view about other countries being able to change their conditions. So they believe that initial institutional (and cultural) conditions are almost perfectly binding and therefore that countries which do not start with the same kind of initial conditions as did the East Asian countries cannot emulate them. One curious thing here is that most of these people do not seem to believe that the 'initial conditions' may be equally binding when countries aim to imitate the Anglo-Saxon model that they typically recommend.

8. Concluding Remarks

During the last few decades of the twentieth century, the East Asian economies have gone through the fastest economic and social transformation in human history. Their successes and failures have generated many heated debates that have significantly affected the way in which we understand some key issues in development economics. While these economies have moved away from their traditional models to one degree or another (most dramatically in the Korean case), their importance in the world economy can only increase in the conceivable future. Therefore, a correct understanding of their past experience and current situation remains crucial in development economics.

Notes

1 World Bank 1993 is the supreme example of this.
2 Maddison 1989.
3 Sweezy et al. 1976.
4 Morishima 1982.
5 For reviews of this debate, see Thompson 1989; Chang 1994, chapter 3.
6 Magaziner and Hout 1980; Johnson 1982.
7 Schultze 1983; Badaracco and Yoffie 1983.
8 Dosi et al. 1989; Chang 1994; Stiglitz 1996. In the 1980s, growing attention was also being paid to the secrets of Japanese corporate success. Many argued that the structures of corporate governance, financing and production organization that characterize the Japanese firms provide them with distinctive advantages over the 'Western' (or rather Anglo–American) firms, as they encouraged long-term commitment and productive investment (see Dore 1987; Best 1990; Aoki and Dore 1994). While no other country could and did import the Japanese institutions of corporate governance and production organization wholesale, the Japanese corporate success has led to a widespread emulation of certain aspects of Japanese production techniques and management skills all over the world since the 1980s.

9 In this section, like most of the literature, I will focus on Taiwan and Korea, given the exceptional nature of Hong Kong and Singapore as city-states.

10 e.g. Ranis and Fei 1975; Balassa 1982.

11 Jones and Sakong 1980; Amsden 1985; Luedde-Neurath 1986.

12 Chang 1993.

13 Krueger 1980.

14 Little 1982; World Bank 1987.

15 Wade 1990; Chang 1993.

16 Amsden 1985, 1989; Wade 1990; Chang 1993.

17 Johnson 1982. Further works in the tradition are compiled in Woo-Cumings eds, 1999.

18 Evans 1995.

19 World Bank 1993.

20 See Chang 1995, appendix; Fishlow et al. 1994; the special symposium in the April 1994 issue of *World Development*.

21 Lall 1994; Rodrik 1994; Chang 1995.

22 Johnson 1982.

23 Krugman 1994.

24 Abramovitz 1989, chapter 1.

25 I say 'traditional' as this model has gone through quite a lot of changes since the late 1980s and early 1990s.

26 Taiwan was a partial exception. The Kuomintang government that has ruled Taiwan since 1949 has had a political aversion to inflation for historical reasons, as it regarded its failure to control inflation as one of the main reasons why it lost mainland China to the Communists.

27 Chang 1993.

28 Singh 1995, table 5.

29 See Chang 1993 and 1997 for further details.

30 Evans 1987, p. 208.

31 Evans 1995.

32 Krugman 1998 was arguably the most influential article along these lines, despite never having been properly published. For criticisms of this argument, see Singh 1999 and Chang 2000.

33 Chang 1998.

34 Chang 2000.

35 Radelet and Sachs 1998; Chang 2000.

36 Furman and Stiglitz 1998; Radelet and Sachs 1998; Singh 1999; Chang 2000.

37 Kindleberger 1996.

38 On the curious similarities between the early mainstream and the Dependency interpretations of the East Asian experience, see Chang 1990. For criticisms of the 'idiosyncrasy' arguments, see Chang 1995.

39 World Bank 1993 is the best example.

40 There is another type of 'non-replicability' argument, which emphasizes the difficulty of using the East Asian style 'non-market-conforming' trade and industrial policy instruments in the new international trading regime under the WTO. This argument is examined in chapter 12, section 5 of this volume.

41 Krugman 1994 is alluding to this aspect of Confucian culture, when he characterizes the East Asian economic system as 'collectivist'. See section 4.3 above.

42 Cheng et al. 1998.

43 Polanyi 1957 is a classic argument along this line. Also see Chang 2002.
44 Westney 1987.

References

Abramovitz, M, 1989, *Thinking about Growth*, Cambridge, Cambridge University Press.
Amsden, A, 1985, 'The State and Taiwan's Economic Development' in P Evans, D Rueschemeyer and T Skocpol, 1985, eds, *Bringing the State Back In*, Cambridge, Cambridge University Press.
——, 1989, *Asia's Next Giant*, New York, Oxford University Press.
Aoki, M and Dore, R, 1994, eds. *The Japanese Firm*, Oxford, Oxford University Press.
Badaracco, J and Yoffie, D, 1983, '"Industrial Policy": It Can't Happen Here', *Harvard Business Review*, Nov./Dec. 1983.
Balassa, B, 1982, 'Development Strategies and Economic Performance' in B Balassa et al., *Development Strategies in Semi-Industrial Economies*, Baltimore, Johns Hopkins University Press.
Best, M, 1990, *New Competition*, Cambridge, Polity Press.
Chang, H-J, 1990, 'Interpreting the Korean Experience – Heaven or Hell?', Research Paper Series, no. 42, Faculty of Economics and Politics, University of Cambridge.
——, 1993, 'The Political Economy of Industrial Policy in Korea', *Cambridge Journal of Economics*, vol. 17, no. 2.
——, 1994, *The Political Economy of Industrial Policy*, London and Basingstoke, Macmillan.
——, 1995, 'Explaining "Flexible Rigidities" in East Asia', in T Killick, 1995, ed., *The Flexible Economy*, London, Routledge.
——, 1997, 'Luxury Consumption Control and Industrialisation in East Asia', mimeo., a background paper prepared for *Trade and Development Report 1997*, UNCTAD, Geneva.
——, 1998, 'Korea: The Misunderstood Crisis', *World Development*, vol. 26, no. 8.
——, 2000, 'The Hazard of Moral Hazard – Untangling the Asian Crisis', *World Development*, vol. 28, no. 4.
——, 2002, 'Breaking the Mould – An Institutionalist Political Economy Alternative to the Neo-Liberal Theory of the Market and the State', *Cambridge Journal of Economics*, vol. 26, no. 5.
Chang, H-J and Rowthorn, B, 1995, eds, *Role of the State in Economic Change*, Oxford, Oxford University Press.
Cheng, T, Haggard, S and Kang, D, 1998, 'Institutions and Growth in Korea and Taiwan: The Bureaucracy', *Journal of Development Studies*, vol. 34, no. 6.
Dore, R, 1986, *Flexible Rigidities: Industrial Policy and Structural Adjustment in the Japanese Economy 1970–80*, London, The Athlone Press.
——, 1987, *Taking Japan Seriously – A Confucian Perspective on Leading Economic Issues*, London, The Athlone Press.
Dosi, G, Tyson, L and Zysman, J, 1989, 'Trade, Technologies and Development: A Framework for Discussing Japan' in C Johnson, L Tyson and J Zysman, 1989, eds, *Politics and Productivity*, New York, Harper Business.
Evans, P, 1987, 'Class, State, and Dependence in East Asia: Lessons for Latin Americanists' in F Deyo, 1987, ed., *The Political Economy of the New Asian Industrialism*, Ithaca, Cornell University Press.
——, 1995, *Embedded Autonomy – States and Industrial Transformation*, Princeton, Princeton University Press.

Fishlow, A, Gwin, C, Haggard, S, Rodrik, D and Wade, R, 1994, *Miracle or Design? – Lessons from the East Asian Experience*, Washington, DC, Overseas Development Council.

Furman, J and Stiglitz, J, 1998, 'Economic Crises: Evidence and Insights from East Asia', *Brookings Papers on Economic Activity*, 1998, no. 2.

Johnson, C, 1982, *MITI and the Japanese Miracle*, Stanford, Stanford University Press.

Jones, L and Sakong, I, 1980, *Government, Business and Entrepreneurship in Economic Development: The Korean Case*, Cambridge, Massachusetts, Harvard University Press.

Kindleberger, C, 1996, *Manias, Panics, and Crashes*, 3rd ed., London and Basingstoke, Macmillan.

Krueger, A, 1980, 'Trade Policy as an Input to Development', *American Economic Review*, vol. 70, no. 3.

Krugman, P, 1994, 'The Myth of East Asian Miracle', *Foreign Affairs*, Nov./Dec. 1994.

——, 1998, 'What Happened to Asia?', mimeo., Department of Economics, Massachusetts Institute of Technology.

Lall, S, 1994, 'Does the Bell Toll for Industrial Policy?', *World Development*, vol. 22, no. 4.

Little, I, 1982, *Economic Development*, New York, Basic Books.

Luedde-Neurath, R, 1986, *Import Controls and Export-Oriented Development; A Reassessment of the South Korean Case*, Boulder and London, Westview Press.

Maddison, A, 1989, *The World Economy in the 20th Century*, Paris, OECD.

Magaziner, I and Hout, T, 1980, *Japanese Industrial Policy*, London, Policy Studies Institute.

Morishima, M, 1982, *Why Has Japan Succeeded?*, Cambridge, Cambridge University Press.

Polanyi, K, 1957, *The Great Transformation*, Boston, Beacon Press.

Radelet, S and Sachs, J, 1998, 'The East Asian Financial Crisis: Diagnosis, Remedies and Prospects', *Brookings Paper on Economic Activity*, 1998, no. 1.

Ranis, G and Fei, J, 1975, 'A Model of Growth and Employment in the Open Dualistic Economy: The Cases of Korea and Taiwan' in F Stewart, 1975, ed., *Employment, Income Distribution and Development*, London, Frank Cass.

Rodrik, D, 1994, 'King Kong Meets Godzilla' in A Fishlow et al., *Miracle or Design? – Lessons from the East Asian Experience*, Washington, DC, Overseas Development Council.

Schultze, C, 1983, 'Industrial Policy: A Dissent', *The Brookings Review*, Fall, 1983.

Singh, A, 1995, 'How Did East Asia Grow So Fast? – Slow Progress Towards An Analytical Consensus', Discussion Paper no. 97, Geneva, UNCTAD.

——, 1999, ' "Asian Capitalism" and the Financial Crisis' in J Michie and J Grieve Smith, 1999, eds, *Global Instability – The Political Economy of World Economic Governance*, London, Routledge.

Stiglitz, J, 1996, 'Some Lessons from the East Asian Miracle', *The World Bank Research Observer*, vol. 11, no. 2.

Sweezay, P, et al., 1976, *The Transition from Feudalism to Capitalism*, London, New Left Books.

Thompson, G, 1989, 'Introduction' in G. Thompson, 1989, ed., *Industrial Policy – USA and UK Debates*, London, Routledge.

Wade, R, 1990, *Governing the Market*, Princeton, Princeton University Press.

Westney, E. 1987, *Imitation and Innovation: The Transfer of Western Organisational Patterns to Meiji Japan*, Cambridge, Cambridge University Press.

Woo-Cumings, M, 1999, eds., *The Developmental State*, Ithaca, Cornell University Press.

World Bank, 1987, *World Development Report, 1987*, New York, Oxford University Press.

World Bank 1993, *The East Asian Miracle*, New York, Oxford University Press.

6

LATIN AMERICA DURING THE SECOND HALF OF THE TWENTIETH CENTURY:

From the 'age of extremes' to the age of
'end-of-history' uniformity

Gabriel Palma[1]

'[The business of historians] is to remember what others forget.'
E Hobsbawm

1. Introduction

The economic and political history of Latin America during the second half of the twentieth century is divided by Mexico's 1982 default, a crisis that not only sealed three decades of unprecedented growth, but also dominated the political economy of the subsequent 'neoliberal' period.[2]

Between 1950 and 1981, Latin America's output increased fivefold (5.3% annually) and, despite having the world's fastest population growth (2.7%), income per capita more than doubled. Later (1991–2000), GDP only increased at 2.2% annually (just 1.9% if the period is extended to 2002), while income per capita stagnated.[3] It is against this background – and that of the remarkable world politics of the 1980s – that Latin America's unsettled post-1982 political economy must be examined.

However, in Latin America, 'averages' are often deceptive, for growing inequalities made it the region with the worst distribution of income and wealth in the world (Figure 1).

In Latin America, politico-institutional structures uniquely succeeded in concentrating the benefits of development, both during and after import-substituting industrialization (ISI), in small segments of the population that

Figure 1. **Regional income shares of decile 10 and log of income per capita, 1990s**

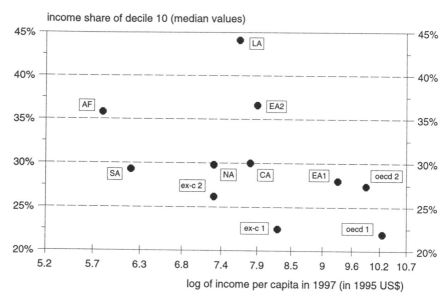

'**LA**'= Latin America; '**AF**'=Sub Saharan Africa; '**EA1**'=first-tier-NICs; '**EA2**'='second-tier-NICs'; '**SA**'=South Asia and low-income South East Asia; '**NA**'=North Africa; '**CA**'=Caribbean; '**oecd 1**'=non-English-speaking-OECD; '**oecd 2**'=English-speaking-OECD; '**ex-c 1**'=Central European ex-communist countries; and '**ex-c 2**'=ex-USSR communist countries.

Source: Palma 2002a.

achieved particularly high living standards. These groups coexisted uneasily with a swelling underclass that endured precarious living conditions, often below basic minimum subsistence levels. Throughout the Third World, political oligarchies would undoubtedly aspire to such a high income share, but the crucial question that still requires an answer is: why is it that only in Latin America do they get away with it?

Figure 2 reinforces the uniqueness of Latin America's income polarization. Unsurprisngly (not only in terms of income but also in wealth and power) Latin America's extreme inequalities have been a major source of tension and in many countries have required repressive military dictatorships for their perpetuation.

Ties between Latin America and the world economy increased during the late nineteenth-century trade boom, consolidating a production structure based on raw materials for export. However, during the 1930s, Latin America

Figure 2. **Regional ratios of deciles 10 and 1 and log of income per capita, 1990s**

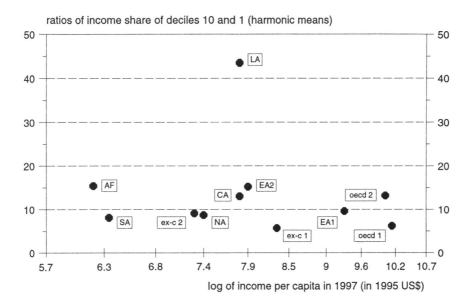

ratios of income share of deciles 10 and 1 (harmonic means)

log of income per capita in 1997 (in 1995 US$)

Abbreviations: as Figure 1.

switched to ISI; its most crucial characteristic – common also to the 1990s' 'neoliberal' model – was that it was implemented in a more ideologically-driven (and less 'Schumpeterian') manner than in other Developing Countries (DCs), for example in East Asia.

Although ISI did deliver a manufacturing growth that had no precedent (or continuity) in Latin America – 6.5% annually in the period 1950–81 – it became increasingly associated with cumbersome policies and foreign-currency shortages. These problems progressively led to constrained investment, lower capacity utilization, 'stop-go' cycles and eventually to excessive foreign borrowing. Although easy access to cheap foreign capital after the 1973 oil-shock did relax short-term constraints, debts accumulated while current-account deficit reached 40% of exports of goods and services in 1981 (70% in oil-rich Mexico). Despite continuous high inflows, the game was over when the FED trebled nominal rates (1977–81).

In sum, between 1950–81 ISI did deliver a growth rate in Latin America that was not only higher than in other developing regions, but also – and for the first time ever – higher than that of the OECD (4.2%).[4] However, as ISI became more mature, it inevitably required continuous readjustments and changes. The crucial problem was that Latin America's capitalist and political elites – never renowned for their versatility and foresight – rather than making the required effort, opted for relatively minor modifications to prolong ISI for as long as possible. Eventually, a combination of domestic and international factors made these elites believe that a change to a different development path was practically inescapable.

Paradoxically, history is repeating itself in the new 'neoliberal' model, which is closely following a similarly myopic political and economic cycle.

2. The rise and fall of the OECD 'Golden Age'

Between 1950 and 1973, the OECD enjoyed unprecedented prosperity: output increased threefold and income per capita 2.4 times. This was twice the rate of any previous period.[5]

The collective memories of the 1930s and of the war played an essential role in shaping this 'Golden Age'. Keynesian demand-management, a growing welfare state, powerful trade unions, different policies to strengthen property rights over human capital, and the compatibility of US internal policy goals with external leadership requirements helped the OECD achieve this unprecedented performance. At first these arrangements worked smoothly. Domestically, they combined to maintain effective demand, 'animal spirits', capacity-utilization, stable profits and low inflation. Internationally, the US recycling trade-related dollar surpluses removed OECD's foreign-exchange bottlenecks.

Not surprisingly, the Keynesian 'revolution' in the North had powerful ideological, politico-institutional and economic repercussions in the South.[6] Although these repercussions were as significant as those of the 1980s' Reagan–Thatcher neoliberal 'counter-revolution', they were certainly absorbed in a more creative way. The longest lasting of these was the shifting away of Latin America from its 'Ricardian' position (which had again been strengthened after the Kemmerer missions of the 1920s), seeking new comparative advantages with greater productivity-growth potential, higher 'technology-ladders', better balance-of-payments prospects and increased chances of 'catching up'.

The five fundamental propositions upon which Latin America's structuralist thinking was built were that: (i.) manufacturing is the best engine of growth; (ii.) ISI is the way to achieve it in middle-income Latin America; (iii.) commodities cannot provide a dynamic export sector; (iv.) inflation results mainly from 'structural' supply-bottlenecks and, (v.) only 'discretionary' government policies could tackle these problems (which include urgently needed 'complementary' investment).[7]

Meanwhile in the OECD, problems began to emerge well *before* the 1973 oil-shock; in particular, there occurred a 'full-employment profit-squeeze' – an imbalance between productivity and wage growth. These were mainly the result of diminishing 'animal spirits', increasingly rigid job security (in the Kaleckian sense) and a change in technological paradigms.[8] The 1970s oil-shocks, of course, exacerbated these problems but were not their original cause.

As these problems appeared first in the USA, they undermined the foundations of the 'Bretton Woods' system (based on US hegemony). When the dollar was transformed from an undervalued into an overvalued currency, Nixon first rescinded gold-convertibility and then (when the US trade balance sustained the first major deficit of the century in 1971) he unilaterally abandoned the fixed-parities system.

In the absence of effective coordination, the new 'floating' system was incapable of resolving increasing global financial disequilibria; and when in 1977–8, Carter tried to stimulate aggregate demand – and US trade deficits reached 1/4 of exports – the rest of the OECD was no longer willing to absorb 'excess' dollars. The resulting dollar weakness, in tandem with rising inflation, set the stage for the (Volker) FED radical monetarist era.

Therefore, the retreat from Keynesianism was based on both domestic and international considerations, including the political weaknesses of the Keynesian camp, characterized by the incompetent Carter–Callaghan duo. What followed was a generalized volte-face in both the economic and the politico-institutional 'paradigms' of the OECD – the Reagan–Thatcher 'neoliberal counter-revolution'. Once again, both domestic and international considerations were inextricably linked in a transformation of this nature. Once again, such an ideological shift in the North, at the very time when a vulnerable Latin America was facing massive internal and external shocks, had powerful influences on the region's ideology, politics, institution-building and economics.

3. The increasing diversity of peripheral capitalism

The 'Golden Age' not only provided the OECD but also developing countires (DCs) with unprecedented prosperity: their output trebled between 1950 and 1973, nearly doubling income per capita. Their growth rate was four times faster than their previous best performance and for the first time was similar to that of the OECD. The strong performance of many DCs is most significant in manufacturing (6.6% in DCs and 3.9% in OECD) and manufactured exports (12% and 5%). Latin America performed best as a region; however, the NICs grew fastest as a subgroup.

Although DCs' exports increased by 5.7% annually, their world share fell by 1/3 and, as Latin America's commodity exports grew at less than 3%, fell by half. This performance compares unfavourably with Latin America's previous commodity-export record, and with its overall growth. Latin America's ISI was implemented in such an inward-looking way, and absorbed such a proportion of resources, that commodities for export and agriculture for the domestic market became its main casualties.[9]

After 1973, the current-account deficit in the average oil-importing, middle-income DCs increased from 1% of GDP (1973) to 5% (1975). However, the mixed blessing of easy access to foreign borrowing helped their 'immunity' to the oil-shock. In fact, their excess borrowing led many *non*-oil currencies to revalue, leading the real economy (certainly in Latin America) to adjust in the opposite direction to that required by their current accounts.[10]

One reason for Latin America's over-borrowing was financial incentives ('over' meaning accumulating more risk than was privately, let alone socially, efficient): even if deflated by Latin America's *non*-oil-export prices, the London Interbank Offer Rate (LIBOR) was negative for seven years between 1972–80 (-5.3% on average).

Thus, on their own terms, the floating exchange-rate regime and financial 'deregulation' were temporarily able to accommodate the 1973–4 financial disequilibria. OPEC's surplus was 'recycled' to balance-of-payments-constrained countries; 'recycling' enabled DCs to maintain growth momentum (thus supporting world aggregate demand); low LIBOR allowed DCs' foreign liabilities to perform; and by 1978, OPEC's surplus had itself disappeared (due to increased absorption).

However, not only had the first oil-shock revealed more OECD rigidities than anticipated – leading to 'stagflation' – but when OPEC added a second shock, the threat of a new international order with some 'power to the (Southern) people' had major political repercussions. Finally, the US trauma after the hostage crisis in Iran is difficult to overestimate. Hence, the political and economic scenes were set for the Reagan–Thatcher neoliberal 'counter-revolution', in which little distinction was made between the crusades against the 'evil empire', domestic trade unions, and the 'ayatollahs' of the Third World. The basic idea was that 'either you are with us, or you are against us'. Most DCs stood up to be counted, and Latin America quickly offered *ex post* public guarantees on unpayable private debts, accepted a one-sided post-1982 debt-rescheduling process and began their long march towards 'neoliberalism'. Those that did not paid dearly for it.

It is this menacing international environment, together with the fact that the 1982 debt crisis was uniquely torturing for Latin America – rather than the powers of persuasion of Freedman or Hayeck, or Latin American politicians suddenly seeing 'the light' on their road to Damascus – that are crucial to understanding not only the degree of orthodoxy of Latin America's new ideological, politico-institutional and economic 'neoliberal' paradigms, but also (following the remarkable collapse of the Soviet Union) its 'end-of-history' uniformity and standardization.

It seems that at a time of high economic uncertainty and radical political change, simplistic discourses tend to strike a chord with large segments of society.

4. The unique 1980s in Latin America

The 1982 crisis had a singularly pernicious effect in Latin America. While Latin America was experiencing a declining income per capita (-0.9% annually), Asia doubled its previous growth rate. Korea (7.8%), China (7.6%), Thailand (5.9%) and India (3.6%) showed a particularly strong 1980s per capita growth rate. Latin America's poor relative performance among DCs was unprecedented, with income differentials between Latin America and Asia declining for the first time since 1820.[11]

Almost every indicator reflects Latin America's 1980s' stagnation. Manufacturing growth fell from 6.6% (1950–81) to 1.1% (1981–90); commodity exports from 3.9% to 0.7%; debt-service ratios increased to about 50% of exports (a level two to three times greater than those found in East Asia); negative transfers abroad (excluding IMF loans) reached (in US dollars of 2000 value) $650 billion (1982–90); per capita investment decreased by 2/3 (1980–90); in some countries urban unemployment even exceeded 20%; and inflation of three, four and even five-digits was common: if 1980 = 100, Latin America's 1990-price level was 4.5 million, while Argentina's was 887 million and Brazil's 70 million.[12] Even Sub Saharan Africa had at least managed a stagnant per capita income and low inflation.

Not surprisingly, ISI and the whole model of state-led development were under enormous strain throughout Latin America; the tension was compounded by fragile transitions to democracy (for example, in Brazil and Argentina). Furthermore, the early recovery – from a massive 13% GDP fall in 1982 – in (already 'neoliberal', and IMF's favourite) Chile was taken as further evidence of the need for and *direction* of change.

Hence, history repeated itself: as in the 1930s, when a massive, persistent and uniquely painful external shock found Latin America in an extremely vulnerable position, both economically and politico-institutionally, and when the North was simultaneously undertaking a paradigmatic change, Latin America not only undertook a very arduous internal and external macroeconomic adjustment, but also a radical change in economic thinking.

Initially, other than in Chile, Latin American leaders actually presented this change as a temporary, but 'unfortunately necessary', step to reverse capital flight, finance exploding foreign debts, reduce runaway inflation and escape from recession. However, once started, there was no going back, and the long-lasting effect was a generalized volte-face in Latin America's economics and politics. As happened in the North, particularly in Anglo-Saxon countries, 'born-again' neoliberalism was characterized by a massive shift in the balance of power towards capital,[13] trade and financial liberalization, wholesale privatization, market deregulation (especially labour), and a substantial reduction in the options open to democratic institutions and economic policy.[14]

In fact, nowhere else in the world did 'neoliberalism' spread so quickly, in such a one-dimensional version, and with such an 'end-of-history' uniformity and standardization. Its discourse had a compass whose 'magnetic north' was simply the reversal of as many aspects of the previous development strategy as possible.[15] The mere idea that alternatives could exist met with a mixture of amusement and contempt.[16]

The neoliberal 'manifesto' comprised six basic propositions: (i) trade and financial liberalization would switch the engine of growth towards domestically-financed private investment in tradeables; (ii) budgetary balance and undistorted market signals would prove sufficient conditions for macroeconomic equilibrium and microeconomic efficiency; (iii) the end of government 'discretionary' policies would not only eliminate state-created rent-seeking activities, but also massively reduce opportunities for corruption; (iv) private imbalances would be self-correcting; (v) market deregulation and trade liberalization would promote private investment and domestic saving; and, (vi) fiscal balances would release savings for more productive use in the private sector. As Argentina has yet again demonstrated, the process of reform turned out to be far more complex and its results certainly more mixed than anticipated.

In sum, Latin America 'threw in the (ISI) towel', moving to a standardized environment in which the only issue at stake was who would best (and most faithfully) implement the 'new' model.[17] As argued in my chapter on financial crises (chapter 16), this contrasts sharply with East Asia, where economic reforms were implemented mainly as a pragmatic mechanism to strengthen the *existing* development model.

The rest of the chapter will briefly discuss the following periods: the 1950s; 1960–73; 1973–82; and 1982–90.[18]

5. The 1950s: postwar instability, ISI, regional diversity and accelerated inflation

With the benefit of hindsight, the main characteristic of the 1950s was the persisting 'twin-collective-memory' of the 1930s and of the war: a (historically justifiable but extreme) pessimism regarding primary commodity-export-led growth, and (the also intellectually-justifiable but extreme) optimism regarding the prospects for ISI. Accordingly, the period is characterized by a progressive disengagement from the international economy and the implementation of ambitious industrialization programmes.

Events in the early 1950s did not help. Externally, the OECD demand for commodities grew very slowly (in part due to the recovery of domestic production), and its markets were closed to Latin America's more processed commodities; the Korean War effect on commodity prices was short lived; and Latin America's terms of trade fell by more than 20%. Furthermore, Latin America had no access to international finance due to continuous default.[19] Internally, political support for ISI also increased rapidly among groups wanting to limit the power of the traditional rural and mining oligarchies.

However, even then, Latin America's postwar reaction to (non-oil) primary-commodity exports seems disproportionate (Figure 3).

Indeed, neglect of exports was such that, when demand for commodities picked up (late 1950s), Latin America had little productive capacity to respond. Thus, when OECD demand increased from 1.9% (1950–5) to 6% (1955–72), exports could only rise from 1.7% to 2.9% – that is to say, from keeping up with market shares to growing at *half* the market's pace. Therefore, as trade theory points out, Latin America was caught in the worst of both worlds: exports grew slowly in a slow-growing market.

Slow export growth and declining terms of trade meant that (while GDP grew by 2/3) the purchasing power of exports (volume of exports multiplied by terms of trade) remained stagnant during the 1950s. Consequently, the trade surplus fell from 3.9% of GDP to 0.7%, while the current account switched from a surplus of $0.7 billion to a deficit of $5.5 billion. As Latin America had little access to international finance, a foreign-exchange constraint began to hinder output growth, investment and fiscal revenues.

Many countries (e.g. Argentina, Brazil, and Chile) used deficit-financing to keep up growth momentum, thus adding an internal imbalance to an emerging external disequilibrium. High inflation led to the first IMF stabilization plans; the conditionality was tight-monetarist macro-policies, which were the subject of heated controversy – there was no 'regimental' intellectual atmosphere in those days![20]

Structuralists were concerned that the IMF emphasis on competitive

Figure 3. LATIN AMERICA (18): **Shares of Manufactures and Exports in GDP (%), 1945–2000**

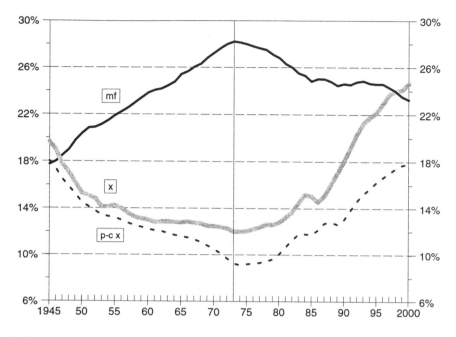

'**mf**'=manufacturing sector; '**x**'=non-oil-exports; and '**p-c x**'=non-oil-primary-commodity exports. 1980 constant-prices. 3-year moving averages. Excludes Venezuela (and Mexico *after* oil-discoveries) – oil is excluded to avoid the highly distorting effect of pricing oil throughout at 1980 prices.

devaluations and reduction of expenditure would at best control inflation at the cost of both deteriorating commodity-terms of trade (fallacy of composition) and of slowing down ISI. Therefore, monetarist-IMF created a false dilemma between price stabilization and economic growth (and would probably be unable to deliver either).

Structuralism instead sought to reduce inflation by attacking its root causes: inelastic supplies, particularly in agriculture, which constrained ISI and increased conflict over real wages. Thus, the modernization of agriculture (particularly land-tenure systems) and public investment were considered to be as important in the long-term fight against inflation as the control of monetary aggregates and the exchange rate.[21]

The 1950s' ISI did succeed on its own terms. The manufacturing growth rate reached 6.6% (steel 13%, and cellulose and oil-derivatives 11%), GDP, 5.1%, and investment, 7.8%. However, there were both high performance diversity among Latin American countries – while the GDPs of Venezuela, Brazil and Mexico grew at 7.6%, 6.8% and 6.1% respectively, Argentina's did so at only 2.8% – and casualties, such as traditional export-commodities and domestic agriculture.

Furthermore, the effectiveness of any economic policy is as much a function of its rationality, the international environment and the consensus that it musters, as of the efficacy of its implementation. Therefore, another casualty was ISI itself; in the long run it suffered greatly from the fact that trade and industrial policies became unnecessarily complicated, obscure and subject to bureaucratic manipulation.[22]

Structuralists tried to 'fine-tune' ISI: domestic markets were too small, and Europe was reaping the benefits of integration. In the early 1960s, LAFTA (Latin American Free Trade Association) and the Central American integration (followed by the Andean Pact) were taking shape.[23] These initiatives achieved some results, but they were modest compared with original expectations – industrial elites were only too happy to continue rent-seeking on captive national markets, and governments were too weak to act.

The Cuban revolution was also having an impact. Political pressure for better distribution of income, wealth and power gathered momentum. Paradoxically, one incentive for change came for the first (and last) time from the USA itself through Kennedy's 'Alliance for Progress': the likelihood of Reagan or Thatcher imposing financial conditionalities on Latin America later in the 1980s based on agrarian reforms was as strong as the likelihood of their conversion to unilateral disarmament. Likewise, to say that Kennedy's 'Weltanschauung' was a far cry from previous, and later, IMF thinking would be something of an understatement.

6. The economic boom of the 1960s and early 1970s

The 1960–73 period is the most dynamic ever for OECD countries and DCs alike. The NICs and some Latin American countries (e.g. Brazil, Mexico and Venezuela) posted the best DC performance. The former benefited from the OECD's growing demand for manufactured imports (12%), which more than doubled the pace of demand for commodities.

Latin America's growth process instead had to keep struggling against a growing balance-of-payments constraint because it continued to commit the twin errors of not making a NIC-style effort to direct new industries towards export markets, and being unwilling to devote enough resources to increase exports of traditional commodities in step with even slow-growing demand. This, combined with weak terms of trade, meant that the purchasing power of non-oil-exports hardly grew at all (Figure 4).

Figure 4. **OECD: imports of manufactures and of primary commodities. LATIN AMERICA: exports of primary commodities and purchasing power of exports**

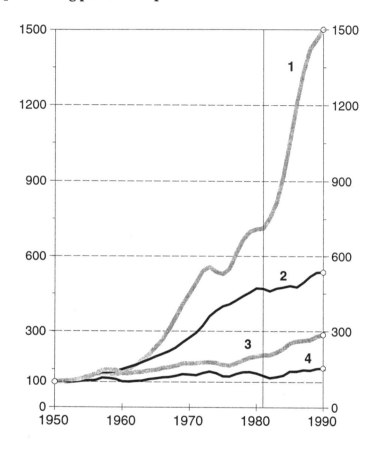

1=OECD's manufactured imports; 2=OECD's non-oil-primary-commodity imports; 3=LA's non-oil primary-commodity exports; and 4=Latin America's purchasing power of non-oil primary-commodity exports. Constant values. 3-year moving averages.[24]

During this period, two major regional trade circuits emerged, one within Europe and between Europe and the US, the other in East Asia: neither included Latin America. As the main engine of these trade zones was manufactured exports, they encouraged 'convergence' through technology transfers – from the US to Europe and from Japan to the NICs. On the tariff front, the NICs used protection at levels often higher than those of Latin America,[25] but the crucial difference was that huge effective protection – and cheap finance – was only granted if producers were able to fulfil specific *export* targets.[26] In this way, ISI and export-led growth were never mutually exclusive alternatives for the NICs: ISI was simply a platform and source of finance (due to 'over-pricing' a captive market) for their export drive. In turn, export orientation forced levels of investment, productivity and product quality that a purely inward-oriented ISI could never deliver.

Instead, Latin America's 'isolationism' brought manufactured-import and commodity-export ratios to almost their absolute minimum. Some countries reacted and tried to incentivize exports and a more selective ISI using subsidies, dual exchange rates, 'crawling-pegs', export zones and regional integration. This policy had some success: manufactured exports expanded by 11.3% yearly (although almost entirely in the larger economies), and intra-regional manufactured exports increased by 15% (1960–73). This contrasts with commodity exports (3.3%).

Within the context in which ISI was *actually* implemented in Latin America, Figure 5 highlights its crucial failure: the trade deficit in manufactures did not drop fast enough to compensate for declining commodity trade surpluses.

Figure 5. **LATIN AMERICA (19): trade balances as a percentage of GDP, 1950–90**

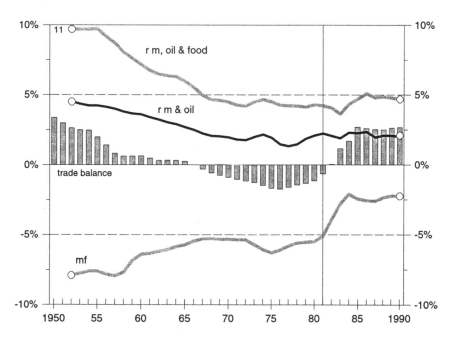

'**mf**'=trade deficit in manufactures; '**rm & oil**'=trade surplus in raw materials and oil; '**rm, oil & food**'= trade surplus in raw materials, oil and agricultural products. Current prices. 3-year moving averages.[27]

What policymakers took time to grasp is that ISI also had a high output elasticity to import manufactures (machinery and manufactured-inputs), particularly in small countries. Consequently, net foreign-exchange savings were not as high as expected. In all, trade balances were reversed by more than five percentage GDP-points to a deficit of 1.2% (1950–72).

Furthermore, Latin America's terms of trade continued to decline until 1967; by then, they had fallen by 30% since 1950. After a short recovery (1967–72), the 1973 oil-shock had an asymmetric impact on oil-importers and oil-exporters (Figure 6).

Figure 6. **LATIN AMERICA (19): terms of trade and real interest rate, 1950–2000**

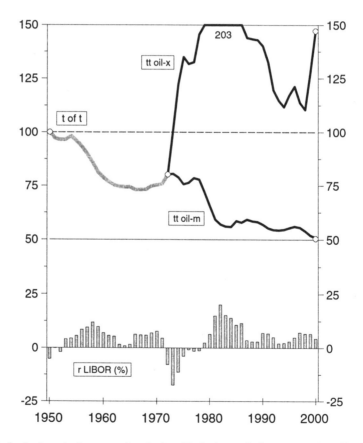

'**t of t**'=Latin America's terms of trade; '**tt oil-x**'=those of oil-exporters; '**tt oil-m**'=those of oil-importers; and '**r LIBOR**'=real LIBOR (deflated by Latin America's non-oil export-prices).

Overall, the 1960–73 period was the most dynamic in Latin America's history. Manufacturing increased at 6.8%, investment at 9% and GDP at 5.9% – doubling output, and increasing income per capita by half. Even the regional diversity decreased, as Argentina accelerated its GDP growth to 4%, while Brazil and Mexico only added one percentage point to their already dynamic growth. However, the end of the OECD 'Golden Age', the problems facing a more mature and complex ISI, the double oil-shocks and the extreme ease with which Latin America could borrow its way out of trouble after 1973 were to radically change its rapid development process.

7. The inter-shock period, 1973–81: the lead-up to financial crisis

The 1973 fourfold oil-price rise came when the 'Golden Age' was winding down, and the new floating exchange-rate system had not yet been firmly established. The new exchange system suddenly had to struggle with abrupt changes – in just one year, the OECD's current account turned from a surplus of $34 billion into a deficit of $47 billion, and that of the non-oil DCs from a deficit of $29 billion into one of $66 billion. Together with the international financial markets, the new floating-rate system was burdened with the largest ever trade-related transfer of resources from the OECD to a group of DCs (OPEC), as well as with the 'recycling' of these resources.

Due to the reemergence of monetarism, most OECD countries attempted to tackle rising inflation with orthodox policies that ignored the fact that inflationary pressures (both old and new) were of a cost-push nature. What followed was 'stagflation' and increased social tension.

In fact, most DCs adjusted to the first oil-shock better than the OECD – while OECD growth fell from 5% (1960–73) to 2.8% (between the oil-shocks), that of DCs only declined from 6% to 5.2%. Latin America's oil exports rose from $7 billion (1972) to $55 billion (1981), but the oil-importers' oil bill increased from $4 billion to $30 billion.

Venezuela followed OPEC's policy of reducing output, but Mexico (not in OPEC) increased its share of Latin America's oil exports from practically zero to 47% (1973–81).[28]

Latin America's oil importers responded to the first oil-shock differently. Some countries, such as Brazil, where the oil bill reached 44% of imports, borrowed heavily thinking it had sufficient *jogo de cintura* to continue with fast growth. This 'debt-led growth' was a response to short-term market signals – highly negative real interest rates, and uncertainties regarding OPEC's capacity to implement strict output-quotas. Others, such as Chile, which still had restricted access to international finance, had to reduce expenditure.

However, after the 1979 shock, the responses were often reversed. Brazil, having already accumulated huge debts, had to adjust, while Chile borrowed heavily.[29] Strangely, oil-*exporters* also borrowed heavily despite massive current-account surpluses – overly liquid lenders needed to push for every possible customer. Oil exporters were thus confronted with cheap and overly abundant funds, highly-overvalued exchange rates, unstable domestic politics and weak property rights (particularly on wealth of doubtful origin). These factors, combined with the proliferation of 'tax havens' led to highly-subsidized capital flights. Amazingly, the IMF regarded them (from invest-ment-constrained and highly-indebted countries) as a 'positive' phenomenon: the resulting reduction in reserves would help 'sterilize' the expansionary effect of higher oil prices and increased international borrowing.

Easy borrowing also encouraged public deficits and imports of luxury con-sumer goods and military hardware. However, it also helped rationalize tariffs and exchange-rate structures. In all, Latin America's imports increased from $77 billion in 1972 to $236 billion in 1981.

An ever-increasing foreign debt tied the fortunes of the region closely to the policies and performance of the OECD. Since 1929, the links had worked mainly through trade flows, with the OECD's demand for commodities being the crucial factor. Now, a strong financial link was again added, characterized by a growing dependency on new loans and the uncertainties of interest rates. Under these circumstances, the second oil-shock, the (Volker) FED monetarist response and the Reagan–Thatcher era was not what Latin America needed. The OECD fiscal position suffered from recession, populis-tic income-tax cuts, and vastly increasing military expenditure; meanwhile, Latin America followed the Reagan and Thatcher populist lead and more than doubled its public sector deficit to $38 billion. By 1981, Latin America's current-account deficit ($80 billion) was as bad as that of the whole of the OECD, yet it could still easily borrow as much as it wanted: Latin America's foreign debt *doubled* to $533 billion between 1976 and 1981. Not the best example for Summer's belief that 'The logic of efficient [financial] markets is compelling'.[30]

The beginning of the end for LA's 'debt-led growth' was the FED trebling nominal rates (1977–81) – in real non-oil-export prices (Figure 6), the LIBOR increased from -11.2% to 22.1%. Non-oil terms of trade also deteriorated (18% between 1980 and 1982). As often happens in times of crisis, the OECD not only halted lending to DCs and contracted imports, but also transferred part of the cost of its own adjustment to the periphery via lower primary-com-modity prices and higher interest rates – this time on a debt with variable interest rates. The resulting recession in many DCs, of course, rebounded on the OECD by lower demand for OECD exports and financial instability.[31]

While it lasted, Latin America's 'debt-led growth' delivered relatively fast growth: GDP increased by 4.7% annually (twice the OECD rate). Investment increased by 1/3 and its GDP share rose from 17% (1960s) to 22% (1976–1981). However, performance diversity increased again, reaching during these years the highest levels of the whole period – from 8% GDP growth in Brazil to the remarkable stagnation of oil-rich Venezuela.

However, 'post-Volker' Latin America could not 'Ponzi-finance' mounting internal and external deficits forever – the debt-service ratio reached 41% of exports in 1981. Mexico's 1982 default stopped 'debt-led growth' dead in its tracks, and drastic adjustment processes desperately tried to reverse massive internal and external imbalances; thus, Latin America moved from its longest period of sustained growth to one of its worst performances ever. In the period 1950–81, Latin America's GDP had grown more than fivefold, manufacturing production sevenfold and manufactured exports twelvefold.[32] Furthermore, as Figure 7 indicates, ISI, and the 'capabilities' it generated (in the Hirschman sense), did provide a useful platform for the very few countries

Figure 7. **MEXICO: growth of manufacturing investment and employment 1970–81 and productivity 1981–2000**

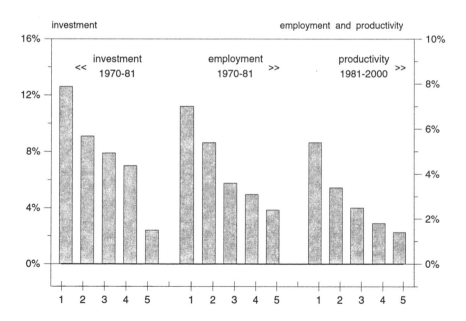

Manufacturing activities are ranked according to exports-output ratios *after* 1981 (group 1 has the highest and group 5 the lowest ratio). Excludes 'maquila'.

Source: Palma 2002b.

that in the 1980s moved their engine of growth towards manufacturing exports.

Mexico's 'non-maquila' post-1981 manufactured-export orientation clearly followed a pattern of selecting activities with previously high levels of both investment and employment growth. That is, during the 1970s, ISI was already allocating both capital and labour to those activities that were to achieve the highest degree of competitiveness after 1981. FDI may have moved into Mexico primarily for reasons to do with the US economy, but the choice of specific non-maquila manufacturing activities as production platforms to the USA also seems closely associated with the 'capabilities' built during ISI. Perhaps ISI was not so irrational after all.

8. From boom to bust: Latin America's 'hyper' stagflation of the 1980s

As mentioned above, both the late-1970s oil and FED shocks, as well as the 1982 debt crisis, had different effects among DCs. While many economies in East and South Asia were able to recover quickly (and then grow faster than previously), these shocks had a devastating impact on the economies of Latin America.

East Asia's much higher export-GDP ratios helped maintain lower debt-service ratios and higher investment levels; also, their export markets remained more dynamic as OECD's manufactured imports still increased by 11% annually during the 1980s (Figure 4). By contrast, Latin America was saddled with huge debt-service ratios and the worst external environment since the 1930s – a stagnant OECD demand for commodities (0.3% yearly growth between 1980 and 1987); a 23% drop in non-oil terms of trade (1979–90); a 22.3 percentage-point increase in real LIBOR in one year (1980–1); and a cessation of voluntary lending.[33] Even including 'virtual' inflows (due to debt rescheduling), net private non-FDI flows switched from $388 billion (1972–82) to a net outflow of $67 billion (1983–9). In fact, as a share of GDP, the negative net transfer of financial resources from Latin America was even larger than that of Germany after World War I.

Furthermore, the desperate effort to generate foreign exchange for debt-servicing was mostly self-defeating: a 30% increase in export volume of goods (1981–7) resulted in export revenues actually dropping by 5% in nominal terms. Therefore, Latin America had to reduce imports by nearly half in just 2 years (1981–3), converting the $29 billion trade deficit (1981) into a $55 billion surplus (1984); the required massive expenditure reductions and devaluations resulting in 'hyper' stagflation – up to 5 digit-inflation together with double-figure GDP declines.

In per capita terms, income fell by 9%, private consumption by 12% and investment by 2/3 (1980–90). Social indicators showed similar declines: up to a 4/5 drop in minimum wages (Argentina); 'open' urban unemployment in double figures, and 'under'-employment at a further 1/3 of the labour force; public expenditure in health and education was severely curtailed; and over half of households below the poverty line in most countries.

The 1980s ended with only four countries (Chile, Colombia, Costa Rica and Uruguay) having recovered basic macro-balances. In the others, despite many years of costly adjustment, 'hyper' stagflation and persistent imbalances were the rule.

9. Latin America's Complex Political Economy: the 1990s and some concluding remarks

After the war, Latin America integrated its economies into the world division of labour in a different way to East Asia. Latin America only resembled East Asia insofar as it refused to accept its traditional 'Ricardian' comparative-advantage position, and struggled to gain an 'endogenously-created' one. However, East Asia did this within the 'flying geese' pattern of manufacturing production and upgrading. Following Japan's example, this was achieved through massive investment and savings efforts, coordinated by strong governments able to implement effective trade and industrial policies, and within a process of regionalization of production that simultaneously aimed at insulating domestic markets and outwardly orienting tradeable production. Their success was helped by an ability to continue upgrading exports, a process facilitated by a positive interaction between productivity and wages growth, and OECD market openness, especially on the part of the USA. This openness was not extended to Latin America, with the exception of Mexico after 1982 (the US fearing that the 1982 debt crisis could turn the usual flow of Mexican immigrants into a tidal wave).

Instead, until the 1982 debt crisis, Latin America tried to improve its chances of 'catching up' with developed countries by attempting to do one thing at a time. In contrast to East Asia, Latin America understood ISI and manufactured-export-led growth as being two successive stages, and found it particularly difficult to switch from the first to the second. Inevitably, excessive reliance on one particular 'engine of growth' leads to highly unbalanced economic and political structures under which the engine itself not only loses its power but also its capacity to transform.

Most Latin American governments (and economists) came to interpret the 1982 debt crisis as evidence that ISI was leading the region into a cul-de-sac. These governments therefore switched to the 'open economy' model, totally abandoning ISI. The East Asian model of simultaneously insulating the domestic markets and outwardly orienting tradeable production was as alien to Latin America's policymaking in its structuralist period as in its neoliberal period.

Thus, before the 1982 debt crisis (i) ISI was almost entirely inward-looking; (ii) the engine of ISI was the high propensity to consume, and the ever-growing diversification of consumption patterns of the high-income groups; (iii) there was a remarkable neglect of primary-commodity exports; (iv) shortages of foreign exchange, inefficient government coordination and the low propensity of the upper-income groups to save money (despite having the world's largest income shares) constrained investment; and (v) despite some success with regional integration, it was expected that FDI (rather than an internal effort) would move the 'upgrading' of the economy on to the second, more open, stage. In fact, a crucial (rent-seeking) similarity between the capitalist elite during ISI on the one hand, and the 'neoliberal' 1990s on the other, is that in both periods they expected that FDI would do the required transformations: in the former they expected that FDI would move the economy toward a more open stage, while in the latter, they expected FDI to pick up where the state had left off.

Another criticism of ISI is that the region was unable to develop an 'endogenous core' of manufacturing activities that might have succeeded in stimulating other sectors of the economy.[34] Others have cited the instability of domestic policies that biased investment efforts towards short-run objectives.[35] FDI itself has also come in for criticism on various counts: (i) until the 1980s (and, again, in 'non-maquila' Latin America in the 1990s) inflows of FDI were mainly oriented towards non-tradeables and tradeable production for the domestic markets, reinforcing ISI-inward orientation;[36] (ii) high-import content led to small shares of value-added in output; and (iii) huge levels of effective protection led to excessively high rates of profit and large profit remittances. Oddly enough, FDI justified this protection with traditional 'infant-industry'-type arguments; therefore, 'infant' corporations such as General Motors, Daimler Benz, ICI, Ford, ITT, Volkswagen, EMI, General Electric, Xerox, du Pont, Unilever, Imperial Tobacco, Nestlé, Siemens and Bayer ended up operating with effective protection that often reached four figures.

Finally, Figure 8 highlights four unique characteristics in Latin America's pattern of ISI.

It is remarkable that the return to a 'Manchester-style' capitalism in the 1990s, other than generating some dynamic export patterns and increased productivity in a few sectors, has only been able to deal with one of these issues: inflation (see chapter 16 on financial crises). As for the others, and

Figure 8. **Latin America and DCs: 'gross' income elasticities to consume and to invest, debt-service ratios and inflation, 1965–1990**

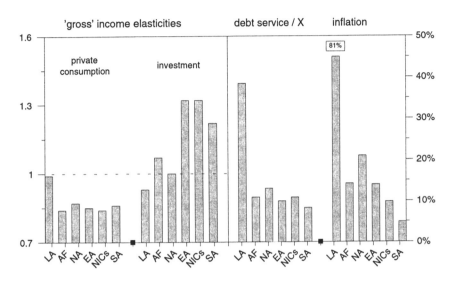

'gross' income elasticities=ratio of the growth-rate of the respective variable to that of national income;[37] and 'debt service/X'=debt service as share of exports.
LA=Latin America; **AF**=Sub Saharan Africa; **NA**=North Africa and the Middle East; **EA**=East Asia (excluding the NICs); **SA**=South Asia.

Source: World Bank (several issues; data only available from 1965.)

indeed for other macroeconomic imbalances more generally, evidence suggests that, despite all the 'neoliberal' fanfare, these are no better today – in fact in many cases are worse – than before the 1982 crisis (except for more diversity between countries, with Chile outperforming the rest of the region); for example, the aggregate current-account deficit for the decade between 1992 and 2001 reached $600 billion – this translates as about $3,000 per economically active person – a figure not so different from that of one-year income per capita. In currency of equal value, this aggregate deficit was more than half as much again that of the decade before the 1982 debt crisis. Furthermore, the 1990s' much larger current account deficits took place alongside a rate of growth of output which was only about half that of the decade before 1982.

In sum, in addition to the well-known – and often over-emphasized – 'external' factors, Latin America's development throughout this period has basically been restricted by two interconnected endogenous factors: one is of an ideological nature; the other is the characteristic of its capitalist elite. The former refers to the predominance – and intensification – of a tendency towards 'fundamentalist' beliefs, characterized in both periods by the obsession with being in every possible aspect the absolute opposite of the previous ideology, and by finding it particularly difficult to evolve even within their own framework (e.g. in the 'neoliberal' period, to be able to absorb, in a practical way, the contributions of information, new-growth and new-trade theories.) The main difference is that in the new orthodoxy – because of its 'end-of-history' attitude – dissent is considered, at best, a sheer eccentricity.

In fact, what characterizes Latin America is not only the extreme form in which new ideologies are taken up, but also the extreme form in which they are subsequently given up: a sort of 'manic-depressive' ideological cycle seems to be the rule – Hirschman once referred to Latin America's 'fracasomania'. It is one thing to acknowledge that all economic policies are, to some extent, ideologically driven; the tendency to take them up – and later, to give them up – in a purely ideological fashion, is a different thing entirely. When serious trouble begins, there is always another 'paradise' to replace the one just 'lost'.

Maybe Latin America is in desperate need of a touch of East Asian 'Confucianism'; i.e., once a development path has been chosen, a significant degree of persistence, pragmatism, effective leadership and self-respect can be of great assistance in policymaking success.[38]

Latin America follows rather in the 'Iberian' tradition, one might say; it was not for nothing that Spain fought a bloody civil war over issues that in other countries would have led to less brutal forms of conflict. Perhaps one reason that 'ideology' is so important in Latin America is because there is little else in the form of social cohesion – such as 'tradition' in the British sense, 'hierarchy' and 'corporatism' in the German sense, 'corporatism' in the Northern Italian sense, a secular but authoritarian state in the French sense, etc.

Regarding the second endogenous development-constraint, that is to say the characteristics of the capitalist elite, little has changed, except that with the 'neoliberal' reforms the distribution of income, wealth and power has deteriorated still further.[39] For example, Latin America's elite continues to believe that it can 'Ponzi-finance' excessive private consumption forever (in the 1990s, the private sector 'gross' income-elasticity to consume actually increased above 1),[40] and that governments should pick up the bill when things go wrong – or as Gore Vidal once put it, 'neoliberalism' is about "socialism for the rich and capitalism for the rest"'.

Latin America's elite also discovered two 'postmodern' economic laws: (i) instead of having to pay taxes to get free public goods, it is much more fun to get them by lending money to the government; and (ii) the lower the taxes (and, therefore, the higher the lending) the higher the interest rate that can be charged. In turn, there is little doubt that Latin America's elite goes on believing (and often getting away with it for long periods of time) that it can always rent-seek on someone else closing the saving-investment and external gaps – namely governments during ISI – and FDI afterwards.[41]

By the beginning of this century, foreign debt had reached $750 billion, many country-risks were in five figures, net transfer of resources had again turned negative (more than $50 billion in 2002), and several domestic debts, most notably Brazil's, were set to burst. Of the four years since 1999, income per capita has already become negative in three (and 2003 is heading in the same direction); and Argentina has probably already beaten Russia to the record for the highest income-per-capita drop in peacetime living memory, although this record may be short-lived. At the time of writing, Venezuela is plunging towards an income per capita drop in 2003 which will be even higher than those of Russia and Argentina. It must certainly take some doing for oil-rich Venezuela to have an income per capita in 2003 below the one it had before the first oil-shock three decades ago, and for Argentina to start the twentieth century with an income per capita among the very top in the world, and to start the 21st with well over half of the population below the poverty line. Unsurprisingly, it had to be a seriously fragmented society, such as Argentina, which imported 'neoliberalism' in its most extreme version.[42]

There remain at least four crucial questions still requiring an answer:

(i) Why was it that the domestic capitalist oligarchies and the 'Washington Consensus' needed individuals such as Pinochet, Collor, Menem, Salinas and Fujimori (to mention only a few) as 'first generation' leaders in order to get the neoliberal show on the road in the first place?[43]

Although these petit-bourgeois parvenu-populists are nothing new in Latin American politics, what is peculiar to 'neoliberalism' is that they initially got into power using an anti-neoliberal discourse and, secondly, that they afterwards switched camp by means of making this populist tradition an artform.[44] Thirdly, for doing this, they were the first political leaders of this tradition since the 1930s that got the support, respect (and admiration) of the oligarchy for having helped create a new structure of property rights from which (as the possibilities of creating new ISI-generated rents were getting exhausted) massive new income streams (rents) could be generated – for example, obscure privatizations, unrestricted monopoly practices, massive bail-outs, 'flexible' labour markets, highly exchange-rate-subsidized capital flight, and so on.[45]

(ii) Why was it necessary to wait for a 'second-generation' type of leader (Aylwin, Cardoso, De la Rua and others) to be elected before some order could be introduced (not always very successfully) into the 'neoliberal' imbroglio?

(iii) Why did these 'second-generation' leaders feel that they were caught in an absolute 'path-dependency' straightjacket; i.e., that they had no option but to offer (though more decently) more reforms from the same basic Washington Consensus programme – including strengthening still further a structure of property rights and incentives that gave all the carrots to (international mobile) capital and all the sticks to human capital)?[46]

(iv) Why are the 'third-generation' political leaders made up mostly of ex-military-plotters, ex-racing drivers, ex-Miss-Universes, Evangelist preachers, Opus-Dei 'super-numerarios', singers, TV-celebrities, ex-football-players, ex-shoe-shine boys, ex-shop-floor workers, and mothers, widows and children of victims of violence and repression? They not only have a rather difficult task ahead, but with the single exception of Lula and his Workers' Party, they are unknown quantities.

Perhaps one answer to all these questions is simply that in Latin America, from time to time, the oligarchy uses massive political and economic change merely as a way of reinforcing the fact that they have succeeded in making the region the world's most paradigmatic case of 'the politics and economics of the *Gattopardo*', in which 'everything has got to change, for everything to stay just as it is'.

Notes

1 This chapter draws on my contribution to Ffrench-Davis, Muñoz and Palma 1994. I would like to thank them and Stephanie Blankenburg, Jonathan Di John and Richard Kozul-Wright for their helpful comments. The ideas of Díaz-Alejandro, Hirschman and Kaldor strongly influence this chapter. The usual caveats apply.

2 See also Wells 1988; Díaz-Alejandro 1989; Fajnzylber 1990; Ffrench-Davis; Muñoz and Palma 1994; Bulmer-Thomas 1995; Thorp 2000; and Cardenas, Ocampo and Thorp 2002.

3 ECLAC Statistical Division; unless otherwise stated, this source, together with ECLAC 2002, IMF 2002a, b and c, World Bank 2002a and b, and the works of footnote 2 are the sources for data. All US-dollar figures throughout are in 2000 values, and all growth rates are real.

4 Dynamic growth also led to social improvements – the mortality rate dropped by half, while life expectancy increased by 1/4 (1950–81).

5 Marglin and Schor 1990.

6 According to Prebisch, he was 'an orthodox economist until he witnessed the 1930s and read *The General Theory*' (which he translated).

7 Palma 1978.

8 Perez 2002.

9 Food production increased at only 0.4% per capita annually (1960–90).

10 On exchange-rate management in a financially liberalized world, see Flassbeck 2001.

11 Only the NICs had been gaining ground since the late 1960s.

12 One of the characteristics of the long-term policy cycle in Latin America, reactivated in

the 1980s, is that bursts of inflation (as they are usually blamed on government and labour) tend to lead to a period of 'sound money – more market' policies. In turn, as these policies are later associated with low growth, high unemployment and inequality, there is a reaction leading to a new period of 'looser money – fewer markets' policies; and so on.

13 In 1971, in the average US corporation the ratio between the CEO-remuneration and that of the lowest-paid worker was 36; after Reagan's presidency it was 400; today it is about 1,000.

14 For example, in the new trade negotiations between the USA and Chile, the USA imposed the condition that Chile should practically renounce its right to use (previously successful) controls on capital inflows and outflows. In a recent interview, Stiglitz remarks that it is conditions like this which fuel discontent with globalization.

15 Even in Brazil, which ISI transformed into one of the fastest growing economies in the world, the attitude was the same. According to Gustavo Franco, President of the Central Bank until the 1999 crisis: '[Our real task] is to undo 40 years of stupidity [*besteira*]...' (Veja 15/11/1996).

16 Franco again: '[The alternative] is to be neo-liberal or neo-idiotic [*neo-burros*].' Adam Smith once said that 'without competition there is no progress' – 1990s 'neoliberalism' in Latin America shows that this certainly applies to ideology as well.

17 In Argentina's 1999 presidential contest, the only dispute among candidates was in whose hands the fixed-parity would be safest; i.e., who would bring the Argentinian 'populistic-taliban' experiment faster to its Wagnerian end.

18 The 1990s are analysed in the financial crises chapter.

19 In 1950, 53% of publicly offered or guaranteed dollar-bonds were still in default; 45% had 'adjusted' debt-service; and only 2% had full service.

20 For a full (annotated) bibliography of this controversy (involving Noyola, Pinto and Sunkel), and other issues discussed in the chapter, see Palma 1995.

21 Austin Robinson (writing on India) had pioneered this view of inflation.

22 Kaldor 1959 emphasized this issue; see Palma and Marcel 1989. History would again repeat itself: inefficient and rigid implementation would end up being neoliberalism's main enemy in the 1990s.

23 See Ffrench-Davis, Muñoz and Palma 1994.

24 Logarithmic regressions confirm that OECD's income elasticity to import manufactures (around 2.5) more than doubles that to import non-oil-commodities (about 1); see, for example, Wells 1988.

25 Someone who got his facts wrong on this was Lall 1984.

26 See Chang 1994. From this perspective, in terms of trade and industrial policies, the real difference between East Asia and Latin America did not lie in the relative volume of 'rents' generated by these polices, but in the fact that in Latin American rents were systematically allocated without performance criteria.

27 See also Wells 1988.

28 New oil riches led a Mexican President to manically declare: 'from now on, Mexico's economic policy is no longer about allocating scarce resources, but one of distributing abundance'!

29 See chapter on financial crises.

30 Summer 1989.

31 For an econometric simulation on the cost for the OECD (in terms of output and employment) of lower DCs' import-demand after 1982, see Marcel and Palma 1988.

32 Of course, regional averages always hide significant performance-diversity: while Brazil's GDP grew at 6.8% and Mexico's at 6.6% during these three decades, Argentina only managed 2.9% (7.6%, 7.4% and 3.1% in manufacturing).

33 As Kindleberger 1996 emphasizes, financial markets can do one thing dumber than irresponsible lending to DCs: bringing that lending to an abrupt halt!

34 Fajnzylber 1983.

35 Díaz-Alejandro 1989.

36 Wells 1988.

37 These ratios are called 'gross elasticity' for pure convenience – the usual caveats apply.

38 Regarding the lack of self-respect of many Latin American countries, see for example endnote 14 (above), which refers to Chile renouncing its right to use capital controls in order to 'appease' the new US administration and get it to sign their latest trade agreement.

39 Post-1982 Latin American politics and economics make one think about what the history of the USA might have been had the South won the Civil War.

40 In *The General Theory*, Keynes stated that 'The fundamental psychological law [...] is that men are disposed, as a rule and on average, to increase their consumption as their income increases, but not by as much as the increase in their income'. Well, perhaps so, but not in Latin America!

41 This rent-seeking attitude was often so extreme that it ended up being a self-defeating process: several econometric works have shown that the surge of FDI that took place in Latin America from the end of the 1980s had a highly negative correlation with domestic investment. In East Asia, by contrast, FDI had a positive 'crowding-in' effect. See, for example, Agosin and Mayer 2000.

42 Something that (as late as 1998) still made the then Brazilian Minister of Labour rather jealous: 'I would like the PT [Lula's Workers' Party] to behave in Brazil like the opposition does in Argentina. There, nobody questions [neoliberal] macroeconomic policies. There, everybody knows that these policies are the true path' (Veja, 14/4/1998).

43 As in Ecuador, for example, with the President who started the 'neoliberal' reforms (with Argentina's Cavallo as his main advisor) running his presidential campaign on the unusually honest slogan 'vote for the madman'. Such individuals could come from a García Màrquez-style novel. However, as late as 1998, in their annual meeting, the IMF and World Bank paraded Menem, of all people, as the perfect 'reformist statesman'.

44 In Argentina, for example, before its 1995 crisis, private consumption reached 93% of GDP; Menem made everybody believe both that this could be achieved in a 'Paretto optimal way' (i.e., nobody had to lose), and that this was perfectly sustainable.

45 For example, in 1998, foreign asset holdings by Argentinean residents amounted to about $100 billion. This figure was equivalent to 3/4 of all outstanding foreign debt, and 125% of all additional foreign debt since the first election of Menem in 1989 (leading to financial liberalization).

46 According to Gramsci, it is in the realm of ideology that people become conscious of social relations; but, if for the majority of them, the social relations of which they have become aware are so disagreeable, perhaps the only alternative to authoritarian regimes is a (fragile) democratic hegemonic control embedded in ideologies which have become 'thin', uniform and 'fundamentalistic' (e.g. 'Latin American-style neoliberalism', and new forms of nationalism and religion).

References

Bulmer-Thomas, V, 1995, *The Economic History of Latin America since Independence*. Cambridge, CUP.

Cárdenas, E, JA Ocampo and R Thorp, eds., *An Economic History of Latin America*, London, Palgrave.

Chang, H-J, 1994, *The Political Economy of Industrial Policy*, London, Macmillan.

Díaz-Alejandro, C, 1989, *Collected Essays*, ed. A Velasco, Oxford, OUP.

ECLAC, 2002, *Statistical Survey*.

Fajnzylber, 1990, *Unavoidable Industrial Restructuring in Latin America*, London, Macmillan.

Ffrench-Davis, R, Muñoz and G Palma, 1994, 'The Latin American Economies, 1950–1990', in *Cambridge History of Latin America*, vol. 6, Cambridge, CUP.

Flassbeck, H, 2001, 'The exchange rate: economic policy tool or market price?', UNCTAD Discussion Paper, 157.

IMF, 2002a, *IFS* Databank.

——, 2002b, *Balance of Payments Statistics*.

——, 2002c, *WEO database*.

Kaldor, N, 1959, 'Economic problems of Chile', *Essays on Policy*, Cambridge, CUP.

Kindleberger, C, 1996, *Manias, Panics, and Crashes*, Chichester, Wiley.

Lall, D, 1984, *The Poverty of Development Economics*, Institute of Economics Affairs.

Marglin, S and J Schor, 1990, *The Golden Age of Capitalism*, Oxford, OUP.

Marcel, M and Palma, G, 1988, 'Third World Debt and its Effects on the British Economy', *Cambridge Journal of Economics*, vol. 12.

Palma, G, 1978, 'Dependency', *World Development*, vol. 6.

——, 1995, 'Bibliographical Essay on Economic Development in Latin America, 1950–1990' in *Cambridge History of Latin America*, vol. 10, Cambridge, CUP.

——, 2002a, 'The Kuznets curve revisited', *International Journal of Development Issues*, vol. 1.

——, 2002b, 'The Mexican Economy since trade liberalisation and NAFTA', UNCTAD.

Palma, G and Marcel, M, 1989, 'Kaldor on the *discreet charm* of the Chilean bourgeoisie', *Cambridge Journal of Economics*, vol. 13.

Perez, C, 2002, *Technological Revolutions and Financial Capital*, Cheltenham, Elgar, 2002.

Summers, L and V Summers, 1989, 'When financial markets work too well', *Financial Services*, vol. 3.

Thorp, R, 2000, *An Economic History of Latin America*, IADB.

TDR, 1993, *Trade and Development Report*, UNCTAD.

Wells, J, 1988, *Latin America at the Cross-roads*, ILO.

World Bank, 2002a, *World Development Indicators*.

——, 2002b, *Global Development Finance*.

——, Several Issues, *World Development Report*.

7

RETHINKING AFRICAN DEVELOPMENT

Howard Stein

1. Introduction

Africa is mired in a developmental crisis, not the common narrow monetary or financial crisis portrayed in the standard literature but a crisis of a more profound and protracted nature. A developmental crisis refers to the generalized incapacity of an economy to generate the conditions necessary for a sustained improvement in the standard of living.

The problem is basically structural in nature. Its antecedents lay in the colonial period and in the inability of postcolonial governments fundamentally to transform the economies inherited at independence. While structural adjustment has exacerbated the underlying weaknesses of African economies, its greatest crime is located in its inherent inability to structurally and institutionally transform African economies. The major reason for this can be found in the roots of structural adjustment, which lie in neoclassical economic theory and its misplaced emphasis on balancing financial variables in a hypothetical axiomatic world.[1] Adjustment is simply incapable of either assessing the nature of Africa's problems or putting in place the policies that will put African countries on a trajectory of sustainable development.

The challenge of the reversal of the African malaise is daunting. Not only are there myriad complex issues that need to be examined, but there are also enormous regional and country variations. Moreover, a proper understanding of the problem requires both contemporary and historical accounts of the transformation of institutions, structures and policies in Africa. There are also a variety of issues at the core of any rethinking of African development. These involve questions of state formation, agricultural development, industrial and export diversification and transformation, and resource mobilization including questions of resource gaps, financial design, foreign direct investment and debt reduction.

While some of these topics will be discussed in this chapter, I will focus on three salient issues, namely, the formation of a developmental state in Africa, and two related areas: the state and agriculture and the state and the manufacturing sector. While some of these subjects echo the titles of other chapters. I will present them in a manner that is more contextually tied to the exigencies of African development. In each case I will attempt to point to theoretical incapacities of neoliberalism to deal with these issues and to highlight alternative approaches utilizing different constructs and concepts. Before I look at these issues I will present a brief empirical overview of the economic crisis in Africa, with a focus on the adjustment period.

2. Statistical dimensions of the crisis

2.1 Capital flows

Sub Saharan Africa's (SSA's) participation in the flows of foreign direct investment (FDI) is minute and has actually been shrinking in recent years.

We can see from Table 1 that FDI flows to developing countries increased sixteenfold between the averages of the mid 1980s to 2000. However, what is evident is that SSA countries, and in particular the least-developed ones, have not been part of this rapid proliferation. The share of FDI going to SSA has fallen by almost 2/3 from the mid-1980s to a very low 2.7% in 2000. For almost all of SSA the decline is apparent through the latter half of the 1990s with the rises in 1995, 1997 and 1999 explained by one-year increases of

Table 1. FDI Inflows 1982–2000 (millions of US dollars, except last two rows which are percentages)

	1982–7	1987–93	1994	1995	1996	1997	1998	1999	2000
1. DCs*	14796	46941	105300	113125	145848	182606	180042	208995	241044
2. SSA*	1122	2106	3700	4734	5125	8357	5781	7334	6459
3. ALDCs**		614	674	1169	1451	1360	1948	1984	2094
2/1 %	7.6		4.5	3.5	4.1	3.5	4.6	3.2	3.5	2.7
3/1 %			1.3	0.6	1.0	1.0	0.7	1.1	0.9	0.9

DC = developing countries and ALDCs = African least developed countries
*Includes South Africa
**Excludes Angola

Source: UNCTAD 1994, 2001

inflows into South Africa (e.g. the 1997 figure was $3 billion higher than the 1996 figure). Excluding South Africa, the SSA share dropped from 7.3% between 1982 and 1987 to 4.4% in the period 1987–93, to a mere 2.9% in 1999, to 2.3% in 2000. Yet these figures in fact overstate the participation of SSA. Most FDI in SSA in the era of adjustment consists of inflows to support oil production. During the 1982–7 period 49% of the total excluding South Africa went to the two major oil producers, Angola and Nigeria. By 1999 the figure had risen to 54% and was still greater than 50% in 2000. In 2000 the other 40 SSA countries in the UNCTAD survey received a meagre $2.8 billion. Similarly the African least developed countries' share of developing country FDI has also fallen significantly compared to the 1987–93 period.

2.2 Trade

A good deal has been written about the globalization of trade in recent years. Between 1983 and 1998, the global level of merchandise exports more than tripled.[2] Table 2 (below), provides information on exports, their structure, terms of trade and current account balances. In 1998 SSA merchandise exports in nominal – not real – dollar terms were actually 13% below the level of 1980.[3] In 2000, exports finally exceeded the 1980 nominal level, due mostly to some recovery in the terms of trade.

What is particularly interesting is the structure of merchandise exports. In 1983, under 10% of exports from SSA (excluding South Africa) comprised

Table 2. Exports, manufactured exports, current account balance and net barter terms of trade for SSA, 1980–2000*

Year	1980	1990	1992	1993	1994	1995	1996	1997	1998	1999	2000
Merch. Exports	53049	45738	42033	38178	39558	48476	56563	56025	46590	50875	64308
Manuf. Exports		3899	3808	3867	4196	5027	5247	5131	5687	5884	5715
Percent		8.5	9.1	10.1	10.6	10.4	9.2	9.1	12.2	11.6	8.8
Bal. On Cur.Act	-4226	-9550	-15084	-15030	-10911	-11527	-5745	-9022	-17022	-17878	-7181
Bal/GDP	-2.3	-5.2								-9.3	-3.6
Terms of Trd.	177.1	113.9	102.4	97.6	96.2	100.0	110.3	101.6	90.1	96.8	119.7

* all figures are in millions of current dollars except for percentages; balance of payments exclude net capital grants; figures exclude South Africa.

Source: World Bank, 2001, 2002a.

manufactured goods. In 2000, the figure was still below 10% (8.8%).[4] This is a remarkable indictment of the orthodox policies of the IMF and World Bank, which have emphasized static comparative advantage and limited the ability of African countries to move up the industrial ladder. By contrast, East Asian and Pacific countries' exports of manufactured goods went from 52% to 78% of total merchandise exports over a comparable period.[5] The advantages of export diversification and moving into manufacturing are significant not only in the domestic economy but in international price movements.

Terms of trade for Africa have been declining at an alarming rate in the past 20 years. In SSA the net barter terms of trade fell by 50% between 1980 and 1998,[6] before rising in 1999 and 2000. In contrast to this Taiwan, which in the 1990s increased the share of manufactured goods in exports to over 90% of the total, saw an increase in its terms of trade by 27% between 1980 and 1996.[7] Arguably the very act of flooding the world with resources in response to IMF pressures has a fallacy of composition effect, thereby exacerbating the export position of resource producing countries.[8]

The relative decline in the terms of trade in Africa is also directly related to the shifting nature of global production. The emphasis on raw material and primary product exports is very problematic in an era in which knowledge becomes a larger proportion of the value-added of commodities. Advances in biotechnology and material sciences are leading to synthetic substitutes for primary products such as vanilla and sugar. Products such as cocoa and palm oil are also being challenged by Western firms, as they undertake genetic research to develop outright synthetic substitutes or alternative methods of production. Natural resources like copper are being replaced by optical fibres or microwaves, contributing to the downward pressure on prices from the demand side. Processing that would provide employment opportunities to African economies is discouraged by tariffs and other forms of protectionism that tend to be higher relative to unprocessed commodities.[9]

Figures on current account balances are also presented in Table 2. The extremely poor performance in exports has led to a deteriorating situation in the balance of payments. Current-account deficits quadrupled between 1980 and 1999, reaching 9.3% of the GDP in 1999 from a previously more manageable 2.3%. The large rise in the terms of trade in 2000 finally helped to reduce the current account deficit. Given the global economic downturn in 2001, however, this is not likely to last.

2.3 Other indicators

Other indicators illustrate that SSA has not done well in the era of adjustment and globalization. Gross national savings and gross domestic investment have

Table 3. **Savings ratio and resource gap for Sub Saharan Africa
1965–99***

Years	1965–70	1970–5	1975–9	1980–4	1990–4	1995–9
Median national savings	8.0	12.9	12.4	8.3	5.9	8.0
Mean national savings	10.0	14.2	13.0	8.2	8.8	8.3
Mean resource gap	-6.1	-2.5	-7.5	-8.4	-10.3	-10.0

* All figures are percentages of GDP for 28 countries in Sub Saharan Africa.

Source: Karshenas 2001, and author's calculations from World Bank 2000b; 2001.

both deteriorated. The resource gap between national savings and domestic investment has also widened. Table 3 presents figures on gross national savings and the resource gap as measured by the difference between national savings and domestic investment from 1964 to 1999.

What is apparent from Table 3 is the collapse in national savings from the pre-adjustment period of the 1970s to the 1990s. The quadrupling of the resource gap from the first half of the 1970s to the 1990s is quite dramatic. Gross domestic investment has also declined from over 20% in the latter 1970s to around 18% in the latter half of the 1990s.

These figures are far below what is needed for a sustained improvement in the standard of living. They are also the lowest regional figures in the world.[10] The contrast to Asia over the same period is striking: while, relative to its GDP, the savings rates in the period 1965–70 in Asia were about four percentage points above those of SSA, by the early 1990s Asia exceeded SSA by a whopping 17.5 percentage points and was able to sustain much higher levels of domestic investment (28.5% in the first half of the 1990s) with very small resource gaps (only 2.2%).[11]

Given the paucity of private capital inflows, SSA has been able to finance these huge resource gaps by assuming large amounts of bilateral and multi-lateral official debt. Table 4 breaks down the debt by type between 1980, 1998 and 2000. Ratios to GDP and exports are also provided. The proliferation of debt over the adjustment period is abundantly evident, with the overall figures increasing nearly fourfold. By 1998 debt to export ratios exceeded 350% with the figures above the nominal GDP level: by the IMF standard anything above 200% is considered to be very onerous, and no country is considered capable of exporting its way out of a debt of this level. Most

Table 4. **External debt of Sub Saharan Africa* (billions of US nominal dollars except for ratios)**

Year	1980	1998	2000
Bilateral	18.0	81.9	83.5
Multilateral Conc.	7.5	57.2	54.5
Private	20.8	27.5	21.9
Short-term	11.2	31.1	23.7
IMF	3.0	7.4	6.7
Total External Debt	60.6	205.3	190.9
Debt/GDP	0.33	1.03	0.97
Debt/Exports	1.1	3.6	2.61

* Figures do not include South Africa.

Source: World Bank 2000b; 2002a; 2002b

African countries are well above this. By far, the overwhelming growth has been in official debt, with private debt nearly stagnant from 1980 to 1998. The impact of debt relief under the HIPC (Heavily Indebted Poor Countries) initiative was having some effect.[12] However the ratios of debt to GDP at around 0.97 and debt/exports at 2.6 were still rather high in 2000. Moreover, the big improvement was on the export side and was due to a one-year (23%) increase in the terms of trade in 2000, which might not be sustainable.

Unsurprisingly GNP has not kept up with population growth. In the period 1965–73 per capita GNP grew by a comfortable rate of 2.9% per annum, falling to only 0.1% between 1973 and 1980, before finally plummeting to -1.2% betwen 1980 and 1991.[13] The figure for 1989–99 is a similarly depressing -0.7% per annum. In real per capita gross national income terms the 2000 level was 39% below the 1980 level.[14]

Daily calorie supply per capita in 1997 was below the 1970 level (and is nearly 16% below the average for all developing countries). It is also the only region that has seen a decline over the period.[15] This has been worsened by the inability of agriculture to generate sufficient food production in line with population increases. Food production per capita in 2000 was 12% below the level of 1980.[16]

The prerequisite for reversing this developmental crisis is not some hypothetical monetary stabilization,[17] but the putting in place of a state formation that can become the agent of transformation and development in Africa.

3. The development of a developmental state in Africa

The conceptualization of the African state development nexus has gone through enormous vicissitudes in the post-independence period. This has included the view of the state as a facilitator of foreign investment in the early post-independent period, to the state-centric mode where the state was both vehicle (the major investor in the economy) and recipient of development (often the most rapidly growing sector) in the 1960s and 1970s, to the neo-liberal mode of the 1980s and 1990s, where the overreaching state was perceived as the impediment to development, and the minimalist state as the solution.

While these intellectual approaches had various influences on and connections with the actual evolution of African states, the growing asymmetries between domestic and bilateral and multilateral sources of finance has increasingly shaped the state in the image of the predominant paradigm. The state has become both subject and predicate (in the sense that the state is obliged to undertake measures against itself), particularly in the 1980s and 1990s when the interstices for alternative strategies were greatly reduced by the collusive singularity of the criteria behind bilateral, multilateral and commercial sources of external finance.

3.1 The World Bank and the state

The World Bank's early conception of the nature of the state under adjustment was heavily influenced by the neoclassical theory of the state. Strictly speaking, in the pure neoclassical model as represented by Walrasian equilibrium, there is no need for a state since society's welfare is maximized. In the less extreme model of structural adjustment, the state is the guarantor of property rights and the money supply. Implicit in this notion is that the state will benignly intervene in these matters. State intervention in any other matter sets up the opportunity for predacity and is less superior than the operation of the market.

Public and rational choice theories have dominated the Bank view of the state.[18] In policy terms the strategy has focused on targets for civil service retrenchment. The pattern was ubiquitous in SSA: between 1981 and 1990, 20 countries undertook World Bank-sponsored retrenchment reforms.[19] In some cases the reductions were a significant portion of the civil service and have been carried through into the 1990s. Between 1993 and 1998/9 Tanzania cut 26% of its labour force under its Civil Service Reform Program, which amounted to 90,600 workers.[20]

The ostensible reason for these cuts was their contribution to reductions in government deficits to help meet adjustment credit targets. However, implicit in this approach was a rather erroneous presumption that curtailing 'bloated' bureaucracies would in some way diminish the dysfunctional nature of the state while releasing scarce human capital for use by the private sector.[21]

A further development of Bank thinking became evident with the release of the Bank's 1992 publication *Governance and Development*.[22] To the Bank, good governance means a state that is accountable in the sense of 'holding public officials responsible for their actions'; 'a legal framework which is known, in force, where one has binding resolution of legal disaccord by independent judicial bodies and proper procedures for amending rules' and 'the improved information and transparency in government to reduce corruption and to make the rationale for policy choices apparent'.[23] Mamadou Dia picks up these themes to explain the poor governance in Africa.[24] To Dia it can be explained by the existence of patrimonialism, which exhibits a pattern contrary to governance that would encourage development. Patrimonialism is a system of leadership characterized by the unwillingness of rulers to distinguish between personal and public property, and in which political and personal loyalties are awarded more than merit. The patrimonial state is one that lacks accountability, transparency and the rule of law.

If we had accountability, transparency and the rule of law, would we have a vibrant developing economy in Africa? It is doubtful. The logic in some senses is an extension of the 'getting the prices right' position at the heart of adjustment in Africa. It follows the general neoclassical notion of an institutional neutrality that will permit an unimpeded space for optimal private decision-making.[25]

In general the Bank's approach to the state is conceptually problematic and incapable of understanding the exigencies of the state and development in Africa. If East Asia is any guide, it will take a much more proactive or developmental state to transform African economies.

3.2 Institutions and the Developmental State

Based partly on the earlier non-neoliberal development literature, Chang lays out four vital economic functions for a developmental state coordination for change, provisions of vision, conflict management and institution building.[26] The fourth function is by far the most important since institutional change is at the core of regenerating growth and development in Africa.

While the World Bank has long recognized the role of the state in guaranteeing property rights, institution building is far more complex than neutrally protecting private property and contracts. Highlighting the organizing of institutions that are consistent with the entrepreneurial vision held by the state, Chang presents examples such as model factories and lifetime employment in Japan or the export-monitoring system in Korea as indicators of the different types of institutions that have been important to Asian economic development.

However the institutional exigencies of the developmental state are much more complex, and are intended not only to meet state visions but also for more general purposes. An economy is a system of interdependent institutions with the government and private sector endogenously intertwined. Economic systems combine legal and financial bodies, formal and informal rules, common values and traditional modes of behaviour. A new network of economic institutions that is required to be formally in place in order to support economic growth and development must be based on a complementary framework of moral values, social traditions and political institutions.[27]

Take the example of markets. Markets, in the neoclassical view that underpins the Bank's vision, are seen as a realm in which rational atomistic individual agents interact in exchange of goods and services. Agents in their utility-maximizing efforts merely respond to the prevailing incentive structure embedded mostly in relative price signals through competitive market interfaces. Markets are then simply impersonal exchanges that involve no transaction costs. By contrast, institutional economics defines markets as social institutions that reduce transaction costs and structures, and organize and legitimate contractual agreements and the exchange of property rights.

Once markets are viewed as institutions and not as neoclassical exchanges, an array of issues, of central importance to any developmental state, are raised. These issues go well beyond simply focusing on correcting market imperfections to arrive at some hypothetical equilibrium to the question of market-construction and -formation. Markets are differentiated and varied in their purpose, further complicating their development.

State and public entities are embedded in even the most rudimentary markets. They provide infrastructure, licensing, regulations and an array of related bodies such as the legal and financial system. These are not simply supporting mechanisms but constructs that are internalized in the operation of markets. While court systems and other political and legal options (e.g. threat of removal of licensing etc.) allow individuals recourse to aid and protect property rights and assure transactional security and informational accuracy, it is frequently the existence, rather than the active utilization, of these organizations, that informs transactions. In this sense these entities become mental constructs that are institutionalized within the daily operation of markets.

The impact may not only be static but also dynamic, allowing for the transformation of markets. State regulations can set quality and health standards, which can alter the characteristics of products. Product improvements can arise not only with the threat of punitive intervention but with a variety of incentive mechanisms, such as access to subsidized financing or support through state organizations that promote access to external markets. However, before designing any path of change, there needs to be a full understanding of both the form and the operational content of existing market institutions and the way they interact with other institutions. In order to achieve a state-assisted transformation of markets, one must first design a parallel track of organizations that have the potential to influence markets. Their internal rules of operation must be carefully designed and institutionalized. However, for these organizations to be effective for dynamic interactive purposes, they must gain legitimacy by building up credibility through the continuity and consistency of their intervention in markets. To avoid being seen as deus ex machinae, which are superficially imposed on existing layers of social production and exchange, such organizations need to be inclusive and interactive in a manner that involves key players and the exchange of information.[28]

Market transformation is a prerequisite for the increasing sophistication of methods of production and exchange. There is little historical evidence for the spontaneous transformation of markets. Structural adjustment has aimed at removing the hypothetical distortions that exist only in the minds of neoclassical economists and have little to do with the challenges of African market transformation. At the same time, there has been a misplaced focus on reorienting the state toward meeting donor-imposed financial targets and retracting state functions away from the support of markets. The post-adjustment agenda needs to focus on the development of the developmental state. Its foremost object should be the return to a view of the state as supporting, and being embedded in, the operation and transformation of markets, particularly in the two vital areas of agriculture and industry.

3.3 The state and agricultural transformation

3.3.1 Structural adjustment and agriculture

After rising by 2.2% per annum in the period 1965–73, agricultural production in Sub Saharan Africa fell by 0.3% (although if Nigeria is excluded it rose by 0.7%) per year between 1973 and 1980.[29] To the designers of structural adjustment, the poor performance in Africa in the 1970s was directly due to urban bias arising from misdirected government policies. Terms of trade were kept deliberately low, thereby reducing the incentive to invest. State-controlled marketing boards disrupted the operation of markets by paying low producer prices, especially for export crops, allocating credit inefficiently, subsidizing inputs which favoured rich farmers, and emphasizing food over cash crops. This has been worsened by overvalued exchange rates, which have reduced the funds available to pay local farmers. The policy recommendations[30] included the following:

1) Flexible prices reflecting demand and supply in local and world markets [which is] the best way to signal to farmers what, how much and when to produce ... if farm gate prices reflect world market conditions when the world price of an export crop is low, farmers will have an incentive to switch their efforts to other crops with relatively higher value.[31]

2) Flexible prices call for a marketing system which private traders are allowed to compete. A vigorous private sector could process and market agricultural produce efficiently and rising investment could combine with new technology to steadily raise yields.[32]

3) Once the bias against agriculture is corrected, the remaining incentives should be neutral between food and export crops and farmers will be guided by their comparative advantage. Countries with a comparative advantage in export crop production should exploit it and import food if necessary.[33]

4) Governments have also tended to maintain below market interest rates. Consequently the demand for credit invariably has exceeded the supply. Credit was rationed. A better approach would let interest rates balance supply and demand. The market could then allocate funds. Higher interest rates would also make the banks less dependent on government for funds and would increase the incentives for savings. The banks would gain the resources needed to strengthen the management of their rural operations. Commercial banks might also be attracted into agricultural lending or encouraged to lend to farmers through intermediaries such as traders ... Banks [should] be allowed to enforce the default clauses on loan agreements.[34]

5) ... there is generally no justification for subsidizing fertilizer use; that only encourages waste. The key is to ensure that reliable supplies are available at full cost ... To reduce supply bottlenecks, private traders and enterprises should be allowed to import, produce and distribute it [fertilizer] themselves.[35]

6) ... many African governments have pursued macroeconomic policies with a distinct urban bias ... Establishing a neutral structure of incentives is an important first step toward a fairer society ... The earlier strategy ... neglected agriculture, a sector in which Africa has a clear comparative advantage. Exploiting Africa's land resources offers the best immediate opportunity for raising incomes ... For farm ... employment

to increase rapidly, external and internal demand for local products must rise ... A devaluation raises the price of imports which switches demand from imports to local goods ... By influencing a country's internal terms of trade – that is by raising the return to domestic producers and prices consumers pay for imports – exchange-rate policy can tackle some of Africa's major barriers to growth.[36]

To what extent does this depiction of Africa's barriers to rural development capture the reality of agriculture on the continent? If the emphasis has been misplaced what impact have these policies had on agriculture in the past twenty years? If the analysis is incorrect then what are the alternative policies, particularly in the context of a developmental state? These are complex questions that can only be addressed briefly here; after presenting some data and arguments, I will return to the six points at the heart of adjustment.

The urban bias argument that originated in the work of Michael Lipton was heavily emphasized in African literature in the early 1980s by Bob Bates.[37] The position gained research and policy prominence in the 1980s under the auspices of Anne Krueger when she was chief economist at the World Bank, and culminated in a five-volume study on the political economy of agricultural pricing.[38]

Liberalization to remove urban bias was widespread by the 1980s. By 1992 16 marketing boards covering cash crops in 23 countries had given up their monopoly positions or had been eliminated. While 25 out of 28 countries had price setting of export crops in the pre-adjustment period, only 11 were still setting prices by the mid-1990s.[39]

3.3.2 Agricultural performance under adjustment

Table Five looks more systematically at the 'urban bias' argument, and the impact of liberalization and its attempt to reverse 'urban bias'. Growth rates in v-ratios measuring labour productivity in agriculture compared to non-agricultural sectors are provided, along with a breakdown of growth of the components of productivity in Asia and Sub Saharan Africa.

Contrary to the urban bias arguments of neoliberal orthodoxy, in the pre-adjustment period for agriculture terms of trade were actually rising at a rate that exceeded the sample of Asian countries (1.3% vs. 0.8%). However, in the period of liberalization the reverse occurred, with relative prices declining by an average 0.6% per year.

While the v-ratio has been rising at a constant rate for SSA over the entire period, the main reason for this increase of sample countires in SSA is due to the collapse of the non-agricultural productivity (e.g. falling denominator)

Table 5. **Trends in Value-Added Ratios in Asia and Sub Saharan Africa 1965–95***

Region	V-ratio 1965–80	Agric. Prod. 1965–80	N-Agr. Prod. 1965–80	Rel. Prices 1965–80	V-ratio 1980–95	Agric. Prod. 1980–95	N-Agr. Prod. 1980–95	Rel. Prices 1980–95
Mean SSA	1.9	0.2	-0.3	1.3	1.9	0.4	-2.1	-0.6
Mean Asia	-0.5	1.6	3.0	0.8	-0.2	2.4	2.8	0.2
Percent Negative growth rates SSA	27	48	52	24	25	46	82	50
Percent Negative growth rates Asia	50	10	0	30	50	0	20	30

* V-ratios refer to value-added per agricultural worker relative to the same for non-agricultural workers; terms of trade are calculated as a residual of trend growth rates in other variables at individual country levels; data from 28 countries in SSA and 10 in Asia.

Source: Karshenas 2001.

particularly during the adjustment period (82% had negative growth). Particularly striking is the extremely low productivity growth of agriculture compared to Asia. Adjustment, with its emphasis on privatization and price control liberalization, has done nothing to encourage productivity. Roughly half the countries were experiencing negative productivity growth both before and after adjustment.

This should not come as a surprise since, even in World Bank and IMF studies, it has been shown that the price elasticity of aggregate supply is very low compared to technical change, weather, infrastructure and other public goods.[40]

The contrast between the levels of mechanization, infrastructure and inputs in SSA compared to Asia is striking. This is illustrated in Table Six, which again compares fertilizer use, irrigation ratios and tractors in use at points from 1965 to 1994.

Table 6. **Mean Fertilizer Consumption, Irrigation Ratio and Tractors in Use, 1965–94 in Asia and SSA***

Years	1965	1980	1994
Fertilizer Consumption in SSA	4.8	12.9	12.7
Fertilizer Consumption in Asia	46.3	147.1	237.3
Irrigation Ratio in SSA	2.2	3.8	4.6
Irrigation Ratio in Asia	29.5	38.3	43.8
Tractors in use SSA	14.5	19.9	22.3
Tractors in use Asia	15.4	55.6	146.4

* kg per hectare of fertilizer use, percentage of irrigated land and tractors per 10,000 ha.

Source: Karshenas 2001.

Fertilizer use has traditionally been much greater and has grown more rapidly in Asia compared to Africa. While in 1965 its use was ten times greater per hectare in Asia, by 1994 it was twenty times greater. In mechanization the difference in strategies is also striking. In 1964 both Africa and Asia used approximately the same number of tractors per 10,000 hectares. By 1994 Asia's usage had increased tenfold, while Africa's had barely shown an increase. Asian countries also have had much greater irrigation compared to African countries. Particularly interesting is the comparison of growth in mechanization, infrastructure and inputs between the pre-adjustment and adjustment periods. Subsidies in the pre-adjustment period clearly helped triple the usage of fertilization per hectare. By contrast, the post-1980 decline in fertilization application per hectare is an indicator of the impact of input liberalization and the dismantling of marketing boards, which often supplied credit support for inputs. The World Bank figures on gross annual usage of fertilizer are also quite revealing: for most years between 1989 and 1998 actual tonnage of fertilizer used was below the 1980 level. The figure peaked in 1993 at only 10% above 1980, falling thereafter.[41] Mechanization growth also slowed to 12% in the adjustment period (as compared to 37% growth in the pre-adjustment period), as did the rate of irrigation growth (21% compared to 73%).

What of the return farmers have received under adjustment compared to earlier periods? Neoliberal proponents have argued that food crops have been subsidized and export crops taxed. In a recent article Boratov investigates the movements of these relative prices and compares the impact of interventionist against non-interventionist regimes in Africa. He shows that deregulation has not been associated with improvements in real producer prices or in terms of trade. For export prices except cocoa, the ratio of producer prices to border prices actually fell faster or rose less rapidly than the border prices in countries with greater liberalization, meaning that liberalization is associated with greater taxation or exploitation of farmers. Since 1984, the overall terms of trade have actually fallen less rapidly in governments with greater intervention. Overall real producer prices have fallen by 40–50% for cocoa, coffee, cotton and tea. This is largely due to the collapse of world commodity prices, which overwhelmed even the improvements in cocoa farmers' shares of prices in places like Ghana. It is interesting that Boratav points to the very positive impact of the bias toward food over this period, since the rate of decline of the terms of trade for food has in fact been far less than for cash crops.

3.3.3 Alternatives to adjustment: rediscovering the role of the state

With this empirical background in mind, let us briefly return to the major policy points of adjustment and agriculture and propose some alternative approaches proactively to reverse the malaise in Africa:

1) The focus on price flexibility arises out of an axiomatic belief that all that is needed to make efficient decisions are undistorted prices. Farmers will costlessly invest in new crops in reaction to shifting prices that reflect the opportunity costs of production. In reality, we have seen that prices play a minor role in the overall supply response compared to non-price variables. The pareto efficient world of neoclassical farmers is very different to the real world in which credit is unavailable: new crops require information which is costly and difficult to obtain; there are time lags for returns – such as the investment in tree crops – which are too long for farmers so close to subsistence; yields are closely tied to weather, leading to hesitation to take on new crops that might be riskier; transportation is so poor that the access to markets for new crops may be impeded by bad weather, and so on. Moreover, the notion that farmers simply flexibly react to changing international prices ignores the enormous volatility of these prices. In a world without future markets or other insurance schemes, prices that might be profitable at the moment of a new planting might have fallen dramatically by the time of harvest. This notion also ignores the fallacy of composition problem I discussed above (footnote 8). In a world of poorly-formed markets, adverse global conditions and weak infrastructure, price supports must be a central part of any agricultural strategy.

2) The view that marketing should be privatized also arises from the neo-classical axiom about the superiority of the private sector over the state. As we have seen, the privatization of marketing has in many cases actually led to a decline in producer prices relative to the world price of commodities.[42] In addition, privatizing the input side and removing subsidies has led to a decline of the usage of inputs like fertilizer, with consequences to yields. Where the road system is well developed, credit is readily available, transportation options exist and there is an abundance of private traders, private marketing may be viable. However that is not the case in most of rural Africa. State or cooperative marketing must continue to be a central component of agriculture.

3) We have seen that the bias toward food production during the adjustment period has been economically beneficial given the adverse movement of cash crop prices relative to those of food crops. Inexpensive food has always been a vital part of keeping wage costs down in order to allow the manufacturing sector to expand in the early stages of industrialization. Food must continue to be emphasized in any agricultural strategy. There is not a single country that has developed on the basis of cash crop exports.

4) The view of freeing up interest rates as an incentive for private commercial banks to loan money to agricultural producers is based on the pre-Keynesian monetary theory that savings and investments are balanced by interest rates. The same reasoning has been behind the disastrous exercises in financial liberalization in Africa and elsewhere. In the rural sector, where information is scarce, collateral weak, and transaction costs high, credit will be largely unavailable and when available well beyond the means of all but a handful of very large-scale farmers. Unsurprisingly, with the privatization of marketing boards – the main source of financing for farmers – the system of seasonal credit has broken down.[43] State provisions or guarantees of credit will be needed in agriculture for the foreseeable future.

5) I have already discussed the declining usage of fertilizer under the privatized system. Given the vicissitudes of weather, farmers have been reluctant to take on the financial liabilities linked to fully priced fertilizer. Moreover, as we noted above in Boratav's work, the dual liberalization of output and input prices has often led to a squeeze on the net or real returns for producers.

6) We have seen that, overall, liberalization has led to a decline not a rise in returns to producers. The belief that removing urban bias and creating neutral incentives will *ipso facto* lead to the development of agriculture is erroneous both in theory and practice. Agriculture needs more than the

price supports discussed above. It also needs large-scale investment in research and infrastructure. However, research has been declining under adjustment and amounted to a mere 0.7% of GDP in 1991, while external aid has also been declining just when it is needed. Between 1987 and 1994, real aid in agriculture declined by almost 2/3, from $4609 million to $1322 million in constant 1990 dollars.[44] This needs to be reversed.

The bigger issue is the overall strategy for economic transformation. While agriculture is important, its continuing emphasis in IFI documents arises out of their static comparative advantage world. Any developmental state must go beyond agriculture to design a strategy of industrial transformation. This has been sadly lacking over the last twenty years.

3.4 The state and industrial transformation

At the core of Asian development has been a thriving manufacturing capacity with considerable export ability. It would appear to be unlikely that sustainable development can be achieved in Africa without considerable focus on manufacturing. Manufactured goods are associated with higher income elasticities, can act as a conduit for the transfer of technology, are very tradeable, are generally heterogeneous allowing for greater market segmentation with higher potential returns, and can stimulate extensive backward, forward and demand linkages. However, during the period of adjustment (post-1985), manufacturing has done poorly in Africa. We have already seen this from the statistics on the composition in exports. Other indicators show rather weak performance.[45]

Take Ghana, until recently the Bank's showcase of adjustment. The logic behind adjustment as it affects industry is that import liberalization, devaluation, the reduction of protectionism and positive real interest rates will punish inefficient industries and reward the efficient ones, which are export-oriented, more labour-intensive and use more local raw materials, allowing the country to exploit its comparative advantage. The result will be a prosperous and growing sector, which will greatly contribute to an increase in exports while using fewer imports. Unfortunately in practice it has not worked this way.

Ghana implemented a standard package of policies and overall manufacturing expanded in the first few years of adjustment, due primarily to an increased availability of foreign exchange. Since 1989, however, manufacturing has badly stagnated, falling from from 10% of GDP in 1987 to only 8% in 1993, while employment declined by 2/3 over the same period to a paltry 27,000 people. By 1999, manufacturing had recovered slightly to 9% of GDP.

It is worth noting that in 1965, manufacturing already accounted for 10% of GDP. Manufacturing export levels have been rather disappointing, reaching only $14.7 million in 1991, with the bulk of exports in the traditional areas of aluminum and wood products.[46] In 1981, 24% of Ghana's exports were in manufactured goods. By 2000 the figure had dropped to only 15%.[47] As in other parts of Africa, the lack of structural transformation has contributed to declining terms of trade (falling by 51% between 1980 and 2000).[48]

3.4.1 Weaknesses of the concept of manufacturing under adjustment

Adjustment has not worked as anticipated because the real world of manufacturing does not look anything like the imaginary one living inside the neoclassical mind. In that world, perfectly competitive firms, operating with full knowledge and accessibility to all possible technologies, choose the most efficient process given market-determined prices of inputs and outputs which reflect their relative scarcity value. The international technology market is assumed to work efficiently with firms buying the right technology off the shelves without costs or barriers. Capital and technology must flow freely without state interference. Markets must be allowed to generate the correct prices without disruption, such as that caused by protectionist distortions.

In the real world, in a place like Ghana, management and labour skills are in very limited supply, finance is difficult to secure, information is costly, relations between firms are poorly developed, technology is difficult to obtain and costly to use, transaction costs are high, public goods are poorly developed, property rights are not always clearly defined, products are not standardized and so on. Opening up industries to the full force of international markets will hardly lead to the desired results when institutions and capacities are so weak. If Asia is any indicator, what is needed is a nurturing environment that will permit industries to mature and prosper.

The way forward, in my view, is the creation of industrial and trade policies that focus on institutionally-centred economic strategies. Their purpose would be to put in place new norms, capacities, incentives, organizations and regulations, aimed at supporting private sector or joint private–state entrepreneurship and accumulation with the goal of enhancing developmental competitiveness.[49] The starting point is to organize state–private sector frameworks of dialogue for industrial development. The focal point of the dialogue should be to choose strategic industrial needs, and to develop plans to meet those needs. Ultimately, the aim is to build state capacities and resources that support industrial entrepreneurship, investment and growth in a manner that is transparent and embedded in the private sector. Once priorities are set, then a framework can be formulated to attract FDI and to provide the climate and incentives for FDI to undertake developmentally-enhancing investment activities.

In the industrial context, capacities encompass supply-side dimensions like entrepreneurship, skills and technological capabilities. Incentives focus on the conditions that motivate companies to engage in sustainable industrial activities. Norms focus on elements, such as trust, that allow the development of clusters and networks that have become increasingly important to the new economy. Regulations deal with creating the legal boundaries to encourage companies' investment in a way that is developmentally enhancing. Organizations include business and professional groups that both create pressure for change and act as a conduit for information to its constituents. Policies can be designed to enhance the development of these five areas at the micro, meso and macro levels.

Take the question of incentives for exports. Governments in East Asia at various points have provided: reductions in corporate and private income tax; tariff exemptions and tax rebates on materials imported for the production of exports; financing of imports needed for producing exports; business tax exemptions; accelerated depreciation allowances; creation of various reserve funds; subsidized interest rates to promote export industries and to encourage firms to enter into exporting; foreign currency loans to finance exports on long-term credits; various export–import linked systems; differential treatment of traders based on export performance; export insurance; etc. South Korea, at various points, subsidized interest rates from 40 to 60% of the commercial loan level. The government set annual targets and used a combination of moral incentives and augmented subsidization when actual levels fell below their targets.[50] Other measures were taken to influence the organizations, capacities, regulations and norms to support export-oriented industrialization.

4. Conclusions

The chapter began with an empirical presentation of the developmental crisis in Africa. By developmental crisis we mean the generalized incapacity of an economy to generate the conditions necessary for a sustained improvement in the standard of living. The evidence of economic deterioration in the era of structural adjustment is quite extensive and includes declining per capita income and food production, worsening balance of payments, growing domestic resources gaps, diminishing participation in foreign direct investment flows and rising foreign debt.

These trends point to the pressing need to rethink development strategies in Africa. The remainder of the paper explored some possibilities in the context of developing developmental states that can put in place institutional-centric strategies to nurture private-sector development and accumulation. The last two sections critically examine the failure of adjustment in agriculture and industry, and point to alternative approaches in these two vital areas. Adding 'poverty reduction' to the latest packaging and labelling of standard policies will do little to generate new strategies to reverse the African developmental crisis.[51]

Notes

1 By neoclassical economics I mean a reliance on methodological individualism, homo-economicus, equilibrium as a natural state, rational deductivity and a reliance on axiomatic reasoning. Adjustment is based on a hodgepodge of neoclassical theories, McKinnon-Shaw financial repression theory, the Swan-Salter Australian model of macroeconomic adjustment in a small and open economy, the IMF financial programming model, traditional trade theory, publicchoice models of government behaviour etc., which rely on the most extreme micro-foundations. The theoretical weaknesses of adjustment have been explored in Stein and Nissanke 1999.

2 World Bank 2000a.

3 World Bank 1999; 2000b; 2002a.

4 World Bank 2002a.

5 World Bank 1999, 2000a.

6 World Bank 2002a.

7 World Bank 1999.

8 Generally, fallacy of composition refers to a situation where if one country increases exports, revenues might rise, but if more than one country undertakes the same strategy, revenues might fall when export quantities increase. This is particularly acute with commodity exports like beverage crops, which have particularly low demand elasticities, and where African countries control a significant portion of the world market share.

9 Adesida 1998.

10 World Bank 2000a; 2000b.

11 Karshenas 2001.

12 As indicated by the small decrease in debt, progress has been quite slow on HIPC. While 20 African countries reached decision point by December 2001, only three countries, Tanzania, Uganda and Mozambique, achieved the more significant completion point where more serious relief is provided (World Bank 2002b).

13 Stein 1999.

14 World Bank 2002a.

15 UNDP 2000.

16 World Bank 2002a. Identifying trends in Africa says nothing about causal factors. There has been considerable debate concerning the impact of adjustment in Africa and the role that it has played in some of the negative economic trends. Five approaches have been used in assessing the impact of structural adjustment the 'before and after' method, the 'control-group' approach and the 'modified control' group, the

'decomposition' approach and the 'with and without' simulations based on CGE (Computable General Equilibrium) models and SAMS (Social Accounting Matrices) The latter category has included some strong assertions by Sahn et al. 1998, that poverty has been reduced by adjustment. However, they utilize absurd neoclassical assumptions such as perfectly-clearing labour markets and circular reasoning, in which the wealthy are defined in terms of their accessibility to economic rents, to prove that they are worse off after liberalization when rents by definition diminish. By contrast, the poor are better off after adjustment because they proportionately have more access to income from tradeables which will rise in price in an adjustment world. For the most part, statistical testing has been unable to show with any consistency that adjustment has improved the economies of Africa. Recently, instead of denying these trends the neoclassicals have attempted to explain them, not by challenging the neoliberal model, but by running large-scale cross-country regressions and using variables outside the model, such as ethnicity. Critical assessments of this literature can be found in Englebert 2000 and Kenny and Williams 2001. Critiques of the CGE models on poverty can be found in De Maio et al. 1999 and Stein 2000. Examples of earlier reviews on the adjustment testing literature include Ajayi 1994; Mosley 1994; Mosley, Subasat and Weeks; and Stein 1997.

17 In the fragile economies of the many African countries that are subject to the vicissitudes of international commodity prices, rapid shifts in financial flows and frequent transformation of political regimes, periods of macroinstability are common. Equilibrium has in practice been aimed at constraining government spending and money supply at a level that would maintain momentary macrostability. However, given the underlying structural weaknesses of these economies few African countries are able to escape constant stabilization policies.

18 This was very evident in World Bank documents from the early 1980s. For example, the WDR (World Development Report) 1983 report argues that 'compelling political and social pressures' push governments to do more than can be accomplished efficiently. The results are economically disastrous. 'In most instances ... price distortions are introduced by government directly or indirectly in pursuit of some social or economic objective, sometimes deliberately and sometimes incidentally.' Pointing out that public service employment was growing very rapidly in developing countries in the 1970s, the report warns that: 'Overstaffing imposes a financial burden on the state, undermines moral and obstructs efficient management'. With relief the report states: 'Several countries have therefore started to reduce the number of staff members ...' (World Bank 1983, pp. 56, 57, 102, 103).

19 These came in the form of the removal of ghost workers through civil service census taking, recruitment freezes, early retirement schemes or termination of services.

20 Valentine 2002.

21 These policies were undertaken despite contrary evidence in some of the World Bank and IMF studies. For instance, looking at data from the 1970s and early 1980s, Heller and Tait 1983 generate an International Government Employment Index, which measures the average number of government employees that would be predicted in countries given their population, per capital income etc. The average score for a sample of 17 African countries was 8 points below the expected level. Botswana and Mauritius were two exceptions above the norm expected. By most estimates, these countries were the most successful in Africa during the 1980s and 1990s. They both avoided harsh civil service retrenchment.

22 World Bank 1992. In a series of papers, memoranda and public pronouncements the Bank began to question the state retrenchment approach and to begin searching for alternatives. There was little evidence of financial savings, private sector employment of laid-off workers, while there was considerable indication of state capacity erosion. See for example Jaycox, 1993 and Dia 1994.

23 World Bank 1992, pp. 13, 5, 39.

24 Dia 1994.

25 In operational terms the new approach is referred to as 'Second Generation' reforms (see Lienert 1998 for a discussion), which move beyond the first stage focus on wage-bill reductions. Given the more recent nature of this focus there are few studies of its impact. The evidence is so far not very positive. Therkildsen 2000 critically examines the impact of these measures in Tanzania, which have included reducing the core functions of the state, emphasizing efficiency, strengthening accountability and staff reorganizations. There is little evidence of service improvements and little domestic support due partly to its externally-imposed nature. In line with the arguments here he finds the conceptual basis of the reform measures to be very weak.

26 Chang 1999.

27 Kozul-Wright and Rayment 1997.

28 Sindzingre and Stein 2001.

29 World Bank 1989.

30 World Bank 1989.

31 World Bank 1989, p. 91.

32 World Bank 1989, pp. 91–2.

33 World Bank 1989, p. 92.

34 World Bank 1989, p. 92.

35 World Bank 1989, p. 96.

36 World Bank 1989, pp.38–9, 43, 45, 47.

37 Lipton 1977; Bates 1981, 1983. Writers in the neoclassical vein simply adopted it as an axiomatic truth. For example David Sahn presents the following argument:

> The criticisms that adjustment reduced subsidies, raised prices, slowed down increases in minimum wages, and so forth overlooks the fact that subsidies and rent-seeking opportunities were rarely enjoyed by the poor. Rather, the politically powerful urban elite were the primary beneficiaries of distortions that both hurt the poor in the short term as manifested in shortages of goods and services and scarcity prices as well as in the medium and long term by retarding the pace of economic growth ... it is generally the case that removing subsidies in Africa, has small, if any, harmful effects on the nutritionally vulnerable. Instead, eliminating highly rationed, urban-based food distribution schemes adversely affected the less needy households more proficient at rent-seeking, while the vast majority of poor, already reliant on parallel free markets, faced little dislocation. (Sahn 1994, pp. 284, 296).

Here the argument illustrates the belief that the urban bias was the driving force behind policies at the expense of the poor. This leads to the kind of syllogistic reasoning deductively posited by neoliberals like Sahn in the African context. Simply put, the government's food subsidies, like any other form of state intervention, will create rent-seeking. Since on balance the poor do not receive the benefits of subsidies, the removal of subsidies will not hurt the poor, but will improve efficiency due to the decline of rent-seeking activities. These assertions are not supported by evidence such as budget household surveys covering the period before and after subsidization. Instead the author relies on the kind of problematic CGE studies discussed in the footnote above.

38 Krueger et al 1991. Karshanas 1998 provides a critique of their methodology. There is an extensive literature criticizing the urban bias argument. For example Jamal 1995, using detailed empirical studies of Sierra Leone, Tanzania and Zambia, shows that there is little evidence of urban bias. In Sierra Leone, for example, the wage-to-farm income ratio fell by 2/3 between 1970–1 and 1982–3. Under adjustment, there has been a further erosion of real earnings with evidence of declining wage to rural income levels.

39 Boratav 2001.

40 For example, Bond 1983, in an IMF study of nine countries in Sub Saharan Africa, found that prices were insignificant in seven cases when using a Nerlovian functional form which takes into account weather and technological change. In the other two cases, Kenya and Ghana, the elasticities were very low (0.34 and (0.16). By contrast, studies in places like India indicate that infrastructural variables like irrigation have an elasticity that exceeds unity (see for example Chhibber 1989).

41 World Bank 2002a.

42 Ponte 2001 also points to the impact of the shifting nature of the global marketing chain. In coffee the diminishing margin is partly due to the breakdown of the International Coffee Agreement and the loss of bargaining power from the dismantling of marketing boards and coffee stabilization funds in many African countries. At the same time there has been a growing concentration of power on the purchasing side among traders and roasters. Privatization of boards has also led to a decline in quality control, with private traders often mixing high and lower quality coffee together. Producers then receive the price of the lower quality product, contributing to a further erosion in farm gate prices.

43 Poulton et al. 1998.

44 Akyuz and Gore 2001. This follows the general downward trend in aid. Net ODA to Sub Saharan Africa, which fell by nearly a third in nominal terms from 1990 to 1999 (World Bank 2002a).

45 There were also declines in the rates of growth of manufacturing value-added, manu-facturing employment and labour productivity, as we saw in the general figures for non-agricultural productivity in Table 5. There was little technological transfer as represented by the ratio of imported machinery and transport equipment relative to total imports, a worsening of industrial non-diversification and stagnancy in invest-ment levels (Noorbakhsh and Paloni 2000).

46 World Bank 2002a; Lall 1994.

47 Tribe 2000; UNDP 2002.

48 World Bank 2002a.

49 Developmental competitiveness is 'an institutional continuum which generates a dynamic process of accumulation aimed at increasing the market share, diversity, depth and linkages of an economy' (Stein 2002).

50 Stein 1995.

51 In September 1999, structural adjustment facilities became Poverty Reduction Growth Funds, IMF, and Poverty Reduction Support Credits, World Bank. In countries like Tanzania, visited by this author in April 2002, the new facilities largely amount to

standard neoliberal policies plus some added social spending as part of the HIPC debt relief initiative.

References

Adesida, Olugbenga, 1998, 'Creating the African Information and Knowledge Society', *African Development Review*, vol. 10, no. 1.

Akyuz, Yilmaz and Gore, Charles, 2001, 'African Economic Development in a Comparative Perspective', *Cambridge Journal of Economics*, vol. 25, no. 3.

Ajayi, Simeon Ibi, 1994, 'The State of Research on the Macroeconomic Effectiveness of Structural Adjustment Programs in Sub-Saharan Africa' in R van der Hoeven and F van der Kraaij, eds, *Structural Adjustment and Beyond in Sub-Saharan Africa*, Portsmouth, NH, Heinemann.

Bates, Robert H, 1981, *Markets and States in Tropical Africa: The Political Basis of Agricultural Policies*, Berkeley, University of California Press.

——, 1983, *Essays on the Political Economy of Rural Africa*, Berkeley, University of California Press.

Bond, ME, 1983, 'Agricultural Response to Prices in Sub-Saharan African Countries', *IMF Staff Papers*.

Boratav, K, 2001, 'Movements of Relative Agricultural Prices in Sub-Saharan Africa', *Cambridge Journal of Economics*, vol. 25, no. 3.

Chang, Ha-Joon, 1999, 'The Economic Theory of the Developmental State' in Meredith Woo-Cuming ed., *The Developmental State*, New York, Cornell University Press.

Chhibber, Ajay, 1989, 'The Aggregate Supply Response: A Survey' in Simon Commander, ed., *Structural Adjustment in Agriculture; Theory and Practice in Africa and Latin America*, London, Heinemann.

Das, DK, 1998, *Civil Service Reform and Structural Adjustment*, Delhi, Oxford University Press.

De Maio, Lorenzo et al., 1999, 'Computable General Equilibrium Models, Adjustment and the Poor in Africa', *World Development*, vol. 27, no. 3.

Dia, Mamadou, 1994, *A Governance Approach to Civil Service Reform in Sub-Saharan Africa*, World Bank Technical Paper, no. 225, Africa Technical Department Series, Washington, World Bank.

Englebert, Pierre, 2000, *State Legitimacy and Development in Africa*, Bolder, Lynne Rienner Publishers.

Heller, Peter S and Tait, Alan A, 1983, 'Government Employment and Pay: Some International Comparisons', International Monetary Fund Comparative Paper, no. 24.

Jamal, V, ed., 1995, *Structural Adjustment and Rural Labor Markets in Africa*, London, Macmillan.

Jayxox, Edward, 1993, 'Capacity Building: The Missing Link in African Development', speech given at the African American Institute Conference on Capacity Building, 20 May 20, mimeo, reprinted in Annex II, of Ali, 1994, '"Capacity Building and Donor Coordination in Sub-Saharan Africa", paper presented at the African Studies Association Meeting, Nov. 3–6', mimeo.

Karshenas, M, 2001, 'Agriculture and Economic Development in Sub-Saharan Africa and Asia', *Cambridge Journal of Economics*, vol. 25, no. 3.

Kenny, Charles and Williams, David, 2001, 'What do We Know About Economic Growth? Or, Why Don't We Know Very Much?', *World Development*, vol. 29, no. 1.

Kozul-Wright, Richard and Rayment, Paul, 1997, 'The Institutional Hiatus in Economies in Transition and its Policy Consequences', *Cambridge Journal of Economics*, vol. 21.

Krueger, Anne et al, eds, 1991, *The Political Economy of Agricultural Pricing*, Baltimore, Johns Hopkins Press (5 vols).

Lall, Sanjaya et al., 1994, *Technology and Enterprise Development, Ghana Under Structural Adjustment*, New York, St. Martin's Press.

Lienert, Ian, 1998, 'Civil Service Reform in Africa: Mixed Results After 10 Years', *Finance and Development*, vol. 35, no. 3.

Lipton, Michael, 1977, *Why Poor People Stay Poor: A Study of Urban Bias in World Development*, London, Maurice Temple Smith.

Mosley, Paul, 1994, 'Decomposing the Effects of Structural Adjustment' in R van der Hoeven and F van der Kraaij, eds., *Structural Adjustment and Beyond in Sub-Saharan Africa*, Portsmouth, NH, Heinemann.

Mosley, P, Subasat, T and Weeks J, 1995, 'Assessing Adjustment in Africa', *World Development*, vol. 23, no. 9.

Noorbakhsh, Farhad and Paloni, Alberto, 2000, 'The De-industrialization Hypothesis, Structural Adjustment and Programs and the Sub-Saharan African Dimension' in Hossein Julian et al., *Industrial Development and Policy in Africa: Issues in Deindustrialization and Devlopment Strategy*, Cheltenham, Edward Elgar.

Ponte, Stefano, 2001, 'The "Latte Revolution"? Winners and Losers in the Restructuring of the Global Coffee Marketing Chain', Center for Development Research Working Paper 1.3 (June).

Poulton et al.,1998, 'The Revival of Smallholder Cash Crops in Africa: Public and Private Roles in the Provision of Finance', *Journal of International Development*, vol. 10, no. 1.

Sahn, David, 1994, 'The Impact of Macroeconomic Adjustment on Incomes, Health and Nutrition' in Cornea, Giovanni and Helleiner, Gerald, *From Adjustment to Development in Africa: Conflict, Convergence and Consensus?*, London, Macmillan.

Sahn, David et al., 1997, *Structural Adjustment Reconsidered: Economic Policy and Poverty in Africa*, Cambridge, Cambridge University Press.

Sindzingre, Alice and Stein, Howard, 2001, 'Institutions, Development and Global Integration: A Theoretical Contribution', paper presented at the 2001 African Studies Association, Houston, Texas, November.

Stein, Howard, ed., 1995, *Asian Industrialization and Africa: Studies in Policy Alternatives to Structural Adjustment*, Basingstoke, Palgrave/Macmillan.

———, 1997, 'Adjustment and Development in Africa: Toward an Assessment', *African Studies Review*, vol. 40, no. 1.

———, 1999, 'Globalization, Adjustment and the Structural Transformation of African Economies: The Role of International Financial Institutions', Centre for the Study of Globalization and Regionalization at the University of Warwick, CSGR Working Paper, no. 32/99 (May).

———, 2000, 'Review' of David Sahn et al., 'Structural Adjustment Reconsidered: Economic Policy and Poverty in Africa', *Economic Development and Cultural Change*, vol. 48, no. 5.

———, 2002, 'Globalization and Industrial and Trade Policy in Vietnam: Creating Developmental Competitiveness', Proceedings of International Conference, 'Legal and Economic Perspectives of Vietnam's Integration into the World Economy', Danang City, Vietnam, July.

Stein, Howard and Nissanke, Machiko, 1999, 'Structural Adjustment and the African Crisis: A Theoretical Appraisal', *Eastern Economic Journal*, vol. 25, no. 4.

Therkildsen, Ole, 2000, 'Public Sector Reform in a Poor, Aid-Dependent Country, Tanzania', *Public Administration and Development*, vol. 20.

Tribe, Michael, 2000, 'A Review of Recent Manufacturing Sector Development in Sub-Saharan Africa', in Hossein Julian et al., *Industrial Development and Policy in Africa: Issues in Deindustrialization and Devlopment Strategy*, Cheltenham, Edward Elgar.

United Nations Development Program, UNDP, 2000, *Human Development Report, 2000*, Oxford, OUP.

United Nations Development Program, UNDP, 2002, *Human Development Report, 2002*, Oxford, OUP.

Valentine, Ted, 2002, *Revisiting and Revising Tanzania's Medium-Term Pay Reform Strategy: Final Report*, Dar Es Salaam: United Republic of Tanzania Public Service Reform Program.

World Bank, 1983, *World Development Report, 1983*, New York, Oxford University Press.

World Bank, 1989, *Sub-Saharan Africa, From Crisis to Sustainable Growth*, World Bank, Washington.

World Bank, 1992, *Governance and Development*, World Bank, Washington.

World Bank, 1999, *World Development Report, 1999*, New York, Oxford University Press.

World Bank, 2000a, *World Development Report, 2000*, New York, Oxford University Press.

World Bank, 2000b, *African Development Indicators, 2000*, Washington, DC, World Bank.

World Bank, 2001, *African Development Indicators, 2001*, Washington, DC, World Bank.

World Bank, 2002a, *African Development Indicators, 2002*, Washington, DC, World Bank.

World Bank, 2002b, *Global Development Finance*, Washington, DC, World Bank.

8

TRANSITION ECONOMIES[1]

Michael Ellman

1. The political economy of transformation[2]

The transformation process has made great progress in a number of countries. In them, central planning is a matter of economic history, there exist functioning markets for goods and factors of production, the legal and administrative framework for a market economy is in place, a large part of the economy is now in private hands, economic growth has resumed after initial depression, and the countries concerned have demonstrated their attractiveness to foreign private capital. Four transformation countries (Czech Republic, Hungary, Poland and Slovakia) joined the OECD in the period 1995–2000 and eight of them are currently scheduled to join the EU in 2004.

The transformation has been marked by a sharp polarization, both between and within countries. Not all countries have made great progress with transformation. Even in relatively successful countries, not all the population has enjoyed the fruits of this success. The end to shortages, the increased variety of goods and services available, and the increased ownership of consumer durables, are all real and important phenomena contributing to higher living standards for those with sufficient incomes to benefit from them. On the other hand, the worsening social indicators in many countries, – to which UNICEF has repeatedly drawn attention – and the increased poverty highlighted by the World Bank, are also unfortunately very real phenomena. The winners are the new business elite (owners of profitable firms, specialists in business services such as law, marketing, advertising, financial services) and those members of the political and criminal elites who have been able to enrich themselves. The losers have tended to include older (former) employees, those working in agriculture, manufacturing, coal mining, and the state sector, the newly unemployed, ethnic minorities (e.g. Romanis or Russians living outside Russia), children, large families and the less educated.

The existence of both winners and losers led to a sharp increase in inequality. According to the World Bank,[3] between the late Communist period (1987–90) and the situation after less than a decade of 'transition' (1996–9), inequality had increased, frequently massively, throughout the region (with the exception of Croatia). Using the Gini coefficient as the measuring rod, it increased relatively modestly in Central Europe (e.g. from 0.19 to 0.25 in the Czech Republic), but jumped from 0.27 to 0.59 in Armenia: this latter figure was remarkably high by world standards. The course of the transformation has surprised outside observers in a number of important respects.

The first surprise was how much the populations of these countries were prepared to endure. The uprising in Albania in 1997 was exceptional. Although in some countries (e.g. Hungary and Poland) there has been a 'normal' alternation of parties in power, in others (e.g. Russia) so-called reformers have been able to cling on to power despite the widespread suffering which a large part of the population has experienced.

The second surprise was the importance of the banking sector and of financial fragility. With some exceptions, there was little attention in initial policy analysis given to the role of the banks. Experience has shown, however, that banks play a very important role in a transformation. They provide – or fail to provide – the payments transmission system, their bad loans can burden the state budget (as in Hungary) or precipitate a deep economic crisis (as in Bulgaria), while poor supervision and regulation of their activities may give rise to spectacular banking collapses, with negative economic consequences (as in the Baltic states, the Czech Republic and Russia).

The third surprise was the need of a market economy for a strong but limited state, for an effective public administration. The predominant initial tendency among local neoliberals and their international backers was to concentrate on building the market sector and neglect the need to maintain and develop the state. Research on the Hungarian banking sector led Abel and Bonin[4] to point out the dangers of state desertion. By 1997, even the managing director of the IMF had drawn attention to the dangers that state collapse posed to the transformation process.[5] The decay of the state, which has been such a feature of developments in the CIS countries, has been a serious problem in fields ranging from taxation to public health, from education to crime.

The fourth surprise was that transformation was a long and difficult process. (For an illustration of this, see section 2 below.)

The fifth surprise has been the unimportance for economic growth of the rapid privatization of inherited large state-owned enterprises. The need to privatize such enterprises quickly was an article of faith of the Washington Consensus, but turned out to be much less important for economic growth than stimulating the rapid development of new private firms.

From the standpoint of the Washington Consensus, the main issues in the transformation of the former state socialist countries into modern capitalist countries were stabilization, liberalization and privatization.

Stabilization turned out to be full of pitfalls and trade-offs. A fixed exchange rate turned out to be a useful element in stabilization packages but one which, if adhered to for too long a period, led to real appreciation, undermining the current account and economic growth. In Russia it took eight years to reduce inflation sustainably to a more or less civilized level (20%). This resulted from inadequate political support for rapid stabilization and structural features of the economy (a market-incompatible geographical location of economic activity, large sectors of the economy for whose output there was little or no demand in a market economy, e.g. the defence and space sectors, the small size of the pre-existing private sector, and the lack of a market-friendly system of economic institutions and public administration).

There was a trade-off between instant convertibility and inflation, since instant convertibility required deeply undervalued exchange rates, and these contributed to inflationary explosions at the beginning of many 'stabilization programmes'. Nevertheless, IMF-backed stabilization programmes, if persisted in, eventually led to a sharp decline in inflation levels everywhere.

Liberalization of prices, of internal and external trade, and of the rules governing the establishment of private firms, were essential elements of the initial steps towards a market economy. Nevertheless, this process also involved trade-offs and pitfalls: the more complete the initial price liberalization, the bigger the initial price explosion; liberalization of internal trade contributed to criminalization; and complete liberalization of international trade was often followed by the reintroduction of some protectionist measures.

As far as privatization was concerned, a trade-off between speed and effectiveness emerged. In countries where emphasis was placed on speed of privatization (e.g. Russia or the Czech Republic), restructuring tended to lag behind. Furthermore, in Poland, the transformation country which was quickest to regain the pre-transformation level of GDP, growth has come mainly from newly-created private enterprises (sometimes using assets which had previously been in the state sector) rather than from the privatization of existing large state-owned enterprises (which turned out to be a lengthy and complex process). Furthermore, there is a trade-off between speed of privatization and fiscal receipts. Quick – voucher – privatization is possible, but does not bring the benefits to the budget of a slower process of sale.

The problem with 'shock therapy' was not the idea of ending very rapid inflation quickly (indeed, this is desirable), nor its stress on the introduction of free prices and free enterprise (which are also desirable), but rather its neglect of the interrelationship between monetary and real variables, and its application to issues that inevitably take time (e.g. institution-building). Further problems inherent in it were the neglect of social policy, of the need to maintain and develop state capacity, and of the importance for economic policy of the differences between countries (e.g. between resource-rich and resource-poor countries, between developed and underdeveloped countries).[6]

What was wrong with 'gradualism', on the other hand, was that in some cases (e.g. in Ukraine) it was a euphemism for postponement, which spread the pain over a long period, postponed recovery, and contributed to a deep depression.

The result of the experience of many countries and of the international policy debate has been the gradual emergence of a new conventional wisdom.[7] This recognizes the surprises, pitfalls, and trade-offs mentioned above. It has dropped the insistence on rapid privatization of inherited large state-owned enterprises and a positive real interest rate. It has also dropped the goal of a sudden transition to single digit annual inflation for high-inflation countries. It continues to stress the need for fiscal discipline, rapid price and trade liberalization, and for quickly bringing inflation below, say, 40% p.a. This new conventional wisdom also recognizes the importance of an efficient public administration, effective corporate governance, an efficient and solvent banking system, new private enterprises, the usefulness in some circumstances of modest tariff protection, and the importance of public goods and affordable transfer payments or wealth transfers (e.g. agricultural land). It recognizes the importance of political, geographical and institutional factors in determing economic outcomes, and is also more conscious of the relevant economic-policy differences between countries.

Russia is the largest, most populous, most heavily armed and most politically important, of the successor states of the former Soviet Union and the former eastern Europe. Its emergence as an independent state from the ashes of the USSR played a key role in creating the conditions for the whole 'transition' process to take place. Accordingly, it is worth while examining its experience in detail. This is done in the rest of this chapter.

2. Economic developments in Russia under Yeltsin

2.1 Systemic change

Between 1992 and 1999 there was a major change in the Russian economic system. Up until 1988 Russia was the classic land of the Soviet economic system. In the period 1989–91 that system decayed and between 1992 and 1999 vigorous efforts were made to introduce a civilized market economy. These efforts were backed by the G7 and its agencies (such as the IMF), and by the international business community. However, these efforts were a failure, and

Russia ended up with a mutant economic system. Eight aspects of this mutant system were of particular importance.

First, the lack of an efficient state apparatus and, in its place, the presence of a parasitic one. The collapse of the USSR and the creation of an independent Russia did not spawn an efficient state apparatus. At the end of the Yeltsin period, Russia lacked a state that could reasonably be seen as the defender of the public interest. It had officials, who temporarily held particular positions, but they saw their offices largely as their private fiefdoms from which they could temporarily enrich themselves. In their well known comparison of retail trade in Warsaw and Moscow, Frye and Shleifer[8] showed that the 'grabbing hand' model was much more applicable in the context of Moscow than Warsaw. They suggested that this was an important reason why the formation of new businesses had been much less dynamic in Russia than in Poland. The role of the grabbing hand was such that the Russian political system in the Yeltsin period acquired significant elements of kleptocracy.

Secondly, the importance of opportunistic behaviour. At all levels the important thing was control over economic resources (rather than formal ownership); of particular significance was control over cash flow, and the concomitant possibilities of diverting it into one's personal (foreign) bank account (or that of an entity under one's control) or using it to finance one's own luxury consumption. It is characteristic of the situation that in 1998, prior to the 17 August crisis, the banks exported capital on a large scale, and immediately after the crisis transferred their remaining assets to other entities controlled by the banks' controllers, thereby robbing creditors.

Thirdly, the enormous importance of the subsistence sector in agriculture. According to official statistics, in 1999 (the final year of the Yeltsin period), the household sector contributed the following shares of the entire Russian agricultural produce: 92% of the potatoes, 77% of the vegetables, 59% of the meat, 50% of the milk, 57% of the wool and 88% of the honey. The fact that in 1999 57% of total agricultural output was produced in the household sector – as against only 43% in the commercial sector – is remarkable evidence of the decreasing importance of the division of labour in Russia and the general primitivization of its economy. (It should be noted, however, that the more productive households in the household sector are gradually making the transition from subsidiary farming to peasant/smallholder agriculture.) Another aspect of this primitivization is the increased ownership of horses in the household sector: this more than doubled in the period 1991–7. Although horses are very useful in Russian agriculture, their growing importance is a sign of technical regress.

Fourthly, the large and increasing (till 1998) importance of barter transactions in industry and agriculture. Barter in industry steadily grew in importance in the period 1992–8: by March 1998 it was estimated to have reached 50% of industrial sales. As far as agriculture is concerned, Wegren reported that 'barter trade has virtually replaced monetarised exchange'.[9] The growth of barter was a clear sign that Russia did not make the transition to a modern market economy during the Yeltsin period.

Fifthly, the non-payment of wages (and pensions) on time. A particularly bad payer has been the state, whose employees – e.g. teachers, doctors, policemen and army officers – have experienced long delays in payment.

Sixthly, the criminalization of the economy. A very high proportion of firms are forced to pay protection money. Murdering one's rival is a well known form of 'competition', and debt collection relies heavily on strong-arm methods. Criminalization worsened significantly in the Yeltsin period. An important feature of Russian society in the 1990s were the close links between the criminal, political and business worlds. It is characteristic of the situation that when Yeltsin resigned in December 1999 he and his family were immediately granted an amnesty from prosecution for any crimes they might have committed while in office.

Seventhly, the absence of private bank accounts. Although individuals and private firms have bank accounts, according to Russian law certain entities, notably the tax authorities and some public utilities, are entitled to remove money from these accounts without the prior permission of the account

Table 1. **Russian GDP, 1991–9 (% change)**

	Official data	Khanin–Suslov
1991	-5	-5
1992	-15	-15
1993	-9	-13
1994	-13	-16
1995	-4	-5
1996	-3	-7
1997	1	n.a.
1998	-5	n.a.
1999	3	n.a.
1990–6	-41	-48
1990–9	-41	n.a.

Source: Official statistics/ Khanin and Suslov 1999.

holder. Hence they cannot really be considered 'private bank accounts'. This naturally encourages capital flight, and offshore, cash and barter transactions.

Eighthly, the importance of reciprocity. Reciprocity is a pre-capitalist form of economic relations, which was important in the USSR and which remains important in Russia, both for individuals and for firms.

Although the Russian economy may be a mutant one, it is nevertheless a mutant *market* economy. This is shown on the microeconomic level by the end of shortages and queues, and the wide availability of goods and services, much greater than in Soviet times, and on the macroeconomic level by its reaction to the rouble depreciation of 1998–9. A price change (the fall in the external value of the rouble) produced the sort of response (a decline in imports, an increase in exports, and an increase in import-substituting domestic production) that one would expect in a market economy. How should the economic system which Yeltsin bequeathed be described? Borrowing from Chinese terminology one can call it 'a market economy with Russian characteristics'.

2.2 Macroeconomic changes

The years 1992–8 were marked by a very deep depression, high but declining inflation, declining living standards, declining employment, increased unemployment, primitivization, and a very sharp deterioration in Russia's relative economic position. In 1999 the macroeconomic situation improved but living standards declined. Some relevant data are set out in Table 1.

The table shows a deep depression in 1991–8, interrupted only by a slight upswing in 1997. What explains this depression? This question has given rise to an extensive literature. Particularly important factors seem to have been the adverse inherited structure of the economy, state collapse and the resulting institutional vacuum, the real appreciation of the currency between 1992 and 1997, and the IMF-inspired stress on reducing inflation, even in the period 1996 to the first half of 1998 when the inflation level was quite moderate.

Therefore, a significant feature of Yeltsin's legacy was an economy only about half the size of the one he inherited. Since much of the world made rapid progress in the 1990s, Russia at the beginning of the 21st century has the same – purely economic – need to catch up with the advanced countries as did the Russia of Peter the Great or Witte, or the USSR of Stalin.

An interesting feature of 1999 was economic recovery, under the influence of import substitution and export growth (as a result of the currency depreciation), and rising world energy prices (gas and oil being Russia's chief exports). The currency depreciation and rising energy prices led to a redistribution of the national income in favour of profits. This improved the financial position of firms and the government, enabling firms to reduce their tax and wages arrears, and the proportion of barter in their turnover. However, it also further impoverished the mass of the population. The real exchange rate and world energy prices remain important factors influencing Russia's future economic development. (The continued economic growth in 2000, 2001 and 2002, owed much to the maintenance of favourable prices on the world energy market.)

Inflation was very high, but rapidly declining in the period 1992–5 (it was 2500% in 1992 and 840% in 1993); it fell further in 1996 and 1997 under the influence of the IMF stabilization programme, jumped in 1998 as a result of the depreciation of the external value of the currency and then declined again in 1999. As long as world energy prices remain at current levels (in Russia energy prices are very important not only as a source of export revenue but also as a source of fiscal revenue), Russia should be able to keep inflation below the World Bank's 40% danger line.

During the Yeltsin period the Russian government proved itself a most unreliable debtor. It wiped out most of its internal debts in 1992 by inflation, a move which caused widespread popular discontent, rescheduled its external debts inherited from the USSR but then largely failed to meet these rescheduled commitments, and in August 1998 once more defaulted on its external and internal debts. Although in the period 1996 to the first half of 1998 the credit rating of Russia was sufficient for the central and local governments and some private firms to borrow on the international capital market, at the end of the Yeltsin period Russia's credit rating was extremely poor.

In view of its 1998 default, Russia rescheduled its external commitments in the post-Yeltsin period, reaching new agreements with the London and Paris clubs. By late 2002, as a result of meeting its rescheduled commitments, its large and rising gold and foreign exchange reserves, and its continued economic growth, its credit rating had improved significantly.

2.3 Structural change

The Yeltsin years saw a major change in the structure of the economy. There was a dramatic demilitarization of the economy and the production of manufactured consumer goods also fell sharply. Agriculture also declined. The share of services in GDP rose massively. In general, the export (gas, oil, nonferrous metals, steel) and non-internationally traded sectors (e.g. services and subsistence agriculture) developed relatively favourably, while in the period between 1992 and the first half of 1998 the import-competing sectors, such as television, clothing and footwear production and commercial agriculture, were hit badly. The car industry only survived because of heavy protection. The decline of manufacturing, hit by reduced government orders, increased raw material prices, import competition and lack of investment, was particularly striking.

Within industry, the sector producing finished products rapidly declined, and the oil, gas and metals sectors grew in importance. There was a sharp decline in light industry, which reflected both difficulties with raw materials (e.g. inability to pay attractive prices for Uzbek cotton) and competition from foreign clothes and footwear, which have captured a large share of the Russian market. There was also a significant decline in engineering, reflecting both the demilitarization of the economy and the sharp decline in investment. According to Khanin and Suslov there was significant net disinvestment in Russia in 1990–6.[10] They estimate that fixed capital in the production sphere declined in that period by 18%. It seems that the capital stock, both in industry and in public services (railways, schools, water supply, sewage, housing) worsened. There was some investment (in private housing, consumer durables, retail trade) but it was probably not enough to offset the disinvestment in industry and public services. This disinvestment has left the economy much more badly equipped, relative to the advanced countries, than it was at the end of the Soviet period.

Besides changes in the structure of production, there were also important changes in the location of the population. The general tendency was for the population in the far north and far east to decline, as subsidies to these areas came to an end, and for the population of the North Caucasus, Volga, Central Black Earth, Urals and West Siberian regions to grow. Overall, during the Yeltsin era the population distribution became more economically rational.

A striking feature of the Yeltsin years was the rise and fall of the banking sector. Numerous so-called banks sprouted in the late Gorbachev and early Yeltsin years. The number of active registered banks reached a peak of 2300 in 1996, and from 1997 to the first half of 1998 Russian banks had international credibility. However, Russian banks in the Yeltsin era were not normal financial intermediaries, financing business with deposits collected from the public. Their main activities were to prey on the state sector by, for example, getting loans from the Central Bank, deposits from state institutions, or attractive assets which were privatized. Other activities were own-account foreign exchange and treasury bill trading, and delaying money transfers in order to pocket the interest that money in transit could earn. Some of the resulting cash flow was used to support firms that had their own pocket banks, and sometimes even for the purpose for which the Central Bank credits were officially intended, but much of it was transferred overseas. The banking sector was hit very badly by the crisis of 1998 and by 1999 the number of active banks had declined to about 1400. Their international credit rating had also declined sharply. At the end of the Yeltsin period the overwhelming majority of Russian household bank deposits were held in Sberbank, the state-owned savings bank, where they benefited from familiarity, a very wide branch network and an anticipated de facto state guarantee. The failure to establish a healthy private banking system in the period 1992–9 was one of the biggest failures of the Yeltsin period.

The political uncertainty, depression, absence of private bank accounts, criminalization and generally poor investment climate, led to large-scale capital flight. Estimates of the sums involved vary sharply and are inherently uncertain. According to a conservative estimate,[11] capital flight in 1992–6 totalled 63 billion dollars; according to Kosarev,[12] in the 1996–8 period it was about $25 billion p.a. Not all the capital exported is lost to the Russian economy; some comes back disguised as 'foreign investment'. In addition to the money exported abroad, substantial sums circulate in Russia in the form of cash dollars. By just before the 1998 crisis perhaps $55–60 billion cash was held by the population (in addition to foreign currency bank deposits of about $15 billion). Part of this sum is the working capital of shuttle traders, whose activities played an important role in meeting consumer demand in 1992–8. In 1992 a major part of the resources lost to Russia consisted of the terms of trade loss from trading with CIS countries at below world market prices.

2.4 Social changes

An important and very positive development in the Yeltsin period was the growth of self-employment and of the new private sector. The growth of productive entrepreneurship in Russia in the 1990s was of great importance for the future. Even in 1999, however, the proportion of the labour force that was self-employed or in the new private sector was far below the proportion of the labour force that was self-employed or working for small firms in the EU countries. It was also below the proportion of the labour force in the new private sector in a more successful transition economy such as Poland. The growth of this sector in Russia was hindered by the grabbing hand, high taxes and social security charges, criminals, the depression and foreign competition.

Total (officially recorded) employment between 1991 and 1999 fell by 12%. Some of those who officially remained employed were given unwanted and unpaid (or partially-paid) leave, or were frequently absent without leave. Of those who ceased to be employed, some took up work in the household or informal sectors, some left the labour force altogether and some became unemployed. Unemployment (ILO) definition grew substantially in the 1990s, reaching a peak of 14.2% in the spring of 1999, in the wake of the August 1998 crisis, and then declined. By the end of 2001 the unemployment rate (ILO definition) at 9% was approximately the same as in the Czech Republic and only about half that in Poland. Unemployment was a new and disagreeable experience for the Russian labour force. It normally meant impoverishment for those concerned and for their dependants (unemployment benefits are very low, are only paid to a minority of the unemployed, and have frequently been many months in arrears).

Another very disagreeable feature of the Russian labour market in the 1990s was delayed payment, payment in kind and non payment. Tens of millions of people found that their wages were not paid in money and on time, some were paid in kind, and millions had their wages delayed for months. These phenomena affected both industrial workers and budget sector employees (teachers, doctors, police, etc). The fall in the absolute and relative pay of budget sector employees, and the fact that they frequently did not receive their pay on time, were important reasons for the spread of corruption in this sector.

A major feature of Russian life in the 1990s was mass impoverishment. Using the data provided by Milanovic,[13] the World Bank's income distribution specialist, it would seem that between 1987–88 and 1993–5 the proportion of the Russian population in poverty rose from 2% to 39%, or from 2.2 million to 57.8 million. Because of the sensitivity to measurement problems of such estimates of the number of poor, not too much weight should be placed on the precision of these numbers. For example, if one defines poverty as half the official poverty (*prozhitochnyi minimum*) line, then according to official data the number of poor in Russia would be not 57.8 million but about 15 million.[14] Nevertheless, the general picture painted by Milanovic of a substantial increase in poverty under 'transition' and of a large number of people currently in poverty, is obviously accurate.

One important development in the 1990s was a decline in average food consumption. Clarke concluded that in the late 1990s at least 10% of households were chronically undernourished.[15] Particularly serious seems to have been protein underconsumption in poor households with children. According to UNDP,[16] stunting in children under two increased from 9.4% in 1992 to 15.2% in 1994. Some decline in food consumption, in response to the change in relative prices and to the increased availability of goods and services, was to be expected and was welfare-enhancing. The former 'sausage–vodka model of consumption' was neither healthy nor desirable. However, it seems that the decline in average food consumption, combined with the sharp increase in income inequality, the worsening of the position of households with dependent children, and the fact that the groups with the lowest incomes get relatively little benefit from self-produced food, has led to some malnutrition, especially among children in poor households.

Besides mass impoverishment, another feature of the Russian income distribution in the 1990s was a large increase in inequality. According to the World Bank,[17] the Gini coefficient of per capita income rose from 0.26 in 1987–90 to 0.47 in 1996–9. The latter would make Russia one of the most unequal countries in the world, on a par with Latin American countries such as Brazil. It may be that these figures exaggerate income inequality by excluding housing income (implicit housing subsidies and the imputed incomes of owner occupiers). In addition, it is possible that the World Bank figures exaggerate the *increase* in inequality by underestimating the *level* of inequality in the Soviet period. Nevertheless, it seems certain that inequality increased substantially in the Yeltsin period.

During the Yeltsin period the provision of public goods worsened in some respects. The police were unable to provide order (the political system provided many laws, but their implementation left much to be desired) and crime increased significantly. The number of registered and attempted murders doubled in the 1990s, rising from 15,600 in 1990 to 31,100 in 1999. The number of deaths from homicide more than doubled in 1990–4, fell in 1994–8 to a level 'only' 59% above that of 1990, and then again rose sharply in 1999–2000. The death rate from homicides in 1999 was 25.9 per hundred thousand of the population, which was about three times the rate in the USA, 15 times the rate in Italy, 25 times the rate in the UK and more than 40 times the rate in Japan. As far as education is concerned, the state of school buildings seems to have generally declined and a significant proportion of school age children appear not to have been attending school. The microcensus of 1994 showed that, in that year, 21% of young people between the ages of 15 and 19 who had not completed secondary school were neither at school nor attending any kind of educational institution (in 1989 this figure had been 17%). This decline in enrolments may lead to a decline in human capital analogous to the decline in physical capital noted above. Another contribution to the decline in human capital comes from the so-called 'brain drain'; the departure of many gifted people to better-paying jobs in other countries is a gain to the receiving countries but a loss for Russia. It is also an example of how 'globalization' works to the advantage of the rich countries.

In the early 1990s there was a significant worsening of the morbidity situation. There was a diphtheria epidemic (which was brought under control) and tuberculosis, syphilis and hepatitis grew substantially (although officially registered syphilis declined in the late 1990s). The danger of a further spread of tuberculosis generated international attention and international assistance programmes. On the other hand, polio was virtually eliminated by the end of the 1990s. Alarming warnings were uttered at the end of the decade about the prospects of the rapid growth in the number of HIV-infected people leading to a large absolute number of AIDS victims at the beginning of the 21st century. The combination of state collapse, kleptocracy, fiscal crisis and declining living standards created a fertile environment for the spread of disease.

During the 1990s there seems to have been an increase in alcoholism, smoking and the consumption of narcotics. The group with the highest per capita alcohol consumption seems to be low-income men. Commenting on the adult male mortality figures for 1998, a Russian sociologist has cited 'the alcoholisation of the population' as the main cause.[18] As far as smoking is concerned, the proportion of men in the age range 30–39 who were smokers increased from 51% to 71% between 1987 and 1999. Similarly, in the period 1990–7 the number of 15 to 17 year olds registered at medical institutions as narcotics users rose twelvefold.

During the Yeltsin period fertility fell. The crude birth rate fell from 12.1 per thousand in 1991 to 8.4 per thousand in 1999, and the total fertility rate from 1.73 in 1991 to 1.17 in 1999. The latter figure is well below that which is necessary to stabilize the size of the population in the long run (not taking account of migration). In addition the crude death rate rose sharply. It increased from 11.4 in 1991 to 14.7 in 1999 (and the estimated rate for 2002 is about 16.3). As a result, the life expectancy of Russian teenage boys fell to what it had been at the end of the nineteenth century.

During the Yeltsin period, Russia became a significant net immigration country. This shows that many people (mainly Russian-speakers) regard the socio-economic situation in Russia as better for themselves and their children than that of other CIS countries, from which most of the migrants come.

The combined result of the developments in the fields of fertility, mortality and migration is that, according to official statistics (which understate immigration) Russia has become a country experiencing depopulation. According to official statistics, in the period 1992–9, the population of Russia fell by 2.8 million or almost 2%.[19]

3. Russian economic policy and western economic advice, 1988–98

Western economic advice to the authorities in Moscow seems to have begun with the 1988–9 Soros mission.[20] The main thrust of this group's advice was to facilitate the transition to a market economy by permitting the existence of an 'open sector' where market economy rules would apply. Given the circumstances of rapidly increasing macroeconomic disequilibrium this was not very sensible advice. It would have been much better to stress the need to reduce the fiscal deficit and finance it in a non-inflationary way. What the USSR needed in 1988–9 was financial control and gradual liberalization, not complete liberalization in one small area in a national economy heading towards acute shortages combined with massive open inflation.[21]

The sad story of the advice given by the Harvard Institute for International Development (HIID), financed by USAID, and the conflicts of interests associated with it, has been told by Wedel.[22] The rapid privatization favoured by these advisors may have been favourable for themselves and their partners (who, in their private capacity, were active in the Russian securities market), but its contribution to economic growth in Russia was less evident. In 1996 the US economist Millar referred to voucher privatization as 'a de facto fraud'.[23] In 1998, in a criticism of the economic policies that had been pursued in Russia, the mayor of Moscow Yuri Luzhkov, 'singled out Harvard for the harm inflicted on the Russian economy by its advisors who encouraged Chubais's misguided approach to privatization and monetarism.'[24] Luzhkov said that 'Harvard was in fact harmful to us by having proposed one of the models for privatization in Russia. Moreover this was a substantive harm.' Wedel herself criticized the USAID-financed HIID for cooperating exclusively with one clique and failing to contribute to building institutions which are transparent and non-exclusive. Wedel's reporting led to the cancellation of USAID financing for HIID, official US investigations, and eventually the closing of HIID.

The interaction between the IMF and the USSR/Russia is a long story with various facets. The USSR declined to join the Bretton Woods organizations when they were set up. Although it was interested in loans on concessionary terms, it did not wish to supply information about its economy to foreign organizations, nor to obtain foreign approval for its economic policy. As USSR–USA relations deteriorated, so too did the Soviet attitude to the US-dominated IMF. The latter was denounced by the USSR and Communists throughout the world as an instrument of the imperialists. In the late 1980s, when Gorbachev was the leader of the USSR and the USSR was running a large and increasing current-account deficit, Western governments had to respond to the USSR's requests for Western loans. In July 1990, the G7 at their Houston summit asked four international financial institutions (IFIs), the IMF, World Bank, EBRD and OECD, to undertake a study of the Soviet economy. This was intended both to prevent the waste of Western money and to formulate sensible economic-policy proposals for the USSR. The four organizations quickly set to work and in December 1990 sent to the participants in the Houston meeting a document entitled *The Economy of the USSR: Summary and Recommendations*, which was published in January 1991. Three detailed volumes of background papers, which underpinned the conclusions reached in the summary volume were published in February 1991. The *Summary and Recommendations* rejected the 'conservative' approach to reform and argued for a 'radical' approach. It stressed that Western balance of payments assistance (i.e. substantial foreign loans) should be conditional on 'the introduction of a major and comprehensive reform program'.

In May 1991 the Soviet Security Council approved Prime Minister Pavlov's proposal that the USSR should apply for membership of the IMF, with only KGB chief Kryuchkov opposing it. In October 1991, in connection with the country's forthcoming entry into the IMF, the managing director of the IMF, M Camdessus, told Gorbachev that if the right policies were pursued, 'the USSR, not some time or other in the indefinite future, but within a few years, will become an economic superpower.'[25] This idea, which was essentially used as a bait to encourage the USSR to enter the IMF and pursue IMF-supported policies, was a complete illusion. The USSR never became an economic superpower. After the USSR's collapse, the FSU countries experienced high inflation, depression, criminalization and state collapse.

Two countries, the USA and Germany, played an important role in formulating Western policy towards the USSR and its successor states, and in both cases political motives were important. For the USA, a 'new Marshall plan' was ruled out because of the hostility of the Congress to foreign aid. Since there was little chance of getting a substantial programme of aid to the USSR and its successor states through the Congress, the US administration was forced to act through the IFIs (such as the IMF and World Bank) which it controlled and whose lending activity was not directly subject to approval by the US Congress. This is why the IMF played a much bigger role in the relationship between the USA and the USSR and its successor states than it had between the USA and Western Europe in the Marshall plan era. For the US administration, the international financial institutions were an alternative source of policy advice and loans for the FSU that avoided the need for Congressional approval. Germany was primarily interested in obtaining Soviet agreement to German reunification within NATO and the withdrawal of Soviet/Russian troops from Germany, which took until the mid 1990s. To help achieve these goals it made extensive loans to the USSR/Russia. It also played an important role in setting up the EBRD, which was partly based on the German tradition of the financing of investment via the banking system. The advice and loans given by the IMF to the FSU in the 1990s were influenced both by the judgements of its own personnel, and also by the wishes of its principal shareholders.

It is possible to make technical criticisms of the IMF's money-based stabilization policy proposals, and argue instead for exchange-rate based stabilization policies.[26] Here we will look instead at some concrete issues in the saga of the interaction between the IMF and the FSU.

In the winter of 1991–2, as the USSR was breaking up, IMF economic advisors were disoriented by the situation and made two policy mistakes. First, they advocated retention of the rouble area. Of course, the introduction of several currencies in what had previously been a unified currency area, was bound to bring about economic disruption and a loss of what suddenly became 'international trade' but which had previously been internal Soviet trade (or barter). However, to suppose that newly independent countries would wish to continue to use the Russian currency was politically naïve. Furthermore, the export of Russian commodities for roubles at subsidized prices, and the ability of the central banks in the non-Russian parts of the rouble zone to create roubles, caused a substantial loss to Russia, particularly in 1992. It would have been more useful if the IMF economists had immediately seen the inevitability of the introduction of national currencies and devoted their attention to the monetary conditions for a civilized divorce.

Secondly, the IMF 'experts' underestimated the level of corrective inflation which would follow price liberalization. At the end of 1991 there were discussions within the Gaidar team and with their advisors about the likely level of inflation in the first month after price liberalization. The Ministry of the Economy (the old Gosplan) estimated it at 200%. Gaidar thought this an exaggeration and estimated it at 100%. The IMF 'experts' thought even this an exaggeration and estimated it at 50%. The outcome was 245%. The IMF 'experts' had turned out to be less knowledgeable about the Russian economy than the old Gosplan specialists on the Soviet economy.

In the mid 1990s the IMF supported in Russia, with both advice and substantial loans, a disinflation policy in which a slowly depreciating nominal exchange-rate range meant a rapidly appreciating real exchange rate. This policy was successful in reducing inflation, which fell sharply in 1995 to the first half of 1998. However, persistence in this policy, even when inflation had fallen to quite civilized levels, had an adverse effect on economic growth and required a state-organized Ponzi scheme to sustain it. It finally collapsed amidst the macroeconomic crisis of August 1998. In July 1998 the IMF tried to maintain the exchange rate with a 'confidence-building' loan, but market participants used this as an opportunity to export capital at the old exchange rate. The currency depreciation of 1998–9, which the IMF had tried so hard to avoid, led to a sharp fall in living standards but also led (together with favourable developments in the prices of Russia's commodity exports) to sustained economic growth.

Looking back on the record of the IMF–Russia interaction, one must note that not everything in it was negative. IMF advice did help reduce the rate of inflation, which in 1992–3 was very high and disorganized the economy. In addition, the technical advice provided by the IMF (e.g. concerning the compilation of internationally-comparable balance of payments statistics) was useful.

Another of the IFIs active in Russia in the 1990s was the World Bank. This made a number of seemingly well-intentioned project loans. For example, it made loans to soften the social costs of reducing the employment of coal miners, and a loan to assist the victims of financial fraud (such as the notorious MMM scam). However, the extent to which the ostensible beneficiaries actually benefited from these programmes is questionable. It seems, for example, that although the World Bank provided $30 million for the victims of financial fraud, not a single casualty ever received any compensation. Such World Bank programmes – which eventually have to be repaid by Russian taxpayers – seem to be better understood not in terms of their ostensible purposes but as bribes to Russian politicians and officials for them to continue supporting the integration of Russia in the global capitalist system.

Looking back at the World Bank's activities in Russia, a 2002 report prepared for the World Bank's own Operations Evaluation Department (OED) came to the conclusion that the verdict on the Bank's activities in Russia up to the crisis of 1998 could only be 'unsatisfactory'. The Bank's work at the project level was characterized as 'poor'. Its social protection programmes in the two areas deemed most important, pension reform and modernization of the labour code, were described as having 'failed'. Some successes were recorded, such as its coal industry loans and an increase in oil production.[27] The idea of evaluating the World Bank's record is a good one, and an advance on the practice of many bureaucratic bodies. In addition, some positive results of its activities were discerned. Nevertheless, the overall picture is negative, and an evaluation by an independent external body might well have been even more so.

As far as the overall assessment of the interaction between Russian economic policy and Western economic advice is concerned, it was a success story from a Western point of view. The Soviet system has been dismantled. The Russian economy has been stabilized, liberalized (to a considerable extent), and extensively privatized. After a decade of 'transition', Russia is negotiating for membership of the WTO and thus for full participation in the globalized world economy, and is also exporting raw materials (particularly oil, natural gas and various metals) on a large scale to the West. In October 2002, as it prepared for war against Iraq, the USA was able to add Russian crude oil to its Strategic Petroleum Reserve.[28] Although on the whole Russia has not been very attractive for Western investment, some investors (e.g. some large Western oil companies) have made significant investments and are hoping for large profits.

However, experience also shows the need for humility when giving economic advice. The increase in poverty and corruption in Russia and other transition countries, the criminalization of these countries, state collapse in many of them, the growth of the informal sector, large-scale capital flight, and the 'democratic-deficit' throughout the CIS, were unforeseen and undesirable developments. They even threaten the G7 themselves, with everything from drugs trafficking via arms smuggling to the spread of infectious diseases such as AIDS. The authoritarian regimes in Central Asia may turn out to have provided a fertile environment for the spread of Jihadism. The West needs to be aware of the full spectrum of the impact of its advice and its responsibility both for some achievements and some failures. As far as the recipients of Western advice are concerned, the following points are particularly important.

First, the need to discriminate between useful and harmful advice. Some of the advice from the IFIs is useful and should be adopted. Some is harmful and should be rejected. It is important that recipient countries have the in-house intellectual and administrative capacity to assess which is which. Secondly, the dangers of debt-dependency. During the 1990s, despite a large current account surplus, Russia fell into a humiliating dependence on Western financial assistance. This contributed to decisions (such as a steadily appreciating real exchange rate in 1997 and the first half of 1998) that had harmful economic effects. Thirdly, the dangers of developing a comprador class/elite. In the 1990s Russia developed such a stratum. These people were at least as concerned to please the West as they were with developing the Russian economy. Fourthly, the primacy of internal factors. Naturally Western advice, and the realities of the global economy, were of great importance to the FSU countries in the 1990s. Nevertheless, internal factors, ranging from the availability of natural resources in Russia to the political orientation of the Estonian people, were probably of greater importance in determining the outcome in those countries.

Notes

1 This chapter draws heavily from two previously published papers: M Ellman, 1997, 'The Political Economy of Transition', *Oxford Review of Economic Policy*, vol. 13 no.2; and M Ellman, 2000, 'The Russian Economy under Yeltsin', *Europe–Asia Studies*, December.

2 'Transition' gives the impression of a process with a uniform starting position, uniform and known end position, and progress according to an accurate recipe known in advance. Since the countries concerned differed significantly in their starting positions (though sharing certain elements in common), seem to be moving towards different goals, and have been through a process not foreseen by anyone, I prefer the term 'transformation'. This stresses the process of change, but emphasizes the decisions that have to be made en route, and leaves open the endpoint.

3 World Bank 2000, p. 140.

4 Abel and Bonin 1993.

5 He stated, with special reference to Russia, that 'No-one measured the true depth of the collapse of all administrative structures, the decomposition of the state which accompanied the collapse of the communist system' (*Financial Times*, 10 January 1997).

6 A key idea of the Washington Consensus was that, as Lawrence Summers, then chief economist of the World Bank, proclaimed in October 1991, 'Spread the truth – the laws of economics are like the laws of engineering. One set of laws works everywhere.' As a result, when for example advising Russia on such matters as taxation and privatization, little attention was given to the crucial importance of natural resource rents in Russia for the budget, the distribution of wealth, and the social acceptability of private enterprise. Similarly, when advising Kyrkyzia, little attention was paid to the special situation of a land-locked underdeveloped country.

7 World Bank 1996; Stiglitz 1998; Kolodko 2000; Dabrowski et al. 2001; World Bank 2002.

8 Fryc and Shleifer 1997.

9 Wegren 2000, p. 242.

10 Khanin and Suslov 1999.

11 Tikhomirov 1997.

12 Kosarev 2000.

13 Milanovic 1998.

14 Clarke 1999a.

15 Clarke 1999b, p. 186.

16 UNDP 1999 p. 23.

17 World Bank 2000, p. 140.

18 Rimashevskaya 1999, p. 66.

19 Preliminary estimates from the 2002 census suggest that these official statistics overstate depopulation (presumably because of unrecorded immigration). However, the accuracy of the initial census data is uncertain. There are suspicions that some regions overstated their population in order to increase their claim for resources.

20 Hanson 1998.

21 McKinnon 1993, especially pp. 155–6.

22 Wedel 1998.

23 Wedel 1998, p. 132.

24 Wedel 1998, pp. 133–4.

25 Chernyaev 1997, p. 224.

26 Bofinger 1997.

27 See the report of a meeting at the Carnegie Endowment for International Peace of 12 September 2002 (*Johnson's Russia List* #6489, 12 October 2002).

28 *The Wall Street Journal Europe*, 2 October 2002, p. A5.

References

Abel, I and Bonin, J, 1993, 'State desertion and convertibility: the case of Hungary', in I Szekely and D Newbery, 1993, eds, *Hungary: An Economy in Transition*, Cambridge, Cambridge University Press.

Bofinger, P et al., 1997, 'Orthodox money-based stabilization (OMBS) versus heterodox exchange rate-based stabilization (HERBS): The case of Russia, the Ukraine and Kazakhstan', *Economic Systems*, vol 21 no.1.

Chernyaev, A, 1997, *1991 god: Dnevnik pomoshchnika Prezidenta SSSR*, Moscow, Respublika.

Clarke, S, 1999a, 'Poverty in Russia' in P Stavrakis, ed, *Problems of Economic Transition*, Armonk NY, ME Sharpe.

Clarke, S, 1999b, *New Forms of Employment and Household Survival Strategies in Russia*, Coventry, ISITO.

Dabrowski, M et al., 2001, 'Whence reform ? A critique of the Stiglitz Perspective', *Journal of Policy Reform* vol. 4, issue 4.

Frye, T and Shleifer, A, 1997, 'The invisible hand and the grabbing hand', *American Economic Review* vol. 87, no. 2.

Hanson, P, 1998, 'Foreign advice' in M Ellman and V Kontorovich, eds, *The Destruction of the Soviet Economic System*, New York, ME Sharpe, chapter 8.5.

Khanin, G and Suslov, N, 1999, 'The Real Sector of the Russian economy: Estimation and Analysis', *Europe–Asia Studies*, vol. 51, no. 8, December.

Kolodko, G, 2000, *From Shock to Therapy*, Oxford, Oxford University Press.

Kosarev, A, 2000, 'Voprosy makroekonomicheskoi otsenki begstva kapitala iz rossii', *Voprosy statistiki*, no. 2.

McKinnon, R, 1993, *The Order of Economic Liberalization*, 2nd ed., Baltimore, John Hopkins University Press.

Milanovic, B, 1998, *Income, Inequality and Poverty During the Transition from Planned to Market Economy*, Washington DC, World Bank.

Rimashevskaya, N, 1999, *Rossiya-1998*, Moscow, Institute of Socio-Economic Problems of the Population, Russian Academy of Sciences.

Stiglitz, J, 1998, *More Instruments and Broader Goals: Moving Towards the post-Washington Consensus*, Helsinki, WIDER.

Tikhomirov, V, 1997, 'Capital flight from post-Soviet Russia, *Europe–Asia Studies*, vol. 49, no. 4, June.

UNDP, 1999, *Human Development Report for Central and Eastern Europe and the CIS*, New York, UNDP.

Wedel, J, 1998, *Collision and Collusion*, Basingstoke, Macmillan.

Wegren, S, 2000, 'Socioeconomic Transformation in Russia: Where is the Rural Elite?', *Europe–Asia Studies*, vol. 52, no. 2, March.

World Bank, 1996, *From Plan to Market*, New York, Oxford University Press.

World Bank, 2000, *Making Transition Work for Everyone. Poverty and Inequality in Europe and Central Asia* (Washington DC, World Bank).

World Bank, 2002, *Building Institutions for Markets*, New York, Oxford University Press.

PART III

STRUCTURAL AND SECTORAL ISSUES

9

NEW GROWTH THEORY

Ben Fine

1. Introduction

The relationship between (economic) growth and development remains controversial. Is growth a cause or consequence of development, and to what extent and in what way is it a core component of the wider economic and social processes that characterize the elusive notion of development itself? For the vast majority of mainstream development economics, these conundrums are a peripheral luxury. Its focus is upon increases of per capita income, and the latest theories and techniques for modelling it. Memory of past contributions is both short and selective, both in terms of their context as well as their content and motivation.

Such are the general circumstances that have given rise to the new or endogenous growth theory, NGT, the subject of this chapter. The next section outlines the old or exogenous growth theory, OGT, that is supposedly superseded and enhanced by the new. Section 3 provides an account of NGT, in part highlighting its continuities with OGT, in part pinpointing where it differs, and in part revealing its legion theoretical and empirical deficiencies, many of which were previously exposed for OGT whether in detail or in principle. The final section places the discussion in a broader context, arguing that NGT reflects the following factors: an absolute commitment to the powers of policy as economic and social engineering; an absolute commitment to the fallible market, albeit one to be corrected alongside other non-market imperfections; and the general extension of economics to non-economic applications, economics imperialism, of which the shift from Washington to post-Washington consensus is in the vanguard of development studies. Hints at an alternative treatment are provided by emphasizing a historically- and country-specific approach that focuses upon economic and social relations, structures and processes, in which some attention – as opposed to none – is directed towards questions of power, conflict and development as transformation.

2. Old Growth Theory

In addressing NGT, it is standard and appropriate to take OGT as a point of departure, especially in its neoclassical one sector (Solow–Swan) version. This is a special case of the Harrod–Domar model of growth, for which steady state balanced growth (SSBG) requires equality between warranted and natural rates of growth. SSBG as a form of equilibrium over time means that the economy just gets bigger but otherwise remains the same in all respects. The natural rate of growth is given exogenously by n, the rate of growth of population. The warranted rate of growth is given by that of the capital stock, K. It is increased each period by sY where s is (constant) saving rate and Y is output. As a result, K grows at sY/K or s/v, where v is the capital-output ratio. For Harrod, there is a problem of existence, for SSBG as s/v and n may not equal one another – one of capital or labour is liable to outstrip the other. The neoclassical model gets round this by allowing the capital-output ratio to vary, with higher per capita output with higher per capital per worker.

This works in per capita terms, assuming constant returns to scale. For output per capita, y, there is a production function for capital per worker, k, so that $y = f(k)$. With constant saving rate s, all assumed to be invested, saving per head is sy. This equals $sf(k)$. In order for the economy to satisfy Harrod–Domar conditions for SSBG, $s/v = n$, or $sf(k)/k = $ n; or $sf(k) = nk$. This last equation is readily interpreted. It says on the LHS that saving/investment per head must match on the RHS the new investment required for n new workers for capital and labour to remain in the same proportions over time and for the growth rate to be constant.

Figure 1 (p. 203) illustrates these points. SSBG is guaranteed by adjusting the capital/labour ratio, k. Two different equilibria are shown by A and B. If n decreases (s increases), the equilibrium moves from A to B, and from lower k_1 to higher k_2. This is not surprising, as with higher saving or lower population growth there is more capital per worker available. It is crucial to recognize that the new equilibrium raises output per capita from y_1 to y_2 but does not affect the equilibrium growth rate; it is given exogenously by n for any SSBG path. Equally important is the observation that per capita output remains constant. As a result, productivity increase can only be added on as an afterthought and explained outside the model as exogenous: 'manna from heaven' was the famous expression used.

In conceptual and contextual terms, the model originated in the 1950s. It was attached to the idea of development as modernization, with the developing countries needing to go through the same stylized transformations as the then-developed. This is not and cannot be made explicit in the model itself, since developing and developed countries look identical to one another but

Figure 1.

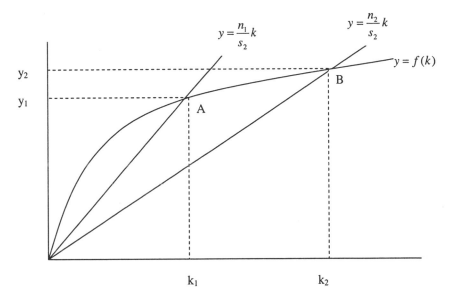

for differences in exogenous parameters s, n and f (and, paradoxically, reducing n would, *ceteris paribus*, lead to a lower growth rate despite the demographic transition to lower birth and death rates being characteristic of the developed countries). But in the then extraordinarily influential approach of the economic historian WW Rostow,[1] the connections between development and modernization were made explicit. Developing countries need to go through the five stages of development that had been experienced by the developed. The presumption is that the growth model lay at the core of these shifts even if it was unable to explain them: increases in productivity, increasing saving rates, development of industry, and so on, would depend upon cultural changes, not least entrepreneurial spirit and the cultural embracing of market and western norms.

Significantly, the subtitle to Rostow's book, *A Non-Communist Manifesto*, indicates its ideological purpose during the Cold War in terms of the political challenge from the Soviet Union (and its claims for its own growth performance and influence over the Third World) and the intellectual challenge from Marxism (dismissed for being too deterministic and reductionist to the economy). In the early 1950s, Rostow enraged his fellow economic historians by suggesting that their primary, almost exclusive, preoccupation should be with economic growth.[2] Also subject to fierce debate was the relationship between economic theory and history, with Rostow's stance acknowledging that the theory is useful but that it needs to be supplemented by the non-economic.[3]

In short, taken in context, OGT could not and did not claim to be a complete explanation for growth, let alone development. Its limitations were understood both in economic and non-economic terms. Significantly, Harrod sought to add a theory of instability to the model through an accelerator-multiplier model. He argued that, even if a SSBG path does exist with s/v fortuitously equalling n, it is liable to be unstable as optimistic (pessimistic) expectations will prove to be more than self-sustaining, sending the economy into explosive growth (decay). Domar also focused upon the mechanisms of growth, suggesting that 'old' investments would not release markets and resources to the 'new'. This would depress capacity utilization on more productive investments and reduce the rate of growth.

In pointing to its modest aims, this commentary and these examples temper what would otherwise appear to be devastating criticisms of OGT, especially for its ability to address development. These are, first, that growth in practice, is neither 'steady' (constant over time) nor balanced (with unchanging composition of output). Second is the presumption of full employment at all times and the effortless matching of all capital and labour to one another in any proportion through the production function. Third is the absence of explanation for changing levels of productivity as well as for saving and population (f, s and n). Fourth is the absence of account for the broader economic and social changes that accompany growth and development as both cause and effect. Essentially, the model can only favourably be interpreted by seeing its growth as embedded within, but extracted from, a process of development that goes through stages, cycles, parameter shifts and social and economic transitions. These all lie outside its analytical embrace.

Irrespective of the merits of this crude separation between the narrowest notion of growth and the widest understanding of development, there are severe weaknesses of the model as economics on its own terms, both theoretically and empirically. First, the model only allows for one sector in the economy, a good that serves all, and both investment and consumption. The crucial issue, although it can be put in a number of different ways, is whether a one-sector model can reasonably be taken to represent models with more than one sector. This is purely a theoretical issue – a property of models. But, as it can be safely assumed that any economy does have more than one sector, there is a problem if the model with one sector only misrepresents those with more than one sector. As shown through the Cambridge Controversy or Critique of Capital Theory, this is the case. For the one-sector model, distribution between capital and labour is determined by the simple device of taking marginal products. Concretely, the rate of profit equals $f'(k)$ and the wage rate equals $f(k) - kf'(k)$. As a result, there are strict algebraic relations between profit (and wages) and k. For profit falls (wages rise) as k grows because of diminishing (increasing) marginal products.

By contrast, in a two or more sector model, these results cannot be replicated. First of all, capital as such cannot be measured and placed within a production function f with the properties required. Essentially, capital now has both a physical aspect (quantities of machines) *and* a price aspect – at the very least $k = pm$ where p is price and m quantity of physical capital. The quantity k depends on p, and this cannot be derived from within the one-sector model, as there is only one good and so no (relative) prices. Mainstream economics reluctantly accepted this in the Controversy, and would seek to deal with it, or close the system, by adding demand to the supply conditions. Be this as it may, the aggregate production function, f, is invalid: distribution cannot be determined by it, and the intuitive relations connecting movements in wages and profits to 'capital' do not hold. Samuelson, as a leading proponent of the neoclassical view, was forced to eat humble pie and, ineffectually in the event, concludes his summing up with this advice:

> If all this causes headaches for those nostalgic for the old time parables of neoclassical writing, we must remind ourselves that scholars are not born to live an easy existence. We must respect, and appraise, the facts of life.[4]

Second, the one-sector model has consequences over and above those attached to its SSBG path. Out of equilibrium, there are implications for wages and profits (as the value of k is too high or low relative to its equilibrium value). In a downturn, when capital is in short supply, the profit rate should rise. This does not correspond to experience but posts the more general warning, to be taken up later, that all the implications of a model should be tested, not just one or two selectively on the basis of a few favoured results.

Third, not so far raised, is the role played by the model in *measuring* technological progress or the contribution of exogenous productivity increases to increases in output. For the neoclassical production function, $Y = F(K, L, t)$ where Y, K and L are now output, capital and labour in aggregate terms and t is a parameter representing shifts of F over time, take differentials:

$$dY = F_K dK + F_L dL + F_t dt$$

Hence $(dY/dt)/Y = (KF_K/Y)dK/dt/K + (LF_L/Y)dL/dt/L + F_t/F$

So $F_t/F = (dY/dt)/Y - (KF_K/Y)dK/dt/K - (LF_L/Y)dL/dt/L$

And $F_t/F = (dY/dt)/Y - adK/dt/K - (1-a)dL/L$, where a is capital's share in output and $1-a$ is labour's share. In words, the final equation shows in the RHS the increase in output (first term), minus contribution to output from increase in capital (second term as growth in capital weighted by its share in output), minus contribution to output from increase in labour (third term as growth in labour weighted by its share in output). This is the output increase that is not explained by increases in inputs and so is designated as due to technological progress and named total factor productivity, TFP. Note that TFP is recognized to be a *residual* after the contribution of increases in inputs have been netted out from increases in output. It is unexplained, just measured.

The major problem with this approach in defining the residual or TFP in principle, and in measuring it in practice, derives from the Cambridge Critique, which renders it totally invalid. This is because changes in K are a combination of changes in both the evaluation and the quantity of capital. To put an extreme case, if relative prices alone were to change (in response to exogenous demand shift towards more physically capital-intensive goods for example), increasing the price of physcial capital, K would be measured as having changed (increased), and a change in TFP would occur in the residual. This is so even though there has been no change in available technologies and techniques. In a nutshell, changes in K involve at least two dimensions (physical quantity and price) but the TFP measures associated with the one-sector growth model must treat changes in each as if a change in physical quantity. It is as though we try and measure the area of a rectangle whilst only knowing its perimeter but not its shape!

The measurement of TFP has, however, continued to be a significant, almost exclusive, method in measuring economic performance at firm, sector and national levels. Rather than acknowledge the deficiency in method, most attention has been drawn to refining the measurement of inputs and interpreting the reasons for patterns of TFP, whether over time or comparatively. As more inputs are added to include skills and so on, the residual TFP tends to be pared down (since other inputs grow disproportionately more). Howsoever TFP has been measured though, the next step is to explain the empirical results by appeal to a further set of factors that have previously been omitted. For example, reference might be made to recession and excess capacity or the power of trade unions as depressing TFP. Doing so gives rise to a striking inconsistency, once again only rarely, if at all, remarked upon. This is that the explanation for TFP is inconsistent with the assumptions on which it has been calculated! For measurement of the residual depends upon assuming full employment and perfect competition (in order that contributions to output from inputs can be measured by marginal products and factor shares).

Leaving aside all of these problems, there remains the question of why some countries should have so much greater levels of TFP than others. If technology, f, is freely available to all, possibly with a lag, it is to be expected that per capita output would converge over time across countries if there is also free flow of capital. For those countries with low s and high n would have low marginal product of labour but high marginal product of capital, inducing an inflow of capital seeking highest return. Even if technology and capital do not flow freely, this should not simply be assumed from the empirical evidence but should be explained in terms of the rational behaviour of economic agents. Why do they not locate technology and capital at the site of its highest levels of productivity? So, the presence or not of convergence in per capita income across countries, especially between developed and developing, is one point of departure for NGT, opening up the possibility that productivity increase is both endogenous and unequal across countries.

3. New Growth for Old?

From modest origins in the classic articles of Romer and Lucas,[5] there has been an explosive growth in contributions to NGT, both in theoretical and empirical content. Although, as will become apparent, there is considerable diversity across models, they have all settled down to have common theoretical elements. First is their dependence on increasing returns to scale. As a result, the bigger the economy, the higher is its level of productivity (IRS) explaining why the developed have an advantage over the developing countries. Further, the higher is the saving rate and investment, the quicker will economies of scale accrue. Choosing a higher saving rate raises – thereby endogenizing – the rate of growth, in sharp contrast to OGT, in which the growth rate is given by n and exogenously given productivity increase, TFP.

Second, though, is the issue of why there should be increasing returns to scale. Most models depend upon the presence of positive externalities. There may be constant returns to scale for the individual producer but positive spillover effects for the economy as a whole – as education, invention, learning, networks such as industrial districts and so on spread individual gains more widely.

Third, then, is the dependence of NGT on market imperfections, for which increasing returns and externalities have long been recognized to be broad examples. Any market imperfection can be used to generate a model for NGT as long as it generates increasing returns (for which the saving rate is liable to be important and the private below social returns). Moreover, almost any aspect of the economy can be perceived to experience market imperfections. For example, research and development can be 'produced' by use of resources dedicated to the purpose, with outcomes dependent upon how benefits accrue through the patent system. Economies can learn by producing or by doing, and so by importing, exporting, adopting, adapting and so on. Education and innovation, and other elements in economic and social infrastructure (the increasing returns of natural monopolies), contribute to productivity increase. And there may be greater or lesser coordination, or mismatch, across skills, finance and investment. In short, the analytical highway from market imperfections through increasing returns to endogenous growth has many lanes, and they have been heavily trodden. Often contributors to NGT simply speculate on some mechanism for raising productivity and bang it into a model without regard whatsoever to the processes in practice (or to the vast literature on the history of technology).

In assessing NGT it is natural, in order to bring out its distinctiveness, to take OGT as a point of comparison along a number of dimensions. First, market imperfections are notably absent from OGT, relegated to the (explanation of the) residual or presumed to be corrected in the long run. Even so, market imperfections are more generally far from new to economic theory, and are standard fare for courses in (applied) *micro*economics, for which they are perceived to lead to static deadweight losses (measured by triangles of lost consumer surplus). What is remarkable is that NGT has taken such static, microeconomic deadweight losses (that might affect the base for growth but not its rate for OGT) and transformed them into a *macro*economic influence on the growth rate.

Second, NGT like OGT is organized around SSBG as equilibrium, although the mathematical models for NGT are sufficiently complicated and diverse that they can, or can be designed to, generate both multiple equilibria and complex, not necessarily stable, paths out of equilibrium. In addition, NGT models usually rely upon economies with a single output for consumption and investment (although there might be a separate sector for education, R&D or whatever as a source for IRS and TFP). With single sector SSBG at the heart of NGT, the question remains of whether this is capable of adequately capturing, let alone explaining, the patterns of growth and economic and social change associated with development.

Third, as a striking case of reinforced collective, academic amnesia, NGT proceeds as if the results of the Cambridge Critique simply do not exist. The aggregate production function is deployed both for theoretical and empirical purposes even though doing so is simply invalid in representing growth macroeconomics for an economy with more than one good. Further, in a point that can only be touched upon, the Cambridge Critique is essentially a debate over value theory (how prices and distribution are determined usually in the context of perfectly working markets). As Arrow has observed,[6] neoclassical value theory falls into disarray and reinvents itself every time once in the presence of increasing returns to scale. Not surprisingly, then, NGT proceeds in the absence of value/price theory even though it depends upon *market* imperfections and emphasizes how the *market* is liable to generate too low a saving rate.

Fourth, reference to Arrow in this context is a coincidence insofar as he is recognized to have contributed the classic article on learning-by-doing as a source of productivity increase. He did so for the example of reduction in manual labour time taken to construct timber aircraft frames with cumulative experience. This indicates that the ideas underlying NGT are far from new, and there are other precedents in the literature on technical change that anticipate NGT. With some exceptions, notably Kaldor's model of cumulative growth, it seems that these earlier contributions recognized their grounding in diverse *microeconomic* case studies or factors that would only be inappropriately extrapolated to the macroeconomy. No such caution is displayed by NGT.

Fifth, it might be thought that the various microeconomic theories underlying endogenous growth might be combined with one another to yield more 'realistic' models in some sense, rather than simply extracting from a few more or less speculative micro-insights to the economy as a whole. Unfortunately, the models become mathematically intractable and to some extent arbitrary once different effects are combined, for economic agents are optimizing into the indefinite future over market imperfections, and some view has to be taken about what they do or do not correct in view of persistent market imperfections.

Sixth, the mathematical properties of the models are often problematic even where they are manageable. As mentioned, it is possible to generate a rich portfolio of outcomes, incorporating multiple equilibria and complex dynamics. But restrictions have to be made in order to be able to obtain acceptable results. Consider Lucas' model of the production of skills (human capital). Output is a function of capital, labour and skills:

$$Y = AK^{\alpha}(LH)^{1-\alpha}$$

for some parameter $\alpha < 1$, where H is level of skill or efficiency units of labour. If H remains constant, then we have normal Cobb–Douglas constant returns to scale and $H^{1-\alpha}$ can be absorbed into the constant term A. But if H varies as an input, we have increasing returns to scale (equal to $2-\alpha$). Lucas assumes that skills can be produced by trading off time spent at work, L, with time spent acquiring skills, $1-L$, say, for unit time available. The production function for skills is:

$$H = B(1-L)^\varepsilon$$

for parameters B and ε. Lucas' concern is to provide a trade-off between more work (or less creation of skills) now and less growth later, or vice versa, depending on how much time you choose to put into work/education.

The concern here is not so much with the speculative and simplistic way in which skills are seen as being created as the formal properties of the model itself. As Solow[7] shows, these depend in an extremely sensitive way on the value of ε that Lucas, without comment, takes to be equal to one. By chance, this is the only value of ε that allows the model to be sensible. For if $\varepsilon < 1$, the productivity effect from skills declines to zero over time. On the other hand, if $\varepsilon > 1$, the model has the remarkable property of generating infinite levels of growth in finite time! Whether by luck or design, or some combination of the two, Lucas chose the only value for ε that allows the model to behave itself. And there seems no reason why there should be constant returns to scale in the provision of skills in this way. More generally, and quite independently of this particular model and growth models in general, the Solow insight can be seen to be indicative of the very powerful constraints imposed on parameters by the presumption of SSBG ($s/v = n$, by analogy for Harrod–Domar OGT, for example). Thus SSBG is a bit of a straitjacket both in terms of technical properties of models and in its descriptive content for growth and development.

Finally, there is the statistical work associated with NGT. Its major starting point has been to test the hypothesis of convergence suggested by OGT, the idea that free flow of capital and technology should lead to the closing of the gap between per capita output across countries. Accordingly, regressions are run on the growth rate and *earlier* levels of per capita income, y_0, posing the hypothesis of a *negative* coefficient as latecomers catch up through gains in capital and technology. This is presumed to give a test of absolute convergence:

$$g = \alpha_0 y_0 + \dots$$

The test for absolute convergence is by the (negative) sign on α_0.

However, it is reasonably recognized that other variables will affect endogenous growth, not least differences in saving rates as well as the host of economic and social factors that have been deployed in NGT. Consequently, the regression is augmented by any number and combination of variables – a hundred or more – from R&D expenditure to levels of democracy and trust, or indeed any variable that might be deemed to affect economic performance. This gives rise to what are termed Barro-type regressions:

$$g = \alpha_0 y_0 + \alpha_1 X_1 + \alpha_2 X_2 + \alpha_3 X_3 + \ldots.$$

Now there can be a test of *conditional* convergence depending on the sign of α_0 – correcting the test for convergence for differences in other variables X_i. In addition, each of the variables X_i can be tested for significance in promoting (endogenous) growth depending on the sign of α_i.

There are, however, a whole series of problems with this testing and esti-mation. First, suppose in testing either absolute or conditional convergence that the coefficient α_0 does indeed turn out to be negative. Is this indicative of convergence? Not necessarily, as can be seen by assuming for the sake of argument that (the processes underlying) growth rates are equally but ran-domly distributed across countries from one period to the next. Now suppose, by chance, that one country has a high (low) rate of growth in one period. Then, on average, it will tend to have a lower (higher) rate of growth in the following period, automatically tending towards generating an inverse rela-tionship between low and high growth rates in successive periods. In other words, as should be recognised in such circumstances by reference to what is known as Galton's regression to the mean, there is some bias within use of Barro-type regressions towards supporting the hypothesis of convergence even where growth rates are randomly distributed.

Second, there is the whole question of how well the overall model is being tested. It is scarcely credible that the hundred or more conditional variables are independent of one another and in their effects on growth. So a full model of interactions ought to be laid out and its empirical implications tested (as for wages and profits over the cycle for OGT). As already observed, such a model is mathematically intractable, and the simple ad hoc device of adding vari-ables to the regression has been used in the absence of any rationale other than to test for them. To put it bluntly, once Barro-type regressions are in use, it is far from clear how they depend upon theory at all. At a deeper analytical level, growth as a process of development involving complex interactions between the factors attached to economic and social transformation are being flattened and separated out to satisfy the needs of the regression.

Third, of importance in use of panel data is the issue of whether compar-isons of SSBG paths are being made across countries or comparisons are of adjustments to those paths. In other words, care needs to be taken in distin-guishing movements along different steady states and movements towards those paths, between equilibria and dynamics. Barro-type regressions do not do so. Figure 2 (p. 212) illustrates the point particularly well. The first SSBG has lower rate of growth than the second. But, in this case, the initial adjust-ments to them are entirely misleading, giving the impression that the second path – where growth adjustment is down and flattish – is for a lower growth

Figure 2.

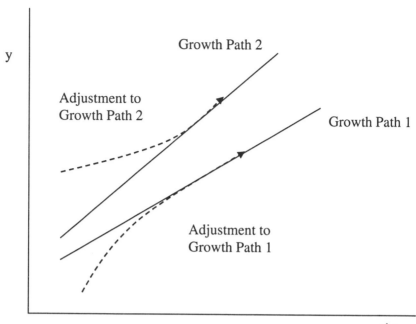

path than for the first, in which the adjustment is upwards and steep. With the arrowed lines indicating adjustment to the unobserved respective SSBG paths for two different countries, it will appear as if there is convergence. But, perversely, the unobserved long-run paths themselves diverge from one another, although adjustment to them seems to indicate otherwise.

Last is the problem of what is known as the stability of the regression itself. With so many (potential) variables, X_i, from which to choose, there are many different regressions that could be run depending upon which of the X_i are included and which excluded. However, the values on the coefficients α_i will change with the portfolio of variables used, not only in absolute magnitude but also in sign. It might be thought that a way round this could be to choose the 'best' regression by some statistical criteria. However, once again assuming for sake of argument that growth rates are randomly distributed, then there is bound to be some regression that is best and a set of coefficients significant for growth. An apparently ingenious, but flawed and indicative, way round this difficulty has been proposed by Barro's collaborator, Sala-i-Martin.[8] He suggests running millions of regressions on different batches of variables, and selecting variables as significant for endogenous growth if they appear as such statistically more often than others. As before, this is bound to yield results even if growth is randomly distributed because of random correlations arising out of random variation. It does, however, reflect the mindless application of statistical techniques in place of analysis, explanation and more rounded consideration of the empirical evidence. In short, Barro-type regressions, from an explanatory point of view, might be considered to the equivalent of the graph drawing of an earlier era, brought up to date by desk or laptop computers.

4. The broader context

In a nutshell, NGT shares some features with OGT: its vulnerability to the Cambridge Critique; the lack of realism in being organized around SSBG; its lack of sound statistical foundations; and its universal use despite these devastating weaknesses. Where NGT − not surprisingly − differs from OGT is in its endogenizing what OGT takes as exogenous, drawing upon those economic and social factors that arise as cause and/or consequence of growth and development. It also shifts from a notion of the economy based on a perfectly working market to one more or less riddled with market imperfections, and it raises micro-insights to macro-conclusions. Whatever the considerable weaknesses of OGT, its goals were quite limited.

Crudely, this shift in approach to growth and development does reflect a changing political and ideological climate. From the mid-1980s, the threat of the Soviet system as an alternative source of support for development was already on the wane. By the 1990s, it had collapsed as an alternative model. Also during the 1980s, the modernization approach to development had given way to the neoliberal Washington consensus, with its emphasis on market forces and a minimal role for the state. But from the mid-1980s onwards, opposition to the Washington consensus mounted, leading to a crisis of legitimacy around the IMF and the World Bank by the mid-1990s.

In short, at its birth and subsequently, NGT has prospered in an intellectual and policy environment seeking both to explain differences in economic performance between developed and developing countries (and the success of the east Asian NICs) and to recognize the virtues if not the infallibility of the market. In these respects, NGT has also conformed and contributed to more general developments within and around mainstream economics. For, over the past two decades, the new information-theoretic approach and the corresponding new microfoundations of macroeconomics have prospered. These emphasize the role of market imperfections, and the responses to them, in analysing and formulating economic policy. New growth theory is an exemplary illustration of this, alongside the emergence of other 'new' fields such as the new economic geography, the new financial economics and the new development economics.

But more, and possibly of more importance, than this is involved. For the new emphasis upon market imperfections, in part a reaction against neo-liberal ideology and the extreme monetarism of the new classical economics, has had profound implications for the relationship between economics and the other social sciences, what has been termed economic(s) imperialism. Over the past century, economics has sought, with greater or lesser success and energy, to extend its methods to the other social sciences. More recently, the most prominent approach has been that most closely associated with Gary Becker, with phenomena such as education and skills, crime, the house-hold and even addiction being treated as if the outcome of rational (utility-maximizing) behaviour by individuals, albeit in what are often non-market contexts. By contrast, the new micro-foundations treat the economy as subject to imperfections to which non-market responses are a rational, if not necessar-ily efficient, response. In this light, institutions, norms and customs are seen as the path dependent, collective response to market imperfections. As a result, institutions etc, are neither taken as exogenous nor reduced to an as if market approach characteristic of earlier versions of economics imperialism. On this basis, old forms of economics imperialism have been reinvigorated and new ones have emerged with the new political economy, the new institutional eco-nomics, the new economic sociology, and attention to new topics such as social capital, governance, ethnicity and democratization.

Within the World Bank and, later and lesser, the IMF, these developments have been marked by the shift from the Washington to the post-Washington consensus. The impact has been uneven in timing and extent across discus-sion of the various policy issues. Whilst, for example, it has been extremely rapid and prominent for social capital, NGT has not figured particularly prominently. Nonetheless, it does appear on one of the few papers to address the *theoretical* underpinnings of the poverty reduction strategy programmes (PRSPs) by Devarajan et al.[9] This remarkable document seeks to address poverty alleviation through the short-run Financial Programming framework of the IMF. It does so by assuming there is full employment at all times and that there is a single labour market! Leaving aside the total lack of realism for developing countries, the perverse effect is more or less to assume away the object of enquiry. For the poor in developing countries are, especially in rural areas, either the unemployed or those in employment at extremely low wages. For full employment and a single labour market, everyone is on the same income with all poor or all rich (except for dependants and those with other sources of income).

The previous paragraph is tangential to NGT except that, within the paper cited, it sets the short-run perspective through which endogenous growth can impact on long-run results. The results of Barro-type regressions are used to draw conclusions about the impact of shifts in government expenditure on the growth rate, so that these can then trickle down to the poor through the short-run segment of the model. The shaky grounds on which such calculations are made has already been discussed, yet, policy outcomes are nevertheless determined in this way across each and every economic and social measure.

But this use of NGT reflects a more general feature of the policies adopted by the IMF and the World Bank, their limited attention to the relationship between the short and long runs, and how they do or do not interact to give rise to development. This issue is explored in detail in Fine and Hailu,[10] in which it is shown that the standard theoretical rationale for stabilization and structural adjustment, once combined across short and long runs, leads either to zero growth or chronic instability. This is hardly conducive to development even on the limited SSBG basis on which it has been defined.

But why should development economics have so mechanically addressed the relationship between poverty and growth, with policy itself ranging over so many economic and social measures? An interesting answer is suggested by one of the leading pioneers of the new political economy who had begun to have grave doubts about how far neoclassical economics could be applied beyond the market. For McKenzie,[11] the rise of the axiomatic and predictive method at the expense of others is a consequence of the rise of the state and the corresponding need for a belief in the power to manipulate behavioural outcomes:

> Because control has become more specific, the need for more predictive theories has grown, and ever more specific (and debatable) arguments have been introduced into the individual's utility function. The demands for social policy, in other words, have required the scientific community of economists to accept more specific, but less realistic, descriptions of behavior.[12]

The NGT represents a perverse response to McKenzie's reservations. All manner of variables are brought within the scope of rational behaviour; corresponding policy measures allow for comprehensive economic and social engineering; and the uncertainties over behaviour and outcomes, over which McKenzie worries, are reduced to the error terms attached to statistical estimation. The rise of NGT, and the post-Washington consensus' reaction against neoliberalism, draws upon the idea that the impact of a very wide range of state interventions can be more or less precisely measured. There is little regard to country-specific details and interactions with other factors other than as the incidence and impact of market imperfections.

The weaknesses of NGT that have been exposed here point towards alternatives that can only be briefly outlined. In broad terms, they derive from two major deficiencies that need to be rectified. One is a belief in the theory vastly out of proportion to its actual reach. It is unrealistic to try to find a general theory of growth applicable across all times and places, for the differences between countries and the determinants of growth (and development) are too varied in their elements and in how they combine with one another to admit such a theory.

The second deficiency is in method. NGT, like OGT in that it at least allows for factors lying outside its analytical embrace, is purely mechanical and deterministic (subject to stochastic variation). It seeks correlations between sets of variables that necessarily set in stone the nature of both growth and development (again subject to the variations arising out of given initial conditions and path dependence). But growth and development have a habit of revolting against such imposed perspectives, and this is hardly surprising. For growth and development depend upon relations (such as those attached to classes and their underlying economic, political and ideological interests), structures (between rural and urban and finance and industry) and processes (industrialization, modernization, urbanization and proletarianization) that are neither deterministic nor reducible to a framework based on SSBG. This is not to suggest that nothing is to be learned from the evidence, only that comparative experience needs to be wedded to close, even prior, attention to local specifics.

Notes

1 See Rostow 1960.
2 See Rostow 1957.
3 McCloskey 1971.
4 Samuelson 1960, p. 582.
5 See Romer 1986 and Lucas 1988.
6 See Arrow 2000.
7 Solow 1992.
8 Sala-i-Martin 1997.
9 Devarajan et al. 2000.
10 Fine and Hailu 2003.
11 McKenzie 1978, p. 640.
12 McKenzie 1978, pp. 640–1.

References and Select Reading

For outline of old growth theory, see Sen 1970, especially his introduction. For an excellent overview of new growth theory, from within its own perspective, see Aghion and Howitt 1998, with the chapter summaries being particularly helpful. A more critical and circumspect assessment is provided in Fine 2000. Kenny and Williams 2001 carefully discusses what has been contributed to the understanding of growth and development. See also Pio 1994. For entertaining and informative accounts in the context of history of economic thought, see Kurz 1997 and Nelson 1997.

Aghion, P and P Howitt, 1998, *Endogenous Growth Theory*, Cambridge, Mass., MIT Press.

Arrow, K, 2000 'Increasing Returns: Histographic Issues and Path Dependence', *European Journal of History of Economic Thought*, vol. 7, no. 2, pp. 171–80.

Barro, R and X Sala-i-Martin, 1995, *Economic Growth*, New York, McGraw-Hill.

Devarajan, S, W Easterly, H Fofack, D Go, A Izquierdo, C Petersen, L Pizzati, C Scott, and L Serven, 2000, 'A Macroeconomic Framework for Poverty Reduction Strategy Papers', http://www.worldbank.org/research/growth/pdfiles/devarajan%20etal.pdf.

Fine, B, 2000, 'Endogenous Growth Theory: A Critical Assessment', *Cambridge Journal of Economics*, vol. 24, no. 2, pp. 245–65.

Fine, B and D Hailu, 2003, 'Convergence and Consensus: The Political Economy of Stabilisation, Poverty and Growth', mimeo.

Kenny, C and D Williams, 2001, 'What Do We Know about Economic Growth? Or, Why Don't We Know Very Much?', *World Development*, vol. 29, no. 1, pp. 1–22.

Kurz, H, 1997, 'What Could the "New" Growth Theory Teach Smith or Ricardo?', *Economic Issues*, vol. 2, part 2, pp. 1–20.

Lucas, R, 1988, 'On the Mechanics of Economic Development', *Journal of Monetary Economics*, vol. 22, no. 1, pp. 3–42.

McCloskey, D, 1971, ed., *Essays in a Mature Economy, Britain after 1840*, London, Methuen.

McKenzie, R, 1978, 'On the Methodological Boundaries of Economic Analysis', *Journal of Economic Issues*, vol. xii, no 3, pp. 627–45.

Nelson, R, 1997, 'How New is New Growth Theory?', *Challenge*, Sept/Oct, pp. 29–58.

Pio, A, 1994, 'New Growth Theory and Old Development Problems: How Recent Developments in Endogenous Growth Apply to Developing Countries', *Development Policy Review*, vol. 12, no. 3, pp. 277–300.

Romer, P, 1986, 'Increasing Returns and Long-Run Growth', *Journal of Political Economy*, vol. 94, no. 5, pp. 1002–37.

Rostow, W, 1957, 'The Interrelation of Theory and Economic History', *Journal of Economic History*, vol. xvii, no. 4, pp. 509–23.

Rostow, W, 1960, *The Stages of Economic Growth: A Non-Communist Manifesto*, Cambridge, Cambridge University Press, third revised edition, 1990.

Sala-i-Martin, X, 1997, 'I Just Ran Four Million Regressions', mimeo.

Sen, A, ed, 1970, *Growth Economics*, Harmondsworth, Penguin.

Solow, R, 1992, *Siena Lectures on Endogenous Growth Theory*, Siena, University of Siena.

10

STRUCTURAL CHANGE AND ECONOMIC DEVELOPMENT: ON THE RELATIVE ROLES OF EFFECTIVE DEMAND AND THE PRICE MECHANISM IN A 'DUAL' ECONOMY*

Amit Bhaduri

1. Structural Change and Development: some stylized facts

One of the most robust facts in development economics, exhibited by cross-section data among countries as well as time series data of individual countries, is an inverse relationship between per capita GDP and the percentage of labour force engaged in agriculture. Richer countries have a smaller percentage of their labour force in agriculture, and in the primary sector.[1] This is reinforced by time series data; as countries become richer over time, the relative importance of the primary sector declines in terms of both its percentage contribution to GDP and the proportion of labour force employed. The numbers are indeed strikingly systematic in this respect: towards the end of the last century, in 1995, older industrialized countries like the UK and the USA had less than 3% of their total labour force engaged in agriculture, producing less than 2% of the GDP. Japan, which industrialized more recently, had less than 6% of the labour force, while (South) Korea still had 12.5% employed in agriculture, contributing 2% and 6% respectively to GDP. Brazil had nearly 20% of its workforce in agriculture, contributing 9% of the GDP, while Mexico had 24% in agricultural employment, contributing only 5% of the GDP. At the other end of the spectrum, poorer countries like China, India or

* Research support from the 'Globalisation and Marginalisation' programme of the Research Council of Norway (NFR) is gratefully acknowledged.

Bangladesh, all had more than half of their labour force engaged in agriculture (China 54%, India 67% and Bangladesh 63%), while agriculture's contribution to GDP was 20% in China, 28% in India and 25% in Bangladesh.[2] Although these numbers are merely illustrative (and there are a few statistical 'outliers'), they reveal the pattern of structural changes that typically accompany economic development. Three propositions roughly sum up that pattern:

1. The relative importance of the agricultural (and the primary) sector declines in terms of both the percentage of labour force employed there, and its percentage contribution to GDP, as per capita GDP increases in the course of economic development.[3]
2. However, the percentage of labour engaged in agriculture is usually considerably higher than the percentage contribution made by the agricultural sector to the GDP, implying that labour productivity is lower in agriculture compared to the national average. This holds for both the developed and the developing countries. Thus, from the above figures, we may calculate that, in relation to their respective national averages, the labour productivity in agriculture was about 67% in the UK and in the USA, 33% in Japan, 48% in South Korea, 45% in Brazil, 21% in Mexico, 35% in China, 42% in India and 40% in Bangladesh.[4]
3. Available data (not presented here) also tend to show that intersectoral differences in labour productivity are in the ratio of 1 to 2.5 for the developed economies, i.e. labour productivity in industry or in the service sector is about 2.5 times higher than that in agriculture. However, in developing countries, the same ratio tends to be much greater, perhaps as high as 8 to 10 times.[5]

The main thrust of these propositions, based on stylized facts, is to emphasize the pressure typically put on developing countries to industrialize at a rapid pace. Not only is agriculture marked by a considerably lower labour productivity than the national average, but the intersectoral productivity gap also tends to be especially large in developing countries. Therefore, transferring labour from the agricultural to the non-agricultural sectors entails large gains in overall labour productivity and in per capita income, propelling the process of economic development through structural change.[6] Nevertheless, this is merely an arithmetical truism. The real economic issues are to identify the nature of constraints and the processes that operate on the demand and on the supply side of a developing economy to regulate the process by which these structural changes occur. To this central problem we now turn.

2. Agriculture–Industry Interaction: Price and Quantity Adjustment in a Dual Economy

It has been an old idea in the history of economic thought to link the '*social division* of labour', that is to say the extent of diversification of the economy into different branches of activity with agriculture generating the *surplus* needed to support the consumption by workers in the non-agricultural activities. This link was seen as early as in the seventeenth century by Sir William Petty,[7] and became a central tenet in later Physiocratic writings. François Quesnay's *Tableau Economique* exhibited how agricultural surplus supports through intersectoral exchanges other non-agricultural activities.[8] From the point of view of later theoretical developments in this area, at least two contributions of the Physiocrats seem to be of lasting value. First, they defined agricultural surplus as the 'gross produce' of agriculture *minus* 'productive consumption' by the farmers. 'Productive consumption' consists of agricultural raw materials required in its own production, and the subsistence, self-consumption by the farmers. The really fruitful Physiocratic idea was not the identification of agricultural surplus with rent and land revenue, which might have been valid in their particular socio-economic context, but their view that, rather the total agricultural product, only the surplus – a predetermined quantity, or an exogenous variable obtained by deducting the self-consumption of the peasants from agricultural value-added – enters the process of intersectoral exchange to support the consumption by workers and artisans engaged in the non-agricultural sectors for diversifying the economy.

Second, the Physiocratic notion of agricultural surplus as exogenous was justified insofar as both agricultural output and the self-consumption by the farmers are considered as given, the latter coinciding with subsistence consumption. In principle, however, this notion could be used for a more flexible formulation. Not only might higher agricultural price provide stronger incentive to increase agricultural output in the manner taught usually by textbooks (although empirical evidence on this point is ambiguous in developing countries) but more interestingly the availability of industrial goods, as well as their relative price in terms of agricultural goods, might also influence the amount the farmers decide to retain for self-consumption. And when these considerations are deemed to be important, the level of agricultural surplus becomes an endogenous variable, influenced by other factors within the system, for example the level of availability of industrially-produced consumer goods and their relative price in terms of agricultural goods.[9]

As reconstruction and decolonization became part of the international agenda after the Second World War, many of the Physiocratic and classical economists' concerns with economic development through structural change began receiving greater attention. Lewis' seminal paper on the dual economy[10] – a concept used earlier by Boeke[11] – was meant to capture the economic process through which the traditional, largely subsistence sector of a developing economy gets modernized. Lewis distinguished the 'modern' from the 'traditional' sector on the basis of the different methods by which production is organized in them. This corresponds only roughly to the division between agriculture as the traditional, and industry as the modern, sector of a 'dual' economy; but it echoes an old Physiocratic idea insofar as the Physiocrats were the first to recognize that production in agriculture is organized differently from that in industry, requiring an analytical division between the two sectors.[12]

Both in Lewis' own model, and in a whole series of models of the 'dual' economy that it subsequently inspired,[13] a pivotal role is played by the assumption that the *supply* of agricultural surplus is exogenously given, while the real wage rate in terms of agricultural goods (e.g. 'food') for which labour supply is unlimited remains constant. The consequence of this assumption is to determine the level of industrial employment sustainable from the supply side simply as the ratio of agricultural surplus divided by the real wage rate. Any attempt to raise the level of industrial employment beyond that point would be thwarted, according to Lewis and his followers, by the price mechanism, namely the intersectoral terms of trade, or the price of industrial goods in terms of agricultural goods, because a faster pace of industrialization would raise further the demand for 'food' and therefore the price of agricultural goods. Real wages in terms of food, which is assumed to be constant, can remain constant only if the money wage rate also rises in the same proportion as the price of food. With industrial prices unaffected, this increase in money wages would squeeze profit in industry, while the terms of trade would move against industry. Using a version of 'Say's Law', in the form of the pre-Keynesian assumption that industrial profit as saving determines industrial investment, Lewis argued that the squeeze on industrial profit would slow down industrial investment and growth, until industrial employment returns to the level sustainable by the exogenously given agricultural surplus and the real wage rate.[14]

Using this Lewis-type dual economy framework as the benchmark, one can see how the argument could be developed further in two almost diametrically opposite directions. On the one hand, all the special structuralist assumptions of the dual economy model could be removed to make it look like the textbook competitive market economy. In that case, higher industrial growth, creating greater demand for 'food', would raise the relative price of agricultural goods, only to create stronger incentives to supply more agricultural surplus. With agricultural surplus no longer exogenously given, higher industrial growth through the working of the price incentives could become feasible. Moreover, the higher price of agricultural goods at any given rate of money wage would imply lower real wage. Thus, if labour supply is unlimited at a given money, rather than real wage, rate, a higher level of industrial employment could be sustained through agricultural price rise for any given amount of agricultural surplus. Thus, both through the price incentive to agricultural suppliers, and through a reduction in the real wage rate, the structural constraints on industrial growth in the economy may be relaxed considerably. It would not be too much of an exaggeration to claim that this sort of reasoning often underlies the emphasis that the 'Washington Consensus' of the IMF and the World Bank placed on 'getting prices right', particularly for the agricultural sector, and making the labour market 'flexible'.

The main problem with this view is that it makes the developing economy look almost like the perfectly competitive market economy of the text books. However, this is achieved only by assumptions, ignoring the peculiar structural characteristics that the dual economy model was meant to highlight. As a matter of fact, one could enrich the model by proceeding in the opposite direction, through incorporating additional, relevant structural features. Perhaps the most important feature, originally due to Kelecki,[15] is to recognize that in agriculture, isolated peasants and farmers carry out production. Their supplies arrive in the market after harvest, prior to price formation. Given the level of supply, prices are formed subsequently in relation to the state of demand. In this sense, agricultural prices tend to be flexible in response to variations in demand, and can be claimed to be largely demand-determined. This flexibility of agricultural prices has been a well-documented fact in both developing and developed countries. For instance, 'with the exception of 1958, US wholesale prices of domestically produced food crops fell (absolutely) in every recession year since the World War II'.[16]

In contrast to agricultural prices, industrial prices tend to be markedly less flexible in response to variations in demand. This is because, unlike in the case of agriculture, industrial prices are usually set prior to sales, while variations in demand are absorbed mostly through inventory changes. Since industrial prices are set prior to sales, i.e. without prior accurate knowledge of the state of demand, the standard procedure is to cover unit variable cost with some (usually fixed percentage) mark-up on that cost to allow for profit net of depreciation, interest payment on loans etc. In this sense, industrial prices tend to be largely *cost-determined*, on the assumption that the state of demand would be 'normal', while deviations from this normal state are usually met through inventory rather than price change in the short run.

This distinction between relatively flexible, demand-determined agricultural price, and relatively inflexible, cost-determined industrial price, when incorporated as a further structural feature of the dual economy model, has important economic consequences. Perhaps the most important consequence is the possibility of 'stagflation' in a dual economic structure.[17] With agricultural surplus assumed to be exogenously given, and a constant (subsistence) real wage rate in terms of 'food' as postulated in Lewis' original model, industrial growth at a pace faster than that sustainable by the available supply of agricultural surplus would lead to higher demand for 'food', and therefore higher demand-determined agricultural price, as had been argued by Lewis. The higher price of 'food' would raise the *money* wage rate proportionately in industry to keep the subsistence real wage rate constant. However, unlike the 'profit squeeze' in industry postulated in the Lewis model, the higher money wage will be transmitted to higher cost-determined industrial price. If mark-up is a fixed percentage on unit variable cost, assumed to be equal to wage cost per unit of output in a closed economy, the percentage rise in industrial price (as well as in agricultural price) will be equal to the rise in the money wage rate. Thus, the consequence would *not* be a squeeze on industrial profit, as Lewis had argued in the context of rising food prices, because industrial profits would be maintained by rising industrial price at that fixed mark-up, making the terms of trade between industrial and agricultural price inflexible in contrast to the Lewis model. The consequence would be stagflationary price rise in both sectors at a rate equal to the rise in the money wage rate.

A further interesting variation on this theme of stagflation in a dual economy occurs by combining it with another important fact of economic life, namely Engel's Law. This postulates that the demand for food tends to be inelastic with respect of variation in income. It can be argued plausibly that a rise in the price of food would typically result in a higher proportion of the money wage of the industrial worker being spent on food if the increase in money wage is proportionally less than that in food price. This would reduce the proportion of money wage left for spending on industrial goods. Consequently, higher food price could reduce overall effective demand for industrial goods, unless it is compensated by a correspondingly higher level of expenditure by the farmers from the higher income they earn from the higher price of food.[18]

The empirically-robust assumption that industrial prices tend to be highly sensitive to cost but not to demand also casts doubt on the efficacy of the terms of trade mechanism in maintaining balance between expansion in both the agricultural and industrial sectors. As we already saw, it can result in almost completely inflexible terms of trade and stagflation in a dual economy. Even more significantly, this opens the way for output rather than price adjustment in the industrial sector in response to excess demand, when that sector is operating under excess capacity. Note, however, that the existence of excess capacity in industry is usually assumed, and this tends to reinforce the rationale for the rule of mark-up pricing widely observed in industry.[19] In this context it becomes especially important to examine how the dual economy operates, when demand-determined price adjusts in the agricultural sector, but quantity adjusts in the industrial sector with excess capacity and cost-determined mark-up pricing. This indeed was the route pursued particularly by Kaldor to bring to the forefront Keynesian considerations for revising our understanding of the role of demand in a dual economy framework.[20]

Kaldor suggested that agricultural surplus plays a critical role in the process of industrialization, not so much by providing the supply of essential wage goods emphasized by Lewis and Kalecki, but by creating demand for industrial goods.[21] A larger volume of agricultural surplus entails a larger market for industry, bringing into operation the (trade) multiplier mechanism for the industrial sector. Thus, by treating agricultural surplus as largely autonomous, its role can be compared analytically to that of exogenous investment or export in the standard Keynesian model of income determination.

However, while this argument is suggestive, it has a serious lacuna.[22] Agricultural surplus creates demand for industrial goods by first being converted into monetary purchasing power. Thus, there is the problem of realizing monetary income from agricultural surplus. In a closed economy without government, it is industry which provides this market for the conversion through the industrial wage bill spent on 'food'. As a result, a greater degree of interdependence from the demand side exists between agriculture and industry in a closed economy than Kaldor's argument suggests. Note that this interdependence arises because all transactions have to be made in terms of money, and not through barter, i.e. as a result of money's being used as a universal medium of exchange.

The importance of this argument relating to monetary exchange becomes all the more apparent if we consider the role of the government in maintaining a minimum 'support price' for agricultural products. Since any amount of agricultural surplus can be sold at that price, there is no problem of realization of that surplus into monetary purchasing power. However, this resolves the problem of realization of surplus only insofar as the agricultural sector is concerned. Viewed from the perspective of industry, the problem of demand still remains unresolved. Unless this monetary purchasing power of agriculture is spent on industrial goods, industry would suffer from insufficient demand, although there is no problem of the realization of agricultural surplus. That this problem can be serious has become clear, for instance, by recent experiences in post-Green Revolution India. In 2001, India had a stock of some 60 million tonnes of foodgrains in government godowns, while

325 million people lived below the 'poverty line', and some 50 million people were on the brink of starvation.

The Indian experience in recent years has yielded a shameful paradox, in that 'too much' food is procured through the support price system, while too many people remain on the brink of starvation.[23] While this simply means that the poor have too little purchasing power, it assumes further significance in the context of a closed, dual economy model of agriculture–industry interaction. It shows why the realization of agricultural surplus into monetary purchasing power through government intervention is merely one facet of the more complex problem of managing effective demand in a sectorally-interdependent monetary economy. Because, unless this purchasing power is spent on domestic industrial goods, industry might suffer from insufficient demand and excess capacity, while the excess purchasing power is held by the agricultural sector in monetary assets. This may raise (agricultural) households' savings, without matching investment demand. In short, it is an illustration of the Keynesian 'paradox of thrift' in a dual economy: the use of money as a 'store of value' by the farmers leads to the failure of Say's law in a monetary economy.

Viewed from the opposite perspective, in the dual economy it is the slow pace of expansion of the industrial sector which can be said to result in insufficient demand for agricultural goods or for 'food', through insufficient expansion of the industrial wage bill. While this provides the rationale of a support price system for agricultural goods, it could obversely be argued that a faster pace of expansion of the industrial sector (e.g. through public investment in infrastructure etc.) would have tended to alleviate the same problem. Thus, assuming the 'fiscal discipline' of a given government budget, the problem of the *composition* of public expenditure between the support price system for agricultural goods on the one hand, and the need for increased public investment for stimulating the demand for agricultural goods on the other, remains an important issue for the management of demand.

Outside the simplest dual economy model, at least two additional complications must be reckoned with in this context of managing demand. First, the incidence of (direct and indirect) tax tends to vary between the incomes of the two sectors; typically, the tax rate turns out to be higher for industry than for agriculture. Consequently, the support price system for agriculture tends to place a greater stain on the public finance position insofar as, through this policy, less money usually returns to the government as tax revenue, compared to an equivalent amount spent on industry to raise its capacity utilization. Second, in an open economy, with trade in goods and services largely liberalized, serious administrative and political problems might arise concerning the maintenance of the agricultural support price at a level different from the international price.[24] Moreover, there is a further problem, in that the monetized purchasing power of agricultural surplus through the support price policy may largely leak out into imported goods without creating the necessary demand for domestic goods. Expansion through public investment might also involve a similar problem, especially because demand may leak out through the import of capital goods. It is worth noting that the less developed the industrial sector of a country is, the more generally pressing is the problem of managing demand due to import leakage. An oft-presented counter argument is that agricultural surplus may be exported to alleviate simultaneously the problem of effective demand through the 'foreign trade multiplier' and the foreign exchange constraint. The plausibility of this argument depends on whether agricultural goods can be sold at all in the international market, and in particular without affecting too adversely the export price (i.e. the 'small country' assumption). Indeed, the very rationale for managing demand at home arises from the fact that most developing countries capable of exporting mostly primary agriculture-based products have grounds for 'export pessimism'.[25]

3. The Terms of Trade as Policy Instrument

So far, we have shown that the dual economy framework emphasizes how excess demand, arising from an imbalance between the different rates of expansion of 'traditional' agriculture and 'modern' industry, might typically lead to price adjustment in agriculture, but to quantity adjustment in industry. Although simple, this is a particularly useful framework of analysis insofar as several controversial policy issues in development economics hinge largely on whether excess demand affects mostly quantity, as is postulated in Keynesian economics, or price, as presumed in neoclassical economics. Consequently, the importance assigned to the 'terms of trade', i.e. the relative price of industrial goods in terms of agricultural goods, could be very different depending on how price and quantity adjustment are woven into the analysis. As we already saw, the Lewis-type analysis relies on price adjustment through *flexible* terms of trade to calibrate intersectoral imbalances in demand or supply. By contrast, the 'stagflation' phenomenon emphasized first by Kalecki, or the role of agricultural surplus in generating effective demand for industrial goods emphasised by Kaldor, have in common the idea of a 'structurally' determined terms of trade, which is relatively *inflexible* to the pressures of excess demand or supply. Insofar as the terms of trade shows any secular tendency to move, in this framework it is influenced mostly by structural factors like different rates of labour productivity growth in industry and griculture, segmentation of the labour market along the sectors, and other factors that are not directly related to excess demand.

However, one could consider the same problem from the opposite angle insofar as the terms of trade might be considered not as an endogenous but as an exogenous variable. It could be treated as an instrument of policy, i.e. an exogenous policy parameter (especially in the context of planning), rather than an endogenous variable determined within the model.[26] This approach to the terms of trade has played a significantly important role in the past, for example in the Soviet Industrialization Debate of the 1920s.

Following the introduction of the New Economic Policy in the spring of 1921, Preobrazhensky[27] criticized it on the ground that it opened the Soviet economy to the risk of a relapse into a dominant private economy. The new state sector, he felt, would not be able to generate sufficient investible surplus to finance its growth at a decisively faster pace than the private sector. When 'taxing' a private sector consisting mostly of agriculture, Preobrazhensky suggested that the terms of trade should be made so unfavourable to agriculture that farmers would be forced to exchange an 'unequally' large amount of agricultural goods for a few essential industrial consumption items like salt, fuel or cloth. Thus, the amount of agricultural surplus made available for industrialization could be increased by changing the terms of trade *against* agriculture. This strategy of extracting agricultural surplus forcibly through the price mechanism would have the additional advantage that relatively few resources would need to be devoted to the production of only those few essential consumption goods, while the growth of heavy, capital goods industries could proceed faster with more resources devoted to them.

This strategy of forcibly extracting agricultural surplus by turning the terms of trade against agriculture runs contrary to the normal role of the price mechanism, because it adversely affects the price incentive to the agricultural suppliers. At the same time, however, it might also increase the demand for essential industrial goods through the operation of Engel's Law on those particular industries.

The strategy of extracting agricultural surplus by deliberately turning the terms of trade against agriculture did not go unopposed in the Soviet Debate on industrialization of that period. Bukharin, in particular, opposed it on the ground that the peasants might simply withdraw from such unfavourable exchange, if this policy were followed too rigorously. Instead, he advocated a more moderate policy of expanding light consumer goods industries, which would provide sufficient consumer goods as well as reasonable terms of trade in order that peasants could engage voluntarily in intersectoral exchange. Bukharin's strategy was also meant to strengthen the political alliance between the industrial workers and the peasants, while Preobrazhensky's policy would have put it under considerable strain.

It is now a matter for history that Soviet industrialization continued at a rapid pace while agriculture got collectivized, at least partly to overcome the problem of extracting agricultural surplus. In the process, an almost laboratory experiment of how the interaction between industry and agriculture may go wrong due to forced industrialization, took place. It is best summed up in the words of an experienced journalist-traveller to the Soviet Union in the 1950s:

Hundreds of thousands of peasants partake steadily in what is a kind of passive revolt against the collective system. They concentrate on their private plots, at the expense of the work of the collective as a whole, sabotage procedures, and are careless of procedures and state property. They resent the rigidity of the system, taxes, and the prices they get for obligatory delivery quotas, and hence produce just enough to support themselves. Some say that they are worse off than their grandfathers who were serfs. Above all, they lack incentive. The peasant does not produce more, because even if he gets a substantial cash income as many do, he has no 'spending power'. Nothing worth buying is in the shops. This brings up one of the dramatic paradoxes of the Soviet economy. The government must, in order to improve the standard of living of the country as a whole get more out of the farmer, but at the same time is unwilling or unable to release more consumer goods to the farmer in order to stimulate him to more production[28]

If the Soviet experience with forced industrialization highlighted the damaging consequences of treating agriculture merely as a passive sector that would adjust easily to the needs of an unwarrantedly high rate of industrial growth, the post-Green Revolution experience in some developing countries like India warns, albeit less dramatically, against committing an error of the opposite type. This results in an overemphasis on generating surplus in agriculture without creating adequate conditions for the expansion of domestic industries at a sufficiently rapid pace to absorb that surplus. The Soviet example highlights the mistake of trying to extract agricultural surplus, without engaging the peasants voluntarily in intersectoral exchange through reasonable terms of trade, and availability of industrial consumers' goods. By not providing adequate incentives, it failed to generate a sufficiently high volume of agricultural surplus to cope with the rising demand from industry. In this sense it highlights the basic concern of the Lewis-type model, in which the supply of an adequate level of agricultural surplus plays the central role.

Consequently forcible extraction, rather than voluntary generation of agricultural surplus, became an unfortunate feature of Soviet planning and collectivized agriculture.

By contrast, rapid growth in agricultural production was promoted by the technology of the Green Revolution, while the minimum support price system provided the necessary price incentive to agricultural producers. In some cases, agricultural surplus grew more rapidly than agricultural production, because the new technology was concentrated mostly in selected regions (in particular those with good access to water), and in the hands of relatively well-off, surplus farmers. In a situation of balanced intersectoral 'trade', the rapidly growing volume of agricultural surplus would have translated into correspondingly rapid growth in the demand for industrial goods. In turn, this would have also led to a rapid expansion in industrial production by relaxing the demand-constraint. In contrast to Lewis, this was the type of scenario that was emphasized by Kaldor. It rightly underscores the equally important aspect of agricultural surplus as a generator of *demand* for industrial goods, in addition to its role as a supplier of 'food' to the industrial workers. Nevertheless, when industry does not expand at a sufficient pace to absorb the growing agricultural surplus, the support price system has to be relied on to provide price incentive for farmers, and to convert their surplus into monetary income. And yet, as observed in the Indian case, this incentive system for agriculture alone may not be sufficient, insofar as it lacks a complimentary policy instrument to ensure that the monetary purchasing power created through the support price system is actually spent on domestic industrial goods. If the farmers tend to hold too high a proportion of their money income either as a 'store of value', or spend it on imported goods – unlike the scenario painted by Kaldor, and in stark contrast to the Soviet case, the economy would run into a persistent problem of apparent 'over-production' of surplus foodgrains. In a dual economy, the Keynesian 'paradox of thrift' might manifest itself as the 'paradox of poverty amidst plenty'. This is a scene of widespread under-nutrition, even starvation, coexisting with rising inventories of foodgrains in government storage, while industry languishes due to insufficient demand. Unfortunately, this is a paradox not altogether unknown in some developing countries.

Notes

1 'Primary' sector includes agriculture, mining, fishing and animal husbandry. We use the term 'primary' sector and 'agriculture' interchangeably, implicitly referring to countries where agriculture is the predominant form of activity in the primary sector.

2 International Labour Office (ILO, 1999) is the source of the employment data, while the World Bank (WB, 2000) is the source of the value-added data.

3 Strictly speaking, this statement applies to the time series data of individual countries, rather than to the international cross section data. However, this proposition is consistent with both cross section and time series data. Limitation of space forces us only to mention this in passing, without going into the details of the historical time series of individual countries.

4 Let, Y=GDP, L=Labour force, $Y/_L = X$ = national average labour productivity and, X_a = labour productivity in the agricultural sector. Then, for example, in the case of Brazil, we have $X_a = (0.09Y/_{0.2L}) = 0.45X$ etc, as the basis of the calculations given in the text.

5 Bhaduri 1993, p. 173, table 6 A.2; based on 1980 data.

6 See Johnston 1970 for a survey.

7 Petty 1963.

8 See Meek 1962.

9 As we shall discuss later, this point is particularly relevant in understanding certain aspects of the Soviet experience with the agricultural sector.

10 Lewis 1954.

11 Boeke 1942.

12 Bharadwaj 1987.

13 e.g. Fei and Ranis 1964; Jorgenson 1961; Zarembka 1970; Dixit 1973.

14 A slight variation on this argument is to use the assumption of profit maximization in industry. With given real wage in terms of agricultural goods, we have in self-evident notations, by assumption (W/P_a) = constant. As the terms of trade (P_i/P_a) moves in favour of agriculture, i.e. (P_i/P_a) falls, the product wage in terms of industrial goods (W/P_i) has to rise to keep real wage (W/P_a) constant; because $(W/P_i) = (W/P_a) \times (P_a/P_i)$, a relation which is satisfied if (W/P_i) and (P_a/P_i) rise proportionately. The higher product wage in industry which equals under profit maximization the marginal product of labour in industry is attained by reducing the level of industrial employment and output.

15 Kelecki 1971.

16 Okun 1981, p. 136.

17 Kalecki 1976; Kaldor 1976.

18 Taylor 1983; Krishnaji 1992; Storm 1993. See in particular Krishnaji (1992, p. 105), who argued empirically that, 'other things remaining the same, rising cereal prices depress the demand for manufactures' in the context of the widespread poverty in India.

19 cf. Bhaduri and Falkinger 1990.

20 Kaldor 1967, 1978, 1989; also Taylor 1983.

21 So long as the terms of trade are relatively inflexible (under conditions discussed earlier), the demand for industrial goods in real terms is provided for any given level of agricultural surplus.

22 Bhaduri and Skarstein 2001.

23 That this is not merely a problem of 'food security', or maintaining a buffer stock of essential food, is clear for two reasons. First, with so many people near starvation, it is not apparent what 'food security" is supposed to mean, unless it is defined exclusively in terms of protecting the interest of only that section of the urban population which is covered by the public distribution system. Second, reported estimates suggest that

around 20% of the stock of procured foodgrains is lost every year through poor storage (a substantial quantity of which is said to be eaten by rats).

24 In a global system, developing countries face considerable international pressure to liberalize their agricultural markets. At the same time, however, the lower income and purchasing power of the average consumer in developing countries create political, even humanitarian, pressures at home to maintain lower food prices more in line with that lower, average income, while paying the farmers a 'politically acceptable' price. The support price system with subsidy on food emerges as a compromise.

25 Despite lower wages, lower land and labour productivity in many developing countries result in their unit cost of production in agriculture being higher than that in many developed countries.

26 Important price-like, macroeconomic variables – e.g. the interest rate, the exchange rate or the wage rate – are often treated as instruments for policy formulation. The terms of trade between agriculture and industry could also be thought of as one such macroeconomic policy instrument.

27 Preobrazhensky 1965.

28 Gunther 1958, p. 394.

References

Bhaduri, A and Falkinger, J, 1990, 'Optimal price adjustment under imperfect information', *European Economic Review*, 34 (4), pp. 941–52.

Bhaduri, A, 1993, 'Alternative development strategies and the rural sector' in A Singh and H Tabatabai, eds, *Economic Crisis and the Third World Agriculture*, Cambridge, Cambridge University Press, pp. 149–78.

Bhaduri, A and Skarstein, R, 2001, 'Effective demand and the terms of trade in a dual economy: a Kaldorian perspective', *Cambridge Journal of Economics* (forthcoming).

Bharadwaj, K, 1987, 'Analytics of agriculture–industry relation', *Economic and Political Weekly*, 17, pp. 19–21: AN15–AN20.

Boeke, JH, 1942, *Economies and Economic Policy in Dual Societies*, Haarlem, Tjeenk Willnik.

Dixit, A, 1973, 'Models of dual economies' in JA Mirrlees and NH Stern, eds, *Models of Economic Growth*, London, Macmillan, pp. 325–52.

Fei, JCH and Ranis, G, 1964, *Development of the Labour Surplus Economy*, Homewood Illinois, Richard D Irwin.

Gunther, J, 1958, *Inside Russia Today*, London, Hamish Hamilton.

International Labour Office (ILO), 1999, '1999 Key Indicators and the Labour Market CD-Rom', Geneva, ILO.

Johnston, DF, 1970, 'Agriculture and structural transformation in developing countries: a survey of research', *Journal of Economic Literature*, 8 (2), pp. 369–404.

Jorgenson, DW, 1961, 'The development of a dual economy', *Economic Journal*, 71 (2), pp. 309–34.

Kaldor, N, 1967, *Strategic Factors in Economic Development*, Ithaca, Cornell University Press.

——, 1976, 'Inflation and recession in the world economy', *Economic Journal*, 86 (4), pp. 703–14.

——, 1978, 'What is wrong with economic theory' in his *Further Essays on Economic Theory*, London, Duckworth, pp. 202–13.

——, 1989, 'Equilibrium theory and growth theory' in F Targetti and AP Thirlwall, eds, *The Essential Kaldor*, London, Duckworth, pp. 411–33.

Kalecki, M, 1971, 'Costs and Prices' in his *Selected Essays on the Dyunamics of the Capitalist Economy*, Cambridge, Cambridge University Press, pp. 43–61.

——, 1976, 'The problem of financing economic development in a mixed economy', in his *Essays on Developing Economies*, Hassocks, Harvester Press.

Krishnaji, N, 1992, 'The demand constraint: a note on the role of foodgrain prices and income inequality' in his *Pauperising Agriculture: Studies in Agrarian Change and Demographic Structure*, Bombay, Sameeska Trust.

Lewis, WA, 1954, 'Economic development with unlimited supplies of labour', *The Manchester School*, 22 (2), pp. 139–91.

Meek, RL, 1962, *The Economics of Physiocracy* (Essays and translations by Ronald Meek), London, George Allen and Unwin.

Okun, AM, 1981, *Prices and Quantities: A Macroeconomic Analysis*, Washington DC, Brookings Institution.

Petty, W, 1662, *A Treatise on Taxes and Contributions* in CH Hull, ed., *The Economic Writings of Sir William Petty*, Cambridge, Cambridge University Press, 1899; New York, revised Augustins M Kelly edition, 1963.

Preobrazhensky, E, 1965, *The New Economics*, London, Oxford University Press, (first published in Russian in 1926).

Storm, S, 1993, *Macroeconomic Considerations in the Choice of an Agricultural Policy*: a study into sectoral interdependence with reference to India, Hants, Avebury.

Taylor, L, 1983, *Structuralist Macroeconomics*, New York, Basic Books

World Bank, 2000, 'World Development Indicators, 2000 CD-Rom', Washington DC, World Bank.

Zarembka, P, 1970, 'Marketable surplus and growth in a dual economy', *Journal of Economic Theory*, 2(2), pp. 107–21.

11

AGRICULTURE AND DEVELOPMENT: THE DOMINANT ORTHODOXY AND AN ALTERNATIVE VIEW

Terence J Byres

1. Introduction

The title of this collection is 'Rethinking Development Economics'. Different people will interpret this in different ways. My interpretation is not to propose that there is some dramatic new way of approaching development economics, which might be held to be implicit in the notion of 'rethinking'. My purpose, rather, is to suggest that there is as alternative to the dominant orthodoxy, an alternative that has an established lineage, and that is powerful and illuminating.

My remit is to address the issue of 'Agriculture and Development', and consider something of what the editor has referred to as 'heterodox views' on this subject. To do this comprehensively, in the short compass allowed, is impossible. To simplify matters I will consider most closely the most recent strand in the dominant orthodoxy, that of the so-called 'new development economics' and, in opposition to this, I will deploy one variant of the heterodoxy: Marxist political economy.

Development Economics and Switching Hegemony: From Classical to Neoclassical Dominance

In development economics, in the first two decades after 1945, a modern variant of classical political economy was hegemonic. The two decisive texts were Rosenstein-Rodan's 'Problems of Industrialisation of Eastern and South-eastern Europe' (1943) and Arthur Lewis's 'Economic Development with Unlimited Supplies of Labour' (1954). Indeed, if one wished to date the birth of modern development economics one might do so with the publication of the former; while if one wanted to identify the beginnings of its remarkable growth one would locate them with the appearance of the latter. Both conceived of a 'developmentalist state' as essential.

Both were clearly in the tradition of classical political economy. Recall Lewis's opening paragraph: 'This essay is written in the classical tradition, making the classical assumption, and asking the classical question. The classics, from Smith to Marx, all assumed, or argued, that an unlimited supply of labour was available at subsistence wages'.[1] Neoclassical economics was, Lewis insisted, irrelevant for the analysis of underdeveloped economies. Rosenstein-Rodan, for his part, when he came to assess his views as one of the 'pioneers in development' some forty years after the publication of his celebrated article, entitled his paper, in continuing defiance of the relevance of neoclassical economics, 'Natura Facit Saltum: Analysis of the Disequilibrium Growth Process' (1984) – *Natura Non Facit Saltum* (Nature does not make a jump) being the motto that Marshall placed on the frontispiece of his *Principles*, the first polished statement of neoclassical economics.

Neither Rosenstein-Rodan nor Lewis was dismissive of neoclassical economics in any general sense. It would come back into its own when development had been secured.[2] Nor was either sympathetic to Marxism. Nevertheless, here was a profoundly non-neoclassical approach. The classical approach remained dominant probably until the end of the 1960s. By this time, however, the centre of gravity had already begun to move quite decisively from classical political economy to neoclassical economics, and this was as true in relation to agriculture as it was with respect to everything else.

For the purposes of this chapter, I will distinguish four distinct manifestations of the neoclassical paradigm in the postwar era with respect to 'development'. The exponents of each had distinctive and differing views on agriculture, which I will explore later. First, I will outline their more general views.

The first is the 'old neoclassical development economics' – henceforth ONCE. Until the late 1960s neoclassical economics had lived perfectly happily, on the whole, with development planning in poor countries; indeed, many of its practitioners were closely associated with such planning. Markets did not work and the state needed to intervene to ensure that the initial steps towards development might be taken before the market could come into its own.

The second is, to use Williamson's expression, the 'Washington consensus' (WC) view.[3] From the late 1960s, this consolidated, hardened and became hegemonic, reaching its full flowering in the 1980s. It was relentlessly anti-planning, anti-state and pro-market. With state withdrawal, and a leaner and meaner, non-interventionist state, an untrammelled market would deliver the goods. With the state dismantled, all that was necessary for development was 'getting prices right'. Many of the former neoclassical advocates of planning adopted this view and metamorphosed into fervent proponents of liberalization. It became, most certainly, the dominant view within both the IMF and the World Bank and among neoclassical development economists, and remained so until the late 1990s.

The third variant is so-called 'new development economics', which set the terms for the 'post-Washington consensus', and whose major proponent has been Joseph Stiglitz; it was Stiglitz who coined the term 'the new development economics' in 1986. In so doing, he was clearly not referring to the replacement of any non-neoclassical development economics, but rather to a marked revision of the WC view. He might, more appropriately, have coined the phrase 'the new neoclassical development economics' (henceforth NNCDE). This, as it happens, has taken agriculture very much as its focus. In this revised view, the state is not lambasted with such ferocity. Indeed, there is something of a case for positive state intervention, as the market, unaided, will not necessarily deliver the goods. 'Getting prices right' may not be enough.

A final neoclassical form is what has been termed 'neoclassical populism'.[4] Here, via the deployment of the standard apparatus of neoclassical economics, a radical egalitarianism, with the advocacy of extreme redistributive land reform, is embraced. Its major exponents have been Michael Lipton and Keith Griffin. A full treatment of the neoclassical view of 'development' would certainly have to include this.[5]

My focus in this chapter will be on the third variant, which I will question in terms of Marxist political economy. Heteredoxy, of course, has other variants: structuralism, dependency theory; variants of Keynesianism (Harrod-Domar type theorizing) . These are not my concern here.

2. The 'old' and the 'new' neoclassical economics

During the 1960s, in the growing literature on 'agriculture and development', a powerful challenge was mounted against the dominance of the classical paradigm by neoclassical economists. As this happened, so ONCE was replaced by a new neoclassical variant, one which would become the standard orthodoxy. The WC view became predominant, but there were already elements in it that would eventually form part of NNCDE.

For example, exponents of ONCE did not demur at the central classical postulate of a vast amount of surplus labour. They also saw high rates of rural interest in informal markets as 'unreasonable'; roundly condemned share-cropping within a Marshallian framework; and perceived peasants as possibly not responding to price movements. While stressing the importance of markets/prices, they were preoccupied with market imperfections, to the extent of seeing them as a possible justification for planning. For exponents of ONCE, planning might clear the way for the ultimate operation of the market. To use the later vocabulary of NNCDE, they viewed existing 'agrarian institutions' as thoroughly dysfunctional with respect to development, and did not necessarily see relationships between economic agents as being mutually advantageous. The state might play a positive and beneficent role.

A new, and fundamentally different neoclassical view emerged. Exponents of this new view departed from all of the foregoing. The first 'revision' was over surplus labour. The existence of surplus labour was already being questioned in the 1950s. Schultz, who had appeared to subscribe to the surplus labour view in 1951 (as a signatory of the landmark UN document of the same year, which stressed the existence of a large quantum of under-employment), now repudiated it;[6] he was quickly joined by other neoclassicals.[7] The assumption of widespread under-employment was, quite simply, not a good neoclassical premise. When Jorgenson, in 1961, threw down the gauntlet to the exponents of the classical two-sector model – the 'Lewis model' – with a very new phenomenon, a neoclassical two-sector model, he assumed that disguised unemployment was non-existent.

In 1964, Schultz's *Transforming Traditional Agriculture*, a key text in the questioning of ONCE, was published; it included a dismissive chapter entitled 'The Doctrine of Agricultural Labor of Zero Value'. The neoclassicals were on the march: Chicago had had enough of classical political economy, with its absurd assumptions. What we witness in neoclassical economics is resistance to the idea that economic agents in poor countries are anything other than allocatively efficient. If they are not, then the state might have to step in on a significant scale. We see the embracing of 'the economic efficiency hypothesis',[8] and resistance to the strongly held classical position that state intervention was necessary to get development going: in this instance, to mobilize surplus labour, but also in a more general sense. That could not be so, since there *was no* surplus labour.

A further blow was struck in the 1960s on relative price movements. The Indian economist, Raj Krishna, 'put to a test the widely prevalent notion that peasants in poor countries do not respond, or respond very little, or negatively, to price movements'. Using data for the inter-war period, Krishna was able to show that 'while the elasticity of acreage of wheat in the Punjab was much lower than that in the United States, the elasticities of cotton and maize acreage in the Punjab were significantly higher'.[9] So here were rational actors – rational peasants – behaving every bit as rationally as North American farmers. Such evidence would later be used as part of the argument that the strategy of 'getting prices right' had a sound basis in poor countries, and should replace the hopelessly inefficient government intervention and planning, with its accompanying, rampant rent-seeking. That, certainly, was part of WC.

In that WC view, what Stiglitz has referred to as 'the efficient markets hypothesis and the Coase theorem' prevail. This is the proposition that, left to themselves, 'individuals would quickly get together to eliminate any inefficient resource allocation (or inefficient institutional arrangement)', and are prevented from so acting only by '(harmful) governmental intervention since economic forces naturally lead to economic efficiency'.[10] Stiglitz took exception to this argument, something to which I will return later in this chapter.

Very important, such evidence – and a large amount of it followed in the wake of Krishna's classic article – would be much cited by the exponents of NNCDE in support of their positing of peasant rationality. Here, it seemed, the 'commercial rationality' of peasants was demonstrated beyond doubt.

The next major assault on the classical approach and on ONCE related to rural interest rates. Bottomley, in a series of articles in the 1960s,[11] challenged the idea that the very high interest rates observed in informal credit markets were exploitative. They could, he argued, be explained in terms of the costs associated with making loans (administrative costs, opportunity costs etc.), and although he did not use the term 'transaction costs', this was implicit in his argument, as, significantly, were the risks associated with such costs – i.e. risk of default. He stressed the significance of so-called 'lender's risk'. Rural interest rates were not to be seen as 'unreasonably' high. The 'institution' of unorganized money markets, or the 'village moneylender', supplies credit at interest rates that are perfectly reasonable, in the given circumstances.

We see the beginnings of an approach to 'agrarian institutions' that views them in a far more favourable light. *Contra* the ONCE view, unorganized money markets are desirable and efficient: they supply credit that would not otherwise be supplied, at rates that reflect relevant costs. They are to the mutual advantage of both parties and are the best available solution to the problem of scarce credit.

The next battleground was over sharecropping. Such a tenancy form was observed to be widespread in poor countries. Not only that, but the practice was known to have been prevalent historically in the now developed economies, and to have endured until well into the twentieth century. Until the late 1960s it had been condemned as inefficient by a line of economists running from Adam Smith down through Alfred Marshall to those who considered it in postwar Less Developed Countries (LDCs). Until then the standard neoclassical view of sharecropping was that suggested by Marshall.[12] It was seen as inefficient because of the disincentive associated with the share, and the Marshallian proposition was maintained that share tenancy would yield lower input per acre and lower output per acre than peasant proprietor-

ship or fixed money rent or wage-based agriculture. But if sharecropping were
so inefficient, how did one explain its prevalence and its tenacity? In 1969,
Cheung gave an answer: in his opinion, transaction costs were important, but
it was sharecropping's remarkable risk-dispersing property, more or less
ignored earlier, that was crucial. According to Stiglitz, its prevalence and its
tenacity might be explained in a dramatically new 'view that it represented an
efficient institutional arrangement for risk-sharing in an environment in which
other forms of insurance were not available: the landlord and the tenant
shared in the risks associated with the fluctuations in output caused by
weather, disease and so on, as well as those associated with the vicissitudes in
the prices of marketed commodities'.[13] To this, Stiglitz added a novel argument: 'that contrary to the standard view that criticized sharecropping as
inefficient because it dampened incentives, sharecropping was desirable
because it increased incentives'.[14]

Risk was a new element in the explanation; and sharecropping was seen to
be mutually advantageous, to landlord and tenant, as was rural credit in informal markets. Risk had already been given central emphasis by Bottomley, in
the context of interest rates; now it was seen to be of primary significance in
tenancy markets. This emphasis on risk was taken up by Stiglitz, and was a
crucial part of NNCDE.

Then another phenomenon that lent itself to the new approach, that had
not been addressed by ONCE, was 'discovered'. Previously, a recurring phenomenon had been observed in the countryside: those from whom loans were
taken might be landlords, or traders, as well as moneylenders. Not only that,
but these activities might be formally linked: a landlord, for example, might
insist, as part of the tenancy, that the tenant must supply labour at a particular
wage, or for no wages. Or, a landlord who was also a moneylender might
stipulate what crops were to be grown, or might insist, as part of the loan, that
all the crop above the rent must be sold to him. Or a moneylender-cum-
trader might insist, as a condition of the loan, that the crop be sold to him at
pre-fixed prices. Until the late 1960s, although this had been observed, it had
not attracted any great attention from economists, and certainly not from
neoclassicals. That now changed, as practitioners of NNCDE took to it like
ducks to water.

It was, in fact, the distinguished Indian political economist, Krishna
Bharadwaj, an outstanding economist in the classical tradition, who first paid
rigorous attention to this relationship. It was Bharadwaj who first conceived it
in terms of 'interlocking of markets';[15]she would later develop her analysis,
and provide a magisterial treatment.[16] Bhaduri, too, analysed it.[17] Neoclassical economists were attracted to the issue, although they would give it a
very different treatment. The phenomenon was given analytical attention in

NNCDE. Inter-linkage was seen to be the outcome of market imperfections, which came with associated costs for both parties. Interlinked markets were a way of minimizing these costs, to the mutual advantage of both parties. One particular cost derived from risk: high risks, rooted in endemic uncertainty, are characteristic of poor agrarian economies. Interlinkage serves to disperse those risks, and is the preferred solution for both parties. This includes: the risks associated with agricultural production itself, the risks involved in seeking employment, the risks involved in seeking a loan, the risks involved in seeking a labour force, the risks of default on interest on loans (or the loans themselves), the risk of rent not being paid.

We have identified some of the building blocks of NNCDE. We may briefly state Stiglitz's rendering of this variant of the neoclassical paradigm, before turning to a critique. Stiglitz conveniently provides a lucid and brief statement in his two texts, that theory is encapsulated in seven tenets.[18]

Firstly, the land in poor countries is worked by peasants, whether they are tenants or owner-cultivators, who are rational in that 'they act in a (reasonably) consistent manner, one which adapts to changes in circumstances'. There is much 'econometric evidence, showing that peasants respond to market forces': not least the large amount of evidence on price responsiveness. That much is a central part of the WC view. Stiglitz works with the category 'peasants', or 'individuals'.[19] In this neoclassical universe, classes do not exist, and there is no hint that peasantries might be socially differentiated. That is as true of Stiglitz's work as it is of practitioners of the WC view.

Secondly, 'while ... peasants may be rational, responding to market forces, they are not fully informed about the consequences either of their actions, or of the institutions through which they operate'.[20] Information is costly and 'individuals do not acquire perfect information, and hence their behavior may differ markedly from what it would have been if they had perfect information'.[21] Not only that, but there is likely to be information asymmetry – for example a landlord or a moneylender may be in possession of information that a peasant does not have, or *vice versa*. There is no suggestion that rich and poor peasants may differ significantly in their access to information or in the quality of information they have.

Thirdly, 'one of the distinguishing characteristics of LDCs is the absence of certain markets ... [or the existence of markets that are] thin'.[22] What this means is the absence of a central driving force in the economy. Stiglitz, indeed, denies the 'efficient markets hypothesis', noted above. While certain kinds of government intervention may indeed be an 'impediment to development', he insists that the stark view of the Coase theorem that 'markets by themselves would take care of matters ... have done a disservice ... for they fail to take note of the important, seemingly positive, role of government in the case of so many of the developed countries'.[23] The distance from the WC position widens.

The fourth tenet encompasses a positive view of 'agrarian institutions'. Previously denounced as 'inefficient' by old-style neoclassicals, these are now seen as 'functional but imperfect'. They are far more flexible than previously thought. Thus: 'Institutions adapt to reflect these information (and other transaction) costs. Thus, institutions are not to be taken as exogenous, and changes in the environment may lead with a lag to changes in institutional structure'.[24] This remarkable 'flexibility', of advantage to all parties involved, seems to be a powerful attribute. Unfortunately, not many examples are given other than cost-share leasing.

These 'agrarian institutions' have a further powerful feature, enshrined in the fifth tenet: their capacity to deal with risk. Stiglitz stresses: 'in the absence of insurance markets (other markets for risk), this is clearly an important function'. This is one of the major 'discoveries' of the NNCDE school. These institutions are far more effective and efficient than was previously thought. In the given objective circumstances, they probably produce the optimum solution. They perform important economic functions 'better than alternative institutional arrangements'.[25]

The sixth tenet is: 'The fact that individuals are rational and that institutions are adaptable does not, however, imply that the economy is (Pareto) efficient'. One wonders, indeed, who might have thought such a thing. After all, it would require 'a complete set of markets and perfect information'. Absurd as that might be in an advanced economy, it is *a fortiori* so in a poor one. Anyway, from this Stiglitz derives the standard neoclassical conclusion: that 'there exists a set of taxes and subsidies which can make everyone better off'.[26]

Stiglitz uses this, along with the third tenet, to derive the seventh one: that 'there is a potential role for the government'.[27] It is, however, a cautious endorsement of a circumscribed role. He stresses that the market itself cannot, necessarily, eradicate economic backwardness and generate development. But he remains more than a little suspicious of government. The following may seem bold and radical, in the company of extreme, pro-market, anti-state neoclassical economists of the WC persuasion, but it is hardly a clarion call for a developmentalist state: '...the government could effect a Pareto improvement if (i) it had sufficient knowledge of the structure of the economy; (ii) those responsible for implementing government policy had at least as much information as those in the private sector; (iii) those responsible for designing and implementing government policy had the incentives to direct policies to effect Pareto improvements, rather than, for instance, to redistribute income (either from the poor to the rich or vice versa, or from everyone else, to themselves), often at considerable loss to national output'.[28]

3. Questioning the dominant orthodoxy

3.1 Differentiated versus homogeneous peasantries

There are, in the NNCDE universe, divisions: between producers with land, landless labourers, landlords, traders, moneylenders. These are not, however, antagonistic divisions: divisions of class. Moreover, it is further assumed that the peasantry is homogeneous, a premise evident in the literature on price responsiveness, rural credit markets, inter-linked markets, sharecropping, and so on.

The appropriate assumption, however, is that of antagonistic class relations, and of socially differentiated peasantries. It is useful to think in terms of a poor peasantry, a middle peasantry and a rich peasantry. In concrete historical situations, these strata need to be identified with care. Their precise characteristics will vary with time, place and circumstance, and according to the degree of capitalist penetration in the countryside.

They may be identified in terms of holding size; whether they produce a regular surplus and what kind of surplus; whether they are net hirers in or out of labour, or are family-based with the need to do neither; whether they are heavily indebted, at usurious rates of interest; whether they are compulsively involved in inter-linked markets, and so on. Size of holding will be a useful, if imperfect, stratifying variable. Of all this NNCDE is innocent.

One thorny issue arises. Rich peasants may have to be distinguished from capitalist farmers. Great caution is necessary, but among the criteria by which one might identify the latter are the following. Rich peasants will tend to use elements of the productive forces that are not qualitatively different from those used by other sections of the peasantry (the same kind of 'traditional' inputs and tools). A capitalist farmer will, however, be quite distinct in this respect. He will probably be in a wage relationship with free wage labour, extracting surplus value via the wage relation and reinvesting it productively in agriculture on an increasing scale. That capital intensification may involve mechanization of farm operations, especially tractorization. Moreover, a capitalist farmer will be able to hold and control his marketable surplus. Yet, the notion of capitalist agriculture, which we need, is not to be found in the neoclassical lexicon.

Although one might illustrate the need to proceed in terms of socially-differentiated peasantries and antagonistic relations of production with regard to any of the major issues addressed by NNCDE, let us single out price responsiveness. The literature on price responsiveness is one that the NNCDE economists cite favourably. What it seems to show is the 'commercial rationality' of *all* peasants.[29] It is taken to support the postulate of peasant rationality that is central to NNCDE.

The price responsiveness studies all operate at the aggregate supply response level. The responsiveness of *all* producers with respect to particular crops is considered econometrically. In so proceeding, much of significance is indeed missed. The questions that lie at the heart of agrarian political economy cannot be addressed at this level. They are simply ignored, and lie hidden in the aggregates that are the stuff of orthodox econometric treatment.

What do the NNCDE economists ignore/abstract from? Bhaduri suggests 'a hypothesis of differential "supply response", depending on the class situation of the peasants: both large and small producers at two ends of the spectrum [rich peasants, on the one hand, poor peasants on the other] may be expected to respond ... strongly to "market forces" by changing suitably the ratio of subsistence crop to cash crop'.[30] But they do so for completely different reasons: reasons associated with their class position. Social differentiation is ignored, and this oversight must be deemed a fundamental weakness of 'orthodox' treatment.

Following the suggested class divisions within the peasantry, at one end of the class spectrum 'large producers'/rich peasants/capitalist farmers 'react due to their voluntary market involvement guided by the "gains from trade" motive'. They choose freely to be involved in the market; and set out to produce in order to earn profit from that production via the marketing, regularly, of a 'true commercial surplus'. At the other end of the class spectrum, however, 'small producers'/poor peasants 'respond only because of their involuntary market involvement through debt'.[31] They are forced/coerced on to the market, because of the relations of production into which they are locked; these may include interlocked markets. This is Bhaduri's 'forced commerce'. Small producers do not produce a 'true commercial surplus' but rather what in 1961 another Indian economist, Narain, has termed a 'distress surplus'. So, '[I]t is only the middle peasants with relative economic independence who may still be in a position to respond relatively sluggishly to "market forces" in changing their cropping patterns'. This is a reality that we need to disentangle: 'the question of differential class response in terms of cropping pattern changes'.[32] It is not an issue addressed by NNCDE, but there is no reason, in principle, why econometric analysis cannot proceed at a more disaggregated level.

3.2 Relationships of exploitation rather than mutuality

The second questionable assumption of NNCDE is that concerning mutuality between producers and non-producers, and among producers themselves, with the relevant 'agrarian institutions' acting powerfully to disperse risk for all parties. Stiglitz strongly resists the idea of exploitation. But in considering those 'agrarian institutions', exploitation/surplus appropriation is far more important than risk in explaining their operation.

In a capitalist situation, a relationship between a capitalist employer and wage labour involves exploitation, that is, appropriation of surplus value. This, of course, is vehemently denied by the neoclassical economist. In the circumstances of economic backwardness, exploitation is equally emphatically denied. But a tenancy relationship, relationship with a moneylender, a relationship with a trader, or a relationship between an employer and labour, all involve exploitation. Even more starkly than in the capitalist situation, these are relationships of exploitation: in which there are relentless pressures to appropriate all surplus above bare subsistence. These will be intensified where there are interlinked modes of exploitation. Thus, the essence of the share-cropping relationship, in which a percentage of the crop, gross or net, of 50% or more, automatically goes to the landlord, is the appropriation of surplus. If, for whatever reason, a poor peasant takes loans at very high rates of interest that he is unable to repay – is saddled with debt – then the moneylender is appropriating surplus. If a poor peasant is locked into a relationship with a trader, whereby he is paid for his produce less than the market price, then surplus is being appropriated. If a poor peasant supplies labour to a landlord at less than the market wage, or at no wage at all, then surplus is being appropriated. It is very difficult to see these as relationships of mutuality. Moral judgements aside, dominant classes are quite simply able to appropriate much of the surplus above subsistence.

One may pursue this with reference to interlinked markets. In the heterodox view, this must clearly be analysed in class terms. It is, in essence, a particular form of exploitation: a particular way of securing and maximizing surplus extraction. A dominant class (whether in the shape of a landlord, a moneylender, or a trader, or one who combines some or all of these activities) is in a particular class relationship with a subordinate class (usually a poor peasant). In Bharadwaj's words, the defining characteristic of these 'interlinked markets' is that '[a] dominant party conjointly exploits the weaker parties in two or more markets by interlinking the terms of contracts'.[33] Although the language of 'contracts' and 'markets' is invoked, it would be quite inappropriate to analyse such a phenomenon in terms of 'market imperfections'. Class relationships, and exploitation, proceed on the basis of a set of 'personalised relationships' and a set of 'personal values', rather than 'market values'. These are not determined by the market: 'The exchanges are set not only in terms of "prices" but there can be non-price factors, explicit and/or implicit, which mainly rely on personal dominance and power equations'.[34] The subordinate class does not have free access to markets: entry will be on a personal basis.

The class relationship allows the dominant party/class to insist that the weaker party/subordinate class accept a manifestly unfavourable 'contract' in one market as a condition of access to another. That 'contract' is unfavourable inasmuch as its terms are clearly inferior to those which would be accepted, or negotiated, in an open or free market, and which others may be observed to obtain. There is a perceived compelling need for the 'weaker party', the subordinate class, to secure access to one market: for survival, reproduction, for cash to permit this, and so on. The 'dominant party' takes advantage of this in order to force compliance with the terms in the other market (or markets). So it is that exploitation is secured, cemented, and, in the given circumstances, maximized.

3.3 Asymmetry of economic power

Embedded in the assumption of mutuality is the assumption of parity of economic power among the different agents/classes. This is clearly quite inappropriate. NNCDE makes much of information asymmetry, and the remarkable ability of 'agrarian institutions' to deal with it. What it ignores completely is asymmetry of economic power.

One might illustrate this with reference to many examples, but I will concentrate on one instance: Cheung's treatment of sharecropping, which is a crucial landmark in the development of NNCDE. When Cheung analyses sharecropping, he considers the significance of risk in relation to transaction costs. He postulates that individual, risk-averse producers will seek to minimize risk subject to the costs involved in doing so, and will choose sharecropping where the cost of doing so is less than the gain achieved from the risk averted. His argument is that although transaction costs are high, this is more than compensated for by considerable risk-dispersing gains. It is those supposedly high transaction costs that attract our attention. In fact, it is the very *low* transaction costs that make sharecropping attractive to landowners, while subordinate classes have little choice at all in the matter. Cheung includes, as part of transaction costs, negotiation costs and enforcement costs.

First, let us consider negotiation costs. A universe is portrayed in which there is active negotiation of 'the rental percentage, the ratio of nonland input to land, and the types of crops to be grown'; and in which there may be quite complicated 'contractual renegotiation' consequent upon, for example, 'changes in relative product prices which call for shifts to different crops, or innovations which call for the adoption of new seeds or new methods of cultivation'.[35] It is an apparently formidable list. But it is all very much in the abstract: no concrete evidence is given of the actual manifestation of such 'negotiation costs'. This picture, of an active bargaining process conducted between parties of more or less equal bargaining power, is not a convincing one. As Bhaduri has observed: 'bargaining is a meaningful concept only if both parties enjoy more or less symmetrical economic power. This is hardly the case when a landlord confronts a pure landless tenant with meagre and uncertain alternative employment opportunities'.[36] When a powerful landlord confronts either a landless tenant, or a heavily-indebted poor peasant with a tiny holding, over whom he has considerable power – perhaps as moneylender as well as landlord – 'negotiation costs' will be minimal, or non-existent. They are a neoclassical fiction.

This is also the case with respect to 'the cost of enforcement'. This supposedly represents the costs associated with 'enforcing the stipulations of the contract' and the 'costs of controlling inputs and distributing input according to the terms of the contract'.[37] Therefore, the landlord has to ensure that the tenant actually supplies the amount of 'nonland input' agreed upon (seed, water etc.); that, in particular there is no 'shirking of labour input'. Not only that, but the landlord must also ensure that he obtains the agreed-upon rental percentage, which will involve 'efforts ... by the landlord to ascertain the harvest yield' and, of course, to see to its division. Thus: 'within a specified lease duration, the violation of the contracted terms ... may call for increasing enforcement efforts, or for revoking the contract before its termination date through court action or other means'.[38] Again, we are provided with an apparently formidable list, and not a shred of evidence. High enforcement costs of the kind suggested again imply some parity of bargaining power and economic strength. If, however, there is no 'symmetry of economic power', if, indeed, we have a powerful landlord, in relationship with a poor peasant, desperately fearful of losing his land, then 'enforcement costs' will be very low. The fear itself of losing the land will be sufficient enforcement. Again, we are in the presence of a neoclassical fiction. Indeed, Cheung himself discusses the proclivity of landlords for relatively short leases, which 'facilitate tenancy dismissal', a procedure, highlighted long ago by Johnson, of 'enforcing the desired intensity of cultivation'.[39] Another oft-mentioned device (also emphasized by Johnson) to secure 'the desired intensity of cultivation' is the leasing of land by landlords to tenants in plots of land of such a size that in order to attain subsistence levels after the landlord's share has been taken, they must apply the maximum amount of labour. These enforcement devices involve limited costs for the landlord. Moreover, there is abundant evidence to show that far from there being a danger of the landlord receiving less than his agreed upon share of the crop, the opposite is commonly true. Again, the underlying asymmetry of economic power is crucial. Indeed, just as Bhaduri suggests, with respect to loans in the countryside, that 'borrower's risk' might be a more meaningful concept than the neoclassical 'lender's risk', so in this context one might think of the need for 'enforcement' far more for the share-cropper than the landlord.

3.4 The causes of backwardness

Stiglitz himself raises 'that most fundamental of questions with which we as development economists are concerned, the persistence of massive differences in standards of living and the means by which those differences may be reduced'.[40] There is a prior, and more fundamental, question: wherein lie the causal roots of economic backwardness and why is that backwardness repro-duced? The practitioners of NNCDE have remarkably little to say about the causes and reproduction of economic backwardness. Indeed, if what they say about the relevant agrarian institutions is valid, it is difficult to see why there is any economic backwardness at all. Within these remarkably functioning agrarian institutions – with their flexible adjustment to 'thin' markets, their capacity to deal with risk, and so on – economic backwardness should have disappeared long ago. Or so it would appear.

There is, by contrast, within the agrarian political economy approach, a marked preoccupation with the roots of economic backwardness and how it is reproduced. Thus, to stay with inter-linked markets, the effects in relation to the generation of surplus, its form and the character and pace of accumula-tion, are clear. This is central to the heterodox approach, but is quite absent in that of NNCDE. Thus, the poverty that prevails in a 'backward agricul-ture', and which is intensified by interlinking of modes of exploitation and the dependency that interlinking secures are crucial. They encourage particular forms of capital investment, a specific pattern of investment. Accumulation takes on a particular character. 'Unproductive', 'usurious', 'mercantile' and 'speculative' forms of investment are the norm, because for dominant classes – those who extract and control the surplus – tenancy, usury, trade and specu-lation pay handsomely. Poverty and dependency make high rents and very high rates of interest possible; they make profit on trade high, because of the low prices at which commodities can be bought; they make speculation attractive, because commodity markets are 'unformed'. The rate of return on these is far higher than any alternative rate of return. The consequences are that 'investment goes into unproductive channels. Productive investment, meaning investment that enhances output growth is at a disadvantage ... Where possibilities of exploiting labour become almost limitless there is less incentive to improve productive forces, that is, undertake productive invest-ment'.[41] So it is that the rate of reinvestment of surplus, and hence 'the growth of surplus itself',[42] are influenced. They are far less than they would be if a greater incentive to undertake productive investment existed. These are powerfully sustained by interlinked modes of exploitation. The central question – the 'agrarian question' – then becomes: under what circumstances might these conditions be overcome and a transition to a capitalist agriculture be secured, whether that transition is via a capitalism from above or a capitalism from below?[43] This kind of transition is well under way in many LDCs. That is the question addressed by agrarian political economy.

One might question the aforementioned causality, but at least those who have suggested it have made a serious effort to address the causes of economic backwardness and its reproduction.

3.5 The State

The NNCDE economists have a problematic and ambiguous view of the state. We may focus upon Stiglitz, as the major intellectual force in NNCDE and as one who has been preoccupied with this issue. With Stiglitz, indeed, his positive view of the state seems promising enough to attract the ire of extreme neoclassical marketeers.

But how 'state-friendly' is NNCDE? One must, Stiglitz insists, be 'cautious in recommending particular government actions as remedies for certain observed deficiencies in the market'.[44] Is it simply 'a set of taxes and subsidies' that can make everyone better off? If that is so, it is not very much. While, indeed, Stiglitz wishes to stress government's potential role, he never really spells that out. Regarding government's role in the earlier phases of capitalist development in the now advanced countries, he comments that '[t]hough Japan is the case that inevitably comes to mind, one should not forget the role of the federal government in the development of American railroads'.[45] That is inadequate, and needs to be replaced with a more positive, nuanced and informed view of the state.

Stiglitz's view on state intervention is ambivalent. Even as he warms to the task of identifying the ways in which intervention is essential and must be substantive, he seriously qualifies his argument and distances himself from anything resembling advocacy of a 'developmentalist state'. In a recent essay, Sender deals incisively with Stiglitz's view of the state Addressing Stiglitz's apparently fundamental critique of the WC, Sender observes: 'In sum, the post-Washington consensus, like the old Washington Consensus, retains a very limited conception of the role of the state in promoting growth in poor economies'.[46] He then notes of the architect of that post-Washington consensus: 'The grudging and qualified tone of the critique is evident in the following speculative conclusion: "Perhaps had these [East Asian] countries followed all of the dictums of liberalization and privatization, they would have grown even faster"'.[47] That conclusion is not a new one. A very similar argument was made long ago by Milton Friedman.

The heterodox view of the state is an altogether more positive one. It does not deny the problems associated with an interventionist state, not least those deriving from the state's representation of the interests of dominant classes to the detriment of subordinate classes. Yet, both in agriculture and more generally, there are certain essential tasks that only the state can undertake. Sender points out that Stiglitz and other representatives of NNCDE in effect focus upon 'the familiar limited menu...[of] education, health, roads and education'.[48] But the state has a far wider, and crucial part to play. This includes the pursuit of protectionist trade policies and import-substituting industrialization, which allow the structural transformation that has been a critical part of all major historical instances of capitalist development. In agriculture, it can be seen in the pursuit of land reform, which, deriving from the very different view of the nature and functioning of 'agrarian institutions', would include the replacement of much-vaunted, flexible 'agrarian institutions' such as sharecropping and interlinked markets. It further entails a massive programme of formal credit, with credit provided at non-usurious interest rates. And it is so, with respect, for example, to substantial initiatives in the creation of modern irrigation facilities, the generating and dissemination of other forms of new technology, the control of inter-sectoral prices and comprehensive poverty alleviation schemes. Without such an interventionist state, it is difficult to conceive of dynamic agrarian transformation in economically backward economies, or transformation in which the interests of subordinate classes are served.

Notes

1 Lewis 1958, p. 400.
2 Cf. Lewis 1958, p. 401.
3 Williamson 1990.
4 This is Chris Scott's phrase, used with respect to Keith Griffin's writing on the 'green revolution'. See Scott's review (1977) of Griffin's *The Political Economy of Agrarian Change* (1974).
5 See Lipton 1968 and 1977; Griffin 1974, 1979; Griffin et al. 2002. For a critique of Lipton see Byres 1979; and of Griffin see Byres (forthcoming, 2003).
6 Schultz 1956a and b.
7 See, for example, Viner 1957; Haberler 1957 and 1959.
8 Schultz 1964, p. 36.
9 Krishna 1963, p. 486.
10 Stiglitz 1989b, p. 20.
11 See Bottomley 1963a; 1963b; 1964a; 1964b; and Bottomley and Nudds 1969, all reprinted in Bottomley 1971.

12 Marshall 1979, pp. 534–7.
13 Stiglitz 1989a, p. 309.
14 Stiglitz 1989b, p. 21.
15 Bharadwaj 1969; 1974.
16 Respectively, Bharadwaj 1979; Bharadwaj 1985.
17 See Bhaduri 1973.
18 Stiglitz 1986 and 1989b.
19 Stiglitz 1986, p. 257; Stiglitz 1989b, p. 257.
20 Stiglitz 1989b, p. 23.
21 Stiglitz 1986, p. 257.
22 Stiglitz 1989b, p. 23.
23 Stiglitz 1989b, p. 20.
24 Stiglitz 1986, p. 257.
25 Stiglitz 1989b, p. 21.
26 Stiglitz 1986, p. 257.
27 Stiglitz 1986, p. 257.
28 Stiglitz 1986, pp. 257–8.
29 Cf. Bhaduri 1983, p. 33.
30 Bhaduri 1983, p. 33.
31 Bhaduri 1983, p. 33.
32 Bhaduri 1983, p. 33.
33 Bharadwaj 1985, p. 12.
34 Bharadwaj 1980, p. 11.
35 Cheung 1969, pp. 67, 84.
36 Bhaduri 1983b, 88
37 Cheung 1969, pp. 62, 63, 67.
38 Cheung 1969, pp. 67, 83.
39 Cheung 1969, p. 83; Johnson 1950, p. 118.
40 Stiglitz 1989b, p. 27.
41 Bharadwaj 1985, p. 15.
42 Bharadwah 1985, p. 15.
43 Byres 1996.
44 Stiglitz 1986, p. 258.
45 Stiglitz 1989b, p.27, n. 4.
46 Sender 2002, p. 197.
47 Stiglitz 1998, p. 120.
48 Sender 2002, p. 192.

References

Bhaduri, Amit, 1973, 'Agricultural Backwardness Under Semi-Feudalism', *Economic Journal*, March, vol. 83, no. 329, pp. 120–37.
——, 1983, *The Economic Structure of Backward Agriculture*, London, Academic Press.
Bharadwaj, Krishna, 1969, *Production Conditions in Indian Agriculture. A Study Based on Farm Management Surveys*, Cambridge: Department of Applied Economics. Mimeo.
——, 1974, *Production Conditions in Indian Agriculture. A Study Based on Farm Management Surveys*, University of Cambridge Department of Applied Economics Occasional Paper 33, London, Cambridge University Press.

Bharadwaj, Krishna, 1979, 'Towards A Macro-Economic Framework for a Developing Economy: The Indian Case', *Manchester School*, September, 47 (3), pp. 270–301.

——, 1985, 'A View on Commercialisation in Indian Agriculture and the Development of Capitalism', *Journal of Peasant Studies*, July, 12 (4), pp. 7–25.

Bottomley, Anthony, 1963a, 'The Cost of Administering Private Loans in Underdeveloped Rural Areas', *Oxford Economic Papers*, July, vol. 15, pp. 154–63.

——, 1963b, 'The Premium for Risk as a Determinant of Interest Rates in Underdeveloped Rural Areas', *Quarterly Journal of Economics*, November, vol. 77, pp. 638–47.

——, 1964a, 'The Structure of Interest Rates in Underdeveloped Rural Areas', *Journal of Farm Economics*, May, vol. 46, no. 2, pp. 313–22.

——, 1964b, 'Monopoly Profit as a Determinant of Interest Rates in Underdeveloped Rural Areas', *Oxford Economic Papers*, July, vol. 16, pp. 432–7.

——, 1969, with D Nudds, 'A Widow's Cause Theory of Capital Supply in Underdeveloped Rural Areas', *Manchester School*, June, vol. 37, no. 2, pp. 131–40.

——, 1971, *Factor Pricing and Economic Growth in the Underdeveloped Rural Areas*, London, Crosby, Lockwood and Son, 1971, especially section 3, which reproduces the articles by Bottomley noted above.

Byres, Terence J, 1979, 'Of Neo-Populist Pipe Dreams: Daedalus in the Third World and the Myth of Urban Bias', *Journal of Peasant Studies*, January, vol. 6, no. 2, pp. 210–44.

——, 1988, 'Charan Singh (1902–87): An Assessment', *Journal of Peasant Studies*, January, vol. 15, no. 2, 139–89.

——, 1996, *Capitalism from Above and Capitalism from Below. An Essay in Comparative Political Economy*. Basingstoke and London, Macmillan.

——, forthcoming, 2003, 'Neo-Classical Neo-Populism 25 Years on; *Déjà Vu* and *Déjà Passé*. Towards A Critique', Paper presented to international conference on *Labour and Capitalist Transformation in Asia*, Trivandrum, India, 13–15 December, 2001. To appear in forthcoming conference volume, *Labour and Transformation in Asia. Critical Reflections and Empirical Studies*, eds KP Kannan and Mario Ruttan.

Cheung, Stephen NS, 1969, *The Theory of Share Tenancy*, Chicago and London, University of Chicago Press.

Griffin, Keith, 1974, *The Political Economy of Agrarian Change* London, Macmillan, 2nd edition, 1979.

Griffin, Keith, Azizur Rahman Khan and Amy Ickowitz, 2002, 'Poverty and Distribution of Land', *Journal of Agrarian Change*, July, vol. 2, no. 3, pp. 279–330.

Haberler, Gottfried, 1957, 'Critical Observations on Some Current Notions in the Theory of Economic Development', *L'Industria*, no. 2, pp. 3–13.

——, 1959, 'International Trade and Economic Development', Fiftieth Anniversary Commemoration Lectures, Lecture 3, Cairo, National Bank of Egypt.

Johnson, D Gale, 1950, 'Resource Allocation Under Share Contracts', *Journal of Political Economy*, vol. 58, April, pp. 111–23.

Jorgenson, Dale W, 1961, 'The Development of a Dual Economy', *Economic Journal*, March, vol. 71, no. 282, pp. 309–34.

Krishna, Raj, 1963, 'Farm Supply Response in India-Pakistan: A Case Study of the Punjab Region', *Economic Journal*, vol. 73, no. 291, pp. 477–87.

Lewis, W Arthur, 1954, 'Economic Development with Unlimited Supplies of Labour', *The Manchester School*, vol. 22, no. 2, May, 1954, pp. 139–91.

Lipton, Michael, 1968, 'Strategy for Agriculture: Urban Bias and Rural Planning' in *The*

Crisis of Indian Planning, eds Paul Streeten and Michael Lipton, London, Oxford University Press, pp. 83–147.

——, 1977, *Why Poor People Stay Poor. A Study of Urban Bias in World Development*, London, Temple Smith.

Marshall, Alfred, [1920] 1979, *Principles of Economics*, London and Basingstoke, Macmillan.

Narain, Dharm, 1961, *Distribution of the Marketed Surplus of Agricultural produce by Size-Level of Holding in India, 1950–51*, Bombay, Asia Publishing House.

Rosenstein-Rodan, PN, 1943, 'Problems of Industrialisation of Eastern and Southeastern Europe', *Economic Journal*, vol. 53, June–September, pp. 202–11. Reprinted in *The Economics of Underdevelopment*, eds AN Agarwala and SP Singh, London: Oxford University Press, 1958, pp. 245–55.

——, 1984, 'Natura Facit Saltum: Analysis of the Disequilibrium Growth Process' in *Pioneers in Development*, eds. Gerald M Meier and Dudley Seers, Oxford, Oxford University Press for the World Bank, pp. 207–21.

Schultz, Theodore W, 1956a, 'The Economic Test in Latin America', *New York State School of Industrial and Labor Relations Bulletin*, 35, pp. 14–15, Cornell University, Ithaca.

——, 1956b, 'The Role of Government in Promoting Economic Growth' in *The State of the Social Sciences*, ed. Leonard D White, Chicago, University of Chicago Press, pp. 372–83.

——, 1964, *Transforming Traditional Agriculture*, New Haven and London, Yale University Press.

Scott, CD, 1977, 'Review' of Griffin 1974, *Journal of Peasant Studies*, January, vol. 4, no. 2, pp. 244–8.

Sender, John, 2002, 'Reassessing the Role of the World Bank in Sub-Saharan Africa' in *Reinventing the World Bank*, eds Jonathan Pincus and Jeffrey A Winters, Ithaca and London, Cornell University Press, pp. 185–202.

Stiglitz, Joseph E, 1986, 'The New Development Economics', *World Development*, vol. 14, no. 2, pp. 257–65.

——, [1987] 1989a, 'Sharecropping' in *The New Palgrave. Economic Development*, eds. John Eatwell et al, London, Macmillan, pp. 308–15.

——, 1989b, 'Rational Peasants, Efficient Institutions, and a Theory of Rural Organization: Methodological Remarks for Development Economics' in *The Economic Theory of Agrarian Institutions*, ed. Pranab Bardhan, Oxford, Clarendon Press, pp. 18–29.

——, 1998, 'Towards a new Paradigm for Development Strategies, Policies and Processes', 1998 Prebisch Lecture, 19th October, UNCTAD, Geneva.

United Nations, 1951, *Measures for the Economic Development of Under-Developed Countries*. New York, United Nations.

Viner, Jacob, 1957, 'Some Reflections on the Concept of Disguised Unemployment', *Indian Journal of Economics*, July, vol. 38, pp. 17–23.

Williamson, John, 1990, 'What Washington Means by Policy Reform' in *Latin American Adjustment: How Much Has Happened*, ed. John Williamson, Washington, Institute for International Economics.

PART IV

TRADE, INDUSTRY AND TECHNOLOGY

12

TRADE AND INDUSTRIAL POLICY ISSUES

Ha-Joon Chang

1. Introduction

The debates surrounding trade and industrial policies are arguably the most contentious in development economics. There are many complex theoretical and empirical issues involved, and it is therefore not possible to review all the important topics in these areas. The issues discussed in this chapter are therefore highly selective. First, I will briefly review some main issues in trade and industrial policies and then critically examine a number of 'new issues'. These include policies concerning foreign direct investment (FDI) in the context of globalization, the implications of the new world trading order instituted through the World Trade Organization (WTO), and the trade-related intellectual property rights (TRIPS) agreement of the WTO.

2. Trade Policy: inward vs. outward orientation in trade policy

In the early postwar years, the debate on trade policy in developing countries focused on whether international trade benefits developing countries at all.[1] The then dominant mode of economic activity in the developing countries – that is, relying on primary commodity exports to finance the import of manufactured products – was believed to be a dangerous strategy, for a number of reasons. First, the collapse of international trade following the Great Depression during the 1930s demonstrated the fragility of the international economic system and the consequent danger of relying too heavily on international trade. Second, the volatility of their prices made primary commodities an unreliable source of foreign exchange. Third, the experience between the late nineteenth century and the Second World War seemed to confirm the so-called Singer–Prebisch hypothesis of falling terms of trade for primary commodity export. Fourth, given the low-income elasticity of demand of primary commodities, the scope for increase in their exports was in the long run regarded as small in any case.

However, since the 1970s, the terms of debate has shifted in line with the overall changes in development thinking. The resurgent neoclassical school produced a large number of empirical (mostly, but not exclusively, econometric) studies, which supposedly proved the positive relationship between trade openness and economic development. It was argued that countries with 'outward orientation' in trade policy perform better than those with 'inward orientation'. On the basis of this, countries were recommended to adopt a free trade regime with neutral incentive system, which in practice means low and uniform rate of tariff and minimal quantitative restrictions. Despite its dominance, and support by the financial muscles of the World Bank and the IMF, this view has numerous theoretical and empirical problems.[2]

The first problem is that the definition of trade policy orientation itself is a very difficult exercise. The most widely-used method of defining a country's trade orientation is to do so in terms of its trade profile, such as the share of export in its GDP, or the rate of its export growth. The reasoning behind this is that a more pro-trade policy will result in a more rapid growth of trade (especially exports) and eventually in a greater trade dependence.

The obvious problem with this approach is that a country's 'revealed' trade strategy, as measured in these ways, may not be the same as a conscious trade strategy. A country may have a high share of export in GDP or a high export growth, which will classify it as a country with a strong outward orientation in its trade policy, for reasons other than trade policy. For example, if trade orientation is defined in terms of share of export in GDP, a smaller country is more likely to be classified as outward-oriented than a larger country, even when there is no difference in their policies, as typically small countries have high share of export in GDP. This approach will also automatically exclude 'failed' cases of outward-oriented trade policy. If trade orientation is defined in terms of export growth, a country that had pursued an outward-oriented trade policy but failed to increase its export fast will be classified as a country with an inward-oriented trade policy, thus systematically introducing a bias in favour of outward orientation.

Recognizing these problems, some studies have tried to classify trade orientation according to the incentive structure that defines the relative attractiveness of export and production for the domestic market.[3] Those who adopt this approach construct an 'index of protection' commonly known as a 'distortion index' – usually an average nominal or effective rate of protection – and classify as inward-oriented countries that register high numbers on such an index.[4]

These indexes are, however, very difficult to construct. Tariff figures may be relatively easy to obtain through official tariff schedules, but they do not reflect the full extent of protection, as it is extremely difficult to collect comprehensive data for the likes of quantitative restrictions (quotas), tax exemptions, tariff rebates and *ad hoc* subsidies. Even when a reasonable 'distortion index' can be constructed it has a critical limitation for it is an 'average' across commodities and does not therefore reflect the incentive effects of differential protection across commodities. Therefore, two countries could score similarly on the 'distortion index' but their respective producers may face very different incentives in different industries.

In practice, moreover, a fundamentally biased definition is often used. Many mainstream economists see outward orientation as characterized by an incentive neutrality between export and domestic production, and inward orientation as characterized by an incentive system biased towards domestic production.[5] If we follow this definition, outward orientation will be by definition better than inward orientation at least in terms of allocative efficiency as far as world prices reflect correct opportunity costs – this is of course a big assumption.[6]

More recently, Lant Pritchett, then a World Bank economist, pointed out that there is no robust correlation between the rankings of countries in terms of outward orientation constructed using different methods of defining trade orientation. This casts a serious doubt on the whole exercise itself.[7]

Despite these underlying theoretical problems, many studies have attempted to measure the relationship between a country's degree of outward orientation and its economic growth through econometric methods. Although the result depends on how trade policy orientation is defined – for example, there is little correlation between the two variables, if outward orientation is defined in terms of the share of export in GDP – many of these studies find a correlation between a country's trade policy orientation and its economic growth. This statistical 'evidence' is often presented by free-trade economists as incontrovertible proof that outward-oriented trade strategy is superior to the inward-oriented one, but their interpretation is not as watertight as they argue.

First of all, we should not forget the simple but fundamental point that statistical correlation does not mean causality.[8] For example, it is possible that both a country's high export growth rate and its high overall economic growth are caused by a third factor, say, a high investment in education, which is *not* related to trade policy *per se*. Moreover, as far as causality is concerned, the converse may also be true: a country's export may be growing fast because the overall economy is growing fast, rather than the other way around (therefore, a case of growth-led export, rather than export-led growth).

Second, cross-section studies assume a lot about the underlying structures of different economies.[9] An obvious alternative is a time-series study of a country with changing trade orientation, but in this case there is a problem of identifying the exact 'response lag'.[10] For example, many studies have shown that the improved growth performance following the shift towards an outward-oriented trade strategy in countries like Korea and Taiwan in the 1960s would not have been possible without the import-substitution policies adopted in the previous period, that had helped to build their underlying export capabilities.

Moreover, there is considerable arbitrariness in classifying the countries, especially when it involves 'out-lier' cases that can skew the statistical outcome. For example, the 'statistical evidence' that the World Bank used in its supposedly 'definitive' work on trade policy of the 1980s[11] depended – critically – on how Korea is classified.[12]

Finally, some studies show that, even when disregarding all the above-mentioned problems, evidence for the superiority of outward-oriented strategy is not universal. For example, Singer and Gray[13] show that, while there is some positive correlation between a country's outward orientation and its growth, the performance gap is much smaller in periods of lower world demand, suggesting that the best trade strategy undoubtedly depends on the state of the world economy. They also point out that the correlation almost disappears for the poorest countries, suggesting that a country may have to reach a minimum level of development to exploit the liberalization of trade.

The evolution of the literature on trade policy over the last few decades shows how the debate in this important area has been marred by mainstream economists' use of biased definitions, dubious statistical evidence and unwarranted generalization. A more critical examination of this work reveals a set of highly complex theoretical and empirical issues that call for a more nuanced approach to the question of the role played by international trade and trade policy in economic development.

3. Industrial Policy – Some Neglected but Important Issues[14]

Closely related to, but distinct from, the trade policy argument is the debate on industrial policy – or 'selective' industrial policy – particularly (but not exclusively) in the context of the East Asian development success. The main bone of contention in this debate has been whether 'selective' state intervention at the industry, or even the firm, level can improve the performance of not only the industry/firm concerned, but also that of the overall economy.

As discussed in Chapter 5, the current mainstream view on industrial policy and economic development is well summarized by the *East Asian Miracle* report (henceforth EAM) of the World Bank.[15] The problems with the faulty methodologies that led to the EAM's conclusion on this issue – namely, that industrial policy may have some theoretical justifications but has never worked except in Japan – are rather well known by now. However, less well known is the EAM's limited notion of industrial policy, which has allowed it to ignore a number of important aspects of *real-life* industrial policy.[16]

The EAM acknowledged three important justifications for industrial policy. The first, and most important from the EAM's point of view, is the 'big push' argument, that is, the need to coordinate complementary investments in the presence of significant scale economies and capital market imperfection. Second is the role that the state is able to play as the organizer of domestic firms into implicit cartels in their negotiations with foreign firms or governments. And, last but not least, policies to deal with learning externalities (e.g., subsidies to industrial training) are mentioned.

In my view, while these reasons for industrial policy are indeed important, policies that emanate from them do not exhaust the gamut of industrial policy – indeed, they do not even necessarily constitute the most important aspects of it. There are at least three more aspects of industrial policy that are more or less completely ignored by the EAM but are in my view even more important than the ones that the EAM discuss.

The first of the neglected aspects of industrial policy is coordination not only of complementary investments but also between competing investments – what is known as 'managed competition'.[17] The logic here is that the oligopolistic competition which characterizes many modern industries often leads to excess capacity, unless there is a coordination of investment activities across the competitor firms. Excess capacity leads to price wars, which damage the profit of the firms concerned and may force them to scrap some of their assets and even to go bankrupt. Needless to say, asset scrapping and bankruptcy are necessary and costless ways of reallocating resources in a world without what Williamson calls 'specific assets'[18] – namely, assets which are built for their current use, so that they generate little or no value in alternative uses. However, when there are specific assets involved, the process of *ex post* coordination through asset scrapping and transfer involves social costs, as those assets have to be scrapped or transferred to alternative uses, in which they generate much less value. *Ex ante* coordination of investment by the state can minimize such costs.[19]

This is not just a theoretical quibble, because coordination of competing investments had been one of the most important components in the industrial policy regime of the East Asian countries. By ignoring this key aspect of industrial policy, the EAM ended up neglecting a huge, and arguably the most important, chunk of industrial policy.

The second aspect of industrial policy that has been generally neglected are the policies that try to deal with the consequences of scale economy. Of course, scale economy plays an important, if somewhat implicit, role in the mainstream understanding of industrial policy as shown in the EAM, as without scale economy there is no need for a 'big push': complementary industries can simply be built in a piecemeal manner. However this is not the only, and in my view not necessarily the most important, way in which scale economy matters for industrial policymakers.

First of all, scale economy has a critical implication for the cost competitiveness of an industry. Economists may have traditionally debated whether the social costs from monopoly constitute 1 or 2% of total output, but in industries with significant scale economy, choosing too small a scale of capacity can often mean a 30–50% fall in production efficiency. It is for this reason that the East Asian governments did everything to ensure that capacities installed were as close to the minimum efficient scale as possible through policy measures such as investment licencing, forced mergers and export requirements.

Second, scale economy also has a hitherto-ignored relationship with luxury consumption control.[20] Luxury consumption control has frequently been denounced as meddlesome government intrusion on individual choice, but it is an important industrial policy tool in certain durable consumer goods industries. For example, by restricting the production of luxury models, the Japanese and Korean governments ensured that there are fewer models, and therefore lower unit costs, in their passenger car industries.

In the end, while it may not sound as fancy as the 'big push', ensuring the achievement of scale economy in key industries was in practice probably a much more important aspect of industrial policy actions of the East Asian governments than the former.

The third theoretical justification for industrial policy that has received little recognition is industrial policy's role as a mechanism to promote structural change by reducing resistance by the 'losers' from such change.[21]

Industrial policy is often equated with 'picking the winners', but it also has an important 'protective' element – that is 'helping losers' by temporarily shielding them from the full forces of the market. The logic behind this is as follows.

When there exist specific assets, those who invested in them may have incentives to block structural changes that are socially beneficial but will make their own assets worthless (e.g. firms which invest in expensive custom-made machinery, workers with particular skills). In such a situation, policies that protect the potential 'losers' may help, rather than hinder, structural change by reducing their incentives for the losers to wreck the process. For example, the East Asian countries implemented industrial policy measures such as orderly capacity-scrapping arrangement between competing firms and retraining programmes in order to reduce such resistance, thus facilitating the structural change.

4. FDI Policy[22]

One of the distinguishing features of the recent – especially post-1980 – phase of globalization is the growing importance of transnational corporations (TNCs), and foreign direct investment (FDI) as its main mode of operation. Reflecting this change, the consensus view on the role of TNCs in economic development has changed radically since the 1980s.

In the 1960s and 1970s, a highly negative view of the TNCs prevailed. There were concerns about: (i) transfer pricing (subsidiaries of a TNC exporting to or importing from other subsidiaries at 'internal' prices so that profits accrue to subsidiaries operating in countries with the lowest corporate taxes); (ii) restrictive clauses (restrictions on exports or R&D activities by their subsidiaries); (iii) crowding-out of domestic investors in the domestic capital market; (iv) excessive royalty charged on technology- or brand-licencing; (v) monopolistic practices; (vi) retardation of local technological development; (vii) the introduction of inappropriate technology (excessively capital-intensive production methods often producing 'non-essential' outputs); (viii) undue political influence (as often witnessed in the support that US TNCs gave to 'friendly' Latin American military dictators).

In contrast to this, the opposing view has prevailed since the 1980s, and in particular with the rise of the globalization discourse from the mid-1990s onward. Now, many people argue that there is essentially no conflict between TNCs and the host countries, and therefore that TNCs are indispensable agents of development. Developing countries are therefore recommended to dismantle regulations on FDI in order to maximize FDI inflows. And there is now even a move to institutionalize this procedure internationally by establishing a multilateral investment agreement in the WTO.

This argument is made up of three key theses. The first thesis is that FDI is playing an increasingly important role in the world economy, especially for developing countries. The second is that TNCs are becoming more and more 'transnational' and therefore are losing loyalties to their home countries. This opens up the possibility that even the high value-added 'core' activities of TNCs (e.g. R&D, even headquarters) may be relocated to any potential host country that is willing to accommodate them. In this regard, the case of Nestlé, which produces only about 5% of its output in its home country of Switzerland, is frequently cited. The third thesis is that countries which have had 'liberal' policies towards FDI have performed better. The East and the South East Asian countries are often given as examples.

How true are these theses? To take the first thesis, it is true that the importance of FDI has been increasing recently, and that the absolute amount of FDI going into developing countries has increased considerably. However in proportional terms the vast bulk (70–80%) of FDI still occurs among the developed countries. The share of FDI going to developing countries has increased throughout the 1990s, but, when China is excluded from the equation, the increase has in fact been very small. Indeed, it returned to the 1980s level during the 1999–2000 international mega-merger boom, which saw a marked increase in the FDI flows among the developed countries (see table 1). And even this small share of FDI is highly concentrated in about a dozen countries, which takes 70–80% of the share coming to the developing world.[23]

As far as the second thesis is concerned, it should be pointed out that most TNCs remain international firms with a strong base in their home countries, rather than truly transnational firms. Typically, 70–80% of their assets and production activities are located in home countries. Nestlé is, then, still the exception rather than the rule. Even when TNCs relocate some of their core activities abroad, these are usually to other developed countries, and even then, countries with a heavy 'regional' bias – Europe, North America, and Japan acting as three regional blocs in this respect. When it comes to the nationality of their top decision-makers, the picture is even more stark. Very

Table 1. **Share of developing countries in world's total Foreign Direct Investment inflows, including and excluding China, 1983–2000**

(in millions of dollars; figures in parentheses are shares in world total)

	1983–9 (annual average)	1990–4 (annual average)	1995–8 (annual average)	1999–2000 (annual average)
World Total	107,134	202,636	448,988	1,172,907
Developing Countries	21,023 (19.6%)	62,067 (30.6%)	145,009 (33.2%)	231,089 (19.7%)
China	2,047 (1.9%)	16,062 (7.9%)	41,431 (9.7%)	40,546 (3.5%)
Developing Countries excluding China	18,976 (17.7%)	46,005 (22.7%)	103,578 (23.6%)	191,043 (16.3%)

Source: UNCTAD, *World Investment Report*, 1995, 1999 and 2002.

few TNCs have more than a token presence of foreign citizens in their top decision-making bodies.[24]

The third thesis also needs to be questioned. Contrary to conventional wisdom, many East and South East Asian countries have had rather restrictive policies towards FDI. Only Malaysia and Hong Kong had predominantly liberal attitudes towards TNCs. Singapore did rely on TNCs very heavily, but deliberately directed FDI towards government-designated priority sectors through targeted investments in infrastructure, education, training, and investment incentives. Among the seven East Asian developing countries, it was only in these three economies that the contribution of FDI as a source of capital accumulation has been exceptionally high by international standards (see table 2). In Thailand, which is usually regarded as a model 'FDI-driven' economy, the corresponding ratio was not much above the developing-

Table 2. **Ratio of FDI inflows to Gross Domestic Capital formation for various regions and selected countries, 1971–99**
(annual average)

	1971–5	1976–80	1981–5	1986–90	1991–5	1996–9
All Countries	n.a.	n.a.	2.3%	4.1%	4.3%	10.2%
Developed	n.a.	n.a.	2.2%	4.6%	3.7%	9.6%
European Union	n.a.	n.a.	2.6%	5.9%	6.0%	14.5%
USA	0.9%	2.0%	2.9%	6.9%	4.2%	11.0%
Japan	0.1%	0.1%	0.1%	0.0%	n.a.	n.a.[1]
Developing	n.a.	n.a.	3.3%	3.2%	6.4%	11.4%
Africa	n.a.	n.a.	2.3%	3.5%	5.8%	9.0%
Latin America	n.a.	n.a.	4.1%	4.2%	7.5%	18.3%
Asia	n.a.	n.a.	3.1%	2.8%	5.9%	9.2%
China	0.0%	0.1%	0.9%	2.1%	11.1%	13.3%
Hong Kong	5.9%	4.2%	6.9%	12.9%	8.0%	32.9%
Indonesia	4.6%	2.4%	0.9%	2.1%	4.7%	1.1%
Korea	1.9%	0.4%	0.5%	1.2%	0.7%	4.5%
Malaysia	15.2%	11.9%	10.8%	11.7%	19.3%	16.5%
Singapore	15.0%	16.6%	17.4%	35.0%	30.7%	28.0%
Taiwan	1.4%	1.2%	1.5%	3.7%	2.4%	3.6%[2]
Thailand	3.0%	1.5%	3.0%	6.5%	3.9%	11.2%
Eastern Europe	n.a.	n.a.	0.0%	0.1%	8.4%	12.5%

Source: UNCTAD, *World Investment Report*, 1993, 1995, 1999 and 2002.

Notes: 1. 1.1% in 1999. 2. The data for 1998 is not available.

country average in the 1970s and 1980s, and was well below the average during the first half of the 1990s, although it shot up in the second half due to the post-financial crisis 'fire-sale' of assets. The table also shows that in Taiwan, Indonesia and especially Korea, the contribution of FDI to capital accumulation has been well below the developing-country average.[25]

Those who argue for the liberalization of policies towards TNCs have a very strong belief that what is good for TNCs is also good for their host countries. However, while there are few justifications for the extreme anti-TNC view that was once popular, this does not mean that TNCs are unambiguously beneficial for the economic development of host countries (all of the worries about TNCs that I mention above are not groundless). Indeed, many of the most successful cases of economic development during the twentieth century were founded on policies that strategically restricted and strictly controlled FDI in terms of entry, ownership, technology transfer and local contents requirement – so not just Japan, Korea and Taiwan but also that unrecognized case of economic miracle, Finland, which was the second fastest growing economy in the world after Japan during the twentieth century.[26]

Of course, some argue that, even if TNCs do not always bring benefits, developing countries should adopt a liberal policy towards them, because TNCs have now become so footloose that they will relocate to countries with the least restrictions. How true is this?

There are certainly some industries (for example, garments, shoes and toys) in which there are very low sunk costs involved in investments and therefore the firms are very footloose. However, there are many other industries in which there exists a high element of sunk costs, not only in terms of dedicated physical equipment (e.g. chemicals, pharmaceuticals) but also in terms of the supplier network that firms have to build over time in order to attain a high level of productivity (e.g., advanced electronics, automobiles). In such industries, TNCs are not entirely footloose, and therefore, once they have made the investments in a country, they will not be able to pull out at the slightest adverse changes in the host country government policies.[27]

More importantly, it should be pointed out that those who argue for liberal policies towards TNCs assume that FDI decisions are mainly affected by the amount of business freedom that is granted to them. However, empirical studies show that FDI decisions are much more strongly affected by the overall performance of the economy, especially the prospect for growth, than the regulatory regime. Moreover, surveys among top managers show that the larger TNCs are able and often willing to accommodate a lot of restrictive policy measures, as far as they are stable and the changes in them predictable.[28]

Many argue that developing country governments should liberalize their FDI policies. This argument holds that there is essentially no conflict of interests between TNCs and the host country, and that globalization has maximized the bargaining power of TNCs by giving them the ability to relocate freely away from countries that pursue 'wrong' policies. However, the costs and benefits of FDI, as well as the relative bargaining power of the foreign investors, vary considerably across countries, industries and contexts. This calls for a strategic approach, in which a country may adopt a very liberal FDI policy in certain areas while adopting a highly restrictive one in others, depending on its long-term development goals, its level of development and the shape of international competitive struggle in the industry concerned.

5. The WTO and the New International Trading Order

In 1995 the Uruguay Round of talks by the GATT (General Agreement on Trade and Tariffs) resulted in worldwide tariff cuts, tougher restrictions on trade-related subsidies, strengthening of trade-related intellectual property rights, and, most importantly, the transformation of the GATT into the more powerful World Trade Organization (WTO). This has made many people argue that the world trading order has irreversibly moved to free trade, and that, whatever its merits may have been, activist trade policy of the kind used by the East Asian countries is now 'out'. Is this a correct assessment?

First of all, we have to note that the launch of the WTO by no means heralds the start of full-blown free trade on a global scale. Even on paper, the WTO agreement by no means obliges countries to abolish all tariffs and protections (more on this later). Moreover, many countries have been dragging their feet in meeting their own promises. In particular, the developed countries have been doing little to reduce their protection in areas like agriculture, textile and clothing. Given this reality, it would be foolish to assume that the WTO rules mean free trade.

Second, and much more serious than the problem of feet-dragging, is the fundamental disagreements that countries have with regard to the definition of 'free trade'. For example, developed countries are accusing many developing countries of engaging in 'unfair competition' by using child labour, allowing 'inhumane' working conditions and destroying the environment. In return, developing countries argue that attempts to impose first-world labour and environmental standards on them are in fact disguised protectionist measures by the developed countries. These are just some examples of the important but neglected fact that the definition of free trade depends on our conception of what constitutes minimum acceptable human rights, and that as a result there cannot be one universal definition of 'free trade'.[29] This will constitute a permanent source of dispute in the WTO as long as there are countries with differences in income levels, moral values and political systems.

Another important point to think about in relation to the WTO is the difficulty of building international organizations.[30] The WTO is a very interesting example in this regard. In terms of its formal structure, it is the first fully democratic international organization in the sense of having the 'one country, one vote' rule – in the WB and the IMF, the principle of 'one dollar one vote' rules, while in the UN the permanent members of the Security Council have veto power. This democratic structure was set up because the developed countries felt the need to get a greater legitimacy, and hence a wider support, for the new trading regime. However, in practice, votes are almost never taken, because the organization is supposed to work through 'consensus', which means that powerful countries like the USA have *de facto* veto power. Indeed, many things are decided in the backroom meetings in which only the most important countries participate.[31] Despite all this, the principle of 'one country, one vote' enables developing countries to exercise some influence in the running of the WTO, and it will be interesting to see exactly how this will affect the way in which the new world trading order shapes up over the coming years.

Finally, we also need to examine the widespread claim that the WTO, in forcing tariff cuts and banning trade-related subsidies, has made the use of interventionist trade policy impossible.

To begin with, it is not as if everything was permitted under the old regime. There existed a lot of restrictions on what countries could do, and countries such as Korea often exploited grey areas in the GATT. It is true that, under the WTO, rules on the use of tariffs, subsidies and quantitative restrictions have become tighter, but it is not as though we are now living in a 'brave new world'.

Second, tariff reduction under the WTO does not mean a total abolition of tariffs. What countries have done is to announce the level below which they will keep their tariffs. And although such ceilings were at times substantially reduced (for example, India cut its trade-weighted average tariff from 71% to 32%), they were still fixed quite high by other standards. Brazil cut trade-weighted average tariff from 41% to 27%, Chile from 35% to 25%, Turkey from 25% to 22%, and so on.[32] Moreover, this tariff cut is supposed to be done over a period of 5 to 10 years, so there is still a breathing space (although this has run out for those who were not classified as 'least developed' countries by 2000). The sad thing is that some countries have gone overboard and reduced the tariffs much quicker than they needed to.

Third, infant industry protection up to eight years is still allowed, although it must be pointed out that infant industry protection was *not* the clause invoked by countries like Korea in protecting their infant industries under the old GATT regime. What they usually used was the balance-of-payments clause, which also still exists under the WTO. This clause allows countries to impose emergency tariff increase (import surcharge) on the grounds of either a sudden surge in sectoral imports or of an overall balance-of-payments problem, for which almost all developing countries qualify. It should also be noted that, while the overall amount of import surcharge should be commensurate to the balance-of-payments problem that the country is facing, where exactly the surcharge is imposed is left to the discretion of the country. This provides vital space for policy manoeuvre.

Fourth, not all subsidies are 'illegal' for everyone. For example, the least developed countries are allowed to use export subsidies, which other countries are not supposed to do. Subsidies for agriculture, regional development, basic R&D, environment-related technology upgrading are still allowed – indeed, the developed countries have actively used these provisions to pursue their industrial policies. For example, the EU and the US state governments have employed regional development subsidies, while the US federal government has aggressively used its R&D budget to influence national technological and industrial developments.

Fifth, it is often forgotten that the WTO restrictions only cover 'trade-related' policies. Although defining exactly which policies are 'trade-related' is controversial, this means that there are many 'domestic' policies which can be used for infant industry promotion purposes. For example, subsidies for equipment investment, tax exemptions for certain types of industries, support for start-up enterprises, subsidies for investment in particular skills and so forth, are tools over which the WTO does not have the jurisdiction.

The birth of the WTO has therefore certainly increased the constraints put on the conduct of trade and industrial policies, especially those of developing countries. However, the constraints are not as completely overwhelming as many people assume, and there is still some important room for manoeuvre for those who are willing to use it.

6. Intellectual Property Rights Issues[33]

The issue of intellectual property rights has recently come to prominence as a result of the debates surrounding the trade-related intellectual property rights (TRIPS) agreement in the WTO.

The TRIPS agreement enables countries to impose trade sanctions on other countries who violate their intellectual property rights. Initially, when TRIPS was enforced on the Koreans producing fake Chanel bags and the Chinese producing pirate CDs, the issue was less contentious. However, more recently the debate has become very heated as it has touched on some extremely sensitive issues. For example, there was a general outcry over attempts by developed country firms to patent products that embody knowledge commonly known in some developing countries on the back of the TRIPS provision (e.g., turmeric, basmati rice). The recent attempts by developed country pharmaceutical companies to block the exports of cheap AIDS/HIV drugs to Sub Saharan Africa by some developing countries (such as Argentina, India, Thailand and Brazil) using TRIPS has highlighted the potential conflict between TRIPS and greater human well-being.

The defenders of TRIPS argue that, despite these problems, TRIPS is good for the world, because without a strong protection of intellectual property rights (henceforth IPR), no one will have the incentive to invest in the generation of new ideas. While they admit that much of this investment will be in developed countries, they argue that developing countries will also benefit from stronger protection of IPR. A stronger protection of IPR by developing countries, they argue, will encourage technology transfer and FDI from developed countries while promoting R&D activities aimed for developing-country markets by firms based in the developed countries. How valid are these claims?

One interesting way to look at this problem is to see whether the US-based National Law Center for Inter-American Free Trade is right in claiming, like many other proponents of TRIPS, that '[t]he historical record in the industrialized countries, which began as developing countries, demonstrates that intellectual property protection has been one of the most powerful instruments for economic development, export growth, and the diffusion of new technologies, art and culture'.[34]

Even a cursory look at the historical evidence shows that a strong IPR regime, in the sense of providing strong protection for *private* intellectual property rights (henceforth PIPR), was *not* an essential condition for their economic development.[35] Most of these countries accorded only very incomplete and weak protection to PIPR, especially those of foreigners, until quite late in their stages of development. They were, often with government support, engaged in poaching skilled workers, smuggling machinery, and industrial espionage. Violation of trademark laws and copyrights was widespread: in the late nineteenth century, there was a widespread German production of fake 'made-in-England' goods, while the USA, despite considering itself as a champion of patentee rights, refused to protect foreigners' copyrights until 1891, as it then was a net importer of copyright materials.

Most importantly, many of today's developed countries had very lax patent laws. Many of them – including Britain (before the 1852 reform), the Netherlands, Austria and France – openly allowed patenting of imported inventions. In the USA, before the 1836 overhaul of its patent law, patents were granted without any proof of originality. This not only led to the patenting of imported technologies but encouraged racketeers to engage in 'rent-seeking' by patenting devices already in use ('phony patents') and by demanding money from their users under threat of suit for infringement.[36] In the most extreme cases, countries such as the Netherlands and Switzerland refused to introduce a patent law until the early twentieth century, when they were among the most developed countries in the world (see Schiff, 1971, for details).

In sum, historical evidence actually proves that today's developed countries did *not* provide a strong protection of IPR until they became capable of generating original inventions, trademarks and copyright materials.

But, irrespective of the the historical evidence, the pro-IPR commentators would ask, isn't there a good reason to say that we need a strong PIPR, mainly in the form of patents, to generate new knowledge? The answer is actually no.

Contrary to what the defenders of strong private intellectual property rights (PIPR) believe, people often pursue knowledge for its own sake or for the 'public good', so they do not always need the monetary incentives conferred by PIPR in order to generate new knowledge. This is indeed a view put forward by the 13 eminent scientists (all fellows of the Royal Society, the most prominent scientific society in the UK) in an open letter to the *Financial Times* arguing against TRIPS. They argue: 'Patents are only one means for promoting discovery and invention. Scientific curiosity, coupled with the desire to benefit humanity, has been of far greater importance throughout history'.[37]

More importantly, even without patents, the innovator can enjoy many 'natural' protective mechanisms and therefore will be able to reap substantial financial gains from his innovation. These natural protective mechanisms include the following. First, there is the 'imitation lag', namely, the lag between the introduction of an innovation and the emergence of imitations of such innovation. Second, there exists the 'reputational advantage', which refers to the phenomenon that simply because the innovator was the first person to come up with a new product, consumers know his product better and tend to associate it with superior quality, even if it is in fact not the case. Third, the innovator has a head start in racing down 'learning curves'. Unit production costs tend to come down as production experience accumulates, and therefore the firm that started production earlier, at a given point of time, tends to have lower unit costs.

That innovators enjoy the above-mentioned natural protective mechanisms was in fact a popular argument deployed by the anti-patent movement in Europe during the nineteenth century,[38] and the idea behind the famous early twentieth-century Austrian–American economist Joseph Schumpeter's vision of capitalist development through the 'creative destruction' of innovation.[39] Indeed, a number of studies confirm that in most industries such natural protection mechanism is much more important than patents in motivating innovation.[40]

In addition to the fact that it is not necessary for knowledge generation, the patent system is also known for its wastefulness due to its 'winner takes it all' nature, which results in duplication of efforts and a waste of resources in 'getting around' existing patents. Also, it can become a hindrance to technological progress, given interdependence between technologies. And as increasingly minute pieces of knowledge (say, down to the gene level) become patentable, the risk of patents hindering, rather than promoting, progress is becoming greater.

People have also raised issues over the granting of patents to inventions that were created using ideas generated at least in part by publicly-funded research.[41] For example, even according to the information provided by the US pharmaceutical industry association, only 43% of pharmaceutical R&D is funded by the industry itself, while 29% is funded by the from the US government's National Institute of Health (NIH).[42]

Addressing the TRIPS agreement specifically, the following criticisms may be made of the pro-TRIPS argument.

First of all, its proponents argue that, by encouraging a stronger system of international PIPR protection, TRIPS will encourage technology transfer to developing countries. While this is theoretically possible, there is no evidence for it happening. Moreover, TRIPS will reduce developing countries' ability to assimilate advanced technologies through 'informal' channels (e.g. reverse engineering, developing alternative processes for patented chemical substances), which has to be set against the alleged (non-existent) increase in formal technology transfers.

The second argument in support of TRIPS is that a better protection of PIPR promotes FDI. However, patents are often used as substitutes for FDI, and therefore the impact of stronger protection of PIPR on FDI is not clear. Moreover, the IPR regime is only one of many considerations in FDI decisions, and a minor one at that. Given these, it is not surprising that there is no evidence for this line of argument. And all of these have to be set against the fact that the impact of FDI is generally ambiguous and highly context-dependent (see above, section 4).

The third argument is that stronger PIPR in the developing countries may encourage innovative activities by developed country firms targeted at developing country markets. Unfortunately, the developing country markets are usually marginal, and therefore the extra profit from them is unlikely to significantly affect the R&D decisions of developed country firms. Once again, there is little evidence for this – the fact that more R&D money is spent on slimming drugs than on malaria is a telling example in this regard.

Now, if it is simply that TRIPS is unlikely to bring much benefit to developing countries, we may not be too worried, but the problem is that that it also imposes substantial costs on these countries. First, running the 'sophisticated' IPR system demanded by TRIPS will require a large amount of scarce human and administrative resources (scientists and lawyers to man the patent office, patent lawyers). It will also increase royalty payments to the outside world, which will harm the countries' balance of payments positions. And it will increase the abuse of monopoly power by large TNCs holding patents and other IPR, given the limited anti-trust capability that developing country governments have. There is also an increased possibility of theft of 'traditional knowledge system'.

My view is that TRIPS should be radically reformed or even abolished. First of all, there should be greater recognition on the part of the developed countries that, when they were themselves developing economies, they were engaged in all kinds of 'illegitimate' practices in order to acquire advanced technology, including the violation of PIPR (especially that of foreign nationals). Second, there should be a greater acceptance that developing countries need fundamentally different IPR regimes from the ones that the developed countries have today. Developing countries should be allowed to grant weaker PIPR (e.g., shorter patent life, easier compulsory licensing and compulsory working, easier parallel imports) and to pay lower licensing royalty rates (probably graduated according to a country's ability to pay). Third, TRIPS should be reformed (or abolished) in such a way that it does not merely lead to greater and cheaper transfer of technologies but also develops the long-term technological capabilities of developing countries, without which an easier access to technology means little. We could also institute an international tax on patent royalties and use at least parts of it for improving technological capabilities in developing countries.

Notes

1 See Smith and Toye 1983.
2 For the two best critical reviews, see Helleiner 1990; Rodriguez and Rodrik 1999.
3 World Bank 1987.
4 Effective rate of protection takes into account the fact that tariff rates on final products overstate protection accorded to the products, because they do not consider the fact that their producers may be using expensive inputs because of protection on the inputs.
5 World Bank 1987 is the best example.
6 Singer 1988.
7 Pritchett 1996.
8 Singer 1988.

 9 Helleiner 1990.
10 Pack 1988.
11 World Bank 1987.
12 See also Evans 1991.
13 See Singer and Gray 1988.
14 This section draws heavily on Chang 2003.
15 World Bank 1993.
16 These issues, unfortunately, are sometimes ignored even by the critics of the World Bank.
17 Amsden and Singh 1994.
18 Williamson 1985.
19 Chang 1994, ch. 3.
20 Chang 1997.
21 Dore 1986 is a pioneering work emphasizing this aspect of industrial policy. See Chang and Rowthorn 1995 for further theoretical developments.
22 This section draws on Chang 1998.
23 Part of this concentration is obviously due to the fact that many of the largest recipients of FDI are also large economies (in terms of GDP). However, even after adjusting for the size of the economy, the concentration still remains high. For example, during the 1980s (1980–91), the 10 largest developing country recipients of FDI received 16.5% of world's total FDI, even though they accounted for only about 7.3% of world's total GDP (for 1980–9). The figures are extracted from Hirst and Thompson 1996, tables 3.2. and 3.4.
24 The takeover by Daimler-Benz (Germany) and of Chrysler (USA) is a very good example in this respect. When the takeover happened, it was presented as a merger of two equals, but the subsequent German domination in the board of directors (12 out of 14 directors are Germans as of 2003) has made it clear that it was nothing of the sort.
25 The rise in the ratio in Korea in the 1996–9 period is also the result of post-crisis 'fire sale' of assets.
26 See Yoshino 1970 on Japan, Chang 1998 on Korea. Wade 1990, pp. 148–56 on Taiwan. Hjerppe and Ahvenainen 1986 on Finland.
27 Of course, this does not mean that in such industries governments can do anything, as whatever a government does now will affect the future investment decisions by TNCs.
28 Chang 1998.
29 A topic discussed further in Chapter 2 of this volume.
30 See Chang and Evans 2000 for further discussion.
31 See also Chapter 23, this volume.
32 See Amsden 2000 for further details.
33 This section draws on Chang 2001.
34 National Law Center for Inter-American Free Trade, 'Strong Intellectual Property Protection Benefits the Developing Countries', 1997, http://www.natlaw.com/pubs/spmxip11.htm.
35 Note that not all IPR are private. Those who do not distinguish between different forms of IPR implicitly assume that the only alternative to private intellectual property rights (PIPR) is a free-for-all open access regime. However, many pieces of knowledge are in fact publicly or communally owned and are therefore subject to certain rules of use and disposal. For example, the private-sector participants in a publicly-financed research consortium may be obliged to make all their findings public and/or be forced

to share the resulting patents with other participants in the project. Even in a situation that looks to be purely 'open access', there may be certain laws and social norms concerning the use of particular types of knowledge for particular purposes. For example, even if the copyright of a book has expired, we do not allow other people to plagiarize from it. To provide another example, many providers of free web-based softwares demand that the resulting (improved) products cannot be appropriated by individuals (UNDP 1999, p. 73, Box, 2.9).

36 Cochran and Miller 1942, p. 14.
37 'Strong global patent rules increase the cost of medicines', p. 20, *The Financial Times*, 14 February 2001.
38 The classic source on the anti-patent movement is Machlup and Penrose 1950.
39 Schumpeter's view is well set out in Schumpeter 1987.
40 Mansfield 1984; Levine et al. 1987.
41 For further details, see Chang 2001.
42 See http://www.phrma.org/publications/profile00/chap2.phtm#growth.

References

Amsden, A, 2000, 'Industrialisation under New WTO Law', a paper for the UNCTAD X meeting, 12–19 February, 2000, Bangkok.

Amsden, A and Singh, A, 1994, 'Growth in Developing Countries: Lessons from East Asian Countries', *European Economic Review*, vol. 38, nos.3 and 4.

Chang, H-J, 1994, *The Political Economy of Industrial Policy*, Basingstoke, Macmillan.

——, 1995, 'Explaining "Flexible Rigidities" in East Asia' in T Killick, 1995, ed., *The Flexible Economy*, London, Routledge.

——, 1997, 'Luxury Consumption Control and Industrialisation in East Asia', mimeo., a background paper prepared for *Trade and Development Report 1997*, Geneva, UNCTAD.

——, 1998, 'Globalisation, Transnational Corporations, and Economic Development' in D Baker, G Epstein and R Pollin, 1998, eds, *Globalisation and Progressive Economic Policy*, Cambridge, Cambridge University Press.

——, 2001, 'Intellectual Property Rights and Economic Development – Historical Lessons and Emerging Issues', *Journal of Human Development*, 2001, vol. 2, no. 2.

——, 2003, 'Industrial Policy and East Asia – The Miracle, the Crisis, and the Future' in Jomo, KS, 2003, ed., *Manufacturing Competitiveness in Asia – How Internationally Competitive National Firms and Industries Developed in East Asia*, London and New York, Routledge Curzon.

Chang, H-J and Evans, P, 2000, 'The Role of Institutions in Economic Change', a paper prepared for the meeting of the 'Other Canon' Group, Venice, January, 2000, and Oslo, August 2000.

Chang, H-J and Rowthorn, R, 1995, 'Role of the State in Economic Change: Entrepreneurship and Conflict Management' in H-J Chang and B Rowthorn, eds, *The Role of the State in Economic Change*, Oxford, Clarendon Press.

Cochran, T and Miller, W, 1942, *The Age of Enterprise – A Social History of Industrial America*, New York, Macmillan.

Dore, R, 1986, *Flexible Rigidities: Industrial Policy and Structural Adjustment in the Japanese Economy 1970–80*, London, Athlone Press.

Evans, D, 1991, 'Visible and Invisible Hands in Trade Policy Reform' in C Colclough and J Manor, 1991, eds, *States or Markets?*, Oxford, Clarendon Press.

Helleiner, G, 1990,' Trade Strategy in medium-term Adjustment', *World Development*, vol. 18, no. 6.

Hirst, P and Thompson, G, 1996, *Globalization in Question*, Cambridge, Polity Press.

Hjerppe, R and Ahvenainen, J, 1986, 'Foreign Enterprises and Nationalistic Control: The Case of Finland since the End of the Nineteenth Century' in A Teichova, M Lévy-Leboyer and H Nussbaum, 1986, eds, *Multinational Enterprise in Historical Perspective*, Cambridge, Cambridge University Press.

Levin, R, Klevorick, A, Nelson, R and Winter, S, 1987, 'Appropriating the Returns form Industrial Research and Development', *Brookings Papers on Economic Activity*, 1987, no. 3.

Machlup, F and Penrose, E, 1950, 'The Patent Controversy in the Nineteenth Century', *Journal of Economic History*, vol. 10, no. 1.

Mansfield, E, 1984, 'Patents and Innovation: An Empirical Study', *Management Science*, vol. 32, February.

Pack, H, 1988, 'Trade and Industrialisation' in H Chenery and TN Srinivasan, eds, *The Handbook of Development Economics*, vol. 2, Amsterdam, North-Holland.

Pritchett, L, 1996, 'Measuring Outward Orientation in LDCs: Can It Be Done?', *Journal of Development Economics*, vol. 49, no. 2.

Rodriguez, F and Rodrik, D, 1999, 'Trade Policy and Economic Growth – A Sceptic's Guide to the Cross-National Evidence', NBER Working Paper, no. 7081.

Schiff, E, 1971, *Industrialisation without National Patents – the Netherlands, 1860–1912 and Switzerland, 1850–1907*, Princeton, Princeton University Press.

Schumpeter, J, 1987, *Capitalism, Socialism, and Democracy*, 6th edition, London, Unwin.

Singer, H, 1988, '*The World Development Report 1987* on the blessings of "outward orientation": A Necessary Correction', *Journal of Development Studies*, vol. 24, no. 2.

Singer, H, and Gray, P, 1988, 'Trade Policy and Growth of Developing Countries: Some New Data', *World Development*, vol. 16, no, 3.

Smith, S and Toye, J, 1983, 'Three Stories about Trade and Poor Economies' in S Smith and J Toye, 1983, eds, *Trade and Poor Economies*, London, Frank Cass.

UNDP (United Nations Development Program), 1999, *Human Development Report, 1999*, New York, Oxford University Press.

Wade, R, 1990, *Governing the Market*, Princeton, Princeton University Press.

World Bank, 1987, *World Development Report 1987*, Oxford, Oxford University Press.

World Bank, 1993, *The East Asian Miracle*, Oxford, Oxford University Press.

Williamson, O, 1985, *The Economic Institutions of Capitalism*, New York, Free Press.

Yoshino, M Y, 1970, 'Japan as Host to the International Corporation' in C Kindleberger, 1970, ed., *The International Corporation – A Symposium*, Cambridge, Mass., MIT Press.

13

TECHNOLOGY AND INDUSTRIAL DEVELOPMENT IN AN ERA OF GLOBALIZATION

Sanjaya Lall

1. Introduction

Technical progress, liberalization and the spread of globalized production systems are creating new opportunities and challenges for industrializing countries. There are, however, different perspectives on how they affect the Third World. The optimistic view is as follows. Technology is now more mobile internationally. Information is easier to access and the cost of transmitting it has fallen to very low levels. TNCs (transnational corporations), the main creators of technology, are constantly searching for new sites in which to use this technology and so are transmitting it more widely. Older technologies are readily available from smaller companies. Countries are eager to attract technology and foreign investment, particularly into export activities, and are removing barriers to imports of equipment and information. Thus, technology will flow to poor countries as they open up to trade and investment: all they need to do is to liberalize, create 'market friendly' environments and invest in infrastructure and education.

There is a less sanguine view, based on four features of technology, to which this chapter subscribes. First, new technologies are not simply 'transferred' to poor countries and used efficiently by them in response to market forces. Considerable effort is needed to access, master, adapt and use them at competitive levels. Thus, while greater openness to technologies and trade is desirable for most of the developing countries that have pursued strongly inward-oriented policies in the past, full and rapid exposure to world markets may not be beneficial. When markets suffer from diffuse failures,[1] liberalization can be costly and damaging, and needs to be carefully managed to conserve and improve domestic capabilities. This calls for government strategy and intervention, but the liberalization that accompanies globalization constrains the freedom of governments to intervene.

Second, technologies are improving in terms of their skill, technology and organizational demands, making the development of capabilities more difficult for new entrants. The newest industrial entrants are disadvantaged, in that capabilities develop cumulatively, so that countries with a head start can pull further away. There may thus be growing divergence, even within the developing world, between countries that have launched effective learning and those that have not.[2] 'Cumulativeness' and 'path-dependence' are ominous terms for latecomers that have not yet mounted effective technology strategies.

Third, the growth of integrated production systems, with facilities at different levels of technological complexity spread over countries, reduces the need for building local capabilities in low-wage countries. However, given economies of scale and cumulative learning, production systems are likely to concentrate in a few sites. There are likely to emerge a few major centres in each region with core industrial activities – say, one or two each in Latin America, East Asia, South Asia, Sub Saharan Africa and the Middle East – and countries outside these centres are likely to be increasingly marginal to production and related activities. In a world of shrinking economic distance and fewer barriers to trade and investment, global production systems are likely to be increasingly inequitably spread.[3]

Fourth, economies of agglomeration exacerbate the inequitable spread of global production. As 'new economic geography'[4] shows, cluster economies are important determinants of industrial location. These economies raise the threat of divergence.

Thus, while the mobility of knowledge and production makes it theoretically easier for all countries to access technologies and markets, it does not mean that all countries will benefit. On the contrary, there are inexorable technological forces making for divergence, not just between developed and developing countries, but also between first movers and laggards in the developing world. The pressures for liberalization that accompany globalization make it more difficult for the laggards to catch up, and this is the issue explored in this essay.

2. The Emerging Setting

The structural changes noted above are not really new. What is new today is their pace and spread, creating a qualitatively different setting for industrial activity compared to the time when most developing countries launched industrial strategies, or to the early twentieth century when the world was relatively open. The information revolution and falling transport costs have brought economies much closer. Technical change is more rapid and pervasive by activity and location. Its nature is different, as are its (tighter) links to the education and science base. Its diffusion now takes place through different mechanisms, and more stringent property rights protect it.

Technology intensive activities, with high rates of R&D spending, are growing much faster than others.[5] We examine their export performance by looking at different technological categories.[6] We separate primary products from manufactures, dividing the latter into four: resource-based (RB), low technology (LT), medium technology (MT) and high technology (HT). In broad terms, resource-based and low technology can be regarded as technologically 'simple', and 'medium' and high technology as 'complex'. Table 1 shows the growth rates of exports in the period 1985–2000 in these categories.

The salient points are as follows:

- Manufactured products are the engine of global export expansion, growing nearly three times faster than primary products.
- Within the main groups of manufactures, RB products grow the slowest and HT the fastest for all groups of countries. Products with 'natural' advantages (i.e. primary and RB manufactures together) are not dynamic; their combined share declined from 43% to 26% over the period 1985–98. HT products are the most dynamic, while LT and MT products grew at almost the same pace.

Table 1. **Structure and growth of world exports, 1985–2000 ($ (in millions) and %)**

Products	1985	2000	Annual growth rate	Distri- bution 1985	Distri- bution 2000
All sectors	1,703,582,494	5,534,008,649	8.17	100	100
Primary Products	394,190,554	684,751,141	3.75	23.1	12.4
Manufactures	1,252,573,675	4,620,266,770	9.09	73.5	83.5
Resource based	330,863,869	863,503,545	6.60	19.4	15.6
Low Technology	241,796,065	862,998,972	8.85	14.2	15.6
Medium Technology	485,784,011	1,639,871,870	8.45	28.5	29.6
High Technology	198,029,682	1,269,587,194	13.19	11.6	22.9
(of which, ICT)	90,151,843	773,119,244	15.40	5.3	14.0

Source: Calculations based on UN Comtrade database, using classification developed by Lall 2001.

- In terms of value, MT products remain the largest category in manufactured exports, with about 1/3 of the total, but at current rates of growth HT products (now at over 1/5 of the total) will soon overtake them. The 'complex' categories (MT and HT) comprise 54% of total world and 64% of manufactured exports in 1998.
- Developing countries grew slower than developed countries in primary exports and RB manufactures. However, they grew faster in manufacturing as a whole and in most technological subcategories apart from RB. What is more interesting is that their growth lead over developed countries rose with technological intensity.

This picture is intriguing. While the HT group is the most dynamic, growth rates do not rise uniformly with technological sophistication. Technology is not, in other words, the only 'driver' of trade dynamism, though it is a powerful force in export growth. The other important driver is the relocation of production (of labour-intensive processes) from rich to poor countries. The relocation has gathered momentum recently because of falling transport costs, trade liberalization and the aggressive search by some developing countries for export-processing FDI. To the extent that it is a once-and-for-all adjustment, however, the trade dynamism it engenders is likely to weaken. Long-term dynamism is expected to depend on such factors as demand growth, innovation and substitution – all strongly related to innovation.

Consider now distribution of manufactured exports by developing countries (Table 2). East Asia dominates all manufactured exports and all categories apart from resource-based products. Its share is growing in all categories except for LT; in HT, it commands over 85%. The other outstanding performer is Mexico, with NAFTA driving rapid export growth in all categories; the rest of Latin America does rather poorly despite massive liberalization. Sub Saharan Africa is practically absent, with the minor exception of RB products, but even in this category it has a tiny presence relative to its strong resource base. Again, such liberalization that has taken place has done nothing to its export dynamism.

Exports in the developing world are also concentrated nationally. The largest 10 exporters account for over 80% of total manufactured exports, their dominance rising over time:[8]

- Overall concentration is very high: in 1998, 5 countries accounted for 60% and 10 for over 80% of total manufactured exports by developing countries.
- Concentration rises with technological sophistication, reaching 96% for the leading 10 HT exporters in 1998.
- Concentration tends to rise over time. This suggests that entry barriers are rising: the ability to compete is not growing in response to liberalization.

Table 2: **Regional shares of developing countries' manufactured exports**

(% of developing world total)[7]

	Year	East Asia	South Asia	Middle East, North Africa	Latin America incl. Mexico	Latin America excl. Mexico	Mexico	Africa incl. South Africa	Africa excl. South Africa
All Manu-	1985	56.9	4.5	12.9	23.1	16.9	6.2	N/A	2.6
factures	1998	69.0	3.8	6.0	19.3	8.9	10.4	1.8	0.8
RB	1985	34.6	3.8	23.8	32.9	30.7	2.2	N/A	4.9
	1998	47.5	4.7	15.0	28.0	24.0	4.0	4.8	1.4
LT	1985	71.7	8.3	7.3	11.9	10.2	1.7	N/A	1.8
	1998	70.2	8.5	7.2	12.6	5.4	7.2	1.5	0.2
MT	1985	63.4	2.0	7.1	25.8	17.5	8.3	N/A	1.8
	1998	63.8	1.8	4.4	28.1	10.2	17.9	1.9	0.2
HT	1985	81.0	1.1	1.8	14.8	6.6	8.2	N/A	1.3
	1998	85.5	0.6	0.7	12.9	2.1	10.8	0.4	0.0

Source: Lall 2001.

Note: 'Africa' denotes Sub Saharan Africa only.

This uneven distribution cannot be explained by differences in trade or investment policies, and it cannot be reversed by persisting with liberalization. It is based on evolutionary processes of building industrial capabilities, and the structural factors involved are difficult to change. Liberalization does not have any in-built forces to reverse cumulative causation.

Trade is also concentrated at the enterprise level, with a relatively small number of firms dominating in most industries. Of these, TNCs are the dominant force, accounting for around 2/3 of world trade.[9] The role of giant firms from the mature industrial countries is particularly large in products with significant economies of scale in production, marketing and innovation. Of the visible trade handled by TNCs, around 1/3 is within TNC systems, between affiliates and parents, or among affiliates. Such internalized trade contains the most dynamic form of exports today: integrated international production systems, in which TNCs locate different functions or stages of production in different countries and link them tightly together.

Affiliates participating in such systems tend to produce on a massive scale (thereby realizing enormous economies of scale) and use the latest technologies, skills and managerial techniques. However, other global industries (now commonly called 'global value chains') are also more tightly organized than before. Even in the field of low technology activities, where FDI is not important (clothing is a good example), there are a few lead players that manage production and marketing; many are international buyers without significant overseas direct investment.

Large companies with transnational operations also increasingly dominate *innovation*: the creation of new technologies and organizational methods that drives competitiveness in all but the simplest activities. Despite innovation by smaller enterprises in new information-based industries, large TNCs account for growing shares of business-funded R&D spending in mature industrial countries. About 90% of world R&D expenditure is in the OECD countries. Within this group, seven countries (led by the USA) account for 90% of R&D, the USA alone for 40%.[10] In the USA, just 50 firms (of a total of over 41,000) account for nearly half of industry-funded R&D.[11] Access to new technologies thus involves access to the knowledge and skills of these leaders, which are increasingly unwilling to part with their most valuable technologies without a substantial equity stake. Thus, FDI becomes the most important – often the only – way of obtaining cutting-edge technologies.

FDI has become a major driver of export competitiveness. In the developing world, the highest shares of affiliates in manufactured exports are in Singapore, Malaysia and Philippines (over 70% each), but TNCs also account for substantial shares in Thailand, Indonesia and China (50% or more). In Latin America, foreign affiliates account for 38% of exports by Argentina and 37% by Mexico (although the foreign share of manufactured exports in Mexico is much higher, given the TNCs' dominant role in *maquiladora* exports).

However, FDI is highly concentrated. At the regional level, South and East Asia and Latin America together account for 93% of total FDI flows to developing countries. The 43 least developed countries receive only half of 1% in the period, and their share does not increase over time. By contrast, the 10 leading host countries raise their shares over the period from 64 to 76%, with Asia and Latin America attracting most inflows to the developing world.

3. Technology in developing countries

Developing countries do not 'innovate' in the sense of creating new products or processes. They do invest in technological effort, but this involves acquiring, mastering and improving upon existing technologies rather than shifting the frontiers of knowledge. In fact, they often have to undertake greater effort than their counterparts in advanced economies, because their absorptive capacities are much lower. Absorbing technologies is not a trivial or costless task, and industrial success depends on how well the process is managed. Since all countries have access to the same international technical knowledge, a critical determinant of industrial performance is technological 'learning' by different countries. The understanding of this phenomenon is critical to the argument of this chapter.

This is not how received economic theory depicts technology in developing countries. By contrast, it assumes that firms in developing countries operate with full knowledge of all technologies: they are on a universal, well-specified and well-behaved production function. Given the right market prices for inputs and outputs, they pick the technologies appropriate to national factor endowments. By definition, all firms in an industry facing the same prices choose the same technologies. There are no tacit elements in the transfer, no learning costs and no need to adapt. All firms immediately use technologies with the same efficiency. Technical inefficiency *must* be due to managerial slack or incompetence, since there are no learning costs.

According to this argument, there is no meaningful technological activity in countries that use existing knowledge. There is, at most, a simple learning process: costs decline as a new plant is 'run in' and productivity rises from repetitive production. Such processes are relatively trivial, predictable and similar across industries. The learning process is passive, and does not involve investment, risk or long maturation periods. There is no need to build the capability to use new technology, or to distinguish between industries in learning.

Firms are believed to acquire and use technologies as individual units, essentially in isolation. There are no linkages between them, and no external-ities resulting from individual efforts to generate skills and information. The development of specialization among firms and industries relics solely on information exchanged in anonymous market transactions. The setting for technology acquisition and deployment has no historical, institutional or social context and is the same everywhere. Since there are no technological externalities, there is also no need to coordinate investments across activities in the same locality or value chain. Nor are some sets of activities more significant for industrial development than others: none offers greater or more beneficial externalities and learning potential does not differ.

Where learning exists, firms are assumed to have the information and fore-sight to finance the (predictable) process by borrowing in capital markets. If capital markets are not fully efficient, infant industry protection may be a second-best measure. However, any protection must be moderate and uniform across activities to minimize resource misallocation. Since no technologies are more difficult, or involve more externalities, than others, there is no need to be selective in promoting particular industries. There is also no need for different policies by countries at different levels of development. A uniform approach across countries, as well as within them, is the least distortionary.

In this framework, the evolution of competitive advantage depends on the accumulation of factors rather than the building of new capabilities. As endowments grow, firms automatically and costlessly shift across technologies. There is no need for policy to dynamize competitive advantage. 'Getting prices right' is necessary and sufficient to promote development.

A large body of research suggests that this picture is wrong and misleading.[12] While technological hardware (equipment) is available to all countries, the disembodied elements of technology are not transferred like physical products. Technical knowledge is difficult to locate, price and evaluate. Its transfer cannot be embodied in equipment or instructions, designs or blueprints. Unlike the sale of goods, in which transactions are complete when physical delivery has taken place, the successful transfer of technology is a prolonged process, involving local learning to complete the transaction. The embodied elements can be used at best practice levels only if they are complemented by a number of *tacit* elements that must be developed locally.

The need for learning exists in all cases, even when the seller of the technology provides assistance, though the costs vary by technology, firm and country.[13] Learning calls for conscious, purposive efforts – to collect new information, 'try things out', create new skills and operational routines and strike new external relationships.[14] This process has to be located at the production facility and embodied in the institutional setting of the enterprise. This process is strikingly different from textbook depictions of technology transfer. We will summarize the ten most important features of technology capability development.[15]

First, learning is a real and significant process. It is vital to industrial development, and is primarily conscious and purposive rather than automatic and passive.

Second, firms do not have full information on technical alternatives; rather, they function with imperfect, variable and rather hazy knowledge of technologies. There is no uniform, predictable learning curve: each firm has a unique learning path depending on its initial situation and subsequent efforts. Each faces risk, uncertainty and additional cost in learning. Differences between learning are larger between firms in countries at differing levels of development.

Third, firms may not know how to build up the necessary capabilities –

learning itself has to be learned. Enterprises may not be able to predict if, when, how and at what cost they learn enough to become competitive, even where the technology is well known elsewhere. This adds to the uncertainty of learning.

Fourth, firms cope not by maximizing a well-defined objective function but by developing organizational and managerial satisfying 'routines', which they adapt over time as they collect new information, learn from experience and imitate other firms.[16] Thus, learning tends to be 'path dependent' and cumulative. Once embarked on, technological trajectories are difficult to change suddenly, and patterns of specialization persist over long periods.

Fifth, the learning process is technology specific. Some technologies are more embodied in equipment while others have greater tacit elements. Process technologies (like chemicals) are more embodied than engineering technologies (machinery or electronics), and demand different (often less) effort. Different technologies involve different learning costs, risks and duration, and differ in their linkages: there are 'easy' and 'difficult' technologies (garment assembly is 'easier' than textile manufacture, which is 'easier' than making textile machinery). Capabilities in one activity may not be easily transferable to another, and policies to promote learning in one may not be very useful in another. Different technologies involve different breadth of skills and knowledge, some needing a narrow range of specialization and others a wide range.

Sixth, different technologies have different degrees of interaction with outside sources of knowledge (firms, consultants, equipment suppliers or technological institutions). These differences lead to different costs, risks and duration.

Seventh, capability building involves effort at all levels: procurement, production, process or product engineering, quality management, maintenance, inventory control, outbound logistics, marketing and external links. 'Innovation' in terms of formal R&D is at one end of the spectrum of technological activity. It does not exhaust it. Most learning in developing countries arises in mundane technical activities, but formal R&D becomes important in complex technologies where efficient absorption requires experimentation.

Eighth, technological development can take place to different 'depths'. The deeper the levels of technological capabilities, the higher the cost, risk and duration involved. It is possible for an enterprise to become, and remain, a good user of imported technologies without developing the ability to 'decode' the processes in order to significantly adapt, improve or reproduce them, or to create new products or processes. This is not optimal for long-term capability development. Without technological deepening, the enterprise or country remains dependent on external sources for major expansion or improvement to its technologies – a costly and possibly inefficient outcome.

Ninth, enterprise technological learning does not take place in isolation: it is rife with externalities and interlinkages. The most important interactions are those between suppliers of inputs or capital goods, competitors, customers, consultants and technology suppliers. Linkages also occur between firms in unrelated industries, technology institutes, extension services and universities, industry associations and training institutions. Many linkages are informal and not mediated by markets. Not all are deliberate or cooperative: some involve imitating and stealing knowledge. Where information and skill flows cohere around a set of related activities, 'clusters' of industries emerge, with collective learning in the group.

Finally, technological interactions occur within and across countries. Imported technology provides a vital initial input into learning in developing countries. Since technologies change constantly, moreover, access to foreign sources of innovation remains crucial to technological progress. Technology import is not, however, a substitute for capability development – domestic technological effort and technology imports are largely complementary.

However, not all *modes of technology import* are equally conducive to indigenous learning. Much depends on how the technology is 'packaged' with complementary factors, whether or not it is available from other sources, how fast it is changing, how developed are the local capabilities and the policies adopted to stimulate transfer and deepening. Transfers that are completely internalized within a firm, e.g. from a TNC parent to its affiliate, are efficient means of providing the latest know-how, but slow in building innovative capabilities in host countries.

4. Structural determinants of technology development

The ability of a country to undertake effective technological effort depends on a complex interaction between its incentive system, factor markets and institutions.[17] The interaction is context specific. It reflects national (regional) policies, resources, support institutions, infrastructure, the inherited skill base, business practices, culture and history. Policies on trade, competition and labour, for instance, affect a firm's learning by influencing the signals it receives from the market. The resource base affects the relative cost and benefit of different learning trajectories. Support institutions affect how firms meet the information, skill, finance and other needs that are difficult to satisfy in open markets. Infrastructure determines the cost of operation and interaction with the outside world. The skill base that firms draw upon determines what and how they learn. The social and business setting, the product of past experience and tradition, is also very important: it affects how firms relate to, and cooperate with, each other.

We now consider the main structural determinants of technology development in the Third World, starting with skills. Skills arise from a variety of sources: formal education, vocational training, in-firm training, specialized training outside the firm and learning on the job. The relative importance of these sources varies according to economic structure, the nature of knowledge utilized and the level of development. Basic schooling and literacy may be sufficient to absorb simple industrial technologies. Advanced schooling and tertiary education become important as more complex knowledge is tackled. Sophisticated modern technologies require high levels of numeracy and a broad base of skills on the shopfloor. They also need a high proportion of technical personnel.

It is difficult to compare skill formation across countries. Informal skill creation on the job is difficult to measure. Data on enterprise training are patchy and incomplete. The available data only allow us to compare enrolments across countries for formal education. Even this has problems. Definitions of education levels are not uniform. The quality of education differs greatly, as does the relevance of the curriculum. Enrolment rates do not show differences in completion rates. Nevertheless, enrolment data are available on a comparable basis, and the rates reveal something about the *base* for skill acquisition.

Table 3 shows broad enrolment patterns for the main groups of countries, including developed and transition economies. The regional enrolment rates are simple averages, not weighted by the relevant populations. They show increases in enrolment rates in all regions. They also show large disparities. Sub Saharan Africa lags at all, particularly tertiary, levels of education. The four mature Tiger economies of Asia (Korea, Taiwan, Singapore and Hong Kong) lead the developing world at higher levels, just slightly lagging behind the developed economies. The new Tigers (Malaysia, Indonesia, Thailand and the Philippines), Latin America and Middle East/North Africa are roughly similar in their secondary and tertiary level enrolments, just behind the levels reached in the transition economies. South Asia and China have low levels of tertiary enrolment, but China is considerably stronger at the secondary level. To the extent that these indicators are valid, they show large gaps in the skill base for competitiveness.

The breakdown of tertiary enrolments in technical subjects is more relevant for the assessment of capabilities to absorb technological knowledge and, of these, enrolments in engineering are the most significant. Table 4 shows the total numbers enrolled in tertiary education and in the three main technical subjects (science, mathematics/computing and engineering) by region in 1995, with regional averages weighted by population. The figures show much wider dispersion in skill creation than the general enrolment rates.

Table 3: **Enrolment Ratios**
(percentage of age groups)

Mean for group (unweighted)	Enrolment Ratios (1980)			Enrolment Ratios (1995)		
	1 level	2 level	3 level	1 level	2 level	3 level
Developing countries	**88**	**34**	**7**	**91**	**44**	**11**
Sub Saharan Africa	74	17	1.3	78	23	2.9
MENA	88	42	9.7	92	59	14.3
Latin America	102	45	14.1	103	53	18.1
Asia	95	44	7.4	99	54	14.4
4 Tigers	106	72	13.0	100	82	36.4
4 new Tigers	103	43	12.3	102	60	17.3
S Asia	75	28	4.0	93	42	4.8
China	112	46	1.3	120	69	5.7
Others	96	37	3.7	98	35	5.9
Transition economies	**100**	**77**	**14.6**	**95**	**76**	**22.2**
Developed Economies	**102**	**84**	**27.2**	**104**	**113**	**50.6**
Europe	101	82	24.5	104	113	44.6
N America	101	91	49.1	102	102	92.0
Japan	101	93	30.5	102	99	40.3
Australia/ N Zealand	111	84	27.0	106	132	65.0

Source: Calculated from UNESCO, *Statistical Yearbooks*, various.

The Asian NIEs enrol over 33 times the proportion of their population in technical subjects than Sub Saharan Africa (including South Africa). The ratio is twice that of industrial countries, nearly 5 times that of Latin America and the new NIEs, and over 10 times that of South Asia and China.

Much technological effort is informal, consisting of tinkering, improvements, adaptations and copying, rather than formal R&D. Over time, R&D becomes more important as countries use increasingly complex technologies and have to use formal R&D to understand, absorb and adapt such technologies and develop new technologies. The R&D data (Table 5) show the same unevenness as skill formation – unsurprisingly, both are strongly linked. The best measure of industrial technology is productive enterprise financed R&D.[18] As a percentage of GNP, this is nearly 400 times higher in the mature Asian Tigers is than it is in Sub Saharan Africa, and around 10 times higher than in the new NIEs and Latin America.

Table 4: **Tertiary level enrolments and enrolments in technical subjects (1995)**

| | 3 level enrolment | | Technical enrolments, numbers & % of population | | | | | | | |
| | Total | % pop. | Natural Science | | Maths, computing | | Engineering | | All Technical subjects | |
	No. students		Numbers	%	Numbers	%	Numbers	%	Numbers	%
Developing countries	*35,345,800*	*0.82*	*2,046,566*	*0.05*	*780,930*	*0.02*	*4,194,433*	*0.10*	*7,021,929*	*0.16*
Sub Saharan Africa	1,542,700	0.28	111,500	0.02	39,330	0.01	69,830	0.01	220,660	0.04
MENA	4,571,900	1.26	209,065	0.06	114,200	0.03	489,302	0.14	812,567	0.22
Latin America	7,677,800	1.64	212,901	0.05	188,800	0.04	1,002,701	0.21	1,404,402	0.30
Asia	21,553,400	0.72	1,513,100	0.05	438,600	0.01	2,632,600	0.09	4,584,300	0.15
4 Tigers	3,031,400	4.00	195,200	0.26	34,200	0.05	786,100	1.04	1,015,500	1.34
4 new Tigers	5,547,900	1.61	83,600	0.02	280,700	0.08	591,000	0.17	955,300	0.28
S Asia	6,545,800	0.54	996,200	0.08	7,800	0.00	272,600	0.02	1,276,600	0.10
China	5,826,600	0.60	167,700	0.02	99,400	0.01	971,000	0.10	1,238,100	0.13
Others	601,700	0.46	70,400	0.05	16,500	0.01	11,900	0.01	98,800	0.08
Transition economies	*2,025,800*	*1.95*	*55,500*	*0.05*	*30,600*	*0.03*	*354,700*	*0.34*	*440,800*	*0.42*
Developed economies	*33,774,800*	*4.06*	*1,509,334*	*0.18*	*1,053,913*	*0.13*	*3,191,172*	*0.38*	*5,754,419*	*0.69*
Europe	12,297,400	3.17	876,734	0.23	448,113	0.12	1,363,772	0.35	2,688,619	0.69
N America	16,430,800	5.54	543,600	0.18	577,900	0.19	904,600	0.31	2,026,100	0.68
Japan	3,917,700	0.49					805,800	0.10	805,800	0.10
Australia, NZ	1,128,900	5.27	89,000	0.42	27,900	0.13	117,000	0.55	233,900	1.09

Source: Calculated from UNESCO (1997) and national sources

Table 5: **R&D propensities and manpower in major country groups**
(simple averages, latest year available)

Countries and regions (a)	Scientists/engineers in R&D		Total R&D (% of GNP)	Sector of performance (%)		Source of Financing (% distribution)		Source of financing (% of GNP)	
	Per million Population	Numbers		Productive sector	Higher education	Productive enterprises	Government	Productive enterprises	Productive sector
Industrialized market economies (b)	**1,102**	**2,704,205**	**1.94**	**53.7**	**22.9**	**53.5**	**38.0**	**1.037**	**1.043**
Developing economies (c)	**514**	**1,034,333**	**0.39**	**13.7**	**22.2**	**10.5**	**55.0**	**0.041**	**0.054**
Sub Saharan Africa (excl. South Africa)	83	3,193	0.28	0.0	38.7	0.6	60.9	0.002	0.000
North Africa	423	29,675	0.40	N/A	N/A	N/A	N/A	N/A	N/A
Latin America & Caribbean	339	107,508	0.45	18.2	23.4	9.0	78.0	0.041	0.082
Asia (excluding Japan)	**783**	**893,957**	**0.72**	**32.1**	**25.8**	**33.9**	**57.9**	**0.244**	**0.231**
NIEs (d)	2,121	189,212	1.50	50.1	36.6	51.2	45.8	0.768	0.751
New NIEs (e)	121	18,492	0.20	27.7	15.0	38.7	46.5	0.077	0.055
South Asia (f)	125	145,919	0.85	13.3	10.5	7.7	91.8	0.065	0.113
Middle East	296	50,528	0.47	9.7	45.9	11.0	51.0	0.051	0.045
China	350	422,700	0.50	31.9	13.7	N/A	N/A	N/A	0.160
European transition economies (g)	**1,857**	**946,162**	**0.77**	**35.7**	**21.4**	**37.3**	**47.8**	**0.288**	**0.275**
World (79–84 countries)	**1,304**	**4,684,700**	**0.92**	**36.6**	**24.7**	**34.5**	**53.2**	**0.318**	**0.337**

Source: Lall 2001.

Notes: (a) Only including countries with data and with over 1 million inhabitants in 1995. (b) USA, Canada, Western Europe, Japan, Australia and New Zealand. (c) Including Middle East oil states, Turkey, Israel, South Africa, and formerly socialist economies in Asia. (d) Hong Kong, Korea, Singapore, Taiwan Province. (e) Indonesia, Malaysia, Thailand, Philippines. (f) India, Pakistan, Bangladesh, Nepal (g) including Russian Federation.

These averages conceal large national differences. The leader in the developing world is Korea, which is neck-and-neck with Japan (and is second in the world after Sweden). Taiwan comes next, spending the same proportion as the UK and a higher proportion than the Netherlands or Italy. Singapore follows, with TNC affiliates conducting the bulk of industrial R&D. These three Tigers are in a different class from other developing countries. Some successful exporters (like Mexico, Thailand, Philippines or Indonesia) conduct little R&D and depend heavily on TNCs to provide innovative inputs. This may be viable in the short-term but not in the long-term. Some, like India, have significant industrial R&D, but lag technologically because of obsolete trade strategies or infrastructure problems. Most others, with weak industrial sectors, make little or no technological effort. They risk being caught in a vicious spiral of industrial backwardness, low skills, low FDI inflows and little ability to absorb or improve on modern technologies.

We have remarked on the skewed distribution of FDI. Figure 1 shows FDI as a percentage of gross domestic investment in 1997 (the picture is similar over the longer term). Reliance on FDI differs sharply among the newly-industrializing countries, with very high reliance in Malaysia and Singapore of the East Asian countries, and in most of Latin America. There is low reliance in Korea and Taiwan, which deliberately restricted inward FDI at the critical stage of building local innovative capabilities. This suggests a trade-off between deepening technological capabilities and relying on ready-made technology from TNCs.

Figure 1. **Foreign direct investment as % of gross domestic investment, 1997**

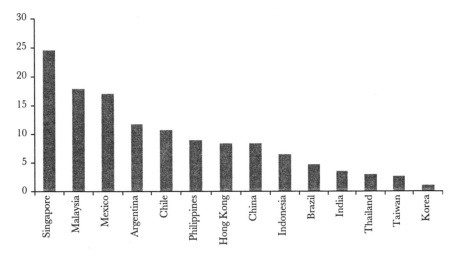

Note that in Latin America, unlike East Asia, much of recent FDI has (with the exceptions of Mexico and Costa Rica) gone into resource-based activities and services, and not into export-oriented manufacturing. Thus, Latin America has not entered dynamic value chains; its lag in electronics is particularly striking. With local firms unable to mount the technological effort to become competitive in hi-tech activities, Latin America now has a low-growth export structure with less spillover and learning benefits from FDI than in East Asia.

We noted the conflict between relying on technology transfers via FDI and developing innovative capabilities. FDI is an effective means of transferring new technologies rapidly and deploying them in production. It is a less effective means of building local capabilities (beyond those needed for production). It is not in the economic interest of TNCs to launch R&D in all affiliates and, where they do start R&D, to go beyond adaptive work in most developing countries. However, host countries have to promote innovation as industrialization continues to take place. It is for this reason that Korea and Taiwan promoted local R&D by restricting FDI.

5. Trade policy for industrial development

Current wisdom eschews trade interventions for industrial development. Its reasoning is based on neoclassical trade theory: free trade promotes the optimal allocation of resources (except when a country has monopoly power in trade). This is based on stringent assumptions, including no scale economies, 'well-behaved' production functions, full information, identical technologies across countries, no learning costs, no risk or uncertainty and so on. All these assumptions are unrealistic and theorists have relaxed several over time. However, perhaps the most unrealistic assumption – and the one most ignored in subsequent refinements – is that there are no capabilities involved in using technologies in developing countries.

The capability approach suggests that free markets cannot give the right signals for resource allocation in the presence of market failures. Free trade leads to latecomers under-investing in 'difficult' technologies, because firms cannot fully recoup their costs when faced with competitors that have already undergone learning or have stronger national learning systems. The market failures arise in encouraging entry into difficult technologies or those with widespread externalities, and in coordinating decisions by numerous enterprises that engage in independent learning but that draw heavily on each other.

On its own, protection does not consitute adequate industrial policy: it will not lead to competitive capabilities if factor markets facing firms are deficient. If the labour market cannot provide the new skills needed, the financial market the capital to finance learning, or the technology market the information needed to master new technologies, protection will result in inefficiency. It is vital to combine protection with improvements in the relevant factor markets – trade policy must be part of a larger strategy.

Intervention to restore efficient allocation must vary by activity according to technology and linkages. Uniform support across activities makes as little sense as non-intervention. However, industrial policy can only work if enterprises take advantage of protection to invest in building capabilities. If they simply collect rents in protected markets they will end up with inadequate capabilities. The secret of effective trade policy lies in combining the sheltering of learning with a stimulus to build capabilities. The best stimulus comes from international competition. It is perfectly possible to combine protection with international competition through the provision of limited protection or the offsetting protection by strong export incentives; indeed, this is exactly what was done by the most successful Asian Tigers.

Trade interventions must be geared to remedying market failures, and should be removed once the failures have been overcome. They should not be the kind of haphazard, open-ended and non-selective protection used by import-substituting regimes. These regimes did not offset the cushion offered by protection with the sharp edge of competition.

Similar arguments apply to the liberalization of protected regimes. Industries set up behind protective barriers are often technically inefficient. The remedy is not to expose them rapidly to international competition. Activities are not 'efficient' or 'inefficient' in some absolute sense; many can be *made* efficient if supported in 'relearning' capabilities. This needs time and support. Liberalization has to be gradual and coordinated with factor market interventions.

All good economists admit the case for trade interventions, but many argue that practical difficulties make them unfeasible. To the committed neoliberal, market failures are always less costly than government failures. While many governments have certainly 'failed' with industrial policy in the past, there is sufficient evidence that this is neither universal nor necessary.

Effective industrial policy *was* mounted successfully in several East Asian economies,[19] as it was earlier by most currently developed countries.[20] Korea started with light industry, but protected, subsidized and intervened in various ways to deepen its industrial structure. It directed (and often subsidized) credit to promote entry into complex technologies. It forced firms to raise local content. It restricted FDI and intervened in the technology transfer process to raise local capabilities. It created giant conglomerates (the *chaebol*) to lead its export and technological push. It guided and promoted R&D and skill formation. It set up a massive technology infrastructure geared to the needs of selected industries. It ignored intellectual property rights to promote copying and reverse engineering.

All these measures constituted a coherent package aimed at the objective of entering difficult industries with significant local integration under national ownership, and with a steady upgrading of innovative capabilities. The same strategic approach guided its liberalization. Korea opened its economy gradually and in a controlled manner, behind a sustained export push that enabled firms to restructure and expand while building the ability to compete in world markets. The opening-up during the 1980s did not result in dislocation or unemployment. It was only much later when Korea adopted the ill-advised policy of premature and rapid financial liberalization that the crash came.

6. Conclusions

Successful industrialization depends vitally on the ability of each country to cope effectively with technical change. Globalization does not reduce the role of local capabilities. On the contrary, it raises it because technical efficiency in each location becomes the final determinant of success. Technical efficiency requires access to new technologies from across the world, but simply exposing value chain to international trade, investment and other flows is not enough. Various measures must be undertaken – by enterprises and by supporting factor markets, institutions and governments – to ensure that knowledge and other resources are used properly.

The evidence reveals growing diversity in the developing world's industrial performance in the face of liberalization and globalization: an unfortunate but intrinsic feature of the new technology-driven economy. Skill development, industrial specialization, enterprise learning and institutional change create cumulative and self-reinforcing processes that promote or retard further learning. Countries set on a pattern with a low technology, low skill and low learning specialization find it increasingly difficult to change course without a concerted shift in a large number of interacting markets and institutions. Economic liberalization may help them to realise their static comparative advantages based on inherited 'endowments' such as natural resources and cheap unskilled labour. However, it may not lead them to develop the more dynamic (skill- and technology-based) advantages needed to sustain growth. Thus, they risk becoming outsiders in a world of rapid technological change, new skill needs and integrated production systems. They may suffer from long-term 'immiserizing' growth, having to export larger amounts of products facing static or declining prices in order to import given amounts of foreign products.

The 'insiders' are the relatively few developing countries that have been able to launch themselves on a high-learning path. The insiders also differ, depending on the strategies adopted. We may distinguish two general strategies: autonomous and FDI dependent.[21] Autonomous strategies – Korea and Taiwan – entail massive industrial policy and accompanying interventions in factor markets and institutions. They lead to rapid development and deepening of indigenous skills and technological capabilities, with the ability to keep abreast of new technologies and become significant global players.

FDI-dependent strategies comprise two sub-strategies, targeted and passive. Targeted strategies – e.g. those in Singapore – also entail considerable industrial policy, but the intensity of interventions is lower than in those with autonomous strategies.[22] The sources of technical change remain largely outside, in the hands of TNCs; for this reason, there is less need to intervene to promote learning in infant industries. However, industrial policy is needed to ensure the development of the relevant skills, capabilities and institutions required to ensure that TNCs keep transferring new technologies and functions.

Passive FDI strategies – as in Malaysia, Thailand or Mexico – involve less industrial policy in export-oriented activities (though there may be intervention in domestic-oriented activity). TNCs are attracted mainly by low wages for unskilled or semi-skilled labour, and good infrastructure, given a conducive macro environment and welcoming policies to FDI. Subsequent dynamism and upgrading does need more intervention, since with rising wages continued growth depends on whether TNCs can be induced to upgrade from simple assembly into more advanced activities with greater local content. The government has to help deepen the local skill and supplier base, and to target FDI. Without such capability development, the initial spurt of growth may peter out. Countries, like Malaysia, that have attracted high-technology assembly activities are better placed than those (like Bangladesh, Mauritius or Sri Lanka) that have only attracted low-technology clothing. High-technology assembly creates a stronger base (with higher sunk costs) than low technology assembly, though it is also vulnerable if skills do not rise *pari passu* with the changing demands of the industry. The 'new Tigers' of East Asia (Malaysia, Thailand and the Philippines) are extremely susceptible to competition from lower-wage China, which offers a more attractive domestic market, highly productive labour and a large supply of technical skills.

Simply opening up to trade and investment flows is not an adequate strategy for countries at the low end of the technology ladder. Stabilization and liberalization can remove the constraints to growth caused by poor macro management, inefficient public enterprises, high entry costs for private enterprises and restrictions on FDI. However, it cannot allow the economy to build more advanced capabilities, to escape a low-level equilibrium trap. Evidence on Kenya, Tanzania, Zimbabwe and Ghana shows that after an initial spurt of growth, liberalizing economies with static capabilities slow down as their initial advantages are exhausted.[23] The spurt that comes from using underutilized capacity as imported inputs and spares become available. As import competition in product markets increases, enterprises find it difficult to cope, closing down or withdrawing into non-traded activities. Without strategic support from the government, they find it difficult to bridge the gap between their skills and capabilities and those needed for international competitiveness. New enterprises find it even more difficult to enter complex activities with even more stringent skill and technology requirements.

There is a danger, therefore, that industrial structures in low-income countries with passive industrial policy regress into simple activities that do not provide a basis for rapid growth. This is one reason why liberalization has had poor results in Sub Saharan Africa. Liberalization has also led to technological regression in many countries of Latin America, with relatively weak growth and competitive performance. These countries often have a large base of capabilities in such industries as food processing and automobile manufacture, but find it difficult to move into dynamic high-tech activities.

The rule-setting part of the international system that deals most directly with development (the Bretton Woods institutions and increasingly the WTO) has so far been more concerned with facilitating globalization rather than helping countries cope with its demands. This approach has been based on the implicit premise that markets and rules to promote market forces will accomplish both objectives: liberalization is the best policy response for all countries. As a result of external pressures, as well as domestic strategic changes, there has been considerable liberalization in the developing and transition worlds. Governments are withdrawing from direct ownership of productive resources and also from the provision of a number of infrastructure services. They play a steadily diminishing role in the allocation of productive resources. The ultimate objective of the current phase of reforms is a liberal production, trading and investment framework where the driving force comes from private enterprises responding to market signals.

There is much to welcome in these trends. Many government interventions to promote development have done poorly, and have constrained rather than helped growth and welfare. Giving greater play to market forces will contain many of the inefficiencies and rent seeking inherent in government intervention. However, as noted, simply opening up to market forces does not deal with many structural problems of development. The most successful developing countries in recent economic history (the Asian NIEs) intervened intensively in markets, with many different strategies to build up their competitive capabilities. Their experience suggests that there is a significant role for government in providing the 'collective goods' needed for sustained development. The issue is not whether, but how, governments should intervene.

In the absence of renewed international support for (new forms of) industrial policy, current global forces will lead to further divergence in industrial and income growth. This will cause intolerable pressures in a world thrust closer together – the same technological forces that are causing structural divergence also lead to more intense social and political interactions. Many policy makers and analysts see that inequities are rising, but so widespread and insidious are the neoliberal arguments that they are unable to understand the structural forces at work. The first step for the development economics profession must be to understand and explain these; the next must be to devise an appropriate policy response.

Notes

1　Stiglitz 1996.
2　UNIDO 2002.
3　Radosevic 1999.
4　Krugman 1995; Venables 1996.
5　NSF 2000.
6　Lall 2001.
7　'East Asia' includes all countries in Asia east of Myanmar, including Myanmar and Vietnam (but not Laos or Cambodia for lack of reported data) and China, and excludes Japan and Central Asian transition countries. 'South Asia' comprises India, Pakistan, Bangladesh, Sri Lanka, Maldives, Nepal and Bhutan. 'MENA' (Middle East and North Africa) includes Afghanistan and Turkey as well as all Arab countries (Sudan is counted under SSA). 'SSA' (Sub Saharan Africa) includes South Africa (SSA1) unless specified (SSA2). 'LAC' (Latin America and the Caribbean) includes Mexico (LAC1) and excludes it (LAC2) when specified.
8　UNIDO 2002.
9　UNCTAD 1999.
10　OECD 1999.
11　NSF 2000.
12　For a recent review see Lall 2001.
13　Ernst et al. 1999.
14　The theoretical antecedents are 'evolutionary' theories developed by Nelson and Winter 1982, and Metcalfe 1995.
15　Lall 2002.
16　Nelson and Winter 1982.
17　Lall 1992.
18　UNIDO 2002.
19　Their interventions were mounted under certain conditions: strong leadership commitment to competitiveness, flexibility in policy making, skilled and insulated bureaucracy, supporting interventions in factor markets, close interaction with industry and exposure to export competition to discipline both firms and the government. On

Korea see Amsden 1989; Chang 1994; Westphal 2002; and on Taiwan see Wade 1990.
20 Chang 2002.
21 Mathews and Cho 2000 provide a fascinating case study of the strategies used by Asian Tigers to build competitive semiconductor industries.
22 Lall 1996.
23 Lall 1999.

References

Amsden, A, 1989, *Asia's Next Giant: South Korea and Late Industrialization*, New York, Oxford University Press.

Chang, H-J, 1994, *The Political Economy of Industrial Policy*, London, Macmillan.

Chang, H-J, 2002, *Kicking Away the Ladder: Development Strategy in Historical Perspective*, London, Anthem Press.

Ernst, D, Ganiatsos, T and Mytelka, L, 1995, eds, *Technological Capabilities and Export Performance: Lessons from East Asia*, Cambridge, Cambridge University Press.

Krugman, P, 1995, *Development, Geography and Economic Theory*, Cambridge, Mass., MIT Press.

Lall, S, 1992, 'Technological capabilities and industrialization', *World Development*, 20(2), pp. 165–86.

——, 1996, *Learning from the Asian Tigers: Studies in Technology and Industrial Policy*, London, Macmillan.

——, 1999, ed., *The Technological Response to Import Liberalization in Sub-Saharan Africa*, London, Macmillan.

——, 2001, *Competitiveness, Technology and Skills*, Cheltenham, Edward Elgar.

Mathews, JA and Cho, DS, 2000, *Tiger Technology: The Creation of a Semiconductor Industry in East Asia*, Cambridge, Cambridge University Press.

Metcalfe, JS, 1995, 'Technology systems and technology policy in an evolutionary framework', *Cambridge Journal of Economics*, 19:1, pp. 25–46.

Nelson, RR and Winter, SJ, 1982, *An Evolutionary Theory of Economic Change*, Cambridge, Mass., Harvard University Press.

NSF, 2000, *Science and Engineering Indicators 2000*, Washington DC, National Science Foundation.

OECD, 1999, *OECD Science, Technology and Industry Scoreboard 1999: Benchmarking Knowledge-Based Economies*, Paris, OECD.

Stiglitz, JE, 1996, 'Some lessons from the East Asian miracle', *The World Bank Research Observer*, 11(2), pp. 151–77.

UNCTAD, 1999, *World Investment Report 1999*, Geneva, UN Conference on Trade and Development.

UNIDO, 2002, *Industrial Development Report 2002/2003*, Vienna, UN Industrial Development Organization.

Venables, AJ, 1996, 'Localization of industry and trade performance', *Oxford Review of Economic Policy*, 12(3), pp. 52–60.

Wade, R, 1990, *Governing the Market*, Princeton, Princeton University Press.

Westphal, LE, 2002, 'Technology strategies for economic development in a fast changing global economy', *Economics of Innovation and New Technology*, 11(4–5), pp. 275–320.

World Bank, 1993, *The East Asian Miracle*, Oxford, Oxford University Press.

World Bank, 1999, *World Development Report 1999*, Washington, DC, World Bank.

14

INDUSTRIAL POLICY IN THE EARLY 21ST CENTURY: THE CHALLENGE OF THE GLOBAL BUSINESS REVOLUTION[1]

Peter Nolan

Suppose giant multinational corporations (say 300 from the US and 200 from Europe and Japan) succeed in establishing themselves as the dominant form of international enterprise and come to control a significant share of industry (especially modern industry) in each country. The world economy will resemble more and more the United States economy, where each of the large corporations tends to spread over the entire continent, and to penetrate almost every nook and cranny.[2]

Introduction

In the 1990s, the global business revolution produced an unprecedented concentration of business power in large corporations headquartered in the high-income countries. This period saw the full flowering of the in-built tendency of the capitalist system to concentration. There was a high-speed firm-level concentration across the value chain on a global scale in a wide range of industrial sectors. The world's leading companies established competitive advantages with high global market share, global brands, high R&D and IT expenditure, and core business focus. They are able to sustain their competitive advantages well into the 21st century.

At the heart of the global business revolution is a new form of 'separation of ownership and control'. In the epoch of the global business revolution, facilitated by advances in IT, core firms within the value chain exercise tight control over firms across the whole value chain, both upstream and downstream. Firms that wish to be selected as 'aligned' or 'partner' suppliers to the leading systems integrators must agree to cooperate with the core firms within the sector in opening their books, planning their new plants, organizing their R&D, planning their production schedules and delivering their products to the core firms. This is a new form of industrial planning which extends across the boundaries of formal ownership structures and radically undermines old ideas of the size and nature of the firm.

The global business revolution presents a fundamental challenge for mainstream economic theory, especially the theory of the firm, and for industrial policy in developing countries.

1. Features of the global business revolution

Drivers

In the 1990s, several forces interacted to drive forward the global big business revolution. These include the liberalization of trade and capital flows, privatization, the collapse of communism, and advances in information technology and migration. First, the 1990s saw a significant widening of the scope of trade liberalization measures, including trade and foreign investment in services. By the late 1990s, 47% of service sectors in industrialized countries and 16% in developing countries had been liberalized.[3] Despite the large rise in capital flows to developing countries, the vast bulk of FDI flows were between the advanced economies. The developed countries have consistently accounted for over 90% of world FDI outflows (93% in the period 1987–92, and 92% in 1998) and their share of inflows is typically around three quarters of the world total.[4] The US has been by far the largest recipient of FDI inflows, accounting for 30% of the world total in 1998.[5] Secondly, the enormous extent of privatization, and the collapse of communism, have opened up huge areas of the economy to private capital in large parts of Europe, the former Communist countries and developing countries. This provided an important stimulus to the 'animal spirits' of Western investors and production enterprises. Thirdly, information technology is central to the facilitation of institutional change in global firms in the epoch of the big business revolution. Finally, a key feature of the global business revolution is that a significant proportion of the most highly-skilled workers in developing countries have migrated to work in the knowledge-intensive industries of the high-income countries.

Competitive advantage

In the epoch of the global big business revolution, successful firms have secured their competitive advantage through a number of interrelated mechanisms:

Core business

The global business revolution witnessed a widespread narrowing of the range of business activity undertaken by the individual large firm. There took place a massive restructuring of assets, with firms extensively selling off 'non-core businesses' in order to develop their 'core businesses'. The goal for most large capitalist firms became the maintenance or establishment of their position as one of the top two or three companies in the global marketplace. The mantra for globally-successful business became: 'If you're not number one, two or three in the world, you shouldn't stay in the business.'

Brand

The epoch of the global big business revolution has seen for the first time the emergence of truly global brands. Their penetration of consumers' consciousness across the world has been facilitated not only by the spread of production centres across the world, but also by the explosion of global culture through the globalized mass media. Successful brands spend billions of dollars on marketing. This includes not only the obvious forms of brand building, notably advertising, but also less obvious forms, such as building a global network of marketing machinery to distribute branded goods in close proximity to customers. It includes constant promotion of new forms of packaging. Moreover, in their search for ever more effective brand building, some of the world's most successful branded goods companies are sharply narrowing their range of products to obtain greater impact from their marketing outlays. The prime movers in the great race for the global marketplace of branded consumer goods are able to shape the consumption habits of the world's population for a long period to come.

R&D

Spending on R&D by the world's leading firms rose at high speed alongside the acceleration in mergers and acquisitions. From a plateau of around $160–170 billion in the early 1990s, R&D spending by the world's top 300 firms accelerated to over $240 billion in 1998,[6] growing at 13% per annum from 1995 to 1998. However, these data fail to capture the full extent of the real increase. A large fraction of the increased expenditure was on information technology hardware to facilitate R&D that was dramatically falling in price in terms of the functional capability being purchased for a given investment. The technical capability of the world's leading firms advanced at high speed in this epoch. Large multinational companies are the chief repositories of the world's stock of economically useful knowledge and skills.

IT expenditure

The period of the big business revolution saw a massive increase in expenditure by the world's leading firms on IT hardware, software and services. For globally successful firms, the ability to undertake larger investment in IT systems facilitates numerous competitive advantages. These include deeper and more effective interactions with suppliers and consumers, centralized global procurement, downsizing of the number of employees, more effective interactions between remaining employees, deeper research using data that can be analyzed by new IT systems, better and more effective R&D programmes, and better monitoring of performance of complex equipment installed by customers. In sectors from soft drinks through to complex aerospace machinery, a striking common characteristic of competitive advantage for the world's leading corporations is their ability to use information technology to integrate the entire value chain, binding together whole swathes of business activity within their sphere of influence. This is a modern form of planning, guided by the market and the pursuit of profit, and facilitated by technical progress in information technology.

Financial resources

The big business revolution has coincided with the largest and most prolonged boom ever seen in Western, and, especially US, stock markets. This process has been fed by, and in turn has fed, the explosion in mergers and acquisitions. Investors, especially the fast-rising institutional investors, have increasingly shifted their portfolios to the world's leading companies, with high global market share, global brands, high R&D, and core business focus that enable the businesses to be transparently analyzed. The lift in share values has facilitated further mergers by enabling mergers to take place by offering shares in the dominant partner's company. Companies with a global competitive edge are able to support their growth through bank borrowing at lower rates of interest than are available to smaller competitors, and through large-scale corporate bond issuance.

Industrial concentration

By the late 1990s there was a very high degree of firm level concentration on a global scale in a wide range of sectors. The process of concentration was most visible at the level of the global system integrators. A powerful trend increase in the extent of firm level concentration of global market share could be observed in industries as diverse as aerospace and defence, pharmaceuticals, automobiles, trucks, power equipment, farm equipment, oil and petrochemicals, mining, pulp and paper, brewing, banking, insurance, advertising and mass media (see Table 1).

Merger frenzy

Mergers played a central role in the growth of the large capitalist corporation. Merger activity has typically intensified in the final phase of a bull market on the stock exchange, as firms use their increased stock market 'wealth' to finance takeovers.[7] The speed of transnational merger and acquisition in the 1990s has increased at an extraordinary rate. From $156 billion in transactions in 1992, the global total nearly doubled to $290 billion in 1994, and then soared to $1,100 billion in 1997.[8] Eight of the world's ten largest mergers took place in 1998, with a total value of $563 billion. The total value of mergers and acquisitions in 1998 was over $2,000 billion.[9] In 1999, the total value of mergers and acquisitions was over $3,300 billion. The merger and acquisition explosion of the 1990s will shape the fundamental features of the global business structure well into the 21st century.

'Cascade effect'

The process of concentration through simultaneous de-merger of non-core businesses and merger of core businesses is cascading across the value chain at high speed. In sector after sector, leading firms, with powerful technologies and marketing capabilities, were actively selecting the most capable among their numerous suppliers, in a form of 'industrial planning' to select 'aligned suppliers' who could work with them across the world. Thus, across a wide range of activities a 'cascade effect' began to work in which intense pressures were brought to bear on first-tier suppliers of goods and services to the global giants to themselves merge and acquire, and develop leading global positions. These, in their turn, passed on intense pressure upon their own supplier networks. The result was a fast-developing process of concentration at a global level in numerous industries supplying goods and services to the systems integrators. The process was most visible in the auto components industry, but was taking place in numerous sectors that supplied the systems integrators, including such diverse activities as metal cans, high value-added steel, aerospace components and print machinery. Across a wide range of business activity, instead of competition between anonymous firms, competition had become oligopolistic at a global level, not only among the systems integrators, but, increasingly, among the first tier suppliers. Leading firms at a global level increasingly competed with the clearly-identified firms that occupied the commanding heights in a wide range of business activities.

Table 1. **Reported market shares for various business activities**

Firm	Business activity	Market share %	Source
Aerospace			
Boeing	Commercial aircraft over 100 seats	70	MSDW 1998
Airbus	Commercial aircraft over 100 seats	30	MSDW 1998
Bombardier	20–90 seat aircraft	38	*FT*, Aerospace 2000
Embraer	20–90 seat aircraft	36	*FT*, Aerospace 2000
Rolls-Royce	aero-engine orders	34	*FT*, 6 Mar. 1998
GE	aero-engine orders	53	*FT*, 6 Mar. 1998
Pratt & Whitney	aero-engine orders	13	*FT*, 6 Mar. 1998
Pechiney	aluminium aerospace products	40	7 Feb. 2001
Loral Space and Communications	commercial satellite construction	25	*Business Wire*, 14 Feb. 2002
Arianespace	satellite launches/launch rockets	50+	*FT*, 12 Nov. 1997
Autos			
Ford/Mazda/Volvo	automobiles	16	MSDW 1999
GM	automobiles	15	MSDW 1999
Daimler-Chrysler	automobiles	10	MSDW 1999
VW	automobiles	9	MSDW 1999
Toyota	automobiles	9	MSDW 1999
Renault/Nissan	automobiles	9	MSDW 1999
Auto components			
Pilkington	auto glass	25	*FT*, 21 May 1996
Denso	air conditioning units	22	*FT*, 28 Nov. 2000
GKN	constant velocity joints	40	*FT*, 22 July 1996
Tenneco	shock absorbers/exhaust systems	25	*FT*, 28 Oct. 1996
Delphi	ride control products	21	*JAC*, 31 Aug. 2000
Kayaba	ride control products	14	*JAC*, 31 Aug. 2000
Lear	Seat systems	22	Annual report, 1997
Lear	door panels	7	Annual report, 1997
Lear	floor and acoustic systems	14	Annual report, 1997
Lear	full interior	19	Lear.com
Kelsey Hayes	ABS brake systems	16	*WAW*, Dec. 1997
Lucas	brake systems	25	*FT*, 8 May 1996
Bosch(Zexel)	diesel fuel injection pumps	52	*WAW*, January 2000
Delphi	diesel fuel injection pumps	21	*WAW*, January 2000
ITT	ABS brake systems	25	*WAW*, December 1997
Bosch	ABS brake systems	31	*FT*, 8 May 1996
Bridgestone	tires	19	*FT*, 19 Jan. 1996
Michelin	tires	18	*FT*, 19 Jan. 1996
Goodyear	tires	14	*FT*, 19 Jan. 1996
Beru AG	diesel cold start systems	40	PR Newswire, 30 Jan. 2002
Knorr Bremse AG	commercial vehicle breaking systems	45	*FAZ*, 25 Jan. 2002
Wabasto	sunroofs	45	*FT*, 11 Feb. 2002

Firm	Business activity	Market share %	Source
Beverages			
Heineken	beers, lagers	6	Lehman Brothers, 2001
Anheuser-Busch	beers, lagers	10	Lehman Brothers, 2001
Interbrew	beers, lagers	4	Lehman Brothers, 2001
Building Materials			
Lafarge	cement	8	*FT*, 21 Aug. 2001
Holcim	cement	6	*FT*, 21 Aug. 2001
Chemicals/Petrochemicals			
BP Amoco	PTA	37	Annual report
BP Amoco	acetic acid (technology licenses)	70	Annual report
BP Amoco	acrylonite (technology licenses)	90	Annual report
Dupont	auto paint coating	30	*FT*, 30 Oct. 1998
Dupont	titanium dioxide	21	*CMR*, 29 Dec. 1997
Tioxide	titanium dioxide	15	*CMR*, 29 Dec. 1997
Shell	bitumen	10	Shell.com
Complex equipment			
Invensys	control/automation equipment	11	*FT*, 24 Nov. 1998
Siemens	control/automation equipment	10	*FT*, 24 Nov. 1998
ABB	control/automation equipment	9	*FT*, 24 Nov. 1998
Emerson	control/automation equipment	8	*FT*, 24 Nov. 1998
Fanuc	machine tool controls	45	*FT*, 11 Sep. 1996
Heidelberger Drucksmeschinen	printing presses	20	*FT*, 18 Apr. 2000
Heidelberger Drucksmeschinen	non-newspaper offset printers	30	*FT*, 18 Apr. 2000
Xerox	printing presses	15	*FT*, 18 Apr. 2000
MAN Roland	printing presses	9	*FT*, 18 Apr. 2000
KBA	printing presses	5	*FT*, 18 Apr. 2000
CNH (Case/ New Holland)	farm equipment	31	*FT*, 5 Jul. 2000
Deere	farm equipment	26	*FT*, 5 Jul. 2000
Agco	farm equipment	12	*FT*, 5 Jul. 2000
TAL/BT Industries	warehouse forklift trucks	22	*FT*, 4 Apr. 2000
Rational	professional ovens	40	*FT*, 19 Sept. 2000
Strix	thermostats and switch on kettles	70	*FT*, 1 Dec. 2000
Schindler	lifts	25	*FT*, 30 Mar. 1999
Otis	lifts	18	*FT*, 30 Mar. 1999
Mitsubishi	lifts	13	*FT*, 30 Mar. 1999
Kone	lifts	9	*FT*, 30 Mar. 1999
Pinguely-Haulotte	elevator nacelles	13	*La Tribune*, 24 Jan. 2002
Ina/FAG	rolling bearings	15	*FT*, 15 Oct. 2001
SKF	rolling bearings	16	*FT*, 15 Oct. 2001
Timberjack	forest machinery	30	*FT*, 14 Dec. 1999
Agusta-Westland	helicopters	20	*FT*, 5 Mar. 1999
Knorr Bremse AG	railway breaking systems	42	*FAZ*, 25 Jan. 2002
Bowe Systec	high speed paper management equipment	17	*FT*, 7 Jan. 1999

Firm	Business activity	Market share %	Source
Fast-moving/branded consumer goods			
Coca-Cola	carbonated soft drinks	51	Annual report, 1998
Unilever	ice cream	20	*FT*, 19 Jan. 1998
Nestle	ice cream	6	*FT*, 19 Jan. 1998
Reckitt Benckiser	wash fabric care	23	*NST*, 10 Feb. 2000
Reckitt Benckiser	dish washing powder	38	Reckitt.com
Proctor and Gamble	tampons	48	MSDW 1998
Gillette	razors	70	MSDW 1998
Fuji Film	camera films	35	MSDW 1998
Chupa Chups	lollipops	34	*FT*, 31 Mar. 2000
Nike	sneakers	36	MSDW, 1998
Fuji	camera film	32	*Business China*, 30 July 2001
Kodak	camera film	35	*Business China*, 30 July 2001
Konika	camera film	11	*Business China*, 30 July 2001
Japan Tobacco	cigarettes	7	*FT*, 8 Mar. 2002
Imperial Tobacco	cigarettes	3.5	*FT*, 8 Mar. 2002
Philip Morris	cigarettes	14	*FT*, 8 Mar. 2002
BAT	cigarettes	12	*FT*, 8 Mar. 2002
Industrial Gases			
Air Liquide	industrial gases	12	*FT*, 3 July 2000
Air Products	industrial gases	12	*FT*, 3 July 2000
Praxair	industrial gases	12	*FT*, 3 July 2000
Nippon Sanso	industrial gases	6	*FT*, 3 July 2000
Air Liquide, Air Products, BOC[29]	industrial gases	40	*FT*, 17 Aug. 1999
IT/Electronics hardware and software			
Lucent	Internet/telecoms equipment	17	*FT*, 27 Oct. 1999
Lucent	ATM carriers for ISPs	34	*FT*, 6 June 2000
Cisco	ATM carriers for ISPs	20	*FT*, 6 June 2000
Alcatel/Newbridge	ATM carriers for ISPs	15	*FT*, 6 June 2000
Nortel	ATM carriers for ISPs	15	*FT*, 6 June 2000
Alcatel	DSL	41	*FT*, 19 May 2001
Lucent	DSL	16	*FT*, 19 May 2001
Intel	microprocessors	85	MSDW, 1998
AMD	PC micro processors	20	*FT*, 1 Feb. 2002
Advantest	semiconductor test equipment	25	*FT*, 15 Dec. 1997
Advantest	memory chip test equipment	45	*FT*, 15 Dec. 1997
Advantest	logic test equipment	15	*FT*, 15 Dec. 1997
Microsoft	PC operating systems	85	*FT*, 29 Apr. 2000
Microsoft	word processing applications	90	*FT*, 24 Jun. 1998
Microsoft	business desktop computer applications	90	*FT*, 29 Apr. 2000
SurfControl	internet security	12	*FT*, 24 Feb. 2001
Trend Micro	overall server anti-virus software	33	PR Newswire, 6 Feb. 2002
Trend Micro	internet gateway anti-virus software	63	PR Newswire, 6 Feb. 2002

Firm	Business activity	Market share %	Source
Trend Micro	groupware anti-virus software	31	PR Newswire, 6 Feb. 2002
Quadstone	customer behaviour modelling software	6	*FT*, 21 May 1999
Amadeus/Worldspan	computerised reservation systems	35	*FT*, 23 June 1998
Sabre	computerised reservation systems	33	*FT*, 23 June 1998
Cisco	computer routers	66	MSDW 1998
Cisco	high end routers	80	MSDW 1998
Corning	optical fibres	50	*FT*, 15 Nov. 1999
Hynix	DRAMS	17	*FT*, 9 Oct. 2001
Samsung Electronics	DRAMS	29	*FT*, 17 Jan. 2002
Eng Teknologi Holdings Bhd	disk drives	13	*NST*, 13 Oct. 1999
Maxtor	disk drives	34	*Gulf News*, 10 Feb. 2002
Compaq	servers	20	*NST*, 23 Nov. 2000
HP	notebooks and desktop PCs	11	*FT*, 8 Mar. 2002
Dell	notebooks and desktop PCs	9	*FT*, 8 Mar. 2002
Palm	hand-held computers	32	*FT*, 7 Aug. 2001
Compaq	hand-held computers	16	*FT*, 7 Aug. 2001
Sony	electronic games	67	*FT*, 29 Mar. 2000
Nintendo	electronic games	29	*FT*, 29 Mar. 2000
Ericsson	mobile phones	15	*FT*, 8 Feb. 1999
Nokia	mobile phones	23	*FT*, 8 Feb. 1999
Motorola	mobile phones	20	*FT*, 8 Feb. 1999
LG Philips Displays	TV and monitor tubes	26	*Business Korea*, 21 Nov. 2001
Oberthur[30]	smart cards	19	*FT*, 1 Sept. 1999
Shlumberger	smart cards	19	*FT*, 1 Sept. 1999
Gemplus	smart cards	25	*FT*, 1 Sept. 1999
Shell Solar	solar cells	15	*FT* Germany, 24 Jan. 2002
BP	solar cells	20	Annual report, 2001

Metals and mining

Firm	Business activity	Market share %	Source
Codelco	copper mining	15	*FT*, 29 Oct. 1999
Penoles	silver mine production	7	*FT*, 22 Jun 1998
Arcelor	blast furnace steel makers	7	*FT*, 2 Jan. 2002
Posco	blast furnace steel makers	3–4	*FT*, 7 Aug. 2000
Nippon Steel	blast furnace steel makers	3–4	*FT*, 7 Aug. 2000
Alcoa	free market alumina supplies	50	*FT*, 31 Oct. 2001
Alcoa	primary production smelted aluminium	15	*FT*, 31 Oct. 2001
Alcan	primary production smelted aluminum	8	*FT*, 31 Oct. 2001

Packaging

Firm	Business activity	Market share %	Source
Toray	Polyester film	60	*FT*, 15 May 1998
Sidel	PET plastic packaging machines	55	Annual report, 1998
Alcoa/Reynolds	aluminium	24	*FT*, 27 Oct. 1999
Alcan/Pechiney/Alsuisse	aluminium	16	*FT*, 27 Oct. 1999
ICI	waterborne lacquer for cans	21	*FT*, 21 Nov. 2000

Firm	Business activity	Market share %	Source
Paper and Board			
Stora Enso	magazine paper	20	Annual report, 2000
Stora Enso	newsprint	7	Annual report, 2000
Stora Enso	graphic paper/office paper	10	Annual report
StoraEnso	aseptic packaging	40	Storaenso.com
UPM Kymmene	magazine paper	20	Annual report, 2000
Pharmaceuticals/life sciences/cosmetics			
Glaxo-Wellcome/ SKB	prescription drugs:	7	*FT*, 18 Jan. 2000
	central nervous system	12	
	anti-infection	17	Annual report, 1999
	respiratory	17	
	anti-asthma	31	
	anti-herpes	49	
Merck	prescription drugs:	5	*FT*, 18 Jan. 2000
	statin anti-cholesterol	40	Annual report, 1998
	angiotension converting enzyme inhibitors	30	
Medtronic	Implantable/interventional therapy technologies:[31]	45	MSDW 1998
	pacemakers	50+	MSDW 1998
Pfizer Warner Lambert	prescription drugs	6	*FT*, 26 June 2000
Novozymes	industrial enzymes	40	*FT*, 20 Nov. 2000
Astra/Novartis	agrochemicals	25	*FT*, 2 Dec. 1999
Bausch and Lomb	contact lenses	17	ft.com, 6 Jan. 2001
Gambro Renal Products	dialysis machines, blood lines and dialysis concentrates	15	*Business Wire*, 13 Feb. 2002
L'Oreal	mass market hair colorants	32	*Economist*, 26 May 2001
Procter and Gamble	mass market hair colorants	13	*Economist*, 26 May 2001
IFF	chemical flavours/fragrances	17	*Chemical Week*, 23 Jan. 2002
Givaudan	chemical flavours/fragrances	15	*Chemical Week*, 23 Jan. 2002
Power equipment			
GE	gas turbines (1993–8)	34	*FT*, 24 Mar. 1999
Siemens/ Westinghouse	gas turbines (1993–8)	32	*FT*, 24 Mar. 1999
ABB/Alstom	gas turbines (1993–8)	21	*FT*, 24 Mar. 1999
Alstom	heavy duty turbines	15	*FT*, 13 Feb. 2002
Others (including services)			
Barry Callebaut	industrial chocolate	33	*FT*, 5 June 1998
Whirlpool	major household appliances	36	*Le Blanc*, 2000
Enodis	fast food cookers/supermarket display units	6	*FT*, 15 June 2001
Shimano	mountain bike parts	30	Forbes, 21 Jan. 1991
Top Glove Corporation	rubber gloves	8	*FT*, 19 Jan. 2002

Firm	Business activity	Market share %	Source
Brita	point of use water filters	85	Simon 1991
Stihl	chainsaws	30	Simon 1991
Assa Abloy	security locks	12	*FT*, 8 Mar. 2000
Ingersoll Rand	security locks	6	*FT*, 8 Mar. 2000
United Airlines	passenger traffic	6	*FT*, 24 July 2000
British/Airways KLM[32]	passenger traffic	10	*FT*, 24 July 2000
Star Alliance	passenger traffic	22	*FT*, 25 May 2000
Goldman Sachs	announced global M&A	40	*FT*, 28 Jan. 2000
MSDW	announced global M&A	33	*FT*, 28 Jan 2000
Gerling NCM Credit and Finance	credit insurance	25	*FT*, 23 Aug. 2001
Marsh	insurance broking	32	ft.com, 11 June 2001
Aon	insurance broking	25	ft.com, 11 June 2001
Willis	insurance broking	7	ft.com, 11 June 2001
Reuters	financial information	30	*FT*, 12 May 2000
Bloomberg	financial information	30	*FT*, 12 May 2000
WPP/Young and Rubicon	advertising	20	*FT*, 12 May 2000
Omnicom	advertising	18	*FT*, 12 May 2000
Interpublic	advertising	18	*FT*, 12 May 2000
Polygram	recorded music	19	Herman and McChesney 2001, p. 218
Time Warner	recorded music	18	Herman and McChesney 2001, p. 218
Sony	recorded music	17	Herman and McChesney 2001, p. 218.
EMI	recorded music	15	Herman and McChesney 2001, p. 218.
Bertelsman	recorded music	13	Herman and McChesney 2001, p. 218.
Frontline	VLCC	11	*FT*, 26 Oct. 2001
Frontline	Suezemax	15	*FT*, 26 Oct. 2001
Boskalis/BHG	dredging services	30–5	*FT*, 22 June 2001
Carnival Corporation	cruise line berths	28	*FT*, 23 Jan. 2002
Royal Caribbean	cruise line berths	20	*FT*, 23 Jan. 2002
Manpower	temporary staffing	9	*FT*, 19 Aug. 1999
Adecco	temporary staffing	12	*FT*, 19 Aug. 1999
Randstad	temporary staffing	4	*FT*, 19 Aug. 1999
Securitas	guarding operations	7	*FT*, 3 Aug. 2000

Sources: CMR (Chemical Market Reporter); MSDW (Morgan Stanley Dean Witter); *NST* (New Straits Times); *FAZ* (Franindustrie Allgemeine Zeitung); *FT* (Financial Times); *WAW* (Ward's Auto World).

Notes: the market share figures given are by various types of measures (volumes, sales etc.)

Market share

The 1990s saw a sharp increase in the global market share of leading companies in a wide range of sectors. A small number of firms accounts for over half of global sales in different sectors (see Table 1). Not only do the world's top two aerospace companies account for 100% of world commercial aircraft sales of planes with over 100 seats, but three engine makers account for 100% of the engines that power these planes. Not only do six firms account for 68% of world auto sales, but two firms alone account for over half of total world brake systems sales and three firms account for over half of total global sales of tyres. Not only do the top two carbonated soft drinks firms account for as much as three quarters of world sales, but the top two suppliers of aluminium, a key packaging material, account for around two fifths of global aluminium supplies. One firm alone accounts for over half of the world total of plastic bottle machinery.

2. The external firm

If we define the firm not by the entity that is the legal owner, but rather by the sphere over which conscious coordination of resource allocation takes place, then, far from becoming 'hollowed out' and much smaller in scope, the large firm can be seen to have enormously increased in size during the global business revolution. As the large firm has 'disintegrated', the extent of conscious coordination over the surrounding value chain has increased. In a wide range of business activities, the organization of the value chain has developed into a comprehensively planned and coordinated activity. At its centre is the core systems integrator. This firm typically possesses some combination of a number of key attributes. These include the ability to raise finance for large new projects, and the resources necessary to fund a high level of R&D spending to sustain technological leadership, to develop a global brand, to invest in state-of-the-art information technology and to attract the best human resources. Across a wide range of business types, from fast-moving consumer goods to aircraft manufacture, the core systems integrator interacts in the deepest, most intimate fashion with the major segments of the value chain, both upstream and downstream.

Upstream

The relationship of the core systems integrator with the upstream first tier suppliers extends far beyond the price relationship. Increasingly, leading first tier suppliers across a wide range of industries have established long-term 'partner' or 'aligned supplier' relationships with the core systems integrators. There are some key aspects of the intimate relationship between systems integrators and upstream firms. First, leading first tier suppliers plan in minute detail the location of their plants in relation to the location of the core systems integrator. This can apply as much to a leading auto component maker as to a leading packaging supplier to a fast-moving consumer goods firm. Secondly, it is increasingly the case that the aligned supplier produces goods within the systems integrator itself. It is common for leading suppliers of specialist services, such as data systems or even travel agents, to physically work within the premises of the systems integrator. Thirdly, leading first tier suppliers plan their R&D in close consultation with the projected needs of the core systems integrator. An increasing part of R&D is contracted out to small and medium-sized firms. This is typically under the close control of the systems integrator. Fourthly, product development is intimately coordinated with the systems integrator. This can apply as much to the development of a new packaging design for a fast-moving consumer goods firm, such as a new design of plastic bottle or can, as to the design of an aircraft engine for a huge airliner. Finally, precise product specifications are instantaneously communicated to the leading suppliers through newly-developed information technology. The production and supply schedules of leading first tier suppliers are comprehensively coordinated with the systems integrator to ensure that the required inputs arrive exactly when they are needed and the inventory of the systems integrator is kept to a minimum.

Downstream

Planning by systems integrators also extends downstream. Manufacturers of complex capital goods, from aircraft and power stations to autos and earth-moving equipment, are increasingly interested in the revenue stream being derived from the maintenance of their products over the course of their lifetime. New information technology is increasingly being employed to monitor the performance of complex products in use, with continuous feedback to the systems integrator in order to construct optimum-servicing schedules. Through this pervasive process, systems integrators deeply penetrate a wide range of firms that use their products. However, penetration of the downstream network of firms is not confined to complex capital goods. Systems integrators in the fast-moving consumer goods (FMCG) sector increasingly coordinate the distribution process with specialist logistics firms in order to minimize distribution costs. They work closely with grocery chains and other selling outlets, such as theme parks, movie theatres, oil companies (petrol stations have become major locations for retailing non-petrol products), and quick-service restaurants, to raise the technical efficiency in the organization of the selling process. The FMCG systems integrators often have their own experts working within the retail chain.

Moreover, a large corporation may have a total procurement bill of many tens of millions of dollars. The total procurement could involve purchases from firms that employ a much larger number of full-time equivalent employees 'working for' the systems integrator than are employed within the core firm itself. There is typically a large sphere of downstream business activity that is coordinated by the systems integrator. A leading systems integrator with 100,000–200,000 employees could easily have the full-time equivalent of a further 400,000–500,000 employees 'working for' the systems integrator, in the sense that their work is coordinated in important ways by the core firm. In this sense, we may speak of an 'external firm' of coordinated business activity that surrounds, and is coordinated by, the modern global corporation.

An even more dramatic expansion of the realm of planning and coordination by systems integrators has been the establishment of a wide range of online procurement networks by groups of the most powerful firms within given sectors. The first sector to announce such a process was the auto industry. In early 2000, GM, Ford and Daimler-Chrysler announced that they were going to establish the world's largest electronic marketplace to purchase components. Between them they purchase directly several hundred million dollars' worth of components. This announcement was closely followed by many others, including the aerospace, energy and even the steel industry. The implications of these developments were enormous, not least for the competition authorities, in that they signalled a massive extension of the realm of planning and conscious coordination over business activity.

Employment

It is widely thought that the average size of large corporations has sharply declined since the late 1980s due to the impact of downsizing and the relentless pursuit of cost reduction. However, this is far from clear. In 1998, among the *Fortune* 500 companies (ranked by value of sales), the median firm size was 55,000 employees. There were five firms with over 500,000 employees, 27 with 200,000–500,000 employees and 88 with 100,000–200,000 employees.[10] What appears to have happened is that the impact of mergers and acquisitions has frequently stimulated an increase in the total number of employees within the entire merged company, alongside considerable corporate downsizing within each of the merged entities. The functions of the core systems integrator have changed radically, away from direct manufacturing towards 'brain' functions of planning the global development of the firm. The proportion of employees working outside the home market has sharply increased. However, the world's leading firms remain very large entities, not only in terms of their revenues, but also in terms of direct employment. Employment remains large, but slow-growing or even declining somewhat alongside rapid acceleration of revenues.[11]

Internal structure

Within the old 'Fordist', vertically integrated large corporation, the different departments had considerable autonomy and the problem of monitoring performance of subordinate units was a serious and widely-discussed issue. Even more difficult were the problems involved in monitoring performance in foreign branches of multinational companies. National branches of major multinational corporations typically developed a high degree of operational autonomy. Leading multinational firms often likened their structure to a feudal system, within which the local chiefs had high degrees of independence. New information technology has drastically increased the possibilities for close monitoring of performance within the firm, even across the entire globe. The 'business unit' structure adopted by many firms typically involves constant monitoring of performance in way that was quite impossible even a few years ago.

Planning and coordination

Through the hugely increased planning function undertaken by systems integrators, facilitated by recent developments in information technology, the boundaries of the large corporation have become significantly blurred. Core systems integrators across a wide range of sectors have become the coordinators of a vast array of business activity outside the boundaries of the legal entity in terms of ownership. The association extends far beyond the price relationship. In order to develop and maintain their competitive advantage, systems integrators deeply penetrate the value chain both upstream and downstream, becoming closely involved in business activities that range from long-term planning to meticulous control of day-to-day production and delivery schedules. Competitive advantage for the systems integrator requires that it must consider the interests of the whole value chain in order to minimize costs across the entire system.

Moreover, the realm of planning and conscious coordination extends beyond the individual large systems integrator. Coordination with leading first tier suppliers and downstream processes, such as logistics, involves systems integrators from totally different sectors coordinating their business activities with the same firms. For example, a leading FMCG firm may work closely with leading aluminium or steel can makers. At the same time, the same aluminium makers may work in close coordination with the world's systems integrators in aircraft and autos. In the steel industry, a leading high-value-added steel maker may work in close coordination with, on the one hand, a leading FMCG firm in the supply of high quality steel cans; on the other hand it may work in close coordination with a leading global auto assembler.

3. Inequality in the regional distribution of firms that lead the global big business revolution

Dominance of firms based in advanced economies

Regions containing a small fraction of the world's population have massively dominated the global big business revolution. The high-income economies contain just 16% of the world's total population. In 1997 they accounted for 91% of the world's total stock market capitalization, 95% of the *Fortune* 500 list of companies, which ranks companies by value of sales, 97% of the *FT* 500, which ranks companies by value of stock market capitalization, and 99% of the world's top 300 companies by value of R&D spending (Table 2). In sharp contrast, developing countries are massively disadvantaged in the race to compete on the global level playing field of international big business. The starting points in the race to dominate global markets could not be more uneven. The whole of the developing world, containing 84% of the world's population, contains just 26 *Fortune* 500 companies (ranked by sales revenue), 16 *FT* 500 companies, ranked by market capitalization and 15 'competitive edge' companies.[12]

US leadership of the global business revolution

Not only is there a massive imbalance between the 'starting points' in the great globalization race on the global level playing field, but there is also a deeply uneven distribution of business power within the advanced capitalist economies in the big business revolution. Dominant in this process are the large firms of the USA.

US-based companies have been at the forefront of the acceleration of foreign direct investment since the mid-1980s. American FDI outflows rose from an annual average of $25 billion in the period 1986–91 to $115 billion in 1997, and the USA's share of total world FDI outflows rose from 14% in the period 1986–91 to 27% in 1997.[13] Moreover, the process had a powerful

Table 2. **Dominance of firms based in high income countries of the global big business revolution**

	Population		GNP, 1997 (a)		GNP, 1997 (b)		Fortune 500 companies (1998) (c)		*FT* 500 companies (1998) (d)		Top 300 companies by R&D spend (1997)		Stock market capital- ization (1997)	
	billion	%	$b.	%	$b.	%	No.	%	No.	%	No.	%	$b.	%
HIEs	926	16	23,802	80	21,091	57	474	95	484	97	298	99	18,452	91
L/MIEs	4,903	84	6,123	20	15,861	43	26 (e)	5	16 (f)	3	2	1	1,725	9

Sources: Financial Times, 28 January 1999; World Bank 1998, pp. 190–1, 220–1; *Fortune,* 2 August 1999; DTI 1998, pp. 70–80

***Notes*:**
(a) at prevailing rate of exchange
(b) at PPP dollars
(c) ranked by sales revenue
(d) ranked by market capitalization
(e) of which: Korea = 9, China =6, Brazil =4, Taiwan =2, Venezuela =1, Russia =1, India =1, Mexico =1, Malaysia =1
(f) of which: Hong Kong =7, Brazil =2, Taiwan =2, Singapore =1, Mexico =1, India =1, Korea =1, Argentina =1

HIEs = High Income Economies
L/MIEs = Low/Middle Income Economies

element of cumulative causation, with successful investment generating further investment: around 60% of US 'outflows' of FDI in 1994/5 was financed out of reinvested profits.[14] In the period 1986–91, Japan's outflows of FDI were 28% greater than those of the US, but by 1997, the outflows of direct FDI from Japan had declined to only 23% of those of the USA.[15]

The leading US-based companies have led the way in the resurgence of big business investment in R&D. In 1997 no less than 135 of the top 300 companies by R&D spending were based in North America,[16] compared with 93 in Europe, 69 in Japan and only 3 in developing countries. The pace of growth of US companies' investment in R&D was much faster than across the rest of the world, rising by 15% in 1997 and 19% in 1998.[17] Moreover, the USA dramatically dominated the high-technology sectors. The IT hardware sector is much the most important single category of R&D expenditure, with no fewer than 57 of the top 300 companies by R&D spending in 1998.[18] Of these, 37 are US-based companies. Furthermore, the role of the state is also crucially important in the overall technical progress of the US economy. 36% of total US expenditure on R&D is funded by the Federal Government. For the fiscal year 2001, 51% ($44 billion) of Federal Government outlays on R&D was allocated to the civilian sector and 49% ($42 billion) to the military sector.[19] A large fraction of this funding for R&D is channelled to the giant corporations that dominate private R&D spending.

In 1996, the USA had 28 of the top 100 companies ranked by value of overseas assets.[20] By 1998, North American firms accounted for 37% of the *Fortune* 500 ranking of the world's leading firms, ranked by sales value.[21] US dominance of the big business revolution is reflected also in the *Competitive Edge* studies published by Morgan Stanley Dean Witter.[22] These studies ranked companies by their capacity to have a sustainable 'competitive edge' in the global economy.[23] In 1998 MSDW identified a total of 238 companies that were 'world leaders'. Of these, 134 were North American, compared with 18 from Japan. In the *FT*'s listing of the world's top 500 companies, ranked by market capitalization, North America had 254 companies in 1998, accounting for more than half of the total.

The USA's dominance of world stock market capitalization is crucially important in the epoch of explosive concentration through merger and acquisition. In a virtuous circle of growth and concentration, firms with high stock market capitalization can more easily take over and merge with those with lower stock market capitalization. Well-focused mergers further enhance stock market capitalization, paving the way for further expansion through merger and acquisition. Even the largest European companies have often found it hard to match the merger and acquisition capability this provides for leading US firms. For Japanese companies to be seriously lagging in stock market capitalization is a deep disadvantage for the long-term positioning of large Japanese firms in the 21st-century global economy. With trivial market capitalizations compared to the global giants (Table 2), it is inconceivable that the vast majority of developing country firms can participate in the global merger explosion in a serious fashion. They are almost entirely passive observers of the revolutionary reshaping of the world's big businesses.

4. Conclusion

Big business has been, and still is, central to the development of capitalism

The normal path of development in advanced capitalist countries has been for oligopolistic business organizations to stand at the centre of the system. Big businesses have been at the centre of the advanced capitalist economies since the late nineteenth century.[24] Big businesses have played a central role in the generation of high rates of investment and in stimulating technical progress.

Oligopolistic competition can be at least as intense as small-scale competition. The top three or four firms in sector after sector are now engaged in competition of unprecedented intensity. They are investing ever-increasing amounts in R&D, information technology and marketing systems, and procuring ever-increasing quantities of inputs across the global economy. In sector after sector, from aircraft to coal, ferocious price-cutting battles are taking place. Firms are fighting intensely to improve product quality and lower system costs across the whole value chain, including the entire supplier network.

The role played by big business is even more important in the early 21st century than it has been at any previous point in the history of capitalism. Large capitalist firms now stand at the centre of a vast network of outsourced businesses which are highly dependent on the core system integrators for their survival. The system integrators possess the technology and/or brand name which indirectly provides sales to the supplier firms. They are therefore able to ensure that it obtains the lion's share of the profits from the transactions between the two sets of firms. The 'external firm' is typically substantially larger in terms of employment than the core firm.

The growth of global big businesses alongside the liberalization of global markets has brought many gains. Typically, globalizing large firms are linked closely to an 'external firm' comprising a group of powerful, globalizing first-tier suppliers. These are, in turn, closely linked to a group of local small and medium-sized enterprises dispersed across the world. Intense pressure cascades down from the core globalizing companies, through the first-tier suppliers, to the myriads of small and medium-sized local businesses that supply the first-tier components and sub-systems suppliers. This process drives forward technical progress, product quality and management skills across the value chain. Across the world, individual consumers and firms can have access to lower cost and higher quality products, benefiting from the massive investment in research and development by the global oligopolists and their increasingly powerful first-tier suppliers. They can profit from the ferocious price competition and pressure to provide high-quality products that has developed among the leading companies across the world. Not only the price of primary products has fallen, but also the price of a wide range of complex manufactured goods and services. The real price of IT goods and services is falling at high speed producing enormous developmental benefits.

The gap between big business in the advanced economies and the businesses of developing countries is wide and sustainable

It is much harder today for a developing country to establish a business that can compete with the most advanced capitalist big businesses than it was only a decade ago. In the new world of global oligopoly, for a long period ahead, the 'distribution of the gains' will be highly uneven in terms of the geographical distribution of the core big businesses and powerful second-tier suppliers that are emerging as the global winners. The world of the 'global level playing field' is likely to result in success for those large firms that already have a head start in the global competition. It has been suggested that the 'global level playing field' is the 'protectionism of the strong'. There is little doubt in the minds of the proponents of the global level playing field that the main beneficiaries among large firms will be those that are based in the advanced economies. Their shareholders are mainly from the advanced economies, as are their owners. As recently as the early 1990s the senior managers of the world's leading multinationals still came chiefly from the company's home country.[25]

We have seen that, in terms of several different criteria, developing large firms from developing countries are almost insignificant within the global business revolution. Table 2 (p. 315) showed that large firms from developing countries, which contain 84% of the world's population, account for just 5% of *Fortune* 500 companies, 3% of *FT* 500 companies, and a mere 1% of the world's top 300 firms by R&D expenditure. Morgan Stanley's selection of 250 'competitive edge' companies includes 133 from North America, 77 from Europe, and 21 from Japan. It includes just 19 from the whole of the 'emerging market' world. Of these there are six from the whole of Latin America, three of which are from Brazil and three from Mexico. The whole of the rest of Latin America has none. The entire area of South Asia has just one representative. The whole of non-Japan Asia has 12. There are none from Eastern Europe, the former Soviet Union, the Middle East or Africa.[26] In other words, in the view of the most brutally honest evaluation available, almost the entire developing world has virtually no representation in the list of the world's most competitive companies. The race for position in the coming struggle for the world's global marketplace begins with the runners in a most uneven position.

It is hardest to catch up in the sectors that are most technically complex, and those which have high R&D outlays. Such sectors in which catch-up is especially difficult include pharmaceutical products, defence and aerospace, and complex machinery such as power equipment, construction machinery, large machine tools, farm machinery and aircraft engines. Morgan Stanley estimate that it will take well over 20 years for an 'aggressive and well-financed competitor' to establish a similar business to the global leaders in the aerospace and defence industry. They believe that it would take an average of 16 years in the complex machinery sector and 11 years in the pharmaceutical and medical products sector.[27] Even in the branded consumer goods sector, the barriers to entry are especially high with 14 years.

'Mid-tech' industries such as steel, chemicals, automobiles and transport equipment appear to offer the best opportunities for emerging big businesses in developing countries to catch up. Within these broad categories, the sub-sectors in which it is easiest to catch up are basic 'commoditized' goods, in which the basic technology is relatively old and non-proprietary, and in which margins and value-added are low. These include products such as coal, low grade tyres, construction steel, chlorine, ethylene, aspirin, vitamin C and nylon. However, even within these commoditized sectors there are massive technical advances in process technology, which greatly reduce production costs and increase profitability. Moreover, within these sectors, in which there is on average a lower degree of sustainability for cutting-edge companies, there are still huge and growing barriers to entry in the high value-added, high R&D subsectors. These include such products as speciality chemicals, stainless steel, and high-carbon steel. High value-added creates high margin pricing, which creates high profitability; this in turn creates further enhancement of competitive advantage through investment in R&D.

The policy challenge

The global business revolution has thrown up a series of deep questions about industrial policy in developing countries. Does the global business revolution signal the end of state-led industrial policy to construct large, globally-competitive firms?

Given that capital has no nationality, is there any point in attempting to construct one's own 'national big business'? If a given country, even a huge one such as China, attempts to do so, what are the costs that might be involved in the attempt, in terms of sheltering inefficient industries? In the long run, will globalizing big business possess any 'nationality'? Will the ownership and the core of operations naturally gravitate in the long-term towards the main locations of the market and global income? Is it conceivable that within a relatively short period of time, quintessential 'American' companies, such as Coca-Cola, or 'British' companies such as British Petroleum (now plain 'BP'), may become more and more Asian, as East Asia's share of the global market and global stock ownership steadily rises? Why fight the process? Is it time to follow the advice of Sun Wu ('Take action only when it is useful to do so. Otherwise do nothing.')?[28] The challenge for policymakers in developing countries is to determine the degree to which it is desirable to attempt to construct indigenously owned businesses, which can challenge the global giants.

Notes

1 In this short article, these ideas are presented in only a schematic form. More detailed analyses of the arguments advanced are presented in Nolan, 2001a, and Nolan, 2001b. These works examine the evidence at a general level and also through the detailed analysis of a number of different sectors: aerospace, oil and petrochemicals, automobiles, pharmaceuticals, heavy electrical engineering, steel, mining, IT hardware and software and financial services. Peter Nolan is extremely grateful to both Dylan Sutherland for discussion of the ideas contained in this paper, and for assistance in collecting information used in it.
2 Hymer 1972.
3 World Bank 2000, p. 65.
4 UNCTAD 1999, pp. 477–87.
5 UNCTAD 1999, pp. 478.
6 DTI 1996; 1999.
7 Schmitz 1993, p. 47.
8 MSDW 1998, p. 4.
9 *Fortune*, 11 January 1999.
10 *Fortune*, 2 August 1999, F-14.
11 For example, between 1992 and 1997, revenues rose by 59% at GE, 53% at Ford, 33% at Shell and 34% at GM. Employment in these giant firms rose by just 19% at GE, 12% at Ford, and fell 17% at Shell and 19% at GM (UNCTAD, 1995, 1999).
12 MSDW 1999, pp. 18–19.
13 UNCTAD 1998, p. 367.
14 UNCTAD, 1996, p. 44.
15 UNCTAD, 1998, p. 367.
16 DTI, 1998, pp. 70–80.
17 *Financial Times*, 25 June 1999.
18 *Financial Times*, 25 June 1999.
19 The White House web site.
20 UNCTAD 1998, pp. 36–8.
21 *Fortune*, 3 August 1998.
22 MSDW 1997; 1998; 1999; 2000.
23 MSDW ranked large quoted companies in terms of their competitive advantage in their respective sector. A key issue was global market share, which strongly influences the capability of new entrants to catch up: the higher the share, the more sustainable was the firm's leadership judged to be.
24 Chandler 1990.
25 Ruigrok and van Tulder 1995, pp. 170–3.
26 MSDW 1998, p. 16.
27 MSDW 1998a, p. 6.
28 Sun Wu 1996.
29 Merger blocked by competition authorities.
30 Electronic chips that store information. Used in mobile telephones, pay-TV signal unscramblers and in the banking and retail sectors.
31 Including pacemakers, implantable defibrillators, leads, programmers for treatment of patients with irregular heart-beats.
32 Blocked by authorities.

References

Chandler, A, 1990, *Scale and Scope: the Dynamics of Industrial Capitalism*, Cambridge, Mass., Harvard University Press.

Department of Trade and Industry (DTI), 1996, *The UK R&D Scoreboard 1996*, Edinburgh, DTI.

Department of Trade and Industry (DTI), 1998, *The UK R&D Scoreboard 1998*, Edinburgh, DTI.

Department of Trade and Industry (DTI), 1999, *The UK R&D Scoreboard 1998*, Edinburgh, DTI.

Hymer, S, 1972, 'The multinational corporation and the law of uneven development', reprinted in Radice, 1975.

Morgan Stanley Dean Witter (MSDW), 1997, *The Competitive Edge*, New York and London, MSDW.

Morgan Stanley Dean Witter (MSDW), 1998a, *The Competitive Edge*, 14 January 1998, New York, MSDW.

Morgan Stanley Dean Witter (MSDW), 1998, *The Competitive Edge: April Update*, New York, MSDW.

Morgan Stanley Dean Witter (MSDW), 1999, *The Competitive Edge*, 14 January 1998, New York, MSDW.

Morgan Stanley Dean Witter (MSDW), 2000, *The Competitive Edge: April Update*, New York, MSDW.

Nolan, P, 2001a, *China and the Global Business Revolution*, London, Palgrave.

——, 2001b, *China and the Global Economy*, London, Palgrave.

Radice, H, 1975, ed., *International Firms and Modern Imperialism*, Harmondsworth, Penguin Books.

Ruigrok, W and R van Tulder, 1995, *The Logic of International Restructuring*, London and New York, Routledge.

Schmitz, CJ, 1993, *The Growth of Big Business in the United States and Western Europe, 1850–1939*, Basingstoke, Macmillan.

Sun, Wu, 1996, *The Essentials of Warfare*, Beijing, New World Press.

UNCTAD (United Nations Conference on Trade and Development), 1995, *World Investment Report 1995: Transnational Corporations and Competitiveness*, Geneva, UN Publications.

UNCTAD (United Nations Conference on Trade and Development), 1996, *World Investment Report 1996: Investment, Trade and International Policy Arrangements*, Geneva, UN Publications.

UNCTAD (United Nations Conference on Trade and Development), 1998, *World Investment Report 1998: Trends and Determinants*, Geneva, UN Publications.

UNCTAD (United Nations Conference on Trade and Development), 1999, *World Investment Report 1999: Foreign Direct Investment and the Challenge of Development*, Geneva, UN Publications.

World Bank, 1998, *World Development Report*, New York, Oxford University Press.

World Bank, 2000, *World Development Report, 1999/2000: Entering the 21st Century*, New York, Oxford University Press.

PART V

FINANCIAL MARKETS AND CORPORATE GOVERNANCE

15

INTERNATIONAL PRIVATE CAPITAL FLOWS AND DEVELOPING COUNTRIES

Ilene Grabel

1. Introduction[1]

Since the mid-1990s, financial crises have plagued developing countries, including Mexico, South Korea, Thailand, Indonesia, the Philippines, Malaysia, Russia, Brazil, Turkey, Argentina and Uruguay. Several of these had been identified as 'model economies' by the international investment and multilateral communities in the years preceding crisis.

When confronted with the challenge of explaining how so many model economies could morph into basket cases in such a short period of time, neo-classical economists sought refuge in defensive explanations of these crises. Each new crisis stimulated research that explained the relevant country's implosion as the outcome of deeply rooted – but apparently overlooked – problems of cronyism, corruption, malfeasance, unsustainable speculative bubbles and/or ill-conceived programs of state intervention. In work on the Mexican, Asian and Argentinean crises, I term these efforts 'exceptionalist' accounts of crisis.[2]

Along with other heterodox (especially post-Keynesian) economists, I unequivocally reject exceptionalist accounts of the recent crises. In my view, the principal cause of these financial crises is the decision to adopt policies of financial liberalization, a strategy that is known as neoliberal financial reform. Programs of neoliberal financial reform have many components, the most important of which is the removal or loosening of restrictions on domestic and international flows of capital. There were, of course, differences in the degree of neoliberal financial reform among the countries that faced crisis, but it nevertheless played a central causal role in each. In particular, the liberalization of international private capital flows (IPCFs) – especially the most liquid and short-term of these – created and/or aggravated the vulnerabilities that culminated in crises.

The heterodox view of unregulated IPCFs articulated here stands in sharp contrast to the dominant neoclassical theory of the developmental benefits of these flows. Given the largely sceptical stance toward unregulated IPCFs, the heterodox view naturally calls for significant changes in the governance of these flows. In this chapter I articulate the heterodox view of liberalized IPCFs in contradistinction to the dominant neoclassical view.

2. Terminology

International capital flows consist of public and private flows.[3] Bilateral (public) flows involve transfers of capital in the form of loans or foreign aid between governments; multilateral (public) flows involve transfers of capital between multilateral institutions such as the IMF or the Asian Development Bank and governments.

There are four main types of IPCFs: remittances, foreign bank lending, portfolio investment (hereafter PI) and foreign direct investment (hereafter FDI). Private remittances refer to international capital transfers between individuals. The most common type of private remittance occurs when a person working abroad sends funds to a family member in the home country. Foreign bank lending refers to the loans extended by commercial banks or multilateral institutions to domestic public or private sector borrowers. PI refers to the purchase of stocks, bonds, derivatives and other financial instruments issued by the private or public sector in a country other than one in which the purchaser resides. FDI refers to the purchase of a 'controlling interest' (defined as at least 10% of the assets) in a business in a country other than one in which the investor resides.

3. Empirical trends

There are two key trends in IPCFs that should be noted:.

3.1 Trend 1: during the 1990s the importance of private flows increased, and PI and FDI became important components of IPCFs

During the 1990s, there was an increase in the relative importance of private, as opposed to public, capital flows. In this period, many donor governments reduced their foreign aid flows in the context of changes in domestic political sentiments on aid.[4]

At the same time that IPCFs were increasing in importance relative to public flows, the composition of IPCFs was changing as well. Historically, foreign lending by commercial banks was the most significant type of IPCF to developing countries. But during the 1990s, commercial banks curtailed this lending. The reduction in lending stemmed from two developments. Commercial banks became wary of lending to developing countries following the 'debt crisis' of the 1980s (although the largest banks were able to pass on the costs of these loans through various publicly-financed initiatives). Banks also found the speculative opportunities available in the liberalized financial environment of the 1990s far more appealing than lending. The decline in both foreign lending and aid to developing countries in the 1990s elevated the importance of attracting FDI and PI flows, both of which increased significantly during this period.

These fundamental changes in the composition of IPCFs to developing countries are illustrated in the following data.[5] The net flow of long-term bank lending (including bonds and excluding loans extended by the IMF) to developing countries was $US 7 billion in 1970, $65.3 billion in 1980, $43.1 billion in 1990, $13.6 billion in 2000 and $-19.5 billion in 2001. In contrast, net FDI to developing countries was $2.2 billion in 1970, $4.4 billion in 1980, $24.1 billion in 1990, $166.7 billion in 2000 and $168.2 billion in 2001. Net PI grew dramatically during the 1990s as well: it was 0 in 1970 and 1980, $3.7 billion in 1990, $50.9 billion in 2000 and $18.5 billion in 2001.

3.2 Trend 2: despite growth in PI and FDI to developing countries, their share of global flows is rather small and remains highly concentrated in large, middle-income countries

The aggregate figures presented above illustrate key changes in the composition of IPCFs to developing countries during the 1990s. However, these data do not reveal two important facts. Developing countries receive a very small proportion of global IPCFs; and IPCFs are highly concentrated in a small number of middle-income, large developing countries. Thus, despite the changes in IPCFs to developing countries since the 1990s, the fact remains that their share of global PI flows remains rather low. Developing countries received 9.7% of global PI flows in 1991, 9.0% in 1994, 6.2% in 1998 and 5.5% in 2000.

The picture for FDI is somewhat brighter: developing countries received 22.3% of global FDI in 1991, 35.2% in 1994, 25.9% in 1998 and 15.9% in 2000. FDI flows to developing countries, however, are highly concentrated in roughly ten large, middle-income countries. During the period 1991–2000, the top ten recipients of FDI flows were (in descending order of importance)

China, Brazil, Mexico, Argentina, Malaysia, Poland, Chile, South Korea, Thailand and Venezuela. These ten countries received 74% of the FDI flows that went to the developing world in 2000. By contrast, low-income developing countries receive a very small amount of IPCFs. Low-income developing countries received $0.3 billion of net FDI in 1970, $0.2 billion in 1980, $2.2 billion in 1990, $9.7 billion in 2000 and $6.6 billion in 2001; they received no PI in 1970 and 1980, $0.4 billion in 1990, $2.6 billion in 2000 and $2.5 billion in 2001.[6]

Despite unevenness in the distribution of IPCFs, and despite the small share of global IPCFs that actually accrue to developing countries, neo-classical economists maintain that policy must target the attraction of these flows via the creation of open, liberalized markets (and other reforms).

4. Factors driving IPCFs

The growth in FDI and PI flows to developing countries since the 1990s is driven by the interaction of numerous factors.[7]

From the late 1980s onward, money managers in industrialized countries found new opportunities for profitable investments, especially for short-term speculative investments, in the liberalizing financial markets of developing countries. The speculative boom in these markets and the new opportunities presented by privatization and mergers and acquisition activities made both FDI and PI desirable.

The liberalization of IPCFs in developing economies created a self-perpetuating dynamic. Liberalization often led to new inflows and increases in asset prices, a phenomenon that led to further liberalization and asset price inflation. Policymakers in developing countries were eager to take advantage of this dynamic, especially since public capital flows and private bank lending to many countries were being curtailed.

Powerful actors like the US government and the IMF have not hesitated to use material and political capital to press developing countries to liberalize IPCFs. US administrations (from Clinton to Bush II) have conditioned entrance to international organizations like the WTO and the OECD, and international and bilateral trade agreements on developing economies' willingness to implement neoliberal financial reforms.[8] The IMF deserves special mention for its efforts to compel countries to liberalize IPCFs (along with the rest of their economy) as a precondition for financial assistance.

The financial and business communities in both developing and industrialized countries have also actively promoted the liberalization of IPCFs. In addition to the obvious material rewards that accrue to proponents of liberalization, its advocates are also driven by ideological considerations. Specifically, these involve an inaccurate reading of history that claims to demonstrate the failure of earlier development models from socialism to Keynesian state-led capitalism, and by powerful ideological shifts that glorify markets.

5. Neoclassical theory: the benefits of unregulated IPCFs

Neoclassical economic theory makes a rather straightforward case for the developmental benefits of unfettered IPCFs.[9]

5.1 The positive case for liberalizing IPCFs

Unrestricted IPCFs give the public and private sectors in developing countries access to capital and other resources (such as technology) that are not being generated domestically because of low income, low savings, low growth and/or capital flight. Thus, inflows of international private capital will increase the nation's capital stock, productivity, economic growth and income. Domestic resources are also inadequate to the task of financing public expenditure because of problems with tax collection and the myriad demands placed on government budgets. Sales of government bonds to foreign investors also increase the resources available for public expenditure.

In addition to inaugurating a virtuous cycle of capital inflows and economic growth, neoclassical theory maintains that IPCFs can increase efficiency and policy discipline in developing countries. The need to attract IPCFs and the threat of capital flight (by domestic and/or foreign investors) are powerful incentives for the government and firms to maintain international standards for policy design, macroeconomic performance and corporate governance. For example, governments that seek to attract IPCFs will be more likely to pursue anti-inflationary economic policies and anti-corruption measures because investors place a high value on price stability and transparency.

Moreover, the liberalization of IPCFs means that these flows will be allocated by markets rather than by governments. According to neoclassical theory, this shift in the allocation mechanism increases efficiency and ensures that finance will be directed towards those projects that promise the greatest net contribution to social welfare. These, of course, will be the projects promising the highest rates of return.

Given this range of developmental benefits, it is not difficult to comprehend the zeal with which neoclassical theorists promote the liberalization of IPCFs. Indeed, had the Asian financial crisis not intervened, the IMF was poised to modify Article 6 of its Articles of Agreement to make the liberalization of all IPCFs a central purpose of the Fund, and to extend its jurisdiction to capital movements.[10]

5.2 The debate over sequencing[11]

A small number of neoclassical economists hold a more nuanced view regarding the liberalization of IPCFs. Some neoclassicals argue that the liberalization of IPCFs should be undertaken only *after* successful liberalization of other sectors of the economy (such as the industrial sector), appropriate institution building and/or attainment of a minimal degree of financial development. This is known as the 'sequencing' argument. Advocates of sequencing generally find their case strengthened following financial crises, as these are seen as a consequence of premature financial liberalization.

It is important to recognize that even among those neoclassical economists who advocate sequencing there is no question that the liberalization of IPCFs remains the ultimate goal for *all* developing countries. Moreover, the case for sequencing is controversial, even within neoclassical theory. Some neoclassical political economists reject the case for sequencing on the grounds that it introduces problems (such as corruption, inertia in reform, slow growth, high capital costs) that are far worse than any financial instability associated with the liberalization of IPCFs.

6. Heterodox theory: the problems with unregulated IPCFs

The neoclassical case for unfettered IPCFs fails on both theoretical and empirical grounds.[12] The liberalization of IPCFs creates a vulnerability to financial crisis, and introduces five distinct, mutually-reinforcing risks to developing economies. These are currency, flight, fragility, contagion and sovereignty risk. The liberalization of all IPCFs is associated with these five problems, albeit to different degrees and through different means.

6.1 Currency risk

Under a system of floating exchange rates, large, sudden inflows of capital can put pressure on the domestic currency to appreciate. A large appreciation of the domestic currency is problematic because it can undermine net export performance. Alternatively, large, sudden capital outflows (termed 'capital flight') can place pressure on the domestic currency to depreciate. This risk of currency collapse is an attribute of any type of exchange-rate regime, provided the government maintains full currency convertibility. Events in Asia and Argentina have underscored the fact that pegging a currency (even through a currency board) does not eliminate currency risk.

Developing economies confront the greatest currency risk for two reasons. Governments are unlikely to hold sufficient reserves to protect the value of their currency should they confront a generalized investor exit. An initial exit from the currency is therefore likely to trigger a panic that deepens investors' concerns about reserve adequacy. Moreover, governments in developing economies are rarely able to orchestrate multilateral currency rescues.

6.2 Flight risk

Flight risk refers to the likelihood that, in the face of perceived difficulty, holders of liquid financial assets will sell their holdings *en masse*. Capital flight often induces a vicious cycle of additional flight and currency depreciation, debt-service difficulties and reductions in stock (or other asset) values. This is because panicked investors tend to sell their assets *en masse* to avoid the new capital losses brought about by anticipated future depreciations of currency or asset values. In this manner, capital flight introduces or aggravates existing macroeconomic vulnerabilities and financial instability.

Developing economies face acute flight risk because of the likelihood of investor and lender herding. In this context, investors face greater political and economic risks and are less confident about the information they receive. Moreover, since investors and lenders often fail to differentiate among developing economies, these economies are more vulnerable to generalized investor and lender exits. Flight risk is most severe when governments fail to restrict the kinds of IPCFs that are subject to rapid reversal (namely, PI, short-term foreign loans and liquid forms of FDI).

6.3 Fragility risk

Fragility risk refers to the vulnerability of an economy's private and public borrowers to internal or external shocks that jeopardize their ability to meet current obligations. Fragility risk arises in a number of ways. Borrowers might finance long-term obligations with short-term credit, causing 'maturity mismatch' (or what Minsky called 'Ponzi financing'). This leaves borrowers vulnerable to changes in the supply of credit, thereby exacerbating the ambient risk level in the economy. Borrowers might contract debts that are repayable in foreign currency, causing 'locational mismatch.' This leaves borrowers vulnerable to currency depreciation that may frustrate debt repayment. Agents might finance private investment with capital that is prone to flight risk. Investors (domestic and foreign) may overinvest in certain sectors, thereby creating overcapacity and fuelling unsustainable speculative bubbles.

To some extent, fragility risk is unavoidable. But the degree to which the decisions of economic actors induce fragility risk depends very much on whether the institutional and regulatory climate allows the adoption of risky strategies. If regulatory bodies do not seek to coordinate the volume, allocation and/or prudence of lending and investing decisions, then there will exist no mechanisms to dampen maturity,or locational mismatches, or the impulse to overborrow, overlend or overinvest. Financial integration magnifies the possibilities for over-exuberance (and introduces currency-induced fragility) by providing domestic agents with access to external sources of finance in the form of IPCFs.

6.4 Contagion risk

Contagion risk refers to the danger of a country falling victim to financial and macroeconomic instability that originates elsewhere. While financial integration is the carrier of contagion risk, its severity depends on the extent of currency, flight and fragility risk that characterize the economy. Countries can reduce their contagion risk by managing their degree of financial integration and by reducing their vulnerability to currency, flight and fragility risks through a variety of financial controls.

6.5 Sovereignty risk

Sovereignty risk refers to the danger that a government will face constraints on its ability to pursue independent economic and social policies. Unregulated IPCFs increase the influence of domestic and foreign investors over domestic policymaking and raise the spectre of excessive foreign control or ownership of domestic resources.

The four risks discussed above can culminate in a financial crisis, an event that seriously compromises economic performance and living standards (particularly for the poor) and often provides a channel for undue foreign influence over domestic decisionmaking. This influence may be exercised in a number of different ways. Policymakers in developing countries may believe that it is necessary to pursue particularly contractionary economic policy during financial crises in order to rescue a collapsing currency and slow investor flight. Moreover, following a crisis, an especially contractionary policy regime may be deemed necessary in order to induce investors to return to the country.[13] And assistance from the IMF following financial crises comes at the price of having critical domestic policy decisions vetted by the institution.

Although sovereignty risk stems from the structural position of developing countries in the world economy, this does not imply that the risk is unmanageable. The adoption of measures to constrain currency, flight, fragility and contagion risk all render the possibility of financial crisis less likely (or reduce its severity should it occur), and thereby buttress policy sovereignty.

6.6 Summary and empirical findings

The five risks discussed above are deeply interrelated and mutually re-inforcing. Analytically, the key point is that the liberalization of IPCFs in developing countries introduces a constellation of risks. The precise triggering mechanism of any individual crisis is ultimately unimportant and usually unpredictable. Similarly, the exceptional features of a particular country do not themselves induce a vulnerability to crisis. Vulnerability is created instead by the specific and interacting risks induced by the liberalization of IPCFs.

Are the rewards of financial liberalization worth the price of exacerbated risk? To date, there exists no unambiguous cross-country or historical evidence that the liberalization of IPCFs is economically beneficial to developing countries. Numerous recent cross-country and historical studies demonstrate conclusively that there is no reliable empirical relationship between the liberalisation of IPCFs in developing countries and performance in regards to inflation, economic growth or investment.[14] More damaging to the neo-classical case is the fact that there is now a large body of unambiguous empirical evidence which shows that the liberalization of IPCFs introduces and/or aggravates important problems in developing countries. For example, numerous studies find that liberalization is strongly associated with banking, currency and generalized financial crisis.[15] Other studies show that liberalization is associated with an increase in poverty and inequality.[16]

7. The necessity of controls on IPCFs

In view of the arguments advanced above and empirical evidence provided (above and below), I argue that there is a strong case for controlling IPCFs in developing countries.[17] Well-designed controls over IPCFs can achieve – and in many cases have achieved – some or all of the following three objectives. First, capital controls can promote financial stability and thereby prevent the economic and social devastation associated with financial crises. Second, capital controls can promote desirable types of investment and financing arrangements (e.g., long-term, stable and sustainable arrangements, which create employment opportunities, improve living standards, promote income equality, technology transfer and learning-by-doing) and discourage less desirable types of investment/financing strategies. Third, capital controls can enhance democracy and national policy autonomy by reducing the potential for speculators and various external actors to exercise undue influence over domestic decisionmaking and/or control over national resources.

Capital controls refer to measures that manage the volume, composition, or allocation of capital flows and/or maintenance of restrictions on investor exit or entrance opportunities. Nearly all industrialized countries successfully utilized capital controls for long periods of time. For example, continental European countries employed extensive capital controls during the economic reconstruction that followed World War II.

Capital controls played critically important roles during the high-growth eras of Japan and most of the 'Asian tiger' economies. Capital controls were successfully employed in Brazil in the 1950s and 1960s. Chile and Colombia successfully used capital controls during the 1990s. The Malaysian government successfully employed stringent capital controls in 1994 and 1998. Despite the fact that capital controls have fallen out of favour (as a consequence of the hegemony of neoclassical views and other factors discussed in section 4 above), some economically successful countries such as China and India continue to employ extensive controls over a variety of investment and financial activities.

8. Strategies for Controlling IPCFs

I now present examples of three broad approaches to controlling IPCFs.[18] These are: 'trip wires' and 'speed bumps'; the 'Chilean model'; and restrictions on currency convertibility. These measures differ from one another in two respects: according to their tangency with market principles and their degree of permanence (i.e., whether they are to be in place prior to signs of distress, or whether they are activated as needed).

8.1 'Trip wires' and 'speed bumps'[19]

The trip wire–speed bump approach is designed to target the unique risks to which individual countries are most vulnerable, and to prevent these risks from culminating in a financial crisis. Trip wires are simple measures that warn policymakers and investors that a country is approaching high levels of currency risk, investor and lender flight risk and fragility risk. When a trip wire indicates that a country is approaching trouble, policymakers could then immediately take steps to prevent crisis by activating speed bumps. Speed bumps would target the type of risk that is developing with a graduated series of mitigation measures.

Developing economies at the lowest, middle and highest levels of development might require distinct trip wire thresholds. Trip wires must be appropriately sensitive to subtle changes in the risk environment, and adjustable. Sensitive trip wires would allow policymakers to activate graduated speed bumps at the earliest sign of heightened risk well before conditions for investor panic had materialized.

Examples of possible trip wires would include the following. Two indicators of currency risk are the ratio of official reserves to total short-term external obligations; and the ratio of official reserves to the current account deficit. Locational mismatch could be evidenced by the ratio of foreign-currency denominated debt (with short-term obligations receiving a greater weight in the calculation) to domestic-currency denominated debt. A proxy for maturity mismatch could be given by the ratio of short-term debt (with foreign-currency denominated obligations receiving a greater weight in the calculation) to long-term debt. If this ratio and gross capital formation were both rising over time, that would indicate the emergence of maturity mismatch. An indicator of lender flight risk is the ratio of official reserves to private and public foreign-currency denominated debt (with short-term obligations receiving a greater weight in the calculation). The vulnerability to PI flight risk could be measured by the ratio of total accumulated foreign PI to gross equity market capitalization or gross domestic capital formation.

Speed bumps can take many forms. Examples include measures that require borrowers to reduce their exposure to positions that involve locational or maturity mismatches, curb the pace of foreign borrowing, limit the fluctuation or convertibility of the currency, or slow the exit, and particularly the entry, of PI. I emphasize the importance of speed bumps governing *inflows* rather than outflows because measures that merely target outflows are more apt to trigger and exacerbate panic than to prevent it.

The use of the trip wire–speed bump mechanism can be easily illustrated. In the case of PI flight risk, for example, if this trip wire ratio approached a predetermined threshold, new capital inflows would have to 'wait at the gate' until domestic capital formation or gross equity market capitalization increased sufficiently. Thus, speed bumps would slow unsustainable financing patterns until a larger proportion of any increase in investment could be financed domestically. Recent experience suggests that the slower short-term growth these speed bumps might induce is a worthwhile price to pay to avoid the instability created by a sudden exit of IPCFs.

The proposal for trip wires–speed bumps differs sharply from the neoclassical projects to develop an 'early warning system' to predict crises by monitoring an array of crisis indicators.[20] In keeping with neoclassical thought, the early warning system is predicated on the view that crisis results particularly from imperfect information. It therefore proposes increased surveillance to ensure that investors have full information.

In contrast, the trip wire–speed bump approach presumes with Keynes that better information is insufficient to prevent crisis. Given fundamental uncertainty and endogenous expectations, the same information might very well yield increasing investor confidence one day and a full-blown panic the next. From this perspective, warnings of potential danger must be coupled with restrictions on investor behavior – otherwise, the warnings are apt to induce the very crisis that they are designed to prevent.[21]

8.1.1 Effect on risks

Trip wires could indicate to policymakers and investors if and when a country approached high levels of currency, fragility and flight risk. The speed bump mechanism provides policymakers with a means to manage measurable risks, thereby reducing the possibility that policy sovereignty will be constrained by a financial crisis. Those countries that have trip wires and speed bumps in place are also less vulnerable to contagion effects from crises that originate elsewhere. Hence, the combined effect of trip wires and speed bumps is to reduce the likelihood of currency, flight, fragility, or contagion risk sparking full-blown economic crisis.

It is certainly possible that activation of trip wires in one country could aggravate contagion risk in those countries that investors have reason to perceive as being vulnerable to similar difficulties. This risk could be mitigated through the use of 'contagion' trip wires. These would be activated (in 'country B') whenever speed bumps are implemented in a country that investors have reason to view similarly ('country A'). In such circumstances, country B would then implement appropriate speed bumps.

One complication bears mention: at present, off-balance sheet activities such as derivatives are largely non-transparent. Recent research indicates that these transactions played a significant role in the Asian crisis.[22] The trip wire–speed bump approach requires that actors be compelled to disclose these activities. In the absence of the will to enforce transparency, policymakers in developing countries would be well advised to forbid domestic actors from engaging in off-balance sheet activities.

8.1.2 A digression on Malaysian controls, 1994 and 1998

In the context of astounding increases in capital inflows, Malaysian authorities implemented stringent, temporary inflow controls in early 1994. Reaction to these measures was rapid and dramatic, so much so that authorities were able to dismantle them in under a year. During the period that the controls were in place, the volume of net private capital inflows and short-term inflows was reduced severely (falling by 18 and 13 percentage points of GDP respectively), the composition of these flows was altered significantly and the inflation of stock and real estate prices was curtailed.[23]

The Malaysian government again implemented stringent controls over capital inflows and outflows in 1998, in the context of the Asian crisis. The government responded to the crisis by restricting foreigners' access to the domestic currency via restrictions on bank lending and account maintenance, and by declaring currency held outside the country inconvertible, by fixing the value of the domestic currency and restricting international transfer and trading of the currency, by closing the secondary market in equities and by prohibiting non-residents from selling local equities held for less than one year. According to numerous accounts, these rather stringent measures achieved their basic objectives.[24] They stabilized the currency and the stock market; facilitated the recovery of employment, wages and the broader economy; and enabled the government to pursue relatively autonomous policy. The immediate, powerful reaction to the temporary Malaysian controls in 1994 and 1998 underscores the potential of speed bumps to target incipient difficulties.

8.2 The 'Chilean model'

In the aftermath of the Asian crisis, heterodox and even prominent mainstream economists focused a great deal of attention on the 'Chilean model,' a term which refers to a policy regime that Chilean and Colombian authorities began to implement in June 1991 and September 1993 respectively. The backdrop for this policy regime in Chile was an ambitious program of neoliberal reform. Though there were national differences in policy design, Chilean and Colombian policies shared the same objectives. The policy regime sought to balance the challenges and opportunities of financial integration, lengthen the maturity structure and stabilize capital inflows, mitigate the effect of large volumes of inflows on the exchange rate and exports and protect the economy from the instability associated with speculative excess and the sudden withdrawal of external finance.

8.2.1 Chile, 1991–8

Financial integration in Chile was regulated through a number of complementary measures. From June 1991 through early 2000, authorities maintained an exchange rate band that was gradually widened and was modestly revalued several times. The monetary effects of the rapid accumulation of international reserves were also largely sterilized. The only policy that governed capital outflows by Chilean investors was a provision that pension funds could invest a maximum of 12% of their assets abroad.

Central to the success of the Chilean model was a multifaceted program of inflows management. Foreign loans faced a tax of 1.2% per year. FDI and PI faced a one-year residence requirement. And from May 1992 to October 1998, Chilean authorities imposed a non-interest bearing reserve requirement of 30% on all types of external credits and all foreign financial investments in the country. The required reserves were held at the Central Bank for one year, regardless of the maturity of the obligation.

The Central Bank eliminated the management of inflows (and other financial controls) in several steps, beginning in September 1998. This decision was taken because the country confronted a radical reduction in inflows in the post-Asian crisis environment (rendering flight risk not immediately relevant). Chilean authorities determined that the attraction of IPCFs was a regrettable necessity in light of declining copper prices and a rising current account deficit. Critics of the Chilean model heralded its demise as proof of its failure.

But others viewed the dismantling of the model as evidence of its success insofar as the economy had outgrown the need for protections. For example, Eichengreen notes that by the summer of 1998 it was no longer necessary to provide disincentives to foreign funding because the Chilean banking system was on such strong footing.[25] In my view, the decision to terminate inflows management was imprudent, given the substantial risks of a future increase in IPCFs to the country, and the risk that the country could experience contagion from financial instability in Argentina, Brazil, Paraguay and Uruguay. It would have been far more desirable to maintain the controls at a low level while addressing the current account deficit and the need to attract inflows through other means. Indeed, flexible deployment of the inflows policy was a hallmark of the Chilean model (consistent with trip wires–speed bumps), and it is regrettable that authorities abandoned such a successful strategy.

8.2.2 Colombia, 1993–8

Colombia's inflows management policies relating to foreign borrowing were similar to (though blunter than) those in Chile. Beginning in September 1993, the Central Bank required that non-interest bearing reserves of 47% be held for one year against foreign loans with maturities of eighteen months or less (this was extended to loans with a maturity of up to five years in August 1994). Foreign borrowing related to real estate was prohibited. Moreover, foreigners were simply precluded from purchasing debt instruments and corporate equity (there were no comparable restrictions on FDI). Colombian policy also sought to discourage the accretion of external obligations in the form of import payments by increasing the cost of import financing. Authorities experimented with a variety of measures to protect exports from currency appreciation induced by inflows. As in Chile, regulations on IPCFs were gradually phased out following the Asian crisis.

8.2.3 Effect on risks

The Chilean model represents a highly effective means for managing all of the risks under consideration here.

Numerous empirical studies find that inflows management in Chile and Colombia played a constructive role in changing the composition and maturity structure (though not the volume) of net capital inflows, particularly after the controls were strengthened in 1994–5.[26] These studies also find that leakages from these regulations had no macroeconomic significance. Following implementation of these policies in both countries, the maturity structure of foreign debt lengthened and external financing in general moved from debt to FDI. Moreover, Chile received a larger supply of external finance (relative to GDP) than other countries in the region, and FDI became a much larger proportion of inflows than in many other developing economies. Colombia's prohibition on foreign equity and bond market participation dramatically reduced the relative importance of short-term, liquid forms of investment finance. More strikingly, FDI became a major source of finance in the country despite political turbulence and blunt financial controls.

The move toward FDI and away from short-term, highly liquid debt and PI flows is a clear achievement of the Chilean model.[27] The Chilean model also afforded policymakers insulation from potential challenges to policy sovereignty via reduction in the risk of crisis. Furthermore, policymakers were able to implement some growth-oriented economic policies because the risk of foreign investor flight was curtailed.[28] The Chilean model also reduced the vulnerability to contagion by fostering macroeconomic stability.

It is noteworthy that the transmission effects of the Asian crisis in Chile and Colombia were quite mild compared to those in other Latin countries (such as Brazil), let alone elsewhere. The decline in capital flows in Chile and Colombia following the Mexican and Asian crises was rather orderly, and did not trigger currency, asset and investment collapse. Contra the experience in Asia, the decision to float the currency in Chile and Colombia did not induce instability.

8.3 Restrictions on currency convertibility

A convertible currency is a currency that holders may freely exchange for any other currency regardless of the purpose of conversion or the identity of the holder. A government can maintain currency convertibility for current account transactions but impose controls on capital account transactions. Moreover, a government can manage convertibility by requiring that investors apply for a foreign exchange licence, which entitles them to exchange currency for a particular reason. This approach allows the government to influence the pace of currency exchanges and distinguish among transactions based on the degree of currency risk associated with the transaction. The government can also suspend foreign exchange licencing (or convertibility, generally) as a type of speed bump. The government can also control non-resident access to the domestic currency by restricting domestic bank lending to non-residents and/or by preventing non-residents from maintaining bank accounts in the country.

Today over 150 countries maintain fully convertible currencies. Developing countries have been pressed to adopt full convertibility (and liberalization of IPCFs) much earlier in their development than did Western Europe and Japan.

8.3.1 Effect on risks

Maintenance of unrestricted currency convertibility in developing economies is highly problematic from the perspective of financial stability. Investors cannot move their money freely between countries unless they can easily convert capital from one currency into another. But the practice of currency conversion and the exit from assets denominated in the domestic currency places currencies under pressure to depreciate. For this reason, unrestricted convertibility introduces currency, flight and currency-induced fragility risks.

Inconvertible currencies can not be placed under pressure to depreciate because there are substantial obstacles to investors' acquisition of them in the first place. Moreover, to the extent that investors are able to acquire the currency (or assets denominated in it), their ability to liquidate these holdings is ultimately restricted. Thus, the likelihood of a currency collapse is trivial because the currency cannot be attacked. The greater are the restrictions on convertibility, the smaller is the scope for currency risk. Convertibility restrictions also reduce currency-induced fragility risk. This measure decreases the possibility that currency depreciation will lead to an unexpected increase in debt-service costs.

Restricting currency convertibility can curtail flight risk. Restricting convertibility can effectively discourage foreign investors from even buying the kinds of domestic assets that are most prone to flight risk because these holdings cannot be readily converted to their own national currency. To the extent that these restrictions do not discourage foreign investors from purchasing assets subject to flight risk, they nevertheless undermine their ability to liquidate these investments and take their proceeds out of the country. Convertibility restrictions also reduce the ability of domestic investors to engage in flight.

By reducing the overall risk of financial crisis, currency convertibility restrictions can reduce sovereignty risk. This measure protects policy autonomy by slowing the rate of depletion of foreign exchange reserves, thereby giving the government time to implement changes in economic policy without being forced to do so by pressures against the currency.[29] Finally, convertibility restrictions can reduce a country's vulnerability to contagion by rendering the economy overall less vulnerable to financial crisis. Insofar as investors know that the economy is less vulnerable to crisis, they are less likely to engage in actions that induce contagion.

It should be emphasized that crises in Asia emerged in and spread precisely to those countries that failed to restrict convertibility. By contrast, countries that did not maintain convertible currencies – such as China, India and Taiwan – were largely unaffected by the crisis insofar as it was impossible for them to experience a currency collapse (and related currency-induced fragility risk) and the risk of investor flight was minimal. Investors had little reason to fear a collapse of currency and/or asset values in these countries, and they therefore behaved accordingly. It is noteworthy that a recent study of capital account regimes by IMF staff concludes that, despite the efficiency costs and some evasion of Chinese and Indian capital account restrictions, these restrictions are among the factors that can be credited with the performance of these economies during the Asian crisis.[30]

9. Policy considerations and opportunities

I have argued that policymakers have no reason to accept the conventional wisdom that developing countries will benefit from the liberalization of IPCFs. I have also argued that a strong case can be made for capital controls. I conclude with a number of points in this regard.

First, the management of IPCFs is critical to any program of crisis prevention in developing countries.

Second, there is no single form of capital control that is uniformly appropriate. It is the task of policymakers in developing economies to select from a range of controls that represent the most appropriate and feasible means to reduce the specific risks deemed most dangerous to their economy.

Third, policymakers can rely on a package of financial controls rather than any single control (as suggested by experience in Chile, China and India). A program of complementary financial controls can reduce the necessary severity of any one control, and can magnify the effectiveness of the regime of financial control.

Fourth, there is no unambiguous evidence that implementation of capital controls in one or a few developing economies will increase or decrease the hurdle rate necessary to attract IPCFs. The 'hurdle rate' (or the rate of return) necessary to attract IPCFs may increase if investors demand a premium in order to commit funds to an economy in which liquidity or exit options are compromised. But it is just as plausible to assume that the hurdle rate in such economies may be reduced by a policy regime that gives investors less reason to fear that capital losses will be incurred or growth will be sacrificed because of financial crisis. That foreign investors found Chile and East Asian economies attractive when they had controls in place gives some credence to the latter view (as does investors' continued fascination with China). It is also the case that capital costs in Malaysia were not punishing, despite the stringent controls during the 1990s.

As a corollary to the fourth point, it is worth acknowledging that the hurdle rate for developing economies as a whole would be lower in a world in which all or most pursue some type of capital controls. Under a multilateral regime of effective capital controls that reduces ambient volatility and risk, all countries might find it easier and less costly to attract IPCFs.

Fifth and finally, it is far from certain that efforts to reduce the risks of IPCFs will be frustrated by corruption, waste and evasion, and will purchase stability at the cost of stagnation. Contra the claims of the new-political economy, corruption, waste and evasion occur under both liberal and illiberal regimes. Witness, for instance, the accounting scandals that have destabilized US financial markets in recent years. Moreover, a tradeoff between stability and growth has not been established. Indeed, the experiences of Chile, China and Korea seem to contradict this tradeoff. It is at least plausible that foreign investors value stability and predictability (especially in the current environment); hence countries with well functioning financial controls might have a comparative advantage in attracting IPCFs. Finally, it is important always to weigh the actual costs of instability and crisis against the potential costs of slower, sustainable growth.

In conclusion, I argue that regulation of IPCFs is a central component of what can be thought of as a 'developmentalist financial architecture,' by which I mean a financial system that promotes equitable, stable and sustainable economic development.[31] The obstacles that block efforts to regulate IPCFs and to create a developmentalist financial architecture are not technical – they are ideological and political. However, these obstacles are not insurmountable.

We know that on the eve of the Asian crisis the IMF was poised to enshrine the liberalization of IPCFs in its Articles of Agreement. In the crisis environment, the IMF quietly tabled the proposal to revise Article 6. The time is therefore ripe for economists to press the case that developing countries should be encouraged to build on the successes of capital controls, and to avail themselves of their Article 6 right to pursue them.

Notes

1 I am grateful to participants at CAPORDE (2001–2), Ha-Joon Chang and George DeMartino for insightful commentary. Peter Zawadzki provided excellent research assistance.
2 Grabel 2002a; 1999; 1996.
3 Discussion in sections two and three draw heavily on Chang and Grabel (forthcoming, ch. 10).
4 However, strategically important developing countries, such as Turkey and Pakistan, received significant foreign aid from the US following the events of 11 September 2001.
5 World Bank 2002. Note that the data presented are meant to be illustrative. The absence of consistent annual data on all IPCFs frustrates efforts to calculate period averages.
6 The World Bank defines low-income countries as those in which per capita gross national income in 2000 was no more than $755.
7 Discussion in section 4 draws on Grabel 2002a; 2003c.
8 See Caliari 2002 for discussion of the 1994 'Coherence Agreement' and related cooperation between the IMF, World Bank and WTO.
9 Discussion in sections 5–6 draws heavily on Chang and Grabel (forthcoming, ch. 10). Fischer 1998 and Dornbusch 1998 are good examples of the neoclassical view.
10 This proposed reform is debated in Fischer et al. 1998.
11 Edwards 2001 makes a case for sequencing.
12 Sections 6.1–6.5 and 6.6 draw heavily on Grabel 2003a and Grabel 2003b respectively.
13 This strategy is commonly undertaken, particularly when the IMF is involved. However, evidence from the Asian crisis countries shows that contractionary policy did not restore investor confidence (indeed, it had the opposite effect). See Stiglitz 2002, ch. 4.
14 Eichengreen 2001; Rodrik 1998.
15 Arestis and Demetriades 1997; Demirgüc-Kunt and Detragiache 1998; Weller 2001.
16 Weller and Hersh 2002.
17 Section 7 draws heavily on Chang and Grabel (forthcoming, ch. 10).
18 Section 8 draws heavily on Grabel 2003a – see this paper and Chang and Grabel (forthcoming, ch. 10) for discussion of additional approaches to controlling IPCFs. Crotty and Epstein 1996 present an exhaustive discussion of controls; Eatwell and Taylor 1998 propose a new institution, the World Financial Authority, to take leadership on capital controls.
19 This measure is advanced in Grabel 1999 and developed more fully in Grabel 2003a.
20 The gold standard of these early warning models is Goldstein, Kaminsky, Reinhart 2000.
21 Grabel 2003b.
22 Dodd 2000.
23 Palma 2000.
24 Kaplan and Rodrik 2001.
25 Eichengreen 1999 p. 53. Nevertheless, Eichengreen 1999 makes clear that authorities erred in terminating inflows management.
26 e.g. Ffrench-Davis and Reisen 1998; LeFort and Budenvich 1997; Palma 2000.

27 However, it is important to note that FDI is not without its problems. It can and has introduced sovereignty risk and can also aggravate many of the other risks discussed in 6.1–6.4 above if not properly regulated (see Chang and Grabel forthcoming, ch. 10).
28 LeFort and Budenvich 1997.
29 Eichengreen et al. 1995.
30 Ariyoshi et al. 2000, pp. 16–17, pp. 31–4.
31 Grabel 2002b; see also Nissanke and Stein 2003.

References

Arestis, P and Demetriades, P, 1997, 'Financial Development and Economic Growth: Assessing the Evidence', *Economic Journal*, vol. 107, pp. 783–99.

Ariyoshi, A, Habermeier, K, Laurens, B, Otker-Robe, I, Canales-Kriljenko, J and Kirilenko, A, 2000, *County Experience with the Use and Liberalization of Capital Controls*, Washington, DC, IMF.

Caliari, A, 2002, 'Coherence Between Trade and Financial Policies: Summary of Issues and Possible Research and Advocacy Agenda', Center of Concern, Washington, DC, www.coc.org/pdfs/coc/coherence_trade902.pdf.

Chang, H-J and Grabel, I, forthcoming, *Reclaiming Development* (provisional title), London, Zed Books.

Crotty, J, and Epstein, G, 1996, 'In Defence of Capital Controls', in L Panitch, 1996, ed., *Are There Alternatives? Socialist Register 1996*, London, Merlin Press, pp. 118–49.

Demirgüc-Kunt, A and Detragiache, E, 1998, 'Financial Liberalization and Financial Fragility', International Monetary Fund Working Paper, no. 83.

Dodd, R, 2000, 'The Role of Derivatives in the East Asian Financial Crisis,' unpublished paper, Derivatives Study Center, Washington, DC.

Dornbusch, R, 1998, 'Capital Controls: An Idea Whose Time is Past,' in 'Should the IMF Pursue Capital-Account Convertibility', *Princeton Essays in International Finance*, no. 207, pp. 20–7.

Eatwell, J and Taylor, L, 1998, 'International Capital Markets and the Future of Economic Policy', Working Paper, Center for Economic Policy Analysis, no. 9.

Eichengreen, B, 2002, 'Capital Account Liberalization: What Do Cross-Country Studies Tell Us?', *World Bank Economic Review*, vol. 15, no. 3, pp. 341–65.

——, 1999, *Toward a New International Financial Architecture*, Washington, DC, Institute for International Economics.

Eichengreen, B, Rose, A, and Wyplosz, C, 1995, 'Exchange Market Mayhem: The Antecedents and Aftermath of Speculative Attacks', *Economic Policy*, vol. 21, no. 2, pp. 249–312.

Fischer, S, 1998, 'Capital Account Liberalization and the Role of the IMF', in 'Should the IMF Pursue Capital-Account Convertibility', *Princeton Essays in International Finance*, no. 207, pp. 1–10.

Fischer, S, et al., 1998, 'Should the IMF Pursue Capital-Account Convertibility', *Princeton Essays in International Finance*, no. 207.

Ffrench-Davis, R and Reisen, H, eds, 1998, *Capital Flows and Investment Performance*, Paris, UN/ECLAC Development Centre of the OECD.

Goldstein, M, Kaminsky, G and Reinhart, C, 2000, *Assessing Financial Vulnerability: An Early*

Warning System for Emerging Markets, Washington, DC, Institute for International Economics.

Grabel, I, 2003b, 'Predicting Financial Crisis in Developing Economies: Astronomy or Astrology?', *Eastern Economics Journal*, vol. 29, no. 2, pp. 245–60.

——, 2003a, 'Averting Crisis? Assessing Measures to Manage Financial Integration in Emerging Economies', *Cambridge Journal of Economics*, vol. 27, no. 3, pp. 317–36.

——, 2002b, 'Towards a Developmentalist International Financial Architecture,' presentation at the 'NGO Dialogue with Delegates of the Second Committee of the UN General Assembly on the Financing for Development (FfD) Follow-up', UN, NY, 7 November 2002.

——, 2002c, 'Ideology, Power and the Rise of Independent Monetary Institutions in Emerging Economies', in J Kirshner, forthcoming, ed., *Monetary Orders: Ambiguous Economics, Ubiquitous Politics*, Ithaca, Cornell University Press, pp. 25–52.

——, 2002a, 'Neoliberal Finance and Crisis in the Developing World', *Monthly Review*, vol. 53, pp. 34–46.

——, 1999, 'Rejecting Exceptionalism: Reinterpreting the Asian Financial Crises', in J Michie and JG Smith, 1999, eds, *Global Instability: The Political Economy of World Economic Governance*, London, Routledge, pp. 37–67.

——, 1996, 'Marketing the Third World: The Contradictions of Portfolio Investment in the Global Economy', *World Development*, vol. 24, no. 11, pp. 1761–76.

Kaplan, E and Rodrik, D, 2001, 'Did the Malaysian Capital Controls Work?', *NBER Working Paper*, no. 8142.

LeFort, VG and Budenvich, C, 1997, 'Capital-Account Regulations and Macroeconomic Policy: Two Latin American Experiences', *International Monetary and Financial Issues for the 1990s, Research Papers from the Group of Twenty-Four, vol. VIII*.

Nissanke, M and Stein, H, 2003, 'Financial Globalisation and Economic Development: Toward an Institutional Foundation', *Eastern Economics Journal*, forthcoming.

Palma, G, 2000, 'The Three Routes to Financial Crises: The Need for Capital Controls', Mimeograph, Faculty of Economics and Politics, Cambridge University, Cambridge, England.

Rodrik, D, 1998, 'Who Needs Capital-Account Convertibility?', in 'Should the IMF Pursue Capital-Account Convertibility', Princeton Essays in International Finance, no. 207, pp. 55–65.

Stiglitz, J, 2002, *Globalization and Its Discontents*, NY, WW Norton & Co.

Weller, C, 2001, 'Financial Crises After Financial Liberalisation: Exceptional Circumstances or Structural Weakness?', *Journal of Development Studies*, vol. 38, no. 1, pp. 98–127.

Weller, C and Hersh, A, 2002, 'The Long and the Short of It: Global Liberalization, Poverty and Inequality', Economic Policy Institute Technical Working Paper no. 260, Washington, DC.

World Bank, 2002, *Global Development Finance*, Washington, DC, World Bank.

16

THE 'THREE ROUTES' TO FINANCIAL CRISES: CHILE, MEXICO, AND ARGENTINA [1]; BRAZIL [2]; AND KOREA, MALAYSIA AND THAILAND [3]

Gabriel Palma[1]

I can [understand and] calculate the motions of the heavenly bodies, but not the madness of [the South Sea Bubble] people.

Isaac Newton

1. Introduction

Four major financial crises have struck Developing Countries (DCs) since the 1982 debt-crisis: 1994 (Mexico, and the 'Tequila-effect' in Argentina); 1997 (East Asia); 1999 (Brazil); and 2001 (Argentina).

In the case of Latin America, two characteristics of the economies most affected by these crises were that they had undertaken the most radical financial liberalization; and that they had 'liberalized' their capital accounts and domestic financial sectors (and foreign trade) at a time of high liquidity in international financial markets (and slow growth in most OECD economies) – i.e., when a rapidly growing, highly volatile and largely under-regulated international financial market was anxiously seeking new high-yield investment opportunities.

As discussed in my chapter on Latin America (this volume, Chapter 6), a key element in understanding economic reforms in Latin America is the recognition that they were carried out as a result of perceived weaknesses in the previous model of development (a 'throwing in the towel' attitude). As also argued elsewhere,[2] this contrasts sharply with the way in which these reforms were understood in East Asia, where they were implemented as a pragmatic mechanism to strengthen their development process.

In Latin America, instead, the 'magnetic north' of the neoliberal compass was simply to reverse as many aspects of the previous growth strategy as possible.[3] It seems that, at a time of high economic uncertainty and radical political change, simplistic discourses tend to strike a chord with many segments of society.[4]

The first part of this chapter will attempt to show that, no matter how diversely these financially liberalized DCs, which had experienced sudden surges in inflows, tried to deal with the problem of 'inflow-absorption', they invariably ended up in financial crisis. Although there is a clear distinction between the Latin American and the East Asian crisis-building pattern, I have identified different basic ways in which DCs tried (unsuccessfully) to deal with these inflow surges, and have concluded that each of them led to financial crisis via a different 'route'; these are best illustrated by the Mexican (1988–94), the Brazilian (1994–9) and the Korean (1988–97) experiences.

These three routes (from now on called 'route 1' for Mexico, 'route 2' for Brazil, and 'route 3' for Korea) will incorporate the experiences of other crisis-countries, such as the Chilean case leading to its 1982 crisis ('route 1'), the experiences of Malaysia and Thailand leading to their 1997 crises ('route-3', but with some components of 'route-1'), and the Argentinian crisis, which closely follows most of the crucial components of the Mexican 'route-1'.

2. The three routes to financial crisis

Figure 1 shows the crucial issue at stake, common to *all* crisis countries: the remarkable surge in inflows on the heels of financial liberalization.

The turnaround is extraordinary: in the case of Brazil, the difference amounts to about $220 billion, $150 billion in Mexico and Argentina, and in the East Asian countries, $260 billion.[6] These surges are even more impressive in relative terms. In Argentina, net inflows in 1993 (i.e., just before its first crisis, following Mexico's 1994 crisis) achieved a level equivalent to 154% of exports, and in 1999, before its second crisis, net FDI inflows alone were greater than exports and equivalent to half the country's investment. In Chile (1981), net inflows also reached a level similar to exports; in Brazil, net FDI inflows alone were equivalent to 2/3 of exports in three consecutive years; in Malaysia, net private inflows reached 25% of GDP (1993); and in Korea they exceeded $1,200 per capita (1996).

In fact, some of these countries even began to be important players in the newly developed derivatives markets; for example, according to the IMF, in the 'Asia Pacific' market, the 'notional principal amount' outstanding for

Figure 1. **LATIN AMERICA and EAST ASIA: aggregate net capital flows before financial liberalization and between financial liberalization and financial crises**

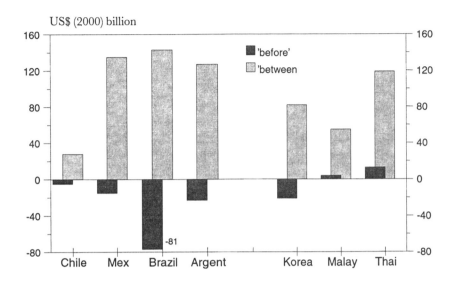

Mex=Mexico; **Argent**=Argentina; **Malay**=Malaysia; **Thai**=Thailand.

In each case the period '**between**' covers the years between financial liberalization and financial crisis: Chile, 1975–82; Mexico, 1988–94; Brazil, 1992–8; Argentina, 1991–2000; and Korea, Malaysia and Thailand, 1988–96. The period '**before**' covers a similar number of years before financial liberalization (in the case of East Asia and Argentina, however, as the period 'before' would have included years preceding the previous 1982 debt crisis, only years since 1982 have been included).

Source: IMF 2002b.[5]

some selected derivatives grew from just over $1 billion in 1986 to $2.4 trillion in 1996.

The key proposition in this chapter is a 'Kindlebergian' one: a massive surge in inflows – and in particular because of its effects on domestic liquidity – is the key to understanding all three 'routes' to financial crises. This is the 'smoking gun'.[7] What is common to all 'routes' is the unsuccessful attempt to absorb these inflows. According to which of the three routes was actually followed, the specific financial 'vulnerabilities' that began to emerge were, of course, varied: for example, in 'route 1' countries, there was a rapid revaluation of real-exchange rates, an explosion of credit to the private sector, consumption booms and asset bubbles and a massive deterioration in current accounts. In 'route 2' (Brazil), high interest rates – mainly necessary for high levels of sterilization, to defend the 'peg', and as a poor substitute for public-sector reforms (i.e., the cost of political stalemate) – help create enormous fragilities in the banking system and in the (Federal and State) public-sector finance, and a deterioration in the term structure of foreign debt. And, in 'route 3' (Korea), corporate debt/equity ratios increased to a level that even in this part of the world should have caused vertigo.

To the key question, 'why did foreign capital swamp these countries so suddenly?', the answer is twofold: the 'push' factor and several 'pull' factors. The former consisted of 'excess' liquidity in international financial markets – DCs have usually played the role of 'market of last resort' [8] – while among the latter undervalued asset markets (artificially created), high interest-rate spreads and expectations of exchange-rate appreciation stood out. Also, optimism regarding the success of economic reforms was in excess supply, partly as a result of the massive 'spin' put on them by those to be found circling around the 'Washington Consensus'. Finally, a crucial 'pull' factor – at least until the last Argentinian crisis – was the 'moral hazard' created by the near certainty in international financial markets that, as in every old Western, the cavalry, in the form of a vast international rescue operation, could be counted upon to arrive in the nick of time, should the 'natives' threaten to default or close their capital account.[9]

As mentioned above, the main 'push' factor was the extraordinary growth in international liquidity. For example, according to IMF data, the value of assets of institutional investors (i.e., the non-banking financial sector) increased between 1988 and 1996 from $12 to $26 trillion. The 'Anglo-Saxon' countries stood out: in the UK, the ratio of these assets to GDP grew by 80 percentage points of GDP over this period; in the US, it grew by 60 points. The average increase for the G7 was 40 percentage points. Needless to say, these are large numbers.

Again according to IMF data, the 'notional' value of outstanding 'over-the-counter' derivative contracts (interest rates, currency and exchange-traded derivatives) reached $72 trillion in 1995; this amount is similar to that of the aggregate value of all bonds, all equity and all bank assets of the G17.[10]

A related problem is that the exposure of these institutional investors to DCs was proportionally so small, that they often believed that it would not pay to invest adequately in information; normal problems of 'asymmetric' information were therefore exacerbated.

Massive international liquidity and the DCs' 'irresistible' magnetic attraction to this liquidity became a lethal cocktail. In fact, some DCs – accustomed to living within a foreign-exchange constraint environment – suddenly saw their fortunes reversed, with the main macroeconomic problem being how to absorb such massive inflows. They found themselves in somewhat uncharted territory: suddenly, it not only rained but it poured.

Furthermore, one of the peculiarities of economic theory is that it is rarely concerned with 'shocks' – although there are of course exceptions like Keynes, Kindleberger, Minsky and Galbraith. It is from the different ways in which these seven DCs tried to deal with the shock of massive inflow-absorption that the three 'routes' to financial crises emerged.

2.1 The Latin American story: to sterilize or not to sterilize an exogenous push of foreign capital (Brazil vs. Chile, Mexico and Argentina)

Figure 2 shows the surges of inflows into LA in the 1970s and 1990s.

The two surges of inflows into LA are not only greater than those into East Asia (and with a more unstable composition), but they are especially large when looked at from the point of view of their respective exports (Figure 3).

Figure 2. **LATIN AMERICA: composition of net capital inflows, 1950–2000**

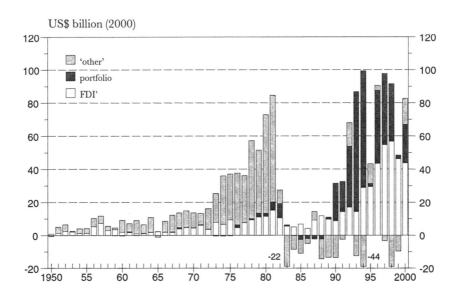

In LA, low levels of inflows go back to 1929.

Figure 3. **LATIN AMERICA and EAST ASIA: financial accounts between the beginning of financial liberalization and respective financial crises**

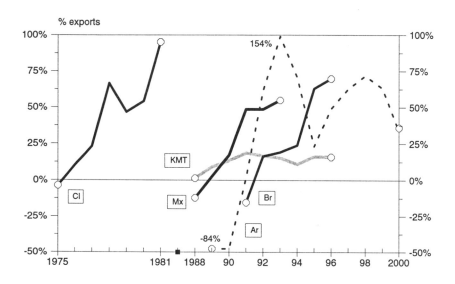

[**CI**]=Chile; [**Mx**]=Mexico; [**Ar**]=Argentina; [**Br**]=Brazil; and [**KMT**]=average of Korea, Malaysia and Thailand. These abbreviations apply to all graphs below.

In Argentina, the turnaround over four years (1989 to 1993) is equivalent to 2.4 times the then level of exports, or from -$11 billion to $24 billion – as the Finance Minister, the legendary Mr Cavallo, once said, the overvaluation of the currency was not then due to fixing the exchange rate; on the contrary, the fixed parity was actually preventing the nominal rate from revaluating.

Not surprisingly, inflows had a totally different effect on real exchange rates in Latin America than in East Asia (Figure 11).

Figure 4 shows the beginning of the major differences in Latin America between Brazil, which decided to make a massive sterilization effort ('route 2'), and Chile, Mexico and Argentina, which did not ('route 1').

One response to the surge in net private inflows ('route 1' in Latin America and 'route 3' in East Asia) was to ride them out by unloading them into the economy via credit expansion;[11] the other response (Brazil) was precisely the reverse: to try to stop their expansionary effect by placing an 'iron curtain' around them.

The crucial factor in understanding the different behaviour of Brazil is the timing of its financial liberalization (second half of 1994); this practically co-

Figure 4. **EAST ASIA and LATIN AMERICA: credit to the private sector between the beginning of financial liberalization and respective financial crises**

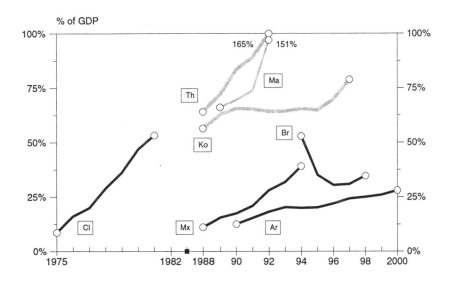

For Latin American countries, see Figure 3. **[Ko]**=Korea; **[Ma]**=Malaysia; and **[Th]**=Thailand. The figures for Thailand and Malaysia shown in the graph correspond to 1997 (those of 1996 are 147% and 137% respectively). The drop in Brazil's figure between 1994 and 1995 (a period of rapidly falling inflation) is mainly due to the fact that the sources used in this graph (World Bank, World Development Indicators) use end-of-year figures for credit and average-of-year figures for GDP.

incided with the Mexican 1994 crisis. Therefore, high degrees of sterilization and high interest rates were explicitly continued after the 'Real Plan' had already succeeded in conquering inflation in order to avoid following a Mexican 'route 1' crisis-path.

Even though there was a similarity in the speed of credit expansion between 'route 1' (part of Latin America) and 'route 3' (East Asia), there also was a crucial difference in the use made of this additional credit expansion: 'route 1' mainly directs it towards increased consumption and asset speculation (Figures 6 to 10); 'route 3' (particularly the paradigmatic case of Korea) towards corporate investment (Figure 18). The difference was also related to the 'magnetism' that first of all attracted these inflows. In 'route 3', it was an 'endogenous pull': additional finance was actually required to sustain high levels of investment at a time of rapidly falling profit levels; in 'route 1', it was rather an 'exogenous push' movement of

Figure 5. LATIN AMERICA and EAST ASIA: domestic real lending rates between the beginning of financial liberalization and respective financial crises

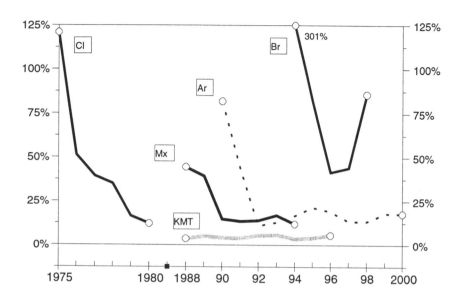

foreign capital into these countries, which then had practically to 'create' a need for itself.

From this point of view, 'route-1' countries could be regarded as a rather peculiar case of Say's Law, in which 'supply has to create demand'. The age-old mechanism was followed: additional inflows increase the amount, reduce the price, ease the access and reduce the transaction costs of liquidity. A (common) side effect of this was to fuel 'expectations'. This process reinforces itself, becoming (for a while) a self-fulfilling prophecy. Easy access to cheap credit fuelled expectations regarding the performance of the economy, a performance that was enhanced by the additional expenditure brought about by extra borrowing and availability of foreign exchange. 'Over lending' and 'over borrowing' were therefore not only the result of a closely interrelated process, but also of one that had a clear direction of causality: the propensity to 'over lend' led to the propensity to 'over borrow'.

Finally, the cases of Malaysia and Thailand are characterized by having one foot in each of these two camps. Their surges in inflows were so large that they followed Korea's 'route 3' using foreign finance to sustain their ambitious private investment programmes – Malaysia actually doubled its share of private investment in GDP (to 30.5%), while Thailand brought its own to

Figure 6. **LATIN AMERICA and EAST ASIA: private consumption between the beginning of financial liberalization and respective financial crises**

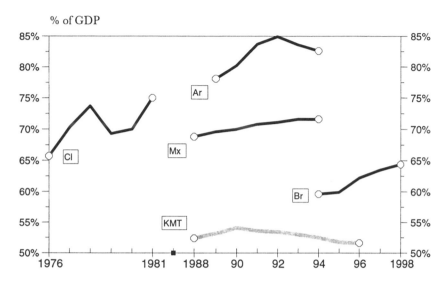

The Argentinian data from this source (WB) are only available until 1994; according to ECLAC (at 1995 prices), the Argentinian ratios for 1992 and 1993 were even higher, reaching 93% of GDP.

34.1%. But, contrary to Korea, there was plenty of spare credit to follow at least *one* element of 'route 1' too – the 'excess' credit fuelled a Latin-style asset bubble in their stock markets and real estate.

Remarkably, however, in these two East Asian countries, massive credit expansion was associated with a *drop* in the share of consumption in GDP – in Thailand, it falls from 56.7% to 54.8%, and in Malaysia from 49.4% to 45.9%. No sign of 'route 1' here.

In sum, these seven DCs chose two different paths to inflow-absorption: one, following the credo of the classical 'efficient-market' theory and the first law of Welfare Economics, was inspired by two simple propositions: [i] keep public finance in balance;[12] and [ii] allow markets to sort out the resulting private imbalances by themselves (routes '1' and '3').[13] Brazil, instead, tried to contain the expansionary effect of surges in capital inflows 'at source' by placing an 'iron curtain' around the Central Bank reserves via a high degree of sterilization. Figures 5 and 15 show the resulting differences in interest-rates policies.

In 'route 1' (Chile, Mexico and Argentina), real interest rates start very high due to their simultaneous stabilization policies, but soon afterwards

Figure 7. **LATIN AMERICA and EAST ASIA: imports of consumer goods between the beginning of financial liberalization and respective financial crises**

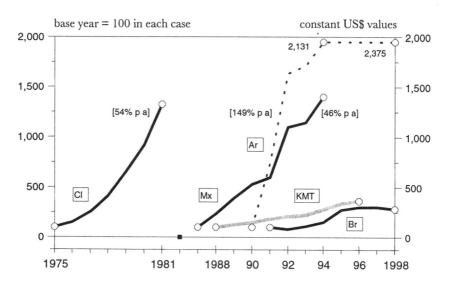

Percentages shown in the graph are average annual rates of growth. The percentage for Argentina corresponds to the period 1990–4 (i.e., between financial liberalization and its first financial crisis).

interest rates are allowed to fall to international levels (plus the corresponding spreads). 'Route 3' countries in East Asia are characterized by a long-term policy of low rates. However, in the case of Brazil, real interest rates are not only set at a much higher level during the price-stabilization programme, but due to the sterilization policy (and other reasons discussed in detail elsewhere[14]), they were never allowed to fall anywhere near the values of 'route 1' countries (let alone 'route 3' countries).

The case of Brazil is very important for the critique of 'moral-hazard-type' crisis-analysis. For example, according to McKinnon and Pill, the main cause of borrowing agents losing their capacity to assess and price their risk properly is that internal and external moral hazards lead to 'artificially' low interest rates; these, in turn, gave a false incentive to agents to accumulate excessive amounts of risk.[15] However, in Brazil, although high interest rates did help to avoid a 'route 1' financial crisis, it did so by creating a different (but equally damaging) type of financial crisis ('route 2').

In turn, Figure 6 shows a crucial difference between routes '1' and '3'.

Figure 8. **LATIN AMERICA and EAST ASIA: annual stock market indices between the beginning of financial liberalization and respective financial crises**

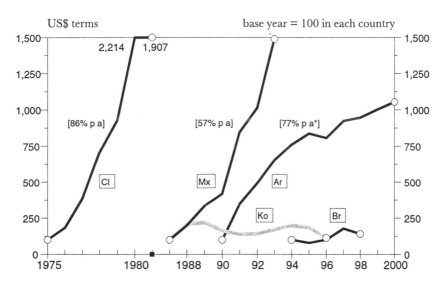

The percentages shown are average annual growth-rates; Chile's rate refers to 1975–80, and Argentina's to the period before its first crisis (1990–4). The Argentinian data are 3-year moving averages of average-of-the-year figures.

Source: DataStream.

Probably no other macroeconomic variable reflects so transparently the different 'models' followed in Latin America and East Asia. Figure 7 shows a related difference between them.

In 'route 1', the expansion of imports of consumer goods (though, from a relatively small initial level) is really exceptional; this is not the case for the other two 'routes' – in Brazil, it is mainly because of higher interest rates and a more cautious trade liberalization.[16]

Figure 8 shows how easy access to credit in 'route 1' countries also led to an asset bubble in the stock market, 'tulip mania' style.

Again, the uniqueness of 'route 1' (Chile, Mexico and Argentina) is clear. What went on in 'route 1' was astonishing, not only when compared with 'route 2' and 'route 3', but also with the OECD. For example, while both the Dow Jones (Industrial and Composite), the S&P-500, the NASDAQ, and the (DataStream dollar-denominated) index for Europe and Asia grew by between 1.4 and 3-fold between 1975 and 1980, the stock market in Chile grew 22-fold in dollar terms[17] – meanwhile, Chile's GDP was growing at a

Figure 9. **Latin America, 'emerging' Asia, Europe, Dow and Nasdaq: stock market indices, 1987–98**

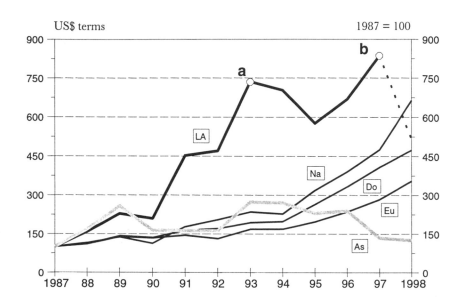

[LA]=Latin America ('**a**'=Mexican crisis; '**b**'=East Asian crisis); [Na]=NASDAQ; [Do]=Dow Jones Industrial; [Eu]=Europe; and [As]='emerging' Asia.

Source: IFC 2002.

modest average of 3.2% (1974–80): this was a (self-fulfilling) 'pull factor' if ever there was one!

As mentioned above, Malaysia and Thailand did follow 'route 1' countries in this respect, but their bubbles are dwarfed in comparison to Chile or Mexico: even when comparing the increase between the lowest quarterly point vis-à-vis the highest one, in Malaysia the expansion is 6-fold and in Thailand is 5.4-fold.

Figure 9 shows the regional differences in stock markets.

The Summers were probably not very well acquainted with Latin America when they stated that: '[In financial markets] prices will always reflect funda-mental values[…]. The logic of efficient markets is compelling.'[18]

Figure 10 shows the other asset bubble of 'route-1' countries, that of real estate.

Once again, the contrast could not be more pronounced – another Kindlebergian 'mania' in Mexico (and Chile), and an actual fall in the indices of Korea and Brazil.[20] Also, Malaysia and Thailand are again much closer to

Figure 10. LATIN AMERICA and EAST ASIA: real estate prices
between the beginning of financial liberalization and respective
financial crises

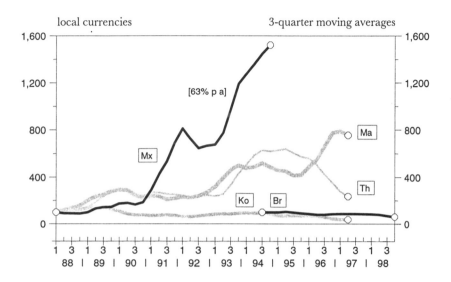

The percentage is Mexico's average annual rate of growth.

Sources: DataStream for East Asia, and 'Jonas Lang LaSalle Index' for Mexico and Brazil
(DataStream does not provide data for Latin America). Neither index provides data on
Chile between 1975 and 1981; however, Chilean Central Bank statistics, though using a
different methodology, show a similar increase to Mexico's.[19]

'route 1' than Korea. In the case of Malaysia, the index between mid-1988
and mid-1997 grows (Latin-style) 12.3-fold, while in Thailand, if one takes the
highest and lowest points of the index, it jumps by almost 8-fold.

It should come as no surprise then that countries in 'route 1' began to
develop several micro and macroeconomic 'distortions' and 'vulnerabilities'.
Figure 11 shows one of the most damaging of these: the overvaluation of
exchange rates.

It is really difficult to fit this picture with the basic postulate of the neoliberal creed of the need to lift distortions and stop governments' 'discretionary'
policies so as to allow the economy to 'get its prices right'. Massive inflows into
Latin America, particularly in relation to exports, and the use of exchange-
rate based stabilization policies – based on the oldest macroeconomic law of
them all: one can only solve a macroeconomic imbalance by creating another
one – brought this most crucial of prices to a level which it would be rather

Figure 11. **LATIN AMERICA and EAST ASIA: real effective rate of exchange between the beginning of financial liberalization and respective financial crises**

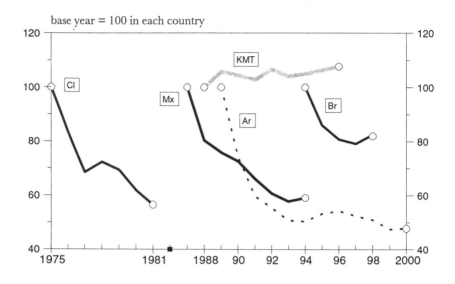

Figure 12. **EAST ASIA and LATIN AMERICA: current account between the beginning of financial liberalization and respective financial crises**

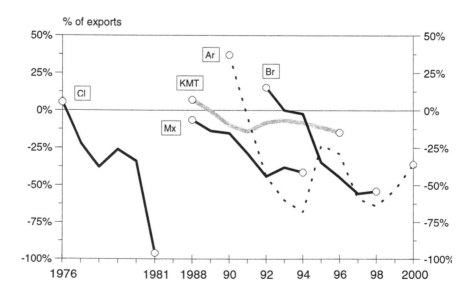

Figure 13. **MEXICO: investment in residential construction, infrastructure, and machinery and equipment, 1981–94**

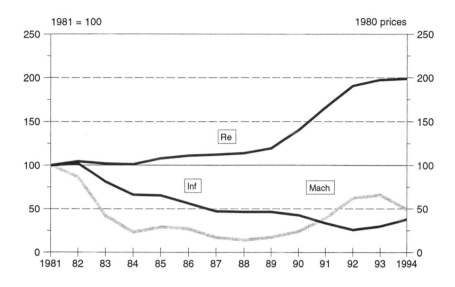

[**Re**]=investment in residential construction; [**Inf**]=in infrastructure; and [**Mach**]=in machinery and equipment. The base year is 1981, as this year represents the peak of the previous (ISI) cycle.

Source: Hofman 2000.

hard to brand as 'right'; particularly in view of the effect it was having in the current account (Figure 12).

As 'route 1' countries (with the partial exception of Argentina) did manage to keep their public-sector accounts in order (Chile, for example, had a surplus of 4.8% of GDP in 1979, 5.4% in 1980 and 2.6% in 1981), these current-account deficits obviously reflect private imbalances. If this was a 'self-correcting' mechanism for the surge in inflows, the resulting accumulation of foreign liabilities was certainly not. In fact, despite continuous high inflows in Mexico, Brazil and Argentina, the increasing cost of servicing foreign debt and the large profit repatriation by FDI led to a situation in which the net transfer of resources into these countries totally evaporated even before their respective financial crises.

Given this evidence, it is difficult to understand how, as late as 1996, the World Bank was still preaching to DCs to continue implementing simultaneously policies of exchange-rate-based sterilization and of trade liberalization

Figure 14. **LATIN AMERICA: private consumption and savings, percentage of GDP**

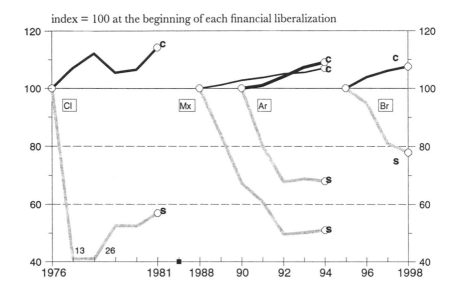

index = 100 at the beginning of each financial liberalization

[**c**]=private consumption as a share of GDP; and [**s**]=private savings as a share of GDP.

even when, at the same time, they explicitly acknowledged that the so-called 'second generation' reforms were still totally lacking.

Moreover, the current account was not the only casualty of the exchange-rate overvaluation; this also distorted the composition of what little investment there was towards the non-tradeable sector (Figure 13).

While residential construction doubles in these 13 years, investment in machinery (despite its recovery in 1991–2) falls by half and that in infrastructure even further.[21] In other words, the distortion in relative prices, easy access to credit, and the asset bubble in real estate set in motion a huge Kuznets' cycle'.[22]

This is a rather odd picture: in fact, 'route 1' economies ended up switching the engine of growth away from their desired aim – domestically financed private investment in tradeable production – towards a more 'post-modernist' goal of externally financed private consumption, asset bubbles, and private investment in non-tradeable activities.

Finally, the contrasting behaviour of private consumption and savings is shown in Figure 14.

This is definitely not the promised land of McKinnon and Shaw's financial liberalization.[23]

Figure 15. **BRAZIL: how to walk into a public-sector 'Ponzi' by over-reacting to external shocks, by the high cost of sterilization (i–r), and by the violation of a 'golden rule' (i>p)**

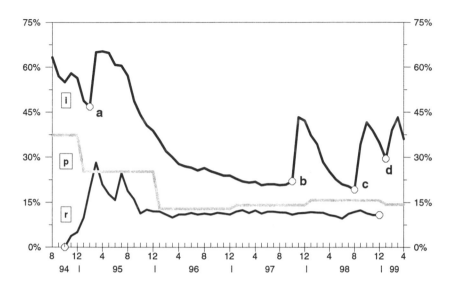

[**i**]=annualized nominal monthly interest rate paid for public debt; [**p**]=annual growth rate of public revenues; and [**r**]=income received for foreign-exchange reserves (assumed equivalent to returns on US Treasury Bills). Domestic currency.[24]

[**a**]=Mexican crisis; [**b**]=East Asian crisis; [**c**]=Russian devaluation and default; and [**d**]=default by the State of Minas Gerais.

Turning to 'route 2', the crucial vulnerability of Brazil lies in massive sterilization and (excessively) high interest rates leading straight into a public-sector 'Ponzi' finance (Figure 15).

First, as has often been argued, the Brazilian Central Bank overreacted to external shocks (an attitude often called 'macho monetarism', or 'sado monetarism').[25] Second, the (unnecessarily) high cost of sterilization becomes evident in the difference between lines 'i' and 'r' – i.e., between what was paid for the paper sold to sterilize and what was recuperated from the return on their holding of foreign-exchange reserves.[26]

Finally, Brazil systematically violated the famous 'fiscal golden rule', by paying a much higher rate for its public debt than the rate at which it managed to increase public revenues (and, certainly, its income per capita). In part, this was the price paid for both the lack of (much needed) public sector reforms and political stalemate – in this sense, the financial crisis in Brazil was more due to a weak public sector than it was in the other two 'routes'.

Figure 16. **LATIN AMERICA and EAST ASIA: spread between lending and deposit rates between the beginning of financial liberalization and respective financial crises**

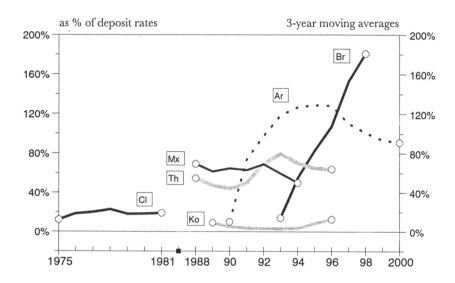

Furthermore, high lending rates followed: the annualized real monthly interest rate paid for working capital peaked at 60% in October 1998, while that for consumer credit did so at 115%. With these rates, of course, hardly any private asset could perform; as discussed elsewhere, non-performing loans (as well as lack of transparency in the banking sector, weak regulatory public institutions and the end of inflation income by the banking system) led to a succession of banking crises, each adding a significant amount to the stock of the public-sector debt due to a policy of indiscriminate bail-outs.[27]

In fact, the ease with which the government could finance its domestic debt was due primarily to private banks falling over themselves to buy public paper, as this was just about the only asset that could perform at such rates. Regarding the rest of their portfolio, not having read – or having read but not understood – Stiglitz, private banks tried to increase profitability by the self-defeating policy of ever increasing spreads (Figure 16).

No prizes for guessing in which countries (in both regions) the crisis of the domestic banking system came before the overall financial crisis (and constituted a major component of the lead-up to it), and in which countries it only followed the crash (when bank-portfolio became non-performing due to falling incomes, sharp devaluations and asset-price deflation).

Figure 17. **EAST ASIA and LATIN AMERICA: private investment between the beginning of financial liberalization and respective financial crises**

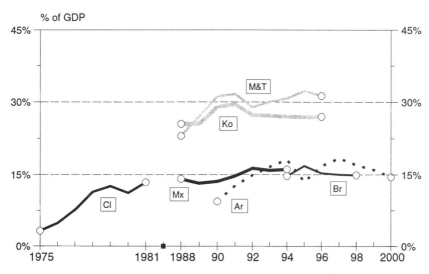

M&T=Malaysia and Thailand

2.2 *The East Asia story of an 'endogenous pull' of foreign capital: the cost of maintaining high levels of investment in the face of falling profits.*

The East Asian story is apparently more complicated than that of Latin America.[28] Inflows – particularly as a share of exports – were not so large, and their composition was more stable; exchange rates were not revalued; interest rates were low and stable, and there was no consumption boom; no collapse of savings; and no deficit in the public sector. So, what about 'overinvestment' – practically the only possible macro-imbalance left?

Figure 17 shows that, while in Latin America private investment seems to find a 'natural' ceiling at around 15% of GDP, in 'Schumpeterian' East Asia it was twice as high. However, the graph also shows that private investment did not really increase in Korea. Therefore, even if it is obvious that routes '1' and '3' countries used their inflows in a different way, the question still needs to be answered as to why the Korean corporate sector suddenly needed such large capital inflows to finance an ambitious but relatively stable investment effort. Figure 18 provides the answer.

As discussed elsewhere,[29] mainly due to declining profitability – a decline

Figure 18. **SOUTH KOREA: sectoral surpluses of the household, government, foreign and corporate sectors, 1987–96**

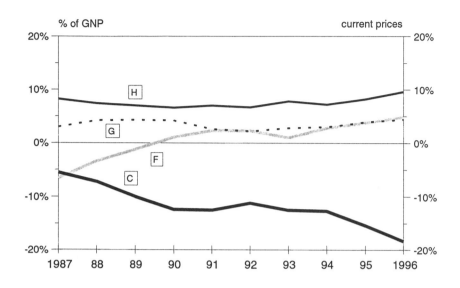

Sectoral surpluses are the differences between sectoral savings and investment.

[**H**]=households; [**G**]=government; [**F**]=financial account balance; and [**C**]=corporate sector.

which had little to do with the Krugman-type critique of Korea, and a lot with collapsing micro-electronic prices[30] – the corporate sector had to finance its high, but relatively stable, levels of investment switching from own-profits to external finance. This process, which caused the sectoral deficit of the corporate sector to increase from about 5% to nearly 20% of GNP, absorbed not only all the increase in the surplus of the 'foreign sector', but that of the household and government sectors as well.[31] Consequently, was there 'over-investment'? The answer – as is so often the case – is more complicated than the typically simplistic 'Washington Consensus' one.[32]

The crucial issue that leads to misunderstandings in the East Asian crisis is to forget that, once you have gone into the type of export structure character-istics of the region, one can only be competitive if able to be at the cutting-edge of technology; and to be able to remain at that level, one has to invest at East Asian levels. Therefore, when prices (and profitability) collapsed, the choice for Korea was not that of 'blackboard economics' – of having the tech-nological choice of being able to produce a given amount of output with different combinations of capital and labour. Rather, it was whether to stay in the microelectronic business or to look for a new type of development pattern altogether, thereby allowing most of its accumulated physical, human and institutional capital to depreciate. The choice was between exporting microchips 'warts and all', or – probably the IMF's preferred solution – switching to the export of potato-chips or returning to silk, Korea's main export product before its massive industrialization drive.

In fact, what might have been an effective solution for East Asian industrialization would have been a Keynesian-style programme of regional investment coordination. For example, what triggered the collapse of the price of the D-Ram memory in 1995 was massive new Taiwanese investment coming into stream at the wrong time. However, the analysis of this issue falls outside the scope of this chapter.

2.3 The day of reckoning

Not surprisingly, financial 'vulnerabilities' quickly began to emerge in each 'route'. Some of these vulnerabilities were specific, and have already been discussed. In 'route 1', they included: overvalued exchange rates; growing current account deficit; asset bubbles threatening to burst; and growing non-performing bank assets.[33] In 'route 2', Brazil, there was public-sector 'Ponzi finance' and repeated private-banking crises, while 'route 3' included exploding corporate debts. However, these countries also had to face at least three common problems: (i) constant changing composition of private inflows; (ii) progressive shortening of the term structure of their debt; and (iii) the constant danger that in a financially liberalized economy the attack could also come from 'within'.

Regarding the first problem, Figure 2 showed that in Latin America there was an erratic changing composition of inflows; this is also found in East Asia, but in a less extreme form. The changing composition made the already difficult matter of absorbing massive inflows even more complicated.[34] Regarding the term-structure of inflows, Figure 19 shows that these shortened significantly over the period. Obviously, this added further fragility and heightened uncertainty to an already difficult situation.

There are two main apparent paradoxes as regards term-structures. The first is that 'route 1' countries – especially Argentina[35] – had the lowest shares of short-term debt.[36] The second is the early high share of Korea's short-term debt. It is really remarkable that this happened much earlier than it did in Latin America, as logic would suggest that it should have been the other way round – in the early 1990s (according to any risk assessment), the likelihood of a financial crisis was so much stronger in Latin America. So, why did this happen?

Figure 19. LATIN AMERICA and EAST ASIA: ratio of short-term debt to total debt between the beginning of financial liberalization and respective financial crises

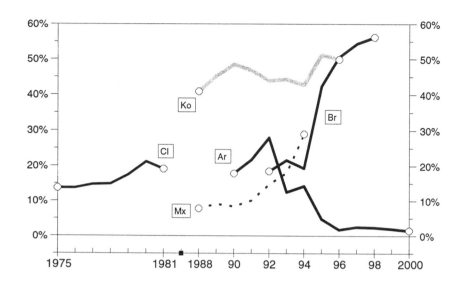

Source: IMF 2002c

The answer is almost as obvious as it is bizarre. Basically, in Korea there was a lot of red tape involved in any form of long-term borrowing, and very little in short-term borrowing (supposedly in order to facilitate trade finance). In other words, it was Korea's own government that gave the incentive to corporations to borrow 'short'. This contrasts sharply with Brazil, where the international financial markets, progressively alarmed at the overall situation, were the ones that imposed a shortening of the term structure of the debt. This is an amazing phenomenon that until now had not been properly picked up by those whose hobby it is to criticize government regulation in East Asia.[37]

Figure 20 shows one of the obvious consequences of increasing short-term debt.

First, in the case of Korea, its main weakness in 1997 – which made it so vulnerable to events in Thailand and Malaysia – was not just its high share of short-term debt, but the combination of such debt with exceptionally low levels of reserves. Figure 20 indicates that Korea's reserves could only cover half its short-term liabilities; in fact, they were not even enough to cover debt with 90 days' maturity or less. Again, as in the case of a large 'self-inflicted'

Figure 20. **LATIN AMERICA and EAST ASIA: ratio of foreign-exchange reserves to short-term debt between the beginning of financial liberalization and respective financial crises**

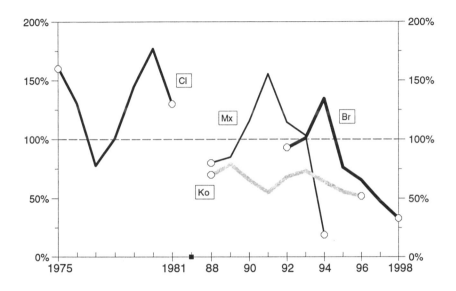

share of short-term debt, Korea's Central Bank authorities operated 'voluntarily' with low levels of reserves, which compounded the short-term debt problem: they paid dearly for these two silly mistakes.[38]

The Korean authorities seemed to have had some sort of schizophrenia vis-à-vis economic planning and regulation. In matters relating to the real economy and in some aspects of domestic finance, they felt the need for strong, detailed and effective intervention, but in areas relating to the capital account and monetary policy, they only seem to have been concerned with *long*-term capital movement, exchange-rate stability and in keeping interest rates as low as possible. This left unchecked what turned out to be two 'suicidal' tendencies in the economy: that of the corporate sector to accumulate short-term debt (as if there was no tomorrow), and that of the Central Bank to keep low levels of reserves (as though international financial markets would never dare to attack).

In Brazil, authorities had a mixed policy on these issues. First, as President Cardoso clearly stated, they were against intervening in the capital account to reduce the share of short-term debt – they were, for example, against capital controls.[39] Nevertheless, authorities did increase the level of reserves; but this seems to have lulled them into a false sense of security because short-term debt grew even faster and, as the 'fundamentals' deteriorated rapidly, the economy was left extremely vulnerable to a sudden collapse of confidence and withdrawal of finance.

Finally, of course, in a financially liberalized economy, the 'attack' could just as easily come from 'within'. Neither Mexico, Brazil nor Korea had significant defences against internal attacks on their exchange rates, as their 'reserves-M2' ratios were also particularly low. In Argentina, where the Currency Board was supposed to provide a self-regulating insurance against such an attack, the Finance Minister, facing a massive capital-flight that was draining the reserves, in 2001 first increased interest rates on deposits from 9% to 16% (and on lending rates from 12% to 24%), and finally imposed a 'corralito' (i.e., a freeze on bank accounts).[40]

Conclusions

In sum, 'route 1' countries, after massive surges in capital inflows, followed a path to financial crisis led by an explosion of credit to the private sector, low levels of interest rates (after stabilization) and a rapid real-exchange re-valuation.

All these produced: consumption booms; asset bubbles; collapse in savings; massive deterioration of current accounts; and distorted the already low levels of investment towards residential construction. In the meantime, the levels of foreign debt exploded, while its term structure deteriorated. It did not take much for this 'route' to encounter a sudden collapse of confidence and withdrawal of finance, leading to major financial crises.

The path to financial crisis in 'route 2' (Brazil) in turn also started with a surge in inflows, but the scene was soon dominated by high interest rates, which were initially necessary for price stabilization, but which later became permanent to avoid another 'Mexico', and to respond to continuous external shocks. These high interest rates were successful in avoiding a repeat of 'route 1', but soon created massive domestic financial fragility in the banking sector and in state-government finance, leading to an increase in public debt through continuous (and indiscriminate) federal-government rescue activities.

This public debt exploded due to high interest rates, which became systematically higher than both the growth in public revenues and the returns on reserves. In the meantime, the real economy imploded because of these rates, which affected the growth of public revenues even further. However, high interest rates became even more necessary as a (poor) substitute for missing public-sector reforms, as a price for political stalemate, and to defend the 'peg', so as to avoid both further domestic banking crises due to high foreign-exchange liabilities and a stampede by restless international fund managers.

The 'Ponzi' finance in the public sector ballooned out of control. Again, it did not take much for this route to end up in a major financial crisis.

Finally, in 'route 3' countries, particularly Korea, again there were massive surges in inflows and increases of private credit but, despite low interest rates, there were no consumption booms or asset bubbles. Rather, in the context of declining profitability, there were high (though stable) levels of investment, and rapid technological change in a world (particularly the sphere of micro-electronics) where there were both collapsing prices and competitiveness only at the cutting edge of technology. This ended up producing corporate debt/equity ratios that reached unprecedented heights. Added to this, there were incomprehensive policy incentives to the corporate and financial sector to borrow abroad 'short', and a Central Bank that seemed to have enjoyed the thrill of living dangerously with low levels of reserves. Again – and despite the growth record of Korea, its degree of competitiveness, and having fundamentals which, if not perfect, were nevertheless the envy of most DCs – it did not take much for this route to also encounter a major financial crisis.

Malaysia and Thailand followed a mix of routes '1' and '3'. After surges in inflows, they followed a path to financial crisis also led by an (even higher) explosion of credit to the private sector, but without the revaluation of exchange rates, consumption booms and declining savings of 'route 1'. However, they did have Latin-style asset bubbles, and most of the problems of Korea as well, plus added difficulties: not only was further upgrading of exports becoming increasingly problematic (in particular breaking away from a 'sub-contracting-type' industrialization), but China was also becoming a formidable competitor. Again, despite a strong growth record, a growing degree of competitiveness, and far better fundamentals than those of Latin America, it was not long before voracious fund managers, eager to profit from long-standing but only precipitately acknowledged 'peccadilloes', had a sudden collapse of confidence that led to bank runs and major financial crises.[41]

So, the moral of the story of the 'three routes' is that, whichever way DCs facing sudden and massive surges in inflows have handled their absorption, they have ended up in major crises. Of course, with hindsight one can always think of hypothetical ways in which the worst excesses could have been avoided, but the fact is that the economic and political dynamics created by these surges in inflows has proved extraordinarily difficult to manage.

Another common element in the genesis of all these crises is the way in which international financial markets and the financial press have interpreted economic news. First, following financial liberalization, good news tends to be exaggerated and bad news totally ignored (the 'turning a blind eye' stage). Second, when bad news cannot be ignored anymore, some is acknowledged but is believed to be easily under control (the 'omnipotent' stage). Finally, there is a sudden turn towards panic, when bad news is – sometimes grossly – exaggerated (the 'hysterical' stage).

Of course, there is a series of other important issues that it has not been possible to analyse here, particularly the politico-institutional framework in which financial liberalization and economic reforms have been carried out.[42] One of these issues is the extraordinary collection of 'first generation' Heads of State that carried them out in Latin America. Although not unfamiliar to Latin American politics, the mélange of Pinochet, Salinas, Collor, Menem, Fujimori, Alemán (and many others), certainly deserves several entries in *The Guinness Book of Records*, particularly under the headings of human rights abuses, electoral fraud, petit-bourgeois parvenu-populism and corruption.[43] After having initially got into power using *anti*-neoliberal discourses, their sudden eagerness to switch to the 'neoliberal' camp was in part related to both their desperate need for an apparently coherent political platform (given their deep ideological emptiness), and the opportunity to create a new structure of property rights from which massive new rents could be generated. Remarkably, they switched camp by using their populist talents to sell 'neoliberalism' successfully as an ideology that could contribute to social cohesion in strongly fragmented societies. And, of course, the more successful they were in selling the 'neoliberal' programme, the more extravagant the predatory capitalism that followed could be.

With these 'first generation' individuals running the show to begin with, financial liberalization and economic reforms (particularly privatizations) probably never really stood a chance.[44]

Again despite previous opposition, when the 'second generation' leaders took office (Aylwin, Cardoso, De la Rua and others), in terms of economic programme – although certainly not in style – 'path-dependency' ruled.[45]

Also, in the face of all the evidence of links between these reforms and financial crises – particularly in their extremely corrupt, populistic and manic 'first round' – how can so many economists still insist that these crises were simply the result of extraneous factors, such as ordinary moral hazards and long standing forms of 'crony' capitalism?[46]

Another explanation seems much more likely:

[Is financial liberalization] being designed on the basis of the best available economic theory and evidence, or is there another agenda, perhaps a special interest agenda? [...] Do those making decisions that affect the lives and livelihood of millions of people throughout the world reflect the interest and concerns, not just of financial markets, but of businesses, small and large, and of workers, and the economy more broadly?[47]

Finally, one additional question – who has misallocated more resources in Latin America since financial liberalization: the often underpaid, at times corrupt and sporadically seriously inefficient government officials, or the excessively-liquid, LTCM-type 'fat-cats' of the international and domestic private financial markets, so prone to oscillating between mania and panic?

Notes

1 An earlier version appeared in Eatwell and Taylor 2002; I would like to thank them and Edna Armendáriz, Alfredo Golcagmo, Antonio David, Daniel Chudnovsky, Carlos Lopes, Jan Kregel, Richard Kozul-Wright, Jose Antonio Ocampo, Arturo O'Connell, Carlota Perez, Bob Sutcliffe, and especially Ha-Joon Chang and Stephanie Blankenburg, and participants at seminars in Bangkok, Bilbao, Cambridge, Cape Town, Chicago, Kuala Lumpur, London, New York, Paris, Santa Cruz, Santiago, Sydney, and Trento for their helpful comments (and hospitality). The ideas of Kindleberger and Minsky strongly influence this chapter. The usual caveats apply.

2 Palma 2001 and 2002c.

3 A case in point is Gustavo Franco, President of the Brazilian Central Bank up to the 1999 financial crisis. According to him: '[Our real task] is to undo forty years of stupidity ('besteira').' (Veja 15/11/1996). The fact that Brazil's previous development strategy had delivered for most of those 40 years one of the fastest growth rates in the world, was, according to Franco, a mere detail of history.

4 Franco again: '[For Brazil, the alternative] is to be neoliberal or neo-idiotic ('neo-burros')[…].'

5 Unless otherwise stated, this source, together with IMF 2002a and c, World Bank 2002a and b, ECLAC Statistical Division and ECLAC 2002 will be the sources for all data in this chapter.

6 All US dollar figures throughout the chapter are expressed in 2000 values.

7 An issue that is absent in most financial crises models, whatever 'generation' they belong to.

8 See Palma 1998.

9 In Argentina, however, despite repeated IMF rescue operations, the government ended up defaulting anyway – a case in which the 'motives' defeated the 'cavalry'.

10 LTCM illustrates the remarkable changes in international financial markets.

11 In Mexico, bank loan portfolio grew from $55 billion (1989) to $200 billion (1994); see Palma 2002b. One insider's 'conspiracy theory' is that higher portfolios allowed Mexican groups to bid up the price at which these banks could be sold to 'gringos'.

12 Only Argentina did not succeed in this; but public imbalances have often been exaggerated (see Kregel 2002).

13 This is sometimes called the 'Lawson law', following the statement of Mrs Thatcher's chancellor that when imbalances are the result of private transactions, no matter how large they are, governments should not intervene.

14 See Palma 2001.

15 McKinnon and Pill 1997. For a critique, see Palma 1999b.

16 The corresponding annual growth rates for Malaysia and Thailand are 16% and 19% respectively.

17 According to the 'efficient capital market theory', stock prices are a random walk –

therefore, in stock markets (particularly those under risk neutrality) there should be no scope for profitable speculation...

18 Summers and Summers 1989

19 Chile 1988.

20 The Brazilian average is a mixture of some increase in Rio, stagnation in Sao Paulo and a fall in Brasilia.

21 From an endogenous-growth point of view, the massive fall in infrastructure investment (necessary to keep the public accounts in balance) should greatly affect future growth by increasing transaction costs and reducing 'complementary' capital.

22 Not surprisingly, the best performing stock was construction.

23 On the effect of stock market behaviour on more durable consumption and savings, see Ludvigan and Steindel 1999. Kelecki also argued that the availability of consumer goods (in the case of these countries highly increased following trade liberalization) was a crucial determinant of savings.

24 Inflation between 1995 and 1998 was relatively low: the wholesale price index increased by 6.4%, 8.1%, 7.8% and 1.5%.

25 At times, and even when there was little fear of devaluation, the Brazilian Central Bank set deposit rates as much as 20 percentage points above international interest rates plus Brazil's country risk.

26 In fact, the 'Ponzi' effect was even larger because some reserves had to be kept liquid, and in 1998 a growing proportion of the public debt was also exchange-rate indexed.

27 See Palma 2002c; Lopes 2002.

28 See TDR 1998.

29 Palma 2002c.

30 The D-Ram price per megabyte, for example, fell from $26 (1995) to $10 (1996), $4 (1997), and less than $1 (1998). Memory chips were one of Korea's main export-items.

31 Daewoo, for example, ended up with an $80 billion debt.

32 See IMF 1998.

33 Non-performing loans in Mexico's banks doubled every year. In 1994 they reached nearly 10% of GDP (see Kregel 1998).

34 See TDR 1991. For the role of long-term financial cycles, see Perez 2002.

35 As problems mounted, in order to reduce both rollover risks and interest payments, Cavallo converted practically all short-term debt into (interest rate back-loaded) long-term claims placed – not very democratically – with domestic banks and pension funds. This action had a double irony: first, it made a mockery of Cavallo's own justification for privatizing pension funds, i.e. to insulate them from the possibility of government plunder. The second one is that, according to 'crisis-probability' models, post-debt-exchange Argentina should have had a low crisis probability, as most models place a high premium on the share of short-term debt.

36 In 1991, for example, while 70% of BIS-reporting banks' assets in Korea and Thailand were in short-term maturities, the figure for Mexico, Argentina and Brazil was only about half that level (see BIS 2001).

37 In the case of the 'second-tier' NICs, part of the reason for their high share of short-term debt was that Japan withdrew long-term finance from the region after its own financial crisis.

38 'Voluntarily' means that Korea's Central Bank had no external constraint to increase reserves; had they done so, they would have only paid less than one percentage point above US Treasury bills.

39 He once famously said: 'We will never use capital controls: we want to be a First World nation'; see Palma 2002c. Obviously, his knowledge of financial history was rather limited...

40 That is, instead of trying to stop the capital flight with Malaysian-style outflow-controls, his 'swan song' was to freeze bank accounts, provoking the collapse of banks, the whole economy and himself. In 2001, before the 'corralito', deposit accounts in domestic currency fell by 20%, and those in dollar accounts by 30% (Chudnovsky 2002).

41 On bank-runs, see Chang and Velasco 1999.

42 For an analysis of how 'neoliberal' reforms in Latin America were part of a new politi-co-institutional settlement, characterized by new distributional coalitions and a different structure of property rights and incentives, see Palma 2002a; 2003; and chapter 6.

43 In an interview, Otto Reich, then in charge of Latin America at the State Department, mentioned Menem, Salinas and Alemán as examples of Latin America's worst type of corruption. However, when reminded that they had been the US's closest allies in the region, he replied 'The State Department did not know that they were corrupt until they had left office[...]' (El País, 30/9/02). According to the 'Transparency International Subjective Corruption Index' and the 'International Country Risk Guide', the level of corruption in Latin America has increased significantly since the beginning of the 'neoliberal' reforms.

44 However, as late as 1998, in their annual meeting, the IMF and World Bank paraded Menem, of all people, as the perfect example of a 'reformist Statesman'. In fact, the only two presidents that gave a speech in the main session were Clinton and Menem.

45 Although, in some countries, previously untouchable issues, such as capital account controls, were taken seriously – at least for a while: in the latest trade negotiations between the US and Chile the US has imposed as a condition for the treaty that Chile should practically renounce the use of inflows and outflows controls for ever! For an analysis of capital controls in the 1990s in Colombia, see Ocampo and Tovar 1999; for in Chile and Malaysia, see Palma 2002d.

46 Among 'political-economy-sanitized' naïve crisis-models – agents have perfect fore-sight, financial intermediation is done by totally efficient and perfectly competitive banks (free of 'agency' problems), governments (and only out of sheer amusement) are mechanically-inducing moral-hazard-machines, unable to learn from past mistakes, etc. – see Dooley 2000. For a critique of the 'moral-hazard approach', see Chang 2000.

47 Stiglitz 2000, p. 1085. For related works of Stiglitz, see Chang 2001.

References

Only includes works not already in the bibliography of the chapter on Latin America (see Chapter 6, p. 151).

BIS, 2001, 'Consolidated Banking Statistics'.

Chang, H-J, 2000, ''The Hazard of Moral Hazard', World Development, p. 28.

——, 2001, The Rebel Within: Joseph Stiglitz at the World Bank, London, Anthem Press.

Chang, H-J, G Palma and H Whittaker, 2001, Financial Liberalisation and the Asian Crisis, Basingstoke, Palgrave.

Chang, R and A Velasco, 1999, 'Illiquidity and Crises in Emerging Markets', NBER.

Chudnovsky, D, 2002, 'La Gestación de la Crisis Argentina', CENIT.

Chile, 1988, *Indicadores Economicos, 1968–86*, Banco Central.

Dooley, M, 2000, 'A Model of Crises in Emerging markets, *Economic Journal*, no. 110.

Galbraith, J, 2000, *A Short History of Financial Euphoria*, Penguin.

Hofman, A, 2000, 'Standardised capital stock for Latin America', *Cambridge Journal of Economics*, no. 24.

IFC, 2002, *Emerging Stock Markets Factbook.*

IMF, 1998, *World Economic Outlook.*

Kregel, J, 1998, 'East Asia is not Mexico: the difference between balance of payments crises and debt deflation', UNCTAD.

——, 2002, 'An alternative view of the Argentine crisis', UNCTAD.

Kuczynski, M, 1998, 'How Asian has the Asian crisis been?', mimeo.

Lopes, C, 2002, 'Public debt and the Brazilian crisis', mimeo.

Ludvigson, S and Steindel, C, 1999, 'How Important is the Stock Market Effect on Consumption?' Federal Reserve Bank of New York Economic Policy Review, 50.

McKinnon, R and Pill, H, 1997, 'Credible economic liberalizations and overborrowing', *American Economic Review*, no. 87.

Ocampo, JA and C Tovar, 1999, 'Price-Based Capital Account Regulations: The Colombian Experience', ECLAC.

Palma, G, 1995, 'UK Lending to the Third World ' in P Arestis and V Chick, eds, *Finance, Development and Structural Change*, Elgar.

——, 1998, 'Three and a half cycles of "mania, panic and [asymmetric] crash": East Asia and Latin America Compared', *Cambridge Journal of Economics*, no. 22.

——, 1999a, 'Spin-doctoring or preventive medicine? The role of the World Bank in economic reform', mimeo.

——, 1999b, 'The over-borrowing syndrome: structural reforms, institutional failures and exuberant expectations. A critique of McKinnon and Pill', mimeo.

——, 2001, 'A Brazilian-style Ponzi', in P Arestis, M Baddeley and J McCombie, eds, *What Global Economic Crisis?*, Palgrave.

——, 2002c, The magical realism of Brazilian economics: how to create a financial crisis by trying to avoid one', in J Eatwell and L Taylor, eds, *International Capital Markets*, OUP.

——, 2002d, 'The three routes to financial crises: the need for capital controls', in J Eatwell and L Taylor, eds., *International Capital Markets*, OUP.

——, 2003, 'National Inequality in the Era of Globalisation' in J Michie, *Handbook of Globalisation*, Elgar.

Stiglitz, J, 2000, 'Capital market liberalization, economic growth, and instability', *World Development*, no. 28.

17

THE NEW INTERNATIONAL FINANCIAL ARCHITECTURE, CORPORATE GOVERNANCE AND COMPETITION IN EMERGING MARKETS: EMPIRICAL ANOMALIES AND POLICY ISSUES

Ajit Singh

'The proper governance of companies will become as crucial to the world economy as the proper governing of countries.' James Wolfensohn, President, World Bank.[1]

1. Introduction

Since the financial crises in Asia, Russia, and Brazil, and the associated difficulties with the highly-leveraged US hedge fund Long Term Capital Management (LTCM), there has been widespread concern about the stability of the international financial system. In the immediate aftermath of the crisis, many initiatives were launched to reform the system and establish a New International Financial Architecture (NIFA). With the abatement of the crisis, any interest in a serious or fundamental reform of the international financial system rapidly evaporated. Nevertheless, with the ostensible objective of preventing future crises, G-7 countries are continuing to press for reforms in developing countries with respect to their financial and economic systems. Whether or not the G-7 analysis is correct, developing countries need to acquire a full understanding of the nature of the reforms being proposed and their implications for long-term economic development.

This chapter concentrates on two of the subjects of reform: (a) the question of corporate governance in developing countries; (b) the closely connected questions of the intensity of domestic and international competition in these countries in an environment of liberalization and globalization.[2] These topics have received much less public and academic attention than those of the banking and financial sector reform under NIFA. Yet they are extremely important, for in essence they involve nothing less than changing the day-to-day microeconomic behaviour of economic agents in emerging countries.

This chapter is organized as follows. Section 2 provides the essential background to the G-7 proposals on corporate governance and competition, which have their origins in the perceived structural weaknesses of the Asian economies on the eve of their acute economic crisis of 1997 to 1999. Sections 3 to 5 discuss issues of corporate governance; sections 6 to 8 consider those on the nature and degree of competition in emerging markets.

2. The Asian financial crisis and corporate governance

The impetus behind the quest for a NIFA came from the 1997 Asian crisis. Whereas previous crises had struck economies with a history of financial instability and low growth, such as Mexico in 1995, the Asian crisis devastated countries that were the fastest growing in the world economy, and that had solid achievements in technological upgrading and poverty reduction. The shock among policymakers and market participants was therefore acute.

After the initial shock of the crisis had worn off, however, there emerged an influential theory of the crisis, which argued that the deeper reasons of the crisis could be found in the institutional structures of the Asian model.[3] This 'structuralist' interpretation of the Asian crisis was highly influential in the design of the IMF policy response, which went far beyond the usual stabilization measures, encompassing fundamental changes in labour regulations, corporate governance and the relationship between government and business.[4]

The 'structuralist' view consists of several interlinked arguments. First, it proposes that fragile financial systems resulted from relationship banking, weak corporate governance structures and lack of competition.[5] Furthermore, the cronyistic relations between financial institutions, business and government shielded the system from market discipline and encouraged the over-investment that led to the crisis. Second, and related to the first point, the high leverage ratios of Asian firms heightened their vulnerability and created the conditions that led to a sudden crisis. Thirdly, the lack of transparency and the poor quality of information in such an insider-dominated system led to informational asymmetries that exacerbated the crisis.[6]

To remedy these alleged faults in the Asian system, reformers sought to dissolve the close links between the state and business, to create an arm's-length relationship between banks and business and to promote greater transparency in economic relations.

The 'structuralist' interpretation is not, however, the only account of the Asian crisis, nor the most persuasive. Singh and Weisse[7] have argued that the 'structuralist' interpretation is not credible for several reasons. First, it does not explain the previous exemplary success of the Asian economies. Second, it does not explain why countries with similar systems such as China, and especially India, did not have a crisis.

A more credible explanation of the crisis that encompasses these facts is that the afflicted economies dismantled their controls over the borrowing of the private sector and embraced financial liberalization. As a consequence, the private sector built up short-term foreign currency debt, which often found its way into the non-tradable sector and into speculative real estate ventures. Accompanying financial liberalization was the irrational exuberance and contagion that are always latent in private international financial flows. In sum, Singh and Weisse argue that the crisis occurred not because the Asian model has been flawed but precisely because it was not being followed. Thus, while Edmund Phelps identifies the crisis with the failure of Asian corporatism,[8] it can be argued that in reality this system underpinned the most successful industrialization drive in history and dramatically reduced poverty. The system, however, was vulnerable to the forces unleashed by financial liberalization.[9]

In this chapter, the two key premises of the 'structuralist' interpretation – the issue of poor corporate governance resulting from crony capitalism and the alleged lack of competition in product markets – will, *inter alia*, be examined in some detail. It is nonetheless important to emphasize that, whether or not one accepts the structuralist interpretation of the Asian crisis, these issues are today also significant for the developing countries in their own right. Even before the crisis, because of the privatization, deregulation and the increasing role of the private sector in these countries, corporate governance and competition were emerging as key issues for assessing the efficiency and for enhancing the developmental contribution of the private resources. What the Asian crisis, the new international financial architecture and the recent WTO ministerial meeting in Doha have done is to make these issues not just matters of national policy significance but to place them squarely on the international agenda as well.[10]

3. Corporate governance in emerging markets: the facts

The analysis of corporate governance structures in developing countries has long been hindered by a lack of detailed information. One benefit to arise from the Asian crisis and the focus of the international financial institutions on governance structures has been the assembling of a large body of evidence on corporate governance structures in developing countries at the World Bank. Thus, we are now in a position to construct a more informed picture of the governance structures in a wide range of developing countries.

One of the key insights to emerge from the new empirical studies is that the widely-held corporation[11] described in the classic study by Berle and Means[12] is an Anglo-Saxon phenomenon. As Table 1 indicates, among developing countries the share of family-controlled[13] firms in the top 20 publicly-traded companies in Mexico, Hong Kong and Argentina are 100%, 70% and 65% respectively. In the UK, by contrast, the top 20 quoted companies are 100% widely held. However, there is a diversity of structures among developed countries. In Sweden and Portugal, 45% of the top 20 publicly-traded firms are family-controlled, while in Greece and Belgium the figure is 50%. Even in the United States the share of family-controlled firms in the top 20 publicly traded firms is 20%.

Evidence also suggests that in Asia firms controlled by families are most likely to have a separation between cash flow and control rights, that is to say, a greater degree of corporate 'pyramiding'. The pattern across company size is less clear, but it appears that small firms are most likely to have a larger wedge between cash flow and control rights, regardless of the type of ownership.[14]

Table 2 presents evidence on the concentration of family ownership of corporate assets. As noted earlier, the orthodox argument in the wake of the Asian crisis was the suggestion that 'crony capitalism' created the conditions for economic collapse. However, the evidence indicates that there is no direct link between economic and financial crises and the share of GDP controlled by family firms. In Hong Kong, the top 15 families controlled 84.2% of GDP in 1996, while in Singapore and Malaysia the figures were 48.3% and 76.2% respectively. In 1997, Hong Kong and Singapore were both able to weather the financial crisis in Asia, while Malaysia experienced a sharp downturn and currency crash. Similarly, Taiwan's avoided the financial crisis with its top 15 families controlling 17% of GDP; on the other hand Korea, a country in which the top 15 families account for 12.9% of GDP, experienced a sharp contraction and currency depreciation in late 1997 and early 1998.

A broadly similar story applies when we measure ownership concentration in terms of the proportion of total corporate assets controlled by the top 15 families, rather than expressing these as a proportion of GDP. It should be noted that such concentrations of economic power in a set of families is not necessarily antithetical to the efficient functioning, transparency and democratic accountability of the industrial system, as indicated by the case of the

Table 1. **Control of publicly traded firms around the world, 1996 (per cent)**

Economy	Widely-held	Family owned	State-owned	Widely-held financial	Widely-held corporation
OECD countries (non-Bank borrower)					
Australia	65	5	5		25
Austria	5	15	70		
Belgium	5	50	5	30	
Canada	60	25			15
Denmark	40	35	15		
Finland	35	10	35	5	5
France	60	20	15	5	
Germany	50	10	25	15	
Greece	10	50	30	10	
Ireland	65	10			10
Italy	20	15	40	5	10
Japan	90	5	5		
Netherlands	30	20	5		10
New Zealand	30	25	25		20
Norway	25	25	35	5	
Portugal	10	45	25	15	0
Spain	35	15	30	10	10
Sweden	25	45	10	15	
Switzerland	60	3		5	
UK	100				
USA	80	20			
Bank borrowers and others					
Argentina		65	15	5	15
Hong Kong	10	70	5	5	
Israel	5	50	40		5
Mexico		100			
Singapore	15	30	45	5	5
Korea, Rep. of	55	20	15		5

Source: Iskander and Chamlou 2001

Table 2. **How concentrated is family control?**

Country	Average number of firms per family	% of total value of listed corporate assets that families control (1996)				% of GDP 1996
		Top 1 family	Top 5 families	Top 10 families	Top 15 families	Top 15 families
Hong Kong	2.36	6.5	26.2	32.2	34.4	84.2
Indonesia	4.09	16.6	40.7	57.7	61.7	21.5
Japan	1.04	0.5	1.8	2.4	2.8	2.1
Korea	2.07	11.4	29.7	36.8	38.4	12.9
Malaysia	1.97	7.4	17.3	24.8	28.3	76.2
Philippines	2.68	17.1	42.8	52.5	55.1	46.7
Singapore	1.26	6.4	19.5	26.6	29.9	48.3
Taiwan	1.17	4.0	14.5	18.4	20.1	17.0
Thailand	1.68	9.4	32.2	46.2	53.3	39.3

Note: Newly asembled data for 2,980 publicly traded corporations (including both financial and non-financial institutions). The data was collected from Worldscope and supplemented with information from country-specific sources. In all cases, we collect the ownership structure as of the end of fiscal year 1996 or the closest possible date. The 'average number of firms per family' refers only to firms in the sample. To avoid discrepancies in the cross-country comparison due to different sample coverage, we have scaled down the control holdings of each family group in the last four columns by assuming that the firms missing from our sample are not controlled by any of the largest 15 families. The % of total GDP is calculated using market capitalization and GDP data from the World Bank.

Source: Claessens et al. (2000), p.108.

highly influential Wallenberg family in Sweden. It is believed that the Wallenbergs control up to 60% of Sweden's industrial capital; consequently, little is done in the business sphere in the country which does not have their approval. Furthermore, as Berglof and von Thadden note, crony capitalism is not strictly a corporate governance problem, since family owners are likely to have the right incentives in their firms.[15] Crony capitalism is rather a product of the complex of relations between the business and political elites and could in principle arise in systems with widely dispersed ownership. Overall the experience of Asian countries with family-controlled firms and strong economic growth suggests that they are an effective vehicle of late development and industrialization.[16]

4. Corporate governance and corporate finance in emerging markets 1990s versus 1980s[17]

In order to ensure a smooth flow of external finance to meet corporate investment requirements, there clearly needs to be an appropriate relationship between corporate governance and corporate finance. Indeed, Shleifer and Vishny[18] define corporate governance in terms of the rules and procedures, ensuring that external investors and creditors in a company can get their money back and will not simply be expropriated by those who are managing the company.

Two of the first large-scale empirical studies of the financing of corporate growth in emerging markets were those by Singh and Hamid in 1992, and Singh in 1995.[19] The two studies covering the period of the 1980s arrived at surprising conclusions. One would have expected, *a priori*, that because of the underdevelopment and imperfections of developing-country capital markets, firms in these countries would be largely self-financing. However, these two studies produced results that were quite contrary to these expectations. Large developing country firms, it was found, depended overwhelmingly on external rather than internal finance, and used equity financing to a surprisingly large degree (see Table 3).

In a sample of ten emerging markets, Table 3 suggests that during the 1980s the average company among the 100 largest listed manufacturing firms in each country financed merely 40% of its growth of net assets from retained profits. About 60% of corporate growth in the sample of emerging markets was financed by external sources – approximately 40% from new equity capital and about 20% from long-term debt. Even though the equity financing figures were to some extent overstated by virtue of the fact that an indirect method of estimation was used (on account of lack of direct information), these figures were much larger than those observed for advanced countries (AC) with well-organized stock markets.[20]

Table 4, which reports on the financing of corporate growth in advanced countries for the period 1970–89, suggests that in these countries the stock market provides relatively little fresh capital to the corporate sector. Indeed the contribution of new equity to corporate investment was negative in both the USA and the UK, indicating that more company shares were retired either through takeovers or through share buy-backs than were added by new issues during the relevant period. However, even in Germany and Japan, where new equity makes a positive contribution to corporate growth, the proportions are quite small.[21] In this context, the fact that, compared with these well-organized stock markets in advanced countries, the considerably smaller

Table 3. **The financing of corporate growth in ten emerging markets during the 1980s**

Country	Internal finance	External finance (equity)	External finance LTD
Brazil	56.4	36.0	7.7
India	40.5	19.6	39.9
Jordan	66.3	22.1	11.6
Malaysia	35.6	46.6	17.8
Mexico	24.4	66.6	9.0
Pakistan	74.0	1.7	24.3
Republic of Korea	19.5	49.6	30.9
Thailand	27.7	NA	NA
Turkey	15.3	65.1	19.6
Zimbabwe	58.0	38.8	3.2
All	38.8	39.3	20.8
F^1	20.0*	31.4*	21.2*
F^2	16.69*	18.93*	6.38*

Source: Singh 1995a.

Notes:
1 F-statistic for comparison of means across countries. '*' implies rejection of the null hypothesis of the equality of means.
2 Bartlett-Box F-statistic for variance across countries. '*' implies rejection of the null hypothesis of equality of variance.
3 LTD in the last column indicates growth by changes in long-term debt. The three sources of finance in columns 2–4 add up to 100% of the corporate growth of net assets.

less-developed and immature emerging markets make a sizeable contribution to financing corporate investment certainly calls for an explanation.[22]

This is all the more necessary since developing country stock markets suffer not just from market imperfections (for example, a comparative lack of private information-gathering and monitoring of organizations and firms) but also from serious regulatory deficits (such as insider trading, lack of protection for minority shareholders).[23] In addition, as Tirole has argued,[24] the share prices on these emerging markets are likely to be arbitrary and much more volatile than in well-developed and mature stock markets. Evidence indicates that there is indeed a greater share price volatility on emerging markets.[25]

Table 4. Net sources of finance for Germany, Japan, UK and USA, 1970–89 (percentages)

	Germany	Japan	UK	USA
Internal	80.6	69.3	97.3	91.3
Bank finance	11.0	30.5	19.5	16.6
Bonds	-0.6	4.7	3.5	17.1
New equity	0.9	3.7	-10.4	-8.8
Trade Credit	-1.9	-8.1	-1.4	-3.7
Capital transfers	8.5	-	2.5	-
Other	1.5	-0.1	-2.9	-3.8
Statistical adj.	0.0	0.0	-8.0	-8.7

Source: Corbett and Jenkinson 1994.

One would have expected such volatility to discourage developing country firms from raising capital on the stock market, or even to seek a market listing at all. However, as Table 3 suggests, not only did these companies tap the stock market for large amounts of fresh capital, but further data (not reported in Table 3) indicates that during the 1980s there was a big increase in listings in many emerging markets.[26]

Shleifer and Vishny[27] point to another anomaly, this time seen from the perspective of the investing public rather than the corporations. They rightly ask 'Who are the buyers of this equity? If they are dispersed shareholders, why are they buying the equity despite the apparent absence of minority protections?'.

It is important to note that the results for advanced countries reported in Table 4 fully conform to the so-called 'pecking order' theory of financing corporate growth, indicating that firms in these countries overwhelmingly finance their investments from internal sources. When external sources are used debt is much more important than equity in a hierarchy of financial sources.

Singh has reviewed the various theories of corporate finance, including the pecking order theory to explain inter-firm differences in financing patterns.[28] He concludes that, although conditions differ both between emerging countries at various stages of development and between small and large firms, there are good reasons to suggest that the pecking order theory should be applicable at least for large developing country (DC) firms. For emerging countries with reasonably well-developed banking systems and established equity markets,[29] large corporations should follow a pecking order pattern of finance, not only because of the informational asymmetries emphasized by

Myers and Majluf[30] for advanced countries, but also due to the institutional specificities of emerging markets (for example, the desire to maintain family ownership and control of corporations). He concludes that if there are good reasons to expect a pecking order pattern of finance for corporate growth in developed countries, on account of ownership patterns and agency considerations, there are even stronger reasons for expecting such a pattern in emerging markets. Yet the data in Table 3 suggests that the pecking order theory is comprehensively rejected for large firms in many emerging markets.

Singh has provided an economic explanation for these anomalous findings, essentially in terms of conjunctural factors which were specific to the 1980s and were expected eventually to peter out.[31] He ascribed the relatively high use of external finance by developing country corporations to their fast growth rates. He then concentrated on the question of the large reliance of these corporations on equity finance, attributing this phenomenon to financial liberalization, deregulation and privatization, which many developing countries implemented in the 1980s. Specifically he called attention to the following factors:

a) The very fast development of stock markets which was stimulated and encouraged by governments through regulatory changes and other measures, often to facilitate privatization.
b) Equity financing was also encouraged in a number of countries by tax incentives.
c) External and internal financial liberalization, which often lead both to a stock market boom and to higher real interest rates; the former lowered the cost of equity capital while the latter increased the cost of debt finance.[32]

5. Financing patterns in the 1990s

Much more detailed corporate accounting information, albeit for a limited range of countries, is available for the analysis of corporate financing patterns for the 1990s. The World Scope Data Bank which is the source of this information unfortunately does not provide comparable data for the 1980s. Table 5 gives an analysis of sources of financing of corporate growth of total assets for the period 1992 to 1996 for four emerging markets (India, Malaysia, Thailand and Korea) and two advanced countries (UK and the USA).

Together with Table 5, Singh has used other available information to examine in detail the corporate financing patterns in emerging and mature markets during the 1980s and the 1990s.[33] His main conclusions are as follows:

Table 5. **Balanced sample: Sources of financing of growth of Total Assets, 1992–6**

Weighted averages are calculated as the sum (over companies) of each source of finance over the sample period, 1992–6, divided by the sum of the growth in total assets over this period. Unweighted averages are the average of the sum (over companies) of each source of finance in each year, divided by the sum of the growth of total assets. The Balanced samples for the four countries are as follows: India=115, Malaysia=130, Thailand=98, Korea=95, USA = 261, UK =752

	India		Malaysia		Thailand		Korea*		USA		UK	
	Weighted	Un-weighted	Weighted	Un-weighted	Weighted	Un-weighted	Weighted	Un-weighted	Weighted	Un-weighted	Weighted	Un-weighted
Retentions	24.2	23.1	20.4	25.3	13.0	13.3	5.5	5.7	31.8	35.2	12.6	16.7
External finance	75.8	76.9	79.6	74.7	87.0	86.7	94.5	94.3	68.2	64.8	87.3	83.2
Shares	29.3	31.2	13.2	14.6	9.5	9.6	12.7	16.1	8.8	8.6	34.8	60.6
Other**	1.7	2.5	8.3	9.1	6.3	6.3	2.0	-2.3	0.7	1.9	-5.3	-13.5
Debt finance	44.7	43.3	58.1	51.0	71.2	70.8	79.8	80.6	58.7	54.3	57.8	36.1
Long-term debt	12.1	13.2	13.9	12.9	34.0	34.0	33.0	32.4	30.6	31.4	8.9	14.9
Short-term debt	32.7	30.1	44.2	38.1	37.2	36.9	46.8	48.2	28.1	22.9	48.9	21.2
Trade credit	8.3	8.3	7.2	6.4	6.2	6.4	12.5	13.1	9.9	10.9	27.6	33.0

* Unweighted ratios for Korea are calculated over the 3 year period, 1994–6. Some unusually large ratios for 1993 were omitted from the overall average.

** Other includes revaluation reserves, minority interests, preferred shares and non-equity reserves.

Emerging market firms use far more external rather than internal finance, and within external finance employ equity finance to an astonishingly large degree: this same basic finding holds for both the 1980s and the 1990s.

- Evidence suggests that these results are unlikely to be due to possible measurement biases arising from the inadequacies of the available data for the 1980s. The more comprehensive data for the 1990s confirms these conclusions.
- The significant differences observed between the financing patterns of emerging and mature markets arise mainly from the different method-ologies which have been used to examine these issues. When the same methodology is used, the financing patterns are seen to be much closer. However, the theoretical anomalies still remain and are indeed com-pounded in the data for the 1990s.
- When the Singh–Hamid and Singh (hereafter SH) methodology[34] is used for the advanced economies, the widely-held belief that these cor-porations implement a pecking order is not valid for all countries in all periods. The analysis carried out in this chapter suggests that evidence for this pecking order is, at the very least, not robust. With a different methodology which, it is argued here, is conceptually more suitable, the results change quite considerably. The pecking order pattern in advanced economies is most evident when flow of funds data is used and the question of financing is considered from the perspective of the cor-porate sector as a whole rather than that of the individual firm. Since the theoretical foundation of the pecking order theory is the individual firm, rather than the corporate sector as a whole, the SH methodology embodying this perspective is more appropriate.
- The foregoing conclusions are, however, based on relatively limited data. Until these findings are tested for a larger body of data for more countries, these conclusions must remain provisional. However, the fact that the anomalous results for developing country corporations in the 1980s continued to hold for the 1990s does suggest that this phenomenon requires the serious attention of economists and finance theorists.[35]

6. Corporate finance, the stock market and corporate governance

In view of the great recourse to equity financing by developing country firms, stock markets might be expected significantly to affect corporate behaviour (for example, corporate policies regarding the payment of dividends) as well as corporate governance (for example, the extent to which managers run corporations in the interests of the shareholders or themselves).

The stock market can affect corporate governance and behaviour directly as well as indirectly. The direct effect is through the stock market's own rules and regulations, for example requirements for listing and raising new issues. In these areas, emerging stock markets usually display considerable deficits in comparison with advanced country markets. For example, listing and disclosure requirements in advanced countries' stock markets tend to be more stringent and more actively enforced than those in developing country markets.

More significantly, however, the stock market can influence corporate governance indirectly through its allocative and disciplinary mechanisms. Each of these channels is important.

6.1 The pricing mechanism

In traditional textbook treatments of the pricing process, the liquid secondary equity market results in a better allocation of funds. It leads to more efficient and dynamic firms obtaining capital at a lower cost than firms which do not perform as well. The latter firms or those in less dynamic industries face a higher cost of equity capital. The result is the movement of funds to more efficient, productive firms that results in higher degrees of technological progress and economic growth.

However, a more critical literature, originating in the work of John Maynard Keynes, has pointed out that the pricing process may not be as efficient as the textbooks suggest, but may instead be dominated by speculation. James Tobin[36] has distinguished two concepts of share price efficiency on the stock market: *informational* efficiency (in the sense that all currently available information is incorporated into the share price) and *fundamental valuation* efficiency (share prices must accurately reflect the future discounted earnings of the corporation). While real world stock-market prices may reflect the former, the critical school maintains that there are strong reasons to doubt that it attains the latter, more important, criterion of efficiency. The reasons for this are found in the psychology of stock-market participants.[37] As Keynes pointed out in his famous description of the beauty contest in the *General Theory*, often the art of the successful investor does not consist in appreciating fundamental values of corporations, but rather in conjecturing at the likely behaviour and psychology of other stock-market participants. Such a process leads to herding, myopia and fads that can result in stock-market values diverging significantly from underlying values (for a current example, note the rise and fall of technology shares on international stock markets). The volatility associated with this process further reduces the capacity of share prices to transmit efficient signals to market participants.

Experience from advanced countries suggests that the stock market may also encourage managers to pursue short-term profits at the expense of long-term investment, since firms are obliged to meet quarterly or half-yearly earnings per share targets determined by market expectations. Any serious fall in performance will quickly be reflected in a lower share price, making the firm vulnerable to takeover. In the late 1980s and early 1990s, numerous analysts in the USA ascribed that country's relatively poor comparative performance, *vis-à-vis* competitors with bank-based financial systems such as Japan and Germany, to the short-termist demands of Wall Street, resulting in lower investment in technological upgrading and new capacity.[38] In a closely related but more general sense, the dominance of stock markets can also result in the ascendancy of finance over productive enterprise. The rules of the game are constructed in such a way that companies can rise or fall depending on their ability to engage in financial engineering rather than in developing new products or processes. This is often reflected within the firm itself, in the dominance of managers trained in finance over those who come from other backgrounds such as engineering or marketing.

Thus, the benefits of having large corporations dependent on a highly liquid equity market are far from being unambiguous, particularly from the perspective of good corporate governance.[39]

6.2 Corporate governance and takeovers

The market for corporate control is thought to be the evolutionary endpoint of stock-market development. The ability of an outside group of investors to acquire a corporation, often through a hostile bid, is the hallmark of the stock-market-dominated US and UK financial systems. The textbook interpretation of takeovers is that they improve efficiency by transferring corporate assets to those who can manage them more productively. Even if current managers are not replaced, an active market for corporate control presents a credible threat that inefficient managers will be replaced, thus ensuring that the incumbent management will actively seek to maximize shareholder value and thereby raising corporate performance. Further, even if quoted firms were not directly susceptible to changes in share prices because they finance themselves almost exclusively from internal finance, the market for corporate control can still discipline managers; morover, even if all firms are on the efficiency frontier, the amalgamation of some through the act of takeovers may lead to a better social allocation of resources via synergy.

However, one critical school has developed a multifaceted critique that has increasingly questioned the above textbook version of the market for corporate control. First, it emphasizes that in the real world the market for corporate control has an inherent flaw in its operation: it is far easier for a large firm to take over a small one than the other way around.[40] While it is in principle possible that a small efficient firm may take over a larger and less efficient company (and to a degree this occurred in the US takeover wave of the 1980s through 'junk bonds'), its incidence is very small.[41]

This consideration is particularly important for developing countries like India where there are large, potentially predatory conglomerate groups.[42] These could take over smaller, more efficient firms and thereby reduce potential competition, to the detriment of the real economy. In a takeover battle it is the absolute firepower (absolute size) that counts rather than the relative efficiency. Therefore, the development of an active market for corporate control may encourage managers to 'empire-build', not only to increase their monopoly power but also to progressively shield themselves from takeover by becoming larger.[43]

Secondly, the efficient operation of the takeover mechanism requires that enormous amounts of information are widely available. Specifically, market participants require information on a corporation's profitability under its existing management and, in the event of takeover, what its prospective profitability would be under an alternative management. It has been noted that such information is not easily available even in advanced countries, and that this informational deficit is likely to be greater in developing countries.

Thirdly, takeovers are a very expensive way of changing management.[44] In countries such as the US and UK there are huge transactions costs associated with takeovers that hinder the efficiency of the takeover mechanism. Given the lower income levels in the developing countries, these costs are likely to be proportionally heavier in these countries. It should also be borne in mind that highly successful countries such as Japan, Germany and France have not had an active market for corporate control and have thus avoided these costs while still maintaining systems for disciplining managers. Furthermore, there is no evidence that corporate governance necessarily improves after takeovers. This is for the simple reason that all takeovers are not disciplinary; in many of them the acquiring firm is motivated by empire-building considerations or even by asset-stripping.

Fourthly, theoretical work[45] suggests that even if managers wish to maximize shareholder wealth, it would pay them to be myopic in a world of takeovers and signal-jamming. Thus, takeovers could exacerbate the already present tendencies towards short-termism in a stock-market-based system.[46]

Fifthly, it has been argued that takeovers can be used as a device to avoid honouring implicit contracts developed between workers and the former management.[47] This abandonment of implicit contracts can be argued to be socially harmful in that it discourages the accumulation of firm-specific human capital by workers. The absence of strong worker-protection laws in many developing countries means that such considerations may be significant.

These critiques of the market for corporate control have been based on the experience of advanced countries.[48] There is every reason to believe, however, that they are likely to be even more relevant to potential takeover markets in developing countries.[49] At the moment, the takeovers market in developing countries is rudimentary because of the facts noted earlier: shareholding is not widely dispersed and standards of disclosure are not conducive to takeovers. It is therefore not surprising that hostile takeovers are rare in developing countries: e.g. in India, the last decade has seen only five or six such takeover attempts, not all of which were successful. However, this situation may change if large MNCs are allowed to engage in takeovers in developing countries.

There are also other potential factors that could lead financial liberalization and stock markets to have a negative effect on corporate governance. Financial liberalization establishes a strong link between two potentially volatile markets, the stock market and the foreign exchange market. The Asian crisis demonstrated that there could be a strong negative feedback relationship between a falling stock market and a depreciating currency. As the stock market declines, investors pull out of the market and move their funds into foreign currency. The depreciating currency, in turn, lowers real returns on the stock market which in turn propels the cycle.[50] Such a collapse in currency and equity values may of course ultimately encourage 'fire-sale-type FDI' in the form of takeovers, suggesting that the expected rate of return measured in foreign currency has increased sufficiently due to the steep decline in domestic share prices. This may overturn quite successful corporate governance structures and replace them with ones that are less appropriate.

7. Intensity of competition in emerging and mature markets[51]

We turn next to the issue of intensity of competition in emerging markets. As indicated above in the Introduction, research on this subject is important for developing countries for a number of reasons:

• Privatization, deregulation and the institution of market-oriented reforms have led to a large expansion of the private sector. Only vigorous competition in the markets can ensure effective utilization of these resources. It is therefore important to know how strong or intense is the state of competition in these countries.

- Apart from the alleged deficiencies in corporate governance, the lack of competition within emerging market economies has been blamed as one of the deeper reasons for Asian crisis. Is this allegation valid?
- There is very little international comparative information available on the nature and degree of product market competition in emerging and mature markets, or among the emerging markets themselves.

To link the discussion of competition with previous analysis of corporate governance, it will be useful to begin by examining the nature of the relationship between the two variables at a conceptual level.

8. Competition and corporate governance: conceptual issues

Milton Friedman long ago argued that, if there were perfect competition in product markets, economists would not have had to worry about problems of separation of ownership and control in modern corporations, or about the associated difficulties of corporate governance.[52] Natural selection in a competitive market would ensure that only the profit maximizers – and by implication, only the optimal ownership patterns and corporate governance structures – would survive. However, as Winters subsequently demonstrated rigorously,[53] if competition were imperfect, different corporate governance systems could coexist.

The debate then moved to the capital market. In seminal contributions Alchian and Kessel, and Manne, argued that, even if there was imperfect competition in the product markets, firms would still be forced to maximize profit and to adopt the optimal governance structures, otherwise they would be subject to takeover from those who would be willing to maximize monopoly profits.[54] The validity of this assertion depends on the existence of a perfect capital market, including a market for corporate control. In the event, although there have been huge merger waves in the Anglo-Saxon economies during the last century (specifically during the 1960s, 1980s and 1990s), these have not fulfilled the requirement of a perfect market for corporate control. As noted in Section 6, this market suffers from fundamental imperfections.

In the light of these difficulties with the market for corporate control, the wheel has turned full circle. It is now being suggested that the main constraint on the behaviour and governance structure of the large corporations is the intense international competition in product markets. Nevertheless, neo-classical economists now recognize that, in view of the oligopolistic nature of product market competition and imperfections in the market for corporate control, there does exist a governance problem in the modern corporation: this is modelled in the form of a principal–agent problem.[55] In this conception, the separation of ownership and control imposes agency costs on the corporation. The magnitude of this cost varies inversely with the nature and extent of the competition in the product and capital markets. As the relevant aspects of the market for corporate control have already been examined above, we turn now to a discussion of the nature and extent of competition, including international competition in emerging markets.

8. Product market competition in emerging markets

In view of the paucity of systematic information on the state of competition in emerging countries, there is a great deal of disagreement on the topic among economists. For example, the structuralist interpretation of the Asian crisis suggests that the deeper reasons for the crisis lay in part in the poor competitive environment in countries such as Korea leading to over-investment. On the other hand Porter, and Amsden and Singh, suggest that Korean *chaebol* display vigorous rivalry in both national and international markets.[56] However, some support for the IMF position is provided by Table 6, which gives average concentration ratios for different time periods for a small group of emerging markets. Table 6 suggests that concentrations tend to be high in these countries, sometimes being greater than those in advanced countries. However, economists have long recognized that such concentration measures based only on properties of the size distribution of firms at a point of time are inadequate for measuring the intensity of competition in an economy.

Recently, Glen, Lee and Singh[57] have addressed the latter question directly and provided systematic comparative evidence on how the intensity of competition varies between emerging markets, and also between emerging and mature economies. The authors use standard methodology based on the so-called 'persistence of profitability' (PP) studies to measure dynamics of competition in seven emerging markets in 1980s and the early 1990s. The seven countries are Brazil, India, Jordan, Korea, Malaysia, Mexico and Zimbabwe. The sample frame consists normally of the hundred largest-quoted manufacturing corporations in these countries. Profitability is defined as earnings after tax divided by the firm's total assets.

The PP methodology is well established and has been employed in a large number of papers to analyse competition dynamics in advanced country product markets.[58] The basic intuition here is that, if competition were intense, firms would tend to display low persistence of profits as any temporary advantage which a firm may enjoy (either, say, because of good manage-

Table 6. **Concentration ratios in emerging economies**

Economy	*Three-firm concentration ratios*
Japan, 1980	56
Korea, Rep. of, 1981	62
Taiwan, China, 1981	49
	Four-firm concentration ratios
Argentina, 1984	43
Brazil, 1980	51
Chile, 1979	50
India, 1984	46
Indonesia, 1985	56
Mexico, 1980	48
Pakistan, 1985	68
Turkey, 1976	67
United States, 1972	40

Source: World Bank 1993

ment, a new money-making technique or monopoly power) will soon be imitated by competitors and the original innovating firm's profits will be reduced ultimately to zero. On the other hand, if the competition is not so intense then those with above average profits in one period will continue to have above average profits in subsequent periods.

Astonishingly, the results of the Glen, Lee and Singh studies indicate that developing countries have, on the whole, lower persistency coefficients than those observed for advanced countries, even when allowance is made for the shorter time series of corporate profitability available for developing than for advanced countries.[59] Further, the proportion of firms for which long-term profitability is significantly different from the norm, either positively or negatively, is also much lower for developing than for advanced countries. The conventional interpretation of these results would suggest that developing countries are subject to no less, if not greater, competition than advanced countries. The possible sources of statistical bias in these empirical results for emerging economies have been examined in detail by Glen, Lee and Singh, who find that these do not affect their main conclusions.[60]

Evidence complementing that of Glen, Lee and Singh is provided by other research using a different methodology. This work, which systematically analyses turnover and the mobility of firms, provides interesting results.[61] The results indicate that there is greater mobility as well as entry and exit of firms in the small number of emerging markets on which such studies have been carried out than for advanced countries.

Besides these two kinds of studies on the dynamics of the competition process, there are also other types of evidence pertaining to the efficiency of emerging market industries and to scale economies that do not accord with the conventional anecdotal account of the lack of competition in emerging countries. This empirical research has recently been reviewed by Tybout, who sums up the situation as follows:

> Indeed, although the issue remains open, the existing empirical literature does not support the notion that less developed country (LDC) manufacturers are relatively stagnant and inefficient. Turnover rates in plants and jobs are at least as high as those found in the OECD, and the amount of cross-plant dispersion in measured productivity rates is not generally greater. Also, although small-scale production is relatively common in LDCs, there do not appear to be major potential gains from better exploitation of scale economies.[62]

Singh suggests that these results on the comparative intensity of competition in emerging and mature countries are in economic terms totally plausible.[63] This is because although there are many structural features of developing countries and the policies of their governments that are anti-competition, there are also equally strong, if not stronger, structural factors which favour competition. The anti-competition factors typically include transportation and infrastructural deficiencies as well as bureaucratic redtape. However, these may be more than balanced by pro-competition forces which include lower sunk costs for starting businesses in developing countries, a large demand for simple products, and at times a pro-competition government policy stance (for example, some developing countries have made firms compete for government favours by setting specified performance requirements, the so-called 'contest-based' competitions.[64]

9. Summary and conclusions

This chapter has examined two important components of the NIFA: the question of corporate governance and the state of competition in leading emerging countries.

The central conclusion in respect of corporate governance is that the anomalous financing behaviour of emerging market corporations observed in the 1980s has broadly continued into the 1990s: it has not petered out, although it has been attenuated to some degree. These corporations still rely overwhelmingly on external sources rather than retained profits to finance the growth of their net assets. The relative contribution of equity versus debt to total external financing changes over time and between countries in response to economic conditions. The results indicate that when the same methodology is used for comparing financing patterns between advanced and emerging markets, the differences between the two are much less pronounced. The differences as well as the similarities in the financing patterns of the two groups nevertheless remain theoretically anomalous in a number of dimensions.

Whether the large role played by the stock market in financing corporate growth in emerging countries would lead to positive or negative changes in corporate governance and economic efficiency depends on one's views on (a) the efficiency of the pricing mechanism and (b) the takeover mechanisms on the real world stock markets. This chapter reads the evidence on (a) as indicating that the pricing process is often dominated by speculation, herding and fads that undermine its capacity to efficiently direct the allocation of resources. It also suggests that the takeover mechanism is an inherently flawed and expensive method of changing corporate governance. It has been further pointed out that the inadequacies and perverse incentives in both the pricing process and the takeover mechanism are likely to be exacerbated in developing countries.

Concerning the state of competition in leading emerging countries, this chapter provides evidence to suggest that product market competition in manufacturing in these economies is as intense, if not more so, than in advanced countries. A comparative analysis of the relative persistence of corporate rates of return in emerging markets and in advanced economies indicates that the former display lower short-term as well as long-term profits persistency than the latter. These results are supported by studies that use different methodologies. Overall, these new findings indicate that product market competition is intense in leading emerging countries, subjecting their managers to market discipline, no less than in advanced countries. It has been argued here that although such indications may be counterintuitive, there are nevertheless good economic reasons for them.

In view of the domestic and international policy significance of corporate governance and competition issues for emerging countries outlined in the Introduction, it is essential that these issues be investigated objectively so as to provide such countries with a solid analytical and empirical basis for policy. It is hoped that this chapter has made a contribution in this direction. It is also hoped that by documenting the anomalous behaviour of emerging market corporations in a number of dimensions, as well as by its counterintuitive findings on the state of competition in emerging and mature markets, this chapter has also posed some challenging questions for economic theory and analysis, in particular for the theory of the firm and the theory of finance.

Notes

1 Wolfensohn 2000, p. 1.
2 This paper is based on Singh and Weisse 2003; the author is grateful to UNCTAD for permission to use material from that paper.
3 Summers 1998; Greenspan 1998.
4 See Feldstein 1998 for a criticism.
5 See for example Johnson et al. 2000.
6 Camdessus 1998.
7 See Singh and Weisse 1999.
8 Phelps 1999.
9 For critical analysis of the structuralist thesis in either implicit or explicit terms, see also Chang 2002, Sakakibara 2001, Stiglitz 1999 and Singh 2002b.
10 The WTO Doha meeting sanctioned work on the so called Singapore issues, which include competition policy. See further Singh 2002a.
11 A widely held corporation is a corporation which does not have any owners who have significant control rights. Owners are further divided into four categories: families (which includes individuals who have large stakes), the state, widely held financial institutions, such as banks and insurance companies, and widely held corporations.
12 Berle and Means 1933.
13 Note that control is defined as a 20% or higher share of equity.
14 See further Claessens et al. 2000.
15 Berglof and von Thadden 1999.
16 For more detailed discussion of these issues see Singh, Singh and Weisse 2000. See also Amsden 1989, 2000.
17 The discussion of this and the following two sections is based on Singh 2003, forthcoming.
18 Shleifer and Vishny 1997.
19 Singh and Hamid 1992; Singh 1995a.
20 For a fuller discussion of these measurement biases see Whittington, Saporta and Singh 1997.
21 Mayer 1990.
22 Allen and Gale 2001.
23 Such deficits exist, as we know from the recent experience of the United States, in advanced countries as well but they tend to be much larger in emerging markets with new stock market institutions.
24 Tirole 1991.
25 See further El-Erian and Kumar 1994.
26 Singh 1995a; 1997.
27 Shliefer and Vishny 1997.
28 Singh 2003, forthcoming.
29 Such as those included in Singh and Hamid 1992 and Singh 1995a.
30 Myers and Majluf 1984.

31 Singh 1995a.
32 These issues are of course more complex; for a detailed discussion see Singh 1995a; 1997, and Singh and Weisse (1998).
33 See Singh 2003, forthcoming.
34 The methodology laid out in Singh and Hamid 1992; Singh 1995a.
35 Allen and Gale 2001; Shliefer and Vishny 1997 also highlight the significance of these phenomena.
36 Tobin 1984.
37 For a modern treatment and detailed discussion of these issues, see for example, Shiller 2000, Allen and Gale 2001. See also Singh, Singh and Weisse 2000 and the literature cited therein.
38 See collection of studies in Porter 1992.
39 See further, Bhinde 1994.
40 Singh 1971, 1975, 1992.
41 Hughes 1989.
42 Singh 1995; 1995b.
43 See further Singh 1975, 1992.
44 Peacock and Bannock 1991.
45 See for example Stein 1989.
46 Singh 2000.
47 Shleifer and Summers 1988.
48 There is a vast literature on the subject. For reviews, see Hughes 1989; Singh 1992; 1993; Mueller 1997; Tichy 2001; and Singh 2002a.
49 Singh 1998a.
50 Of course, there is also a positive feedback loop between the two markets, with higher stock market valuations leading to capital inflows and an appreciating exchange rate. It is thus possible that a stock market bubble will lead to an overvalued real exchange rate that in turn affects the competitiveness of the tradeable sector.
51 This section is based on Singh 2002a.
52 Friedman 1953.
53 Winters 1964.
54 Alchian and Kessel 1962; Manne 1965.
55 Jensen and Meckeling 1976; Jensen 1988.
56 Porter 1990; Amsden and Singh 1994.
57 Glen, Lee and Singh 2001; 2002.
58 The classic references here are Mueller 1986; 1990, the latter is a collection of studies for a large number of advanced economies. See also Waring 1996; Goddard and Wilson 1999.
59 The evidence on the latter countries can be found in, for example, Goddard and Wilson 1999 and Odagiri and Yamawaki 1990.
60 Glen, Lee and Singh 2002.
61 Studies in this genre have recently been summarized by Tybout 2000 and Caves 1998.
62 Tybout 2000, p. 38.
63 Singh 2002a.
64 World Bank 1993.

References

Aichian, AA and Kessel, RA, 1962, 'Competition, monopoly and the pursuit of pecuniary gain', *Aspects of Labor Economics,* Conference of the Universities National Bureau Committee for Economic Research, Princeton.

Allen, F and Gale, D, 2001, *Comparing Financial Systems,* Cambridge, Mass., MIT Press.

Amsden, A, 1989, *Asia's Next Giant: South Korea and Late Industrialization.,* New York, Oxford University Press.

Amsden, A, 2000, *The Rise of 'The Rest': Challenges to the West from Late-industrializing Economies,* Oxford, Oxford University Press.

Amsden, A and Singh, A, 1994, 'The optimal degree of competition and dynamic efficiency in Japan and Korea', *European Economic Review,* vol. 38, no.3/4, 941–51.

Berglof, E and von Thadden, L ,1999, 'The Changing Corporate Governance Paradigm: Implications for Transition and Developing Countries', Unpublished Working Paper, Stockholm Institute of Transition Economics, Stockholm, Sweden.

Berle, A and Means, G, 1933, *The Modern Corporation and Private Capital,* New York, Macmillan.

Bhinde, A, 1994, 'The hidden cost of stock market liquidity', *Journal of Financial Economics,* pp. 31–51.

Camdessus, M, 1998, Speech to Transparency International reported in the *IMF Survey,* 9 February 1988.

Caves, R, 1998, 'Industrial Organization and New Findings on the Turnover and Mobility of Firms', *Journal of Economic Literature,* vol. 36 (December), pp. 1947–82.

Chang, H-J, 2002, 'The Hazard of Moral Hazard – Untangling the Asian Crisis', World Development, vol. 28, no. 4.

Claessens, S, Djankov, S and Lang, L, 2000, 'The separation of ownership and control in East Asian Corporations', *Journal of Financial Economics,* vol. 58, pp. 81–112.

Corbett, J and Jenkinson, T, 1994, 'The financing of industry, 1970–89: An international comparison', Discussion Paper no. 948, London, Centre for Economic Policy Research.

El-Erian, MA and Kumar, MS, 1994, 'Emerging Equity Markets in Middle Eastern Countries', Paper given at World Bank Conference on Stock Markets, Corporate Finance and Economic Growth, World Bank, Washington, DC, February 16–17.

Feldstein, M, 1998, 'Trying to do too much', *Financial Times,* March 3.

Friedman, M, 1953, *Essays in Positive Economics,* Chicago, University of Chicago Press.

Glen, J, Lee, K and Singh, A, 2000, *Competition, Corporate Governance and Financing of Corporate Growth in Emerging Markets,* Cambridge Discussion Paper in Accounting and Finance no. AF46, Department of Applied Economics, University of Cambridge.

Goddard, JA and Wilson, JOS, 1999, 'The persistence of profit: a new empirical interpretation', *International Journal of Industrial Organisation,* vol. 17, no. 5, pp. 663–87.

Greenspan, A, 1998, Testimony before the Committee on Banking and Financial Services, US House of Representatives, January 30, 1998.

Hughes, A, 1989, 'The Impact of Mergers: A Survey of Empirical Evidence for the UK 1950–90" in J Fairburn and JA Kay, eds, *Mergers and Merger Policy,* 1989, 2nd edition, Oxford, Oxford University Press.

Iskander, MR and Chamlou, N, 2000, *Corporate Governance: A Framework for Implementation,* World Bank, Washington DC.

Jensen, MC, 1988, 'Take-overs: their causes and consequences', *Journal of Economic Perspectives.* vol. 2, no. 1 (Winter), pp. 21–48.

Jensen, M and Meckling, W, 1976, 'Theory of the firm: Managerial behaviour, agency costs and ownership structure', *Journal of Financial Economics*, vol. 3, no. 4, pp. 305–60.

Johnson, S, Boone, P, Breach, A and Friedman, E, 2000, 'Corporate governance in the Asian financial crisis', *Journal of Financial Economics*, vol. 58, pp. 141–86.

Manne, HG, 1965, 'Mergers and the market for corporate control', *Journal of Political Economy*, no. 73, pp. 693–706.

Mayer, C, 1990, 'Financial systems, corporate finance and economic development' in R Glen Hubbard, 1990, ed., *Asymmetric Information, Corporate Finance and Investment*, Chicago, University of Chicago Press.

Mueller, D, 1986, *Profits in the Long Run*, Cambridge, Cambridge University Press.

——, 1990, ed., *The Dynamics of Company Profits: An International Comparison*, Cambridge, Cambridge University Press.

——, 1997, 'Merger Policy in the United States: A Reconsideration', *Review of Industrial Organization*, vol. 12, nos 5–6, pp. 655–85.

Myers, S and Majluf, N, 1984, 'Corporate Financing and Investment Decisions When Firms Have Information that Investors Do Not Have', *Journal of Financial Economics*, vol. 13, no. 2, pp. 187–221.

Odagiri, H and H Yamawaki, 1990, 'The persistence of profits in Japan', in Mueller 1990, pp. 129–46.

Peacock A and Bannock G, 1991, *Corporate Take-overs and the Public Interest*, Aberdeen, Aberdeen University Press.

Phelps ES, 1999, 'The Global Crisis of Corporatism', *Wall Street Journal*, 25 March.

Porter ME, 1990, *The Competitive Advantage of Nations*, New York, Macmillan.

——, 1992, 'Capital disadvantage: America's falling capital investment system', *Harvard Business Review*, September–October, vol. 70, no. 5, pp. 65–82.

Sakakibara, E, 2001, 'The East Asian Crisis – Two Years Later', *Annual World Bank Conference on Development Economics 2000*, pp.243–55, The International Bank Reconstruction and Development/The World Bank.

Shiller, RJ, 2000, *Irrational Exuberance*, Princeton University Press, Princeton.

Shleifer, A and Summers, L, 1988, 'Breach of trust in hostile take-overs' in Alan Auerbach, 1988, ed., *Corporate Take-overs: Causes and Consequences*, Chicago, University of Chicago Press, pp 33–61.

Shleifer, A and Vishny, RW, 1997, 'A survey of corporate governance', *Journal of Finance*, 52, pp. 737–83.

Singh, A, 1971, *Take-overs, Their Relevance to the Stock Market and the Theory of the Firm*. Cambridge, Cambridge University Press.

——, 1975, 'Take-overs, Economic Natural Selection and the Theory of the Firm', *Economic Journal*, September, vol. 85, pp. 497–515.

——, 1992, 'Corporate Takeovers", in J Eatwell, M Milgate and P Newman, 1992, eds, *The New Palgrave Dictionary of Money and Finance*, London, Macmillan, pp. 480–6.

——, 1993, 'Regulation of Mergers: A New Agenda', in Roger Sugden, 1993, ed., *Industrial Economic Regulation: A Framework and Exploration*, London, Routledge, pp. 141–58.

——, 1995a, *Corporate Financial Patterns in Industrializing Economies: A Comparative International Study*, IFC Technical Paper, Washington, DC, IFC.

——, 1995b, 'The causes of fast economic growth in East Asia', *UNCTAD* Review, pp. 91–127.

Singh, A, 1997, '"Financial liberalisation, stock markets and economic development', *Economic Journal*, May, vol. 107, no. 442, pp. 771–82.

——, 1998a, 'Liberalisation, the stock market and the market for corporate control: a bridge too far for the Indian economy?' in Ahluwalia, IJ and Little, IMD, 1998, eds, *India's Economic Reforms and Development: Essays for Manmohan Singh*. Oxford, Oxford University Press, pp. 169–96.

——, 2000, 'The Anglo-Saxon market for corporate control: The financial system and international competitiveness' in Candice Howes and Ajit Singh, 2000, eds., *Competitiveness Matters: Industry and Economic Performance in the US*, Ann Arbor, University of Michigan Press, pp. 89–105.

——, 2002a, 'Competition and Competition Policy in Emerging Markets: International and Developmental Dimensions', ESRC Centre for Business Research, University of Cambridge, Working Paper no.246.

——, 2002b, 'Asian Capitalism and the Financial Crisis' in Eatwell, J and L Taylor, eds, *International Capital Markets: Systems in Transition*, Oxford, Oxford University Press, Inc., pp. 339–67.

——, 2003, forthcoming, 'Corporate Governance, Corporate Finance and Stock markets in Emerging Countries', forthcoming in *Journal of Corporate Law*.

Singh, A and Hamid, J, 1992, *Corporate Financial Structures in Developing Countries*, Technical Paper 1, IFC, Washington DC.

Singh, A, Singh, A and Weisse, B, 2003, 'Corporate Governance Competition, the New International Financial Architecture and Large Corporations in Emerging Markets', forthcoming in Yilmaz Akyuz (ed.), *Management of Capital Flows*, UHCTAD, Geneva.

——, 1998, 'Emerging stock markets, portfolio capital flows and long-term economic growth: Micro and Macro Perspectives', *World Development*, vol. 26, no. 4, pp. 607–622.

——, 1999, 'The Asian model: A crisis foretold?', *International Social Science Journal*, no. 160.

Summers, LH, 1998, quoted in an article by Gerard Baker, 'US looks to G7 backing on Asia crisis', *Financial Times*, February 19, 1998.

——, 2000, *Information Technology, Venture Capital and the Stock Market*, Cambridge Discussion Paper in Accounting and Finance, no. AF47, Department of Applied Economics, University of Cambridge.

Stein, JC, 1989, 'Efficient stock markets, inefficient firms: A model of myopic corporate behaviour', *Quarterly Journal of Economics*, November.

Stiglitz, J, 1999, 'Reforming the Global Financial Architecture: Lessons from Recent Crises', *Journal of Finance* vol. 54, no. 4), pp. 1508–22.

Tichy, G, 2001, 'What do we know about success and failure of mergers?', Paper presented at UNIP Conference in Vienna, December.

Tirole, J, 1991, 'Privatisation in Eastern Europe: Incentives and the Economics of Transition', in OJ Blanchard and SS Fisher, 1991, eds, NBER Macroeconomics Annual 1991, Cambridge, Mass., MIT Press.

Tobin, J, 1984, 'On the efficiency of the financial system', *Lloyds Bank Review*, 1–15 July.

Tybout, J, 2000, 'Manufacturing firms in developing countries: How well do they do and why?', *Journal of Economic Literature*, vol. 38, no. 1 (March), pp. 11–44.

Waring, G, 1996, 'Industry Differences in the Persistence of Firm-Specific Returns', *American Economic Review*, December, vol.86, no. 4, pp. 1253–65.

Whittington, G, Saporta, V and Singh, A, 1997, *The Effects of Hyper-Inflation on Accounting Ratios: Financing of Corporate Growth in Industrialising Economies*, Technical Paper 3, IFC, Washington.

Winters, SG Jr, 1964, 'Economic 'natural selection' and the theory of the firm", *Yale Economic Essays,* Spring, vol. 4, no. 1, pp. 225–72.

Wolfensohn, J, 2000, quoted on worldbank.org in 'Remarks by Mark Baird, Transparency and Corporate Governance', April 25, 2000, http://lnweb18.worldbank.org/eap/eap.nsf/6ab4a442217f81de852567c9006b5ef9/7c4308a14b3d9ab9852568cc004ea1e3?OpenDocument

World Bank, 1993, *The East Asian Miracle: Economic Growth and Public Policy,* New York, Oxford University Press.

PART VI

POVERTY AND INEQUALITY

18

RURAL POVERTY AND GENDER: ANALYTICAL FRAMEWORKS AND POLICY PROPOSALS

John Sender

The rapidly expanding literature on rural poverty is now far too large to be summarized in a short chapter.[1] It may appear rash to suggest that some common themes are discernible, or that a consensus on rural poverty had emerged by the end of the 1990s. Nevertheless, many academic development economists, the majority of NGOs, the World Bank, the International Food Policy Research Institute, as well as UN agencies and major bilateral donors, do appear to share a common set of assumptions and to recommend a remarkably similar range of policies addressing the issue of rural poverty and female deprivation in low-income countries.

This chapter begins by attempting to identify a few hegemonic assumptions concerning the characteristics of the poor, as well as the related policies that have recently been funded by official development assistance, by a great many NGOs and by governments in rural Asia and Africa. The validity of these assumptions, and the quality of the evidence used to support them, are then questioned. The chapter concludes by arguing that alternative, more realistic assumptions would lead to a radically different analysis of the prospects for escaping rural poverty and that, unfortunately, the relevant policy options have been ignored in the mainstream literature.

1. Identifying the Poor

Most literature on rural poverty takes as its starting point three assumptions concerning the characteristics of the poorest rural people.[2]

1. They are usually farmers and self-employed. Many of them, especially in Africa, are small 'subsistence' farmers, which means that they mainly

survive by relying on *direct* (non-market mediated) consumption of those items produced on their own farms.

2. A very high proportion of all the people living in rural Africa (60 to 80%), and a similarly high proportion of all rural Asians are usually defined as 'poor'. The vast majority of all Africans identified as poor are assumed to fall into the 'smallholder', 'subsistence', 'peasant' category. Thus, virtually all smallholders in these low-income countries may safely be regarded as poor; and the 'small farmer' category, containing many hundreds of millions of people, may be considered as *homogeneous*: sharing the characteristics of poverty.

3. The assumption of homogeneity is relaxed to a limited extent when it is admitted that one dimension of differentiation may be a significant feature of the smallholder group. It is sometimes claimed that it is possible to identify a sub-group of small farm households that contains poorer people than other rural households. This sub-group consists of Female Headed Households.

These three assumptions prove to be convenient in addressing current concerns with poverty and gender in developing countries. They facilitate an analytical focus on: a) women as self-employed farmers, including women working on their own family's farm; or b) Female Headed Households in rural areas.

2. Policy conclusions

Partly on the basis of these assumptions, two policy conclusions are usually drawn. First, that the poor will benefit when policies are introduced to provide them with price incentives to expand production on their farms – that is to say, when policy reforms create an appropriate set of relative prices, especially higher relative prices for those agricultural commodities that are produced by the poorest smallholders, including basic foods that are typically consumed (as well as produced) by the poor.

Secondly, the markets providing poor smallholders with access to inputs need to be improved. Smallholder producers need timely and realistically priced inputs into farming operations if they are to respond to price incentives and escape poverty through increasing farm output. Apart from seeds, planting material, fertilizers and agro-chemicals, smallholders need improved access to seasonal and medium-term production credit, which micro-credit programmes can provide. If micro-credit is focused on rural females, then the gender dimension of rural poverty can be tackled. Similarly, smallholders need timely access to appropriate information concerning production opportunities, new techniques, improved varieties, pest and disease threats, etc. If extension services are reformed, perhaps privatized, and advice is relevant to and directed towards those farming operations performed by women, poverty will be reduced. Many of the problems of input supply can, it is believed, be explained in terms of the distortions that are so pervasive a feature of rural markets. Bureaucratic, inefficient and corrupt state-subsidized agencies responsible for delivering fertilizers or credit, for example, distort markets and are responsible for inappropriate relative prices and a pattern of incentives that favour larger and less efficient farm enterprises using capital-intensive techniques. In general, undistorted market mechanisms are regarded as the best institutional form for the delivery of inputs to smallholders.

These broad policy conclusions have underpinned the funding of agricultural sector loans and the conditions attached to much donor support for rural policy in developing countries. Thus, it has been argued that,

> In retrospect, it is evident that one major body of thought, albeit with plenty of side excursions and add-ons, has dominated the landscape of rural development thinking throughout the last half-century. This is the 'agricultural growth based on small-farm efficiency' paradigm ... both growth and equity goals appear to be satisfied simultaneously via the emphasis on small-farm agriculture. Much rests on the rural poor being poor small farmers.[3]

However, the impact of the prescribed reforms has increasingly been seen as disappointing. In the 1990s, unsubsidized private-sector agents did not rush in to fill the gaps in the supply of inputs and financial services that limited the production potential of smallholders and female farmers.[4] Attempts to reduce market distortion failed to deliver the anticipated benefits in terms of rapid-output growth on small farms; too many markets were missing in the rural areas of low-income countries, especially markets to insure against pervasive, covariant agricultural risk, while information costs and asymmetries, as well as the imperfection of land markets, were used to explain the inability of the poor to access credit despite their good potential to service loans through efficient small-scale farming.

Moreover, in the period following relative price and input supply reforms, a growing volume of rural micro research highlighted unanticipated negative consequences for poor farmers and women. These field researchers argue that the pattern of benefits has been extremely skewed. The principal beneficiaries continue to be men, who – directly or indirectly – obtain much of the credit, monopolize contacts with extension agents, and are more likely to have access to increasingly scarce production inputs such as fertilizer.[5] At the same time, the work intensity of female family members increases and/or the intra-household distribution of income deteriorates as cropping patterns change in response to new price incentives. Thus, only a small subset of male-headed rural households in favourable locations, with the best political connections and owning most of the livestock, draft equipment, means of transport and land, benefit in the new policy regime. One policy conclusion was to modify the general advice to improve smallholder access to inputs (the second policy conclusion noted above), to insist that the same inputs need to be focused to a much greater extent on Female Headed Households, or directed towards those specific farming enterprises within all households that are undertaken and 'controlled' by women.

It has also been recognized, belatedly and with some reluctance, especially in Sub Saharan Africa, that many rural women lack secure – or indeed any – access to sufficient fertile, well-watered land to enable them to farm effectively; that a very large number of the rural poor in both Africa and Asia are landless, or only have access to such tiny parcels of land that it will never be possible for them to survive on the basis of consumption derived from production on their own plots. Even if it is assumed that redistributive land reforms and radical improvements in the legal status and tenurial rights of women could be imposed by an imaginary, 'pro-poor', benevolent state, increasing the amount of land and the security of access to land for the poorest, the ratios of cultivable land to the labour force are so very low in Bangladesh, Bihar, North East Ethiopia and the Kenyan Highlands, for example, that tens of millions would remain effectively landless. Unprecedented and massive shifts in the allocation of farm inputs and credit, if these could be achieved in the real political context of these heavily populated regions, could not establish sustainable farm enterprises.

Recognition of the increasing significance of landlessness has prompted further modification of the second policy conclusion. Faced with the difficulties of offering rural women an exit route from poverty that depends on rising levels of production on their own or their family's farms, it is widely recommended that other forms of rural self-employment, especially *non-farm* self-employment, will provide a solution to acute problems of female deprivation. Therefore, the policy mix advocated by the vast majority of agencies (and implemented by the NGOs that they fund) has become dominated by initiatives to promote various forms of off-farm female self-employment: the promotion of retailing enterprises, food processing/catering stalls, hairdressing, handicraft (baskets, mats, pottery, soft toys), sewing/tailoring and small livestock enterprises (chickens, ducks, rabbits, stall-fed goats, etc.) that do *not* require access to large areas of land.

Some intellectual legitimacy for these initiatives has been offered by the 'livelihoods approach' literature, which accepts the evidence that poor rural people may not be small farmers, but usually have to combine *non-agricultural* assets and activities in 'diversified livelihood packages', in a 'coping' or survival strategy.[6] It is assumed that the distorted, discriminatory rural credit market remains a key constraint on female success in the strategy of diversifying income sources, the main barrier to entering non-farm enterprises. Thus, micro-credit programmes have proliferated, together with expenditures to train women in the modern business skills required to establish off-farm enterprises. Unsurprisingly, it is also argued that it is necessary to remove the red tape and regulatory impediments faced by 'informal' enterprises, to deregulate the markets in which small-scale entrepreneurs operate, and to remove the inefficient hand of the state agencies that constrain the dynamism of women's 'income-generating projects', e.g. through the licensing requirements they place on small businesses. Therefore, the international aid bureaucracy now insists on reforms designed to promote 'an enabling environment for start-up non-farm activities'.[7]

As in the case of small farmers, any processes or operations that cannot be undertaken efficiently because of the tiny scale of women's enterprises, such as marketing, transport or the purchase of bulky items of equipment, can nevertheless be successfully achieved through new institutional arrangements. Through the vociferous promotion of groups or associations of rural women it is hoped not only that that scale diseconomies will be overcome, but also that female 'empowerment' will be achieved. Facilitated by NGOs, the demands of a rising rural petty bourgeoisie will become more forcefully articulated through these associations, holding developing country states accountable for the market distorting and rent-seeking misdemeanours to which they are prone.

To summarize, hegemonic development theory proposes that poor rural women can escape from poverty if official development assistance is channelled through NGOs to promote self-employment. The problems of state inefficiency and distorted markets that constrain the viability of small farm and non-farm enterprises can be tackled politically by nurturing participatory associations of the self-employed and by making market deregulation, as well as the fragmentation (or decentralization) of the state, a condition for capital inflows.

3. Identifying the poor: an alternative approach

There are a number of problems surrounding the assumptions underlying mainstream policy conclusions. These difficulties arise partly as a result of ahistorical and unexamined ideological beliefs concerning the role of the market and individual choice in explaining capitalist accumulation and distribution processes in agrarian economies. Although the assumptions may appear to find some support in the results of household survey evidence, many of these surveys are actually extremely unreliable as sources of evidence on rural poverty and dynamic processes. Some of the most misleading features of these surveys will be discussed below.

It is possible to develop a more appropriate and realistic set of assumptions with which to begin an analysis of rural poverty and gender relations in developing countries. This alternative analysis is based on 'stylized facts' that capture, using a wealth of interdisciplinary micro research and national level secondary sources, what is known with some confidence about the characteristics of the poorest rural people and the dynamic processes through which they enter, and could conceivably escape from, poverty. [8] These stylized facts are not, for the most part, controversial or disputed in the current literature on the subject. They are summarized below.

The characteristics of the poorest rural households – the bottom 15 to 20% of the distribution – can usually be identified fairly easily by examining some simple demographic, anthropometric and asset indices.

1. These households contain women who have failed to complete many years of education; in fact, they are unlikely to contain an adult woman who is literate.
2. A relatively high proportion of the women in these households will have started to have children as teenagers.
3. A relatively high proportion of their children will have a low weight at birth and will have died before the age of five; their surviving children will have relatively low heights-for-age.
4. The ratio of adult females to males in these households will be relatively high and many of the women living in these households will have had *no* access to the income of an adult male for a period of several years, because they are divorced, abandoned, widowed or attached to males who are unhealthy, disabled, or unable to earn or remit income for other reasons.
5. The types of houses in which they live will clearly be inferior to those of other rural households, in terms of the materials with which floors and roofs are constructed, the number of rooms, quality of sanitation and lighting facilities. They will not have access to radios, bicycles, watches or other basic assets, including livestock, that are found in less destitute rural households.

Purposive samples of households with the above characteristics are far more likely to provide insights into the nature of rural poverty than the costly random surveys designed to describe the characteristics of the 'average' rural household that are promoted by the World Bank's Living Standards Measurement Programme (LSMS).[9] Besides, the simple indices derived from these stylized facts are likely to be far more robust and collected with far less measurement error than those used in mainstream poverty analyses of rural households, which continue to rely on absurdly lengthy questionnaires that attempt to elicit a huge volume of recall information to compute monthly per capita household expenditure as a proxy for income and the main metric for poverty.

Where purposive samples have been drawn, and the biases of conventional sampling techniques have been avoided, an important additional stylized fact can clearly be identified. The evidence for this stylized fact, which is particularly damaging to key assumptions in the conventional literature, is very strong indeed in Asia and is rapidly accumulating for Sub Saharan Africa.[10] This evidence suggests that the poorest rural households contain women who are performing manual agricultural wage labour, and that such households rely upon these female wages to survive.[11]

The proportion of these poor households' income that is derived from self-employment, whether agricultural or non-agricultural, is insignificant. Their survival strategy may include foraging or an attempt to grow some foodstuffs on miniscule homestead plots, but the total contribution to annual consumption of such desperate efforts is negligible. Only in far wealthier rural households, with far more access to land, male incomes, and other inputs, is self-employment a feasible option for women. Wives and daughters in these wealthier households would not contemplate seeking arduous and demeaning manual work for wages on their neighbours' fields, nor would their male relatives allow them to engage in such labour for others.

The literature on 'diversified livelihood packages', as well as most of the available LSMS or other analyses of Household Budget Surveys, often fails to identify the critical difference between various forms of off-farm income. But women who make a contribution to household income through the regular salary they earn as teachers, nurses or secretaries should obviously not be lumped into the same category as women who depend on seasonal wages as unskilled agricultural workers or on payment in kind as rural domestic servants. Thus in some crude tabulations of survey evidence it is suggested that rural households in receipt of wage incomes are *not* poorer than other rural households. This impression is the result of failing to disaggregate. For typically, no attempt is made to distinguish between income derived from salaried state employment, for example, and from seasonal agricultural wage labour.[12]

Similarly, while survey tabulations may suggest that most rural households obtain some income from various forms of off-farm self-employment, the *average* contribution of this source of income masks key differences between types of off-farm enterprise operated by poor and richer households and the absolute amounts of income they are capable of generating. Therefore, a rural woman managing the family shop and trucking business (employing half a dozen shop assistants, cleaners, drivers, loaders and mechanics) cannot easily be distinguished from a desperately poor woman, who is also misleadingly categorized as 'employed in retailing' because she occasionally sells (on commission) a few items of fruit from a basket at the side of the road. The tiny minority of women living in the wealthiest rural households, who can accumulate on the basis of retailing, do not provide evidence that poor rural women can depend on 'similar' enterprises to survive, or to lift themselves out of poverty in the future.

Thus, LSMS and other Household Budget Surveys regularly fail to recognize the importance of specific types of female wage labour to the survival prospects of the poor, partly because the precise sources of household income in the poorest and richest households, including remittance income, are not described in sufficient detail or classified appropriately. More importantly, this failure to focus on the relationship between poverty and unskilled rural wage labour can also be explained by a bias that is a common feature of allegedly 'random' samples. If the sample is drawn from a population list that *excludes* 'unregistered' people, such as seasonal and temporary migrants, hostel dwellers, workers living in compounds or 'pondoks' serving construction sites, workers in barracks, lines or temporary accommodation on farms, squatters and those living in illegal housing, sleeping rough, or engaged in the sexual services industry, then the poorest people will be under-represented.[13] While LSMS pays attention to the minutiae of statistical sampling and weighting in an effort to ensure that rural sample averages are nationally 'representative', far too little attention is paid to problems arising from the use of officially-produced lists of arbitrarily defined 'households', and the need to move beyond these if the sample is to include poor people.[14] The exclusion of so many poor people from 'nationally representative random sample surveys of households' produces results that help to justify both the assumption that the rural poor are self-employed farmers and the policy focus on self-employment as a viable strategy for the poor.

4. Dynamic processes and the determinants of rural poverty

While Household Budget Surveys may provide a more or less misleading picture of the characteristics of rural households at one or – more rarely in developing countries – at a few points in time, there are very few cohort studies or sets of panel data that can be used to study dynamic processes. Besides, since poverty is conventionally defined in terms of household per capita expenditure levels, attempts to identify *real* changes in standards of living over time face serious problems in choosing appropriate deflators.[15] Sometimes available are regional price data series which can be used in attempts to apply a price index that is considered appropriate to a particular region within a country, but the markets faced by rural people are often so fragmented that the average prices they pay for basic commodities will not only vary by region or district but even within villages, depending on who is purchasing from whom and on fluctuations in the relative bargaining power of the individuals concerned. Even if the choice of an appropriate deflator for household expenditure could readily be made, these data do not provide any information on the intra-household patterns and consequences of expenditures, which would be required for assessing trends in female welfare. Therefore, statements about the scale, timing and determinants of women's transitions out of poverty in developing countries are difficult to justify on the basis of national household survey data. Certainly, there is little evidence in support of the proposition that large numbers of poor women have escaped from poverty by increasing the incomes they earn through self-employment on their own farms or elsewhere in rural areas.

It is perhaps not surprising, therefore, that only rather vague conclusions could be reached in a recent survey of the largest body of evidence on changes in poverty over time, published by the World Bank:

> Households moved in and out of poverty in response to price changes, harvest levels, and the partitioning of household lands ... movement can be attributed to fluctuations in harvest quality and to personal calamities[16]

An even more recent survey of the Indian evidence, also sponsored by the World Bank, attempts to explain why the standard mainstream prediction linking farm output growth to poverty reduction was not as strongly supported by the experience of some Indian states as by others.[17] The explanatory equation found that higher farm yields and higher non-agricultural output per person in particular states did have significant, if widely varying, effects in reducing the incidence of household poverty, while higher rates of inflation increased poverty. These results can, of course, be interpreted as directly supporting some orthodox economic policy prescriptions. But an additional variable was also found to have a significant effect on poverty reduction in India, namely the level of state expenditure on development. While the policy implications of this finding are not discussed in the World Bank article, state expenditure has also been found to be a significant determinant of trends in poverty reduction in another, more interesting study of the causal mechanisms that underlie trends in female rural poverty.

The starting point for this study is the recognition that rural real wage rates in India, both for agricultural and non-agricultural wage workers, increased in the period since the mid-1970s, albeit at different rates in different states.[18] Moreover, this wage increase took place in a context of growing feminization and casualization of the rural labour market, so that the welfare of the poorest rural women and households in India, who depend on this labour market, improved. Therefore, an analysis of the factors influencing rates of growth in female rural real wages in different Indian states is of crucial importance if policies to reduce rural poverty are to be developed.[19]

Contrary to what might be expected on the basis of conventional analyses, Sen and Ghosh show that some states with very rapid rates of growth in farm output only achieved mediocre growth rates in female rural wages, or even failed to reduce the gap between the levels of female and male rural wages. However, strong rates of growth in rural female wages were associated with fast rates of growth in state expenditure, which resulted – directly or indirectly – in the creation of new rural wage employment opportunities and a tightening of agricultural labour markets.

The causal link between state expenditure and rising rural female wage rates is plausible: the majority of the new rural jobs that became available in Indian states towards the end of the 1980s were non-agricultural jobs; and a high proportion of all rural non-agricultural regular employment (about 60%) is accounted for by government employees, such as teachers, nurses, primary health care staff, construction workers, cleaners, office staff and so on. The direct and indirect effects on the labour market of an expansion in government activity, and hence in the number of these types of job in the rural areas of India's states, were extremely important. Even if males and the educated children of relatively wealthy households are the first to obtain these regular non-agricultural positions, one consequence is that fewer of them will compete in the more poorly-paid, irregular and low-status casual agricultural labour markets. The number of days of employment in the casual labour market that are available for unskilled women will increase, while this market is also likely to tighten for another reason. State expenditure on education has the effect of increasing the proportion of teenage girls attending school, therefore limiting the size of the female labour force available for casual agricultural wage labour. In addition, rural women's real wages may increase as a result of improvements in female bargaining power and mobility that are associated with higher levels of female literacy.

It is difficult to reconcile this analysis and the disaggregated evidence from India's states with the orthodox view that the distorting affects of the growth of state expenditure are generally harmful to poor rural women. Moreover, it is important to note that evidence of a positive relationship between state intervention/regulation and higher female rural wages has also been found outside India.[20] There are, besides, many other ways in which state intervention in rural markets – an anathema to the mainstream view – can be seen to have contributed to poverty reduction in developing countries. Again, the prime example is India, where state intervention to stabilize the prices of basic food grains has played a key role in reducing rural poverty since the 1950s.

Basic food grains constitute the largest component of the consumption basket of the poor, accounting for 75 to 80% of consumption expenditure among rural wage labourers in India, a far higher percentage than that found in any other group. It follows that if there are large, unanticipated fluctuations in food grain prices, then the poorest rural people – i.e. those unable to hold stocks of food, employed in non-unionized markets characterized by excess labour supply, with weak bargaining power, organizational skills and literacy – will be particularly vulnerable and most likely to suffer from worsening poverty when their money wage rates fail to keep pace with rising food prices.[21]

In India, it appears that periods of sharp decline in agricultural output have been associated with significant increases in the price of agricultural products relative to manufactures. But the price-formation mechanism is asymmetrical. In those periods when there were large increases in agricultural output, there were only moderate declines in the relative price of agricultural products.[22] Therefore, those states in India that experienced the fastest rates of growth in agricultural output were not necessarily those with the fastest reductions in poverty. The policy conclusion reached by Ghose is that reductions in Indian poverty depended upon state intervention in basic food grain markets, e.g. state procurement and fair trade shops, designed to limit the range of fluctuations in basic food grain prices.[23] He also concludes that there is an important role for state investment geared to increasing the stability of the rate of growth of agricultural production, particularly in those states most subject to crop failures where there has been inadequate investment in water control and irrigation. Of course, since irrigated land allows multiple cropping and uses far more hired labour per hectare than unirrigated land, there is a general case (throughout most of Asia and Africa) for state-supported investment in irrigation and other rural infrastructure, if the demand for rural female wage labour is to increase with positive consequences for poor women's annual real-wage earnings and for poverty reduction.

To summarize, it is not possible to use the available evidence to provide a simple or straightforward account of trends in female poverty in developing countries, even in India where the survey data and analytical work are particularly rich. However, it is clear that an account which stresses the role of self-employment and price incentives to increase farm output in reducing female poverty is unsatisfactory. The implications for the poor of reducing state expenditure and limiting the scope of state interventions in rural areas may also be very different from those predicted in the hegemonic literature. More research is required at a disaggregated level to examine the determin- ants of trends in rural female wages. These vary quite dramatically within rural areas of developing countries, and the real wages that rural women can earn have a decisive impact on the poorest children and households. Unfortunately, in most developing economies no efforts at all are made to collect time-series data on the wages of those employed in small-scale farm and non-farm rural enterprises, especially on the wages of those who are irregularly, seasonally, or casually employed. In most of these economies, in fact, there is no reliable data on the number of people or households that depend upon earnings from these types of employment; it is simply assumed that the rural poor are, or will, become self-employed, and that proletarian- ization is not a feature of capitalist growth in developing countries.

4. Contrasting perspectives and policy conclusions

A clear contrast may be drawn between the medium-term perspective on poverty reduction offered in the mainstream literature, and a perspective that is based on historical analyses of processes of poverty reduction in developed and developing countries. The mainstream scenario appears to be that, in a context of minimal state intervention, the poor rural self-employed labour force will over time succeed in developing increasingly successful agricultural and non-agricultural rural businesses. A growing proportion of rural house- hold income will be provided by these expanding enterprises, and absolute standards of living of both female and male household members engaged in these small businesses will increase.

In contrast to this petty bourgeois utopian vision, an alternative perspective is that, over time, a growing proportion of poor rural people, and of the total rural labour force, will become wage workers. They will initially work for wages on farms and in the non-farm rural sector as domestic servants, cleaners, waiters, construction and transport workers in small district towns. An increasing number will migrate in search of similar forms of unskilled wage employment, both to other rural areas and to larger towns and cities. Wage levels will determine their standards of living and the rate at which they can escape from poverty. The history of most economies in which the percentage of the labour force living in absolute poverty has declined shows that an increasing proportion of the labour force became employed for wages, and that the percentage of the labour force employed for wages in large enterprises increased. Certainly, in the OECD context, 'the predominant trend in self-employment is downward' and 'increases in the proportion of self-employment appear to produce *lower* not higher GDP'.[24] Higher wages and growing labour productivity are a feature of economies in which a relatively large proportion of the labour force is employed for wages in technologically dynamic and rather large enterprises, while only a small percentage of the labour force is self-employed or employed in small family businesses.

If the poorest women now rely, and will increasingly depend in the future, upon wage incomes to survive and to escape from poverty, then it is not clear that fashionable policies providing them with training to make baskets, or offering them micro-credit to facilitate start-up enterprises in rural environments already over-supplied with similar and failing enterprises,[25] are sensible. Aid agency policies now focus on 'capacity building' in all manner of ineffective, small-scale and corrupt decentralized organizations – NGOs, CBOs, Group Credit and other financial institutions,[26] but any organization that has a realistic prospect of increasing the political and economic bargaining power of the lowest-paid wage workers is shunned, or dismissed as potentially 'market distorting' and, *ipso facto*, harmful to the poor. There is, for example no support for, or even discussion of, the need to allocate resources to support the formation of trade unions by seasonal agricultural labourers. Nor is there support in the mainstream literature for effective legislation to monitor and enforce the rights of migrant domestic servants or women employed in garment sweat shops. Indeed, any state intervention that might create an 'enabling environment' for more effective struggles by such workers is likely to be rejected on the grounds that it might compromise the viability of small enterprises. In fact, the voluminous literature on poverty published by the aid bureaucracy and its consultants studiously avoids mentioning the specific organizations, the legislation, or institutions that have historically been most significant in defending the human rights and living standards of the poor in capitalist labour markets.

At the same time, there is no discussion of the economic policies and the precise forms of state investment and intervention that might be capable of promoting the growth of female-wage labour-intensive enterprises. There is clear evidence that particular crops, agro-processing and other export industries employ relatively large numbers of women for wages.[27] However, appropriate sectoral policies and industrial strategies are unlikely to be developed, if the most influential development economists insist that poverty can be reduced only when markets are deregulated and when states abandon their old-fashioned aspirations to formulate industrial policy.

In the first part of this chapter I outlined the currently fashionable theoretical framework, in which the poor are self-employed 'agents', playing maximizing games in imperfect rural markets. They simply need more 'assets', purchased through access to micro-credit, provided by more perfectly functioning rural financial markets, to smooth the process of their transition into membership of the petty bourgeoisie. Within this framework, it is not easy to identify the rural poor as women who will continue to be forced to depend on earnings in the wage labour market as casual/seasonal farm labourers or domestic servants. The chapter concluded by criticizing the relevance of many of the conventional policy recommendations, by highlighting lacunae in current policy debates, and by offering some brief suggestions concerning topics on which research is required to develop more effective poverty reduction strategies.

Notes

1 The scale of the published output may be seen in the 25 pages of references cited in IFAD 2000; in Lipton and Ravallion 1995; and by searching the library of the World Bank's 'Poverty Net': http://poverty.worldbank.org/library/

2 Of course, influential sources do not make all of these assumptions and they sometimes adopt different and more qualified assumptions to describe the poor in particular regions. Detailed citations emphasizing the nuances of different assumptions and policy recommendations are avoided in this synthetic summary.

3 Ellis and Biggs 2001, p. 440–1

4 Poulson, Dorward and Kydd 1998; Devereux 2002.

5 Saito, Mekonnen and Spurling 1994.

6 Carney 1998; Bryceson and Bank 2001.

7 Ellis and Biggs 2001, p. 445.

8 The use of stylised facts in economic analysis, as developed by Kaldor, is discussed in Boylan and O'Gorman 1997. The most reliable national survey data is often provided by Demographic and Health Surveys, available at http://www.measuredhs.com/. A guide to the most informative micro-level research methods is available in Breman 1996; and Breman and Wiradi 2002.

9 Since 1980 the LSMS programme has carried out well over 40 surveys in about 22 developing countries. The LSMS approach to sampling is described in Grosh and Munoz 1996.

10 Cramer and Sender 1999; Cramer and Pontara 1998; Sender and Smith 1990.

11 Sender 2002.

12 Many surveys report results on the sources of income for the poorest as opposed to other households in such a way that it is impossible to identify precisely the gender of employees, types of wage employment, or the specific sectors offering the wage employment opportunities that are important for the poorest households (Adams and He 1995; Dercon and Krishnan 1996; Tschirley and Weber 1994). For a review of some of the empirical classification issues that have been neglected in African rural household income surveys, see Reardon 1997.

13 It is widely recognised that household surveys are also not a reliable source for measuring the incomes of the very rich (Datt and Ravallion 2002, p. 93). They are therefore an unreliable guide to analysing inequality as well as poverty.

14 Breman 1996; Standing, Sender and Weeks 1996; Sender and Johnston 1996; Sender and Pincus 2001; Sender 2002.

15 The choice of alternative deflators, as well as alternative methods for drawing the poverty line, makes a huge difference to estimates of poverty incidence (Deaton 2001; Said and Widyanti 2001).

16 Jayaraman and Lanjouw 1999, p. 15.

17 Given that India contains such a large proportion of the total number of poor people in the world, these results may be considered to have global significance.

18 Sen and Ghosh 1993; Bhalla 1997.

19 There is now little dispute in the literature that the incidence of poverty in India fell during the 1980s (Datt and Ravillion, 2002, p. 106) and that a large and rising proportion of the poorest rural households (over 40%) depend for their survival on wages earned in the rural sector.

20 Sender 2002.

21 In Egypt, for example, only about 1/10 of a food price increase is normally reflected in the nominal agricultural wage rate after one year (Datt and Olmstead 1998), while in Indonesia rural real wages fell very dramatically indeed following the hike in food prices during the crisis of the late 1990s, and have yet to recover (Levinsohn, Berry and Friedman 1999; Smith et al. 2000.)

22 Ghose 1989.

23 For a positive assessment of the role of state intervention to stabilize prices in food markets in Asia, see Dawe 2001. More generally, Burmesiter 1990 shows the positive contribution of state intervention in explaining farm output growth in South Korea.

24 Blanchflower 2000, p. 12 and p. 22.

25 Dessing 1990; Buckley 1997.

26 UNDP 2000; World Bank 2002; DfID 1999.

27 MERG 1993. There is also evidence on the impact of irrigation on employment growth and poverty reduction, as well as a good case for investment in large-scale irrigation in both Africa and Asia (IFAD, 2001, pp. 92–4).

References

Bhalla, S, 1997, 'Liberalisation, Workforce Restructuring, Wages and Want: the Harayana Story in an All India Context. Workshop on Rural Labour Relations in India', LSE Development Studies Institute, June.

Blanchflower, D, 2000, *Self-Employment in OECD Countries*. Working Paper, 7486, Cambridge, MA, National Bureau of Economic Research.

Boylan, TA and P O'Gorman, 1997, 'Kaldor on Method: a Challenge to Contemporary Methodology', *Cambridge Journal of Economics*, 21, pp. 503–17.

Breman, Jan and Gunawan Wiradi, 2002, *Good Times and Bad Times in Rural Java*, Leiden, KITLV Press.

Bryceson, Deborah Fahy and Leslie Bank, 2001, 'End of an Era: Africa's Development Policy Parallax', *Journal of Contemporary African Studies*, 19(1), pp. 5–23.

Buckley, G, 1997, 'Microfinance in Africa: Is it Either the Problem or the Solution?', *World Development*, July.

Burmeister, L, 1990, 'State, Industrialisation and Agricultural Policy in Korea', *Development and Change*, 21, pp. 197–223.

Carney, D, 1998, *Sustainable Rural Livelihoods*, London, Department for International Development (DfID)).

Cramer, Christopher and John Sender, 1999, *Poverty, Wage Labour and Agricultural Change in Rural Eastern and Southern Africa*, Background Paper for the Rural Poverty Report 2001, Rome, International Fund for Agricultural Development.

Cramer, Christopher and Nicola Pontara, 1998, 'Rural Poverty and Poverty Alleviation in Mozambique: What's Missing from the Debates?', *Journal of Modern African Studies*, 36(1).

Datt, Gaurav and Jennifer Olmstead, 1998, *Agricultural Wages and Food Prices in Egypt: A Governorate-Level Analysis for 1976–1993*, Discussion Paper, 53, Washington, Food Consumption and Nutrition Division, International Food policy Research Institute.

Datt, Guarav and Martin Ravallion, 2002, 'Is India's Economic Growth Leaving the Poor Behind?', *Journal of Economic Perspectives*, 16(3), pp. 89–108.

Dawe, D, 2001, 'How Far Down the Path to Free Trade? The Importance of Rice Price Stabilization in Developing Asia', *Food Policy*, 26(2), pp. 163–76.

Deaton, A, 2001, 'Counting the World's Poor: Problems and Possible Solutions', *World Bank Research Observer*, 16(2).

Dessing, M, 1990, *Support for Microenterprises: Lessons for Sub-Saharan Africa*. World Bank Technical Paper, WTP122, Washington DC, World Bank.

Devereux, S, 2002, *State of Disaster: Causes, Consequences & Policy Lessons from Malawi*, London, ActionAid.

DfID, 1999, *Economic Well-Being*, International Development Target Strategy Paper Consultation Document, London, DfID.

Ellis, Frank and Stephen Biggs, 2001, 'Evolving Themes in Rural Development 1950s–2000s', *Development Policy Review*, 19(4), pp. 437–48.

Ghose, A, 1989, June, 'Rural Poverty and Relative Prices in India', *Cambridge Journal of Economics*.

Grosh, Margeret and Juan Munoz, 1996, *A Manual for Planning and Implementing the Living Standards Measurement Study Survey*, LSMS Working Paper, 126, Washington DC, World Bank.

IFAD, 2001, *Rural Poverty Report 2001: The Challenge of Ending Rural Poverty*, New York, Oxford University Pres.

Jayaraman, Rajshri and Peter Lanjouw, 1999, The Evolution of Poverty and Inequality in Indian Villages, *The World Bank Research Observer*, 14(1).

Levinsohn, James, Steven Berry and Jay Friedman, 1999, *Impacts of the Indonesian Crisis: Price Changes and the Poor*. Working Paper, 7194, Cambridge, MA, National Bureau of Economic Research.

Lipton Michael and Martin Ravallion, 1995, 'Poverty and Policy' in JTN Behrman, ed., *Handbook of Development Economics, 3b*, Amsterdam, Elsevier.

Macro Economic Research Group (MERG), 1993, *Making Democracy Work: A Macroeconomic Policy Framework for South Africa*, Capetown, Stockholm and London, MERG.

Poulton, C, A. Dorward and J Kydd, 1998, 'The Revival of Smallholder Cash Crops in Africa: Public and Private Roles in the Provision of Finance', *Journal of International Development*, 10(1), pp. 85–103.

Reardon, T, 1997, 'Using Evidence of Household Income Diversification to Inform Study of the Rural Nonfarm Labor Market in Africa', *World Development*, 25(5).

Said, Ali and Wenefrida D Widyanti, 2001, 'The Impact of Economic Crisis on Poverty and Inequality in Indonesia', Symposium on Poverty Analysis and Data Initiatives, 30 April–3 May, Manila, Phillipines.

Saito, Katrine Hailu Mekonnen and Daphne Spurling, 1994, *Raising the Productivity of Women Farmers in Sub-Saharan Africa*, Africa Technical Department Series, 230, Washington DC, World Bank.

Sen, Abhijit and Jayati Ghosh, 1993, *Trends in Rural Employment and the Poverty Employment Linkage*. ILO ARTEP Working Papers, Delhi, International Labour Organisation.

Sender, John and Deborah Johnston, 1996, 'Some Poor and Invisible Women: Farm Labourers in South Africa', *Development Southern Africa*, 13(1), pp. 3–16.

Sender, John and Jonathan Pincus, 2001, 'Preliminary Results from the Indonesian People's Security Survey: Characteristics of the Most Insecure and Vulnerable Households', People's Security Surveys Conference, Geneva, ILO.

Sender, John and Sheila Smith, 1990, *Poverty Class and Gender in Rural Africa: A Tanzanian Case Study*, London, Routledge.

Sender, J, 2002, 'The Struggle to Escape Poverty in South Africa: results from a Purposive Surve', *Journal of Agrarian Change*, 2(1), pp. 1–49.

Smith, JP, EF Duncan Thomas, Kathleen Beegle and Graciela Teruel, 2000, *Wages Employment and Economic Shocks: Evidence from Indonesia*, Working Paper Series: Labor and Population Program, 00-07, California, RAND.

Standing, G, John Sender and John Weeks, 1996, *Restructuring the Labour Market: The South African Challenge*, Geneva, ILO.

UNDP, 2000, *Overcoming Human Poverty*, New York, UNDP.

World Bank, 2000, *Attacking Poverty*, Washington DC, Oxford University Press.

World Bank, 2002, *Poverty Reduction and the World Bank: Progress in Operationalizing the WDR 2000/01*, Washington DC, World Bank.

19

GLOBALIZATION AND THE DISTRIBUTION OF INCOME BETWEEN AND WITHIN COUNTRIES

Giovanni Andrea Cornia

1. Introduction: the neglect of inequality as a key policy issue

The last decade has witnessed a flourishing of research on poverty-related topics as well as growing concern for poverty reduction by governments, the international community and many social scientists. This new awareness has triggered a few potentially important changes, including the United Nations General Assembly's adoption of the Millennium Development Goals on poverty reduction and the creation of new lending facilities explicitly targeted at poverty alleviation. While it is too soon to assess the real impact of these changes, many believe they have the potential to make a dent in the long-lasting problem of poverty.

A similar shift in focus and policy stance has not yet taken place in the case of income inequality. While research in this field has made considerable strides over the last decade,[1] and while the traditional view that inequality is good for growth has been increasingly challenged, the dominant approach to policy reform inspired by the Washington Consensus has by and large ignored the issue of high and growing inequality. Some of its proponents view high inequality as a non-issue or as an important issue about which nothing much can be done, while others see it as a source of incentives and capital accumulation leading to faster growth for all, including the poor, or as a stimulus to upward mobility for low-income groups. Meanwhile, in the countries in transition, rising inequality is seen as a normal side-effect of the unwinding of socialism's artificial compression of incentives.

Ironically, such neglect of the inequality issue has been accompanied by marked changes in the field of income distribution. On one side, the secular trend towards higher relative global inequality has slowed down. On the other, the 'absolute income gap' between the advanced and developing countries has risen, while the income inequality within countries has surged in about 2/3 of the nations with consistent time series in this field.

While the debate is far from over, initial evidence suggests that the causes of these changes are also related to the spread of the new global market paradigm. This paradigm advocates the rapid removal of barriers to international trade, opening up to foreign direct investments and short-term portfolio flows, and the creation of a standardized patent regime regulating technology transfers and intellectual property. Globalization has also generally entailed the prior liberalization of the domestic markets and the privatization of state-owned enterprises. As it will appear in the course of this chapter, empirical evidence mostly contradicts the supposed favourable distributive effects of these measures.

2. Changes in global and between-country inequality

The distribution of per capita income among the citizens of the world can be split into the distribution of average income per capita between countries and the distribution of income per capita within countries. Most studies on global inequality suggest that inequality between countries explains 60–90% of it (depending on the index used) and that inequality within countries explains the remaining 10–40%. Changes in global and between-country inequality are analysed below, while changes within countries are discussed in Section 3.

2.1 Studies of population-weighted changes in the distribution of average GDP per capita converted into US dollars at the market exchange rate

Most of the studies in this group underscore the fact that, while over the last 30 years a few Asian nations converged towards the income per capita of the OECD group, the rest of the developing world further diverged from it, heightening global inequality as a result. An UNCTAD study[2] on 124 countries, representing 93% of the world population, shows that the Gini coefficient of the global income distribution rose from 0.68 in 1980 to 0.74 in 1990, mainly because of a rise in the income share of the countries with the richest 10% of the world population. Similar conclusions were reached by the 1999 Human Development Report,[3] which found that between-country inequality rose in recent years, as the income gap between the fifth of the world's population living in the richest countries and the fifth living in the poorest countries rose from 30:1 in 1960 to 74:1 in 1997.

These studies make use of market exchange rates to convert GDP per capita – expressed in national currencies – into US dollars, and have been criticized because the 'traded sector bias' implicit in this approach raises the estimates of global inequality. Some authors[4] have in fact shown that between-country inequality is lower, and may fall over time, when national-currency GDPs per capita are translated into dollars by means of PPP exchange rates. However, Dowrick and Akmal argue[5] that analyses based on PPP exchange rates are themselves subject to another bias (the 'substitution bias'[6]) that artificially lowers the level of global inequality and its trend over time.[7] Making use of the Afriat true index, they therefore compute a new distribution of GDP per capita and find that the Gini coefficient of such distribution rises slightly over time from 0.615 in 1980 to 0.623 in 1993. By adding a component for changes in inequality within countries, they obtain a Gini coefficient of the global income distribution that rises moderately, from 0.698 to 0.711, over the same period. However, when using other indexes (Theil, the squared coefficient of variation and the variance of logs) they find bigger inequality increases ranging between 5 and 9%.

2.2 Studies of population-weighted changes in the distribution of individual GDP per capita converted into US dollars at the market exchange rate

This methodological improvement is important because, even if between-country inequality rises (falls), world inequality may decline (increase) if within-country inequality falls (rises) in many countries. Most of these analyses, however, do not make use of survey data, which alone can provide precise information on the shape of national income distributions, but rely instead on synthetic indexes (such as the Gini or Theil coefficients) and assumptions about the shape of domestic distributions (the most common assumption being that it is log-normal).

One such analysis by Korzeniewicz and Moran[8] studies changes in the world distribution of GNP per capita in 46 nations accounting for 68% of the world population in the period 1965–92. They concluded that the world income distribution became more skewed, with the Gini index rising from 0.749 to 0.796 and the Theil index soaring from 1.15 to 1.32. A breakdown of the latter index showed that between-country inequality accounted for 79 and 86% of the world inequality in 1965 and 1992, while within-country inequality accounted for the rest. Similar results were arrived at by Schultz[9] for 120 countries in the period 1960–89. However, when converting the GDPs per capita with PPP exchange rates, world inequality increased between 1960 and 1968 but declined between 1968 and 1989. In the later period, convergence in income per capita between countries more than offset the increase in within-country inequality. However, when China was excluded from the sample, the decline in global inequality after 1975 was no longer evident.[10]

Bourguignon and Morisson[11] carried out a study of world income inequality in the period 1820–1992 on the basis of GDP per capita and quantile shares for 15 large countries and 18 aggregates of similar neighbouring nations. As for the last twenty years, the study points to a slow rise in inequality due to a moderate and unstable increase in between-country inequality and a rise of within-country inequality (Table 1). The study also shows that within-country inequality declined between 1950 and 1970 and then surged in the subsequent period – a finding also confirmed by the analysis in section 4.

Finally, Sala-i-Martin[12] generated a global income distribution by adding up the distributions for 125 countries between 1970 and 1998. To do so, he

Table 1. **Evolution of the global distribution of income and of its components, 1820–1992**

	1820	1870	1910	1950	1960	1970	1980	1992
Gini Coefficient (global inequality)	0.500	0.560	0.610	0.640	0.635	0.650	0.657	0.657
Theil Coefficient								
Inequality *within* country groups	0.462	0.484	0.498	0.323	0.318	0.315	0.330	0.342
Inequality *between* country groups	0.061	0.188	0.299	0.482	0.458	0.492	0.499	0.513
Total (global) inequality	0.522	0.672	0.797	0.805	0.776	0.808	0.829	0.855
Mean logarithmic deviation								
Inequality *within* country groups	0.370	0.382	0.399	0.303	0.300	0.304	0.321	0.332
Inequality *between* country groups	0.053	0.162	0.269	0.472	0.466	0.518	0.528	0.495
Total (global) inequality	0.422	0.544	0.668	0.775	0.766	0.823	0.850	0.827

Source: Bourguignon and Morisson 2002

estimates the yearly national income distribution between 1970 and 1998 for 78 countries with several observations on income shares, while making strong assumptions on the shape of the distribution of 57 nations with little or no data. His results (Table 2) show that between-country inequality rose modestly between 1970 and 1980 and has since then declined, as the growth of China and India in the 1980s and 1990s was faster than that of the OECD. Meanwhile, within-country inequality rose steadily over the period. As this increase was smaller than the decline in between-country inequality, global inequality fell since 1980. Also in this case, removing China from the sample raises global inequality and reduces within-country inequality.

Also this second group of studies suffers from important methodological problems. For instance, it is impossible to predict the shape of income distribution on the basis of a single statistic (as a Gini coefficient is compatible with an infinite number of Lorenz curves), nor it is reasonable to assume that all distributions follow a lognormal pattern.

2.3 Analyses based on individual income data derived from household surveys converted by means of PPP exchange rates

This approach permits an accurate estimate of the shape of income distribution for each country and, by aggregation, the distribution of income among world citizens. To the best of our knowledge, there are only four studies of this

Table 2. Evolution of the global income distribution of its components, 1970–98

	1970	1980	1990	1992	1998
Gini Coefficient (global inequality)	0.633	0.638	0.630	0.621	0.609
Theil Coefficient					
Inequality *within* country groups	0.186	0.193	0.194	0.195	0.203
Inequality *between* country groups	0.586	0.593	0.583	0.554	0.513
Total (global) inequality	0.771	0.786	0.776	0.749	0.716
Mean logarithmic deviation					
Inequality *within* country groups	0.170	0.181	0.201	0.206	0.226
Inequality *between* country groups	0.634	0.647	0.586	0.557	0.513
Total (global) inequality	0.805	0.828	0.787	0.763	0.739

Source: derived from Sala-i-Martin 2002

Table 3. **Findings of changes in global inequality and its components over the recent decades**

	Period Covered	Exchange rate used	Inequality measure	Within countries inequality	Between countries inequality	Total (global) inequality	Approach followed and main assumptions
UNCTAD 1997	1980–90	Market	Gini	...	Up	...	Uses GDP/c and income shares
UNDP 1999	1960–97	Market	Quintile ratio	...	Up	...	Uses GDP/c
Korzeniewicz and Moran 1997	1965–92	Market	Gini	...	Up	...	Uses GDP/c
			Theil	...	Up	...	Uses GDP/c
Schultz 1998	1968–89	PPP	Gini	Up	Down	Down	Uses GDP/c and income shares
			Gini (excl. China)	Up	Stable	Up	
Sala-i-Martin 2002	1970–98	PPP	7 ineq. indexes	Up	Down	Down	Uses GDP/c and quintile shares for 125 countries (for 57 of them assumptions are made on the shape/stability of distribution) National trends in quintile shares are obtained through linear regression.
			7 ineq. indexes (excl. China)	Stable	Slightly up	Slightly up	
Bourguignon and Morisson 2002	1980–92	PPP	Gini	...	...	Stable	Uses GDP/c and income shares to proxy the distribution of 33 large countries/country groups
			Theil	Up	Up	Up	
			MLD	Up	Down	Down	

Study	Years	Method	Measure				Notes
Dowrick and Akmal 2001	1980–93	Afriat	Gini	Up	Slightly up	Up	Uses GDP/c and income shares
			Theil	Up	Up	Up	
			SCV	Up	Up	Up	
Milanovic 2000	1988–93	PPP	Gini	Up	Up	Up	Uses *Income/c* and *original distributions* from 91 nations. Large Asian countries are separated into rural and urban
			Theil	Up	Up	Up	
Li, Squire, Zou 1998	1980–92	n.a.	Gini	Stable	…	…	49 countries linear trend regression
Cornia 2002	1980–95	n.a.	Gini	Up	…	…	73 countries quadratic trend regression

Source: author's compilation

type. The first two comprise only developing countries, while the third also includes the transitional economies. The fourth and most complete, by Milanovic,[13] also covers the developed countries – this is significant, as their exclusion would sharply alter the shape of global distribution. The study uses PPP-adjusted survey data on the distribution of income per capita in 1988 and 1993 for 88 countries, accounting for 84 and 93 percent of the world population and GDP respectively. The study treats the rural and urban sectors of China, India, Bangladesh, Pakistan and Egypt as separate economies, owing to their huge size and the recent widening of the income gap between their urban and rural areas. The study finds that the Gini coefficient of world income distribution rose from 0.628 in 1988 to 0.670 in 1993 as a result of a surge in both within- and between-country inequality. Milanovic ends his analysis noting that '...slow growth of rural per capita incomes in populous Asian countries (China, India and Bangladesh) compared to income growth of several large and rich OECD countries, plus fast growth in urban China compared to rural China and India, were the main reasons why world Gini increased'. However, the main problem with this class of study is that the limited number of household surveys for the earlier years impedes obtaining a sufficiently long trend of global inequality and its components.

2.4 Summing up the evidence

The results of these three groups of studies and of the analyses of within-country inequality discussed in section 4 are summarized in Table 4. They suggest the following tentative conclusions:

- The measurement of the level and trend of global inequality depends to a considerable extent on a long and important series of statistical choices;[14] the use of synthetic statistics or micro data from surveys to proxy the national distributions; the inequality index chosen; the period considered; the 'correct measurement' of the (presumably overstated) Chinese rate of growth in the 1990s; and the treatment of China, India and other poor and populous countries as single nations or as two nations each comprised of the urban and rural sector. Different methodologies lead to different conclusions.
- Bearing these considerations in mind, the evidence suggests – on balance – that between the early 1980s and 1993 (few analyses extend beyond that year) global inequality stagnated, or increased at a slower pace than during the first wave of globalization due to a stagnation or modest rise in between-country inequality and a rise in within-country inequality (see next section); this, however, affected global inequality less than in the past.

Table 4. Gini coefficients of the distribution of net per capita disposable household income between 1989 and 1994–95

Moderate Increases	1989 Gini	1989–95 Increase	Large Increases	1989 Gini	1989–95 Increase
Slovenia	23.7	1.3	Lithuania	27.5	8.5
Hungary	21.4	1.6	Latvia	22.5[a]	8.5
Slovakia	19.5	3.0	Estonia	27.7	11.9
Romania	23.5	4.9	Bulgaria	25.0[b]	12.0
Czech Republic	18.5	4.9	Moldova	26.7	13.3
Poland	24.9	5.1	Russia	25.7	15.2
			Ucraine	23.3[a]	24.1

Source: Cornia with Kiiski (2001)

Notes:
a 1988. The data are not always directly comparable over time due to changes in the sampling framework. For a few countries and years the data refer to gross household income per capita.
b 1990.

- The rise in global inequality was more pronounced during the 1990s, a period in which the US expanded rapidly while rural incomes in India and China did not grow as quickly as in the 1980s. By contrast, during the 1980s, fast agricultural growth in China and India and sluggish growth in the OECD probably led to a drop in global inequality;
- Finally, if inequality is assessed not as a ratio of but as the absolute differences between the GDP per capita of the countries involved, the picture clearly points to a growing North–South polarization. As noted by Wade, 'The other strong conclusion is that *absolute* income gaps between the West and the rest are widening, even in the case of relatively fast growing countries like China and India, and are likely to go on widening for another half century at least. No one disputes this, but globalists tend to focus on *relative* incomes only [italics mine].'[15]

3. Changes in within-country inequality

In this section we briefly summarize the findings of a comprehensive review of changes in domestic income inequality carried out recently by Cornia with Kiiski.[16] These authors found that in several countries inequality declined during the first 20–25 years of the post World War II period following a decline in unemployment, stable earnings inequality and growing redistribution in the OECD and socialist countries and the introduction of programs of land reform, educational enlargement and some redistribution in developing countries. In India, for instance, the Gini coefficient of household consumption expenditure per capita fell from 0.36 to 0.31 over 1951–61 and then fluctuated in the 0.29–0.32 range until 1991.

This trend towards lower inequality came gradually to a halt in many countries. Starting from the mid 1970s, and increasingly so since the early 1980s, frequent reversals in national inequality trends were observed in the OECD countries (beginning with the USA and UK) and the Latin American nations. In the latter region, for instance, in the 1980s inequality declined in only three countries (Colombia, Uruguay and Costarica) out of eleven while in the 1990s inequality worsened in eight cases and stagnated in seven despite the return to full-capacity growth.[17] The 1990s also witnessed growing income polarization in the economies in transition. The rise in inequality was limited in the countries of Central Europe but explosive in those of the former USSR and South Eastern Europe, as shown by Table 4. Meanwhile, in China inequality rose slowly over 1978–84 but rapidly between 1985 and 1990 and very fast after 1990.

A reversal of the inequality trend was observed also in the East Asian economies known for having achieved in the past rapid growth with falling inequality. However, this reversal took place later and was less marked than in other regions. For instance, in South Korea earnings inequality declined steadily over three decades but rose again in the aftermath of the 1997 crisis, as full-capacity unemployment rose from 1–2 to 4–5 percent and the share of part-time and daily workers jumped from 42.5 to 52.5 percent.[18]

This brief summary suggests that the declines in income inequality observed (with some exceptions) during the Golden Age were reversed over the last two decades, as country after country experienced an upsurge in income inequality. As a result, the trend of the domestic Gini coefficients has taken a more or less pronounced U-shape, with the turn-around year placed most commonly between 1980 and 1990. It is important to note with Atkinson[19] that '... these recent changes should not be extrapolated into an inexorable rise in inequality in the future. ... the empirical evidence suggests ... that in some countries the U appears only in attenuated form ... as a bird in flight rather than a sans serif U. In other countries, ... there are signs that it [the inequality increase] reached cruising altitude.' This may imply that some of these reversals are associated with shifts in policy regimes from a Keynesian to a neoliberal stance, and that – when such shift has taken place fully – the right arm of the U stabilizes at the 'steady state inequality level' typical of the new policy regime, as observed for instance in the UK where –

after a sharp rise of 11 points over 1979–90 – the Gini coefficient of equivalized disposable income stabilized over the subsequent decade.

The conclusions of the above literature review contradicts the findings of prior research in this area that suggests that within-country inequality remained stable over 1950–1990. For instance, after fitting linear trends to 49 country data, Li, et al.[20] concluded that '... there is no evidence of a time trend in 32 countries or 65% of our sample'. Examination of the estimation procedure followed in their and similar studies suggest, however, that these conclusions are dependent on the methodology adopted. Indeed, their sample did not include most economies in transition (which experienced a universal rise in inequality), extended only up to 1991–3 (thus missing the disequalizing impact of globalization and the financial crises), its datapoints were interpolated only with linear trends (a functional form that does not permit to capture U-shaped trends) and country results were not weighted by population and GDP.

To overcome this methodological limitations, Cornia with Kiiski[21] extracted from the November 1998 version of WIDER's World Income Inequality Database (WIID) 770 'reliable observations' of Gini coefficients for 73 countries[22] accounting for 80 and 91 percent of the world population and GDP-PPP. These coefficients are derived from fully documented, comparable and representative surveys of the entire economy covering the period from the mid 1950s to 1994–5.[23] For each country, the best functional form was selected on the basis of the most significant statistics and highest R2. The results summarized in Table 5 confirm formally the conclusions reached above about the reversal of inequality trends. Indeed, inequality was found to have risen – though by different extents and with different timing – in 48 of the 73 countries analyzed, including most large economies such as China, the USA and Russia. Only in nine small and medium-sized countries (such as Honduras, Jamaica, France and Malaysia) is there evidence of a decline in inequality over time. Inequality remained constant in 16 countries including Germany, as well as in countries for which data from 1995 to 1999 show a perceptible deterioration of their inequality trend.

To take care of these recent inequality changes, we thus moved India, Indonesia, South Korea, Tanzania and the Philippines to the 'rising inequality' category of Table 5. In this way, of the 73 countries in our sample, 53 experienced a surge in income concentration over the last 20 years. Region-wise, this increase was universal in the economies in transition, almost universal in Latin America and the OECD and increasingly frequent, if less pronounced in South, South East and East Asia. In Sub Saharan Africa, the picture is mixed. The size of the observed rises in Gini coefficients varied but was substantial in many cases. Out of the 53 countries affected, the rise was of

Table 5. Trends in within-country income inequality in 73 countries, 1950s to the mid 1990s

	Sample countries in each group				Share of population of total sample countries	Share of GDP–PPP of total sample countries
	Developed	**Developing**	**Transitional**	**Total**		
Rising inequality	12	15	21	48	59	78
of which:						
U shaped	...	...	...	29	55	73
Constant inequality	2	14	0	16	36	13
Falling inequality	2	5	2	9	5	9
Total	16	34	23	73	100	100

Source: Cornia with Kiiski (2001) based on the November 1998 version of WIDER's WIID.

less than 5 Gini points in 20 cases, between 5 and 10 points in 11 nations, 10–20 points in 14 countries and more than 20 in three countries of the former Soviet Union.

4. Sources of the recent changes in inequality

As noted by Atkinson,[24] there is a remarkable consensus among scholars on both sides of the Atlantic in ascribing the recent growth of inequality to a single uniform cause, i.e. a shift of demand away from unskilled and towards skilled labour. Some, like Wood,[25] attribute such demand shift to trade with low-wage developing countries, others put more emphasis on technology. An additional argument put forward in the transitional and some developing countries focuses on the scarcity rents paid for undersupplied professionals such as bankers and other specialists and to a physiological rise in returns to education following the liberalization of the labour market. Yet, the changes in inequality trends reviewed in section 3 reflect more complex distributional shifts including:

4.1 Changes in the factoral distribution of income

Data on the size and distribution of capital incomes are limited. The few data available in income surveys are massively and increasingly underreported – especially in transitional and developing countries – as suggested by the growing discrepancy between the estimate of their share on survey data versus that obtained from national accounts, banking sources and tax returns. Despite these limitations, there is scattered but compelling evidence that the capital share has risen in several countries over the last two decades.

In the OECD countries, an indirect measure of the rise of the capital share comes from the analysis of the incomes of the top 1% of income earners. As over 60% of the their incomes is constituted by capital incomes, a sharp rise in the share of this group implies a rise in the capital share. For instance, the shift from 21 to 34% in the income share of the top 1% observed in the UK between 1979 and 2001[26] entailed an estimated rise of 8 points in the capital share.

Additional evidence about the rise of capital income comes from five country studies included in Cornia (forthcoming). In India, the share of the operating surplus in the net domestic income rose from 9.9 to 16.2% over 1988–96. In turn, in Turkey the share of interest payments on the public debt rose from close to zero in 1980 to 15.2% of GDP in 1998, a figure similar to the value-added of agriculture, a sector that employs 45% of the labour force. In Thailand the share of non-farm profits and property incomes rose from 19.5

to 24.9 between 1988 and 1996, while in oil-dominated and capital-intensive Venezuela the capital share rose from 58 in 1978 to 78% in 1996. Also in the non-oil sector, there was a transfer of 11 points from labour to capital income between the 1970s and the 1990s. Finally, in South Africa income from property rose steadily from 18% to nearly 30% between 1981 and 2000, while the labour share fell 11 points. Other analyses point in the same direction. Sainz and Calcagno,[27] for instance, indicate that between 1980 and the late 1980s, the labour share declined by 5–6 percentage points in Argentina and Chile and by ten in Mexico.

Capital incomes include profits, distributed dividends, capital gains, interests and various types of rents. A rise in the profit share may derive, for instance, from a compression of formal sector wages, the spread of informal employment[28] or a reduction in corporate taxes. Changes along these lines were repeatedly observed during the last decade. UNCTAD,[29] for instance, indicates that the profit share in industry, transport and communication rose since the middle 1970s–early 1980s in all industrialized countries. In other countries – as in Chile during the military dictatorship – the rise in the capital share was due to the relaxation of laws on workers dismissals, the limitation of trade unions powers, the suspension of wage indexation, cuts in public employment, a more restrictive application of the minimum wage legislation, the elimination of wealth and capital gains taxes and the substantial reduction of profit taxes.

The rise of interest payments on the corporate, private and public debt was also an important contributor to the rise of the capital share. Several factors affected interest payments during the last two decades, including the growth of the financial sector following financial deregulation, past policies leading to a strong debt accumulation, the IMF demand to raise interest rates in crisis countries and the trend in international interest rates. The latter were affected by factors such as the monetary stance of US (which followed a high interest rate policy over 1982–93[30]) and trends in country premiums. Last, realized capital gains emerged as a growing source of capital income, as suggested by the rapid increase in capitalization observed in the 1990s in most stock markets, including those of low income countries such as India.

Finally, an increase in the capital share may be explained by changes in norms on the accumulation and transmission of wealth via inheritance or influencing the net returns on assets. For instance, in the post World War II period many advanced countries witnessed a decline in the capital share due to high inheritance taxes while progressive taxation and inflation reduced the net returns on such assets. This trend came to a halt during the last two decades that saw a recovery in the net returns on financial assets thanks to the reduction in inflation and tax rates on top incomes while the intergenerational transmission of accumulated wealth was facilitated by the sharp reduction of inheritance taxes or, as in Italy, by their outright abolition.

4.2 Explanations of rising wage inequality not based on the human capital approach

Explanations based on the standard approach referred to above account for only part of the increases in wage differentials observed during the past twenty years. Other factors appear to have plaid a greater role. To start with, changes in social norms affected the level of both bottom and top wages. With rare exceptions, the real minimum wage and its ratio to the average wage fell in most countries of Latin America and Africa, Eastern and Central Europe and the OECD countries.[31] The latter argue for instance that in the US 30 percent of the rise in earnings concentration over the 1980-mid 1990s period was explained by a 44% fall in the minimum wage. Changes of this nature were observed on a limited scale in countries with centralized wage-setting institutions (Germany) and high minimum wages (France).

Greater wage dispersion was also due to a sharp increase in top earnings relative to the average. Atkinson (2002) shows that the ratio of the remuneration of CEOs and other top professions to the average wage rose rapidly over the last twenty years, including because of the spread of remuneration packages based on stock options. In the US, for instance the average real compensation of CEOs rose by 109 percent over 1984–99, well ahead of the increase of the average wage. Among the theories that explain such phenomenon, Atkinson cites those on executive remuneration in a hierarchical structure which show that the size of the income increment per promotion fell during the first half of the postwar period and then rose steadily between 1970 and 1999. Another explanation is based on the 'superstar theory' according to which improvements in information and communication technology have enlarged the markets and rents of those with the very highest abilities. Because of the growing concentration of demand on the superstars, the income of the second, third and n-th best performers declined and the earnings gradient became much steeper than earlier.

4.3 Changes in redistribution

Inequality in the distribution of disposable income has also been affected by policies that reduced the redistributive role of the state. Atkinson[32] notes that between 1980 and the mid-1990s the distribution of market incomes deteriorated in the six OECD countries he analyzed. While in three of them an increase in redistribution offset such impact, the other three recorded a decline in redistribution and a rise in the concentration of disposable income greater than that of market incomes. In all six countries the generosity, coverage and redistributivness of the unemployment benefit declined and the personal income tax schedule became less progressive, though in three of them a broadening of the tax base offset in part this effect.

A systematic survey of tax incidence studies conducted in the developing and transitional economies from the mid 1970s to the mid 1990s[33] comes to somewhat similar conclusions. In the 36 countries reviewed, taxation was found to be regressive only in 7 and direct taxes appeared to be progressive in 12 out of 14 studies. The survey points also to the one percentage point average drop recorded in the tax/GDP ratio between the 1980s and 1990s (as opposed to a rise by 1.6 points between the 1970s and 1980s), a decline in the importance of direct taxes in the total, a fall in overall tax progressivity and a negative effect of the latter change on inequality.

4.4 Rising spatial inequality

An often ignored aspect of aggregate inequality is regional inequality. In this regard, the divergence of average provincial incomes was a main factor in the rise in overall income inequality observed in China since 1984 (see the last three columns of Table 6). The fiscal decentralization introduced in 1978 substantially reduced the capacity of the central government to contain the divergence through transfers to poorer provinces. The industrial and export promotion policies plaid an even greater disequalizing role, as they favored the coastal over the interior and remote provinces through the granting of special administrative and economic powers, tax privileges and other benefits which facilitated the development of export industries and the inflow of foreign direct investments.

A similar story can be told for Thailand where the ratio of the regional product per capita of the Bangkok region to that of the poor North East rose from 6.1 to 9.1 from 1973 to 1992 to fall mildly to 8.5 in 1996 due to government efforts to develop the Eastern Seaboard Area. In India, with the onset of market-oriented reforms, government transfers, public investment and industrial licensing used in the past to promote a balanced regional development declined in importance, so that disparities due to differences in factor endowments and social structure were no longer kept under control.[34]

Table 6. **Evolution of the Gini coefficients and income gap in China, 1978–98**

Year	Overall Gini	Urban Gini	Rural Gini	Inter-Provincial Income gap (rural)[a]	Inter-Provincial Income gap (urban)[a]	Inter-Provincial Income gap (total)[a]
1978	0.32	0.16	0.21	...	...	...
1981	...	0.15	0.24	2.80	1.81	12.62
1984	0.28[b]	0.16	0.26	3.16[c]	1.59[c]	9.22[c]
1990	...	0.23	0.31	4.17	2.03	7.50
1995	0.43	0.28	0.34	4.82	2.34	9.79

Source: Cornia with Kiiski (2001).

Notes:
a Ratio between the average income of the highest to the lowest province, by rural, urban and total area.
b Refers to 1983.
c Refers to 1985.

5. Causes of the recent changes in inequality

What factors account for the reversal of the aggregate inequality trends illustrated in section 3 and the distributive shifts discussed in section 4? One can in principle propose three sets of explanations based on: (i) an aggravation of the traditional causes of inequality, such as high asset concentration, the urban bias of public policy, inequality in education and increasing dependence on natural resources; (ii) the distributive impact of ICT, and (iii) the impact of liberalization and globalization policies.

As for the first set of factors, Cornia with Kiiski[35] find that while these are still responsible for much of the variation in inequality across countries they are unable to explain its recent surge, with the exception of the worsening of educational achievements in Latin America in the 1980s and 1990s. Similar conclusions apply to technological change (*ibid*). Thus, with the exception of a few middle income countries, the claim that technological change is the main factor behind the inequality rises of the last two decades seems, on balance, weak. The third – and most relevant – set of explanations pivots around the impact of liberalization and globalization. Standard theory suggests that, in labour abundant countries, trade liberalization and the freeing of capital movements have an equalizing effect. The real impact of these reforms is, however, more complex than suggested by these textbook arguments. Conclusions about their impact depend on the regions analysed, the policy mixes considered and the methodology used for their evaluation. Conscious of all this, we first review the literature on the impact of the overall reform package, then examine the impact of trade and financial liberalization and of their accompanying reforms.

5.1 Impact of the overall liberalization–globalization package

There are only few multi-country studies on the distributive effect of these reforms. Behrman et al.[36] assess the impact on wage differentials of reform packages introduced in 18 Latin American countries over 1980–98. They focus on six types of economy-wide reforms, i.e. trade liberalization, capital account liberalization, domestic financial liberalization, privatization and tax and labour market reform. They found that the overall package had a significant short-term disequalizing effect on wage differentials,[37] the intensity of which, however, declined over time. The strongest disequalizing impact was due to domestic financial reform, capital account liberalization and tax reform. Trade openness had, on balance, no clear impact, possibly because its many effects cancelled each other out.

Similar evidence is provided by a review of the impact of 21 reform episodes in 18 countries during the last two decades.[38] Income inequality was found to have risen in 13 cases, remained constant in 6 and improved in two. Virtually without exception, wage differentials by skill level rose as a result of a reduction of employment in the modern sector, a rise in productivity and wage concentration by skill within the same, the reallocation of excess labour to the low-paying non-traded sector (informal trade, services and traditional agriculture) and a rise of inequality within the latter. Of the 18 countries analysed, only El Salvador and Costa Rica reduced inequality on occasion of liberalization thanks to a surge in the employment of unskilled workers in the export sector.

Cornia with Kiiski[39] regressed the changes in income inequality over 1980–1995 in 32 developing and transitional economies on the intensity of their liberalization policies (proxied by a synthetic reform index); the initial value of the Gini coefficient, as even sharp reforms are likely to affect equity less where inequality is already high; a dummy variable for the countries of the former Soviet Union where weak institutions and the low quality of policy heightened the impact of liberalization; and a dummy variable for Latin America where the pervasive effect of financial liberalization is not adequately captured by the overall reform index. The regression results confirmed the disequalizing effect of the overall package which was however less discernible in countries with high initial inequality. A *ceteris paribus* simulation shows that in a country with an initial Gini coefficient of 0.35, a shift of the liberalization index from 'no reform' to 'medium intensity reforms' raises the Gini coefficient by 3 points while a shift to 'strong liberalization' raises it by 5.5 Gini points, with stronger effects in the former Soviet Union and Latin America.

In a careful study of the poverty impact of IMF-World Bank programs, Easterly[40] found that these moderated the rise of poverty during output contractions, possibly because of the cushioning effects of adjustment-related 'social safety nets'. But he also found that, during spells of economic expansion, these programs reduced the poverty alleviation elasticity of growth relative to 'home-grown' programs. For instance, in China – a country with medium inequality and no Fund-Bank program – poverty incidence fell over 1990–2 by 3.8% for every point of GDP growth, while in 1995–6 Colombia – a country with high inequality and a Fund-Bank adjustment loan – experienced zero poverty reduction for every point of GDP growth (Table 7). This suggests that Fund-Bank programs worsened the income distribution, at least the part of it near the poverty line.

These reduced-form analyses do not permit to arrive to firm conclusions about the inequality impact of the policy reforms inspired by the Washington Consensus, not least because they are unable to trace the key structural linkages between liberalization, globalization and inequality. More work is also needed to refine the indexes of the extent and quality of specific reforms, capture the interaction between policy measures part of the same package, identify their mutually offsetting effects and analyze the time profile of the inequality rise. Yet, these results do not permit to reject the view that there is no association between mainstream reforms and distributional worsening.

Table 7. Poverty elasticity of growth for different Gini coefficients and IMF–World Bank adjustment loans per year

Gini coefficient	Average number of IMF–World Bank adjustment loans per year during survey spell		
	0	0.5	1.0
30	-3.8	-2.7	-1.7
45	-2.9	-1.9	-0.9
60	-2.1	-1.0	0.0

Source: Easterly (2001), Table 3

5.2 *Trade liberalization*

Standard theory argues that trade liberalization improves between-country inequality, within-country inequality in poor countries and, by implication, global inequality. Some empirical analyses for the 1960s and 1970s (as Wood's seminal 1994 book) have confirmed these predictions. Yet, over the subsequent two decades trade liberalization raised wage inequality in a broad range of countries including the East Asian exporters of manufactures and most Latin American and Eastern European countries.

To explain this contradiction, the 'skill-enhancing trade hypothesis' suggests that trade liberalization facilitates the imports by developing countries of world class investments whose capital-intensive technology raises the demand of skilled rather than unskilled labour. A second explanation argues that the comparative advantages of a country may be valid within a given 'cone of diversification' but not in a global sense, so that the success of its trade liberalization depends on 'third party effects' i.e. the decision of countries with even more favourable labour endowements to enter the world market. Because of this, the formal sector of middle income countries no longer has a comparative advantage in labour-intensive exports and either it informalizes its production or shifts it towards skill-intensive exports. Third, both static and dynamic gains from trade are elusive in countries specializing in the export of primary commodities. This sector is subject to considerable price shocks due to global demand effects as well as because of the increase in the number of suppliers entering a stagnant market. Birdsall and Hamoudi[41] show that in most commodity producing countries such price shocks reduced the trade/GDP ratio, as well as employment and earnings in the import substituting sector, without enjoying a corresponding income rise in the export sector. Finally, in low-tech exporters, trade liberalisation has led to unsatisfactory export growth because of the weak domestic conditions of these countries and persistent protectionism in the OECD nations. In a recent review of protectionist tendencies in Northern countries, Slaughter[42] concludes that current trade barriers in the North cost Southern countries billions of dollars annually.

5.3 *Domestic and international financial deregulation*

The domestic financial liberalization of the 1980s was to lead to financial deepening and the creation of bond and stock markets. But it was instead characterized by inadequate bank supervision, a sizeable rise in interest rates and growing bank failures. The distributive impact of such effects is difficult to capture but the data are suggestive of a negative impact. Indeed, these policy changes, together with the 1982 rise in US interest rates and the IMF policy of demanding large increases in interest rates in countries facing crises, fuelled a worldwide rise in real interest rates in the 1980s. Financial deregulation thus led to an increase in the return on financial assets, a rise in the share of GDP accruing to capital incomes and the redistribution via the budget of labor income to holders of state bonds.

The reform of the domestic sector was followed in the early 1990s by the liberalisation of cross border movements of foreign direct investments, bank loans and portfolio investments. With rare exceptions, the liberalization of portfolio flows generated a negative social impact. This was in part due to the 'disciplining' structural effect such measure had on the decisions of governments in the field of taxation and redistribution and on the demands of organized labour, and partly due to the real appreciation of the exchange rate which shifted resources to the non-tradable sector while encouraging subcontracting and wage cuts in the tradable sector to preserve profit margins.[43] The impact on inequality was also mediated by the tendency of capital account liberalization to increase the frequency of destabilizing financial crises. Left to themselves, deregulated financial systems cannot perform well owing to problems of incomplete information, markets and contracts, herd behavior, panics, weak supervision and speculation on asset prices.

The distributional impact of financial crises has been particularly negative in countries with weak labor institutions and social safety nets, as underscored by Galbraith and Lu[44] who found that in Latin America and Asia financial crises raised inequality in 73 and 62 percent of the time while no impact was evident in Finland and Spain. Diwan[45] arrived at similar conclusions. On the basis of panel data he found that the labor share contracted markedly and permanently in the wake of financial crises while in a subsequent paper, he showed that capital account restrictions help maintain the labour share once financial crises occur.[46]

5.4 Domestic 'complementary policy changes' preceding globalization

External liberalization was generally preceded by domestic policy changes that – regardless of their inherent merits– were inspired by the desire to attract foreign investors. Labour markets were liberalized by relaxing norms on workers dismissal, safety at work, minimum wages, social security contributions and collective bargaining. Likewise, policies on corporate taxation, infrastructural development and privatization were influenced by the desire to attract foreign investors seeking low-tax locations endowed with adequate facilities. The distributive impact of these 'complementary policies' is seldom factored in the assessment of the impact of open-door policies.

The liberalization of the labour market, for instance, is likely to generate a rise in both employment and wage dispersion. The net distributive effect depends on the relative significance of the 'wage inequality' and 'employment-creation' effects as well as on the evolving importance of the informal sector. Outside East Asia and China, the experience of last twenty years points to a dominance of the negative effects over the favorable ones (see section 4). In turn, during the last two decades tax systems moved away from taxes on corporations and trade and towards indirect taxes, while the progressivity of wealth and direct tax rates was reduced though greater accent was placed on eliminating exemptions and improving collection. The net impact of these reforms has varied from country to country but the general trend is towards lower tax progressivity. In reviewing the impact of tax changes in Latin America, for instance, Morley[47] notes that the effect of these changes were to shift the burden of taxation away from the wealthy and towards the middle and lower classes.

Finally, privatization – that was most common in Latin America and Eastern Europe – has had a mixed impact. Privatization of agriculture has often generated a favourable impact, as in the case of the dismembering of the communes land in China and state farms in Armenia and Romania. Privatization of large industrial assets proved more complex and inequality often rose as institutional reforms in the field of anti-monopoly legislation, competition policy and regulation of privatized utilities lagged behind. The worst outcomes were observed in the economies in transition where insider privatization led to rapid concentration of assets in the hands of a small élite of former managers of state enterprises. In Latin America, the acquisition of privatized utilities by multinational firms worsened equity through the low price paid for the assets purchased, the high service prices charged by the privatized utilities, the employment cuts following restructuring and the limited capacity of local regulators to control large transitional corporations. Morley[48] suggests that privatization of utilities in Latin America hurt mainly the middle class.

6. Conclusions

During the last two decades, global inequality continued growing though much less rapidly than before. Meanwhile within-country inequality rose in two thirds of the 73 countries reviewed in this chapter. This finding contradicts the viewpoint dominating the literature which claims that within-country inequality remained stable over the post World War II period.

There are three possible explanations for this widespread rise in within-country inequality. First, contrary to the experience of the first globalization, limited migration to the advanced nations – the main source of convergence last century – did not help equalising the distribution of income in the countries of origin. Second, international financial flows have become more unstable and disequalizing than a century ago. And third, within-country inequality was influenced by domestic policy reforms – such as those concerning the labour market, financial sector and tax system – which were introduced to facilitate the international integration of poor countries but which often caused adverse effects on the labour share and wage distribution.

Of the six components of the liberal package, capital account liberalization appears to have had the strongest impact on within-country inequality, followed by domestic financial liberalization, labor market deregulation and tax reform. Privatization of state land was found to improve equity and growth in many cases while that of industrial assets and utilities was associated with rising inequality. Trade liberalization appears to have been equalizing in East Asia in the 1960s and 1970s, in a few small countries and – at the margin – in China and Vietnam, but not in the large Latin American countries, Eastern Europe and most of Africa.

The above conclusions on the adverse distributive effects of liberalization and globalization do not entail their wholesale rejection or the abandonment of the objective of balanced economic integration. But they signal that their premature, poorly-sequenced and unselective implementation under weak institutional and incomplete market conditions can lead to negative distributive results. Unless the orthodox paradigm corrects these flaws and evolves in a distributionally favourable manner, in several countries high inequality might in the years ahead depress growth, reduce its poverty alleviation elasticity and prevent the achievement of the poverty alleviation targets to which the world community is now firmly committed.

Notes

1 See the literature review by Aghion et al. 1999.
2 UNCTAD 1997.
3 UNDP 1999.
4 e.g. Schultz 1998.
5 Dowrick and Akmal 2001.
6 In the PPP conversion method, the many services consumed by people in low-income countries are assigned US prices (which are much higher than those in developing countries). But, in developing countries, these services are consumed not because consumers are rich but because their local price is low. The GDP/c level obtained through the PPP method is thus inconsistent with the observed consumption structure and causes an artificial substitution in the consumption structure of low-income people.
7 The decline in inequality over time does not follow from differences between market and PPP exchange rates. The authors attribute it to the fact that country price struc-

tures between developing countries and the USA have become less and less similar over the last twenty years or so.

8 Korzeniewicz and Moran 1997.

9 Schultz 1998.

10 Several analysts suggest that the Chinese growth over the 1990s has been overstated and that a growth rate of 5–6% a year is closer to reality than the 8–10% indicated by the official statistics (Wade 2002).

11 Bourguignon and Morisson 2002.

12 Sala-i-Martin 2002.

13 Milanovic 2000.

14 Conclusions about the level of and changes in global inequality depend on the statistical conventions adopted for its measurement and, in particular, on whether the comparisons:

- are carried out on the basis of GDP-GNP/capita (that is derived from the National Accounts) or disposable income per capita (that is derived from Household Income and Expenditure Surveys). The two concepts differ considerably. While both include imputations for incomes in kind, GNP/c also comprises undistributed profits and operating surpluses, the depreciation of capital stock, changes in inventories and public expenditure. As a result, estimates of income/c based on GDP/c are always substantially bigger (up to a factor of 3) than survey-based estimates. Thus estimates of global inequality are always much bigger (by up to 15 Gini points) when they are derived from GDP/c data. Finally, the ratio of income/c to GDP/c declines with the increase in GDP/c. Differences over time in inequality estimates based on the two concepts are thus not constant;

- make use of market exchange rates or of Purchasing Power Parity (PPP) exchange rates. It is well known that PPP exchange rates are higher. Thus, conversion of national incomes into US dollars by means of PPP exchange rates leads to a lower estimate of the income gap between developed and developing countries and to lower estimates of global inequality. However, doubts are being raised on the precision of the methodology used in the choice of the 'common basket' of goods and services (too biased towards that of Western countries) for the comparison of price levels across countries, and on the data used for the computation of the Chinese and Indian price levels, as China did not participate in two price surveys organized by the PPP project and India took part only in one;

- on whether international comparisons of GDP/c or income/c take into account the different population size of the countries compared with each other;

- implicitly assume that all citizens of one nation have the same income per capita or use synthetic statistics of the distribution of income (such as the Gini or Theil coefficients), or micro-data depicting in detail the distribution of income/c. The use of synthetic statistics of inequality is common in studies of global income inequality. But this approach does not provide a good approximation of the real distribution of household incomes/c. Indeed, the Gini coefficients are seldom computed on the basis of random samples or account for differences in household composition. In addition, they often rely on expenditure or consumption data, rather than income data, with the result that the shape of the income distribution and overall inequality are being artificially compressed. Evidence suggests that, survey-based Gini coefficients systematically understate the extent of inequality of the distribution of individual incomes in most countries;

- treat large 'highly dualistic' countries such as China and India as a single nation, two separate sub-nations (each comprised of the urban and the rural sector) or as multiple regions (as, for instance, in the case of China which is often separated in this kind of studies into its Inner, Middle and Coastal areas, i.e. regions that have grown at very different rates. Treating these different segments of a large economy as separate entities increases between-country inequality.

15 Wade 2002, p. 23.
16 See Cornia and Kiiski 2001 for more details.
17 Altimir 1996; Székely and Hilgert 1999.
18 KLSI 2001.
19 Atkinson 2002, p.25.
20 Li et al. 1998, p.35.
21 Cornia with Kiiski 2001.
22 Of these 73 countries 34 are developing, 23 transitional economies and 16 from the OECD. Except for Africa, these countries account for 84 to 98 percent of the population and 82 to 98 percent of the GDP–PPP of these regions. For Africa, the six countries included in the analysis account for 18 and 32 percent of the total population and GDP–PPP.
23 See Cornia and Kiiski 2001 for the related statistical information.
24 Atkinson 2002.
25 Wood 1994.
26 Atkinson 2002, Figure 11.
27 Sainz and Calcagno 1992.
28 Taylor (2001) illustrates vividly on the basis of the analysis of 18 developing countries the informalisation of the labour market and other cost-cutting measures introduced on occasion of the appreciation of the exchange rate driven by a surge in capital inflows.
29 UNCTAD 1997.
30 During this period, the real interest rate on dollar assets oscillated around 6%, well above of the secular value of 2–2.5%.
31 Cornia, forthcoming; Cornia 1996; Gottschalk and Smeeding 1997.
32 Atkinson 2003.
33 Chu et al. 2003.
34 Cornia, forthcoming.
35 Cornia with Kiiski 2001.
36 Behrmann et al. 2000.
37 However, a similar review of the impact of policy reform in Latin America during the same period, Morley (2000) arrives to somewhat contradictory conclusions.
38 Taylor 2000.
39 Cornia with Kiiski 2001.
40 Easterly 2001.
41 Birdsall and Hamoudi 2002.
42 Slaughter 2000
43 Taylor 2000.
44 Galbraith and Lu 1999.
45 Diwan 1999.
46 Diwan 2000.
47 Morley 2000.
48 Morley 2000.

References

Aghion, Philippe, Eve Caroli and Cecilia Garcia-Penalosa, 1999, 'Inequality and Economic Growth: The Perspective of the New Growth Theories', *Journal of Economic Literature*, vol. XXXVII (December 1999), 1615–1660.

Altimir, Oscar, 1996, 'Economic Development and Social Equity', *Journal of Interamerican Studies and World Affairs*, Summer/Fall 1996.

Atkinson, Anthony, 2002, '*Income inequality in OECD Countries: Data and Explanations*' paper presented at the CESifo Conference 'Globalisation, Inequality and Well-being', Munich 8–9 November 2002.

——, (2003), '*Increased Income inequality in OECD Countries and the Redistributive Impact of the Government Budget*' in Cornia Giovanni Andrea, ed., 'Inequality, Growth and Poverty in an Era of Liberalisation and Globalisation', forthcoming in 2003.

Behrman, J, Nancy Birdsall and Miguel Székely, 2000, 'Economic Reform, and Wage Differentials in Latin America', *Working Paper of the Research Department* no. 435, Inter-American Development Bank, Washington, DC.

Birdsall, Nancy and Amar Hamoudi, 2002, 'Commodity Dependence, Trade and Growth: When 'openness' is not enough', *Working Paper Number 7*, Centre for Global Development, Washington DC.

Bourguignon, Francois and Christian Morisson, 2002, 'Inequality among World Citizens' *American Economic Review,* vol. 92, no. 4.

Chu, Ke-young, Hamid Davoodi, and Sanjeev Gupta, 2003, '*Income Distribution And Tax and Government Social Spending Policies in Developing Countries*' in Cornia Giovanni Andrea, ed., 'Inequality, Growth and Poverty in an Era of Liberalisation and Globalisation', forthcoming in 2003.

Cornia, Giovanni Andrea, 1996, 'Transition and Income Distribution: Theory, Evidence and Initial Interpretation', *WIDER Research in Progress*, no.1, UNU/WIDER, Helsinki.

Cornia, Giovanni Andrea with Sampsa Kiiski, 2001, 'Trends in Income Distribution in the Post World War II Period: Evidence and Interpretation', *UNU/WIDER Discussion Papers*, UNU/WIDER, Helsinki, Finland.

Cornia Giovanni Andrea, forthcoming, 'Inequality, Growth and Poverty in an Era of Liberalisation and Globalisation'.

Diwan, Ishac, 1999, 'Labour Shares and Financial Crises'. Preliminary draft. The World Bank, Washington, DC.

——, 2000, 'Labour Shares and Globalisation'. paper presented at the Conference on Poverty and Inequality in Developing Countries: A Policy Dialogue on the Effects of Globalisation, 30 November–1 December 2000, OECD Development Centre, Paris.

Dowrick, Steve and Muhammad Akmal, 2001, 'Contradictory Trends in Global Income Inequality: a Tale of Two Biases', http://ecocomm.anu.edu.au/economics/staff/dowrick/worl-ineq.pdf.

Easterly, William, 2001, 'The Effect of IMF and World Bank Programs on Poverty', paper prepared for the WIDER Development Conference 'Growth and Poverty' 25–26 May 2001, Helsinki.

Galbraith James and Lu Jiaqing, 1999, 'Inequality and Financial Crises: Some early Findings' *UTIP Working Paper* Number 9, LBJ School of Public Affairs, The University of Texas at Austin.

Gottshalck, Peter and Timothy Smeeding, 1997, 'Cross-National Comparison of Earnings and Income Inequality', *Journal of Economic Literature,* June.

Korzeniewick, Roberto and Timothy Moran, (1997), 'World-Economic Trends in the Distribution of Income, 1965–1992', *American Journal of Sociology*, vol.102: 1000–39.

Li, Honhyi, Lyn Squire, and Heng-fu Zou, (1998), 'Explaining International and Intertemporal Variations in Income Inequality', *Economic Journal*, Vol. 108 No. 446.

Milanovic, Branko, (2000), 'The true world income distribution, 1988 and 1993: First calculations based on household surveys alone', mimeo (November 2000), The World Bank, Washington DC.

Morley, Samuel, (2000), 'Distribution and Growth in Latin America in an Era of Structural Reform', paper presented at the Conference on Poverty and Inequality in Developing Countries: A Policy Dialogue on the Effects of Globalisation, 30 November–1 December 2000, OECD Development Centre, Paris.

Sainz, Pedro and Alfredo Calcagno, (1992), 'Em Busca de Otra Modalidad de Desarrollo', *CEPAL Review*, No. 48, December.

Sala-i-Martin, Xavier, (2002), 'The Disturbing 'Rise' of Global Income Inequality', *NBER Working Paper Series* 8904, National Bureau of Economic Research, Cambridge, MA.

Schultz, T. Paul, (1998), ' Inequality in the distribution of personal income in the world: how it is changing and why', *Journal of Population Economics*, 1998: 307–344.

Slaughter, Matthew, (2000), 'Protectionist Tendencies in the North and Vulnerable Economies in the South' *WIDER Working Paper Series*, No.196, September, UNU/WIDER, Helsinki.

Székely, Miguel and Marianne Hilgert, (1999), 'The 1990s in Latin America: Another Decade of Persistent Inequality', Working Paper 410, Research Department of the Inter-American Development Bank, Washington, DC.

Taylor, Lance, (2000), 'External Liberalisation, Economic Performance and Distribution in Latin America and Elesewhere', *UNU/WIDER Working Paper* N. 215, World Institute for Development Economics Research, Helsinki.

UNCTAD, (1997), '*Trade and Development Report*', United Nations, Geneva.

UNDP, (1999), '*Human Development Report*', Oxford University Press, Oxford.

Wade, Robert, (2002),'Globalization, Poverty and Inequality, paper presented at the CESifo Conference 'Globalisation, Inequality and Well-being', Munich 8–9 November 2002.

Wood, Adrian, (1994), *North-South Trade, Employment and Inequality*, Clarendon Press, Oxford, United Kingdom.

20

INCREASING POVERTY IN A GLOBALIZED WORLD: *MARSHALL PLANS* AND *MORGENTHAU PLANS* AS MECHANISMS OF POLARIZATION OF WORLD INCOMES

Erik S Reinert

1. The Problem: Marshall Plans & Morgenthau Plans

During the 1990s, a majority of the world's nations experienced falling real wages. In many cases real wages declined both rapidly and considerably; a human crisis of large proportions is evolving in some former communist countries, while in most Latin American countries real wages peaked sometime in the late 1970s or early 1980s, and since then have fallen. The term 'state' is hardly applicable to several African countries, and this problem of 'failed states' is growing. In these nations many institutions, such as educational systems, that used to be handled by the nation state, have broken down, and different areas of what used to comprise a nation are ruled over by different warlords. This is a type of political structure that a few years ago was thought of as belonging to a mediaeval past. If there is something called 'progress' and 'modernization', globalization has – particularly for many small and medium-size nations – brought with it the opposite: many are experiencing 'retrogression' and 'primitivization'. Poverty and disease increase sharply in Sub Saharan Africa, and a creeping 'Africanization' in parts of Latin America can be detected.[1]

These events profoundly challenge the present world economic order and the standard textbook economics on which this order rests. This is because the increasingly globalized economy seems to produce opposite effects of what standard economic theory predicts. Instead of a convergence of world income (towards factor-price equalization), we find that a group of rich nations show a tendency to converge, while another convergence group of poor countries gathers at the bottom of the scale. Mainstream logic is that the more backward a nation, the easier it will be to catch up to some imaginary 'frontier'. In effect, what is actually happening is very different: Nations specialize. Some nations specialize in producing continuous flows of innovations that raise their real wages ('innovation rents'), whereas other nations specialize either in economic activities where there is very little or no technological change (*maquila*-type activities), or where technological change takes the form of process innovations (in which technical change is taken out in the form of lower prices to the consumer rather than in higher wages to the workers, who are typically unskilled – particularly in the area of raw material production).[2] We claim that economy-wide differences in wage levels originate in these specialization patterns in key areas of production, and that – as in standard trade theory – free trade reinforces the pattern of specialization: based on these innovation rents some nations specialize in being rich, others specialise in being poor. We shall return to this discussion in more detail later.

The World Bank estimates that a bus driver in Germany enjoys a standard of living 13 times higher than a bus driver in Kenya.[3] In other words, the world market rewards people with exactly the same productivity very differently. The purpose of this paper is to explain the mechanisms and the economic policies that created this type of gap in the living standard of workers in the non-tradeable service sector. This sector, which includes most of the government sector – jobs that are all subject to a natural and total protection from international competition – provides the majority of jobs in most developed nations. Whereas increasing population pressures in an agricultural sector subject to diminishing returns were the causes of historical mass migrations,[4] a main factor behind modern mass migrations are these enormous differences in living standards between people who are essentially equally efficient.

In this paper we shall outline a theory that explains the economic forces which have produced the enormous wage differentials between people with the same level of productivity in different countries. This alternative theory of wealth and poverty – The Other Canon Theory – differs fundamentally from mainstream economic theory. The Other Canon constituted the toolkit of the pre-Smithian mainstream around 1750, and has also been the basis of the economic strategies that have catapulted laggard countries from relative poverty to relative wealth, from fifteenth-century England, to Korea in the period 1960–80 and Ireland between 1980 and 2000.[5]

For practical purposes we have established two ideal types of economic policies. We have named economic policies that create the vortices of, respectively, wealth and poverty after two types of economic strategies that were developed and – like the atomic bomb – tried out in the field in the 1940s: Marshall Plans and Morgenthau Plans. We shall claim that virtual virtuous circles of development are the result of a set of policies that we refer to generically as Marshall Plans. The opposite effect, vicious circles, is the result of Morgenthau Plans.

The purpose of the Morgenthau Plan – named after Henry Morgenthau Jr., the US Secretary of the Treasury from 1934 to 1945 – was to prevent Germany, which had caused two wars in the twentieth century, from ever starting a war again.[6] This was to be achieved by de-industrializing Germany: taking all industrial machinery out of the country and filling the mines with water, thereby turning it into a pastoral state. The plan was approved in an Allied meeting in 1943 and carried out after the German capitulation in May 1945.

The Morgenthau Plan was abruptly stopped in Germany in 1947 when ex-President Herbert Hoover of the United States reported back from Germany: 'There is the illusion that the New Germany left after the annexations can be reduced to a 'pastoral state'. It cannot be done unless we exterminate or move 25.000.000 out of it'.[7] Hoover had rediscovered the wisdom of the mercantilist population theorists: an industrialized nation has a much larger carrying capacity in terms of population than an agricultural state.[8] The deindustrialization process had also led to a sharp fall in agricultural yields and partly to an institutional collapse, providing evidence of the importance of the linkages between the industrial and agricultural sector that were also a hallmark of mercantilist economics.[9] Less than four months after Hoover's alarming reports from Germany, the US government announced the Marshall Plan, which aimed to achieve exactly the opposite of the Morgenthau Plan: Germany's industrial capacity was at all cost to be brought back to its 1938 level. It cannot be emphasized enough that the Marshall Plan was not a financial plan, it was a *reindustrialization plan*.

We shall claim that Morgenthau Plans, after years of neglect, were resurrected by the Washington Consensus starting in the 1980s and, even more strongly, after the end of the Cold War in 1991. De facto Morgenthau Plans came with the label of 'structural adjustment', which very often had the effect of de-industrializing Third World nations.[10] These two ideal types of economic policy, the Marshall Plan and the Morgenthau Plan, explain the 'virtuous' and 'vicious' circles that were fashionable, but not well explained, in the heyday of development economics during the 1950s and 1960s.[11]

This paper can only outline what Schumpeter calls a Vision.[12] Schumpeter describes Vision as a 'preanalytic cognitive act' that supplies the raw material for the analytical effort, which in the case of this theory took place in the late

1970s and was expressed in my 1980 PhD thesis.[13] This particular vision developed from a profound conviction that the sources of uneven economic development had fundamentally to be found in the realm of production rather than in the neoclassical realm of barter, trade and finance. In several articles in the 1990s, I have elaborated on the same basic understanding of the evolution of wealth and poverty.

For nearly 500 years, from the late 1400s to the 1960s, it was common knowledge that a nation with an inefficient manufacturing sector would have a higher standard of living than a nation with no manufacturing sector at all. Such was the common sense behind the reconstruction of Europe after World War II. Everyone knew that world free trade in 1945, because of the superiority of the United States, would have meant a virtual deindustrialization of Europe. Free trade was only a goal that was to be introduced after Europe had been solidly reindustrialized. The essence of the Marshall Plan was to bring back Europe's industrial production – including Germany's – to the pre-war level. Around 1750 it was generally understood that colonialism was in effect what we call a Morgenthau Plan; it was only with the appearance of barter-based economic theory – with Adam Smith and David Ricardo – that colonialism ceased to be understood as a system of poverty creation.

The contrast between the 1950s and the 1990s in terms of economic understanding is abysmal. Many Third World countries were subjected to a de facto Morgenthau Plan – a deindustrialisation – in the 1990s.[14] This is because the economics profession by 1990 – having lost all sense of historical perspective – had come to believe in the Cold War propaganda version of neoclassical economics, a theory in which the market produces automatic harmony. We shall argue that understanding uneven development requires an understanding of imperfect competition, and that the mercantilist policies that laid the foundations for Europe's wealth did indeed have a developed understanding of the same type of mechanisms which created wealth and fame for Boston Consulting Group starting in the 1970s. We shall return to this argument later.

2. The two conflicting theories of globalization

It is generally not remembered that two Nobel laureates in economics have provided two largely conflicting theories of what will happen to world income under globalization.

1. Based on the standard assumptions of neoclassical economic theory, US economist Paul Samuelson 'proved' mathematically that unhindered international trade will produce 'factor-price equalization', i.e. that the

prices paid to the factors of production – capital and labour – will tend to be the same all over the world.[15]

2. Based in an alternative tradition – which we broadly have labelled The Other Canon – Swedish economist Gunnar Myrdal was of the opinion that world trade would tend to increase already existing differences in incomes between rich and poor nations.[16]

The economic policies of the Washington Consensus – the basis for the economic policies imposed by The World Bank and the International Monetary Fund – are exclusively built on the type of theory which is represented by Paul Samuelson. The developments of the 1990s are in sharp conflict with Samuelson's type of theory, but confirm Myrdal's assertion: the rich nations as a group seem to converge into a cluster of wealthy countries, while the poor seem to converge towards poverty, with the gap between the two groups getting wider. Paul Samuelson's theory appears to explain what goes on inside the group of rich nations, while Gunnar Myrdal's theory seems to be able to explain the development of relative wealth between the group of rich nations and the group of poor nations. Samuelson's theory is not harmful to nations which already have established a comparative advantage in increasing returns, or rather in Schumpeterian activities. It is, however, extremely harmful to those nations that have not passed the mandatory passage point of a conscious industrialization policy.

The kind of theory that Myrdal proposes – a type of institutional economic theory that we call The Other Canon – is today almost extinct: it either exists only in fragments or in a perverted form tied to neoclassical economics as 'New Institutional Economics'. In its original form, it is rarely taught in the economics departments in today's leading universities. The economics profession as a group is therefore very reluctant to see that, when it comes to the relationship between rich and poor countries, Myrdal might be right instead of Samuelson.

Seeing only the broad outlines of world development, Samuelson's type of theory can claim a certain degree of success in predicting the developments *within* each group of nations. The rich nations seem to tend towards being more equally rich, while the poor seem to converge towards being equally poor. A result of this is that the 'medium-rich' – or middle income – nations are disappearing, and the two convergence groups, rich and poor, stand out as isolated clusters in a scatter diagram. Myrdal's prediction is definitely correct when it comes to the relationship between rich and poor countries since 1990. We shall argue that the poverty of the Second and Third Worlds was an outcome of a Morgenthau Plan rather than a Marshall Plan.

3. The mechanisms at work

> A paradigm can, for that matter, even insulate the community from
> those socially important problems that are not reducible to the puzzle
> form, because they cannot be stated in terms of the conceptual and
> instrumental tools the paradigm supplies.[17]
>
> Thomas Kuhn, *The Structure of Scientific Revolutions.*

3.1 The absence of taxonomies and categories prevents us from seeing the causes of wealth and poverty

We would assert that the type of theory represented by Paul Samuelson fails
to account for the increasing miseries of the 1990s, in essence because this
standard economic theory does not involve any theory of economic development other than that of adding capital to labour. In standard economic
theory, all inputs – human beings and economic activities – are seen as being
qualitatively identical and equally fit as carriers of economic growth. In this
standard theory Man's wit and will, Man as a spiritual being, is also largely
absent. Not surprisingly, a theory in which all inputs are qualitatively alike, all
outcomes are also qualitatively alike. In other words, this is a type of theory
which can only produce theoretical outcomes where all factors are as they
were when they entered into the model, i.e. perfectly identical. 'Factor-price
equalization' – the prediction that in a globalized economy all wage-earners
will tend to have the same wages – is therefore the only possible outcome of
standard economic theory: the conclusions about equality are already built
into the assumptions that everything is equal.

On this basis Thomas Kuhn – in what is the most-quoted scientific book –
is right when he explains how scientific paradigms may insulate the community from burning social problems such as the increasing poverty of the poor
during the 1990s. The problem at hand is – as Kuhn says – not reducible to
the 'language' of standard economic theory. For this reason the standard
reply of the economics profession to the dramatically diminishing standards of
living in many countries is 'more of the same'. Their type of theory does not
contain the elements that can explain why economic development is, by its
very nature, an uneven process. In this paper we shall attempt to explain the
developments of the 1990s in a 'common sense' language, that of the nearly
defunct Other Canon theory of economics.

Picking up on Kuhn's point, it should be emphasized that standard economics is not a taxonomic science; the theory of the Washington Consensus is
void of any possibility to observe and classify the differences in conditions that
ultimately cause the differences in wealth. 'One must first observe differences
in order to observe attributes', says Rousseau.[18] Its inability to observe such

differences makes standard economics a theory that can only explain even economic growth.

An important explanation as to why the mainstream paradigm insulates the community from the problems created by globalization is the loss of the role of production in economic development. The roots to inequality of wealth are to be found in the realm of production. This loss of production is certainly one of the unfortunate legacies of Adam Smith, who makes no distinction between *commerce* and *industry*. Smith assimilates the process of production to that of exchange, and labour time becomes the common measuring rod of both.[19] In this way economics becomes what Lionel Robins calls a *Harmonielehre*, a system that, if left to itself, creates a system of economic harmony.

During the twentieth century this weakness was exasperated, and economic theory came to lose the very cause of twentieth century wealth: industrialism. Swedish institutional economist Johan Åkerman explains these mechanisms well:

> Capitalism, property rights, income distribution came to be considered the essential features, whereas the core contents of industrialism – technological change, mechanisation, mass production and its economic and social consequences – partly were pushed aside. The reasons for this development are probably found in the following three elements: *Firstly*, Ricardian economic theory … became a theory of 'natural' relations, established once and for all, between economic concepts (price, interest, capital, etc). *Secondly*, the periodic economic crises are important in this respect because the immediate causes of the crises could be found in the monetary sphere. Technological change, the primary source creating growth and transforming society, disappeared behind the theoretical connections which were made between monetary policy and economic fluctuation. *Thirdly*, and most importantly, Marx and his doctrine could capitalise on the discontent of the industrial proletariat. His teachings gave hope of a natural law which led towards the 'final struggle', when the pyramid of income distribution would be turned on its head, the lower classes should be the powerful and mighty. In this ongoing process the technological change came to be considered only as one of the pre-conditions for class struggle.[20]

3.1 Which factors cause economic development?

Austrian Harvard economist Joseph Alois Schumpeter once criticized 'the pedestrian view that it is capital per se that propels the capitalist engine'.[21]

This is indeed the basic mechanism by which standard economic theory sees economic development happening: the addition of more capital to each worker.

We would claim that this perception is fundamentally wrong. Rather, economic development is caused by new ideas and new knowledge, which produce investment opportunities and therefore create a demand for capital to invest. In this view what the Third World lacks is not capital, but investment opportunities that lead to innovations, projects in which capital may be profitably invested. For this reason, among others, we observe capital flight from the poor countries to the rich. By attempting to provide capital for the Third World without creating profitable investment opportunities, we are treating the symptoms of economic development – the lack of capital – instead of its real cause: the lack of certain types of economic activities from which growth and structural change emanate.

Two important fifteenth-century inventions made it possible to increase the supply of investment opportunities: patents and protection. These two features – one so much loved and the other so much hated by present United States trade policy – were brainchildren of the same qualitative understanding of human progress. The first patents were created in Venice in the late 1400s and enabled people to make a living by generating new ideas. When ideas could no longer be immediately copied, investment in new ideas became profitable and a continuous supply of new and steep learning curves became what we now call economic development. In order for these new activities – these productivity explosions and learning curves (see sections 3.2 and 3.3) – to spread to other nations and other labour markets, protective tariffs were created in order to make profitable the introduction of new activities in more backward nations. The protective system prevented economic development from becoming a game where the winner – the first inventing country – could take all.[22] Patents vastly increased what Carlota Perez calls 'windows of opportunity' for profitable investments, and protection made it possible for laggard nations to catch on to the steep learning curves in the industries where technological change was focused. The origins of path-dependent trajectories of economic development are to be found in these early policies. These policies were all products of an administrative tradition based on civic humanism.

3.2 The productivity explosions

To use Nathan Rosenberg's term, technical change and human learning is – at any point in time – 'focused' in certain business areas.[23] A nation with a strong concentration in the economic activities that experience high growth will experience a 'catapult effect' in real wages.

Figure 1. **An early productivity explosion: the mechanization of cotton spinning in the first paradigm**

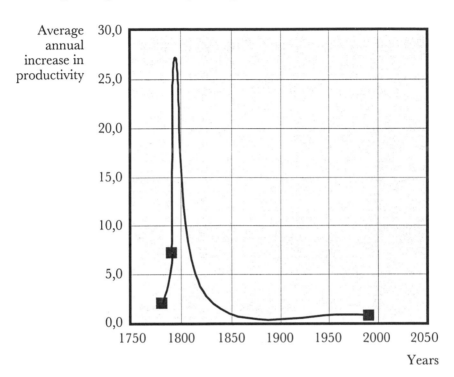

Average annual increase in productivity

Years

Source: Carlota Perez, Calculations from Jenkins 1994

Figure 1 shows the first 'productivity explosion' of the first industrial revolution. In the late eighteenth century, about the time when Adam Smith was writing his *Wealth of Nations,* the productivity of cotton spinning was increasing at an incredible speed in English manufacturing industry, reaching levels of increase up to more than 25% per year.

At that time – in fact since the late fifteenth century – all European nations based their economic policy on the fact that the production from such 'leading sectors' had to take place inside the borders of every nation. From the time of Henry VII's accession to the throne of England, in 1485, the synergies observed between these 'leading sectors' and the rest of the economy (see section 3.3) were accepted wisdom in all nations. In fact, the essential difference between a colony and the Mother Country was that the colony was not allowed to produce any goods from the leading sector – from the manufacturing sector – at all. The English prohibition of most manufactures in the North

American colonies was in fact a major factor behind the American Revolution in 1776. The accepted knowledge of the time – and indeed in practice
until after World War II and into the 1950s – was that the export of manufactured goods and the import of raw materials was 'good trade' for a nation. By
contrast, the export of raw materials and the import of manufactured goods
were considered 'bad trade' for any nation. The latter was the trading pattern
imposed on overseas colonies.

Interestingly, the export and import of manufactured goods was considered
'good trade' for both trading nations. The kind of economic theory which
gives support to this long-practised tradition disappeared in the 1930s because
increasing returns to scale – the key factor explaining the difference between
manufactured goods and the production of raw materials – was not compatible with the equilibrium models that had been voted in as the core
assumption of standard economic theory. It is deeply ironic that the practical
implementation of the standard theory – leading to the deindustrialization of
the Third World – only started in the early 1980s, at a time when the old
models depicting increasing returns had been resurrected under the label of
'New Trade Theory', again 'proving' that the pre-Smithian theories (Paul
Krugman, etc.) were correct. The essential problem with the new models that
'proved' that the old theories were correct, was that they were only seen as
'toy models' by the economics profession. The equilibrium models of the early
twentieth century – where all economic activities are qualitatively alike as carriers of economic growth – became the sole foundations of The Washington
Consensus and the policies which deindustrialized so many Third World
Countries during the 1990s.

Since the 1770s the world has experienced many 'productivity explosions'.
These are described in the works of Christopher Freeman and Carlota Perez.
Recently the so-called IT revolution has given birth to 'Moore's Law', which
essentially explains the same phenomenon that is recorded in Figure 1.
According to Moore's Law the productivity of the silicon chip doubles every
eighteen months. Obviously this is not a development that can go on forever,
but in the decades when this 'law' has been observed to be correct, the nations
engaged in the economic activities subject to this 'productivity explosion'
have moved ahead of the poor nations in fast growth without inflation.
'Productivity explosions' are deflationary: the price decreases recorded in
these industries tend to reduce the general price level.

3.3 Learning and the pattern of international trade

Seen from a different angle, the productivity explosions – when plotted in
terms of labour productivity per unit of product – produce 'learning curves'.

Figure 2. **Learning as the essence of economic growth. USA: learning curve of best-practice productivity in medium grade men's shoes**

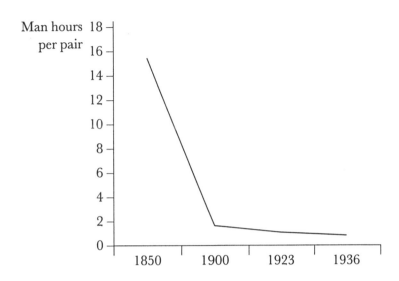

Man hours required by best-practice methods of producing a pair of medium-grade men's shoes at selected dates in the US

Year	Man hours per pair
1850	15.5
1900	1.7
1923	1.1
1936	0.9

Source: Reinert 1980, p. 259

These are curves that show the speed of human learning in economic activities. As a general rule, the faster the speed of learning, the faster is the rate of economic growth. This is because the benefits from productivity improvements not only spread to world consumers as lower prices (a 'classical' spread of the benefits from economic change); they also spread in terms of higher wages to the workers (a 'collusive' spread of the benefits from technical change). See also section 3.4 for these 'collusive' effects.

Figure 2 shows the progress of human productivity, drawn as learning curves, in the production of a standard pair of shoes from 1850 to 1936. While the learning was particularly intense, from 1850 to 1900, the United States was a big producer and exporter of shoes. The United States experienced a 'productivity explosion' in the shoe industry from 1850 to 1900. As the possibilities for productivity improvements fell, the US slowly became a net importer of shoes. This is in effect, the 'product life cycle theory of international trade' associated with Ray Vernon and Lou Wells in the 1970s.[24]

A wealthy nation produces where the learning curve is steep – as it was in the IT industry in the 1990s – and imports products where the possibilities for learning are small and the learning curve correspondingly flat. This is the natural working of the world market: industries with fast learning capabilities use knowledge and skilled and expensive labour intensively. This is the comparative advantage of wealthy nations. Poor nations automatically specialize in economic activities where the potential for learning is low. These economic activities use inexpensive labour intensively. In this way the poor nations automatically develop a comparative advantage in providing cheap and uneducated labour. In other words, within the international division of labour they 'specialize' in being poor. This kind of perspective is lost in standard economic theory, where all economic activities are seen as being qualitatively equal.

The mercantilist economic policy that was carried out in Europe and in the United States for so many centuries found its scientific explanation in the world of business during the 1970s through the work of Boston Consulting Group (BCG). This worldwide consulting firm became famous in the world of business for the creation of two tools which helped companies survive in a world dominated by dynamic Schumpeterian competition. The first tool was 'The Experience Curve', essentially a learning curve plotting total cost rather than labour hours on the vertical axis (Figure 2).[25] The second tool was the product portfolio, a matrix where mature cash-cows continuously finances innovations that in their turn become the cash-cows of the future.[26] In our view this theory emulates the strategy of the best mercantilists; making sure all European nations got into the cash-cows that required new skills, creating national productivity explosions and steep learning curves. The policy towards the colonies, however, caused these nations to be stuck in what BCG calls 'dog industries', activities bereft of increasing returns, with no growth and with the low profitability of commodity competition.

3.4 The Synergies Emanating from the Productivity Explosions

Husbandry ... is never more effectually encouraged than by the increase of manufactures.

David Hume, *History of England,* 1767, vol. III.

The extremely important synergies between the leading sectors with 'productivity explosions' and the rest of the economy have been noted in England since the late 1400s. The quote above, from Adam Smith's closest friend, is typical: efficient agriculture is normally only seen in industrialized nations.

An illustration of the importance of synergies from the manufacturing sector can be observed by studying the wages of barbers or bus drivers around the world. How can we explain why the German bus driver has a standard of living 16 times higher than his counterpart in Kenya or in La Paz, Bolivia? This is essentially because, as the industrialized countries experienced wave after wave of productivity explosions in a sequence of new industries, the wages not only of the industrial workers but of the whole industrial nation were raised with rising productivity. The workers received their part of the productivity improvements not only as lower prices (in the 'classical' way) but to a large extent also as higher wages (the 'collusive' way).[27] In this way, each productivity explosion in the First World also jacked up the real wages of barbers and bus drivers, in this way gaining, step by step, in real wages compared to their equally productive counterparts in the Third World.

In our opinion, the only way to raise living standards in the Third World is to repeat this procedure, the only one that has ever worked from fifteenth-century England to twentieth-century Korea. Today, the application of the rules of the Washington Consensus – essentially disallowing the historically proven procedure of artificially creating a comparative advantage in manufacturing – means that the road to development, which has been followed by all industrialized countries up until now, is completely blocked for the Third World of today. To use a nineteenth-century expression, we have 'pulled up the ladder' preventing new nations from following us on the path to development. In the meantime we address the mere symptoms of development, not the causes, through our development aid.

4. Enters taxonomy: how economic activities differ

We will never be able to understand why economic growth is so uneven unless we understand how economic activities differ. We all intuitively understand that a group of investment brokers make more money than a group of people washing dishes in a restaurant. Once this kind of pre-Ricardian common sense was part of economics. In the nineteenth century the United States in particular emphasized the need for a 'high wage strategy': the logic was that providing the nation with jobs which paid well would make the nation rich. To the United States this meant getting out of cotton growing, which required slavery and could not support wage labour.

4.1 Two different kinds of economic activities

We argue that there are essentially two kinds of economic activities, having very different characteristics. A nation specializing in Schumpeterian activities will find that both increasing returns and technological change will cause production costs to fall, thus opening up the way for technology-based rents that can be divided between capitalists, workers and the government. A nation specializing in Malthusian activities will find that, after a certain point, specialization will cause unit production costs to rise. This is the core of Antonio Serra's 1613 argument, in which he explained the wealth of Venice

Figure 3. How economic activities differ: only the presence of Schumpeterian activities has ever managed to raise a nation out of poverty

Marshall Plans: Produced by focus on **Schumpeterian Activities** (= 'good' export activities)	Morgenthau Plans: Produced by focus on **Malthusian Activities.** (= 'bad' export activities if no Schumpeterian sector present)
Increasing Returns	Diminishing Returns
Dynamic imperfect competition	'Perfect competition' (commodity competition)
High growth activities	Low growth activities
Stable prices	Extreme price fluctuations
Generally skilled labour	Generally unskilled labour
Creates a middle class	Creates 'feudalist' class structure
Irreversible wages ('stickiness' of wages)	Reversible wages
Technical change leads to higher wages to the producer ('Fordist wage regime')	Technical change tends to lower price to consumer
Creates large synergies (linkages, clusters)	Creates few synergies

and the poverty of his native Naples. Reinert[28] showed that the main export activities of Peru, Ecuador and Bolivia were actually producing well into diminishing returns: when production was reduced, production costs were also reduced. Significantly, this mechanism explains why nations exporting raw material – in the absence of a national manufacturing sector – have never managed to get out of their poverty trap.

A nation specializing in Malthusian-type activities will stay poor, while nations that specialize in Schumpeterian-type activities will raise their wage level and standard of living. The growth of Malthusian activities at the expense of Schumpeterian activities is at the core of any Morgenthau Plan, as are those activities unleashed under the label of 'structural adjustment' in the 1990s.[29]

In our opinion Malthus was right when he predicted that human wages would always be around subsistence level. The historical record on this is unanimous: only Schumpeterian-type activities are able to lift nations out of poverty. This type of theory has dominated the history of economic policy, and was first advanced on a theoretical level by Antonio Serra in 1613.

Figure 4 shows how productivity will fall when a nation specializes in a diminishing returns activity. These activities are also subject to technical change, but this example shows how the effects of diminishing returns dwarf the effects of technical change.

Studying four waves of industrialization and deindustrialization in Peru between 1950 and 2000, Roca and Simabuco showed the same mechanism at

Figure 4. **Ecuador: Diminishing Returns in Banana Production 1961–1977**

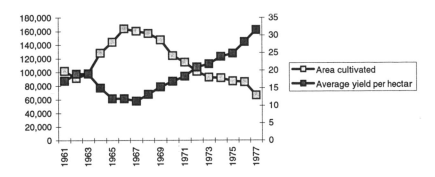

Source: Reinert 1980, page 175. Programa Nacional del Banano y Frutas Tropicales, Guayaquil. Unpublished data.

work.[30] An extra percentage point in the share of manufacturing activities in the Peruvian economy increased white-collar real wages by 10.6% and blue-collar real salaries by 15.5%. This means that a growing manufacturing sector not only provides a 'catapult' for standards of living, but also has a proportionally larger impact on blue-collar salaries, thus leading to a positive impact on income distribution.

4.3 Creating the wage gap: the cumulative effect over time

A central point in the alternative vision of economic growth is how the gap between the rich and poor nations developed over time: the mechanisms which created today's situation in which the Frankfurt bus driver has a standard of living which the World Bank has calculated to be 16 times higher than that of the equally efficient bus driver in Nairobi. The developed nations have captured large rents from a sequence of productivity explosions (Figure 1) that have occurred since before the first industrial revolution. In addition to the obvious impact that these productivity explosions have had in making goods cheaper (what we call the 'classical' mode of distributing productivity gains), it has also had the effect of 'catapulting' the general wage level of the

Figure 5. **How the wage differentials between rich and poor nations were created through sequences of 'productivity explosions' translated into wage rents**

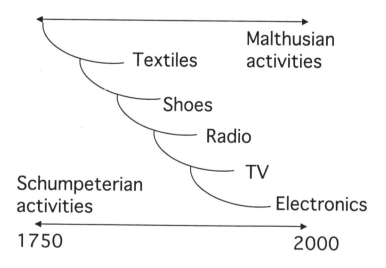

industrial nation to a new and higher level (what we call the 'collusive' mode of distributing productivity gains).[31]

In Malthusian economic activities, for reasons given in Figure 3, technological change is essentially distributed in the classical mode, i.e. in the form of lower prices to the consumer rather than higher wages to the workers, whose flat wages are represented by the top flat line. The Schumpeterian activities, on the other hand, create a sequence of steep learning curves which – every time – jacks up the wage rent in the whole labour market in the respective First World markets.[32]

Man plays two roles in the economy, as a producer and as a consumer. In order to understand the economic policies that previously made it possible for laggard countries – including, in sequence, England, United States, Germany and Korea – to catch up, it is necessary to understand the conflicts between the economic interests of Man-the-Producer vs. Man-the-Consumer. A key feature of today's standard economics is an exclusive focus on Man-the-Consumer. Nineteenth-century US economic policy, based on the path-breaking works of Daniel Raymond in 1820 and Mathew Carey in 1821, explained the trade-off between the two roles. If the industrial nations have managed to jack up their wage levels in the way described in Figure 5, the poor nation will – after a certain point – achieve a higher national wage level by being a relatively inefficient industrial producer, rather than to continue as a supplier of raw materials. Mathew Carey succeeded in convincing US farmers of the United States that even though in the short term they would have to pay more for US-produced industrial goods than for the goods they imported from England, in the longer run they would be more than compensated for this: the rise in the general wage level in the USA would more than compensate for the higher prices which had to be paid for industrial goods. In other words, the benefits accruing to a person as a producer (in the form of higher wages) would more than outweigh the costs accruing to the same person as a consumer.

In the nineteenth-century economic debate between the USA and the UK, the English consistently refused to see the logic of Carey's argument until John Stuart Mill admitted the logic of 'infant industry protection'. Later Alfred Marshall recommended an economic policy subsidising increasing-return activities by taxing diminishing-return activities.[33] This is exactly the kind of policy that is at the core of creating Marshall Plans out of previous Morgenthau Plans. US economic policy was based on this principle throughout the nineteenth century. Today, the vast majority of US economists will be as blind to this argument as their English colleagues were for most of the nineteenth century.

6. Systemic effects: globalization as a Morgenthau Plan for the third world

As a Morgenthau Plan under a different name, deindustrialization has always had the same effect. From the same problems of desperate poverty, the same remedy – industrialization – appears again and again in history. In 1613 Antonio Serra saw the wealth of Venice and the abject poverty of Naples being the result of the lack of manufacturing in Naples. 150 years later an economist in Northern Italy under French rule made the same observation there. Observers in France after the Napoleonic Wars reported the same kind of misery that Hoover saw in Germany in the spring of 1947 and that we see today in Ulaanbaatar, Mongolia or Lima, Peru: where industry is closed down, poverty enters. The 'American System' of protecting manufacturing was born in the early 1820s in a similar difficult situation. It is about time we made the same discovery again.

Figures 6 and 7 show – in circular flow-chart form – the cumulative effects of the vicious circles of deindustrialization and poverty contrasted with the virtuous circles of economic development. The main point here is that economic development is 'activity specific', that is to say it can only occur in certain economic activities (Schumpeterian-type activities), and not in others (Malthusian-type activities). This is why, for a very long time, the term 'industrialized country' was considered synonymous with 'rich country'. The policies of the Washington Institutions have, since the late 1980s, left this traditional understanding behind.

The current fashion is to blame the poverty caused by globalization on the lack of openness on the part of industrialized countries towards agricultural imports from the Third World; in other words, the problems are seen as being created by a lack of openness to free trade. In our opinion, the historical record proves these assertions to be wrong. No nation has ever taken the step from being poor to being wealthy by exporting raw material in the absence of a domestic manufacturing sector. Malthusian activities alone have never and never will in the future be able to lift a nation out of poverty without the presence of a domestic manufacturing sector. The only results of any importance that will be achieved by freeing the imports of foodstuffs from the Third World to the First World are:

a) A destruction of First World farming and of the rural areas of the First World

b) A change to industrialized farming in the Third World, where income will fall to such an extent that the local workers will not be able to afford to purchase the food they produce for the rich. This is in essence the mechanism foreseen already by Malthus.

The only way to achieve a global trading system without hunger is to strike the following deal between the rich and the poor countries: 1) The rich nations selectively commit to nourish, target and protect some of their Malthusian Activities (agriculture) while 2) the Third World is allowed selectively to nourish, target and protect some of their Schumpeterian Activities (industries and advanced services subject to increasing returns) and also to protect their own food production; all under a system of internal competition. This must be done under a system of regional integration of the Third World countries.

The present policy of blind globalization coupled with increasing 'development aid' is essentially a policy of applying palliative economics: economics that addresses the symptoms of poverty without at all attacking its causes. The essence of economic development is a violent structural change leading down steep learning curves towards increased productivity. Providing a better well to subsistence agriculture is purely a palliative medicine, unrelated to the process of economic development in the real sense.

7. Conclusion

> From the raw materials from Spain and the West Indies – particularly silk, iron and *cochinilla* (a red dye) – which cost them only 1 florin, the foreigners produce finished goods which they sell back to Spain for between 10 and 100 florins. Spain is in this way subject to greater humiliations from the rest of Europe than those they themselves impose on the Indians. In exchange for gold and silver the Spaniards offer trinkets of greater or lesser value; but by buying back their own raw materials at an exorbitant price, the Spaniards are made the laughing stock of all Europe.
>
> Luis Ortiz, Spanish Minister of Finance, to Felipe II: 'Memorandum to the King to prevent money from leaving the Kingdom', Madrid, 1558.

The nations that, in sequence, have taken the step from being poor to being rich have all been through a stage of what we could call 'the cult of manufacturing'. As often happens, economic policy came before economic theory, but an early statement of this Other Canon policy is found in the quotation above, from Spain's Minister of Finance in 1558. The funnel of wealth coming from the New World had not been invested in the production sector, and the gold and silver had deindustrialized Spain as if it had been subject to a Morgenthau Plan. The present problems of Venezuela, and the growing problems in the productive economy of Norway, are examples of the same effect produced when monetary wealth crowds out the productive powers of an economy.

Figure 6. **The mechanisms of a Morgenthau Plan: the 'vicious' circle of economic underdevelopment**

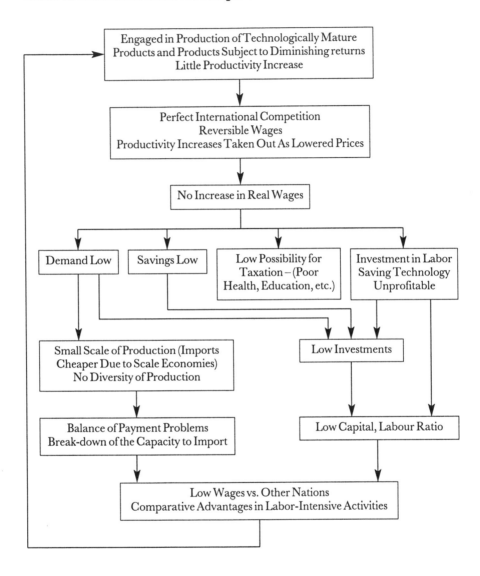

Note: It is futile to attack the system at any one point, e.g., increasing investment when wages are still low and demand is absent. An instance of this is poor capital utilization and excess capacity in Latin American LDCs.

Source: Reinert (1980), *op.cit*, p.41.

Figure 7. **The virtuous systemic effects of a Marshall Plan**

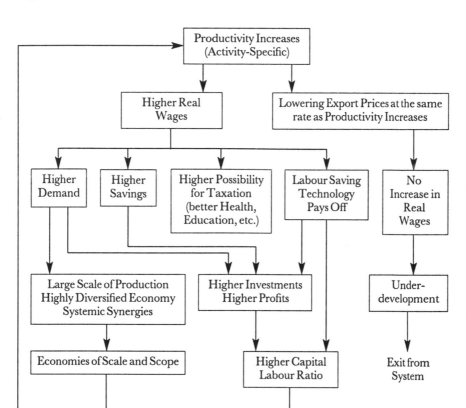

Note: In a closed system, with constant employment rate, the only way GNP per capita can grow is through the 'Virtuous Circle'. However, the system can be cut-off at any one point, e.g., if higher demand goes to foreign goods alone, the circle will break.

Source: Reinert (1980), *op.cit*, p.39.

For most nations today, however, the problems are of a very different nature. As it gradually became clear during the 1990s that the basic Washington Consensus model failed to deliver its promised results, mainstream economics evolved by adding new prescriptions for the poor nations. 'Get the prices right' was initially the whole message, but it was later widened, in sequence, with 'get the property rights right', 'get the institutions right', 'get the governance right', 'get your competitiveness right' and 'get your national innovation systems right'. In our view, however, these prescriptions – these buzz-words of development – all fail on their own to get to the core of the matter. We would claim that the key to understanding unequal development is to be found in the realm of production.

From an Other Canon point of view, one formula we have been waiting for is 'get your economic activities right', i.e. some kind of policy reflecting the fact that, fundamentally, economic development is historically a process of profound structural change in which the presence of activities able to absorb new knowledge, and production under conditions of increasing returns and high barriers to entry, are conditions necessary to the achievement of economic growth. For centuries this type of economic activity was called 'manufacturing' or 'industrialization', but they are not necessarily limited to these activities. Today we have got the causalities wrong; we confuse the symptoms of development with their causes. 'It is known that a primitive people does not improve their customs and institutions later to find useful industries, but the other way around'[34] was almost common sense at the time, an understanding that was not far from that of the 1960s.

Today, there are, broadly speaking, only two possible solutions to solving the increasing poverty problems caused by globalization:

1. We can globalize the labour market, the only main institution that is not yet globalized, by allowing all the poor to move where the 'Schumpeterian' economic activities are located. This will lead to an unprecedented exodus, to enormous social problems, and to a neoclassical type 'factor-price equalization', in which world wages will tend to be equalized downwards. All will tend to get equally poor.
2. We can follow the nineteenth- and early twentieth century path taken by all the currently rich countries – Australia is an interesting prototype for a non-export led model – by creating national Schumpeterian sectors which initially are not competitive in the world markets, and slowly over time let the economy 'graduate' to compete on the world market. This is the only way to create dynamic 'factor-price equalization' upwards. Only in this way can we make poor countries into middle-income countries.

In our opinion option two is the only viable solution. By a mass migration of a large number of the world's poor to the rich countries, there is an overwhelming likelihood of a factor-price equalization downwards: that the wages in the First World will fall towards the wage level of the majority of the world's population, i.e. very close to subsistence level. In this way the world will risk being caught in an underconsumption equilibrium from which the market alone will never free the economy.

The crucial transition from being a poor to being a wealthy country has, in all historical cases, involved a situation in which nations have used the market creatively as a tool to create a comparative advantage for themselves in types of economic activity which we have called 'Schumpeterian' (Figure 3) and 'High Quality Activities' (Figure 6). In this sense, the transition from a poor to a rich nation has always been a totally artificial construct, a 'managed economy' in the sense of using private interest to artificially create a comparative advantage outside the raw materials sector. Once this threshold is overcome, the market can be left pretty much alone again. It is this transition – first made by England after 1485 and lastly by Korea in the 1960s – that is no longer possible under the Washington Consensus.

Only when the Third World has also created a comparative advantage in Schumpeterian activities will free trade be beneficial to all nations involved. This was the essential credo of United States and Continental European economic theory during the nineteenth century; it was the theory behind which Europe and the US industrialized, and is the only theory which will bring the Third World out of poverty. This type of production-based economic theory, which we have labelled the Other Canon (www.othercanon.org), has been used by all currently wealthy nations during their transition from poor to rich countries.

Notes

1 The bright spots in this development are that the two most populous nations on the planet – China and India – have not taken the same road towards increasing misery as have so many of the smaller Third World states. This is no doubt to a large extent a result of their reluctance to follow the recommendations of mainstream economics.
2 See Reinert 1994 for a description of the two different ways technological change spreads in the economy; the classical mode – through lower prices to the consumers – and the collusive mode, through higher wages to the producers.
3 Financial Times 2002.
4 Alfred Marshall quotes the Bible, Genesis xii &, to emphasize this point.
5 Reinert and Daastøl 1997, 2003.
6 Morgenthau 1945.
7 Hoover's Report no. 3, March 18, 1947, quoted in Baade 1955.

8 Stangeland 1966.
9 Reinert 2000.
10 Reinert 2000.
11 The crucial role of the nation state in carrying out the right type of economic policy is discussed in Reinert 1999.
12 Schumpeter 1954, pp. 41–2.
13 Reinert 1980.
14 Reinert 2000.
15 Samuelson and Stolper 1949, 1950.
16 Myrdal 1956.
17 Thomas Kuhn, *The Structure of Scientific Revolutions*, p. 37.
18 Quoted in Lévi-Strauss 1996, p. 247.
19 For an excellent discussion of this, see Biernacki 1995, p. 253.
20 Åkerman 1954, pp. 26–7.
21 Schumpeter 1954, p. 468.
22 England did indeed attempt this winner-takes-it-all strategy – being the only industrial nation – well into the nineteenth century by attempting to 'kill American industry in its cradle' as a Parliamentarian expressed it.
23 Rosenberg 1975.
24 Reinert 1980.
25 Boston Consulting Group 1972; Reinert 1980.
26 Stern and Stalk 1998, pp. 35–7.
27 Reinert 1994.
28 Reinert 1980.
29 See Reinert 2000 for a detailed description of these mechanisms.
30 Roca and Simabuco 2003.
31 Reinert 1996.
32 Reinert 1980, p. 265.
33 Marshall 1890, p. 492.
34 Meyen 1770, p. 11.

References

Åkerman, Johan, 1954, *Politik och Ekonomi i Atomålderens Värld*, Stockholm, Natur och Kultur.

Baade, Fritz, 1955, 'Gruß und Dank an Herbert Hoover', in *Weltwirtschaftliches Archiv*, vol. 74, no. 1, pp. 1–6.

Biernacki, Richard, *Fabrication of Labor*, Berkeley, University of California Press.

Boston Consulting Group, 1972, *Perspectives on Experience*, Boston.

Cecchini, Paolo, 1988, *The European Challenge* (aka 'The Cecchini Report'), Brookfield, Gower Press.

Lévy-Strauss, Claude, 1996, *The Savage Mind*, Oxford, Oxford University Press.

Meyen, Johan Jacob, 1770, *Wie kommt es, dass die Oekonomie bisher so wenig Vortheile von der Physik und Mathematik gewonnen hat; und wie kann man diese Wissenschaften zum gemeinen Nutzen in die Oekonomie einführen, und von dieser Verbindung auf Grundsätze kommen, die in die Ausübung brauchbar sind?*, Berlin, Haude & Spener.

Morgenthau, Henry, Jr, 1945, *Germany is Our Problem. A Plan for Germany,* New York, Harper.

Myrdal, Gunnar, 1956, *Development and Under-development: A Note on the Mechanisms of National and International Economic Inequality,* Cairo, National Bank of Egypt.

Perez, Carlota, 2003, 'Technological Revolutions, Paradigm Shifts and Socio-Institutional Change', in Reinert 2003.

Pigou, AC, ed., 1925, *Memorials of Alfred Marshall,* London, Macmillan.

Reinert, Erik S, 1980, *International Trade and the Economic Mechanisms of Underdevelopment,* Ann Arbor, University Microfilm.

——, 1994, 'Catching-up from way behind – A Third World perspective on First World History' in Fagerberg, Jan et al., eds, *The Dynamics of Technology, Trade, and Growth,* Aldershot, Edward Elgar, 1994.

——, 1995, 'Competitiveness and its predecessors – a 500 year cross-national perspective', in *Structural Change and Economic Dynamics,* vol. 6 (1995), pp. 23–42. Spanish translation: 'El concepto de 'competitividad' y sus predecesores', *Socialismo y Participacion* no. 72, Lima, Peru, December 1995, pp. 21–41.

——, 1996, 'Diminishing Returns and Economic Sustainability: The dilemma of resource-based economies under a free trade regime' in Hansen, Stein, Jan Hesselberg and Helge Hveem, eds, *International Trade Regulation, National Development Strategies and the Environment: Towards Sustainable Development?,* Oslo, Centre for Development and the Environment, University of Oslo, 1996.

——, 1999, 'The Role of the State in Economic Growth.', *Journal of Economic Studies,* vol. 26, no. 4/5, 1999. A shorter version published in Toninelli, Pier Angelo, 2000, ed., *The Rise and Fall of State-Owned Enterprises in the Western World,* Cambridge, Cambridge University Press.

——, 2000, 'Globalisation in the Periphery as a Morgenthau Plan: The Under-development of Mongolia in the 1990's, in Lhagva, Sakhia, 2000, *Mongolian Development Strategy; Capacity Building,* Ulaanbaatar, Mongolian Development Research Center, also in Reinart 2003.

——, 2003, ed., *Evolutionary Economics and Income Inequality,* Cheltenham, Elgar.

Reinert, Erik S and Arno Daastøl, 1997, 'Exploring the Genesis of Economic Innovations: The religious gestalt-switch and the *duty to invent* as preconditions for economic growth', *European Journal of Law and Economics,* vol 4, nos 2/3 (1997), pp. 233–83.

——, 'The Other Canon: The History of Renaissance Economics. Its Role as an Immaterial and Production-based Canon in the History of Economic Thought and in the History of Economic Policy', in Reinert 2003.

Roca, Santiago and Luis Simabuko, 2003, 'Natural Resources, Industrialisation and Fluctuating Standards of Living in Peru from 1950–1997: A Case Study of Activity-Specific Economic Growth' in Reinert, ed., 2003.

Rosenberg, Nathan, 1975, *Perspectives on Technology,* Cambridge, Cambridge University Press.

Samuelson, Paul, 1948, 'International Trade and the Equalisation of Factor Prices', *Economic Journal,* vol. 58, pp. 163–84.

——, 1949, 'International Factor-Price Equalisation Once Again', *Economic Journal,* vol. 59, pp. 181–97.

Schumpeter, Joseph Alois, 1954, *History of Economic Analysis,* New York, Oxford University Press.

Stangeland, Charles Emil, 1966 [1904], *Pre-Malthusian Doctrines of Population. A Study in the History of Economic Theory,* New York, Kelley.

Stern, Carl W and George Stalk Jr, 1998, *Perspectives on Strategy from The Boston Consulting Group,* New York, Wiley.

Wolf, Martin, 2002, 'Location, location, location equals the wealth of nations.', *Financial Times,* Wednesday September 25, 2002, p. 15.

PART VII

INSTITUTIONS AND GOVERNANCE

21

ON UNDERSTANDING MARKETS AS SOCIAL AND POLITICAL INSTITUTIONS IN DEVELOPING ECONOMIES

Barbara Harriss-White

There is no science in the study of markets unless their relevant institutions are incorporated

Penny 1985

To conceive of economic phenomena as embedded is not to renounce theory, certainly not, it is to start theorising differently

Caille 1994

Introduction

The small minority of students of economics who wonder how supply is supplied and demand demanded is asking a question to which the answer certainly cannot be found within the discipline – and a fully satisfactory answer may not be found at all. It is not that the tools of economics have not been used to address institutions. It is that economic markets are vehicles for the exercise of forms of social authority, the origins of which lie outside markets and which operate outside markets as well as inside them. In the same way, economic markets are one of the arenas for struggles between political interests. Markets do not perform 'subject to' institutions, they *are* bundles of institutions and are nested in others. In this brief essay, mindful of the fact that there can be no 'theory of everything', we will consider some of the ways in which markets have been 'theorized differently' as social and political constructs, and will consider the significance for their functioning of social forms of regulation and of continual political contestation.

1. Markets and Institutions

All theories are social constructs. All theories about the economy – not excluding neoclassical ones – embody assumptions about forms of social organization. The default concept of the competitive market has long been known to embody strong and implausible assumptions about society, needing several means by which large numbers of buyers and sellers are equally endowed with (accurate) information and can transact rapidly in one (virtual) space. While some have concluded that economics is 'under-socialized', others have found that its depiction is socialized all right, but in ways inconsistent with that of real, observed economies.

Theories have come into being under particular economic and political conditions and perform political roles. In the last quarter of the twentieth century, neoclassical economics has used its assumptions of ahistorical methodological individualism and of rational, maximizing behaviour to colonize three areas of society and politics – the household, the state and the firm (and the contracts it makes). In the new home economics,[1] the allocation of household labour between productive activity outside the home using land, labour and other markets and reproductive activity inside the home (e.g. the preparation of meals, cleaning or childcare, which are modelled as the production of 'z'-goods) is theorized as an efficient response to the existence of prices for the labour of the different genders, and to the *difference* between those prices, on markets outside the household, subject to constraints (such as a irreducible minimum of z-good production by one gender or a fixed leisure requirement for one or both of the one-generation parents). Whether one parent is a benevolent dictator, or whether and how each individual's interests can be subordinated to a collectively agreed goal, is a bone of contention in this approach.[2] In the new political economy (not so new, and unhistorically political) the state has been modelled as the sum of individual maximizing behaviour by its agents, with parties or policies taking the place of goods, voters proxying for consumers and votes replacing currency.[3] In the new institutional economics (NIE), the (corporate) firm has been cast as a bundle of labour contracts, under continual renegotiation in the light of performance, the institutional boundaries to which are conditioned only by supervision and measurement costs.[4] Further, since spot contracts are rare, especially in developing economies, a variety of non-spot contracts have been theorized (either by means of analysing their existence conditions or by means of pair-wise comparison and contrast) as efficient solutions to the problems of asymmetrical information and differentials in the costs of useful knowledge, of transactions costs (the costs of search, negotiation and enforcement of contracts) and of protection against opportunistic behaviour, moral hazard and adverse selection.[5] The rational solutions to coordination problems in economic land-scapes in which such concepts and tools are deployed result in outcomes which cannot otherwise be explained in economics. The sharecropping contract, actually rather rare, has received such varied attention that it can be studied as a microcosm of the NIE approach to the micro-economics of development.[6]

These acts of theoretical colonization are applied to highly stylized households, states, firms and contracts, overlooking a larger problem for explanation which immediately confronts any student of 'actually existing' households, states, firms and markets in developing economies. This is the simultaneous coexistence of a great range of types of institution, of contracts and of 'technologies', each of which has non-trivial internal variation.[7] This theoretical colonization also isolates institutions and wrenches them from their contexts of property distribution and power.[8] Power is not necessary to explanations couched in transactions or information costs; at best it is reduced to 'opportunism' or 'self interest with guile' and then generally considered to be practised by employees or agents rather than by owners or principals. Allocative and/or contractual behaviour is assumed to have to be devised by agents which are accepted as being imperfectly informed, with limits to their cognitive competence and boundaries to their rationality. Such solutions are theorized as efficient, as minimizing transactions costs, because transaction-cost minimization is their objective. Such reasoning is not only tautological, it also flies in the face of evidence both for the persistence of inefficient tech-nologies and institutions,[9] and for the role of institutions in protecting people from a superabundance of information, rather than from its scarcity.

In fact, it is not possible to evaluate the efficiency of existing institutions because there are in fact no existing deinstitutionalized alternatives with which to compare them. Institutions are also inadequately theorized as con-straints on maximizing behaviour. They are actually the way societies work – indeed, a society cannot exist without them – and are facilitating and enabling. While, in theory, factors driving change in institutions are exogen-ous and/or assumed (typically, these factors are changes in price, technology, population and/or 'subjective preference'), institutions are in practice con-tinually changing. They evolve from within, through the action of individual agents (for a range of motivations), through the consequences of the unavoid-able use and degradation of energy,[10] and from the coercive and competitive creation and defence of wealth and property.[11] Further, the matrix of insti-tutions through which the economy is regulated and controlled replicates itself and evolves over time in interaction with its components in ways that make time, space and society unique.[12] Unfortunately, history is therefore essential to theory. The new home, political and institutional economics tend to dehistoricize markets and all the non-market institutions they touch. Their political role is, first, to reduce capitalism to the interplay of supply and demand, secondly (subject to some specific qualifications), to reduce markets to prices and thirdly to naturalize markets.

Elsewhere, I have reviewed the use of frameworks derived from industrial organization theory and from theories of value chains/ *filières* for the evaluation of the economic efficiency of markets.[13] Although these approaches are concerned with assets structures, competitive conditions, price formation and performance, they do not allow for the non-economic structuring of markets. Alternative, critical, historical methods of conceiving of and analysing markets in developing economies recognize that markets are social and political phenomena. However, they are all also in some ways unsatisfactory. We will consider three approaches here: those of economic sociology, of the politics of markets and of social structures of accumulation.

2. Economic Sociology

At the heart of this approach is the insight that the economy is not the sum of individual maximizing motivation but is a socially embedded phenomenon. Karl Polanyi, one of the most influential exponents of economic sociology,[14] argued that there were three economic principles. These are reciprocity (where price is the product of custom), redistribution (where price is the product of command) and market exchange (where price is the product of supply and demand).[15] Underdeveloped economies are regulated in various combinations by these three principles, in such a way that economic transactions cannot be understood outside their social relations. For instance, it is through relations of kinship or religion that occupation may be regulated;[16] through gender relations. That the terms of participation – firm size, activity, credit, the divisions of task and labour relations – are negotiated or thrashed out.[17] The moral character of goods may affect the structure and performance of markets;[18] and the network may be the means whereby jobs are secured and commodities distributed.[19] In many societies, and until recently, market exchange has been literally marginal. Its sites – marketplaces – may have evolved from a healthy (but economically irrational) distance from the edge of a town; its practitioners may have been migrant and/or stigmatized, and/or have kept themselves socially separate in order to reduce the heavy social obligations that generally come with wealth.[20] As economies evolve, not only do social arrangements cede regulative authority to political, legal procedure (custom gives way to contract), but market exchange also comes to dominate other principles of economic regulation. Polanyi argued that society is thereby transformed to suit the interests of the self-regulating market. The direction of causality reverses, from the economy being embedded in social arrangements to society being embedded in market-serving arrangements. Polanyi realized that, at its extreme, his argument gave rise to a contradiction. For markets are not only principles of allocation driven by supply and demand, but they also have destructive properties. Not only do they destroy other principles of economic allocation, but by themselves they also destroy human life because they cannot protect it. As Sen put it more recently, markets are consistent with any income distribution, including one where some have no income at all.[21] Markets are so inherently destructive that a pure market society (aka pure capitalism) cannot exist. Society and states intervene to protect markets from destroying society. In all markets, there are thus continual political tensions between more and less regulation, between social and state regulation and between market regulation and politically necessary, socially protective redistribution.

So it is not surprising that empirical work in the most *advanced* market economies has revealed that the most developed market exchange is far from being socially disembedded. John Davis, in his study of markets in the UK, discovered 'at least' 80 different forms of non-market exchange – mixtures of price formation that did not owe themselves purely to the interaction of supply and demand.[22] In the UK for example, festive occasions or the rhythm of vehicle registration, not price reductions, are the reasons for huge surges in demand. This increase in demand is not reflected in systematic price hikes. Nicholas Emler's work on social information (gossip) showed that 90% of all corporate transactions are personalised.[23] Geoff Hodgson has stressed the foundational importance in complex systems of production of the routine (or the 'meme').[24] Gender, age, educational history, region and class of origin, religion (if any) and participation in civic associations shape the structures of production, trade and consumption. Habituated behaviour does not necessarily minimize costs – even transactions costs – but it makes production possible. All this work confirms that forms of power originating outside the economy have enduring impacts on economic performance. Furthermore, the spheres of public service and of the production, distribution and consumption of public goods are not only celebrations of a variety of market-limiting values but are also part of the political shield protecting society from market-created casualties.[25]

It is one thing to accept the idea that even modern markets are embedded, to seize the nettle of defining these social institutions and to try to analyse/measure their impacts. It is quite another matter to recognize that exactly the same institutions have been theorized as examples of different economic principles. Moral-economic activity may be interpreted substantively in terms of norms of reciprocity, generosity, the expression of social rules about the siting of spatial arrangements, the sharing of work and co-operative access. Such activity is also open to formalist interpretation in terms of long term self-interest, individual risk-minimization and insurance, or solutions to problems of lack of trust.[26] For the substantivist economic sociologist the economy is moulded by non-economic factors, while for the formalist (for that economic sociology influenced by the new institutional economics) – the economy is shaped by distributions of information, uncertainty and relative factor scarcities. What both approaches have in common is their reliance on norms, norms of social embeddedness in one and norms of individual self interest in the other.

3. The politics of markets

Markets are not just socially embedded phenomena, they are sites of the exercise of power in ways which are not reducible either to the tool kit of the new institutional economics or to norms of social embeddedness. Following Max Weber, market exchange is 'always the resolution of conflicts of interest'[27] and it is this pursuit of interest that we define as politics, rather than the narrow conception of party or electoral power. It is not only the variety of real world markets that has required the development of a framework for the political analysis of markets; it is also the repeated experience of adverse and apparently unintended consequences of that kind of development policy which uses a deinstitutionalized conception of markets that demands such a framework. Basic markets in developing countries have been found not to function well and also to change the way they function according to the seasons, as well as in extreme circumstances.[28] Attempts to regulate them – through consensus, or through democratic governance, or through the narrow legal prescription of proper contract – have often foundered because the interests at play in markets are highly unequal.[29]

Market power, the capacity of one agent to direct the action of another – a capacity which is intrinsic to transactions – is situated in a structure of power which determines the choices available to participants: the choices between tactics and between objectives. What are these structures of power? There appear to be four, and it is to the examination of these which I shall now turn.[30]

First, there is *state power*. State and market are not separate but in practice densely intertwined. In turn, the state's involvement in markets takes two forms. One is direct participation – a form of politics well known to have taken a severe battering from the Bretton Woods financial agencies and from market fundamentalists. Yet the state is bound to be an active player in any market which needs creating and protecting under conditions which deter private capital (e.g. in remote regions, or where marketed surplus is small and sporadic, or where sellers are unable to borrow money against their products); or when a combination of roles are required which the private sector cannot play (e.g. short term profit maximizing trade together with the long-term security and redistribution of food and essential commodities). The second kind of intervention involves the *political regulation* of markets. There are then several layers or kinds of political regulation. One is where the state exercises *parametric* power in markets in order to correct distortions or achieve developmental goals. (Often this kind of politics materializes around *development projects* – in credit to producers or traders, in infrastructure, in the deliberate social targeting of certain products (especially grain), in production conditions (irrigation/land reclamation/ tenurial reform) and so on.) Another is where state power pervades markets through the policies which make markets work (the legal definition of property, sites of trade, licensing laws, the calibration of weights and measures, the regulation of money and contracts, the existence of institutions of adjudication and enforcement of these pervasive laws). Third, redolent of Foucault's notion of the capillary nature of power, states may *saturate* markets, 'even' determining the hours of sale, the description of contents, the proximity of goods to one another, the environmental quality of packaging, the display of brands and prices etc.. These examples are confined to the point of sale. The labelling on a Coke bottle makes the point, but the bureaucratic politics of state saturation behind this labelling is far less visible.

If the complex roles of markets are to be understood, if the effectiveness of markets is to be appreciated, then we have to understand this institutional patterning, because, as markets develop, these are exactly the kinds of regulation which are transferred from custom to contract, from social institutions to legal ones. In this process the law becomes a political resource – the object of determined attempts at capture, of evasion, or of manipulation alongside customary norms in legally pluralist regulative systems.[31]

At the same time the regulators cannot be assumed only to regulate. They also protect their own interests and may themselves embody conflicts of interest (a common example is when regulators discipline *and* represent *and* promote those regulated[32]). The result is markets which are structured so as not to be socially neutral. The analyst must also be aware of differences between procedure and practice – of the existence of incomplete, inconsistent and/or inconsistently amended law, and of the varying scope for improvization in the practice of regulation, such that regulation takes on a local character moulded by the interests of political and social elites.[33]

In the current era, this lack of social neutrality is strikingly due to the influence of corporate capital not only upon a state's regulative capacity but also upon democratic politics at all levels. Markets are exploding in number as a new market-driven politics enables corporate capital to penetrate the public sector (for example in food security, physical protection, insurance, health and education) and other areas of social life (such as broadcasting) previously protected from markets. In this political process of re-regulation, public goods and services are converted into commodities, need and social values have to be transformed into effective demand, domestic labour and public sector employees have the terms and conditions of their work changed so that profit can be extracted from their employment. Finally, through tax concessions, changes in the structure of subsidies, residual infrastructure provision and social security, the state, itself acting increasingly itself like a corporation, underwrites the risk to capital of this proliferation of markets. The impact of market-driven forms of regulation on democratic politics is to replace party politics with countervailing political influence through individual and collective corporate leverage on elected governments, through the co-option of business in consultation and policy advice, through the key positioning of corporately motivated individuals inside state bureaucracies, through the capture of regulatory bodies by the interests regulated such that states are driven to the competitive appeasement of corporate interests and/or leave them to self-regulation through unenforceable voluntary codes of conduct.[34] Corruption is only one component of an armoury of political tactics.[35] Samir Amin has called this 'low intensity democracy'.[36]

The second dimension of the politics of markets is therefore that driven by *association*, by means of which (some) participants act collectively in their own interests, in ways which may be antagonistic to others. The resolution of conflicts of collective interest often leads to endogenous regulation. The latter takes several commonly observable forms, theorized as association, network and hierarchy. *Association* defines formal organizations (trades unions, trade associations and consumer groups). Sometimes lumped together as 'civil society', these groups have formed to create and protect rents and thus evade competition, also to guarantee the collective preconditions for market competition and/or sometimes paternalistically to represent or to control labour.[37] The developmental outcome of the politics of association will depend on the type of rent created.[38] *Networks* are symbols for repeated interactions which counteract the working of competitive markets and are often portrayed theoretically as the manifestation of relations of trust.[39] Regarded as developmentally positive, networks are also exclusive and can operate as 'conspiracies against the public'.[40] A wide range of socio-economic relationships have been reduced by network theory to (layers of) nodes and flows. This is as gross a reductionism as that of the individualism of neoclassical economics. The *hierarchy* is manifest in the firm. Far from being a consensual unit, an 'island of coordination in a sea of market relations',[41] the firm is a governance structure bristling with micro-politics; 'a combat unit designed for doing battle in the market',[42] with hierarchical controls to maintain internal discipline in ways which benefit the owners. However, highly dynamic and synergistic interrelations have now been researched within and between clusters of firms in third-world markets.[43]

The third dimension of markets as political institutions concerns the politics of *economic structure*. Here, the distribution of endowments shapes the exchange between individual elements and affects the relative returns to market engagement.[44] In both advanced and developing economies industrial organization analysis has revealed that the impact on performance of complex competitive conditions (of which monopoly and competition are but the extremes) are inconclusive.[45] In developing countries, under conditions of non-voluntaristic commercialization (induced by the need to repay debt or pay taxes), market exchange is better understood not in terms of allocative efficiency but rather as a mechanism of extraction of surplus by one class from another.[46] The function of exchange is not to clear the market but to gain advantage of producers, a characteristic of markets that Bhaduri has termed 'class efficiency'.[47] Market transactions will then be an expression of the relative power of dominant and subordinate classes. In agriculture, for instance, interlocking and more complex (triadic) contracts in markets for labour, credit, raw materials, products, water and transport may be manipulated to give propertied classes the capacity to benefit from unequal sets of choices. Interlocked contracts have been used to replace the elements of non-contractual obligation in contracts under circumstances where they have been challenged.[48]

In the fourth dimension of the politics of markets, markets are arenas for the expression of forms of social authority and status derived from outside the economy. The distinction between this dimension as conceived of here, and as seen in economic sociology, revolves around the 'politics of markets' insistence on analysis not merely of social embeddedness but also of the exercise of social power. Patriarchal authority is one obvious form. Gender relations regulate market exchange through restrictions on task and work, by screening access to labour markets, through ideologies of subordination, through rules of market participation prejudicial to women.[49] As a result of the way markets are gendered, economic growth may be constrained, competition suppressed and the social piety of the women in the business family may affect the credit-worthiness of the family business.[50] Religious authority is another. Divine authority expressed in the economy can be the basis of the formation of occupationally specialized social groups. Such groups may supply the preconditions for competition (information, skilling, contacts, access to finance, also collective insurance and even livelihood guarantees). They may also be the foundation of apparently secular corporatist regulative institutions. The existence of such groups can be explained in terms of the minimization of information and transactions costs, but the point is that such groups are never merely groups and their purpose never merely confined to the economy. Religion (or sect, denomination or *biradari*) can and does determine the spatial arrangement of residence and marketplace. In developing economies, laws deemed 'personal' or 'customary' are ways in which divine authority regulates property, individual rights to property and the distribution of property on inheritance, marriage or the partition of a business. Religion has also been found capable of defining the rules of transaction with co-religionists and to differentiate them from rules of transaction with 'others'.[51]

Evidently markets achieve order by means other than the purely economic and by forms of politics not restricted to parties or states. These arenas of power are not to be presumed to be developmentally beneficial. They can be the base for market exclusion.

While it should now be evident that markets are political institutions and that their politics can be extremely complicated and multilayered, the approach outlined here is a framework rather than a theory. It is greedy of evidence of a sort that is hard to come by, particularly in official statistics on markets which have very limited purposes (e.g. defininition of eligibility for tax, tracking price fluctuations and the standard of living). The official records show not a shred of interest in the consequences for markets of patriarchal or religious authority. The 'rich description' to be had from the use of such a framework will be specific to place and time. So, we must *expect* generalizations to be falsified.

4. Social Structures of Accumulation (SSA)

This is an approach to market analysis and theory which has emerged from a series of insights gained from economic history. These include the evident lack of equilibria anywhere in the world, the long waves of the business cycle and the debates over their causes (are they due to bunched cycles of innovation, or to the life cycles of capital goods and infrastructure, or to contingent factors such as wars or new technologies?).[52] The SSA school has theorized that business cycles are a result of the structural nature of the cradle of social institutions which support accumulation (or the creation of productive wealth). The relationships between the elements of this matrix of institutions are not fixed but are thought to follow regular and predictable courses. Their unravelling will herald the end of a stable phase of a business cycle and their reconfiguration will consolidate another. The SSA thus has elements which are social, political and even ideological – enabling investment. But the SSA does not simply help to minimize investment risk, it also regulates contradictions and conflicts, and reduces insecurity over the long term so that profit levels can be maintained and sustained.

If we are to understand markets we have to understand their SSAs. What are the key social structures? According to Kotz, they are those governing the control of raw materials, the labour process, consumption and demand, money and credit. They draw our attention away from politics per se towards certain formal institutions hitherto not much discussed in this exploration of markets: the legal constitution of firms, labour laws, the banking system and ideas (especially those ideas which weaken conflict and control the 'unruly tendencies' of labour).[53]

This list has been criticized as arbitrary. In fact it follows from the idea that capitalist development takes place in conflict: that between financial, industrial and mercantile capital; and conflict between firms in specific markets, both of which are conflicts over the distribution of value. Conflict also erupts between capital as a whole and labour, and between capital and peasants.[54] Such conflict belongs to the category of 'contradiction', which refers to institutions with opposing interests which nonetheless cannot function without one another. Social structures of accumulation are those institutions which enable the regulation of such conflict and contradiction. Other aspects of SSA theory are disputed. The rules governing the start, the breakdown or the succession of SSAs have not been established; the debate over the cause of crises of capitalism (whether due to the dynamic of capital itself, or due to the dynamic of SSAs or due to the relationships between capital and its SSAs) is unresolved. The timing of the development of key SSAs have not been shown to accord with the long swings of the macro-economy. Some components, particularly markets for finance, are inherently unstable.[55] The notion of structure has been criticized as mechanical and essentialist; though, while some essentialism is unavoidable, it is analytically useful to examine an element of an SSA in isolation prior to considering its interrelationships. SSAs need to be explored not only historically in relation to the macroeconomy but also with regard to the contemporary microeconomy.

5. In sum

Each of the approaches that has been developed to systematizse our understanding of markets on the ground has evolved so as to privilege certain institutions at the expense of others. The NIE is centred upon contracts, firms, farms and households. Economic sociology focuses upon networks, labour markets, corporations and the state. The politics of markets requires analysis of the state as participant and regulator, of collective institutions, of assets and their relation to tactics of competition or collusion, of the social power in which markets are embedded – and of each in relation to the others. The 'social structure of accumulation' school has revealed the importance of the legal regulation of each stage of transfer of property rights in the process of production, distribution and consumption. In developing economies, this last approach requires extension in order to establish the roles of non-state, social structures which regulate the economy and stabilize accumulation. These include gender, religion, ethnicity, region, age or life cycle status and even language – though language has never to date been researched as a SSA.

Each approach privileges certain modes of explanation at the expense of others: information and transactions costs in the case of the NIE; social norms, types of exchange and network in economic sociology; market-driven politics in the approach considering markets as political phenomena; and the interconnection of state (and non-state) regulative structures in the SSA. While the NIE does not need reference to time or space in order to develop theory, in the other three the insights of history and geography are crucial to any attempt at explanation.

It is hard for the economist to evade the proposition that markets are social and political constructs whose performance is affected and continually changed by relations of authority. These are established outside the economy and act both inside and outside it. The diversity of meso-level theory already generated by the observation of actually existing markets testifies to the complexity of markets. Interdisciplinary work is necessary to understand them.[56] Such work must celebrate local specificities. It must explore the impact on market structure, regulation and behaviour that is brought about by political and social ideologies as well as the material conditions in which exchange takes place.

Notes

1 Folbre 1994; Haddad et al. 1997.
2 See the critical reviews in references in endnote 1; plus the important debates in Young et al. 1981 and Jackson and Pearson 1999.
3 Bates 1981 is paradigmatic for developing countries.
4 Hodgson 1988, p. 178.
5 See Bardhan 1989; Basu 1994; Harriss Hunter and Lewis 1995; and Subramanian 1992.
6 Byres 1983; Majid 1994.

7 See Patnaik 1994 for an attempt to theorize this variation in agricultural production. See Rogaly 1996 for the coexisting diversity of labour contracts and the range of variation within any given contract.
8 Bhaduri 1983 and Subramanian 1992 are rare attempts to theorize power.
9 North 1990.
10 Martinez-Alier 1987.
11 Harriss-White 1996.
12 Harriss-White 2003.
13 Harriss-White 1995a.
14 The great founding father of which is Max Weber 1978 [1922].
15 Polanyi 1957.
16 See van Ufford 1999 on Benin's cattle trade.
17 See Pujo 1997 for its role in Guinee's rice economy.
18 See Harriss-White 1996 for the moral status of garlic, onion and tobacco in the rural Indian economy.
19 See Granovetter 1995 for labour markets in the US; see Meagher 2003 for informal petty commodity production and marketing in southern Nigeria.
20 Evers and Schrader 1994; see Clough 1995 for Hausa Nigeria.
21 Sen 1981, quoted in Mackintosh 1990.
22 Davis 1992.
23 Prof N Emler 1999 (personal communication).
24 Hodgson 2002.
25 Leys 2001.
26 Granovetter and Swedburg 1992.
27 Weber 1978 [1922].
28 See Crow 2001 for seasonal changes in Bangladesh; see Cutler 1988, Keen 1994, and Ravallion 1987 for market behaviour in famine conditions in Ethiopia, Sudan and Bangladesh respectively; see Palaskas and Harriss-White 1993; 1996 for analysis of price behaviour over the medium term in North East and South East India.
29 Harriss-White 1995b.
30 This discussion owes much to White 1993.
31 von Benda Beckmann and van Meijl 1999.
32 Monbiot 2001.
33 Bavinck 2003.
34 Leys 2001; Gupta 2002.
35 Guhan and Paul 1997; Khan and Jomo 2000.
36 Amin 2002.
37 See Harriss-White 1993; 2003 for explorations of this type of market-driven politics in India.
38 Khan and Jomo 2000.
39 Castells 2000; Meagher 2003.
40 Smith 1995.
41 Hodgson 1988.
42 White 1993.
43 Schmitz and Nadvi 1999; Nadvi 1999.
44 Bardhan 1991.
45 Harriss 1979.
46 Crow 2001.

47 Bhaduri 1986.
48 Janakarajan 1993. Agricultural labour contracts involved obligations to maintain irrigation infrastructure. Land sales between upper and lower castes has led to low-caste agricultural labour's refusing to carry out these non-contractual obligations. This change in contractual content has contributed (together with the proliferation of private open wells) to the collapse of the tank irrigation system.
49 See Jackson and Pearson 1998; Pujo 1997; Robson 2002.
50 Laidlaw 1995.
51 Harriss-White 2003, chapter 6.
52 Kotz, McDonough and Reich 1994; Gordon, Edwards and Reich 1982.
53 Kotz 1994.
54 Despite the discussion of market-driven politics in the section on the politics of markets, it must not be assumed that there cannot be conflict between capital and parts of the state.
55 Fitzgerald 2002.
56 In the last four decades, there have been two big waves of interest in rural markets in developing economies. In the 1960s and 1970s, industrial organization methods were used to evaluate the competitiveness of local markets. If they were concluded to be competitive (which by and large they were, even when the detailed ethnographic evidence showed otherwise) there was then no case for extensive state intervention. The second wave of field research was provoked in the 1990s by the failure of structural adjustment conditions to have their predicted impacts upon domestic markets. See Harriss 1979a; 1979b for reviews of the first phase and de Alcantara 1993, Bryceson 1993, Dorward and Kydd 1998 and Crow 2001 for reviews of the second phase.

References

Amin, S, 2002 , 'Economic Globalisation and Political Universalism : Conflicting Issues?', in Harriss-White, 2002, chapter 2.
Bardhan, P, 1989, *The Economic Theory of Agrarian Institutions*, Oxford, Clarendon Press.
——, 1991, 'On the concept of power in economics' *Economics and Politics* vol. 3, no. 3, pp. 265–77.
Basu, K, 1994, ed., *Agrarian Questions*, Delhi, Oxford University Press.
Bates, R, 1981, *Markets and States in Tropical Africa*, Berkeley, University of California Press.
Bavinck, M, 2003, 'The Spatially Fragmented State: Myths and Realities in the Regulation of Marine Fisheries in Tamil Nadu, India', *Development and Change*.
Bernstein, H, B Crow, M Mackintosh and C Martin, 1990, *The Food Question*, London, Earthscan.
Bhaduri, A, 1983, *The Economics of Backward Agriculture*, New York, Academic Press.
——, 1986, 'Forced Commerce and Agrarian Growth', *World Development*, vol. 14, no. 2, pp. 267–72.
Bryceson, D, 1993, *Liberalising Tanzania's Food Trade: The Public and Private Faces of Urban Marketing Policy, 1939–1988*, London, James Currey.
Byres, TJ, 1983, *Sharecropping and Sharecroppers*, London, Frank Cass.
Caille, A, 1994, ' D'une Economie Politique qui aurait pu etre' in Caille et al, 1994.
Caille, A, et al, 1994, *Pour une Autre Economie/ Revue du Mouvement Anti-utilitariste dans les Sciences Sociales*, Paris, La Decouverte.

Castells, M, 2000, *The Rise of the Network Society*, Oxford, Blackwell.

Clough, P, 1995, 'The Economy and Culture of the Talakawa of Marmara', DPhil thesis, Oxford University.

Crow, B, 2001, *Markets Class and Social Change*, London, Palgrave.

Cutler, P, 1988, 'The Development of the 1983–5 Famine in Northern Ethiopia', PhD thesis, London School of Hygiene and Tropical Medicine, London University.

Davis, J, 1992, *Exchange*, London, Open University Press.

Dorward, A and Kydd, J, 1998, *Smallholder cash Crop Production under Market Liberalisation: a New Institutional Economics Perspective* ,Wallingford, CAB International.

Evers, HD and Schrader, N, 1994, *The Moral Economy of Trade : Ethnicity and Developing Markets*, London, Routledge.

Fitzgerald, EVK, 2002, 'The Security of International Finance' in Harriss-White, 2002.

Folbre, N, 1994 *Who pays for the Kids : Gender and the Structures of Constraint*, London, Routledge.

Gordon, D, R Edwards and M Reich, 1982, *Segmented Work, Divided Workers*, Cambridge, Cambridge University Press.

Granovetter, M and Svedberg, R, eds, 1992, *The Sociology of Economic Life*, Boulder, Westview.

——, 1995, *Getting a Job: a Study of Contracts and Careers*, Chicago, University of Chicago Press.

Guhan, S and Paul, S, 1997, *Corruption in India*, New Delhi, Vision Publishers.

Gupta S, 2002, *Corporate Capital and Political Philosophy*, London, Pluto Press.

Haddad, L, et al, 1997, eds. *Intrahousehold Resource Allocation in Developing Countries* Baltimore, Johns Hopkins University Press.

Harriss, B, 1979a, '"There's Method in my Madness, or is it Vice Versa?" Measuring Agricultural Market Performance', *Food Research Institute Studies*, Stanford, vol. xvi, no. 2, pp. 40–56.

——, 1979b, 'Going against the Grain', *Development and Change*, vol. 10, no. 3, pp. 368–84.

Harriss J, J Hunter and C Lewis, 1995, eds, *The New Institutional Economics and Third World Development*, London, Routledge.

Harriss-White, B, 1993, 'The Collective Politics of Foodgrains Markets in South Asia', *Bulletin, Institute of Development Studies* vol. 24, no. 3, pp. 54–63.

——, 1995a, 'Maps and Landscapes of Grain Markets in South Asia', pp 87–108 in Harriss 1995.

——, 1995b, '"Order... order..." Agro-commercial micro-structures and the state: the experience of regulation', pp 275–314 in Stein and Subrahmanyam 1995.

——, 1996, *A Political Economy of Agricultural Markets in South India*, New Delhi, Sage.

——, 2002a, ed., *Globalisation and Insecurity*, London, Palgrave.

——, 2002b, 'India's Religious Pluralism and its Implications for the Economy', QEH Working Paper, no. 82.

——, 2003, *India Working*, Cambridge, Cambridge University Press.

Hewitt de Alcantara, C, 1993 *Real Markets: Social and Political Issues of Food Policy Reform*, London, Frank Cass.

Hodgson, G, 1988, *Economics and Institutions*, London, Polity Press.

——, 2002, 'Is Social Evolution Lamarckian or Darwinian', paper to the International Workshop on Evolutionary Economics, University of Herts, UK.

Jackson, C and Pearson, R, 1998, *Feminist Visions of Development: Gender Analysis and Policy*, London, Routledge.

Janakarajan, S, 1992, 'Interlinked transactions and the Market for Water in the Agrarian Economy of a Tamilnadu Village' in Subramanian, 1992, pp. 151–89.

———, 1993, ' Traidic Exchange Relations: an Illustration from South India', *Bulletin, Institute of Development Studies*, vol. 24, no. 3, pp. 75–82.

Keen, D, 1994, *The Benefits of Famine*, Princeton, Princeton University Press.

Khan, M and Jomo, KS, 2000, *Rents, Rent Seeking and Economic Development in Asia*, Cambridge, Cambridge University Press.

Kotz, D, 1994, 'The Regulation Theory and the Social Structures of Accumulation Approach' in Kotz, McDonough and Reich 1994, pp. 85–98.

Kotz, DM, McDonough, T and Reich, M, 1994, eds, *Social Structures of Accumulation: the Political Economy of Growth and Crisis*, Cambridge, Cambridge University Press.

Laidlaw, J, 1995, *Riches and Renunciation: Religion, Economy and Society among the Jains*, Oxford, Clarendon Press.

Leys, C, 2001, *Market-Driven Politics*, London, Verso.

———, 2002, 'Global Capitalism and National Politics' in Harriss-White, 2002a.

Mackintosh M, 1990, 'Abstract Markets and Real Needs' Bernstein et al., 1990, pp. 43–53.

Majid, N, 1994, 'Contractual Arrangements in Pakistan's Agriculture: A Study of Share Tenure in Sindh', D. Phil. Thesis, Oxford University.

Martinez-Alier, J, 1987, *Ecological Economics: Energy Environment and Society*, Oxford, Blackwell.

Meagher, K, 2003, 'Informalisation and Embeddedness in South Eastern Nigeria', D.Phil. Thesis, Oxford University.

Monbiot, G, 2001, *Captive State: the Corporate Take-over of Britain* , London, Pan Books.

Nadvi, K, 1999, 'Shifting Ties, Social Networks in the Surgical Instruments Cluster of Sialkot, *Development and Change*, vol. 30, no. 1, pp. 143–77.

North, D, 1990, *Institutions, Institutional Change and Economic Performance*, Cambridge, Cambridge University Press.

Palaskas, T and Harriss-White, B, 1993, 'Testing Marketing Integration: New Approaches with Case Material from the West Bengal Food Economy', Jounral of Development Studies, vol. 30, no. 1, pp. 1–57.

———, 1996, Identification of Market Exogeneity and Market Dominance by Tests instead of Assumptions: An Application to Indian Material Journal of International Development, vol. 8, no. 1, pp. 111–23.

Patnaik, U, 1994, 'Tenancy and Accumulation' in Basu, 1994, pp. 155–202.

Penny, D, 1985, *Starvation: A Political Economy*, Canberra, Australian National University.

Polanyi, K, 1957, *The Great Transformation*, Boston, Beacon Press.

Pujo, L, 1997, 'Towards a Methodology for the Analysis of the Embeddedness of Markets in Social Institutions: Application to Gender and the Market for Local Rice in Eastern Guinee', DPhil Thesis, Oxford University.

Ravallion, M, 1987, *Markets and Famines*, Oxford, Clarendon Press.

Robson, E, 2002, 'Gender, Households and Markets: Social reproduction in a Hausa Village, Northern Nigeria', DPhil Thesis, Oxford University.

Rogaly, B, 1996, 'Agricultural Growth and the Structure of "Casual" Labour-hiring in Rural West Bengal', *Journal of Peasant Studies*, vol. 23, no. 4, pp. 141–60.

Schmitz, H and Nadvi, K, 1999, 'Clustering and Industrialisation: Introduction', Special issue on *'Industrial Clusters in Developing Countries' World Development*, vol. 27, no. 9, pp.1503–14.

Sen, AK, 1981, *Poverty and Famines*, Clarendon, Oxford.

Smith, A, 1995, *An Enquiry into the Nature and Causes of the Wealth of Nations*, London, Pickering.

Stein, B and Subrahmanyam, S, 1995, eds, *Institutions and Economic Change in South Asia*, Delhi, Oxford University Press.

Subramanian, S, 1992a, 'Appendix : a Model of Triadic power Relations in the Interlinkage of Agrarian Markets' in Subramanian, 1992b, pp. 190–201.

——, 1992b, ed., *Themes in Development Economics*, Delhi, Oxford University Press.

Van Ufford, PQ, 1999, 'Trade and Traders, The Making of the Cattle Market of Benin', PhD Thesis, Amsterdam University.

Von Benda-Beckmann, F and van Meijl, T, 1999, eds, *Property Rights and Economic Development*, London, Kegan Paul.

Weber, M, 1978 [1922], *Economy and Society : An Outline of Interpretive Sociology*, Berkeley, University of California Press.

White, G, 1993a, 'Towards a Political Analysis of Markets, in White 1993b, pp. 4–11.

——, 1993b, ed., *The Political Analysis of Markets* Special Issues of the *Bulletin, Institute of Development Studies*, vol. 24, no. 3.

Young, K, et al, 1981, *Of Marriage and the Market*, London, CSE Books.

22

INSTITUTIONAL DEVELOPMENT IN HISTORICAL PERSPECTIVE[1]

Ha-Joon Chang

1. Introduction

The issue of institutional development, especially under the slogan of 'good governance', has recently come to occupy the centre stage of development policy debate. During the last decade or so, the international development policy establishment (henceforth IDPE) – comprising the IMF, the World Bank and key donor governments – have come to recognize the limitations of their earlier emphasis on 'getting the prices right' through policy reform and have accepted the importance of the institutional structure that underpins the price system.[2] Increasingly, they are putting emphasis on 'getting the institutions right' and attaching 'governance-related conditionalities', involving things like political democracy, corporate governance reform and reform of the financial system.

On the offensive today are those who believe that every country should adopt a set of 'good institutions' (unfortunately often implicitly equated with US institutions), with some minimal transition provisions (5–10 years) for the poorer countries – various agreements in the WTO being the best example of this. Many of them believe that these institutions are so necessary that they have to be imposed on the developing countries through IMF and World Bank loan conditionalities and irreversible bilateral and multilateral treaties. Backing up such a claim is a rapidly growing body of literature, especially from the World Bank and its associates, which is trying to establish statistical correlation between institutional variables and economic development, with the supposed causality running from the former to the latter.[3]

Naturally, there is widespread unease about these attempts. One obvious reason is that the IMF and World Bank do not have a mandate to intervene in many of these areas[4] – take, for example, the imposition of corporate governance-related conditionality by the IMF during the Asian financial crisis, when the IMF's original mandate is limited to the balance of payments problem. Taken to its extreme, this push for the adoption of institutional global standards amounts to neo-imperialism. Another source of unease is that the standards demanded from developing country institutions seem to be

Table 1. **Introduction of democracy in the NDCs**

Country	Universal Male Suffrage	Universal Suffrage
Australia	1903[1]	1962
Austria	1907	1918
Belgium	1919	1948
Canada	1920[2]	1970
Denmark	1849	1915
Finland	1919[3]	1944
France	1848	1946
Germany	1849[2]	1946
Italy	1919[4]	1946
Japan	1925	1952
Netherlands	1917	1919
New Zealand	1889	1907
Norway	1898	1913
Portugal	n.a.	1970
Spain	n.a.	1977 (1931)**
Sweden	1918	1918
Switzerland	1879	1971
UK	1918[5]	1928
USA	1965 (1870)*	1965

Source: Chang 2002, table 3.1.

1 With racial qualifications
2 With property qualifications
3 Communists excluded
4 With restrictions
5 All men and women over 30
*   Universal male suffrage was introduced in 1870, but reversed between 1890 and 1908 through the disenfranchisement of the blacks in the Southern states. It was only restored in 1965.
** Universal suffrage was introduced in 1931 but reversed by the military coup of General Franco in 1936. It was only restored in 1977, following Franco's death in 1975.

too high – many developing countries, often justly, say that they simply cannot 'afford' the high-quality institutions that are demanded of them.

Such criticism is important, but in the absence of some idea as to which institutions are necessary and/or viable under what conditions, they are in danger of justifying whatever institutional *status quo* that exists in developing countries. Then what is the alternative?

One obvious alternative is for us to find out directly which of the 'best practice' institutions are suitable for particular developing countries by transplanting them and seeing how they fare. However, as the failures of the structural adjustment programmes in many developing countries and of 'transition' in many former Communist economies show, this usually does not work and can be very costly.

Another alternative is for the developing countries to wait for spontaneous institutional evolution. It may be argued that the best way to get the institutions that suit the local conditions is to let them evolve naturally. However, such spontaneous evolution may take a long time, and there is no guarantee that the outcome will be optimal, even from the national point of view.

The third and my preferred alternative is to learn from history by looking at institutional development in the developed countries when they were 'developing countries' themselves. Therefore, in this chapter I try to draw lessons from the *history*, as opposed to the *current state*, of the developed countries.

2. The history of institutional development in the now developed countries

In this section, I discuss the evolution of six categories of institution that are widely regarded as essential components of a 'good governance' structure in the now developed countries (henceforth NDCs) during the period between the early nineteenth and early twentieth centuries, when they were at similar levels of development as that of today's developing countries. They are: democracy; bureaucracy (including the judiciary); property rights; corporate governance institutions; financial institutions; and welfare and labour institutions.

2.1 Democracy

As is well known, there is currently a lively debate on whether democracy is good for economic development.[5] Whatever one's position is in this regard, it is clear that the NDCs did not develop under democracy.

As can be seen in Table 1, it was not until the 1920s that most NDCs adopted universal male suffrage for the majority white population, as they finally abolished property ownership qualification for suffrage that until then had blocked the poorer sections of the society from voting. However, it was not until the late twentieth century that all NDCs fulfilled the minimum definition of 'democracy': granting votes to every adult, regardless of property ownership, educational qualification, gender and race. Spain and Portugal, until this time under military rule, only restored democracy in the 1970s. Votes were given to ethnic minorities in Australia and the USA in 1962 and 1965 respectively, while votes were given to women in many countries after the Second World War and in Switzerland as late as in 1971.

Even when democracy formally arrived, its quality was often extremely poor. Secret balloting was introduced only in the early twentieth century, while corrupt electoral practices (such as vote buying, electoral fraud, legislative corruption) lasted well into the twentieth century in most countries. With such 'expensive' elections, it was no big surprise that elected officials were corrupt. In the late nineteenth century, legislative corruption in the USA, especially in state assemblies, got so bad that the future US president Theodore Roosevelt lamented that New York assemblymen, who engaged in the open selling of votes to lobbying groups, 'had the same idea about Public Life and Civil Service that a vulture has of a dead sheep'.[6]

It is interesting to note that most of today's developing countries adopted universal suffrage at much lower levels of development than the ones at which the now-developed countries adopted it, as can be seen in Table 2. Of course, many developing countries have experienced reversals in their democratic progresses (in just the same way that the NDCs did). However, even as they were suspending elections altogether, none of the non-democratic governments in currently developing countries reintroduced selective disenfranchisement based on things like property ownership, gender, and race – things that had been widely accepted as legitimate criteria for enfranchisement in NDCs in the early days. This shows that the *idea*, if not necessarily the practice, of universal suffrage has been much more widely accepted in today's developing countries than it was in the NDCs when they were at similar stages of development.

2.2 *Bureaucracy and judiciary*

Up until the eighteenth century – and in some cases beyond – the open sale of public offices (and honours), sometimes with widely-publicized price tags, was a common practice in most NDCs.[7] Partly because they were openly bought and sold, public offices were formally regarded as private property in many of these countries. For example, in Britain, prior to the reforms carried out in the early nineteenth century, government ministries were 'private establishments' unaccountable to the Parliament, paid their staff by fees (rather than salaries), and kept many obsolete offices as sinecures.[8]

The 'spoils' system, in which public offices were allocated to the loyalists of the ruling party, became a key component in American politics from the emergence of the two-party system in 1828 with the election of President Jackson. It was also prevalent in Spain and Portugal. In addition, there was widespread nepotism even in countries like Prussia, which was a pioneer of modern bureaucracy. Feuchtwanger argues that, even after the extensive bureaucratic reform under Frederick William I, 'nepotism was still rife and many offices were virtually hereditary'.[9]

With the sales of offices, spoils system, and nepotism, it is hardly surprising that professionalism was conspicuously lacking in the bureaucracies of most NDCs until the late nineteenth century. Until the 1883 Pendleton Act, none of the US federal bureaucrats were competitively recruited. Less than half of them were competitively recruited by the end of the nineteenth century. It was only through a long-drawn-out process of reform, starting with Prussia in the eighteenth century, that the bureaucracies in the NDCs were able to be modernized.

Judiciaries often lacked professionalism and independence. For example, in Italy, up until the late nineteenth century, judges did not usually have a background in law and, according to one historian, 'could not protect themselves, let alone anyone else, against political abuses'.[10] Until the early twentieth century, the judiciary in many countries was prone to dispense 'class justice', in which middle-class crimes were less diligently brought to the court and much more leniently dealt with than working class crimes.[11]

2.3 Property rights

This section does not attempt to chart the evolution of property rights regimes, since it would involve an impossibly wide range of institutions (e.g., contract law, company law, bankruptcy law, inheritance law, tax law, land law, urban planning regulations, etc.). However, one observation that needs to be made is that the current emphasis on strong protection of property rights is misplaced, as the preservation of certain property rights sometimes proved harmful for economic development. Many historical examples demonstrate that the violation of certain existing property rights (and the creation of new property rights) were actually beneficial for economic development. The British enclosure system, squatting in the US midwest in the nineteenth century, East Asian land reform and nationalization in postwar Austria and France are all such examples.

So in this section, I consider only one element of the property rights

Table 2. Income per capita at attainment of universal suffrage

GDP p.c. (in 1990 international dollars)	NDCs (Year universal suffrage was attained; GDP p.c.)	Developing Countries (Year universal suffrage was attained; GDP p.c.)
<$1,000		Bangladesh (1947; $585[1]) Burma (1948; $393[2]) Egypt (1952; $542) Ethiopia (1955; $295) India (1947; $641) Indonesia (1945; $514) Kenya (1963; $713) Pakistan (1947; $631[1]) South Korea (1948; $777) Tanzania (1962; $506) Zaire (1967; $707)
$1,000–$1,999		Bulgaria (1945; $1,073) Ghana (1957; $1,159) Hungary (1945; $1,721) Mexico (1947; $1,882) Nigeria (1979; $1,189) Turkey (1946; $1,129)
$2,000–$2,999	Austria (1918; $2,572) Germany (1946; $2,503) Italy (1946; $2,448) Japan (1952[3]; $2,277) Norway (1913; $2,275) Spain (1931; $2,713) Sweden (1918; $2,533)	Columbia (1957; $2,382) Peru (1956; $2,732) Philippines (1981; $2,526)
$3,000–$3,999	Denmark (1915; $3,635) Finland (1944; $3,578) France (1946; $3,819)	Taiwan (1972; $3,313) Chile (1949; $3,715)
$4,000–$4,999	Belgium (1948; $4,917) Netherlands (1919; $4,022)	Brazil (1977; $4,613)
$5,000–$9,999	Australia (1962; $8,691) New Zealand (1907[4]; $5,367) Portugal (1970; $5,885) UK (1928; $5,115)	Argentina (1947; $5,089) Venezuela (1947; $6,894)

Table 2 **continued**

GDP p.c. (in 1990 international dollars)	NDCs (Year universal suffrage was attained; GDP p.c.)	Developing Countries (Year universal suffrage was attained; GDP p.c.)
>$10,000	Canada (1970[5]; $11,758) Switzerland (1971; $17,142) USA (1965; $13,316)	

Source: Chang 2002, table 3.2.

Notes:
1 GDP p.c. in 1948.
2 GDP p.c. in 1950.
3 Universal suffrage was granted in 1946 under the constitution drawn up by the occupying forces after the Second World War, but did not come into effect until the end of US military rule in 1952.
4 When dominion status was achieved.
5 When the Election Act that year granted full franchise.

system that is comparatively easily examined, namely that of intellectual property rights (henceforth IPR) institutions. The picture that emerges of the NDCs' IPR regimes is that they were 'deficient' by the standards of our time.[12] Patent systems in many countries lacked disclosure requirements, incurred very high costs in filing and processing patent applications, and afforded inadequate protection to the patentees. Most patent laws were very lax on checking the originality of the invention. For example, in the USA, before the 1836 overhaul of the patent law, patents were granted without any proof of originality. Few countries allowed patents on chemical and pharmaceutical substances (as opposed to their processes) until the late twentieth century.[13]

These laws accorded only very inadequate protection, especially in relation to the protection of foreign IPR. In most countries, including Britain (before 1852), the Netherlands, Austria, and France, patenting of 'imported invention' by their nationals was often explicitly allowed. The cases of Switzerland and the Netherlands in relation to their patent laws deserve even greater attention.[14] The Netherlands abolished its 1817 patent law in 1869, partly as a result of the rather deficient nature of the law (even by the standards of the time), but also through having been influenced by the anti-patent movement that swept Europe at the time. Switzerland did not acknowledge any IPR over inventions until 1888, when a patent law, protecting mechanical inventions only, was introduced.[15] Only in 1907, partly prompted by the threat of trade sanction from Germany in retaliation to the Swiss use of its chemical and pharmaceutical inventions, a patent law worth its name came into being. However, chemical substances remained unpatentable until 1978.[16]

In other areas of IPR, such as copyrights and trademarks, the protection fell well short of what is demanded of developing countries today. For example, the USA did not recognize foreign citizens' copyrights until 1891, while there was a widespread violation of the British trademark law by the German firms in the late nineteenth century.

2.4 Corporate governance institutions

Even in the most developed countries (the UK and the US), many key institutions of what is these days regarded as a 'modern corporate governance' system emerged after, rather than before, their industrial development.

In most countries, until the 1860s or the 1870s, limited liability – without which there will be no modern corporations based on stock ownership – was not standard, but rather something granted as a privilege to high-risk projects with good government connections (e.g. the British East India Company). Indeed, until the late nineteenth century, many people, including no less an economist than Adam Smith, objected to the introduction of limited liability on the grounds that it would lead to what modern economists call 'moral hazard' on the part of the dominant owners and managers.

Until the 1930s, there was virtually no effective regulation on company audit and information disclosure, even in the most developed economy of the time, namely, the UK. The UK made the external audit of companies a requirement in 1844, but this was made optional again in 1856. It was only with the introduction of the 1900 Company Act that external audit was again made compulsory. However, there was no explicit requirement for firms to publish the results of audits; the reporting of a balance sheet was finally made compulsory in 1907. Even then, many companies exploited a loophole in the Act, which did not specify the time period for this reporting, and filed the same balance sheet year after year. Although this loophole was closed in 1928, disclosure rules were still poor by modern standards until the Companies Act of 1948. Crafts argues that 'the development of capital markets based on extensive shareholder rights and the threat of hostile takeover is a relatively recent phenomenon in the UK even though the British were pioneers of modern financial reporting and had the Common Law tradition'.[17]

Until the late nineteenth century, bankruptcy laws were geared towards punishing bankrupt businessmen by putting them into debtors' prison, as they were seen as either profligate or dishonest. Only in the late nineteenth century did bankruptcy laws start to be seen as a way of giving them a second chance, and countries began to introduce 'modern' bankruptcy laws.

Competition law did not really exist in any country until the early twentieth century. The USA did introduce the Sherman Antitrust Act in 1890, but it was crippled by the Supreme Court in 1895. Until 1902, when President Theodore Roosevelt used it against JP Morgan's railways holding company, Northern Securities Company, the Act was in fact mainly used against labour unions rather than against large corporations. It was not until the Clayton Antitrust Act of 1914, which banned the use of antitrust legislation against the unions, that the USA acquired a genuine competition law. The European NDCs tended to take a less harsh view on cartels and in any case did not introduce competition law until the mid-twentieth century.

2.5 Financial institutions

Modern financial systems with widespread and well-supervised banking, a central bank, and a well-regulated securities market did not come into being until the mid-twentieth century, even in the most developed countries.

The banking system was only established slowly in the NDCs.[18] Even in England, a country with the most advanced banking system until well into the mid-twentieth century, complete financial integration was only achieved in the 1920s, when deposit rates became uniform for town and country. In France, the development of the banking system was even more delayed, with widespread use of bank notes emerging only in the mid-nineteenth century (as opposed to the eighteenth century in Britain) and with 75% of the population without access to banking until as late as 1863.

In the NDCs, banks became professional lending institutions only from the early twentieth century onwards. Before that time, personal connections strongly influenced bank lending decisions. For example, throughout the nineteenth century, US banks lent the bulk of money to their directors, their relatives, and those they knew. Scottish banks in the eighteenth century and English banks in the nineteenth century were basically self-help associations for merchants wanting credit, rather than banks in the modern sense.

Banking regulation was highly inadequate, with the USA permitting 'wild-cat banking', which was 'little different in principle from counterfeiting operations'.[19] As late as 1929, the US banking system was made up of 'thousands upon thousands of small, amateurishly managed, largely unsupervised banks and brokerage houses'.[20] Even in the relatively advanced economies of Germany and Belgium, banking regulation was only introduced in the 1930s.

Central banks, which many people regard as foundation stones of the modern banking system, were also slow to develop. Although the potential usefulness of a lender-of-last-resort was recognized in some circles from as early as the seventeenth century, many people at the time objected to the creation of a central bank. In the same way in which they were concerned with the 'moral hazard' effect of bankruptcy law and objected to its creation, people believed that central banking would encourage excessive risk-taking by bailing out imprudent borrowers in times of trouble.[21] This sentiment is best summed up in Herbert Spencer's observation that '[t]he ultimate result of shielding man from the effects of folly is to people the world with fools'.[22]

The Swedish Riksbank was nominally the first official central bank in the world (established in 1688), but until the early twentieth century, it could not function as a proper central bank because it did not have, among other things, monopoly over note issue. The Bank of England was established in 1694 and started assuming the role of lender of last resort from the eighteenth century (or from some viewpoints the first half of the nineteenth century). However, it was not until 1844 that it became a real central bank – the first of its kind in the world.

As we can see from Table 3, until the early twentieth century, countries such as Sweden, Germany, Italy, Switzerland and the USA lacked a central bank. The US Federal Reserve System came into being in 1913, but until 1915 only 30% of the banks (with 50% of all banking assets) were in the system; as late as 1929, 65% of the banks were still outside the system, although by this time they accounted for only 20% of total banking assets. This meant that in 1929 the law 'still left some sixteen thousand little banks beyond its jurisdiction. A few hundred of these failed almost every year'.[23] Also, until the Great Depression, the Federal Reserve Board was de facto controlled by Wall Street.[24]

Securities regulations were also late in coming. Serious securities regulations did not come into being until the 1930s, even in the UK and the USA where the securities markets were most developed (the 1939 Prevention of Fraud (Investments) Act of the UK and the 1933 Federal Securities Act of the USA). It was only with the 1986 Financial Services Act that the UK introduced a comprehensive system of securities regulation.

A similar story applies to public finance. The fiscal capacity of the state remained highly inadequate in most NDCs until the early twentieth century, when most countries did not have income tax. Before Britain introduced a permanent income tax in 1842, countries used it only as emergency measures during wartime. Even in Britain, as last as in 1874, Gladstone was fighting his election campaign with a pledge to abolish income tax. Even Sweden, despite its later reputation as a high-income-tax country, did not have income tax until 1932. In the USA, the income tax law of 1894 was overturned as 'uncon-

Table 3. **Development of central banking in the NDCs**

	Year of Establishment	Year when Note Issue Monopoly was gained
Sweden	1688	1904
UK	1694	1844
France	1800	1848[1]
Netherlands	1814	After the 1860s
Spain	1829	1874
Portugal	1847	1891[2]
Belgium	1851	1851
Germany	1871	1905
Italy	1893	1926
Switzerland	1907	1907
USA	1913	After 1929[3]

Source: Chang 2002, table 3.3.

1 Controlled by the bankers themselves until 1936.
2 Legally note issue monopoly was established in 1887, but de facto monopoly was achieved only in 1891 due to the resistance of other note-issuing banks. The bank is still 100% privately owned and cannot intervene in the money market.
3 65% of the banks accounting for 20% of banking assets were outside the Federal Reserve System until 1929.

stitutional' by the Supreme Court. A subsequent bill was defeated in 1898, and the Sixteenth Amendment allowing federal income tax was adopted only in 1913. However, the tax rate was only 1% for taxable net income above $3,000, rising to 7% on incomes above $500,000.

With limited taxation capability, government finance, especially that of local government, was in a mess: telling examples of this is the simultaneous defaults by a number of US state governments on British loans in 1842. After these defaults, British financiers put pressure on the US federal government to assume the liabilities (which reminds us of the events in Brazil following the default of the state of Minas Gerais in 1999). When this pressure came to naught, *The Times* poured scorn on the US federal government's attempt to raise a new loan later in the year by arguing that '[t]he people of the United Sates may be fully persuaded that there is a certain class of securities to which no abundance of money, however great, can give value; and that in this class their own securities stand pre-eminent'.[25]

2.6 *Welfare and labour institutions*

As we can see in Table 4, social welfare institutions (e.g., industrial accident insurance, health insurance, state pension, unemployment insurance) in the NDCs only started to emerge in the late nineteenth century. Their development was spurred on by the increasing political muscle-flexing of the popular classes after the significant extension of suffrage during this time and by union activism. Of course, there was no direct relationship between the extension of suffrage and the extension of welfare institutions. While, in cases like New Zealand, there is a clear link between the early extension of suffrage and the development of welfare institutions, in cases like Germany welfare institutions grew quickly under relatively limited suffrage.

In fact, Germany was the pioneer in this area. It was the first to introduce industrial accident insurance (1871), health insurance (1883) and state pensions (1889), although France was the first country to introduce unemployment insurance (1905). The early German welfare institutions were already very 'modern' in character (e.g. they had universal coverage), and apparently attracted great admiration from the French left at the time.[26]

Once introduced, social welfare institutions diffused quite quickly. In 1875, none of the 19 countries listed below in table 4 had any of the four welfare institutions covered in the table, except for the industrial accident insurance introduced in Germany in 1871. However, by 1925, 16 of these countries had industrial accident insurance, 13 had health insurance, 12 had pension and 12 had unemployment insurance.

Effective labour institutions (e.g., regulations on child labour, working hours, workplace safety) did not emerge until around the same time, even in the most advanced countries. Child labour regulations started emerging in the late eighteenth or early nineteenth centuries, but most of these regulations were extremely mild and poorly enforced until the late nineteenth/early twentieth centuries (see Table 5).

Until the early twentieth century, regulation of working hours or working conditions for adult male workers was considered unthinkable in most countries. In 1905, for example, the US Supreme Court declared in a famous case that a 10-hour act for the bakers introduced by New York state was unconstitutional because 'it deprived the bakers of the liberty of working as long as they wished'.[27]

As a result, even minimal regulations on adult working hours and conditions did not come about in many NDCs until the late nineteenth and early twentieth centuries. It was only well into the twentieth century that we begin to witness 'modern' regulations on working hours. Most countries introduced 48-hour work week in the 1920s and the 1930s.

Table 4. **Introduction of social welfare institutions in the NDCs**

	Industrial Accident	Health	Pension	Unemployment
Germany	1871	1883	1889	1927
Switzerland	1881	1911	1946	1924
Austria	1887	1888	1927	1920
Norway	1894	1909	1936	1906
Finland	1895	1963	1937	1917
UK	1897	1911	1908	1911
Ireland*	1897	1911	1908	1911
Italy	1898	1886	1898	1919
Denmark	1898	1892	1891	1907
France	1898	1898	1895	1905
New Zealand	1900	1938	1898	1938
Spain	1900	1942	1919	n.a.
Sweden	1901	1891	1913	1934
Netherlands	1901	1929	1913	1916
Australia	1902	1945	1909	1945
Belgium	1903	1894	1900	1920
Canada	1930	1971	1927	1940
USA	1930	No	1935	1935
Portugal	1962	1984+	1984+	1984+

Source: Chang 2002, table 3.4.

Notes:
Countries are arranged in the order in which they introduced industrial accident (starting with Germany in 1871). If it was introduced in the same year, the country that introduced health insurance earlier is listed first.

Figures include schemes which were initially voluntary but state-aided as well as those that were compulsory.

* Ireland was a UK colony in the years mentioned.
+ Although some social-welfare institutions were introduced in Portugal from the 1960s onward, they remained a very fragmented system consisting of partial regimes regulating social insurance of certain social groups until 1984.

Table 5. **Introduction of child labour regulation in the NDCs**

	First attempt at Regulation (mostly ineffective)	First 'serious' Regulation	Relatively comprehensive and well-enforced Regulation
Austria	1787	1842?	?
UK	1802	1833	1878
Prussia	1839	1853–4	1878
France	1841	?	?
USA	1842*	1904–14	1938
Sweden	1846	1881	1900
Saxony	1861	?	?
Denmark	1873	1925	?
Spain	1873	1900	?
Holland	1874	?	?
Switzerland	1877	?	?
Belgium	1878	1909	1914?
Norway	1892	?	?
Italy	1902	?	?
Portugal	1913	?	?

Source: Chang 2002, table 3.5.

* When Massachusetts introduced its state regulation.

3. Institutional development in developing countries then and now

The first point that emerges from our historical examination is that it typically took the NDCs decades, if not centuries, to develop institutions from the time when the need for them started to be perceived. It should be also pointed out that the NDCs frequently experienced reversals in this process. Let us provide some examples to illustrate this point.

Democracy took a long time to develop. To give a couple of examples, it took France and Switzerland almost 100 years (1848 to 1946 and 1879 to 1971 respectively) to move from universal male suffrage to universal suffrage. The need for modern professional bureaucracy was widely perceived from the eighteenth century, but it was only by the late nineteenth century that such bureaucracy was instituted in many NDCs. The value of limited liability institutions was already recognized in the sixteenth century, when royal charters permitting limited liability were granted to big, risky ventures (e.g., the British East India Company), but limited liability was not generalized, even in the most advanced countries, until the mid-nineteenth century. The need for central banking was perceived in some circles from as early as the seventeenth century, but the first real central bank, the Bank of England, was instituted only in 1844. And so on.

The diffusion of new institutions from the 'innovator' country to the rest of the NDCs also took considerable time.[28] It took anything between 20 years (e.g., state pension, unemployment insurance) and 1.5 centuries (in the case of modern central banking) between an institutional innovation and its adoption by the majority of the NDCs. When it comes to the time period between an institutional innovation and its adoption as an 'international standard' among the NDCs (that is to say, with all or nearly all of them adopting it), we are talking not in decades, but in generations. The reasons behind this slow pace of institutional development in the NDCs were diverse.

First of all, particularly in the earlier stages of development, many institutions did not get adopted or remained ineffective when adopted, because they were 'unaffordable'. The absence of social welfare and labour regulations are the more obvious examples in this regard; moreover, many institutions of corporate governance and finance remained ineffective in their earlier times because there were not enough resources for their management and enforcement.

Secondly, in many cases institutions did not get accepted, even when they had become 'affordable', because of resistance from those who would (at least in the short run) have lost out from the introduction of such institutions. The resistance to democracy, labour regulation, or income tax by the propertied classes are probably the best examples in this regard.

Thirdly, institutions sometimes did not get adopted because the economic logic behind them was not properly understood at the time. Resistances to limited liability or central banking, even by many of those who would have benefited from such institutions, are good examples of this.

Fourth, there were also institutions that did not get adopted because of certain 'epochal prejudices', even when they had become obviously 'affordable' and the logic behind them was understood. The late introduction of professional bureaucracy in the US as a result of the Jacksonian prejudice against professionalism, or the late introduction of female suffrage in Switzerland are probably the best examples in this regard.

Fifth, institutional development sometimes got delayed because of the interdependence between certain institutions, which required simultaneous developments of related institutions. For example, without the development of public finance institutions to collect taxes, it was difficult properly to pay for a modern professional bureaucracy, but without a developed tax bureaucracy, it was difficult to develop public finance institutions. It is no coincidence that the development of modern bureaucracy went hand in hand with the development of the fiscal capacity of the state.

More detailed historical knowledge will be required in order to explain why a particular institution did not get adopted in a particular country at a particular time, and this is no place to engage in such discussion. However, what seems clear from our discussion is that institutions have typically taken decades, if not generations, to develop. In this light, the currently popular demand that developing countries should adopt 'global standard' institutions right away or at least within the next 5–10 years, or face punishments seems to be at odds with the historical experiences of the NDCs.

Another important point emerges when we compare the levels of institutional development in the NDCs in the earlier period and those in today's developing countries. For example, in 1820, the UK was at a somewhat higher level of development than that of India today (measured by the – admittedly inadequate – income level), but it did not even have many of the most 'basic' institutions possessed by India.[29] It did not have universal suffrage (it did not even have universal *male* suffrage), a central bank, income tax, generalized limited liability, a generalized bankruptcy law, a professional bureaucracy, meaningful securities regulations, or even minimal labour regulations (except for a couple of minimal and hardly-enforced regulations on child labour).

To take another example, Italy in 1875 was at a level of development comparable to that of Pakistan today.[30] However, it did not have universal male suffrage, a professional bureaucracy, an even remotely independent and professional judiciary, a central bank with note-issue monopoly, or competition law. These are all institutions that Pakistan has had for decades, except for periodic disruptions in democracy due to military intervention; even then suffrage, when allowed, has remained universal.

Turning to another example, the USA in 1913 was at a level of development similar to that of Mexico today, yet its level of institutional development was well behind that of Mexico now.[31] Women were still formally disenfranchised, and blacks and other ethnic minorities were de facto disenfranchised in many parts of the country. It had been just over a decade since a federal bankruptcy law was legislated (1898) and barely two decades since the country recognized foreigners' copyrights (1891). A (highly incomplete) central banking system and income tax had only just come into being (1913), and the establishment of a meaningful competition law (the Clayton Act) had to wait another year (1914). There was moreover no federal regulation on securities trading or on child labour, and what little state legislation that existed in these areas was of low quality and very poorly enforced.

Such comparisons could go on. The point is that, in the early days of their economic development, the NDCs were operating with far less developed institutional structures than those which exist in today's developing countries that are at comparable levels of development. It need hardly be said that the level of institutional development in the NDCs fell well short of the higher 'global standards' to which today's developing countries are told to conform.

4. Implications

What are the implications for today's developing countries of our historical examination?

First of all, our discussion suggests that many of the institutions that are currently being promoted as being 'necessary' for development emerged after, not before, economic development in the NDCs. This may not matter much if institutions do not cost anything to establish and run. However, in the real world, demanding that developing countries adopt institutions that are not strictly necessary can have serious opportunity cost implications, as investing resources in establishing and running these institutions means taking resources away from other, more necessary, activities. It is curious that mainstream economists who define economics as a study of allocating 'scarce resources' talk as if there is no scarcity when it comes to the human and financial resources required to establish and run complex institutions.

Secondly, even when we agree that certain institutions are 'necessary', we have to be careful in specifying the exact form that they take. So, for example, we may agree that a 'good' property rights regime is necessary, but we still need to work out what this should in practice mean – how 'debtor-friendly' should the bankruptcy law be?; how strongly should the patent law protect patentee rights?; when should there be land reform? and so on.

Thirdly, we should accept that institutional development takes a long time and be more patient with the process. Seen from this perspective, the five to ten year 'transition periods' currently given to the developing countries to bring their institutional standards up to the 'global standard' are highly inadequate. Asking these countries to install a whole range of new 'global standard' institutions, many of which are not really necessary and some of which are positively harmful for developing countries, in short periods of time seems unrealistic, especially given that today's developing countries are already institutionally more advanced than the NDCs at comparable stages of development.

This, of course, should not mean that developing countries should adopt nineteenth-century institutional standards. Nor should it make us accept whatever 'we-are-not-ready-yet' arguments that is put forward by some developing-country governments. However, it is clear that there should be a keener recognition of the limit to the speed with which institutional development can be achieved in developing countries. At least three objections can be raised against my argument, to which I will now turn.

The first, and most obvious, of these possible objections is the argument that developing countries need to adopt the institutions recommended by developed countries whether they like them or not, because that is how the world is – the strong calling the shots and the weak following them.

At one level, it is difficult to deny the force of this argument. Indeed, there is plenty of evidence that, even in the present age when colonialism and unequal treaties are no longer acceptable, the developed countries can exercise enormous influence on the developing countries. They exercise direct bilateral influence through their aid budgets and trade policies. They maintain collective influence on developing countries through their control of the international financial institutions, on which the latter countries are dependent. And they have disproportionate influence in the running of various international organizations, including even the ostensibly 'democratic' (one-country-one-vote) WTO.[32] The collapse of the Soviet Union, which provided some counterbalance to the power of the developed countries, and the demise of the so-called non-aligned movement among the developing countries have weakened even more the bargaining positions of the developing countries during the last two decades or so.

However, at another level, the argument that developing countries should follow the 'new rules' of the world economy because that is what the developed countries, and the international development policy establishment (IDPE) that they control, want is beside the point. What I am arguing is that it is precisely these 'new rules'' which should be changed. I do agree that the chance of these rules being changed in the near future is slight. However, this does not mean that therefore it is not worth discussing how they should be altered. If we think these rules need changing, we need to debate how best this can be achieved, however low the chance of this happening may be: this chapter is intended precisely to make a contribution to such a debate by identifying the rules by which the NDCs have developed.

The second possible objection to my argument is that the institutions recommended by the IDPE to the developing countries have to be adopted because they are what the international investors want. It is not relevant, it may be argued, whether or not the developing countries like these new rules, or even whether the IDPE is willing to change them, because in this globalized age it is international investors who call the shots. Countries that do not adopt institutions that international investors want, it may be argued, will be shunned by them and suffer as a result. However, this argument has many problems.

First of all, it is not clear whether international investors do necessarily care so much about the institutions promoted by the IDPE. For example, China has been able to attract a huge amount of foreign investments despite having very few of the 'good institutions' as currently defined. This suggests that what investors really want is often different from what they say they want or what the IDPE says they want – democracy and the rule of law being the best examples in this regard. Empirical studies show that most institutional variables are much less important in determining international investment decisions than factors like market size and growth.[33]

Second, even if institutions' conformity to international standards may bring about increased foreign investments, such investments are not going to be the key element in most countries' growth mechanisms.[34] In other words, the potential value of a policy or an institution to a country should be determined more by what it will do to promote internal development rather than by what international investors will think about it. Indeed, I have argued above that many of the institutions that are currently promoted by the proponents of the 'good governance' framework may not be necessary for development. Some of them may not even be good for development at all (e.g., protecting certain property rights). The establishment of such institutions can easily have negative impacts overall – especially when considering their set-up and maintenance costs – even if it leads to higher foreign investments.

Third, unless certain 'good institutions' that get introduced as the result of global pressure can be effectively enforced, they may not deliver the expected results. It is possible to argue that we should welcome a certain degree of external pressure in certain situations where the government of a developing country is resisting the introduction of certain institutions that are obviously 'affordable' and compatible with the prevailing political and cultural norms in the society in question. However, we should also recognize that the introduction of institutions in countries that are not 'ready' can mean that the institutions will not function well, or may even be undermined altogether. Examples of this include democracies undermined by military coups, electoral frauds and vote buying, or income taxes routinely and openly evaded by the rich in many developing countries. There will be also problems with institutional changes that are imposed from outside without 'local ownership', as the current jargon has it. If that is the case, cleverer international investors will figure out that having certain institutions on paper is not the same as really having them, which means that formally introducing 'global standard' institutions will make little difference to the country's attractiveness to foreign investors.

Fourth, as far as the IDPE is able to influence the way in which 'good institutions' are defined, interpreted and promoted, there is still a value in discussing what policies and institutions should be asked of which developing countries. The 'follow the global norm or perish' argument assumes that the IDPE is a weathervane blindly following the winds of international investor sentiments. However, this establishment can, and does, actively decide to a large extent which policies and institutions are pushed for and how strongly.

The third possible objection to my argument is that the 'world standard' in institutions has risen over the last century or so, and therefore that the current developing countries should not consider the NDCs of 100 or 150 years ago as their models.

I wholeheartedly agree with this point. At one level, it would be absurd to argue otherwise. In terms of per capita income, India may be at a similar level of development to that of the USA in 1820,[35] but that should not mean that it should reintroduce slavery, abolish universal suffrage, deprofessionalize its bureaucracy, abolish generalized limited liability, abolish the central bank, abolish income tax, abolish competition law and so on.

Indeed the heightened global standard in institutions has in many ways been a good thing for the developing countries, or at least for reformers in them. Unlike their counterparts in the NDCs of yesterday, the reformers in today's developing countries do not have to struggle (at least, not too hard) with the view that the introduction of things like female suffrage, income tax, restrictions on working hours, and social welfare institutions spells the end of the civilization as we know it. They also don't have to reinvent certain institutions like central banking and limited liability, the logic behind which many people the NDCs in earlier times had found difficult to understand.

Therefore, the developing countries should exploit the advantages of being a latecomer to the maximum, and try to achieve the highest level of institutional development possible. What I am worried about, however, is the view that institutions are simply matters of choice and that all countries should therefore try to reach the very high threshold of the 'minimum global standard' right away or after a minimal transition period. While accepting that latecomer countries do not have to spend as much time as did the pioneer countries in the development of new institutions, we should not forget that it took the NDCs typically decades, and sometimes even generations, in establishing certain institutions whose need had already been perceived; it usually took them another few decades to make them work properly by improving administration, plugging loopholes and strengthening enforcement. In addition we should not forget that, when compared to the NDCs in earlier times, today's developing countries *already* have high standards of institutional development, which in the 1960s and the 1970s proved quite capable of supporting much higher rates of economic growth than those we see today.[36] Given this, it may be unreasonable to ask them to raise the quality of their institutions dramatically in a short time span.

5. Concluding Remarks

The present chapter has shown that the currently popular agenda for 'governance reform' and 'institutional development' needs a serious reexamination. The historical experiences of the NDCs show how some institutions that we take for granted (even for the developing countries of today) are products of lengthy processes of institutional development involving political struggles, ideological battles and legal reforms. While institutional copying is often possible and desirable, institutions are frequently not things that can be easily copied by every country regardless of their conditions, and therefore recommendations for institutional development have to be made with great caution. Unless there is a complete change of perspective among the proponents of the 'good governance' agenda in its present form, the push for 'global standard' institutions will at best remain highly ineffective in addressing the development failure of many developing countries, and at worst will be harmful to their development.

Notes

1 This chapter heavily draws on chapter 3 of Chang 2002.
2 The most important example is World Bank 2002.
3 For a review of these studies, see Aron 2000.
4 Kapur and Webb 2000.
5 See Bardhan 1993 for a concise review.
6 Garraty and Carnes 2000, p. 472.
7 See Kindleberger 1984, pp. 160–1 for England and pp. 168–9 for France.
8 Finer 1989.
9 Feuchtwanger 1970, p. 45.
10 Clark 1996, p. 54.
11 Blackbourn 1997, p. 384.
12 I put quotation marks around the term 'deficient', because what is deficient at least partly depends on one's viewpoint. For example, some people believe that product patents on chemical and pharmaceutical substances should not be allowed, while others argue that they are desirable.
13 Chemical substances remained unpatentable until 1967 in West Germany, 1968 in the

Nordic countries, 1976 in Japan, 1978 in Switzerland and 1992 in Spain. Pharmaceutical products remained unpatentable until 1967 in West Germany and France, 1979 in Italy and 1992 in Spain. Pharmaceutical products were also unpatentable in Canada into the 1990s. For details, see Patel 1989, p. 980.

14 Schiff 1971.

15 Schiff (1971, p. 85), observes that the 1888 patent law protected only 'inventions that can be represented by mechanical models'.

16 Patel 1989, p. 980.

17 Crafts 2000, p. 5.

18 Kindleberger 1984.

19 Atack and Passell 1994, p. 103.

20 Broagan 1985, p. 523.

21 Chang 2000. Indeed this is the line taken by Friedrich von Hayek, when he proposes the scrapping of central banks and argues for free competition among note-issue banks.

22 Quoted in Kindleberger 1996, p. 146. The original source is H Spencer, 'State Tampering with Money and Banks' in *Essays: Scientific, Political, and Speculative* (London, Williams & Northgate, 1891), vol. 3, p. 354.

23 Cochran and Miller 1942, p. 295.

24 Brogan 1985, p. 477. The most telling evidence is the story of Charles E Mitchell, head of the National City Bank and a director of the Federal Reserve Bank of New York. Mitchell, in an attempt to minimize damage on his speculative activities in the run-up to the Great Depression, successfully put pressure on the Federal Reserve Board to reverse its policy of monetary tightening announced in early 1929 (Brogan, 1985, pp. 525–6).

25 Cited in Cochran and Miller 1942, p. 48.

26 Blackbourn 1997, pp. 346–7.

27 Cited in Garraty and Carnes 2000, p. 607.

28 See table 3.6 of Chang 2002 for further details.

29 In 1820, per capita income of the UK in 1990 dollars was $1,756, compared to $1,348 of India in 1992. The data are from Maddison 1995.

30 In 1875, per capita income of Italy in 1990 dollars was $1,516, compared to $1,642 of Pakistan in 1992. The data are from Maddison 1995.

31 In 1913, per capita income of the USA in 1990 dollars was $5,032, compared to $5,098 of Mexico in 1992. The data are from Maddison 1995.

32 See chapters 12 and 23 of this volume for further discussion on the workings of the WTO.

33 Chang 1998.

34 See this volume, chapter 12, section 4.

35 In 1820, per capita income of the USA in 1990 dollars was $1,287, compared to $1,348 of India in 1992. Data from Maddison 1995.

36 The developing countries grew in per capita terms at 3% during the 1960s and the 1970s, while they have grown at half that rate (1.5%) during the 1980s and the 1990s. Note that even this 1.5% average would fall to about 1% or below, if we excluded China and India, which have not followed the orthodox recommendations but have grown very fast in recent years. During the last 20 years, the Sub Saharan African economies have been shrinking (at a rate of about –0.7% per year against 2% growth before), while Latin America has been basically stagnant (growing at 0.6% against 3.1% before). Things are even worse in the former communist countries, most of which

have experienced a dramatic fall in living standards after the fall of communism – in several of these countries, per capita income is still less than half what it was under communism. See Chang 2002, chapter 4, for more detailed data.

References

Aron, J, 2000, 'Growth and Institutions: A Review of the Evidence', *The World Bank Research Observer*, vol. 15, no. 1.

Atack, J and Passell, P, 1994, *A New Economic View of American History*, 2nd ed., New York, Norton.

Bardhan, P, 1993, 'Symposium on Democracy and Development', *Journal of Economic Perspectives*, vol. 7, no. 3.

Blackbourn, D, 1997, *The Fontana History of Germany, 1780–1918*, London, Fontana Press.

Brogan, H, 1985, *The Penguin History of the United States of America*, London, Penguin.

Chang, H-J, 1998, 'Globalisation, Transnational Corporations, and Economic Development' in D Baker, G Epstein and R Pollin, 1998, eds, *Globalisation and Progressive Economic Policy*, Cambridge, Cambridge University Press.

——, 2000, 'The Hazard of Moral Hazard – Untangling the Asian Crisis', *World Development*, vol. 28, no. 4.

——, 2002, *Kicking Away the Ladder – Development Strategy in Historical Perspective*, London, Anthem Press.

Clark, M, 1996, *Modern Italy, 1871–1995*, 2nd ed., London and New York, Longman.

Cochran, T and Miller, W, 1942, *The Age of Enterprise: A Social History of Industrial America*, New York, The Macmillan Company.

Crafts, N, 2000, 'Institutional Quality and European Development before and after the Industrial Revolution', a paper prepared for World Bank Summer Research Workshop on Market Institutions, 17–19 July, 2000, Washington, DC.

Feuchtwanger, E, 1970, *Prussia: Myth and Reality – The Role of Prussia in German History*, London, Oswald Wolff.

Finer, S, 1989, 'Patronage and Public Service in Britain and America' in A Heidenheimer et al., 1989, eds, *Political Corruption: A Handbook*, New Brunswick, Transaction Publishers.

Garraty, J and Carnes, M, 2000, *The American Nation – A History of the United States*, 10th edition, New York, Addison Wesley Longman.

Kapur, D and Webber, R, 2000, 'Governance-related Conditionalities of the IFIs', G-24 Discussion Paper Series, no. 6, Geneva, UNCTAD.

Kindleberger, C, 1984, *A Financial History of Western Europe*, Oxford, Oxford University Press.

——, 1996, *Manias, Panics, and Crashes*, 3rd edition, London and Basingstoke, Macmillan.

Maddison, A, 1995, *Monitoring the World Economy*, Paris, OECD.

Machlup, F and Penrose, E, 1950, 'The Patent Controversy in the Nineteenth Century, *Journal of Economic History*, vol. 10, no. 1.

Patel, S, 1989, 'Intellectual Property Rights in the Uruguay Round – A Disaster for the South?', *Economic and Political Weekly*, 6 May 1989.

Schiff, E, 1971, *Industrialisation without National Patents – the Netherlands, 1869–1912 and Switzerland, 1850–1907*, Princeton, Princeton University Press.

World Bank, 2002, World Development Report 2002 – Building Institutions for Markets, New York, Oxford University Press.

23

GLOBALIZATION, GLOBAL GOVERNANCE AND THE DILEMMAS OF DEVELOPMENT

Martin Khor

1. Introduction

As the twentieth century closes and the twenty-first century begins, the main paradigm influencing or even determining development policy and global economic relations is the phenomenon of globalization. Its effects are most severely felt in the developing countries, for most of them are too small or weak to be active proponents, and are therefore passive recipients of the globalization process.

Many of the policies made by these countries, in an effort to regain economic sovereignty after their political independence, have been eroded as they come under intense pressure to 'integrate' with the world market. As boundaries melt and barriers fall, the local economies (including the small local firms and farms) are made to compete with a deluge of imported products and with large foreign corporations that want to invest in their countries.

Only a few developing countries have successfully found a niche in the pattern of globalization. However, even some stalwart Asian and Latin American developing countries in this category have recently fallen foul of the global financial markets and are now in deep crisis. For the majority of developing countries, the waves of economic globalization have left them marginalized, with few benefits and many costs. The prospects in the new century appear uncertain, frightening, even bleak, especially to many of the least developed countries.

This paper provides a perspective on the problems, dilemmas and options facing developing countries in their interface with the global economy, with the globalization process and with the present system of global governance. It also provides several suggestions for improving the situation.

2. Globalization and its differential effects

Economic globalization is not a new process. Over the past five centuries, firms in the central countries have increasingly extended their outreach through trade and production activities (intensified in the colonial period) to territories all over the world. However, in the past two to three decades, economic globalization has accelerated as a result of various factors, especially the policies of liberalization that have swept across the world. The present globalization process is thus inextricably linked to the policies and practices of liberalization; and in turn it also intensifies liberalization in the developing world.

Of the three main aspects of liberalization (finance, trade and investment), the process of financial liberalization has been the most pronounced. The demise of the Bretton Woods system in 1972–3 opened up an international trade in foreign exchange that has expanded at spectacular rates. The volume traded in the world foreign exchange market has grown from a daily average of $15 billion in 1973 to over $900 billion in 1992; it now far exceeds $1,000 billion. Much of this transaction is speculative in nature, as it is estimated that only a small portion (less than 2%) of the foreign exchange traded is used for facilitating trade. Due to the interconnectedness of financial markets and systems and the vast amounts of financial flows, there is now increasing evidence of the fragility and vulnerability of the system, and of the risk of breakdown in some critical areas or in the general system itself. These concerns have been heightened by the crises in East Asia, Russia, Turkey, Argentina and Brazil in recent years.

Trade liberalization has also gradually increased, but not at such a spectacular pace as that of finance. World exports rose from $61 billion in 1950 to $315 billion in 1970 and $3,447 billion in 1990. The share of world exports in world GDP rose from about 6% in 1950 to 12% in 1973 and 16% in 1992.[1] The increased role of trade has been accompanied by a reduction in tariff barriers in both developed and developing countries, due partly to autonomous policies and partly to the series of multilateral trade rounds under GATT. Trade liberalization is expected to accelerate under the World Trade Organization.

There has also been a steady growth in liberalization of foreign direct investment (FDI), although again on a smaller scale than in international financial flows. Many FDI flows are among the developed countries, but developing countries as a whole have been getting an increased share; this coincides with recent FDI liberalization in most developing countries. However, much of this FDI centres on only a few developing countries, and LDCs in particular are receiving only very small FDI flows. Therefore, FDI is insignificant as a source of external finance to most developing countries, and is likely to remain so in the next several years.

A major feature of globalization is the growing concentration and monopolization of economic resources and power by transnational corporations. In this process, which has been termed 'transnationalization', fewer and fewer transnational corporations are gaining a large and rapidly increasing proportion of world economic resources, production and market shares. Where a multinational company used to dominate the market of a single product, a big transnational company now typically produces or trades in an increasing multitude of products, services and sectors. Through mergers and acquisitions, fewer and fewer of these TNCs now control a larger and larger share of the global market, whether in commodities, manufactures or services. The top 200 global corporations accounted for $3,046 billion of sales in 1982, equivalent to 24% of world GDP ($12,600 billion) that year. By 1992, their sales had reached $5,862 billion, and their equivalent value to world GDP ($21,900 billion) had risen to 26.8%.[2]

Although globalization has generally been associated with liberalization, the reality is in fact more complex. The developed countries have continued to protect sectors and areas in which they are weak. The most outstanding example is agriculture, in which the OECD countries maintain massive subsidies (up to US$1 billion a day) and high tariffs in sensitive products. They also continue to maintain high protection in textiles and clothing, and in some manufactured products in which developing countries have an export potential. Moreover, while capital flows have been liberalized, the flow of labour across borders remains highly restricted. The developed countries have also made use of high levels of intellectual property rights across the world to protect their dominance in technology and to facilitate anti-competitive practices by their corporations. Thus, the globalization process is marked by both liberalization and protectionism. This is explained by the fact that the developed countries have been largely able to determine the rules of the global economy, and to shape them to their advantage.

'Globalization' is a very uneven process, with unequal distribution of benefits and losses. This imbalance leads to polarization between the few countries and groups that gain, and the many countries and groups in society that lose out or are marginalized. Globalization, polarization, wealth concentration and marginalization are therefore linked in a single process.

The globalization process is thus affecting different categories of countries differently. This process can broadly be categorized as follows: growth and expansion in the few leading or fully participating countries; moderate and fluctuating growth in some countries attempting to fit into the globalization/liberalization framework; and marginalization and exclusion experienced by many countries unable to get out of acute problems such as low commodity prices and debt, and unable to cope with problems of liberalization.

The uneven and unequal nature of current globalization is manifested in the fast-widening gaps between the world's rich and poor people and between developed and developing countries; and by the large differences among nations in the distribution of gains and losses in economic growth.

The UNDP *Human Development Report 1992* highlighted the high, and growing, income inequality in the world. It estimated that the 20% of the world's population in the developed countries receive 82.7% of total world income, whilst the 20% of people in the poorest countries receive only 1.4%. In 1989, the average income of the 20% of people living in the richest countries was 60 times higher than that of the 20% living in the poorest countries. This ratio had doubled from 30 times in 1950.

The UNDP's *Human Development Report 1996* showed that over the past three decades only 15 countries have enjoyed high growth, while 89 countries are worse off economically than they were ten or more years ago. In 70 developing countries, income levels in 1996 were less than in the 1960s and 1970s, and the report observed that 'Economic gains have benefited greatly a few countries, at the expense of many'. Since 1980, 15 – mainly Asian – countries have had growth rates much higher than any seen during industrialization in the West. However, economic decline in most parts of the developing world has lasted far longer and gone deeper than during the Great Depression of the 1930s. While the rich countries mostly rebounded from the depression within four to five years, the 'lost decade' of the 1980s is still continuing for hundreds of millions of people in many countries of Asia, Africa and Latin America. In some cases people are poorer than 30 years ago – and there is little hope of rapid improvement.

3. The need for an appropriate approach to the integration of developing countries in the world economy

Among the biggest dilemmas for developing countries is whether they should open their economies to the globalization process (in the hope of obtaining some of the benefits) to a greater extent, or whether they should take a more cautious approach to avoid risks. The challenge to developing countries is whether they can take advantage of the liberalization process – which is being pushed on them externally to a great extent – while at the same time avoiding or minimizing the disruptive consequences on their societies and economies. The ability to manage liberalization and globalization will be a crucial aspect of national policymaking in the years ahead.

At this juncture the danger is that most developing countries, under great pressure from agencies such as the WTO, the IMF and the World Bank, will go along with the trend and institute more, as well as rapid, liberalization policies, without a clear idea of the conditions needed to successfully take the associated risks. Instead of rapid liberalization, a selective approach to liberalization is more appropriate. The aim of this would be to strike a careful balance between opening the domestic market (to benefit consumers) and protecting it to take into account in particular the interests of small producers.

Perhaps the most important, and most difficult, set of development policies that a developing country has to decide, is the interface between domestic policies and the world economy. Whether, how, when, to what extent, in which sectors, and in which sequence, to integrate the domestic economy and society with international economy and society, are simple but big questions and issues that face developing countries.

The dominant view of the past two decades favoured by the 'Washington Consensus', the major developed countries and the agencies under their influence, is that full, rapid and comprehensive integration of developing countries into the global economy is both beneficial and essential for their development. The dominance of this paradigm is now rapidly eroding, due to the empirical record of developing countries that have followed (or attempted to follow) the policies of rapid liberalization. The East Asian financial crisis of 1997–9, and other subsequent crises (including those in Argentina and Uruguay), have undermined the policy prescription that developing countries should rapidly liberalize their financial systems. It is now more widely recognized that financial liberalization is qualitatively different from trade liberalization, and that developing countries should be cautious in deciding how to – or even whether to – open their capital account.

In the area of trade liberalization, there is also empirical evidence that excessive import liberalization has caused dislocation to local industries and farms in several developing countries; at the same time there has not been an increase in export opportunities or performance to offset these adverse developments. There is now an emerging trade-policy paradigm that stresses the importance of addressing other factors (such as the need to tailor the rate of import liberalization to the increase in competitiveness of local firms, and the need to increase the supply-side capacity of local firms in order to realize the country's export potential). Failure to address these needs can lead to serious problems of domestic economic dislocation and worsening trade imbalances, should a country liberalize its imports.[3]

In the area of foreign direct investment, host developing countries are now being cautioned to take an even-handed approach and to have policies that seek to maximize benefits (for example, through equity-sharing and profit-sharing and technology-transfer arrangements) and to take account of and minimize risks (especially of potentially large drains on foreign exchange through high import content and large profit repatriation).

The emerging paradigm calls for developing countries to take a pragmatic approach to globalization and liberalization, and to be selective and deliberate in choosing how and when, in which sectors and to what extent to integrate their domestic economy with the global economy, in the areas of finance, trade and investment. This approach recognizes that interaction with the global economy can benefit (and can potentially be of significant benefit to) a developing country. However, the terms of interaction are crucial if the potential benefits are to be realized, and if costs and damage are to be avoided. Too rapid a rate of integration, or integration in the wrong areas and in the wrong way, can be harmful rather than helpful. The approach of selective integration, done carefully and appropriately, suited to the needs and particular conditions of a country, is therefore of the utmost importance. It should replace the still-dominant approach of 'big-bang' rapid liberalization, done inappropriately in a one-size-fits-all manner.

This change in paradigm and approach should firstly be considered at the national level, when governments choose their development strategies. However, it must be recognized that most developing countries do not have the 'luxury' or space to choose their approach on economic integration, because of the determining influence of loan and aid conditionalities, or because of the rules they had agreed to in the WTO. Thus, reform of the governance of the global economy is urgently required. There is an underlying need for an understanding that developing countries should have the right to take an appropriate and pragmatic approach towards selectively integrating their domestic economy with the world economy. This understanding should be the basis for the systems of international trade, finance, investment, aid and intellectual property rights. The policies, rules and conditionalities arising from these systems should reflect these realities facing developing countries, and their needs. Without this change in attitude and approach at international level, it would be difficult or even impossible for many developing countries to pursue appropriate responses to globalization, or appropriate development strategies.

4. The globalization of national policymaking and the influence of international agencies

Perhaps the most important and unique feature of the current globalization process is the 'globalization' of national policies and policymaking mechanisms. National policies (including in economic, social, cultural and technological areas) that until recently were under the control of states and people within a country have increasingly come under the influence of international agencies and processes, or of big private corporations and economic/financial players. This has led to the erosion of 'national sovereignty' and narrowed the ability of governments and people to make choices from options in economic, social and cultural policies.

Most developing countries have seen their independent policymaking capacity eroded, and instead have to adopt policies made by other entities, which may on balance be detrimental to the countries concerned. The developed countries are better able to maintain control over their own national policies as well as to determine the policies and practices of international institutions and the global system. However, the large corporations have also taken over a large part of the decision-making process in the developed countries, at the expense of the power of the state or political leaders.

Part of the erosion of national policymaking capacity is due to the liberalization of markets and developments in technology. For example, the free flow of capital, the large sums involved, and the unchecked power of big players and speculators, have made it difficult for countries to control the level of their currency and the flows of money in and out of the country. Transnational companies and financial institutions control such huge resources, more than many – indeed most – governments are able to marshal, and are thus able to have great policy influence in many countries. Certain technological developments make it difficult or virtually impossible to formulate policy. For example, the establishment of satellite TV and the availability of small receivers, and the spread of electronic mail (especially the Internet) make it difficult for governments to determine cultural or communications policy, or to control the spread of information and cultural products.

However, an even more important aspect is the recent process by which global institutions have become major makers of an increasingly wide range of policies that are traditionally under the jurisdiction of national governments. These governments now have to implement policies that are in line with decisions and rules of these international institutions. The key institutions concerned are the Bretton Woods institutions (the World Bank and the IMF) and the World Trade Organization.

There are also other influential international organizations, in particular the United Nations, its agencies and its conventions and world conferences. However, in recent years, the UN has lost a lot of its policy and operational influence in economic and social matters, and correspondingly the powers and authority of the World Bank, IMF and GATT/WTO have expanded.

The Bretton Woods institutions wield tremendous authority in a majority of developing countries (and countries in transition) that depend on their loans. In particular, countries requiring debt rescheduling have to adopt structural adjustment policies (SAPs) that are mainly drawn up in the Washington institutions. SAPs cover macroeconomic policies, and have recently also covered social policies such as health services. They have been responsible for the move towards liberalization, privatization, deregulation and a withdrawal of the state from economic and social activities.

The Uruguay Round negotiations greatly expanded the powers of the GATT system, and the Agreements under the GATT's successor organization, the WTO, have established disciplines in new areas beyond the old GATT, including intellectual property rights, services, agriculture and trade-related investment measures. Rules made at the WTO are legally binding on all member states. Non-compliance can result in a state being brought before a panel, and a negative decision will have to be met with compliance. Failure of a country to comply with a panel decision can lead to trade penalties and sanctions by other WTO members. It is the legally-binding nature of rules in the WTO and the strong enforcement capability (through its dispute settlement system) that make the WTO so powerful.

According to several recent analyses, the Uruguay Round has produced an unequal treaty, and the WTO Agreements and system (including the decision-making system) are weighted against the interests of the South. The existing agreements now require domestic legislation and policies of member states to be altered and brought into line with them. Thus, national governments have to comply with the disciplines and obligations in the already wide range of issues under WTO purview. Therefore, many domestic economic policies of developing countries are being made in the WTO negotiations, rather than in parliament, bureaucracy or cabinet at national level.

There are now attempts by Northern governments to expand further the jurisdiction of the WTO to yet more areas, including rights to be granted to foreign investors, competition policy, government procurement practices, labour standards and environmental issues. The greater the range of issues to be taken up by the WTO, the more the space for national policymaking (and development options) in developing countries will be whittled away.

However, while the World Bank, IMF, WTO and the OECD are the most powerful, the United Nations and its agencies also form an alternative set of global institutions. In recent years there have been several UN world conferences: on environment and development (1992); population, social development (1995); women (1995); habitat (1996); genetic resources (1996); food (1996); financing for development (2002); and sustainable development (2002). The UN also has legally-binding conventions. The UN agencies, conferences and conventions, which are much more transparent and democratic, can also potentially influence the nature of globalization as well as national policies.

The UN approach to economic and social issues is different from that of the WTO and Bretton Woods institutions. The latter promote the empowerment of the market, a minimal role for the state and rapid liberalization. Most UN agencies on the other hand operate under the belief that public intervention (internationally and nationally) is necessary to enable basic needs and human rights to be fulfilled and that the market alone cannot do the job – and in many cases hinders the job being done.

The Bretton Woods–WTO institutions have become much more powerful than the UN, whose authority and influence in the social and economic areas have been depleted in recent years. This is a reflection of the nature of the globalization process. The former institutions promote the principles of liberalization and the laissez-faire market model, and give high priority to commercial interests; they are therefore given the role of leading the globalization of policymaking. The UN and its agencies represent the principles of partnership, in which the richer countries are expected to contribute to the development of the poorer countries and which emphasize the rights of people to development, and the fulfilment of social needs. The kind of globalization represented by the UN is not favoured by the powerful nations today, as a result of which the UN's influence has been curtailed.

5. Global economic governance: the United Nations versus the IMF–World Bank–WTO trinity

As the processes of globalization have such significant impact, especially on developing countries, global economic governance has become an even more important topic. Governance includes two key issues: how decisions are taken at the global institutions (the process issue) and whether the policies made there are appropriate (the substance issue).

Global-level decision-making has become much less democratic and transparent. One of the major reasons for this is the transfer of authority and influence of more democratic global institutions (the United Nations and its agencies) to less democratic institutions (especially the IMF, the World Bank and the WTO).

At the UN, decisions are usually taken on a one country–one vote basis (except in the Security Council where the power is concentrated among the five veto-wielding permanent member states). Discussions and negotiations are usually carried out in the open, with member states having the right to take part. Positions of various countries and groupings are stated clearly; these various positions are put on paper, and negotiations are conducted to narrow the differences until a consensus (if possible) is attained. Since the majority of UN members are developing countries, they generally have no little influence.

Of course, the developed country members are able to, and often do, disagree with the developing counties. Voting is carried out at the General Assembly and resolutions based on majority vote are passed. In the important world conferences, the final outcomes (political declarations and programmes of action) are approved by consensus, which usually involves painstaking negotiations in many preparatory meetings.

In the economic and social agencies of the UN, programmes that are deemed to be in the interests of developing countries are adopted, although there are of course problems with the environmental or social impact of several of the projects and programmes. Funds are obtained by the agencies from donor countries, and programmes are carried out in developing countries, usually on a grant basis. The agencies are thus manifestations of a 'redistributive' mechanism, in which a small part of the income of rich countries is given to UN agencies which provide more or less 'free services' to developing countries, e.g. WHO in health, UNEP in environment, UNCTAD on trade and development issues, etc. The declarations and action plans of the UN world conferences (on environment, food, social development, women and so on) are generally, if mildly, favourable to developing countries' interests.

Thus, in both process and substance, the UN operates in a manner that is relatively friendly to developing countries' interests and needs. Aid from donor countries is supposed to be recycled to developing countries to meet their needs.

However, in the 1980s and 1990s there was a massive transfer of authority and influence on economic and social issues away from the UN and towards the IMF, World Bank and GATT/WTO. UNCTAD used to be the major forum for North–South economic negotiations. However, the 'new international economic order' (NIEO) plans, policies and movement declined and died out as Northern countries were not in favour. The producer–consumer commodity agreements that were meant to enable developing countries to have stable and fair prices for their export commodities declined and died out when the Northern countries pulled out of many agreements in the 1980s. This is one reason why commodity prices are now left to market forces to determine and, because of oversupply, these prices have been in continuous decline. The attempt to have a code of conduct on TNCs was abandoned and the secretariat for that effort, the UN Centre on TNCs, was also closed. The attempt by UNCTAD to devise a code on technology transfer to developing countries was also aborted.

The debt crisis of the 1980s, which has stretched into the 1990s and 2000s, gave a new lease of life to the IMF and World Bank. They became the gatekeepers of the rescheduling (involving questions of whether and how to reschedule) of the loans of countries facing debt repayment crises. This gave the Bretton Woods institutions the leverage to impose loan conditions on the indebted countries. The range of conditions has grown through time to encompass fiscal and monetary policy, privatization policy, trade, investment and finance policy, social policy (health, education, land ownership) and even political and corporate governance policies.

Although the IMF and World Bank are widely perceived to be promoting policies that are generally not in the interests of developing countries, those countries that face debt repayment problems do not have much say over these policies; rather, they have to accept them in order to obtain new loans or to roll over old loans. More importantly, the decision-making powers are determined by the votes weighted according to the share of equity in the institutions. Since the quotas for shares are weighted heavily in favour of the developed countries, the developing countries are unable to have much of a say in the decisions.

On trade issues, the relative influence of UNCTAD vis-à-vis GATT changed significantly when UNCTAD's authority in North–South negotiations waned in the 1980s, and the powers of GATT were greatly enhanced when it accumulated a mandate over new areas (services, intellectual property, investment measures) through the Uruguay Round that created the WTO. Whereas the old GATT system's mandate was over narrow trade issues 'at the border' (tariff and non-tariff measures for products), the WTO now has mandate over key areas involving domestic economic and social policies (intellectual property and access to products and technology, services and the liberalization of investments, subsidies provided by government to local enterprises and farmers, etc.). Moreover, it has been found that many of the WTO agreements are imbalanced and skewed in favour of the developed countries; and that they adversely affect the development options and interests of developing countries.

One reason for this bias is the nature of the decision-making process. Although the WTO is supposed to be based on a one country–one vote basis, in practice decisions are taken on the basis of 'consensus'. This consensus system works to the favour of developed countries, as they can decide on a course of action among themselves and then embark on persuading and influencing the developing countries to agree. In this process, those developing countries that have a contrary view are subjected to special persuasion or are marginalized or isolated. In practice, then, the developed countries have usually got their way and have been able to determine the rules, as well as to initiate the process to establish new rules and agreements that favour them.

In summary, global decision-making in economic and social affairs has become much less democratic, participatory and transparent as the resources, mandate and influence of the UN eroded and as the power and mandate of the IMF, World Bank and WTO expanded. The erosion of democracy in process has also adversely affected the appropriateness of the policies' substance. Many of the important policies promoted at the IMF and the WTO have been inappropriate for the development of the developing countries. Their policy options have narrowed, the policies they are influenced or pressurized to adopt are often unsuitable, and their development prospects are in many cases bleak.

Process and substance are thus linked intimately, and reforms in both are needed if the South is to have the chance to develop in the future. In order that they be able to develop, developing countries must be given the space and opportunity to strengthen their economies and to develop their social infrastructure. For this to happen, there has to be a much more favourable international environment, starting with the democratization of international relations and institutions, so that the developing countries can have an active role in decision-making. The role of the United Nations should be strengthened, while the IMF, World Bank and WTO should be made more accountable to the public. There should also be international economic and financial reforms to reduce the widening gap between rich and poor countries. Most importantly, reforms have to be made to structural adjustment policies and to the WTO rules so that adequate space and possibilities are given to developing countries to have macroeconomic and development options between alternative national policies.

The next two parts of the paper deal in greater length with governance and reform of the international financial and trading systems.

6. Governance of the global financial system and the IMF

Two sets of actions are urgently required in order to improve the governance of the international financial system in the interests of developing countries. The first set involves the need to avoid new policies or agreements that would 'lock in' further financial liberalization. Countries should not be pressurized further to liberalize their financial systems, either by the IMF, by investment agreements (at international, regional or bilateral levels) or by the financial services negotiations in the WTO.

The second set of proposals relates to international policies and measures that need to be put in place, including the following:

• Measures and guidelines to help countries prevent debt and financial crises. Included in these are measures that regulate and control the type and extent of foreign loans that the public and private sectors are allowed to obtain; and regulations to prevent speculation and manipulation in the stock market and the currency markets.

- If, notwithstanding these measures, a financial crisis breaks out, in which a country is unable to service its external debt, international measures and mechanisms are required to enable the affected country to manage the crisis effectively, and to allow the debtors and creditors to share the burden equitably. At present there is no systemic treatment for debt workout, rescheduling and relief, and the debtor countries usually end up carrying the overwhelming bulk of the burden, while in many cases the outstanding debt remains or even grows. The measures required include an arrangement in which a country in financial trouble can opt for a debt-standstill arrangement, and have recourse to an international debt arbitration court or panel, which would then arrange for a debt workout that fairly shares the cost and burden between creditors and debtors, and also facilitate the provision of fresh credit to aid the affected country's recovery.
- Meanwhile a comprehensive system of debt elimination and debt relief should be established to cover the countries that have been and are in a debt crisis. Many of these countries have really repaid their debt principals and part of their interest. A comprehensive resolution of the debt problem is necessary if these countries are to have the chance to develop.
- A framework that allows and freely permits countries (especially developing countries, which are more vulnerable than rich countries), without fear of attracting penalties, to establish systems of control over the inflow and outflow of funds, especially of the speculative variety.
- Governments of countries which are the sources of internationally mobile funds should be obliged to discipline and regulate their financial institutions and players to prevent them from causing volatility and speculation abroad.
- International regulation is needed for activities of hedge funds, investment banks and other highly leveraged institutions, offshore centres, the currency markets and the derivatives trade.
- An international monetary system that enables the stability of currency exchange rates is also urgently required.
- A change in the set of conditionalities (structural adjustment policies) that accompany IMF–World Bank loans so that recipient countries can have options to choose among appropriate financial, monetary, fiscal, macroeconomic, trade, ownership and other economic and social policies, instead of being obliged to follow the IMF prescriptions which often do not work but instead lead to disastrous results.

As long as the present system of governance is maintained, there is not much chance of such a system being put in place. Vested interests in many of the developed countries would like to preserve the system as long as possible, however unstable or imbalanced it may be, since it enables them to profit. What is urgently required is a reform of the decision-making system in international institutions like the IMF and the World Bank (as well as the regional development banks), so that the developing countries can have a fair say in the policies and processes of these institutions that so greatly determine the course of their economies and societies. The distribution of quotas in the international financial institutions (IFIs) should be reviewed and reformed, so that developing countries are enabled to have more than half the total shares.

If the IMF and the basis of its decision-making process can be reformed, then it may be possible to base the needed changes in the global financial system on the existing institutions. But whether the IMF can be reformed is a very big question. Meanwhile, developing countries can consider regional-level cooperation arrangements, such as a regional monetary fund to which the region's countries can contribute and draw from, with conditions attached to the loans that may be different from (and more appropriate than) the set of policies associated with the IMF.

In the absence of the kind of international or regional measures outlined above, developing countries should seriously consider domestic measures to protect themselves from falling into debt crises. In particular, they should have regulations that control the extent of public and private sector foreign loans (for example, restricting them to projects that yield the capacity to repay in foreign currency); that prohibit manipulation of their currencies and stock markets; and that treat foreign direct investment in a selective way that avoids buildup of foreign debt.

The array of national policy instruments should include capital controls, which would assist the country to avoid an excessive buildup of external debt, to curb volatility of the flow of funds, and to enable the country to have more scope to adopt macroeconomic policies that can counter recession (such as lower interest rates or budget expansion) while reducing the risks of volatility in the exchange rate and flow of funds.

Capital controls constitute an integral part of a nation's right to economic self-determination and no pressure must be brought to bear on any state to abandon such controls if it has resorted to them. In particular, IFIs must desist from attempts to dissuade developing countries from having recourse to such controls by threats (overt or veiled) of the withdrawal of credits or other financial support.

In short, the crucial question of when or how a state wishes to liberalize its capital account, or whether it wishes to embark on such liberalization at all, should be left to its sole determination, without outside pressure.

7. Trade, Development and Reform of the Multilateral Trading System

The multilateral trading system, and the WTO, are at a crossroads. Decisions made in the next few years at the WTO will have an important effect on the future direction of the trade system. The most important decision is whether the next few years will see the WTO members doing their best to rectify the problems and imbalances in the rules and system, or whether proposals to expand the mandate of the WTO are accepted, in which case more new issues will be added to the WTO, which will distort the trading system and contribute to the already existing imbalances.

The following are the major issues to be resolved:

7.1 The anticipated benefits from the Uruguay Round have not accrued to most developing countries.

The developing countries' main expectation of benefit was that the developed countries would open their protected agriculture and textiles sectors, but both have remained heavily protected. In agriculture, tariffs on many items remain prohibitive, while the total subsidies have not declined but increased, as subsidies allowed by the agreement on agriculture rose even as subsidies under discipline fell.[4] As far as textiles are concerned, very few items which the developing countries export have been taken off the quota list, even though more than half the implementation period has passed.[5]

7.2 Many developing countries have seen the prices of their commodity exports declining very significantly.

The trade system has therefore resulted in losses rather than gains for those countries that remain commodity-dependent. The terms-of-trade decline has led to a bigger trade deficit in many countries, thus adding to the debt problem. The poorer developing countries also continue to suffer from 'supply-side constraints', i.e. their production capacity is low in manufacturing and they are therefore unable to export even if there is greater market access for them.

7.3 Implementing their obligations under the WTO Agreements has brought many problems for developing countries.

These problems include:

- the prohibition of investment measures and subsidies, making it harder to encourage domestic industry;

- import liberalization in agriculture, threatening the viability and livelihoods of small farmers whose products face competition from cheaper imported foods, many of which are artificially cheapened through massive subsidy;[6]
- the effects of a strong intellectual property rights (IPR) regime that has led to exorbitant prices of medicines and other essentials; to the patenting by Northern corporations of biological materials originating in the South; and to higher cost for, and lower access by, developing countries to industrial technology;[7]
- increased pressures to liberalize their services sectors, including banking and insurance, as well as telecommunications, postal, water and health services. These pressures are likely to lead to further privatization and transfer of ownership to foreign firms.[8]

These problems raise the serious issue of whether developing countries can presently or in the future pursue development strategies (including industrialization, technology upgrading, development of local industries and services, food security and maintenance of local farms and agriculture, and fulfillment of health and medicinal needs).

These problems listed above arise from the structural imbalances and weaknesses of the WTO Agreements. There is thus a need to redress the imbalances in the rules and the problems they generate. The developing countries have put forward their problems of implementation, and their proposals for redressal are now on the table at the WTO. Unfortunately the developed countries have so far not responded positively. Their attitude seems to be that the developing countries have entered into legally binding commitments and must therefore abide by them, however painful these commitments may prove; any changes require new concessions on the part of developing countries. Such an attitude does not augur well for the WTO, for it implies that the state of imbalance will have to remain, and if developing countries 'pay twice' or 'pay three or four times', the imbalances will become worse and the burden heavier.

7.4 The biggest immediate problem is that the developed countries are putting immense pressure on developing countries to accept the expansion of the WTO's mandate to non-trade issues, including the establishment of new agreements on investment, competition and transparency in government procurement.

If accepted, these proposals would be equivalent to making developing countries pay two, three or four times in order for the developed countries to consider looking at the implementation problems for developing countries, and to consider giving them more market access in agriculture and textiles. The new agreements and obligations in these new areas would be very detrimental to developing countries, which will find even more of their development options closed off; at the same time (given the poor record of the North in not keeping their commitments) there is no guarantee at all that the implementation problems will be resolved or that there will really be more meaningful access to Northern markets in agriculture, textiles and other sectors.

The three proposed new agreements have a common theme: increasing the rights of the big foreign firms to have much greater access to the markets of developing countries. The aim of the investment agreement is to increase the right of foreign firms to enter, invest and operate in developing countries with minimum regulation (as performance requirements would be prohibited) and to be given 'national treatment' (treated at least as well as locals). The competition agreement is meant to oblige developing countries to adopt competition laws and policies which would result in 'effective equality of opportunity' for foreign firms vis-à-vis local firms. The agreement on transparency in government procurement would be the first stage of an eventual agreement that would grant foreign firms the same right as local firms to bid for the business of government supplies, contracts and projects. These agreements would seriously tie the hands of government, preventing it from regulating foreign firms while also preventing it from providing a boost to local firms. It would severely restrict the ability of developing countries to build the capacity of their domestic sectors, enterprises and farms.

7.5 In order that the trading system does not do further harm but can be oriented to serving the needs of developing countries, the following reforms should be made:

- **Review and reform the existing WTO rules.** Each agreement should be reviewed to remove the imbalances, and to facilitate the operation of special and differential treatment for developing countries. In the meantime, developing countries should not be subjected to dispute settlement action until completion of the review.
- **The problem of low and falling commodity prices should be addressed.** This could be done through establishing a new set of commodity agreements in which the ecological and social values of the commodities are taken fully into account.
- **The developed countries should stop pressurizing developing countries to expand the WTO mandate into new areas such as investment, competition and government procurement.**

- **The process of decision-making in the WTO must be democratized, made more transparent and must enable the full participation of developing countries.** At present, the system of participation is flawed. The so-called consensus system enables the developed countries to pressurize developing countries to accept what has been agreed among the developed countries. Moreover, manipulative devices are used, especially surrounding the Ministerial Conferences during which the key decisions are taken. For example, at the Singapore Ministerial Conference, only 30 countries were invited to the 'informal' meeting in which the major decisions were taken, and the remaining countries were asked to accept the decisions on the last night. At the Doha Ministerial Conference, the proposals of a majority of developing countries on key subjects were not included in the drafts of the Declaration, despite their objections. This put them at a great disadvantage. There has to be a fundamental overhaul of the decision-making processes. At the least: (a) All members must be allowed to be present and participate in the meetings. (b) The views of all members must be adequately reflected in negotiating texts. (c) Pressure should not be applied on members to accept views of other members. (d) Adequate time must be given to all members to consider proposals being put forward. Only if there is a more democratic decision-making system can the other reforms described in this section be made possible.

7.6 Reorienting the WTO and the multilateral trade system towards development needs should also be on the medium-term agenda.

First, there should be a basic rethinking of the nature and timing of liberalization. Many developing countries face declining export prices, and are also unable to export new items. Yet they have been under pressure to rapidly liberalize their imports. If import liberalization goes ahead, these countries are likely to suffer balance-of-payments difficulties and higher debt. Trade liberalization should not be pursued automatically or rapidly as an end in itself. Rather, what is important is the quality, timing, sequencing and scope of liberalization (especially import liberalization), and how the process is accompanied by (or preceded by) other factors. Therefore, developing countries need adequate policy space and freedom, to be able to choose between different options in relation to their trade policies and related policies in the areas of finance, investment and technology, in order to make decisions on the rate and scope of liberalization.

Secondly, the objective of development should become the overriding principle guiding the work of the WTO, and its rules and operations should be designed to produce development as the outcome, given that the developing countries form the majority of the WTO membership. The test of a rule, proposal or policy being considered in the WTO should not be whether it is 'trade-distorting', but rather whether it is 'development-distorting'. Since development is the ultimate objective, while reduction of trade barriers is only a means, the need to avoid development distortions should have primacy over the avoidance of trade distortion.

The reorientation of the WTO towards this perspective and approach is essential if there is to be progress towards a fair and balanced multilateral trading system with more benefits – as opposed to costs – for developing countries. Such a reorientation would make the rules and judgment of future proposals more in line with empirical reality and practical necessities. Taking this approach, the goal for developing countries would be to attain 'appropriate liberalization' rather than to come under the pressure of attaining 'maximum liberalization'. The rules of the WTO should be reviewed to screen out those that are 'development-distorting', and a decision could be formulated that would at the least permit developing countries to be exempted from adhering to rules or measures that prevent them from meeting their development objectives. These exemptions can be on the basis of special and differential treatment.

Thirdly, there should be a rethinking of the scope of the WTO's mandate over issues, and the role of other agencies. It is misleading to equate the WTO with the 'multilateral trading system', as is often done in many discussions. In fact, the WTO is both less than and more than the global trade system. There are key issues regarding world trade that the WTO is not seriously concerned with, including the trends and problems of its members' terms of trade and the problems in primary commodity markets (including low commodity prices). On the other hand, the WTO has become deeply involved in domestic policy issues such as intellectual property laws, and domestic investment and subsidy policies. There are also proposals to bring in other non-trade issues including labour and environment standards.

The WTO and its predecessor the GATT have evolved trade principles (such as non-discrimination, MFN and national treatment) that were formulated in the context of trade in goods. It is by no means assured or agreed that the application of the same principles to areas outside that of trade would lead to positive outcomes. Indeed, the incorporation of non-trade issues into the WTO system could distort the work of the WTO itself and the multilateral trading system.

Therefore, a fundamental rethinking of the mandate and scope of the WTO is required. First, non-trade issues should not be introduced in the

WTO as subjects for rules. This should apply at least until the question of the appropriateness and criteria of proposed issues is dealt with satisfactorily in a systematic manner. Secondly, a review should be made of the issues that are currently in the WTO to determine whether the WTO is in fact the appropriate forum for them. Prominent trade economists such as Jagdish Bhagwati and TN Srinivasan have concluded that it was a mistake to have incorporated intellectual property as an issue in the Uruguay Round and in the WTO. There should be serious consideration, starting with the mandated review process, given to transferring the TRIPS Agreement on intellectual property rights from the WTO to a more suitable forum.

Within its traditional ambit of trade in goods, the WTO should reorientate its primary operational objectives and principles towards development, as elaborated in the sections above. The imbalances in the agreements relating to goods should be ironed out, with the 'rebalancing' designed to meet the development needs of developing countries and to be more in line with the realities of the liberalization and development processes.

The WTO, reformed along the lines above, should then be seen as a key component of the international trading system, complementing, coexisting with and cooperating with other organizations; together the WTO and these other organizations would operate within the framework of the trading system.

8. The search for alternative development strategies

The review of structural adjustment policies, and of the liberal 'free-market' model in general, shows that a reconceptualization of development strategies is required, and that alternative approaches are needed. For example, the recent Asian financial crisis makes it crucial to reflect on the dangers to a country of excessive openness to foreign funds and investors.

An important issue is whether developing countries will be allowed to learn lessons from and adopt key aspects of these alternative approaches. For this to happen, the policy conditions imposed through structural adjustment have to be loosened, and some of the multilateral disciplines on developing countries through the WTO Agreements may have to be reexamined.

In the search for alternative options for developing countries, work also has to be increased on developing economic and development approaches based on the principles of sustainable development. It is crucial that the research in this area is increased.

More work needs to be done – including in developing countries at regional and national levels – to produce evidence that environmental damage is economically harmful, and that environmental protection and eco-friendly technology and practices are themselves economically efficient ways of conducting development. It would also be very useful to highlight, and draw lessons from, elements of the successful implementation of sustainable and human development policies and approaches. The emerging 'sustainable and human development' paradigm could then contribute to the debate on appropriate macroeconomic policies; the appropriate relations between state, markets and people; and appropriate development styles and models.

Notes

1 Nayyar 1995.
2 Clairmont 1996, p. 39.
3 TWN 2001.
4 TWN 2001, OECD 2000.
5 WTO 2000.
6 TWN 2001; FAO 2000, 2001.
7 Khor 2001.
8 TWN 2001.

References

Bhaduri, A and Nayyar, D, 1996, *The Intelligent Person's Guide to Liberalization*, New Delhi, Penguin Books.
Clairmont, FF, 1996, *The Rise and Fall of Economic Liberalism*, Penang, Third World Network.
Das, Bhagirath Lal, 1998, *The WTO Agreements: Deficiencies, Imbalances and Required Changes*, Penang, Malaysia: Third World Network.
——, 1999, *Some Suggestions for Improvements in the WTO Agreements*, Penang, Malaysia: Third World Network.
——, 2002, *The New WTO Work Programme*, Penang, Third World Network.
FAO, 2000, *Agriculture, Trade and Food Security, vol. I*, Rome: Food and Agriculture Organization.
——, 2001, *Agriculture, Trade and Food Security, vol. II*, Rome, Food and Agriculture Organization.
Khor, Martin, 1993, 'South-North Resource Flows', Penang, Third World Network.
——, 2000, *Globalization and the South: Some Critical Issues*, Penang, Third World Network.
——, 2001, *Rethinking IPRs and the TRIPS Agreement*, Penang, Third World Network.
——, 2002, *The WTO, the Post-Doha Agenda and the Future of the Trade System: A Development Perspective*, Penang, Third World Network.
Nayyar, d, 1995, *Globalization: The Past in our Present*, Penang, Third World Network.
OECD, 2000, *Agricultural Policies in OECD Countries: Monitoring and Evaluation 2000*, Paris: OECD Secretariat.
Shafaeddin, SM, 1994, *The Impact of Trade Liberalization on Export and GDP Growth in Least Developed Countries*, Discussion Paper no. 85, Geneva, UNCTAD.
Third World Network, 2001, *The Multilateral Trading System: A Development Perspective*, Report prepared for UNDP.

UNCTAD, 1999, *Trade and Development Report, 1999*, New York and Geneva, United Nations.

———, 2002, *Economic Development in Africa: From Adjustment to Poverty Reduction: What is New?*, Geneva, United Nations.

UNDP, 1992, *Human Development Report 1992*, New York, Oxford University Press.

———, 1996, *Human Development Report 1996*, New York, Oxford University Press.

———, 2000, *Human Development Report 2000*, New York, Oxford University Press.

World Trade Organization (WTO), 1999, Preparation for the 1999 Ministerial Conference: Ministerial Text, Revised Draft, WTO, Geneva, 19 October.

———, 2000, 'Statement by Hong Kong, China at special session of the WTO General Council on 22 June 2000 on behalf of International Textiles and Clothing Bureau' (Document WT/GC/W/405.).

———, 2001a, 'Ministerial Declaration,' adopted 14 November.

———, 2001b, 'Declaration on the TRIPS Agreement and Public Health,' adopted 14 November.

———, 2001c, 'Implementation-Related Issues and Concerns.' Decision of 14 November.

———, 2001d, 'Compilation of Outstanding Implementation Issues Raised by Members', General Council document JOB(01)152/Rev.1, dated 27 October 2001.

———, 2001e, 'Implementation-related Issues and Concerns', General Council document JOB (01)/14 dated 20 Feb 2001.